A Global Perspective

Source Readings from World Civilizations
Volume II

A Global Perspective

Source Readings from World Civilizations

Volume II
1600 to the Present

Edited by
Lynn H. Nelson
University of Kansas

Harcourt Brace College Publishers
Fort Worth   Philadelphia   San Diego
New York   Orlando   Austin   San Antonio
Toronto   Montreal   London   Sydney   Tokyo

To
DOROTHY M. DRUMMOND
with
love and gratitude

Copyright © 1989 by Harcourt Brace & Company

All rights reserved. No part of this publication may be reproduced or transmitted in any form or by any means, electronic or mechanical, including photocopy, recording, or any information storage and retrieval system, without permission in writing from the publisher.

Requests for permission to make copies of any part of the work should be mailed to Permissions Department, Harcourt Brace & Company, Orlando, Florida 32887.

Printed in the United States of America

ISBN: 0-15-529617-5

5 6 7 8 9 0 1 2 3 4 090 13 12 11 10 9 8 7 6 5 4

Preface

The source readings in the present volumes are selected from a variety of genres and represent some of the world's classics of thought and expression. The readings illuminate five basic themes: Love, Death, The Good Life, War and Peace, and Virtue and the Individual. These particular themes were chosen as common concerns of all humanity and, for this reason, as transcending considerations of time and space. Men and women of all cultures and eras have confronted these issues, often with attitudes and values far different from our own. Despite these differences of approach, however, the basic concerns abide, rendering the views of previous ages and other societies worthy of our consideration. It is my hope that these readings will afford the reader not only a better appreciation of the past, but a better awareness of some of the fundamental issues of life.

The two volumes contain an extensive apparatus. The thirty selections in each volume are grouped into three chronological parts, and each part is preceded by a time line that relates the selections to the major events and literary achievements of the period. Moreover, an introduction to each part provides a broad overview of the age, supplementing whatever core text may be exployed and furnishing a context for the better appreciation of the individual selections. Every selection is prefaced by an essay that discusses its historical background, the character of its author, and the nature of the work itself. A set of reading questions directs the reader's attention to major issues within the reading, and the selection is followed by a bibliography of relevant and related works. Finally, each part concludes with a series of ten or more discussion questions framed to encourage the reader to consider the scope and relevance of the issues involved, the interrelationships of the readings, and significant comparisons and contrasts in thought and approach.

The structure of these volumes facilitates comparisons across time and between cultures. Each chronological part contains ten selections, five from Western and five from non-Western sources. Each of the five major themes is represented by two readings, one Western and one non-Western. For every reading, the material presented is both substantial and representative, and, in fact, several of the selections constitute complete works.

This arrangement permits a variety of approaches. One might adopt a chronological approach, for instance, and consider the topic of love in the Western tradition by reading the selections, Molière's *Love's the Best Doctor*, Louisa May Alcott's "The Death of Beth," and D. H. Lawrence's *Sons and Lovers*. Conversely, one might wish to pursue a comparative approach and contrast the treatment of the love between sisters and companions portrayed in "The Death of Beth" with that between the husband and wife in the Chinese memoir, *The Sorrows of Misfortune*.

The various possibilities are enriched by the fact that, although the selections each illustrate a major theme, they usually also relate to more than one topic. "The Death of Beth," for instance, is concerned with the love between two sisters, but it is also the story of how the two face their parting, the ideal of the family in a changing industrial world, and, in the figure of Beth, an ideal of selfless virtue. The discussion questions assist in indicating such connections, and a Topical Table of Contents not only lists each reading under its main area of emphasis but also indicates other, related selections.

This apparatus and structure enable both instructor and student to use the work profitably at a number of levels: readings may be assigned simply to supplement a core text; chronological or topical groups of readings can serve as the bases for reports or classroom discussions; or one or more readings, together with their bibliographies, might serve as the starting point for term papers. The discussion questions raise subjects suitable for student papers or discussions, or even as themes around which the instructor might wish to center classroom presentations. The aim has been to provide the instructor with as powerful a tool as possible, and to offer the student a wide variety of exciting and signficiant expressions of the human spirit.

I acknowledge the valuable assistance and counsel I have received from Steven Drummond in the conception and preparation of these volumes.

I would like to express my appreciation to the following individuals for their advice and suggestions in both the selection of materials and in the preparation of the accompanying apparatus: Professors Daniel Bays and Rose Greaves of the University of Kansas, Professor Albert Hamscher of Kansas State University, Professor Roger Davis of Kearny State College, Professor Fred Krebs of Johnson County Community College. I owe particular thanks to Professors Stanley Chodorow of the University of California, San Diego, and Edward Graham of Michigan State University for their painstaking appraisal of the plan of this work and their many suggestions for its improvement.

I have enjoyed the full support of the editorial staff of Harcourt Brace Jovanovich, Inc., and wish to extend my particular thanks to Paula Bryant, Drake Bush, Eleanor Garner, Rebecca Lytle, Gina Sample, Mandy Van Dusen, and Karl Yambert for their assistance, encouragement, and forbearance.

LYNN H. NELSON
University of Kansas

Table of Contents

Preface   v

Topical Table of Contents   xi

PART I   The Early Modern World: A.D. 1600 to 1789   **1–180**

The Adventures of a Simpleton   **7**

    The Adventures of a Simpleton   9
    From Hans Jacob Christoffel von Grimmelshausen, *The Adventures of a Simpleton* (London: William Heinemann, 1912).

Love's the Best Doctor   **23**

    Love's the Best Doctor   25
    From Molière, *Molière: Five Plays*, trans. John Wood (New York: Penguin Books, 1960).

The Treasury of Loyal Retainers   **43**

    Yuranosuke at His Revels   45
    From Takeda Izumo et al., *Chushingura: The Treasury of Loyal Retainers, A Puppet Play*, trans. Donald Keene (New York: Columbia University Press, 1971).

The Scholars   **60**

    The Scholars   61
    From Wu Ching-tzu, *The Scholars*, trans. Yang Hsien-yi and Gladys Yang (New York: Universal Library, 1972).

Speeches of Minavavana and Pontiac   **83**

    Speeches of Minavavana and Pontiac   85
    From Francis Parkman, *The Conspiracy of Pontiac and the Indian Wars After the Conquest of Canada* (2 Vols.: Boston, MA: Little, Brown and Co., 1898).

Candide   **89**

    Candide   91
    From Voltaire, *Candide*, trans. Richard Aldington, in *The Portable Voltaire*, ed. Ben Ray Redman (New York: Viking Press, 1968).

The Sufferings of Young Werther   **119**

    The Sufferings of Young Werther   121
    From Johann Wolfgang von Goethe, *The Sufferings of Young Werther*, trans. Harry Steinhauer (New York: W. W. Norton, 1970).

The Interesting Narrative of the Life of Olaudah Equiano   130

    The Narrative of Olaudah Equiano   131

    From Oladuah Equiano, *The Interesting Narrative of the Life of Olaudah Equiano*, in *Three Black Writers in Eighteenth-Century England*, ed. Francis Adams and Barry Sanders (Belmont, CA: Wadsworth, 1971).

The Dream of the Red Chamber   140

    The Dream of the Red Chamber   142

    From Tsao Hsueh-ch'in, *The Dream of the Red Chamber*, trans. Chi-chen Wang (Garden City, NY: Doubleday, 1958).

Robespierre's Speech of 17 Pluviôse   158

    Speech of 17 Pluviôse   160

    From *The Ninth of Thermidor: The Fall of Robespierre*, ed. Richard T. Bienvenu (New York: Oxford University Press, 1968).

Discussion Questions   177

PART II   Industrialism and Democracy: 1789 to 1914   181–340

An Essay on the Principle of Population   187

    An Essay on Population   189

    From Thomas Robert Malthus, *An Essay on the Principle of Population*, ed. Philip Appleman (New York: W. W. Norton, 1976).

The Sorrows of Misfortune   208

    The Sorrows of Misfortune   210

    From Shen Fu, *Six Records of a Floating Life*, trans. Leonard Pratt and Chiang Su-hui (New York: Penguin Books, 1983).

The Tale of Kieu   215

    The Tale of Kieu   217

    From Nguyên Du, *The Tale of Kieu*, trans. Huynh Sanh Thông (bilingual edition: New Haven and London: Yale University Press, 1983).

Democracy in America   231

    Democracy in America   233

    From Alexis de Tocqueville, *Democracy in America*, ed. Richard D. Heffner (New York: New American Library, 1956).

War and Peace   253

    War and Peace   255

    From Leo Tolstoy, *War and Peace*, trans. Ann Dunnigan (New York: New American Library, 1968).

Little Women   282

    The Death of Beth   284
    From Louisa May Alcott, *Little Women* (New York: Bantam Books, 1983).

Commentary on the Commentator   294

    Commentary on the Commentator   296
    From Afghani, *An Islamic Response to Imperialism; Political and Religious Writings of Sayyid Jamal Din "al-Afghani,"* ed. and trans. Nikki R. Keddie (Berkeley, CA: University of California Press, 1983).

Stanley and Livingstone   303

    Stanley and Livingstone   305
    From *The Autobiography of Sir Henry Morton Stanley*, ed. Dorothy Stanley (New York: Houghton Mifflin, 1909).

The Gaucho: Martín Fierro   317

    Martín Fierro   319
    From José Hernández, *Martín Fierro*, trans. C. E. Ward (Albany, NY: State University of New York, 1967).

Wounded Knee   327

    Wounded Knee   329
    From John G. Neihardt, *Black Elk Speaks* (Lincoln, NE: University of Nebraska Press, 1961).

Discussion Questions   338

PART III   The Twentieth Century: 1914 to the Present   341–490

Sons and Lovers   347

    Sons and Lovers   348
    From D. H. Lawrence, *Sons and Lovers* (New York: Penguin Books, 1983).

Statement in the Great Trial of 1922   359

    Statement in the Great Trial of 1922   361
    From Mohandas K. Gandhi, *The Selected Works of Mahatma Gandhi: Volume VI*, ed. Shriman Narayan (Ahmedabad-14, India: Navajivan Printing House, 1968).

All Quiet on the Western Front   367

    All Quiet on the Western Front   369
    From Erich Maria Remarque, *All Quiet on the Western Front*, trans. A. W. Wheen (New York: Ballantine Books, 1984).

Brave New World   382

    Brave New World   384
    From Aldous Huxley, *Brave New World* (New York: Harper and Row, 1969).

Guests of the Nation   410

Guests of the Nation   411
From Frank O'Connor, *Frank O'Connor: Collected Stories* (New York: Alfred A. Knopf, 1981).

The Night of a Thousand Suicides   422

The Night of a Thousand Suicides   423
From Teruhiko Asado, *The Night of a Thousand Suicides*, trans. Ray Cowan (New York: St. Martin's Press, 1972).

On the People's Democratic Dictatorship   436

On the People's Democratic Dictatorship   438
From Mao Tse-tung, *Selected Works of Mao Tse-tung* (5 vols.: Peking: Foreign Languages Press, 1969).

Fifteen Poems Out of Africa   451

Fifteen Poems Out of Africa   454
From *The Heritage of African Poetry*, ed. Isidore Okpewho (Essex, UK: Longman Group, 1985).

The Nobel Prize Address of Mother Teresa of Calcutta   467

The Nobel Prize Address   469
From Robert Serrou, *Teresa of Calcutta* (New York: McGraw-Hill, 1980).

One Earth   477

One Earth   479
From Octavio Paz, *One Earth, Four or Five Worlds: Reflections on Contemporary History*, trans. Helen R. Lane (New York: Harcourt Brace Jovanovich, 1985).

Discussion Questions   488

Topical Table of Contents

Each reading is listed here under its major topical area. Related Selections are readings not primarily focused on the major topic but relevant to it.

LOVE

Love's the Best Doctor   25
The Dream of the Red Chamber   142
The Tale of Kieu   217
The Death of Beth   284
Sons and Lovers   348
Fifteen Poems Out of Africa   454

Related Selections

Yuranosuke at His Revels   45
Candide   91
The Sufferings of Young Werther   121
The Sorrows of Misfortune   210
Stanley and Livingstone   305
All Quiet on the Western Front   369
Brave New World   384
The Nobel Prize Address of Mother Teresa of Calcutta   469

DEATH

Yuranosuke at His Revels   45
The Sufferings of Young Werther   121
An Essay on Population   189
The Sorrows of Misfortune   210
Guests of the Nation   411
The Night of a Thousand Suicides   423

Related Selections

The Scholars   61
Candide   91
War and Peace   255
Wounded Knee   329
Sons and Lovers   348
All Quiet on the Western Front   369
Brave New World   384
The Nobel Prize Address of Mother Teresa of Calcutta   469

THE GOOD LIFE

Candide   91
The Narrative of Olaudah Equiano   132
Democracy in America   233
Commentary on the Commentator   296
Brave New World   384
On the People's Democratic Dictatorship   438

Related Selections

The Adventures of a Simpleton   9
The Scholars   61
Speeches of Minavavana and Pontiac   85
Speech of 17 Pluviôse   160
An Essay on Population   189
Commentary on the Commentator   296
Martín Fierro   319

WAR AND PEACE

The Adventures of a Simpleton   9
Speeches of Minavavana and Pontiac   85
War and Peace   255
Wounded Knee   329
All Quiet on the Western Front   369
One Earth   479

Related Selections

Candide   91
The Narrative of Olaudah Equiano   132
Speech of 17 Pluviôse   160
An Essay on Population   189
Guests of the Nation   411
The Night of a Thousand Suicides   423

VIRTUE AND THE INDIVIDUAL

The Scholars   61
Speech of 17 Pluviôse   160
Stanley and Livingstone   305
Martín Fierro   319
Statement in the Great Trial of 1922   361
The Nobel Prize Address of Mother Teresa of Calcutta   469

Related Selections

The Adventures of a Simpleton   9
Yuranosuke at His Revels   45
Candide   91

The Narrative of Olaudah Equiano   132
The Tale of Kieu   217
Democracy in America   233
War and Peace   255
The Death of Beth   284
Commentary on the Commentator   296
All Quiet on the Western Front   369
Brave New World   384
Guests of the Nation   411
The Night of a Thousand Suicides   423

PART I

THE EARLY MODERN WORLD

A.D. 1600 to 1789

	1600	
EUROPE	1600 British East India Company founded 1604 William Shakespeare: *Othello* 1618–1648 Thirty Years' War 1620 Francis Bacon: *New Organon* 1624–1642 Richelieu 1632 Galileo: *Dialogue Concerning the Two Chief World Systems* 1637 Descartes: *Discourse on Method*	1651 Thomas Hobbes: *Leviathan* 1660 THE ADVENTURES OF A SIMPLETON 1665 Molière: LOVE'S THE BEST DOCTOR 1685–1750 Johann Sebastian Bach 1687 Newton's Law of Gravitation 1690 John Locke: *An Essay Concerning Human Understanding*
SOUTHWEST ASIA AND AFRICA	ca. 1600 Fall of Kongo 1626 First French settlements on Madagascar 1638 Turks take Baghdad 1640 Mulla Sadra: *The Wisdom of the Throne* 1601–1677 Mirza Muhammad Ali Sa'ib, Persian poet	1650 Ali Bey becomes Bey of Tunis 1652 Dutch found Cape Colony 1660 Rise of the Bambasa kingdoms 1662 Portugal cedes Tangier to England 1671 Royal African Company founded 1683 Ottoman seige of Vienna
SOUTH AND SOUTHEAST ASIA	1526–1739 Mughal Empire 1532–1623 Tulsi Das, Indian poet 1612 English defeat Portuguese fleet at Surat 1619 Dutch colonize Indonesia 1641 Dutch capture Malacca from Portuguese	1653 Taj Mahal completed r. 1658–1707 Aurangzeb, Mughal ruler 1669 Persecution of Hindus in India 1690 British found Calcutta
EAST ASIA	1600–1868 Tokugawa shogunate, Japan 1610–1695 Huang Tsung-asi: *Plan for the Prince* 1628–1700 Tokugawa Mitsukuni: *The Great History of Japan* 1630 Japan closed to foreigners 1644–1911 Qing dynasty, China	1653–1724 Chikamatsu, Japanese playwright 1662–1722 Kang Xi, Manchu emperor 1672–1734 Kao Ch'i-p'ei, Manchu painter ca. 1675–1725 Golden Age of Edo urban culture, Japan 1683 Bashō: *The Hollow Chestnuts*
THE AMERICAS AND THE PACIFIC	1607 Jamestown settled 1608 Quebec founded 1620 Puritans land in Massachusetts 1636 Harvard College founded 1649 Commercial Company of Brazil founded 1650 *The Works of Anne Bradstreet in Prose and Verse*	1664 British seize New Amsterdam 1673 Father Marquette and Joliet reach the Mississippi 1675–1676 King Philip's War 1679–1683 Explorations of La Salle 1689–1697 King William's War 1692 College of William and Mary chartered in Virginia

1700

EUROPE

1701–1714 War of Spanish Succession
1715–1774 Louis XV
1734 Alexander Pope: *Essay on Man*
1739–1809 Thomas Paine
1740–1780 Maria Theresa
1740–1786 Frederick the Great
1748 Montesquieu: *The Spirit of Laws*

1756–1763 Seven Years' War
1759 Voltaire: CANDIDE
1774 Goethe: THE SUFFERINGS OF YOUNG WERTHER
1776 Adam Smith: *The Wealth of Nations*
1789 French Revolution begins
1793 Robespierre: SPEECH OF 17 PLUVIÔSE

SOUTHWEST ASIA AND AFRICA

ca. 1700 Rise of Ahanti, West Africa
1711 Mir Vais establishes Afghan state
1715 French take Island of Mauritius
1729 *Letters of the Late Ignatius Sancho*
1737–1747 Nadir Shah, Decline of Safavid Empire

r. 1757–1789 Sidi Mohammed of Morocco
1776 Rise of Tukulor power in West Africa
1787 British acquire Sierra Leone
1787 Ottobah Cugoano: *Thoughts and Sentiments on the Evil and Wicked Traffic of Slavery*
1789 THE INTERESTING NARRATIVE OF OLAUDAH EQUIANO

SOUTH AND SOUTHEAST ASIA

ca. 1700 Sikhs form militant order
1739 Maratha northward expansion checked by Persians
1748 Treaty of Aix-la-Chapelle restores Madras to England

1751 French control Deccan
1757 Battle of Plassey
1772–1883 Raja Ram Mohan Roy, Father of Modern India
1782 Rama I founds new Siamese dynasty
1786–1793 Cornwallis in Bengal

EAST ASIA

1700 300,000 Christian converts in China
1716–1797 Yüan Mei, Chinese poet
1723–1777 Tai Chen, Chinese scholar
r. 1736–1795 Emperor Qian Long
1748 THE TREASURY OF LOYAL RETAINERS

1750 Wu Ching-tzu: THE SCHOLARS
1751 China invades Tibet
1754–1806 Kitigawa Utamaro, Japanese artist
1792 Tsao Hsueh-chin: DREAM OF THE RED CHAMBER

THE AMERICAS AND THE PACIFIC

1701 Detroit founded by Cadillac
1728 Bering explores Alaska
1732 Ben Franklin: *Poor Richard's Almanac*
1743–1826 Thomas Jefferson
1750 Treaty of Madrid between Spain and Portugal

1756–1763 French and Indian War
1763 SPEECHES OF MINAVAVANA AND PONTIAC
1768–1780 Cook explores Pacific Ocean
1776–1783 American Revolution
1783–1830 Simón Bolívar
1788 *The Federalist Papers*

By 1600, their superiority in weaponry, metallurgy, and navigation had allowed the Europeans to dominate the world's sea-lanes. Access to raw materials and the opening of new markets to absorb European production produced great changes in the course of the next two centuries. The European standard of living improved markedly, population grew, and greatly increased wealth was available for internal investment. However, much of this new wealth was squandered in warfare among the various European states. A series of savage religious conflicts culminated in the Thirty Years' War, in which virtually all of the European powers took part and in which a third of the population of Germany died. *The Adventures of a Simpleton* suggests the sense of futility aroused by such destructive and pointless conflict. Once the war ended, as much from general exhaustion as from any other factor, it was not until the twentieth century that the Europeans again allowed themselves to be drawn into such unrestricted internal conflict.

There ensued a general relaxation of tension in which it was possible to question established institutions and accepted truths in a way hitherto impossible. The career of the French dramatist Molière is an example of this new spirit. *Love's the Best Doctor* shows Molière holding the medical profession and their traditional practices up to ridicule. The greatest advances, however, were made in mathematics and astronomy, where the realization that the universe appeared to operate in accordance with discoverable, objective laws stimulated the intellectual movement known as the Enlightenment. Enlightenment thinkers proceeded on the assumption that a rational basis existed for all phenomena, and that human society could be perfected by discovering these underlying laws and by shaping institutions to work in harmony with them. During this era, often called the Old Regime, the ideals of rationality, proportion, and measure permeated music, art, literature, and even statecraft. Of course, the ideal and the actual were often at variance, as Voltaire demonstrates with scathing sarcasm in *Candide*.

Near the close of the nineteenth century, the rationalism of the Enlightenment was further challenged by a new intellectual movement known as Romanticism, which generally emphasized the importance of the human will as opposed to the abstract and mechanical laws favored by Enlightenment thinkers. Goethe's *The Sufferings of Young Werther* is an early expression of the Romantic spirit, showing the individual's hopeless but inescapable struggle against formal social constraints. This emphasis upon an active human will that determines events and shapes institutions encouraged increasing demands for greater popular participation in government and society. In Europe itself, this movement was exemplified in the French Revolution, and Robespierre's "Speech of 17 Pluviôse" provides a passionate defense of this new democratic ideal.

Although Europe's economic strength and military superiority grew throughout the period 1600–1789, the power of the established civilizations of the East generally enabled them to define the terms upon which contact with the West was to occur and the degree to which Western influences would be tolerated. Japan, for instance, rejected Western influence almost entirely; *The Treasury of Loyal Retainers* illustrates how feudal practices and attitudes persisted in Japan until a late date. For its part, China, still the richest and most populous nation in the world, restricted the Western presence to a few seaports and limited European imports and influences to those least likely to affect its traditional pattern of life. *The Scholars* and *The Dream of the Red Chamber* show the persistence of a complex traditional society virtually oblivious of the West.

Islamic lands enjoyed relative prosperity during this period. Though the French and British established trading stations along the coast of India and deprived the Muslims of much of the profits they had once gained from Indian Ocean commerce, this had relatively little effect on the Muslim world. The Muslims turned their attention inland and inward, and contrived to reconcile some of the conflicts that had troubled them for so long. This period saw the golden age of the Mughal empire, with the construction of the city of Isfahan, the former magnificent capital of Iran, and monuments such as the Taj Majal, and the abatement of the long struggle between Persia and the Ottoman Empire. With great wealth, a new spiritual dynamism, and internal peace, Islam ignored the challenge of Western expansion and growth and concentrated for the time upon its own affairs.

Among the European powers themselves, the long dominance of Spain and Portugal in commerce and colonization was successfully challenged in a series of wars for empire. Great Britain, France, and the Netherlands emerged as the new colonial powers, transforming the very basis of colonial economics in the process. Instead of simply searching for precious metals, as had the *conquistadores*, the new imperial powers constructed elaborate commercial networks based on the production and exchange of a bewildering variety of commodities. Moreover, these networks were administered according to increasingly sophisticated and standardized business procedures. These expanding colonial systems forcibly absorbed many peoples who had little desire to become part of a world dominated by the Western way of life. *The Interesting Narrative of the Life of Olaudah Equiano* illustrates how the traditional patterns of native life in Africa—even beyond the direct reach of the Europeans—were influenced by the colonial powers' need for additional manpower. Moreover, the "Speeches of Minavavana and Pontiac" provide ominous signs that the Europeans had little interest in protecting or preserving the traditional societies they encountered.

In many ways, the West was in turmoil by the end of the period. Democratic revolutions threatened the relative peace and stability that had characterized the Old Regime. Moreover, the same democratic sentiments spread to European colonies and challenged the philosophy that colonies existed solely for the benefit of the motherland. The outlooks of the Enlightenment and Romanticism were in conflict, and the intellectual unity that had for some time marked European thought and art was broken. And yet, the disruption was that which normally accompanies progress, not that which is the symptom of decay. The Scientific Revolution of the seventeenth century had continued into the eighteenth, stimulating novel applications of many of the new discoveries being made. Advances in machinery, particularly those making mass production possible, together with the utilization of fossil fuels for energy production, laid the foundation for the Industrial Revolution, which would increase the wealth and power of the West to an unprecedented degree.

The Adventures of a Simpleton

Among the consequences of the Protestant Reformation and the development of the centralized state were waves of religio-political conflict that swept over Europe during the sixteenth and seventeenth centuries. Nowhere were the effects of this strife felt more deeply than among the various German states. The region was politically divided, and religious hostilities already ran deep. A revolt in Bohemia in 1618 soon blossomed into a full-scale confrontation between the independent Protestant states of the area on the one hand, and the Catholic Holy Roman Emperor on the other. The other European powers soon chose sides, and eventually a continental war was in progress on German soil, a war that would last until 1648 and enter the history books as the Thirty Years' War.

None of the combatants had either the ability or the desire to maintain permanent national armies in the field; the fighting was carried out instead largely by mercenary bands. These bodies of troops maintained loyalty only to their commanders, replenished their numbers by forced recruitment, lived off the land, and gained their pay primarily through plunder and booty. Hunger drove them to inhuman acts of cruelty, and little in the way of compassion restrained them. The result of the thirty years of conflict was a compromise peace among the great powers and the almost complete devastation of German-speaking lands. The population of the region dropped from thirty to twenty million during the period, many more dying from famine and plague than of wounds. The wealth of the land was dissipated, and the populace suffered a psychological trauma that impeded the course of German development for many years.

Hans Jacob Christoffel von Grimmelshausen (1621?–1676), the author of this selection, was both a chronicler and a product of this period of turmoil. Kidnapped by soldiers at about the age of 14, he fought for various of the opposing armies until peace was declared

From Hans Jacob Christoffel von Grimmelshausen, *The Adventures of a Simpleton* (London: William Heinemann, 1912), pp. 54–61, 202–210.

in 1648. He then moved from job to job until he finally secured a minor official post in a small town. The war had left him little time for education, but he frequented libraries when he could and read avidly. He was particularly captivated by German translations of Spanish picaresque novels. The themes of such novels—the misadventures of young men thrown on their own in a cruel, often immoral, but always exciting world—naturally appealed to him, and he undertook to write a German novel in the picaresque mode. His own career provided ample material for his account, and his semi-biographical work, *The Adventures of a Simpleton*, achieved an immediate and enduring popularity. The work not only provides a firsthand view of German life during the Thirty Years' War, it remains the only German novel of the seventeenth century with significant appeal to a modern audience.

Driven from his home by marauding soldiers, the young hero flees to the woods and lives there with a pious hermit. When this refuge is also overrun, he joins the Swedish Protestant army and learns to make his way in the world. He is captured by imperial troops and eventually becomes an outstanding soldier in the Catholic forces. In the following years, he has many adventures. He gains and loses a number of fortunes, has several love affairs, and at various times tries his hand at farming, banditry, and international travel. Eventually, however, he finds his way back to the hermitage in the Black Forest from which he had set out many years before. Renouncing the temptations and uncertainties of the world, he resolves to become a hermit himself and to devote his life to seeking God.

The following selections present Grimmelshausen's views on war and peace. In the first selection, after the soldiers who had raided his hermitage depart, the Simpleton falls asleep and dreams of a tree that symbolizes how the war has taken root in Germany. This is a particularly pictorial passage and must be read with an eye to visualizing what the author is describing. The reading public of the time was particularly fond of "emblems," allegorical pictures, sometimes quite elaborate, often symbolizing quite complex thoughts. Such emblems were generally found as frontispieces for books and provided a visual key to the main ideas of the work. Grimmelshausen clearly pictured an emblem when writing this passage, an emblem that represented not only the misery that the war was causing but also the degree to which war had become the established order of life in Germany.

The Simpleton has become a veteran soldier and the leader of a small body of troops by the time the second selection begins. In an ambush, he captures a madman who believes himself to be the god Jupiter, come down to earth to put an end to this madness. Under the Simpleton's amused prodding, "Jupiter" proclaims that he will create a German hero who will bring peace and plenty to Germany, punishing the wicked and uniting all factions in fruitful harmony. The soldiers find his idealistic ravings, full of gods, goddesses, and learned allusions, quite laughable, but none sees the terrible yearning for peace and justice that lies behind his words or asks what may have driven the old man mad. They have adapted to their situation and do not quite understand what peace is.

The two selections present Grimmelshausen's view of a world turned upside down. War is a way of life, rooted in the soil, and peace is nothing but the impossible antics of a lunatic. The war did come to an end, but largely as a result of the attrition and exhaustion of the combatants. Looking back, Grimmelshausen could see nothing that redounded to the benefit or credit of the participants. And yet, *The Adventures of a Simpleton* is not a pessimistic work. The Simpleton survives all the carnage of the period and, although he finally retires from the world and its ways, he looks back upon it as a terrible, yet wonderful place.

Questions

1. In the dream of the tree, what people benefit from the war? Who suffers?

2. Does the dream of the tree provide any clue as to why the war has endured so long?

3. Aside from the supernatural powers of his German hero, what is basically unsound with "Jupiter's" plan for peace?

THE ADVENTURES OF A SIMPLETON

Now when I came home I found that my fireplace and all my poor furniture, together with my store of provisions, which I had grown during the summer in my garden and had kept for the coming winter, were all gone. "And whither now?" thought I. And then first did need teach me heartily to pray: and I must summon all my small wits together, to devise what I should do. But as my knowledge of the world was both small and evil, I could come to no proper conclusion, only that 'twas best to commend myself to God and to put my whole confidence in Him: for otherwise I must perish. And besides all this those things which I had heard and seen that day lay heavy on my mind: and I pondered not so much upon my food and my sustenance as upon the enmity which there is ever between soldiers and peasants. Yet could my foolish mind come to no other conclusion than this—that there must of a surety be two races of men in the world, and not one only, descended from Adam, but two, wild and tame, like other unreasoning beasts, and therefore pursuing one another so cruelly.

With such thoughts I fell asleep, for mere misery and cold, with a hungry stomach. Then it seemed to me, as if in a dream, that all the trees which stood round my dwelling suddenly changed and took on another appearance: for on every tree-top sat a trooper, and the trunks were garnished, in place of leaves, with all manner of folk. Of these, some had long lances, others musquets, hangers,[1] halberts,[2] flags, and some drums and fifes. Now this was merry to see, for all was neatly distributed and each according to his rank. The roots, moreover, were made up of folk of little worth, as mechanics and labourers, mostly, however, peasants and the like; and these nevertheless gave its strength to the tree and renewed the same when it was lost: yea more, they repaired the loss of any fallen leaves from among themselves to their own great damage: and all the time they lamented over them that sat on the tree, and that with good reason, for the whole weight of the tree lay upon them and pressed them so that all the money was squeezed out of their pockets, yea, though it was behind seven locks and keys: but if the money would not out, then did the commissaries so handle them with rods (which thing they call military execution) that sighs came from their heart, tears from their eyes, blood from their nails, and the marrow from their bones. Yet among these were some whom men call light o' heart; and these made but little ado, took all with a shrug, and in the midst of their torment had, in place of comfort, mockery for every turn.

So must the roots of these trees suffer and endure toil and misery in the midst of trouble and complaint, and those upon the lower boughs in yet greater hardship: yet were these last mostly merrier than the first named, yea and moreover, insolent and swaggering, and for the most part godless folk, and for the roots a heavy unbearable burden at all times. And this was the rhyme upon them:

> "Hunger and thirst, and cold and heat,
> and work and woe, and all we meet;
> And deeds of blood and deeds of shame,
> all may ye put to the landsknecht's[3] name."

Which rhymes were the less like to be lyingly invented in that they answered to the facts. For gluttony and drunkenness, hunger and thirst, wenching and dicing and playing, riot and roaring, murdering and being murdered, slaying and being slain, torturing and being tortured, hunting and being hunted, harrying and being harried, robbing and being robbed, frighting and being frighted, causing trouble and suffering trouble, beating and being beaten: in a word, hurting and harming, and in turn being hurt and harmed—this was their whole life. And in this career they let nothing hinder

---

[1] Small swords.
[2] Long-handled battle-axes with spear tips; also *halberds*.
[3] Common soldier's.

them: neither winter nor summer, snow nor ice, heat nor cold, rain nor wind, hill nor dale, wet nor dry; ditches, mountain-passes, ramparts and walls, fire and water, were all the same to them. Father nor mother, sister nor brother, no, nor the danger to their own bodies, souls, and consciences, nor even loss of life and of heaven itself, or aught else that can be named, will ever stand in their way, for ever they toil and moil at their own strange work, till at last, little by little, in battles, sieges, attacks, campaigns, yea, and in their winter quarters too (which are the soldiers' earthly paradise, if they can but happen upon fat peasants) they perish, they die, they rot and consume away, save but a few, who in their old age, unless they have been right thrifty reivers and robbers, do furnish us with the best of all beggars and vagabonds.

Next above these hard-worked folks sat old henroost-robbers, who, after some years and much peril of their lives, had climbed up the lowest branches and clung to them, and so far had had the luck to escape death. Now these looked more serious, and somewhat more dignified than the lowest, in that they were a degree higher ascended: yet above them were some yet higher, who had yet loftier imaginings because they had to command the very lowest. And these people did call coat-beaters, because they were wont to dust the jackets of the poor pikemen, and to give the musketeers oil enough to grease their barrels with.

Just above these the trunk of the tree had an interval or stop, which was a smooth place without branches, greased with all manner of ointments and curious soap of disfavour, so that no man save of noble birth could scale it, in spite of courage and skill and knowledge, God knows how clever he might be. For 'twas polished as smooth as a marble pillar or a steel mirror. Just over that smooth spot sat they with the flags: and of these some were young, some pretty well in years: the young folk their kinsmen had raised so far: the older people had either mounted on a silver ladder which is called the Bribery Backstairs or else on a step which Fortune, for want of a better client, had left for them. A little further up sat higher folk, and these had also their toil and care and annoyance: yet had they this advantage, that they could fill their pokes[4] with the fattest slices which they could cut out of the roots, and that with a knife which they called "War-contribution." And these were at their best and happiest when there came a commissary-bird flying overhead, and shook out a whole panfull of gold over the tree to cheer them: for of that they caught as much as they could, and let but little or nothing at all fall to the lowest branches: and so of these last more died of hunger than of the enemy's attacks, from which danger those placed above seemed to be free. Therefore was there a perpetual climbing and swarming going on on those trees; for each would needs sit in those highest

---

[4] Sacks.

and happiest places: yet were there some idle, worthless rascals, not worth their commissariat-bread, who troubled themselves little about higher places, and only did their duty. So the lowest, being ambitious, hoped for the fall of the highest, that they might sit in their place, and if it happened to one among ten thousand of them that he got so far, yet would such good luck come to him only in his miserable old age when he was more fit to sit in the chimney-corner and roast apples than to meet the foe in the field. And if any man dealt honestly and carried himself well, yet was he ever envied by others, and perchance by reason of some unlucky chance of war deprived both of office and of life. And nowhere was this more grievous than at the before-mentioned smooth place on the tree: for there an officer who had had a good sergeant or corporal under him must lose him, however unwillingly, because he was now made an ensign. And for that reason they would take, in place of old soldiers, inkslingers, footmen, overgrown pages, poor noblemen, and at times poor relations, tramps and vagabonds. And these took the very bread out of the mouths of those that had deserved it, and forthwith were made Ensigns.

All this vexed a sergeant so much that he began loudly to complain: whereupon one Nobilis answered him: "Knowst thou not that at all times our rulers have appointed to the highest offices in time of war those of noble birth as being fittest therefore. For greybeards defeat no foe: were it so, one could send a flock of goats for that employ: We say:

"Choose out a bull that's young and strong to lead and keep the herd,
For though the veteran be good, the young must be preferred.
So let the herdsman trust to him, full young though he appears:
'Tis but a saw, and 'tis no law, that wisdom comes with years."

"Tell me," says he, "thou old cripple, "is't not true that nobly born officers be better respected by the soldiery than they that before-time have been but servants? And what discipline in war can ye find where no respect is? Must not a general trust a gentleman more than a peasant lad that had run away from his father at the plough-tail and so done his own parents no good service? For a proper gentleman, rather than bring reproach upon his family by treason or desertion or the like, will sooner die with honour. And so 'tis right the gentles should have the first place. So doth Joannes de Platea plainly lay it down that in furnishing of offices the preference should ever be given to the nobility, and these properly set before the commons. Such usage is to be found in all codes of laws, and is, moreover, confirmed in Holy Writ: for 'happy is the land whose king is of noble family,' saith Sirach[5] in his tenth chapter:

---

[5] Author of the Apocryphal book of Ecclesiasticus.

Frontispiece, first edition of The Adventures of a Simpleton.

which is a noble testimony to the preference belonging to gentle birth. And even if one of your kidney[6] be a good soldier enough that can smell powder and play his part well in every venture, yet is he not therefore capable of command of others: which quality is natural to gentlemen, or at least customary to them from their youth up. And so saith Seneca, 'A hero's soul hath this property, that 'tis ever alert in search of honour: and no lofty spirit hath

[6] One of your kind.

pleasure in small and unworthy things.' Moreover, the nobles have more means to furnish their inferior officers with money and to procure recruits for their weak companies than a peasant. And so to follow the common proverb, it were not well to put the boor above the gentleman; yea, and the boors would soon become too high-minded if they be made lords straightway; for men say:

" 'Where will ye find a sharper sword,
than peasant churl that's made a lord?'

"Now had the peasants, by reason of long and respectable custom, possessed all offices in war and elsewhere, of a surety they would have let no gentleman into such. Yea, and besides, though ye soldiers of Fortune, as ye call yourselves, be often willingly helped to raise yourselves to higher ranks, yet ye are commonly so worn out that when they try you and would find you a better place, they must hesitate to promote you; for the heat of your youth is cooled down and your only thought is how ye can tend and care for your sick bodies which, by reason of much hardships, be crippled and of little use for war: yea, and a young dog is better for hunting than an old lion."

Then answered the old sergeant, "And what fool would be a soldier, if he might not hope by his good conduct to be promoted, and so rewarded for faithful service? Devil take such a war as that! For so 'tis all the same whether a man behave himself well or ill! Often did I hear our old colonel say he wanted no soldier in his regiment that had not the firm intention to become a general by his good conduct. And all the world must acknowledge that 'tis those nations which promote common soldiers, that are good soldiers too, that win victories, as may be seen in the case of the Turks and Persians; so says the verse

" 'Thy lamp is bright: yet feed it well with oil:
an thou dost not the flame sinks down and dies.
So by rewards repay the soldier's toil,
for service brave demands its pay likewise.' "

Then answered Nobilis: "If we see brave qualities and in an honest man, we shall not overlook them: for at this very time see how many there be who from the plough, from the needle, from shoemaking, and from shepherding have done well by themselves, and by such bravery have raised themselves up far above the poorer nobility to the ranks of counts and barons. Who was the Imperialist John de Werth? Who was the Swede Stalhans? Who were the Hessians, Little Jakob and St. André? Of their kind there were many yet well known whom I, for brevity's sake, forbear to mention. So is it nothing new in the present time, nor will it be otherwise in the future, that honest men attain by war to great honours, as happened also among the ancients. Tamburlaine became a mighty king and the terror of the whole world, which was before but a swineherd: Agathocles, King of Sicily, was son of a potter; Emperor Valentinian's father was a ropemaker; Maurice the Cappadocian, a slave, was emperor after Tiberius II.; Justin, that reigned before Justinian, was before he was emperor a swineherd; Hugh Capet, a butcher's son, was afterward King of France; Pizarro likewise a swineherd, which afterwards was marquess in the West Indies, where he had to weigh out his gold in hundred-weights."

The sergeant answered: "All this sounds fair enough for my purpose: yet well I see that the doors by which we might win to many dignities be shut against us by the nobility. For as soon as he is crept out of his shell, forthwith your nobleman is clapped into such a position as we cannot venture to set our thoughts upon, howbeit we have done more than many a noble who is now appointed a colonel. And just as among the peasants many noble talents perish for want of means to keep a lad at his studies, so many a brave soldier grows old under the weight of a musquet, that more properly deserved a regiment and could have tendered great services to his general."

I cared no longer to listen to this old ass, but grudged him not his complaints, for often he himself had beaten poor soldiers like dogs. I turned again to the trees whereof the whole land was full and saw how they swayed and smote against each other: and the fellows tumbled off them in batches. Now a crack; now a fall. One moment quick, the next dead. In a moment one lost an arm, another a leg, the third his head. And as I looked methought all trees I saw were but one tree, at whose top sat the war-god Mars, and which covered with its branches all Europe. It seemed to me this tree could have overshadowed the whole world: but because it was blown about by envy and hate, by suspicion and unfairness, by pride and haughtiness and avarice, and other such fair virtues, as by bitter north winds, therefore it seemed thin and transparent: for which reason one had writ on its trunk these rhymes:

> *"The holmoak[7] by the wind beset and brought to ruin,*
> *Breaks its own branches down and proves its own undoing.*
> *By civil war within and brothers' deadly feud*
> *All's topsy-turvy turned and misery hath ensued."*

By the mighty roaring of these cruel winds and the noise of the breaking of the tree itself I was awoke from my sleep, and found myself alone in my hut.

---

[7] Evergreen oak of southern Europe.

Without a home or food, the Simpleton joins the nearest army. Although badly treated at first, he learns to make his way in the world. He takes up the soldier's trade and, a few years later, has become a seasoned veteran and the leader of a small unit.

Now it happened that I lay with twenty-five musquets not far from Dorsten and waited for a convoy that should come to the town: and as was my wont, I stood sentry myself as being near the enemy. To me there came a man all alone, very well dressed and flourishing a cane he had in his hand in strange wise: nor could I understand aught he said but this, "Once for all will I punish the world, that will not render me divine honours." From that I guessed this might be some mighty prince that went thus disguised to find out his subjects' ways and works, and now proposed duly to punish the same, as not having found them to his liking. So I thought, "If this man be of the opposite party, it means a good ransom; but if not, thou canst treat him so courteously and so charm away his heart that he shall be profitable to thee all thy life long."

With that I leapt out upon him, presented my gun at him at full-cock, and says I, "Your worship will please to walk before me into yonder wood if he will not be treated as an enemy." So he answered very gravely, "To such treatment my likes are not accustomed": but I pushed him very politely along and, "Your honour," said I, "will not for once refuse to bow to the necessities of the times." So when I had brought him safely to my people in the wood and had set my sentries again, I asked him who he was: to which he answered very haughtily I need not ask that, for I knew already he was a great god. I thought he might perhaps know me, and might be a nobleman of Soest that thus spoke to rally me; for 'tis the custom to jeer at the people of Soest about their great idol with the golden apron: but soon I was aware that instead of a prince I had caught a madman, one that had studied too much and gone mad over poetry: for when he grew a little more acquainted with me he told me plainly he was the great god Jupiter himself.

Now did I heartily wish I had never made this capture: but since I had my fool, there I must needs keep him till we should depart: so, as the time otherwise would have been tedious, I thought I would humour the fellow and make his gifts of use to me; so I said to him, "Now, worshipful Jove, how comes it that thy high divinity thus leaves his heavenly throne and descends to earth? Forgive, O Jupiter, my question, which thou mightest deem one of curiosity: for we be also akin to the heavenly gods and nought but wood-spirits, born of fauns and nymphs, to whom this secret shall ever remain a secret." "I swear to thee by the Styx," answered Jupiter, "thou shouldst not know a word of the secret wert thou not so like to my cup-bearer Ganymede, even wert thou Paris's own son: but for his sake I communicate to thee this, that a great outcry concerning the sins of the world is come up to me through the clouds: upon which 'twas decided in the council of all the gods that I could justly destroy all the world with a flood: but inasmuch as I have always had a special favour to the human race, and moreover at all times shew kindness rather than severity, I am now wandering around to learn for myself the ways and works of men: and though I find all worse than I expected, yet am I not minded to destroy all men at once and without distinction, but to punish only those that deserve punishment and thereafter to bend the remainder to my will."

I must needs laugh, yet checked myself, and said, "Alas, Jupiter, thy toil and trouble will be, I fear, all in vain unless thou punish the world with water, as before, or with fire: for if thou sendest a war, thither run together all vile and abandoned rogues that do but torment peaceable and pious men. An thou sendest a famine, 'tis but a godsend for the usurers, for then is their corn most valuable: and if thou sendest a pestilence, then the greedy and all the rest of mankind do find their account, for then do they inherit much. So must thou destroy the whole world root and branch, if thou wilt punish at all."

So Jupiter answered, "Thou speakest of the matter like a mere man, as if thou didst not know that 'tis possible for us gods so to manage things that only the wicked shall be punished and the good saved: I will raise up a German hero that shall accomplish all with the edge of the sword; he shall destroy all evil men and preserve and exalt the righteous." "Yea," said I, "but such a hero must needs have soldiers, and where soldiers are there is war, and where war is there must the innocent suffer as well as the guilty." "Oho;" says Jupiter, "be ye earthly gods minded like earthly men, that ye can understand so little? For I will send such a hero that he shall have need of no soldiers and yet shall reform the whole world; at his birth I will grant to him a body well formed and stronger than had ever Hercules, adorned to the full with princeliness, wisdom, and understanding: to this shall Venus add so comely a face that he shall excel Narcissus, Adonis, and even my Ganymede: and she shall grant to him, besides his other fine parts, dignity, charm, and presence excelling all, and so make him beloved by all the world, for which cause I will look more kindly upon it in the hour of his birth. Mercury, too, shall endow him with incomparable cleverness, and the inconstant moon shall be to him not harmful but useful, for she shall implant in him an invincible swiftness: Pallas Athene shall rear him on Parnassus, and Vulcan shall, under the influence of Mars, forge for him his weapons, and specially a sword with which he shall conquer the whole world and make an end of all the godless, without the help of a single man as a soldier: for he shall need no assistance. Every town shall tremble at his coming, and every fortress otherwise unconquerable he shall have in his power in the first quarter of an hour: in a word, he shall have the rule over the greatest potentates of the world, and so nobly bear sway over earth and sea that both gods and men shall rejoice thereat."

"Yea," said I, "but how can the destruction of all the godless and rule over the whole world be accomplished without specially great power and a strong arm? O Jupiter, I tell thee plainly I can understand these things less than any mere mortal man." "At that," says Jupiter, "I marvel not: for thou knowest not what power my hero's sword will have; Vulcan shall make it of the same materials of which he doth forge my thunderbolts, and so direct its virtues that my hero, if he do but draw it and wave it in the air, can cut off the heads of a whole armada, though they be hidden behind a mountain or be a whole Swiss mile distant from him, and so the poor devils shall lie there without heads before they know what has befallen them. And when he shall begin his triumphal progress and shall come before a town or a fortress, then shall he use Tamburlaine's vein, and for a sign that he is there for peace and for the furthering of all good shall shew a white flag: then if they come forth to him and are content, 'tis well: if not, then will he draw his sword, and by its virtue, as before described, will hew off the heads of all enchanters and sorceresses throughout the town, and then raise a red flag: then if they be still obstinate, he shall destroy all murderers, usurers, thieves, rogues, adulterers, whores, and knaves in the said manner, and then hoist a black flag: whereupon if those that yet remain in the town refuse to come to him and humbly submit, then shall he destroy the whole town as a stiff-necked and disobedient folk: yet shall he only execute them that have hindered the others, and been the cause that the people would not submit. So shall he go from country to country, and give each town the country that lies around it to rule in peace, and from each town in all Germany choose out two of the wisest and learnedest men to form his parliament, shall reconcile the towns with each other for ever, shall do away all villenage,[8] and also all tolls, excises, interest, taxes, and octrois[9] throughout Germany, and take such order that none shall ever again hear of forced work, watch-duties, contributions, benevolences, war-taxes, and other burdens of the people, but that men shall live happier than in the Elysian fields.[10] And

---

[8] Serfdom.
[9] Commercial privileges.
[10] Paradise.

then," says Jupiter, "will I often assemble all Olympus and come down to visit the Germans, to delight myself among their vines and fig-trees: and there will I set Helicon[11] on their borders and establish the Muses anew thereon: Germany will I bless with all plenty, yea, more than Arabia Felix, Mesopotamia, and the land of Damascus: then will I forswear the Greek language, and only speak German; and, in a word, shew myself so good a German that in the end I shall grant to them, as once I did to the Romans, the rule over all the earth."

"But," said I, "great Jupiter, what will princes and lords say to this, if this future hero so violently take from them their rights and hand them over to the towns? Will they not resist with force, or at least protest against it before gods and men?"

"The hero," answered Jupiter, "will trouble himself little on that score: he will divide all the great into three classes: them which have lived wickedly and set an evil example he will punish together with the commons, for no earthly power can withstand his sword: to the rest he will give the choice whether to stay in the land or not. They that love their fatherland and abide must live like the commons, but the German people's way of living shall then be more plentiful and comfortable than is now the life and household of a king; yea, they shall be one and all like Fabricius, that would not share King Pyrrhus his kingdom because he loved his country and honour and virtue too much: and so much for the second class. But as to the third, which will still be lords and rulers, them will he lead through Hungary and Italy into Moldavia, Wallachia, into Macedonia, Thrace and Greece, yea, over the Hellespont into Asia, and conquer these lands for them, give them as helpers all them that live by war in all Germany, and make them all kings. Then will he take Constantinople in one day, and lay the heads of all Turks that will not be converted and become obedient before their feet: then will he again set up the Roman Empire, and so betake himself again to Germany, and with his lords of Parliament (whom, as I have said, he shall choose in pairs from every city in Germany, and name them the chiefs and fathers of his German Father-land) build a city in the midst of Germany that shall be far greater than Manoah[12] in America, and richer than was Jerusalem in Solomon's time, whose walls shall be as high as the mountains of Tirol and its ditches as broad as the sea between Spain and Africa. And there will he build a temple entirely of diamonds, rubies, emeralds, and sapphires, and in the treasury that he shall there build will he gather together rarities from the whole world out of the gifts that the kings in China and in Persia, the great Mogul in the East Indies, the great Khan of Tartary, Prester John in Africa, and the great Czar in Muscovy will send to him. Yea, the Turkish em-

---

[11] Mountain in Greece; home of Apollo and the Muses.
[12] Legendary city of fabulous riches; also *Manoa*.

peror would be yet more ready to serve him if it were not that my hero will have taken his empire from him and given it as a fief to the Roman emperor."

Then I asked my friend Jupiter what in such case would become of the Christian kings. So he answered, "Those of England, Sweden, and Denmark (because they are of German race and descent), and those of Spain, France, and Portugal (because the Germans of old conquered and ruled in those lands), shall receive their crowns, kingdoms, and incorporated lands in fee as fiefs of the German nation, and then will there be, as in Augustus's time, a perpetual peace between all nations."

Now Jump-i'-th'-field, who also listened to us, had wellnigh enraged Jupiter and spoiled the whole affair; for said he, "Yea, yea; and then 'twill be in Germany as in fairyland, where it rains muscatels[13] and nought else, and where twopenny pies grow in the night like mushrooms: and I too shall have to eat with both cheeks full at once like a thresher, and drink myself blind with Malvoisie."[14] "Yea, truly," said Jupiter, "and that the more because I will curse thee with the undying hunger of Erysichthon,[15] for methinks thou art one of them that do deride my majesty," and to me said he, "I deemed I was among wood-spirits only: but meseems I have chanced upon a Momus[16] or a Zoilus,[17] the most envious creatures in the world. Is one to reveal to such traitors the decrees of heaven and so to cast pearls before swine?" So I saw plainly he would not willingly brook laughter, and therefore kept down mine own as best I could, and "Most gracious Jupiter," said I, "thou wilt not, by reason of a rude forest-god's indiscretion, conceal from thy Ganymede how things are further to happen in Germany." "No, no," said he, "but I command this mocker, who is like to Theon,[18] to bridle his evil tongue in future, lest I turn him to a stone as Mercury did Battus. But do thou confess to me thou art truly my Ganymede, and that my jealous Juno hath driven thee from heaven in my absence." So I promised to tell him all when I should have heard what I desired to know. Thereupon, "Dear Ganymede," says he, "for deny not that thou art he—in those days shall gold-making be as common in Germany as is pot-making now, and every horse-boy shall carry the philosophers' stone about with him." "Yea," said I, "but how can Germany be so long in peace with all these different religions? Will not the opposing clergy urge on their flocks and so hatch another war?" "No, no," says Jupiter, "my hero will know how to meet that difficulty cleverly, and before all things to unite all Christian religions in the world." "O wonderful," said I, "that

---

[13] Raisins.
[14] Sweet wine.
[15] Erysichthon cut down a tree sacred to Demeter and was punished with so great a hunger that he ate himself.
[16] Ridicule personified as a mocking god.
[17] Greek critic of the fourth century B.C.
[18] A common soldier who interrupted the council of Greek leaders in the *Iliad* to carp.

were indeed a great work! How could it come about?" "I will with all my heart reveal it to thee," answered Jupiter, "for after my hero hath made peace for all mankind he will address all the heads of the Christian world both spiritual and temporal, in a most moving speech, and so excellently impress upon them their hitherto most pernicious divisions in belief, that of themselves they will desire a general reconciliation and give over to him the accomplishment of such according to his own great wisdom. Then will he gather together the most skilful, most learned, and most pious theologians of all religions and appoint for them a place, as did once Ptolemy for the seventy-two translators,[19] in a cheerful and yet quiet spot, where one can consider weighty matters undisturbed, and there provide them all with meat and drink and all necessaries, and command them so soon as possible, and yet with the ripest and most careful consideration, first to lay aside the strifes that there be between their religions, and next to set down in writing and with full clearness the right, true, holy Christian religion in accordance with Holy Writ; and with most ancient tradition, the recognised sense of the Fathers. At which time Pluto will sorely scratch his head as fearing the lessening of his kingdom: yea, and will devise all manner of plans and tricks to foist in an 'and,' and if not to stop the whole thing, yet at least to postpone it *sine die*,[20] that is for ever. So will he hint to each theologian of his interest, his order, his peaceful life, his wife and child, and his privileges, and aught else that might sway his inclinations. But my brave hero also will not be idle: he will so long as this council shall last have all the bells in Christendom rung, and so call all Christian people to pray without ceasing to the Almighty, and to ask for the sending of the Spirit of Truth. And if he shall see that one or another doth allow himself to be tempted by Pluto,[21] then will he plague the whole assembly with hunger as in a Roman conclave, and if they yet delay to complete so holy a work, then will he preach them all a sermon through the gallows, or shew them his wonderful sword, and so first with kindness, but at last with severity and threats, bring them to come to the business in hand, and no longer as before to befool the world with their stiff-necked false doctrines. So when unity is arrived at, then will he proclaim a great festival and declare to the whole world this purified religion; and whosoever opposes it, him will he torment with pitch and sulphur or smear that heretic with box-grease and present him to Pluto as a New Year's gift.

Further Readings

The history of Europe in the seventeenth century is covered in the classic account by George N. Clark, *The Seventeenth Century* (Oxford: The Claren-

---

[19] Translators of the Jewish Scriptures into Greek.
[20] Literally, "without day"; (to cease) without setting a date to start again.
[21] Personification of wealth and worldly goods.

don Press, 1929), while the complexities of the Thirty Years' War are clarified by Cicely V. Wedgwood, *The Thirty Years' War* (Garden City, NY: Doubleday, 1961). Geoffrey Palmer, *The Thirty Years' War* (London: Routledge and Kegan Paul, 1984), covers the period 1607–1650 with excellent illustrations and good maps. A small collection of contemporary documents in *Germany in the Thirty Years' War*, edited and translated by Gerhard Benecke (New York: St. Martin's Press, 1979), conveys some of the flavor of the times. *The Last Valley* (1971: ABC) is an excellent film, faithful to historic detail, and an engrossing evocation of that turbulent period. Roy Pascal, *German Literature in the Sixteenth and Seventeenth Centuries: Renaissance, Reformation, Baroque* (London: Cressent Press, 1968) offers a brief but thorough survey of the subject, with a compilation of short biographies and bibliographies of the major authors of this period of German literature. Kenneth Negus, *Grimmelshausen* (New York: Twayne Publishers, Inc., 1974), provides an intelligent introduction to Grimmelshausen's life and works, with special emphasis on the literary qualities and relative artistic merits of his prose works.

Love's the Best Doctor

By the middle of the seventeenth century, France had emerged as the dominant power on the continent of Europe. Although almost bankrupted by its exertions in the Thirty Years' War and troubled by internal revolt, France finally gained the upper hand over its rival, Spain. A series of brilliant ministers quickly restored the nation's finances and succeeded to an unprecedented degree in centralizing political power and social prestige in the royal court. During the reign of Louis XIV (1643–1715), the "Sun King," Paris became the intellectual and cultural capital of Europe, attracting nobles, bureaucrats, intellectuals, and artists eager to cultivate the king's patronage. The immense palace of Versailles, constructed a few miles outside of Paris, is an enduring monument to Louis' power and accomplishments. Under Louis' influence, the nobles of his court developed a code of conduct in which learning and artistic accomplishments were appreciated and encouraged to a degree unparalleled since the Italian Renaissance.

Nowhere was this golden age more evident than in the French theater. Historians have recorded the names of over a hundred playwrights active during the period, among them three of the greatest figures of French drama: the tragedians Pierre Corneille (1606–1684) and Jean Racine (1639–1699), and the comedian Jean-Baptiste Poquelin (1622–1673), better known as Molière. Such a concentration of dramatic genius has rarely been equalled.

Molière was born the son of a prosperous Parisian upholsterer and was provided with an excellent education in Classics and Law. His heart was set upon the theater, however, and as soon as his education was complete, he joined a Paris acting troupe in 1642. The venture was a failure, however. The company went bankrupt, and Molière and his fellows went to the provinces to repair their fortunes.

Slightly adapted from *Selected Comedies* by J. B. Poquelin Molière, Vol. II, translated by Henry Baker and James Miller. J. M. Dent and Sons, Ltd. © 1929, reprinted 1948.

Their tour lasted for thirteen years, during which time Molière perfected his art as both actor and playwright, returning to Paris in 1658 as head of the company. They soon appeared before the king, who saw promise in their comedic abilities, gave them leave to perform, and placed a playhouse at their disposal. Molière's 1659 production of *The Folly of Affectation* (*Les Précieuses ridicules*) marked a new era in French comedy, combining as it did farce, realism, and social satire. With this triumph, his position was established. From this time forward, no form of hypocrisy or affectation was safe from his pen; the supercilious manners of some nobles, the boring behavior of others, religious insincerity, male jealousy, female silliness, academic pedantry, medical pomposity, and middle-class pretension were only some of his targets. Although it was always his intention to ridicule the quality and not the individual, his efforts earned him many enemies, and it was only through royal protection and with many difficulties that he was able to continue his work.

Doctors and medicine were among his favorite marks, and no fewer than four of his plays deal with these themes. *Love's the Best Doctor,* produced in 1665, is among the most delightful of these efforts and is offered here in full. It was written in five days for a royal performance at Versailles. When it was published, Molière asked the reader to remember that it was written for the stage, not as a literary effort. One must keep that in mind, mentally supplying the costumes and the cavorting of the actors, picturing the dancing that formed an important part of the presentation, and imagining the music written by the composer Jean-Baptiste Lully for the performance. Only then can the animation and sheer love of fun that characterized Molière's work be appreciated.

Molière died in 1673, shortly after forcing himself to complete a performance of *The Hypochondriac (Le malade imaginaire).* A comic actor, especially one who had mocked the establishment, had no standing in the eyes of the Church, and Molière was denied burial in consecrated ground. In the dark of night, France's greatest comic genius was placed in an unmarked grave in a plot of ground reserved for suicides and unbaptized infants.

Questions

1. What are the real concerns of the doctors called in by Sganarelle? What are their qualifications?

2. Does anyone in the play act altruistically?

3. Why does Lucinde love Clitandre?

4. Why does Lisette help the lovers?

LOVE'S THE BEST DOCTOR

ACTORS

SGANAREL, *Lucinda's father.*
LUCINDA, *daughter to Sganarel.*
CLITANDER, *in love with Lucinda.*
AMINTA, *neighbour to Sganarel.*
LUCRETIA, *niece to Sganarel.*
LYSETTA, *attendant of Lucinda.*
MR. WILLIAM, *a seller of tapestry.*
MR. JOSSE, *a goldsmith.*
MR. THOMÈS,
MR. FONANDRÈS,
MR. MACROTON,   } *physicians.*
MR. BAHYS,
MR. FILLERIN, *a scrivener.*
CHAMPAGNE, *servant to Sganarel.*
THE OPERATOR.

SCENE: *Paris.*

Act I: Scene I

SGANAREL, AMINTA, LUCRETIA, MR. WILLIAM, MR. JOSSE.

SGANAREL.   What a strange thing is life! And how well may I say with the great philosopher of antiquity, that "He who hath wealth hath warfare"; and that "One misfortune never comes without another." I had but one wife, and she is dead.

MR. WILLIAM.   How many then would you have had?

SGANAREL.   She is dead, friend William; this loss is very grievous to me, and I can't think of it without weeping. I was not mighty well satisfied with her conduct, and we had very often disputes together, but in short death settles all things. She is dead, I lament her. If she was alive we should quarrel. Of all the children that Heaven has given me, it has only left me one daughter, and this daughter is all my trouble; for in short she is in the most dismal melancholy in the world, in a terrible sadness, out of which there is no way of getting her, and the cause of which I can't learn. For my part, I'm out of my wits about it, and have need of good advice on this matter.

MR. JOSSE.   For my part, I look upon finery and dress to be the thing which delights young girls the most; and if I was as you, I'd immediately buy her a fine ornament of diamonds, or rubies, or emeralds.

MR. WILLIAM.   And I, if I were in your place, would buy her a fine suit of hangings of landscape tapestry, or imagery, which I would have put up in her chamber to delight her mind and sight with.

AMINTA. For my part, I would not do so, I would marry her well, and as soon as I could, to the person that they say asked her of you some time ago.

LUCRETIA. Now I think that your daughter is not at all fit for marriage; she's of a complexion too delicate and sickly, and 'tis wilfully sending her quickly into the other world to expose her, in the condition she is, to bring forth children. The world won't at all do for her, and I would advise you to put her in a nunnery, where she'll meet with diversions which will be more to her humour.

SGANAREL. All these advices are certainly admirable. But I find a little too much of self-interest in 'em, and think that you advise mighty well—for yourselves. You are a goldsmith, Mr. Josse, and your advice smells of a man who had a mind to get rid of some of his wares. You sell tapestry, Mr. William, and you seem to have some hangings that incommode you. He whom you are in love with, neighbour, has some inclination they say for my daughter, and you would not be sorry to see her the wife of another. And as for you, my dear niece, 'tis not my design, as 'tis well known, to marry my daughter to any one at all, and I have my reasons for that; but the advice you give me to make her a nun, is the advice of one who could very charitably wish to be my sole heiress. Thus, gentlemen and ladies, though your advices are the best in the world, be pleased to give me leave to follow ne'er a one of 'em.

Scene II

LUCINDA, SGANAREL.

SGANAREL. Oh! here comes my daughter to take the air. She does not see me. She sighs. She lifts up her eyes to heaven. [*To* LUCINDA.] Heaven keep thee! Good-morrow, my dear. Well, what's the matter? How d'ye do? What, always thus sad and melancholy; and won't you tell me what ails you? Come, discover they little heart to me; come, my poor dear, tell, tell, tell thy little thoughts to thy dear little papa. Take courage. Shall I kiss thee? Come. [*Aside.*] I'm distracted to see her of this humour. [*To* LUCINDA.] But tell me; wilt thou kill me with vexation, and can't I know whence this great languishment proceeds? Discover the cause of it to me, and I promise thee I'll do everything for thee. You need only tell me the reason of your melancholy, and I here assure thee, and swear to thee, that there's nothing which I'll not do to satisfy thee; that's saying everything. Art thou jealous of any of thy companions that thou seest finer than thyself? And is there any new-fashioned silk thou wouldst have a suit of? No. Dost not think thy chamber well enough furnished, and dost thou long for any little cabinet out of St. Laurence's Fair? 'Tis not that. Hast a mind to learn anything, and wilt have me get thee a master to teach thee to play on the spinet? No. Dost love anybody, and dost wish to be married? [LUCINDA *makes a sign to him that 'tis that.*]

Scene III

SGANAREL, LUCINDA, LYSETTA.

LYSETTA. Well, sir, you have been discoursing your daughter. Have you found out the cause of her melancholy?

SGANAREL. No, the slut makes me mad.

LYSETTA. Sir, let me alone, I'll sound her a little.

SGANAREL. 'Tisn't necessary; since she will be of this humour, I'm resolved to leave her in't.

LYSETTA. Let me alone, I tell you; perhaps she'll discover herself more freely to me than to you. What, madam, won't you tell us what ails you? And will you grieve all the world thus? There's nobody I think acts as you do, and if you have any repugnance to explain yourself to your father, you ought to have none to discover your heart to me. Tell me, do you want anything of him? He has told us more than once that he'll spare nothing to content you. Is it because he does not give you all the liberty you could desire, and don't walks and feasts tempt your fancy? Um? Have you been displeased by anybody? Um? Have you no secret inclination for any one whom you'd have your father marry you to? Ahah! I understand you. There's the thing. What the deuce! Why so much ado? Sir, the mystery is discovered, and—

SGANAREL. Go, ungrateful girl, I'll talk to thee no more, but leave thee in thy obstinacy.

LUCINDA. Since you will have me to tell you the thing, sir—

SGANAREL. Yes, I'll throw off all the affection I had for thee.

LYSETTA. Her melancholy, sir—

SGANAREL. The hussy would kill me.

LUCINDA. Sir, I'll really—

SGANAREL. This is not a fit recompense for bringing thee up as I have done.

LYSETTA. But sir—

SGANAREL. No, I'm in a horrible passion with her.

LUCINDA. But father—

SGANAREL. I have no longer any tenderness for thee.

LYSETTA. But—

SGANAREL. She's a baggage.

LUCINDA. But—

SGANAREL.   An ungrateful hussy.
LYSETTA.   But—
SGANAREL.   A slut, that won't tell me what ails her.
LYSETTA.   She wants a husband.
SGANAREL. [*Pretending not to hear.*]   I abandon her.
LYSETTA.   A husband.
SGANAREL.   I detest her.
LYSETTA.   A husband.
SGANAREL.   And disown her for my daughter.
LYSETTA.   A husband.
SGANAREL.   No, don't speak to me of her.
LYSETTA.   A husband.
SGANAREL.   Don't speak to me of her.
LYSETTA.   A husband.
SGANAREL.   Don't speak to me of her.
LYSETTA.   A husband, a husband, a husband.

Scene IV

LYSETTA, LUCINDA.

LYSETTA.   'Tis a true saying, "That none are so deaf as those that won't hear."
LUCINDA.   Well, Lysetta, I was in the wrong to conceal my disquiet, and I had nothing to do but to speak, and to have all I wished from my father. You see now.
LYSETTA.   Faith, he's a villainous man; and I own that I should take a great deal of pleasure in playing him some trick. But how comes it though, madam, that you hid your distemper till now from me too?
LUCINDA.   Alas! What service would it have done me to have discovered it to you sooner? And should not I have got as much by concealing it all my lifetime? Dost thou think I did not plainly foresee all that you, now find? That I did not thoroughly know all my father's notions, and that the refusal he sent to him who solicited for me by a friend, did not extinguish all hope in my breast?
LYSETTA.   What, is it the stranger who asked you of your father, for whom you—
LUCINDA.   Perhaps 'tis not modest in a girl to explain herself so freely. But in short I must confess to thee, that if I was permitted to choose anything, it would be him that I should choose. We have had no conversation together, nor has his mouth declared the passion he has for me. But in every place where he

has been able to get a sight of me, his looks and actions have always spoken so tenderly, and his demanding me from my father appears to me so very honourable, that my heart could not help being touched with his affection. And yet you see to what the harshness of my father reduces all this tenderness.

LYSETTA. Come, let me alone; whatever reason I have to blame you for making a secret of it to me, I won't fail to assist your love, and, provided you have resolution enough—

LUCINDA. But what would you have me do against the authority of a father? And if he's inexorable to my wishes—

LYSETTA. Come, come, you must not suffer yourself to be led like a goose, and, provided honour be not offended by it, one may free one's self a little from a father's tyranny. What does he intend you shall do? Aren't you of age to be married, and does he think you are marble? Come, once more, I'll serve your passion; I from this present take upon me all the care of its concerns, and you shall see that I understand stratagem.—But I see your father. Go in again, and leave me to act.

Scene V

SGANAREL. [*Alone.*] 'Tis good sometimes to pretend not to hear things which one hears but too well; and I did wisely to ward off the declaration of a desire which I don't mean to satisfy. Is there anything more tyrannical than this custom that people would subject parents to? Anything more impertinent and ridiculous than to heap up riches with great labour, and bring up a daughter with much care and tenderness, in order to strip one's self of both, and give 'em into the hands of a man whom we have no manner of concern with? No, no, that custom's a jest to me, and I'll keep my money and my daughter to myself.

Scene VI

SGANAREL, LYSETTA.

LYSETTA. [*Pretending not to see* SGANAREL.] Oh! misfortune! O disgrace! O poor Mr. Sganarel! Where shall I find you?

SGANAREL. [*Aside.*] What does she say there?

LYSETTA. Ah, unhappy father! What will you do when you know this news?

SGANAREL. [*Aside.*] What can it be?

LYSETTA. My poor mistress!

SGANAREL. [*Aside.*] I'm undone.

LYSETTA. Ah!

SGANAREL. [*Running after* LYSETTA.] Lysetta.

LYSETTA. What a misfortune this is!

SGANAREL. Lysetta.

LYSETTA. What an accident!
SGANAREL. Lysetta.
LYSETTA. What a fatal mischance!
SGANAREL. Lysetta.
LYSETTA. Ah! sir.
SGANAREL. What's the matter?
LYSETTA. Sir!
SGANAREL. What is't?
LYSETTA. Your daughter.
SGANAREL. Oh! Oh!
LYSETTA. Sir, don't cry in that manner, for you'll make me laugh.
SGANAREL. Tell me then quickly.
LYSETTA. Your daughter, quite struck with the words you spoke to her, and with the terrible passion she saw you were in with her, went up immediately to her chamber, and, full of despair, opened the window which looks upon the river.
SGANAREL. Well?
LYSETTA. Then lifting up her eyes to heaven, No, said she, 'tis impossible for me to live under my father's anger; and since he disowns me for his daughter, I must die.
SGANAREL. So threw herself down?
LYSETTA. No, sir, she gently shut the window again, and laid her down on the bed; there she fell a-weeping bitterly, and all at once her face grew pale, her eyes rolled, her heart ceased to beat, and she remained in my arms.
SGANAREL. Oh! my daughter! she's dead then?
LYSETTA. No, sir, by pinching her I brought her to herself again; but this takes her again every moment, and I believe she'll not live out to-day.
SGANAREL. Champagne! Champagne! Champagne!

Scene VII

SGANAREL, CHAMPAGNE, LYSETTA.

SGANAREL. Here quick, let physicians be got, and in abundance; one can't have too many upon such an accident. Ah, my girl! My poor girl!

Act II: Scene I

SGANAREL, LYSETTA

LYSETTA. What will you do, sir, with four physicians? Is not one enough to kill any one body?
SGANAREL. Hold your tongue. Four advices are better than one.
LYSETTA. Why, can't your daughter die well enough without the assistance of these gentlemen?
SGANAREL. Do the physicians kill people?

LYSETTA. Undoubtedly; and I knew a man who proved by good reasons that we should never say, such a one is dead of a fever, or a catarrh, but she is dead of four doctors and two apothecaries.

SGANAREL. Will you hold your tongue, I say? What impertinence is this! Here they come.

LYSETTA. Take care. You are going to be greatly edified; they'll tell you in Latin that your daughter is sick.

Scene II

MESSRS. THOMÈS, FONANDRÈS, MACROTON, BAHYS, SGANAREL, LYSETTA.

SGANAREL. Well, gentlemen!

MR. THOMÈS. We have sufficiently viewed the patient, and there are certainly a great many impurities in her.

SGANAREL. Is my daughter impure?

MR. THOMÈS. I mean that there is much impurity in her body, an abundance of corrupt humours.

SGANAREL. Oh! I understand you.

MR. THOMÈS. But . . . We are going to consult together.

SGANAREL. Come, let chairs be given.

LYSETTA. [*To* MR. THOMÈS.] Oh! sir, are you there?

SGANAREL. [*To* LYSETTA.] How do you know the gentleman?

LYSETTA. By having seen him the other day at a friend of your niece's.

MR. THOMÈS. How does her coachman do?

LYSETTA. Very well. He's dead.

MR. THOMÈS. That can't be.

LYSETTA. I don't know whether it can be or not; but I know well enough that so it is.

MR. THOMÈS. He can't be dead, I tell you.

LYSETTA. And I tell you that he is dead and buried.

MR. THOMÈS. You are deceived.

LYSETTA. I saw it.

MR. THOMÈS. 'Tis impossible. Hippocrates says that these sort of distempers don't terminate till the fourteenth or twenty-first, and he fell sick but six days ago.

LYSETTA. Hippocrates may say what he please; but the coachman is dead.

SGANAREL. Silence, prate-apace, and let us go from hence. Gentlemen, I beg you to consult in the best manner. Though 'tis not the custom to pay beforehand, yet for fear I should forget it, and that the thing may be over, here—

[*He gives them money, and each makes a different gesture*].

Scene III

MESSRS. FONANDRÈS, THOMÈS, MACROTON, AND BAHYS.

[*They sit down and cough.*]

MR. FONANDRÈS. Paris is wonderfully large, and one must make long jaunts when practice comes on a little.

MR. THOMÈS. I must own that I have an admirable mule for that, and the way I make him go very day is scarce to be believed.

MR. FONANDRÈS. I have a wonderful horse, and 'tis an indefatigable animal.

MR. THOMÈS. Do you know the way my mule has gone to-day? I was first over against the arsenal, from the arsenal to the end of the suburb St. Germain, from the suburb St. Germain to the very end of the marshes, from the end of the marshes to the gate St. Honorius, from the gate St. Honorius to the suburb St. James's, from the suburb St. James's to the gate of Richelieu, from the gate of Richelieu hither, and from hence I must go yet to the Palace-Royal.

MR. FONANDRÈS. My horse has done all that to-day, and besides I have been at Ruel to see a patient.

MR. THOMÈS. But well thought on, what side do you take in the dispute betwixt the two physicians, Theophrastus and Artemius? for 'tis an affair which divides all our body.

MR. FONANDRÈS. I am for Artemius.

MR. THOMÈS. And I likewise; not but that his advice killed the patient, and that of Theophrastus was certainly much the better; but he was wrong in the circumstances, and he ought not to have been of a different opinion to his senior. What say you of it?

MR. FONANDRÈS. Without doubt. The formalities should be always preserved whatever may happen.

MR. THOMÈS. For my part I am as severe as a devil in that respect, unless it's amongst friends. And three of us were called in t'other day to a consultation with a strange physician, where I stopped the whole affair, and would not suffer 'em to go on unless things went in order. The people of the house did what they could, and the distemper increased; but I would not bate an inch, and the patient died bravely during this dispute.

MR. FONANDRÈS. 'Twas well done to teach people how to behave, and to show 'em their mistake.

MR. THOMÈS. A dead man is but a dead man, and of no consequence: but one formality neglected does a great prejudice to the whole body of physicians.

Scene IV

SGANAREL, MESSRS. THOMÈS, FONANDRÈS, MACROTON, AND BAHYS.

SGANAREL. Gentlemen, my daughter's oppression increases, pray tell me quickly what you have resolved on.
MR. THOMÈS. [*To* MR. FONANDRÈS.] Come, sir.
MR. FONANDRÈS. No, sir, do you be pleased to speak.
MR. THOMÈS. You jest sure, sir.
MR. FONANDRÈS. I'll not speak the first.
MR. THOMÈS. Sir.
MR. FONANDRÈS. Sir.
SGANAREL. Nay, pray gentlemen, leave all these ceremonies, and consider that things are pressing.
MR. THOMÈS. Your daughter's illness—
MR. FONANDRÈS. The opinion of all these gentlemen together—
MR. MACROTON. Af-ter ha-ving well con-sult-ed—
MR. BAHYS. In order to reason— [*They all four speak together.*]
SGANAREL. Nay, gentlemen, speak one after another, pray now.
MR. THOMÈS. Sir, we have reasoned upon your daughter's distemper; and my opinion, as for my part, is that it proceeds from a great heat of blood: I'd have you bleed her as soon as you can.
MR. FONANDRÈS. And I say that her distemper is a putrefaction of humours, occasioned by too great a repletion, therefore I'd have you give her an emetic.
MR. THOMÈS. I maintain that an emetic will kill her.
MR. FONANDRÈS. And I, that bleeding will be the death of her.
MR. THOMÈS. It belongs to you indeed to set up for a skilful man!
MR. FONANDRÈS. Yes, it does belong to me; and I'll cope with you in all kinds of learning.
MR. THOMÈS. Do you remember the man you killed a few days ago?
MR. FONANDRÈS. Do you remember the lady you sent into the other world three days since?
MR. THOMÈS. [*To* SGANAREL.] I have told you my opinion.
MR. FONANDRÈS. [*To* SGANAREL.] I have told you my thoughts.
MR. THOMÈS. If you don't bleed your daughter out of hand, she's a dead woman. [*Goes out.*]
MR. FONANDRÈS. If you do bleed her, she'll not be alive a quarter of an hour hence. [*Goes out.*]

Scene V

SGANAREL, MESSRS. MACROTON AND BAHYS.

SGANAREL. Which of the two am I to believe, and what resolution shall I take upon such opposite advices? Gentlemen, I conjure you to determine me, and to tell me without passion, what you think the most proper to give my daughter relief.

MR. MACROTON. [*Drawling out his words.*]   Sir, in these mat-ters, we must pro-ceed with cir-cum-spec-ti-on, and do no-thing in-con-si-de-rate-ly, as they say; for-as-much as the faults which may be com-mit-ted in this case are, ac-cor-ding to our ma-ster Hip-po-cra-tes, of a dan-ge-rous con-se-quence.

MR. BAHYS. [*Sputtering out his words hastily.*]   'Tis true. We must really take care what we do; for this is not child's play; and when we have once faltered 'tis not easy to repair the slip, and to re-establish what we have spoilt. *Experimentum periculosum.* Wherefore we should reason first as we ought to do, weigh things seriously, consider the constitutions of people, examine the causes of the distemper, and see what remedies one ought to apply to it.

SGANAREL. [*Aside.*]   One creeps like a tortoise; t'other rides post.

MR. MACROTON.   For, sir, to come to fact, I find your daugh-ter has a chro-ni-cal dis-ease, and that she may be in jeo-par-dy if you don't give her some assis-tance; for-as-much as the symptoms which she has are in-di-ca-tive of a fu-li-gi-nous and mor-di-cant va-pour, which pricks the mem-branes of the brain; for this va-pour, which we call in Greek *at-mos,* is caus-ed by pu-trid, te-na-ci-ous, and con-glu-ti-nous humours, which are con-tain-ed in the abdomen.

MR. BAHYS.   And as these humours were engendered there by a long succession of time; they are over-baked there, and have acquired this malignity, which fumes towards the region of the brain.

MR. MACROTON.   So that to draw a-way, loos-en, ex-pel, e-va-cu-ate the said hu-mours, there must be a vi-go-rous pur-ga-tion. But first of all, I think it proper, and it would not be in-con-ve-ni-ent to make sure of some lit-tle a-no-dyne me-de-cines; that is to say, lit-tle e-mol-li-ent and de-ter-sive cly-sters, and re-fresh-ing ju-leps and sy-rups, which may be mix-ed in her bar-ley wa-ter.

MR. BAHYS.   Afterwards we'll come to purgation and bleeding, which we'll reiterate if there be need of it.

MR. MACROTON.   Not but for all this your daughter may die; but at least you'll have done some-thing, and you'll have the con-so-la-ti-on that she di-ed ac-cord-ing to form.

MR. BAHYS.   It is better to die according to the rules than to re-cover contrary to 'em.

MR. MACROTON.   We tell you our thoughts sin-cere-ly.

MR. BAHYS.   And have spoken to you as we would speak to our own brother.

SGANAREL. [*To* MR. MACROTON, *drawling out his words.*]   I ren-der you most hum-ble thanks. [*To* MR. BAHYS, *sputtering out his words.*] And am infinitely obliged to you for the pains you have taken.

Scene VI

SGANAREL. [*Alone.*] So I'm just a little more uncertain than I was before. S'death, there's a fancy comes into my head, I'll go buy some orvietan,[1] and make her take some of it. Orvietan is a remedy which many people have found good by. Soho!

Scene VII

SGANAREL, THE OPERATOR.

SGANAREL. Sir, pray give me a box of your orvietan, which I'll pay you for.

THE OPERATOR. [*Sings.*]
 The gold in all lands which the sea doth surround,
 Can ne'er pay the worth of my secret profound:
 My remedy cures, by its excellence rare,
 More maladies than you can count in a year.
  The scab,
  The itch,
  The scurf,
  The plague,
  The fever,
  The gout,
  The pox,
  The flux,
  And measles ever,
 Of orvietan such is the excellence rare.

SGANAREL. Sir, I believe all the gold in the world is not sufficient to pay for your medicine, but however here's a half crown-piece which you may take if you please.

THE OPERATOR. [*Sings.*]
 Admire then my bounty, who for thirty poor pence,
 Such a marvellous treasure do so freely dispense.
 With this you may brave, quite devoid of all fear,
 All the ills which poor mortals are subject to here.
  The scab,
  The itch,
  The scurf,
  The plague,
  The fever,
  The gout,
  The pox,
  The flux,
  And measles ever,
 Of orvietan such is the excellence rare.

Act III: Scene I

MESSRS. FILLERIN, THOMÈS, FONANDRÈS.

MR. FILLERIN. Are not you ashamed, gentlemen, to show so little prudence for men of your age, and to quarrel like young hair-brained simpletons? Don't you plainly see what mischief these sort of disputes do us in the world? And is it not enough that the learned see the contrarieties and dissensions which are between our authors and ancient masters, without our discovering the knavery of our art to the people too, by our disputes and quarrels? For my part, I don't at all comprehend this mischievous policy of some of our brethren, and it must be confessed that these contests have disparaged us lately in a strange manner; and that if we don't take care we shall ruin ourselves. I don't speak of this for my own interest, for thank God I have already established my small affairs. Let it blow, rain or hail, those that are dead are dead, and I have wherewith to pass amongst the living; but yet all these disputes do physic no good. Since Heaven does us the favour to let people for so many ages continue infatuated with us, let us not undeceive men by our extravagant cabals, but profit by their folly as quietly as we can. We are not the only people, you know, who try to take advantage of human weakness; the study of the greatest part of the world lies that way, and every one strives to take men on their blind side to get some profit from it. Flatterers, for example, seek to profit from the love men have of praise, by giving 'em all the vain incense they can wish; and 'tis an art that, we see, raises considerable fortunes. The alchymists endeavour to profit from the passion men have for riches, by promising mountains of gold to those that will hearken to 'em; and the conjurers by their deceitful predictions make a profit of the vanity and ambition of credulous minds. But the greatest weakness men have is the love they have for life; and we make a profit of that by our pompous jargon, and know how to make our advantages of the veneration which the fear of death gives 'em for our trade. Let us preserve ourselves then in the degree of esteem wherein their weakness has put us, and let us agree before our patients to attribute to ourselves the happy event of the distemper, and to throw all the blunders of our art upon nature. Let us not, I say, foolishly destroy the happy prepossessions of an error which gives bread to so many people, and by their money whom we have sent to the grave, has raised us up, on all sides, such fine estates.

MR. THOMÈS. You have reason in all you say, but these are heats of blood, which sometimes we are not masters of.

MR. FILLERIN. Come then, gentlemen, lay aside all animosity.

MR. FONANDRÈS. I agree to it. Let him but admit of my emetic for the patient which is now in hand, and I'll admit of anything he

shall please for the first patient he shall be concerned with.
MR. FILLERIN.   Nothing could be said better.
MR. FONANDRÈS.   'Tis done.
MR. FILLERIN.   Shake hands then. Farewell.

Scene II

MR. THOMÈS, MR. FONANDRÈS, LYSETTA.

LYSETTA.   What, gentlemen, are you there? And don't you think of repairing the injury which they have done to physic?
MR. THOMÈS.   How? What's the matter?
LYSETTA.   There's an insolent fellow who has had the impudence to encroach upon your trade, and has, without your order, killed a man by running a sword through his body.
MR. THOMÈS.   Harkee, you make a jest of it now, but you'll come under our hands some day or other.
LYSETTA.   I'll give you leave to kill me when I have recourse to you.

Scene III

CLITANDER (*in the habit of a phsyican*), LYSETTA.

CLITANDER.   Well, Lysetta, what say you of my equipage? Do you believe that I may gull the good man with this habit? Do you think I make a good figure thus?
LYSETTA.   The best in the world, and I impatiently waited for you. Heaven has made me of a nature the most humane in the world, and I can't see two lovers sigh for one another, without having a charitable tenderness, and an ardent desire to relive the ills they suffer. I am resolved, cost what it will, to deliver Lucinda from the tyranny she is under, and put her in your power. You pleased me at first. I am skilful in men, and she could not have made a better choice. Love ventures upon extraordinary things, and we have concerted a kind of stratagem together, which may perhaps succeed for us. All our measures are already taken. The man we have to deal with is not the most crafty in the world; and if this adventure fails us, we shall find a thousand other ways to come at our end. Wait for me only a little here, and I'll return to fetch you.

[CLITANDER *retires to the farther part of the stage.*]

Scene IV

SGANAREL, LYSETTA.

LYSETTA.   Joy! sir, joy!
SGANAREL.   What's the matter?
LYSETTA.   Rejoice!

SGANAREL.   For what?
LYSETTA.   Rejoice, I say.
SGANAREL.   Tell me for what, and then perhaps I may rejoice.
LYSETTA.   No, I'll have you rejoice beforehand, dance and sing.
SGANAREL.   On what account?
LYSETTA.   Upon my word.
SGANAREL.   Come then. [*Sings and dances.*] La, la, la, lera, la. What the deuce!
LYSETTA.   Sir, your daughter's cured.
SGANAREL.   My daughter's cured!
LYSETTA.   Yes, I bring you a physician; but a physican of importance, who does marvellous cures, and who despises other physicians.
SGANAREL.   Who is he?
LYSETTA.   I'll bring him in.
SGANAREL.   [*Alone.*]   I must see if this will do more than the others.

Scene V

CLITANDER *(in the habit of a phsyican)*, SGANAREL, LYSETTA.

LYSETTA.   Here he is.
SGANAREL.   This physician has but a young beard.
LYSETTA.   Knowledge is not measured by the beard; his skill doesn't lie in his chin.
SGANAREL.   Sir, I'm told you have wonderful recipes to make people go to stool.
CLITANDER.   Sir, my remedies are different from those of others; they have emetics, bleedings, purges, clysters;[2] but I cure by words, sounds, letters, talismans, and constellated rings.
LYSETTA.   Did not I tell you?
SGANAREL.   A great man this!
LYSETTA.   Sir, your daughter being yonder in her chair, dressed, I'll bring her to you.
SGANAREL.   Do so.
CLITANDER.   [*Feeling* SGANAREL's *pulse.*]   Your daughter's very bad.
SGANAREL.   Can you tell that here?
CLITANDER.   Yes, by the sympathy there is between father and daughter.

Scene VI

SGANAREL, LUCINDA, CLITANDER, LYSETTA.

LYSETTA. [*To* CLITANDER.]   Sir, here's a chair near her. [*To* SGANAREL.] Come, let's leave 'em both here.
SGANAREL.   Why so? I'll stay here.
LYSETTA.   You jest sure! we must leave 'em; a phsyician has a hundred questions to ask which 'tisn't fit for a man to hear.

[SGANAREL *and* LYSETTA *retire.*

CLITANDER. [*Apart to* LUCINDA.] Ah! madam, how great is my pleasure! and how little do I know in what manner to begin my discourse to you! Whilst I spoke to you only by my eyes, I thought I had a hundred things to say; and now I have the liberty to speak to you as I desired, I am silent, and my excess of joy stifles my words.

LUCINDA. I may say the same, and, like you, I feel movements of joy which hinder me from speaking to you.

CLITANDER. Ah! madam, how happy should I be if you really felt all I feel, and if I were permitted to judge of your heart by my own! But, madam, may I believe that 'tis to you I owe the thought of this happy stratagem, which gives me the enjoyment of your presence?

LUCINDA. If you don't owe the thought of it to me, you are at least obliged to me for having gladly approved the proposition.

SGANAREL. [*To* LYSETTA.] He talks mighty close to her.

LYSETTA. [*To* SGANAREL.] He's observing her physiognomy and the traces of her features.

CLITANDER. [*To* LUCINDA.] Will you be constant, madam, in these favours you show me?

LUCINDA. Will you be firm in the resolutions you have shown me?

CLITANDER. Till death, madam. I desire nothing so much as to be yours, and I'll show it in what I'm going to do.

SGANAREL. [*To* CLITANDER.] Well, how does your patient? She looks a little brisker.

CLITANDER. 'Tis because I have already tried upon her one of the remedies my art teaches me. As the mind has a great influence over the body, and that being often the cause of diseases, my custom is first to cure the mind, before I come to the body. Therefore I observed her looks, her features, and the lines of her hands; and by my knowledge I find that her mind is the part she's sick in; and that all her disease proceeds only from an irregular imagination, from a depraved desire of being married. For my part, I think nothing more extravagant and ridiculous than that desire people have for matrimony.

SGANAREL. [*Aside.*] A skilful man this!

CLITANDER. And I have a horrible aversion to it.

SGANAREL. [*Aside.*] A great physician!

CLITANDER. But as we must flatter the imaginations of our patients, and seeing an alienation of mind in her, and even that 'twould prove dangerous without speedy succour, I took her on her blind side, and told her that I was come to demand her of you in marriage; suddenly her countenance changed, her complexion cleared up, her eyes were animated, and if you would but hold her in this error for some days, you'll see we shall entirely recover her.

SGANAREL. Ay, I'll do it with all my heart.

CLITANDER. Afterwards we'll use other remedies to cure her wholly of this fancy.

SGANAREL. Ay, that will do mighty well. Well, daughter, this gentleman has a mind to marry you, and I have told him that I am willing.

LUCINDA. Alas! Is it possible?

SGANAREL. Yes.

LUCINDA. But really?

SGANAREL. Yes, yes.

LUCINDA. O how happy am I, if this be true!

CLITANDER. Don't doubt it, madam; 'tis not to-day that I began to love you, and burn to be your husband; I came hither for that alone; and if you'd have me tell you the thing just as 'tis, this habit is but a mere pretence, and I acted the physician only to get to you, and the more easily to obtain what I desire.

LUCINDA. That's giving me marks of a very tender love; I am as sensible of it as I ought to be.

SGANAREL. O poor silly girl! silly girl! silly girl!

LUCINDA. Then, sir, do you give me the gentleman for a husband?

SGANAREL. Yes; come, give me your hand; give me yours too.

CLITANDER. But, sir— [*Holding back.*

SGANAREL. No, no, 'tis only to—[*Stifling his laugh.*] to make her easy. Come, take hands.. There, 'tis done.

CLITANDER. As a warrant of my fidelity, accept of this ring. [*Low to* SGANAREL.] 'Tis a constellated ring which cures distractions of the mind.

LUCINDA. Let the contract be made then, that nothing may be wanting.

CLITANDER. Lack-a-day! with all my heart, madam. [*Low to* SGANAREL.] I'll call up the man that writes down my prescriptions, and make her believe 'tis a notary.

SGANAREL. Very well.

CLITANDER. Soho! Call up the notary I brought with me.

LUCINDA. What! did you bring a notary?

CLITANDER. Yes, madam.

LUCINDA. I'm glad on't.

SGANAREL. O poor silly girl! silly girl!

Scene VII

THE NOTARY, CLITANDER, SGANAREL, LUCINDA, LYSETTA.

[CLITANDER *whispers to the* NOTARY.]

SGANAREL. [*To the* NOTARY.] Yes, sir, you are to draw a contract for those two persons. Write. [*To* LUCINDA.] The contract is making, girl. [*To the* NOTARY.] I give her twenty thousand crowns as a portion. Write.

LUCINDA.   I am obliged to you, father.

NOTARY.   'Tis done, you have nothing to do but to sign.

SGANAREL.   Here's a contract soon drawn.

CLITANDER. [*To* SGANAREL.] But, however, sir—

SGANAREL.   Hey, no, no. Don't I know? [*To the* NOTARY.] Come, give him the pen to sign. [*To* LUCINDA.] Come, sign, sign, sign.

LUCINDA.   No, no; I'll have the contract in my own hands.

SGANAREL.   Well, take it. [*After signing it.*] Are you satisfied?

LUCINDA.   More than you can imagine.

SGANAREL.   That's well, that's well.

CLITANDER.   I have not only had the precaution to bring a notary, but I've brought several singers, musicians, and dancers, to celebrate the feast, and make merry. Call 'em in.

Scene VIII

SGANAREL, LUCINDA, CLITANDER, LYSETTA.

Comedy, Music, Dancing, the Sports, the Smiles, and the Pleasures.

Comedy, Dancing, and Music together.

    All humankind, without us three,
     Would soon become diseased;
    Their chief physicians sure are we
     By whom their ills are eased.

Comedy.

    If you by pleasant means would aim
     To cure the vapoured head,
    Leave your Hippocrates, for shame,
     And come to us for aid.

All three.

    All humankind, without us three,
     Would soon become diseased;
    Their chief physicians sure are we
     By whom their ills are eased.

[*Whilst the Sports, the Smiles, and the Pleasures are dancing,* CLITANDER *carries off* LUCINDA.]

Scene IX

SGANAREL, LYSETTA.

Comedy, Music, Dancing, the Sports, the Smiles, and the Pleasures.

SGANAREL. This is a pleasant manner of curing people. Where is my daughter and the physician?
LYSETTA. They're gone to conclude the rest of the marriage.
SGANAREL. What marriage?
LYSETTA. Faith, sir, the woodcock's caught; you imagined you had been in jest, and it proves in earnest.
SGANAREL. [*Endeavours to go after* CLITANDER *and* LUCINDA, *but the dancers hold him.*] What the devil? Let me go; let me go, I say. Again? [*They endeavour to force him to dance.*] Pox take you all!

Dance.

THE END

Further Readings

A detailed and readable account of seventeenth-century France by a gifted writer is provided by Pierre Gaxotte, *The Age of Louis XIV*, translated by Michael Shaw (New York: Macmillan Co., 1970). Life in the royal court is intimately detailed by Jacques Levron, *Daily Life at Versailles in the Seventeenth and Eighteenth Centuries*, translated by Claire Engel (New York: Macmillan Co., 1968). Nancy Mitford, *The Sun King: Louis XIV at Versailles* (New York: Harper and Row Publishers, 1975), presents a richly illustrated survey of the reign of Louis XIV and his great palace. Gertrude Mander, *Molière*, translated by Diane Peters (New York: Frederick Ungar Publishing Co., 1975), is an excellent biography, while Mikhail Bulgakov, *The Life of Monsieur de Molière*, translated by Myrra Ginsberg (New York: Funk and Wagnall's, 1970), builds upon historical evidence in a novelistic approach. Hallam Walker, *Molière* (New York: Twayne Publishers, 1971), summarizes and perceptively analyzes Molière's life and works. There are many translations and editions of various of Molière's plays, but a complete collection may be found in Molière, *Comedies* . . . (2 vols.: New York: Dutton, 1929).

The Treasury of Loyal Retainers

Written in 1748, the *Treasury of Loyal Retainers (Chushingura)* is perhaps the most famous and highly praised drama of popular Japanese theater. Originally written as a puppet play and later adapted for the Kabuki theater, it quickly became the most popular drama in the entire Japanese theatrical repertoire. The story has become part of the traditional heritage of the Japanese people and has continued to captivate Japanese audiences to the present day. Although in many ways peculiarly Japanese, the play's popularity extends to foreign audiences—it was probably the first work of Japanese literature to be translated into English. Its popularity stems both from its remarkable representation of Japanese life, portrayed in its elaborate and detailed character development, and from the intriguing historical events from which the story is drawn.

The play is a dramatization of an actual event known as the Ako vendetta that occurred in the early eighteenth century. Lord Asano of Ako (Enya Hangan), enraged by the conduct of a high official of the shogun (military dictator of Japan), struck the official with his sword. Because of this grave offense, Asano was ordered by the shogun to commit suicide by *seppuku* (ritual disembowelment). Asano's estates were confiscated after his death, resulting in the extinction of his noble house. His armed retainers became *ronin*, or masterless samurai. Their position was extremely difficult. Their honor required that they avenge their lord's death, but he had died by the shogun's order, and vengeance in such a case was illegal. In addition, Kira Yoshinaka (Lord Moronao), the official who had brought about Asano's downfall, was both powerful and suspicious and had the *ronin* closely watched for any sign that they might be planning revenge. Nevertheless, this leaderless band, some forty-seven in number, pledged themselves to avenge their master upon Lord Kira.

From Takeda Izumo, Miyoshi Shoraku, and Namiki Senryu, *Chushingura: A Puppet Play*, translated by Donald Keene (New York: Columbia University Press, 1971), pp. 104–124.

First, however, they had to lull his suspicions by convincing him that they had lost their honor and forgotten their duty and that they presented no danger to him.

After two years of hardship and suffering, playing the drunk and the fool, the *ronin* were ready to strike. On 30 January 1703, they burst into the residence of Lord Kira in Tokyo and killed him. They promptly carried his severed head to the temple where Lord Asano was buried and placed it on his grave. The vendetta was completed and their honor restored.

News of this event spread rapidly. The boldness of the deed and the selfless resolution of the *ronin* captured the imagination of people of all classes, and the forty-seven *ronin* were immediately acclaimed as heroes. Their action expressed the highest standards of samurai courage and loyalty, but it was also illegal. The authorities considered the case for some time, but eventually handed down the death sentence for the entire group. Partly due to public opinion, they were allowed to die honorably by following their lord in committing *seppuku*. They died together on 20 March 1703 and were interred alongside Lord Asano. Their graves continue to the present day to be a popular pilgrimage site.

Over a hundred plays have been written on the theme, but the most popular was that written by Takeda Izumo in collaboration with Namiki Senryu and Miyoshi Shoraku. It was first produced at the Takemoto Doll Theater in Osaka in 1748. The play is lengthy, consisting of eleven acts. Single acts are popular fixtures on Kabuki programs, and the seventh act, "Yuranosuke at His Revels," from which this selection is taken, is a particular favorite. The act opens as Kudayo, a hireling of Lord Moronao, arrives at the stylish Ichiriki teahouse in Kyoto, where Yuranosuke, the chief retainer and hero of the play, debauches himself, apparently forgetful of both honor and revenge. Three samurai also soon arrive with the intention of discussing revenge with Yuranosuke, only to have him put them off. Heiemon, a low-ranking samurai, describes his own efforts to join the vendetta. Again, Yuranosuke refuses to discuss the matter, and the samurai leave, dismayed and disgusted. Rikiya, Yuranosuke's son, then arrives and awakes his father, who is apparently in a drunken stupor. Yuranosuke is immediately wide awake and completely sober. He receives a letter containing information as to when the attack upon Lord Kira should be made, and then sends his son away.

The villainous Kudayu reappears, and Yuranosuke resumes his feigned drunkenness. After testing to see if Yuranosuke has truly forgotten revenge, Kudayu leaves, apparently satisfied, and Yuranosuke reads the letter he received from Rikiya. He discovers that Okaru, Heiemon's sister who has sold herself into servitude to save the family, has been looking over his shoulder. He continues to fein drunkenness, promises Okaru to buy her freedom, and then leaves. Heiemon arrives, and Okaru tells him what has happened. He realizes that Yuranosuke, knowing that she has read his letter and learned the secret of the plot, intends to buy Okaru's freedom only to be able to silence her permanently. Okaru decides to commit suicide, but Yuranosuke returns in time to prevent her. After hearing their story, Yuranosuke praises both brother and sister and allows Heiemon to join in the plot. The act ends with Yuranosuke discovering Kudayu hiding outside, stabbing him, and instructing Heiemon to eliminate him in a discreet fashion.

Yuranosuke is perhaps the greatest role in all of Japanese theater. Although his presence is felt throughout the play, it is only in this seventh act that he emerges as the chief character. His actions clearly illustrate the personal hardships and humiliation he and his comrades are suffering in order to further their cause, and his conduct discloses the fierce sense of honor that sustains them. *The Treasury of Loyal Retainers* for a Japanese audience is an exaltation of the samurai code, but it transcends this cultural limitation. It is a profound study of the meaning of honor and responsibility.

Questions

1. *The Treasury of Loyal Retainers* fascinated both nobles and commoners in Japan. Why do you think that it appealed to two such different classes?

2. Would you consider this play a glorification of warlike attitudes?

3. What are some of the comic elements in "Yuranosuke at His Revels?" What function do they play?

YURANOSUKE AT HIS REVELS

NARRATOR: If you would dally among flowers you will find in Gion a full range of colors. East, south, north, and west, with a glitter as bright as if Amida's Pure Land has been gilded anew, Gion sparkles with courtesans and geishas, so lovely as to steal away the senses of even the most jaded man, and leave him a raving fool.

KUDAYŪ: Is anybody here? Where's the master? Master!

MASTER: Rush, rush, rush! Who's there? Whom have I the pleasure of serving? Why, it's Master Ono Kudayū! How formal of you to ask to be shown in!

KUDAYŪ: I've brought a gentleman with me who's here for the first time. You seem awfully busy, but have you a room you can show this gentleman?

MASTER: Indeed I have, sir. Tonight that big spender Yuranosuke had the bright idea of gathering together all the best-known women of the Quarter. The downstairs rooms are full, but the detached wing is free.

KUDAYŪ: Full of cobwebs, no doubt.

MASTER: More of your usual sarcasm, sir?

KUDAYŪ: No, I'm just being careful not to get entangled at my age in a whore's cobweb.

MASTER: I'd never have guessed it. I can't accommodate you downstairs, then. I'll prepare an upstairs room.—Servants! Light the lamps and bring saké and tobacco.

NARRATOR: He calls out in a loud voice. Drums and samisens[1] resound from the back rooms.

KUDAYŪ: What do you think, Bannai? Do you hear how Yuranosuke is carrying on?

BANNAI: He seems completely out if his head. Of course, we've had a series of private reports from you, Kudayū, but not even my master Moronao suspected how far gone Yuranosuke was. Moronao told me to come up to the capital and look over the situation. He said I should report anything suspicious. I'd never have believed it if I hadn't seen it with my own eyes. It's worse than I imagined. And what has become of his son, Rikiya?

KUDAYŪ: He comes here once in a while and the two of them have a wild time together. It's incredible that they don't feel any embarrassment in each other's presence. But tonight I've come with a plan for worming out the innermost secrets of Yuranosuke's heart. I'll tell you about it when we're alone. Let's go upstairs.

BANNAI: After you.

KUDAYŪ: Well, then, I'll lead the way.

NARRATOR (*sings*):

> *Though in truth your heart*
> *Has no thought for me,*
> *Your lips pretend you are in love,*
> *With great bewitchery—*

JŪTARŌ: Yagorō and Kitahachi—this is the teahouse where Yuranosuke amuses himself. It's called Ichiriki. Oh, Heiemon, we'll call you when the time comes. Go wait in the kitchen.

HEIEMON: At your service, sir. Please do what you can for me.

JŪTARŌ: Is anyone there? I want to talk to somebody.

MAID: Yes, sir. Who is it, please?

JŪTARŌ: We've come on business with Yuranosuke. Go in and tell him that Yazama Jūtarō, Senzaki Yagorō, and Takemori Kitahachi are here. Several times we've sent a man to fetch him, but he never seems to leave this place. So the three of us have come to him. There's something we must discuss with him. We ask that he meet us. Be sure and tell him that.

---

[1] Banjo-like three-stringed instruments.

MAID: I'm sorry to tell you sir, but Yuranosuke has been drinking steadily for the past three days. You won't get much sense out of him, even if you see him. He's not himself.
JŪTARŌ: That may be, but please tell him what I said.
MAID: Yes, sir.
JŪTARŌ: Yagorō, did you hear her?
YAGORŌ: I did, and I'm amazed. At first I thought it was some trick of his to throw the enemy off the track. But he has abandoned himself to his pleasures more than convincingly. I simply don't understand it.
KITAHACHI: It's just as I said. He's not the same man in spirit. Our best plan would be to break in on him—
JŪTARŌ: No, first we'll have a heart-to-heart talk.
YAGORŌ: Very well, we'll wait for him here.
PROSTITUTE (*sings*): Come where my hands clap, hands clap, hands clap. (*Yuranosuke enters. He is blindfolded.*)
YURANOSUKE: I'll catch you! I'll catch you!
PROSTITUTE: Come on, Yura the blind man! We're waiting!
YURANOSUKE: I'll catch you and make you drink.—Here!—Now I've got you! We'll have some saké! Bring on the saké! (*He grabs Jūtarō, taking him for his partner in blind-man's bluff.*)
JŪTARŌ: Come to yourself, Yuranosuke. I'm Yazama Jūtarō. What in the world are you doing?
YURANOSUKE: Good heavens! What an awful mistake!
PROSTITUTE: Oh, the kill-joys! Look at them, Sakae. Have you ever seen such sour-looking samurai? Are they all in the same party, do you think?
SAKAE: It certainly looks that way. They all have the same fierce look.
JŪTARŌ: Girls, we've come on business with Mr. Ōboshi. We'd appreciate it if you left the room for a while.
PROSTITUTES: We guessed as much. Yura, we'll be going to the back room. Come join us soon. This way, everybody.
JŪTARŌ: Yuranosuke, you remember me. I'm Yazama Jūtarō.
KITAHACHI: I'm Takemori Kitahachi.
Yatarō: And I am Senzaki Yatarō. We've come here hoping to have a talk with you. I trust you're awake now?
YURANOSUKE: Thank you all for having come to see me. What have you in mind?
JŪTARŌ: When do we leave for Kamakura?
YURANOSUKE: That's a very important question you've asked me. There's a song in *Yosaku from Tamba*[2] that goes, "When you leave for Edo, oh so far away. . . ." Ha, ha. Forgive me, gentlemen, I'm drunk.
THREE MEN: A man's character stays the same even when he's drunk, they say. If you're not in your right mind, the three of us will sober you up.

---

[2] A famous play.

HEIEMON: Don't do anything rash, please. I hope you'll forgive me, gentlemen, but I'd like a word with him. Please hold off for a while before you start anything. Master Yuranosuke—I am Teraoka Heiemon. I am very glad to see you're in such good spirits.

YURANOSUKE: Teraoka Heiemon? Who might *you* be? Are you that fleet-footed foot soldier who was sent as a courier to the north?

HEIEMON: The same, sir. It was while I was in the north that I learned our master had committed *seppuku,* and I was dumfounded. I started off for home, running so fast I all but flew through the air. On the way I was told that his lordship's mansion had been confiscated and his retainers dispersed. You can imagine what a shock that was. I served his lordship only as a foot soldier, but I am as much indebted to him as anyone. I went to Kamakura, intending to kill Moronao, our master's enemy. For three months I watched for my chance, disguising myself as a beggar, but our enemy is guarded so strongly I couldn't even get close to him. I felt I had no choice but to disembowel myself, but I thought then of my parents in the country, and I went back home, despondent though I was. But then—surely it was a heaven-sent revelation—I learned about the league you gentlemen have formed. How happy and thankful that made me! I didn't even bother to take my things with me, but went to call on these gentlemen at their lodgings. I begged with all my heart for them to intercede in my behalf. They praised me and called me a brave fellow, and promised to plead for me with the chief. So I've come along with them here, encouraged by their assurances. Moronao's mansion—

YURANOSUKE: What's all this? You're not so much light of foot as exceedingly light of tongue. It's quite true that I felt a certain amount of indignation—about as big as a flea's head split by a hatchet—and tried forming a league of forty or fifty men, but what a crazy notion that was! I realized when I thought about it calmly that if we failed in our mission our heads would roll, and if we succeeded we'd have to commit *seppuku* afterwards. Either way, it was certain death. It was like taking expensive medicine, then hanging yourself afterwards because you couldn't pay for the cure. You're a foot soldier with a stipend of three *ryō*[3] and an allowance of three men's rations. Now don't get angry—for you to throw away your life attacking the enemy, in return for a pittance suitable for a beggar priest, would be like putting on a performance of grand *kagura* to express your gratitude for some green *nori.*[4] My stipened was

---

[3] A coin; three *ryō* was a small sum compared to that received by a lord's more prominent followers.

[4] That is, to offer an elaborate ritual of thanks (*kagura*) for only a simple gift of edible seaweed (*nori*).

1,500 *koku*.⁵ Compared to you, I might take enemy heads by the bushel and still not do my share. And that's why I gave up the idea. Do you follow me? At any rate, this uncertain world (*sings*) is just that sort of place. *Tsuten Tsutsuten Tsutsuten.*⁶ Oh, when I hear the samisens playing like that I can't resist.

HEIEMON: I can't believe that is you speaking, Yuranosuke. Each man has only one life in this world, whether he's a wretch like myself with a bare income of three rations, or a rich man like you with 1,500 *koku,* and there is no high or low in the debt of gratitude we owe our master. But there's no disputing family lineage. I know it's presumptuous and rude for a miserable creature like myself to beg to join distinguished gentlemen who could have stood as deputies for our master. It's like a monkey imitating a man. But I want to go with you, even if it is only to carry your shoes or shoulder your baggage. Please take me with you. Sir, please listen to me, sir.—Oh, he seems to have fallen asleep.

KITAHACHI: Come, Heiemon. There's no point in wasting any more breath on him. Yuranosuke is as good as dead. Well, Yazama and Sensaki, have you seen his true character? Shall we act as we agreed?

YAGORŌ: By all means, as a warning to the others in our league. Are you ready?

NARRATOR: They close in on Yuranosuke, but a cry from Heiemon stops them. With calming gestures he comes up beside them.

HEIEMON: It seems to me, as I turn things over in my mind, Yuranosuke has undergone many hardships in his efforts to avenge our master, ever since they were parted by death. He has had to worry, like a hunted man, over every noise and footfall, and stifle his resentment at people's abuse. He couldn't have survived this long if he hadn't taken so heavily to drink. Wait till he's sober before you deal with him.

NARRATOR: Forcibly restraining them, he leads them into the next room. Their shadows on the other side of the sliding door, cast by a light that illuminates the distinction between good and evil, are blotted out as the moon sinks behind the mountains.

Rikiya, Yuranosuke's son, having run the whole *ri*⁷ and a half from Yamashina, arrives breathless. He peeps inside and sees his father lying asleep. Afraid that people may hear, he goes up to his father's pillow and rattles his sword in its scabbard, instead of a horse's bit.⁸ At the clink of the hilt Yuranosuke suddenly rises.

YURANOSUKE: Is that you, Rikiya? Has something urgent come up? Is that why you rattled the scabbard? Keep your voice low.

---

⁵ Samurai were accorded stipends of rice, measured in *koku* (about 5 bushels).
⁶ Sounds intended to suggest the music of the samisen.
⁷ A *ri* is about 2½ miles.
⁸ Samurai dozing on horseback were said to awaken to the sound of the horse's bit.

RIKIYA: An express courier just brought a secret letter from Lady Kaoyo.

YURANOSUKE: Was there no verbal message besides?

RIKIYA: Our enemy Kō no Moronao's petition to return to his province has been granted and he will shortly start for home. Her ladyship said the details would be found in her letter.

YURANOSUKE: Very good. You return home and send a palanquin for me tonight. Be off now.

NARRATOR: Without a flicker of hesitation Rikiya sets off for Yamashina. Yuranosuke, worried about the contents of the letter, is about to cut the seal when a voice calls.

KUDAYŪ: Master Ōboshi! Master Yuranosuke! It's me, Ono Kudayū. I'd like a word with you.

YURANOSUKE: Well! I haven't seen you in a long time. How wrinkled you've become in the year since we last met. Have you come to this house to unfurrow those wrinkles? What an old lecher you are!

KUDAYŪ: Yura—they say little faults are overlooked in a great achievement. The fast life you've led here in the gay quarters, in defiance of people's criticism, will pave the foundation for your achievements. I consider you a hero, a man of great promise.

YURANOSUKE: Ha, ha. What a hard line you take! You've set up a perfect battery of catapults against me. But let's talk about something else.

KUDAYŪ: There's no point in pretending, Yuranosuke. Your dissipation is, in fact—

YURANOSUKE: You think it's a trick to enable me to attack the enemy?

KUDAYŪ: Of course I do.

YURANOSUKE: How you flatter me! I thought you'd laugh at me as a fool, a madman—over forty and still a slave to physical pleasure. But you tell me it's all a scheme to attack the enemy! Thank you, good Kudayū. You've made me happy.

KUDAYŪ: Then you have no intention of avenging our master Enya?

YURANOSUKE: Not in the least. I know that when we were about to turn over the house and the domain I said I would die fighting in the castle, but that was only to please her ladyship. I remember how you stalked out of the room at the time, saying that resistance would make us enemies of the shogun. But we continued our debate in deadly earnest. What idiots we were! In any case, our discussion got nowhere. We said we'd commit *seppuku* before his lordship's tomb, but one after another we stole out the back gate. I have you to thank for being able to enjoy these pleasures here, and I haven't forgotten our old friendship. Don't act so stiff! Relax with me.

KUDAYŪ: Yes, I see now, when I think back on the old days, that I used to be quite a fraud myself. Shall I show you my true nature and have a drink with you? How about it, Yuranosuke? The first cup we've shared in a long time.
YURANOSUKE: Are you going to ask for the cup back, as at a formal banquet?
KUDAYŪ: Pour the liquor and I'll drink.
YURANOSUKE: Drink up and I'll pour.
KUDAYŪ: Have a full cup. Here, I'll give you something to eat with it.
NARRATOR: He picks up in his chopsticks a piece of octopus that happens to be near him and holds it out to Yuranosuke.
YURANOSUKE: Putting out my hand, I accept an octopus foot. Thank you!
KUDAYŪ: Yuranosuke—tomorrow is the anniversary of the death of our master, Enya Hangan. The night before the anniversary is supposed to be especially important. Are you going to eat that octopus and think nothing of it?[9]
YURANOSUKE: Of course I'll eat it. Or have you had word that Lord Enya has turned into an octopus? What foolish ideas you get into your head! You and I are *rōnin* now, thanks to Lord Hangan's recklessness. That's why I hold a grudge against him. I haven't the faintest intention of becoming a vegetarian for his sake, and I'm delighted to sample the fish you've so kindly provided.
NARRATOR: With the greatest aplomb he gulps down the fish in a single mouthful, a sight that stuns even the crafty Kudayū into silence.
YURANOSUKE: This fish is no good for drinking. We'll get them to wring a chicken's neck and give us chicken in the pot. Let's go to the back room. Come along, girls, and sing for us.
KUDAYŪ (*sings*):

> On uncertain legs he staggers off
> To the lively beat of the samisens
> Tere tsuku teretsuku tsutsuten tsutsuten . . .

YURANOSUKE (*to jesters*): Hey, you small fry! Do you expect to be let off without getting soused?
NARRATOR: Amid all the bustle he goes within. Sagisaka Bannai, who has been observing everything from beginning to end, comes down from the second floor.
BANNAI: I've kept close watch on him, Kudayū, and I can't believe a man so rotten at the core he'd even eat animal food on the

---

[9] The offer of octopus is significant as a test of Yuranosuke's attitude because those in mourning must abstain from animal food.

anniversary of his master's death will ever attack his enemy. I intend to report this to my master Moronao, and to recommend that he relax his precautions and open his gates.

KUDAYŪ: You're right. Lord Moronao need not take such precautions any more.

BANNAI: Look here—he's forgotten his sword!

KUDAYŪ: Yes, that really proves what a nitwit he's become. Let's examine this symbol of his samurai spirit. Why, it's rusty as a red sardine!

BANNAI: Ha, ha, ha!

KUDAYŪ: This certainly shows us his true nature. Your master can set his mind at rest. (*Calls.*) Where are my servants? I'm leaving. Bring my palanquin!

NARRATOR: With a shout they bring it forth.

KUDAYŪ: Now, Bannai, please get in.

BANNAI: No, sir, you're older than I. After you, please.

KUDAYŪ: In that case, by your leave.

NARRATOR: He gets in.

BANNAI: By the way, Kudayū, I hear that Kampei's wife is working in this place. Have you run into her here?

NARRATOR: Surprised not to receive a reply, he lifts the bamboo blinds of the palanquin and sees inside a fair-sized stone.

BANNAI: Good heavens! Kudayū has turned into a stone, like Lady Sayo of Matsuura![10]

NARRATOR: He looks around him. A voice calls from under the veranda.

KUDAYŪ: Here I am, Bannai. I've played a trick and slipped out of the palanquin. I'm worried about the letter Rikiya brought a while ago. I'll watch what happens and let you know later on. Follow along beside the palanquin. Act as if we were leaving together.

BANNAI: I will.

NARRATOR: He nods in agreement and slowly walks beside the palanquin, pretending someone is inside.

Meanwhile, Kampei's wife Okaru is recovering in her upstairs room from intoxication; familiar now with the Quarter, she lets the blowing breezes dispel her sadness.

YURANOSUKE (*to women in back room*): I'll be back in a moment. Yuranosuke's supposed to be a samurai, but he's forgotten his precious sword. I'll go and fetch it. In the meantime, straighten the kakemono[11] and put some charcoal on the stove.—Oh, I must be careful not to step on that samisen and break it. Well, that's a surprise! It looks as if Kudayū's gone. (*Sings.*)

---

[10] The Lady Sayo waved her scarf so long at the ship bearing her husband away that she finally turned to stone.
[11] Wall-hanging.

He hears a tearful voice that cries,
"Father! Mother!" and to his surprise,
The words came from a parrot's beak:
His wife had taught the bird to speak!

NARRATOR: Yuranosuke looks around the room; then, standing under the light of a lantern hanging from the eaves, he reads the long letter from Lady Kaoyo describing in detail the enemy's situation. The letter is in woman's language, full of polite phrases, and not easy to follow. Okaru, envious of other people happily in love, tries to read the letter from upstairs, but it is dark and the letter far away and the writing indistinct. It occurs to her that by holding out her mirror to reflect the writing she can read the message. Under the veranda, by the light of the moon, Kudayū reads the letter as it unrolls and hangs, but Yuranosuke, being no god, is unaware of this. Okaru's hair ornament suddenly comes loose and falls. Yuranosuke looks up at the sound and hides the letter behind him. Kudayū, under the veranda, is still in smiles; Okaru in the upstairs room hides her mirror.

OKARU: Is that you, Yura?

YURANOSUKE: Oh, it's you, Okaru. What are you doing there?

OKARU: You got me completely drunk. It was so painful I've been cooling myself in the breeze, trying to sober up.

YURANOSUKE: You're lucky to have such a good breeze. But Okaru, there's a little matter I'd like to discuss with you. I can't talk from here, across the rooftops, like the two stars across the Milky Way—won't you come down here for a moment?

OKARU: Is this matter you'd like to discuss some favor you want to ask me?

YURANOSUKE: Yes, something like that.

OKARU: I'll go around and come down.

YURANOSUKE: No, if you go by the staircase some maid is sure to catch you and make you drink.

OKARU: What shall I do, then?

YURANOSUKE: Look—luckily there's a nine-runged ladder lying here. You can use it to come down.

NARRATOR: He leans the ladder against the eaves of the lower floor.

OKARU: What a funny ladder! Oh, I'm afraid! It feels dangerous somehow.

YURANOSUKE: Don't worry. You're way past the age for feeling afraid or in danger. You could come down three rungs at a time and still not open any new wounds.

OKARU: Don't be silly. I'm afraid. It feels like I'm on a boat.

YURANOSUKE: Of course it does. I can see your little boat god from here.

OKARU: Ohh—you mustn't peep!

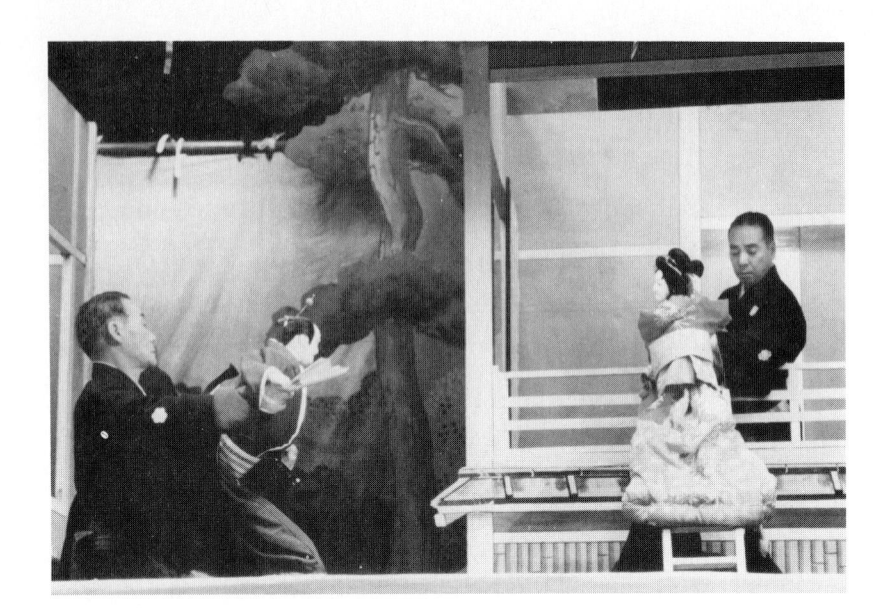

Yuranosuke and Okaru.

YURANOSUKE: I'm admiring the autumn moon over Lake T'ung-t'ing.
OKARU: I won't come down if you're going to act that way.
YURANOSUKE: If you won't come down, I'll knock you up.
OKARU: There you go again with your awful language.
YURANOSUKE: You make such a fuss anybody would think you were a virgin. I'll take you from behind.
NARRATOR: He catches her in his arms from behind and sets her on the ground.
YURANOSUKE: Tell me, did you see anything?
OKARU: No, no, I didn't.
YURANOSUKE: I'm sure you did.
OKARU: It looked like a letter from a girl friend.
YURANOSUKE: Did you read the whole thing from up there?
OKARU: Why are you grilling me so?
YURANOSUKE: It's a matter of life and death.
OKARU: What in the world are you talking about?
YURANOSUKE: I mean—I know it's an old story, Okaru, but I've fallen for you. Will you be my wife?
OKARU: Now stop it! You're lying to me.
YURANOSUKE: The truth may have started as a lie, but if I didn't really mean it, I couldn't go through with it. Say yes, please.
OKARU: No, I won't.
YURANOSUKE: But why?
OKARU: Because what you say is not truth that started as a lie, but a lie that started as truth.
YURANOSUKE: Okaru, I'll redeem your contract.

OKARU: Will you?

YURANOSUKE: I'll prove to you I'm not lying. I'll buy out your contract tonight.

OKARU: No, I have a—

YURANOSUKE: If you have a lover, you can live with him.

OKARU: Do you really mean it?

YURANOSUKE: I swear, by the providence that made me a samurai. As long as I can keep you for three days, you are at liberty to do what you please afterwards.

OKARU: I'm sure you just want me to say how happy I am before you laugh at me.

YURANOSUKE: Absolutely not. I'll give the master the money at once and settle things here and now. You wait here and don't worry about anything.

OKARU: Then I'll wait for you. I promise.

YURANOSUKE: Don't move from the spot until I get back from paying the money. You're my wife now.

OKARU: And just for three days.

YURANOSUKE: Yes, I've agreed.

OKARU: I'm most grateful.

NARRATOR (*sings*):

> *If ever woman was born*
> *Unlucky, I'm the one.*
> *How many pangs I've suffered*
> *For the man I love, alas.*
> *I cry alone with muffled notes*
> *Like a plover of the night.*

Okaru, hearing this song from the back room, is sunk in thought as she feels how closely its words fit herself. At that moment Heiemon suddenly appears.

HEIEMON: Okaru—is that you?

OKARU: Heiemon! How shaming to meet you here!

NARRATOR: She hides her face.

HEIEMON: There's nothing to feel ashamed about. I stopped to see Mother on my way back from the East and she told me everything. It was noble of you to have sold yourself for your husband and our master. I'm proud of you.

OKARU: I am happy if you can think so kindly of me. But I have good news for you. Tonight, most unexpectedly, my contract is to be redeemed.

HEIEMON: No news could please me more. Whom have we to thank for this?

OKARU: Someone you know, Ōboshi Yuranosuke.

HEIEMON: What did you say? Your contract is to be redeemed by Ōboshi Yuranosuke? Have you been intimate with him for a long time?

OKARU: How could I have been? I've occasionally, perhaps two or three times, drunk with him. He said that if I had a husband I could stay with him, and if I wanted to be free he would let me go. It's almost too good to be true.

HEIEMON: You mean, he doesn't know you're married to Hayano Kampei?

OKARU: No, he doesn't. How could I tell him, when my being here is a disgrace to my parents and my husband?

HEIEMON: It would seem, then, he's a libertine at heart. Obviously he has no intention of avenging our master.

OKARU: No, that's not so. He has, I know it. I can't say it aloud, but I'll whisper it. (*Whispers.*)

HEIEMON: Then you definitely saw what the letter said?

OKARU: I read every word. Then we happened to look each other in the face and he began to flirt with me. Finally he talked about redeeming me.

HEIEMON: This was after you read the whole letter?

OKARU: Yes.

HEIEMON: I understand everything, then. My sister, you're doomed. You can't escape. Let me take your life.

NARRATOR: He draws his sword and slashes at her, but she jumps nimbly aside.

OKARU: What is it, Heiemon? What have I done wrong? You're not free to kill me as you please. I have my husband Kampei and both my parents too. I've been looking forward so much to seeing my parents and my husband as soon as my contract is redeemed. Whatever my offense may be, I apologize. Please forgive me, pardon me.

NARRATOR: She clasps her hands in supplication. Heiemon flings down his naked sword and gives way to bitter tears.

HEIEMON: My poor dear sister. I see you know nothing of what happened. Our father, Yoichibei, was stabbed to death by a stranger on the night of the twenty-ninth of the sixth month.

OKARU: It's not possible!

HEIEMON: You haven't heard the worst. You say you want to join Kampei as soon as you're redeemed. But he committed *seppuku* and is dead.

OKARU: Oh, no! Is it true? Tell me!

NARRATOR: She clutches him and, with a cry, collapses in tears.

HEIEMON: I understand. No wonder you cry. But it would make too long a story to tell you everything. I feel sorriest for Mother. Every time she mentions what happened she weeps, every time she remembers she weeps again. She begged me not to tell you, saying you'd cry yourself to death if you knew. I made up my mind not to tell you, but you can't escape death now. Yuranosuke is singlemindedly, fanatically motivated by loyalty. He'd have had no reason to ransom you if he didn't know you were Kampei's wife. Certainly it wasn't because he's infatuated with you. The letter you saw was of the greatest importance. He will redeem your contract only to kill you. I'm sure that's what he has in mind. Even if you tell no one about the letter, the walls have ears, and any word of the plan leaking from somebody else is sure to be blamed on you. You were wrong to have peeped into a secret letter, and you must be killed for it. Rather than let you die at a stranger's hands, I will kill you with my own hands. I can't allow any woman with knowledge of the great secret to escape, even if she's my own sister. On the strength of having killed a person dangerous to our plot I shall ask to join the league and go with the others. The sad thing about being of the lower ranks is that unless you prove to the other samurai your spirit is better than theirs, they won't let you join them. Show you understand by giving me your life. Die for my sake, sister.

NARRATOR: Okaru sobs again and again as she listens to her brother's carefully reasoned words.

OKARU: I kept thinking all the while that the reason why he didn't write me was that he'd used the money I raised as the price of my body and started on his journey. I was resentful because he hadn't even come to say good-by. It's a dreadful thing for me to say, but though Father met a horrible death he was, after all, an old man. But how sad and humiliating it must have been for Kampei to die when he was hardly thirty! I'm sure he must have wanted to see me. Why didn't anyone take me to him? What a terrible fate never even to have abstained from animal food in mourning for my husband and father. What reason have I to go on living? But if I died at your hands I'm sure Mother would hate you for it. I'll kill myself. After I'm dead, if my head or my body can bring you credit, please use it for that purpose. Now I must say farewell to you, my brother.

NARRATOR: She takes up the sword.

YURANOSUKE: Stop! Wait a moment!

NARRATOR: Yuranosuke restrains her. Heiemon jumps in astonishment. Okaru cries out.

OKARU: Let me go! Let me die!

NARRATOR: Yuranosuke holds her back and she struggles, impatient for death.

YURANOSUKE: You are an admirable brother and sister. All my doubts have been resolved. Heiemon, you may join us on our eastward journey. You, Okaru, must live on so you can offer prayers for the future repose of his soul.

OKARU: I'll pray for him by going with him to the afterworld.

NARRATOR: Yuranosuke holds firmly the sword he has twisted from her grasp.

YURANOSUKE: We admitted your husband Kampei to our league, but he was never able to kill a single enemy. What excuse will he be able to offer our master when he meets him in the afterworld? This may serve as his apology!

NARRATOR: He drives the sword hard between the mats. Underneath the floor Kudayū, his shoulder run through, writhes in agony.

YURANOSUKE: Drag him out!

NARRATOR: Even before the command leaves Yuranosuke's mouth, Heiemon leaps from the veranda and resolutely drags out Kudayū, dripping with blood.

HEIEMON: Kudayū! It serves you right!

NARRATOR: He hauls him up and throws him before Yuranosuke, who grabs Kudayū by the topknot, not letting him rise, and pulls him over.

YURANOSUKE: The worm that feeds on the lion's body—that's you! You received a large stipend from our master and benefited by innumerable other kindnesses, and yet you became a spy for his enemy Moronao and secretly informed him of everything, true and false alike. The forty and more of us have left our parents and separated from our children, and have even forced our wives, who should have been our lifelong companions, to work as prostitutes, all out of the desire to avenge our late master. As soon as we wake up in the morning, then all through the day, we think about how he committed *seppuku*, and the remembrances arouse tears of impotent rage. We have racked ourselves with pain, mind and body. Tonight especially, the night before our master's anniversary, I spoke vile words of every sort, but in my heart I was practicing the most profound abstention. How dared you thrust fish before my face? What anguish I felt in my heart, not being able to accept or refuse. And how do you think I felt on the night before the anniversary of a master whose family my family has served for three generations, when the fish passed my throat? My whole body seemed to crumble to pieces all at once, and my bones felt as though they were breaking. Ahh—you fiend, you diabolical monster!

NARRATOR: He rubs and twists Kudayū's body into the ground, then breaks into tears of despair.

YURANOSUKE: Heiemon, I forgot my rusty sword a while ago. It was a sign I was meant to torture him to death with it. Make him suffer, but don't kill him.

HEIEMON: Yes, sir.

NARRATOR: He unsheathes his sword and at once leaps and pounces on Kudayū, slashing him again and again, though the wounds are superficial. He scores Kudayū's body until no part is left unscathed.

KUDAYŪ: Heiemon, Okaru, please intercede for me!

NARRATOR: He joins his hands in entreaty. What a repulsive sight—Kudayū, who always despised Teraoka as a lowly foot

soldier, and refused to favor him with so much as a glance, now prostrates himself humbly.
YURANOSUKE: If we kill him here we'll have trouble explaining it. Pretend he's drunk and take him home.
NARRATOR: He throws his cloak over Kudayū to hide the wounds. Yazama, Senzaki, and Takemori, who have been listening in secret, fling open the sliding doors.
THREE MEN: Yuranosuke, we humbly apologize.
YURANOSUKE: Heiemon—this customer has had too much to drink. Give him some watery gruel for his stomach in the Kamo River.
HEIEMON: Yes, sir.
YURANOSUKE: Go!

Further Readings

E. Matsushima, *Chushingura* (Tokyo: Iwanami Shoten, 1964), provides a helpful treatment of both the historical background and composition of the play. *Chushingura: Studies in Kabuki and Puppet Theater*, edited by James R. Brandon (Honolulu: University of Hawaii Press, 1982), includes four articles focusing on the play and concludes with a text of the *Forty-Seven Ronin*. Sakae Shioya, *Chushingura, an Exposition* (Tokyo: The Hokuseido Press, 1940), is a retelling of the historical events followed by a summary of the action of the play. Yasuji Toita, *Chushingura* (Tokyo: Sogensha, 1957), is a useful discussion of the different traditions in the performance of the play.

Three worthwhile surveys of Kabuki theater are A. C. Scott, *The Kabuki Theater of Japan* (New York: Macmillan Co., 1966); Earl Ernst, *The Kabuki Theater* (New York: Oxford University Press, 1956); and Yasuji Toita, *Kabuki, the Popular Theater*, translated by D. Kenny (New York and Tokyo: Walker/Weatherhill, 1970). Donald Keene, *Bunraku: The Puppet Theater of Japan* (Tokyo and Palo Alto, CA: Kodansha International Ltd., 1965), presents an interesting discussion of Japanese puppet theater.

Peter Arnett, *The Theatres of Japan* (New York: Macmillan Co., 1969), traces the development of classical Japanese theatrical forms and their influence on modern productions. English translations of some Kabuki plays are available in Samuel L. Leiter, *The Art of Kabuki* (Berkeley, CA: University of California Press, 1979), and in *Kabuki: Five Classic Plays*, translated by James R. Brandon (Cambridge, MA: Harvard University Press, 1975). William Malm, *Nagauta: The Heart of Kabuki Music* (Tokyo: Tuttle, 1963), is an informative study of the music of the Kabuki theater.

The Scholars

The Scholars (Ju-lin wai-shih), completed around 1750 and first published two or three decades later, is considered one of the great novels of the Chinese tradition. A loosely connected series of satirical stories revolving about various members of the scholar class, it is the first Chinese novel of significant scope that does not borrow its characters from history and legend. Its author drew heavily upon his own experiences; many of the characters of *The Scholars* were modelled upon his friends and acquaintances, and his descriptions of people and places are recollections of his own observations.

A member of a scholarly family that had distinguished itself in government service during late Ming and early Ch'ing times, Wu Ching-tzu (1701–1754) appears to have been poorly prepared for a competitive official life. Although he succeeded in gaining the preliminary academic degree, he failed in subsequent civil-service examinations. Having squandered his fortune, he moved his family from his native town to the city of Nanking in 1734. Here he lived the life of an idle scholar until composing his great novel.

Wu's continual failures to pass the civil-service examinations embittered him toward this highly competitive system that lay at the heart of imperial government. Designed to attract the most talented individuals into government service and to weed out those less fit for service, the examination system allowed the ambitious and able scholar entry to a well-defined ladder of advancement that led to prestige, power, and wealth. *The Scholars* is primarily an attack upon the absurdities of this system and the shortcomings of those involved in it. It is notable not only for its satiric portrayal of scholars and pseudo-scholars, however, but also for its descriptions of ordinary men and women functioning within their normal surroundings.

The autobiographical hero of the piece is Tu Shao-ch'ing, an aristocrat who refuses to take advantage of others. Tu foolishly

From Wu Ching-tzu, *The Scholars,* translated by Yang Hsien-yi and Gladys Yang (New York: Universal Library, 1972), pp. 387–413.

squanders his family fortunes through his extravagant generosity to a number of individuals who have no scruples about compromising their own honor to take advantage of the noble hero. Tu rejects the opportunity to enter government service and, with all his proud nonconformity, moves to the metropolis of Nanking to live among more congenial friends. Here he spends the remaining years of his life enjoying the scenic spots and engaging in intellectual conversation.

The excerpt provided here presents Tu as an appealing person, a proud and honest scholar, but prone to reckless generosity. He is not blind to the lack of character of the petitioners who besiege him. He is certainly aware that his steward Wang is corrupt and that many of his guests are dishonest flatterers. He is moved to tears when the dying Mr. Lou advises him to end his indiscriminate generosity and to pattern his conduct upon that of his virtuous father. He cannot control himself, however, and is eventually impoverished.

The Scholars was the first Chinese work of satiric realism to detach itself from the common religious beliefs of its day. Popular Buddhist writings of the time generally depicted the virtuous as rewarded and the wicked as punished. Wu shunned this facile didacticism. In the world of *The Scholars,* as in the real world, a virtuous individual is not necessarily rewarded and the wicked often prosper precisely because they are unscrupulous.

Questions

1. The Western reader often prefers a hero dedicated to a life of action. Describe Tu Shao-ch'ing's character. Do you find him admirable and virtuous? Why or why not?

2. Which does the author consider the more blameworthy, ignorance or immorality?

3. What relationship exists between learning and the attainment of worldly success?

4. The cornerstone of *The Scholars* is the attainment of true virtue. What constitutes true virtue for the author?

THE SCHOLARS

LIST OF PRINCIPAL CHARACTERS

TU-SHAO-CHING, *brilliant scholar who squanders his fortune*
TU SHEN-CHING, *his cousin*
PAO TING-HSI, *adopted son of Pao Wen-ching, son of Ni Shuang-feng*
WEI SSU-HSUAN (Fourth Mr. Wei), *Tu Shao-ching's friend*
WHISKERS WANG, *Tu Shao-ching's steward*

CHANG CHUN-MIN (Iron-armed Chang), *swordsman and charlatan*
TSANG LIAO-CHAI, *licentiate*
HSIANG TING, *magistrate of Antung, later intendant of Ting-chang Circuit*
MR LOU, *an old retainer of Tu Shao-ching's family*

VISITORS CALL ON A GALLANT IN TIENCHANG COUNTY.
GOOD FRIENDS DRINK WINE IN TU SHAO-CHING'S LIBRARY

Pao Ting-hsi was amazed at the amount of money Tu Shen-ching had spent on the contest.

"Why don't I take advantage of his generosity to borrow a few hundred taels?"[1] he thought. "Then I can start another opera company, and make enough to live on."

Having reached this decision, he made himself so useful every day in the house by the river that Tu began to feel under an obligation to him. And late one night, when none of the servants were in the room, they had a frank talk.

"What do you live on, Mr. Pao?" inquired Tu. "You ought to go into some kind of business, you know."

At this question, Ting-hsi plumped down on both knees. Quite taken aback, Tu helped him up.

"What is the meaning of this?" he asked.

"You are as kind as heaven and as generous as the earth to put that question to your humble servant, sir!" cried Ting-hsi. "But I used to manage an opera company, and that is the only trade I know. If you want to befriend me, sir, will you be good enough to lend me a few hundred taels, so that I can start another company? As soon as I have money, I will repay you."

"That should be easy," said Tu. "Sit down, and let's talk it over. A few hundred taels isn't enough to start an opera company—you'll need at least a thousand. Between ourselves, I don't mind telling you that although I have a few thousand taels of ready money, I don't want to spend it at the moment. Why not? In the next year or two I expect to pass the palace examination, and after that, of course, I'll need a lot of money; so for the time being I must hold on to what I have. Regarding this company of yours, I can tell you somebody who can help. It will be the same as if I helped you myself. But you mustn't let him know I put you up to this."

"Who else but you will help me, sir?" demanded Ting-hsi.

"Steady on. Listen to me. There are seven main branches to my family. The Minister of Ceremony belonged to the fifth branch. Two generations ago, the head of the seventh branch passed first in the palace examination, and his son was prefect of Kanchow in Kiangsi. He was my uncle, and his son is my twenty-fifth cousin, Shao-ching. He's two years younger than I am, and has passed the district examination too. My uncle was an honest officer, who didn't

---

[1] A unit of value, based on a weight of silver equal to about $\frac{1}{12}$ pound.

add anything to the family estate and left no more than ten thousand taels at his death. But, like a fool, Shao-ching acts as if he had hundreds of thousands. He doesn't know the difference between good silver and bad, yet he loves to act the patron. Anyone with a bad luck story can be sure of substantial help from him. Why don't you stay and help me out till autumn, when it's cooler? Then I'll give you your fare to Tienchang. I guarantee you'll get your thousand taels."

"I hope you will write a letter of introduction for me, sir, when the time comes."

"No, no. That would never do. He likes to be the one and only patron helping anybody—he doesn't like others to join in. If I were to write, he would think I'd already helped you, and wouldn't trouble to do anything for you. You must apply to someone else first."

"To whom?"

"My cousin used to have an old steward called Shao, whom you ought to know."

"He came one year when my father was alive," said Ting-hsi after thinking hard. "He arranged for us to give a performance for the old mistress's birthday! I saw the Prefect of Kanchow too."

"Excellent! Old Shao is dead now, and the present steward is a thoroughgoing scoundrel called Whiskers Wang, whom his master trusts implicitly. My cousin's weakness is this: anybody who claims to have known his father—even a dog—wins his respect. You must call on Whiskers Wang first. The rascal likes drinking and, if you treat him to wine and persuade him to tell his master that you were a favourite with the old prefect, then Shao-ching will shower you with silver. He doesn't like to be addressed as the master, so call him 'the young master.' Another of his peculiarities is that he can't stand talk about officials or rich men. Don't tell him, for instance, how good Prefect Hsiang was to you. Keep on harping on the fact that he is the only true patron in the world. And if he asks you whether you know me, tell him you don't."

This conversation left Pao Ting-hsi overjoyed. He made himself useful in Tu's household for another two months, until the end of the seventh month when the weather began to grow cooler. Then he borrowed a few taels from Tu Shen-ching, packed his luggage, and crossed the river to travel to Tien-chang.

The day that he crossed the Yangtse, he put up for the night at Liuho. The next morning he rose early and travelled a dozen miles or more to a place called Fourth Mount, where he went into an inn and sat down. He was just going to ask for water to wash when a sedan-chair stopped at the gate. From it alighted an old man in a square cap, white gauze gown and red silk slippers who had the red nose of a heavy drinker, and a long, silky, silvery beard. As this old man came in, the inn-keeper hastened to take his luggage.

"So it is the fourth Mr. Wei!" he cried. "Please take a seat inside, sir!"

Wu Ching-tzu, author of The Scholars.

As Mr. Wei entered the main room, Ting-hsi stood up and bowed. Mr. Wei returned his greeting. Ting-hsi urged him to take the seat of honour, and sat down himself in a lower place.

"I believe your name is Wei, sir," he said. "May I venture to ask your honourable district?"

"My name is Wei, and I come from Wuyi in Chuchow. What are your name and district, sir? And where are you bound for?"

"My name is Pao, and I am a native of Nanking. I am on my way to Tienchang, to visit the Mr. Tu whose grandfather was a Number One Scholar."

"Which Mr. Tu? Shen-ching or Shao-ching?"

"Shao-ching."

"There are sixty or seventy young men in the Tu family, but those are the only two who keep open house. The rest stay behind closed doors at home to prepare for the examination and look after their estates. That's why I asked straight away which of the two you meant. They are both well known all down the Yangtse Valley. Shen-ching is a most cultivated individual, but a little too effeminate for my taste. Shao-ching is a true gentleman of the old school. I'm on my way to see him too. We can travel together after we've eaten."

"Are you related to the Tu family, sir?"

"I was a classmate and sworn brother of Prefect Tu's. We were very close friends."

Upon hearing this, Ting-hsi's manner became even more respectful.

After their meal, Mr. Wei mounted his chair again. Ting-hsi hired a donkey, and trotted along beside the chair. When they reached Tienchang city gate, Mr. Wei dismounted.

"Let us walk to the house together, Mr. Pao," he said.

"Pray go on ahead in your chair, sir," replied Ting-hsi. "I want to see his steward first, before paying my respects to Mr. Tu."

"Very well," said Mr. Wei, and mounted his chair again.

When he reached Tu's house, his arrival was announced by the gate-keeper. Tu Shao-ching hastened out to meet him, and invited him into the hall, where they exchanged greetings.

"We have not seen each other for half a year, uncle," said Shao-ching. "I ought to have called to inquire after your health and that of your wife. Have you been well?"

"Quite well, thank you. There is nothing to do at home at the beginning of autumn, and I remembered your garden and reckoned the cassia must be in full blossom now. So I came to pay you a visit and drink with you."

"When tea has been served, I will invite you to have a rest in the library."

When a boy brought in tea, Tu Shao-ching gave him the order:

"Bring in Mr. Wei's baggage, and put it in the library. Then pay the chair-bearers and send them away."

Presently he led Mr. Wei by a passage from the back along a winding path to the garden. As you went in you saw three rooms with an eastern exposure. A two-storeyed building on the left was the library built by the Number One Scholar, overlooking a large courtyard with one bed of *moutan* peonies and another of tree peonies. There were two huge cassia trees as well, in full bloom. On the other side were three summer houses, with a three-roomed library behind them overlooking a great lotus pool. A bridge across this pool led you to three secluded chambers where Tu Shao-ching used to retire to study.

He invited Mr. Wei into the library with the southern exposure. The two cassia trees were just outside the window.

"Is old Lou still here?" asked Mr. Wei as he sat down.

"Mr. Lou's health has been very poor recently," replied Shao-ching, "so I have made him move into the inner library. He has just gone to sleep after taking his medicine. I'm afraid he won't be able to come out to greet you, uncle."

"If he is ill, why don't you send him home?"

"I have brought his sons and grandsons here to prepare his medicine. In this way I can inquire after his health morning and evening."

"After being with your family for thirty-odd years, hasn't the old man put by a substantial sum of money? Hasn't he bought any property?"

"After my father was appointed Prefect of Kanchow, he gave the books for the entire property to Mr. Lou. Mr. Lou was in complete charge of all financial transactions, and my father never questioned him. Apart from his salary of forty taels of silver a year, Mr. Lou didn't touch a cent. When the time came for collecting rent, he would go down to the country to visit the tenants himself; and if they prepared two dishes for him, he would send one away and eat one only. Whenever his sons or grandsons came to see him, he would pack them off after two days, and would never allow them to take a cent beyond their travelling money. In fact, he used to search them as they were leaving, to make sure none of the stewards had given them any silver. But in collecting rents or interest, if he discovered any of our friends or relatives were in difficulties, he would do his best to help them. My father knew this, but didn't query it. Sometimes when my father's debtors were unable to pay, Mr. Lou would burn their notes of hand. Though he is an old man now with two sons and four grandsons, he is still no richer than before. I feel very bad about it!"

"A true gentleman of the old school!" exclaimed Mr. Wei admiringly. "Is Shen-ching at home and well?"

"My cousin has gone to Nanking."

Just then Whiskers Wang took up his stand outside the window with a red card in his hand, but did not presume to enter.

"What is it, Wang?" asked Shao-ching, catching sight of him. "What's that in your hand?"

The steward came in and handed the card to his master.

"A man called Pao is here from Nanking," he announced. "He's a theatre manager, who has been away from home for the last few years and has only just come back. Now he's crossed the river to pay his respects to you, sir."

"If he's in the theatre, tell him I have guests and can't see him. Keep his card, and ask him to leave."

"He says he was very kindly treated by our late master, sir. He wants very much to see you to thank you."

"Did my father help him out?"

"Yes, sir. One year Mr. Shao fetched his company across the river, and the prefect took a great fancy to this Pao Ting-hsi. He promised to look after him."

"In that case, show him in."

"I met this fellow Pao from Nanking on the road," said Mr. Wei.

Whiskers Wang went out to fetch Pao Ting-hsi, who advanced reverently. He looked round the spacious garden, and could see no end to it. Upon reaching the library door, he saw Tu Shao-ching sitting there with a guest. Tu was wearing a square cap, jade-coloured lined gauze gown, and pearl-decked shoes. He had a rather sallow complexion and eyebrows which rose obliquely, like a portrait of the God of War.

"That is our young master," said Whiskers Wang. "You can go in."

Pao Ting-hsi went in, knelt down and kowtowed.

"We are old friends," said Tu, helping him up. "Don't stand on ceremony."

Ting-hsi rose to his feet and exchanged greetings, first with Tu, then with Mr. Wei. Tu Shao-ching invited him to be seated on a lower seat.

"I owe your father such a debt of gratitude that even if my bones are ground to powder it will be hard to repay him," said Ting-hsi. "Because things have not gone well with me these last few years and I have been busy touring with my players, I did not come to pay my respects to the young master. Only today have I come to inquire after the young master's health. I hope you will forgive me, sir, for being so remiss."

"Just now," said Tu, "my steward Wang told me that my father took a great fancy to you, and meant to look after you. Since you are here, you must stay, and I will see what I can do for you."

"Dinner is ready, sir," announced Whiskers Wang. "Where would you like it served?"

"Why not here?" suggested Mr. Wei.

"We need a fourth," said Tu, and after a moment's hesitation called the library boy, Chia Chueh.

"Go out through the back gate and invite Dr. Chang over," he ordered.

Chia Chueh assented and left.

Presently the boy returned accompanied by a man with large eyes and a brownish moustache, who was wearing a tile-shaped cap and a wide cloth gown. Swaying as he walked in imitation of a scholar's gait, he came in, greeted them, sat down, and asked Mr. Wei's name.

"And what is your honourable name, sir?" inquired Mr. Wei, after giving his own.

"I am Chang Chun-min," was the reply, "and have served the Tu family for many years. I have a smattering of medical knowledge, and the young master does me the honour of calling me in every day to attend to Mr. Lou. How has the old gentleman been since he took his medicine today?"

Tu Shao-ching ordered Chia Chueh to go and find out.

"Mr. Lou had a nap after his medicine," reported the boy on his return. "He is awake now, and feels rather better."

"Who is *this* gentleman?" asked Chang, indicating Ting-hsi.

"This is my friend Pao from Nanking," replied Tu.

While they were speaking the table was spread, and they sat down: Mr. Wei in the seat of honour, Chang Chun-min opposite him, Tu Shao-ching in the place of host, and Pao Ting-hsi in the lowest seat. Their cups were filled, and they began to drink. The dishes to go with the wine had all been prepared at home, and were delicious. There was ham that had been hung for three years, and crabs weighing half a catty[2] each, removed from their shells before cooking.

"I have no doubt you have attained great skill in your calling," said Mr. Wei to Chang Chun-min while they were eating.

"A thorough knowledge of Wang Shu-ho[3] is not as good as experience of many diseases," quoted the doctor. "I won't deceive you, sir. I have knocked about a good deal outside without reading many books, but seeing plenty of patients. Only recently, thanks to the young master's advice, have I learned the need for book knowledge. So I am not teaching my son medicine, but have engaged a tutor for him; and he is writing compositions which he brings to show Mr. Tu. The young master always comments on them for him, and I also study these comments carefully at home, in this way learning something about literary composition. In another year or two I'll send my son in for the district examination, and he will get his share of dumplings as a candidate. Then, when he sets up in practice, he can call himself a scholarly physician!"

Mr. Wei laughed long and loud at this speech.

Then Whiskers Wang brought in another visiting card.

"Mr. Wang, the salt merchant at the North Gate, is celebrating his birthday tomorrow," he announced. "He has asked the magistrate as guest of honour, and invites you too, sir. He begs you to be sure to go."

"Tell him I have guests and cannot go," replied Tu. "How ridiculous the fellow is! If he wants a good party, why doesn't he invite those newly-rich scholars who have passed the provincial and metropolitan examinations? What time do I have to keep officials company for him?"

Whiskers Wang assented and left.

"You are a great drinker, uncle," said Tu to Mr. Wei. "You used to sit up half the night drinking with my father. We must have a good drinking session today too."

---

[2] Unit of weight equalling 16 taels, or about 1⅓ pounds.
[3] A physician of the Tsin Dynasty, whose books are medical classics.

"Yes," replied Mr. Wei. "I hope you don't mind my saying this, friend; but though your food is first-rate, this wine bought in the market is too new. You have one jar of wine in your house which must be eight or nine years old by now. Assuming, that is, you still have it."

"I didn't know that," said Tu.

"You wouldn't know," rejoined Mr. Wei. "The year that your father went to take up his post in Kiangsi, I saw him to the boat, and he told me: 'I've buried a jar of wine in my house. When my term of office is up and I come home, we'll do some serious drinking together.' That's why I remember. Why don't you ask your household?"

"The young master couldn't have known this." Chang Chun-min smiled.

Tu Shao-ching went to the inner chambers.

"Though Mr. Tu is young, he is one of the most gallant gentlemen in these parts," declared Mr. Wei.

"The young master is so good to everyone too!" put in the doctor. "If anything, he's too open-handed. No matter who makes a request of him, he gives the fellow taels and taels of silver."

"I've never seen such a generous, noble gentleman in all my life!" chimed in Ting-hsi.

Tu Shao-ching went to the inner chambers to ask his wife if she knew anything about this wine, but she did not. He asked all the servants and maids, but none of them knew. Last of all he questioned his wet-nurse, Shao.

"There *was* such a jar," she recalled. "The year that our late master became prefect he brewed a jar of wine and buried it in a small room at the back of the seventh court-yard. He said it was to be kept for Mr. Wei. The wine was made of two pecks of glutinous rice and twenty catties of fermented rice. Twenty catties of alcohol went into it too, but not a drop of water. It was buried nine years and seven months ago, so it must be strong enough now to blow your head off. When it's dug up, don't drink it, sir!"

"Very good," said Tu.

He ordered the wet-nurse to unlock the door of the room where wine was stored, and went in with two servants. They dug up the wine jar, and carried it to the library.

"I've found your wine, uncle!" he cried.

Mr. Wei and the two guests stood up to look at it.

"That's it!" cried Mr. Wei.

The jar was opened, and they ladled out a cupful. It stood as thick as gruel in the cup, and had a rich bouquet.

"This is capital!" exclaimed Mr. Wei. "I'll tell you how we must drink this, friend. Send out for another ten catties of wine to mix with it. We can't drink it today, so just leave it there for the present. We'll drink all day tomorrow. These two gentlemen must join us."

"We will certainly keep you company," said Chang.

"Who am I," asked Ting-hsi, "to drink this fine wine the prefect has left? Tomorrow will be the happiest day of my life!"

Presently Chia Chueh was told to fetch a lantern and escort the doctor home. Ting-hsi slept in the library with Mr. Wei, and Tu Shao-ching waited till the latter had gone to bed before retiring himself.

The next morning Pao Ting-hsi rose early and went to Whiskers Wang's room. Chia Chueh was sitting there with another servant.

"Is Mr. Wei up yet?" asked Whiskers Wang.

"He's up and washing his face," said Chia Chueh.

"Is the young master up?" the steward asked the other servant.

"He's been up a long time. He's in Mr. Lou's room, watching them prepare the medicine."

"Our master is an extraordinary man," declared Whiskers Wang. "Mr. Lou is only one of the prefect's employees! When he fell ill, our master should have given him a few taels of silver and sent him home—why keep him here and treat him as one of the family, waiting on him hand and foot?"

"How can you say that, Mr. Wang!" protested the servant. "When we prepare gruel or dishes for Mr. Lou, it's not enough for his sons and grandsons to inspect them—our master has to see them too before they can be given Mr. Lou! The ginseng pot is kept in the mistress's room, and of course she prepares the ginseng and other medicines herself. Every morning and evening, if our master can't take in the ginseng himself, it's the mistress who takes it in to the patient. If the master hears you talking like that, he'll give you a good dressing down!"

Just then the gate-keeper came in.

"Go in, Uncle Wang, and announce that the third Mr. Tsang is here," he said. "He's sitting in the hall, waiting to see the young master."

"Go and fetch the master from Mr. Lou's room," said Whiskers Wang to the servant. "I'm not going there to ask after Lou's health!"

"This just shows how good your master is," declared Ting-hsi.

Presently Tu Shao-ching came out to see Mr. Tsang, and after exchanging greetings they sat down.

"I haven't seen you for some days, Third Brother," remarked Tu. "What have you been doing in your literary groups?"

"Your gateman told me you had a guest from some distance," said Tsang. "Shen-ching seems to be enjoying himself so much in Nanking that he doesn't want to come back."

"Uncle Wei from Wuyi is here," said Tu. 'I'm preparing a feast for him today, and you must stay to it too. Let's both go to the library now."

"Wait a little," said Tsang. "I have something to say to you. Magistrate Wang here is my patron, and he's told me many times how much he admires your talent. When are you coming with me to see him?"

"I must leave it to you, Third Brother, to call on magistrates and pay your respects as a student," replied Tu. "Why, in my father's time—to say nothing of my grandfather's and great-grandfather's—heaven knows how many magistrates came here! If he really respects me, why doesn't he call on me first? Why should I call on him? I'm sorry I passed the district examination, since it means I have to address the local magistrate as my patron! As for this Magistrate Wang, who crawled out of some dust-heap to pass the metropolitan examination—I wouldn't even want him as my student! Why should I meet him? So when the salt merchant who lives at the North Gate invited me to a feast today to meet the magistrate, I refused to go."

"That's why I'm here," said Tsang. "Magistrate Wang wouldn't have accepted the invitation if the salt merchant hadn't told him you would be there too; but he wants to meet you. If you don't go, he will be very disappointed. Besides, your guest is staying here, so you can keep him company tomorrow if you go out today. Or, if you like, I'll keep your friend company today while you go to the salt merchant's."

"Please don't insist, Third Brother," said Tu. "Your patron is no lover of worth or talent; he likes to accept students simply in order to collect presents from them. He wants me as his student, does he? He must be dreaming! In any case, I have guests today; and we've cooked a seven-catty duck, and unearthed some nine-year-old wine. The salt merchant will have nothing so good to offer me! I won't hear another word about going! Come with me now to the library."

He started marching Tsang off.

"Stop a minute!" cried Tsang. "What's the hurry? I've never met Mr. Wei. I must write a card."

"All right."

Tu ordered a servant to bring an inkstone and card, and Mr. Tsang wrote: "Your kinsman and fellow candidate, Tsang Tu."

He bade the servant take this to the library, then went in with Tu Shao-ching. Mr. Wei came to the door to greet them, and they took seats. Chang Chun-min and Pao Ting-hsi, who were also there, sat down too.

"May I inquire your second name?" Mr. Wei asked Tsang.

"Mr. Tsang's second name is Liao-chai," said Tu. "He was one of the best students of my year, and is a good friend of Shen-ching's as well."

"I am delighted to make your acquaintance," said Mr. Wei.

"I have long wanted to meet you, sir," rejoined Tsang.

Tsang knew the doctor, but looking at Pao Ting-hsi he asked: "Who is *this* gentleman?"

"My name is Pao," replied Ting-hsi. "I have just arrived from Nanking."

"If you come from Nanking, do you know Mr. Tu Shen-ching?"

"I have met the seventeenth master."

When they had breakfasted, Mr. Wei brought out the wine and added ten catties of new wine to it, then ordered the servants to light plenty of charcoal and pile it when it was red by the cassia trees, setting the jar of wine on top. After the time it takes for a meal, the wine was hot. Chang Chun-min helped the servant take down the six window frames and move the table to under the eaves. They then took seats, and fresh dishes were served. Tu Shao-ching called for one gold and four jade cups, which he filled by dipping them into the wine. Mr. Wei had the gold cup, and after each drink exclaimed: "Marvellous! They had feasted for some time when Whiskers Wang led in four servants carrying a chest. Tu asked what it was.

"This is a chestful of new autumn clothes for you, sir, and for the mistress and young gentleman. They have just been made, and I've brought them for you to check. I've already paid the tailor."

"Leave them there," said Tu. "I'll look at them when we've finished drinking."

No sooner had the chest been set down than the tailor came in.

"Tailor Yang is here," announced Whiskers Wang.

"What does he want?" asked Tu.

He stood up and saw the tailor walk into the courtyard, kneel down and kowtow, then burst out sobbing.

"What is the matter, Mr. Yang?" demanded Tu, much surprised.

"I've been working all this time in your house, sir," said the tailor. "This morning when I received my pay, I didn't know that my mother would suddenly be taken ill and die. I didn't foresee this when I went home, so I used all the money to pay my fuel and rice bills. And now I haven't got a coffin for my mother, or mourning. There's nothing I can do but come back and beg you to lend me a few taels of silver. I'll work off the debt gradually."

"How much do you want?"

"I'm a poor man. I dare not ask for a lot. Six taels, if that's not too much, sir. Otherwise four taels. I must be able to pay it back by tailoring."

"I don't want you to repay it," said Tu, much moved. "You may be in a small way of business, but you can't treat your mother's funeral casually, or you will regret it all your life. What good are a few taels? You must buy a sixteen-tael coffin at the very least; and with clothes and miscellaneous expenses you will need twenty taels altogether. I haven't got a cent in the house at the moment—wait though! This chest of clothes can be pawned for twenty taels.

Wang, you take this chest for Mr. Yang, and give him all the money you can raise on it. . . . I don't want this to prey on your mind, Mr. Yang. Just forget it. You aren't drinking or gambling with my silver, but seeing to the most important event of your mother's funeral. We all have mothers, don't we? It's only right for me to help you."

The tailor carried out the chest with Whiskers Wang's help, crying as he did so. Tu Shao-ching came back to the table and sat down.

"That was a fine deed, friend!" said Mr. Wei.

Ting-hsi shot out his tongue.

"Amida Buddha!" he exclaimed. "I didn't know such a good man existed!"

They feasted all day. Since Tsang was not a heavy drinker, by the afternoon he was sick and had to be helped home. Mr. Wei and the others drank till the third watch, and broke up only when the jar of wine was empty.

But to know what followed, you must read the next chapter.

IN WHICH ARE DESCRIBED THE GALLANT DEEDS OF TU SHAO-CHING,
AND THE LAST WORDS OF MR. LOU

After the party broke up, Mr. Wei slept till late the next morning, then told Tu Shao-ching that he must be leaving.

"I mean to call on your uncle and cousin," he said. "I enjoyed myself enormously at the feast you so kindly prepared yesterday! I don't suppose I shall have such a good time anywhere else. Well, I must be going. I haven't even returned your friend Tsang's call, but please give him my best regards."

Shao-ching kept him for another day. The day after that he hired chair-bearers, then took a jade cup and two costumes which had belonged to the prefect of Kanchow to Mr. Wei's room.

"You are the only sworn brother my father had, uncle," he said. "I hope you will often come to see me, and I shall visit you more often to inquire after your health. I want you to take this jade cup to drink from. And please accept these two costumes which belonged to my father, for when you wear them I shall feel I am seeing him again."

Mr. Wei accepted these gifts with pleasure. Pao Ting-hsi joined them over another pot of wine, after which rice was served. Then Tu and Ting-hsi saw Mr. Wei out of the city and bowed before his sedan-chair as he left. Upon their return, Tu went to Mr. Lou's room to see how he was. The old man affirmed that he was better, and that he would send his grandson home, keeping his son only to tend him.

Tu Shao-ching agreed with this. Then, remembering that he had no money, he sent for Whiskers Wang.

"I want you to sell my land within the dyke to that man," he told him.

"That fellow wants to get it cheap," objected Whiskers Wang. "You asked for one thousand five hundred taels, sir, but he's offered one thousand three hundred only. So I don't dare make a deal with him."

"One thousand three hundred will do."

"I just wanted to be clear on that before leaving, sir. Otherwise you might abuse me for selling it too cheaply."

"Who's going to abuse you? Hurry up and sell it. I need money right away."

"There's another thing I wanted to say, sir. When you've got the silver, I hope you'll put it to good use. It's a pity to sell your property, if you're only going to give hundreds and thousands of taels away for no reason."

"Have you seen me give silver away for no reason? You want to get something out of it, I know; but you can stow all that hypocritical talk. Be off with you now!"

"I was only making a suggestion," said Whiskers Wang.

Upon leaving the room, the steward whispered to Ting-hsi:

"Good! There's hope for you. I'm going to the dyke now to sell some land, and when I come back I'll think up a plan for you."

Whiskers Wang returned several days later having sold the land for one thousand and several hundred taels, which he brought home in a small bag.

"This is only ninety-five per cent pure silver, sir," he reported to his master. "It was weighed by the market balance, which gives thirteen and a half cents less to the tael than the official balance. And he deducted twenty-three taels forty cents for the middleman there, while the witnesses to the contract took another twenty to thirty taels. We had to foot both those bills. Here is the silver, sir. Let me fetch the scales so that you can weigh it."

"Who's got the patience to listen to your fiddling accounts! Since the silver's here, why weigh it? Take it aside and have done with it!"

"I simply wanted to make it clear," said the steward.

Now that Tu Shao-ching had this silver, he called Mr. Lou's grandson to the library.

"Are you leaving tomorrow?" he asked.

"Yes, sir. Grandfather told me to go."

"I have a hundred taels of silver here for you, but you mustn't let your grandfather know about it. You have a widowed mother to keep; so take this silver home and set up in some small business which can support you both. If your grandfather recovers and your second uncle is able to leave, I shall give him a hundred taels too."

Delighted, Mr. Lou's grandson took the silver and concealed it on his person, then thanked the young master. The next day, when he took his leave, Mr. Lou would not let him be given more than thirty cents of silver for the road. When Tu Shao-ching returned from seeing him off, he found a country-man standing in the hall who knelt down and kowtowed as soon as he saw the young master.

"Aren't you Huang Ta, who looks after our ancestral temple?" asked Tu. "What are you doing here?"

"I used to live in a cottage by the ancestral temple which your father bought me," replied Huang Ta. "After all these years the place needed repairing, and I made bold to take some dead trees from your graveyard to replace the beams and pillars. But some gentlemen of your family found out, and said I'd stolen the trees. They thrashed me within an inch of my life, and sent a dozen stewards to my cottage to take back the trees, who pulled down even those parts which were all right before. Now I've nowhere to live; so I've come to beg you to speak to your clan, sir, and ask them to give me a little money for repairs from the communal fund, so that I can go on living there."

"My clan!" exclaimed Tu. "It's no use speaking to them. If my father bought you the cottage, it's obviously up to me to repair it. Since it's in ruins, how much will you need to build a new one?"

"A new one would cost a hundred taels. If I make do by repairing it, forty to fifty taels should be enough."

"Very well," said Tu. "I'm short of money at the moment, so just take fifty taels. When that's spent you can come back."

He fetched fifty taels for Huang Ta, who took the silver and left.

Then the gate-keeper came in with two cards.

"The third Mr. Tsang invites you to a feast tomorrow, sir," he announced. "This other card is to ask Mr. Pao to go along too."

"Tell the messenger to give my compliments to the third master," said Tu. "I will certainly go."

The next day he went with Pao Ting-hsi to Tsang's house. Tsang Liao-chai had prepared a good meal, and he invited Tu very respectfully to be seated and poured him wine, after which they chatted at random. Towards the end of the meal Tsang filled a cup with wine, raised it high in both hands and walked round the table to bow and present the cup to Tu. Then he knelt down.

"Brother!" he said. "I have a favour to ask."

With a start, Tu hastily set the wine on the table and knelt down to take Tsang's arm.

"Are you out of your mind, Third Brother?" he demanded. "What do you mean by this?"

"I won't get up till you've drunk that cup and promised to help me."

"I don't know what you're talking about. Get up and tell me."

Ting-hsi also tried to raise Tsang to his feet.

"Will you promise?" asked Tsang.

"Of course!" replied Tu.

"Then drink this cup of wine."

"I will drink it in a minute."

"I'm waiting for you to drain it."

Only then did Tsang stand up and resume his seat.

"Go ahead with whatever you have to say," prompted Tu.

"The examiner is at Luchow now, and it will be our turn next. The other day I tried to buy a licentiate's degree for someone, and paid the examiner's agent three hundred taels of silver. But later he told me: 'Our superiors are very strict, and I dare not sell this degree. Let me sell you a salaried scholar's rank instead, since you have already passed the preliminary test.' So I gave him my own name, and that is how I became a salaried scholar this year. But now the man who wanted to buy the licentiate's degree is demanding his money back; and if I don't return him three hundred taels, the whole business will be made public. This is a matter of life and death! You must help me, brother! If you will lend me three hundred taels of the money you got for your land to settle this business, I'll pay you back gradually. You promised just now to help."

"Pah!" exclaimed Tu. "I thought you were in real trouble when it was nothing but this all the time! You didn't have to put on such an act—kowtowing and pleading—for such a trifle! I'll give you the silver tomorrow."

"Well said!" cried Ting-hsi, clapping his hands. "Let's have large cups to drink to this!"

At once large cups were brought, and they drank until Tu was tipsy.

"Tell me, Third Brother," he said, "what made you so set on this salaried scholar's rank?"

"You wouldn't understand!" retorted Tsang. "A salaried scholar has a better chance of passing the next examination, and once you pass that you become an official. Even if you don't pass, after a dozen years you become a senior licentiate, and when you've taken the palace examination you'll be appointed a magistrate or a judge. Then I shall wear boots with knotted soles, hold court, pass sentence and have people beaten. And if gentlemen like you come to raise the wind, I'll have you locked up and fed on beancurd for a month, till you choke to death!"

"You ruffian!" cried Tu with a laugh. "You are utterly contemptible!"

"What a joke!" chuckled Ting-hsi. "You two gentlemen should each drain a cup after that."

Later that evening they parted.

The next morning Tu told Whiskers Wang to take a casket of silver over, and the steward received another six taels as his tip. On his way back he stopped at the fish shop for a bowl of noodles, and found Chang Chun-min there.

"Come over here, Mr. Whiskers, and sit with me!" called the doctor.

Whiskers Wang went over to his table, and when the noodles were brought started eating.

"I want you to do something for me," said Chang.

"What is it? Do you want a present because you've cured old Lou?"

"No, old Lou's disease is incurable."

"How much longer has he got?"

"Not more than a hundred days, probably. But you needn't tell him that. I want you to do something for me."

"Go on."

"The examiner will soon be here, and my son wants to take the examination; but I'm afraid the college authorities will say I'm an outsider. I'd like your young master to speak to them."

"That's no use." Whiskers Wang made a sign of dissent. "Our young master has never had anything to do with that lot. And he doesn't like to hear of people sitting for the examinations. If you ask him that, he'll advise you not to enter the boy!"

"What's to be done then?"

"There *is* a way. I'll tell Mr. Tu your son isn't allowed to sit; but the examination school in Fengyang was built by our young master's father, and if Mr. Tu wants to send in a candidate, who's to stop him? That'll goad him into doing something for you—he'll be willing even to spend money!"

"Handle it as you think best, Whiskers. If you pull it off, I'll not fail to thank you."

"As if I wanted thanks from you! Your son is my nephew. I'll be quite satisfied if he kowtows a few times to his old uncle when he's entered the college and is wearing a brand-new square cap and blue gown!"

This said, Chang Chun-min paid for the noodles and they left.

Whiskers Wang went home and asked the servants: "Where is the young master?"

"In the library," was the answer.

He went straight to the library, where he found Tu Shao-ching.

"I delivered the silver to the third Mr. Tsang," announced the steward. "He is very grateful to you, sir. He says you've saved him from serious trouble, and made it possible for him to become an official. Nobody else would be willing to do such a thing."

"A mere trifle," said Tu. "Why come here and gabble about it?"

"I've something else to report, sir," said the steward. "You've paid for Mr. Tsang's degree, and built a cottage for the caretaker of the ancestral temple. Very soon now the examinations are going to be held, and they'll be asking you to repair the examination school. Your father spent thousands of taels building that school, but other people have had all the advantage of it. If you were to send in a candidate, who would dare oppose him?"

"Candidates can enter themselves. Why should I send one?"

"If I had a son and you sent him in, would they dare say anything?"

"Of course not. Those college scholars are no better than slaves themselves."

"The son of Dr. Chang at the back gate has been studying. Why don't you tell him to sit for the examination?"

"Does he want to?"

"His father is an outsider—he dares not enter."

"Tell him to enter. If any scholar says anything, tell the fellow *I* sent him."

"Very good, sir."

With this, Whiskers Wang left.

Mr. Lou's illness was taking a turn for the worse, and Tu Shao-ching, who had invited a second physician to attend him, stayed at home in low spirits.

One day Tsang called.

"Have you heard the news?" he asked, without waiting to sit down. "Magistrate Wang is in trouble. Yesterday evening they took away his seal, and his successor is pressing him to move out of the yamen.[4] But because everyone says he is a corrupt official, no one will put him up. He's at his wit's end!"

"What is he doing?"

"He just stayed in the yamen last night. But if he doesn't move out tomorrow, he'll be in for a big loss of face! Who's going to lend him rooms, though? He'll have to move into the Old Men's Home!"

"Really?"

Tu ordered the servant to fetch Whiskers Wang.

"I want you to go at once to the yamen," he said, "and ask the attendants to inform Magistrate Wang that if he has nowhere to stay, he is welcome to come here. He needs rooms badly—hurry up!"

The steward hastened off.

"You refused to meet him before," said Tsang. "What makes you offer him accommodation today? Just think, you may find yourself involved in his trouble; and if there's a riot the mob may destroy your garden!"

"Everybody knows the good my father did for this district," replied Tu. "Even if I hid bandits here, no one would break into my house. Don't worry about that, brother. As for this Mr. Wang, it's lucky for him he knew enough to respect me. To have called on him the other day would have been making up to the local magistrate; but now that he's been removed from office and has nowhere to live, it's my duty to help him. When he receives my message, he's sure to come. Wait till he arrives, and you can talk to him."

Just then the gate-keeper came in to announce: "Dr. Chang is here."

---

[4] Headquarters of a public official or department.

Chang Chun-min walked in, knelt down and kowtowed.

"What is it this time?" asked Tu.

"It's about this business of my son taking the examination, sir. I'm extremely grateful to you."

"I have already promised to help."

"When the scholars knew it was your wish, sir, they had no objections, but they insisted that I raise a hundred and twenty taels to help repair the college; and where can I get so much money? That's why I've come to beg your help, sir."

"Will a hundred and twenty be enough? You won't need more later?"

"I won't need any more."

"That's easy. I'll pay it for you. All you have to do is write an application to enter the college, promising to contribute towards the repairs, and bring it here. You take it to the college for him, Third Brother. You can get the silver here."

"I am busy today," said Tsang to the doctor. "I'll go with you tomorrow."

Having expressed his thanks, Chang Chun-min left. The next moment Whiskers Wang came flying in.

"Magistrate Wang has come to call!" he announced. "He's at the gate and has left his chair."

Tu and Tsang went out to meet him. The magistrate was wearing a gauze cap and the clothes of a private citizen. He came in and bowed.

"I have long wished to make your acquaintance, sir, but lacked the opportunity," he said. "It is exceedingly good of you to put me up in your distinguished residence during my present difficulties, and I feel ashamed to trespass on your hospitality; I have therefore come to express my thanks before profiting more fully by your instructions. It is lucky my friend Tsang is here too!"

"A trifle like this is beneath Your Honour's notice," replied Tu. "Since my poor house is empty, I hope you will move in at your earliest convenience."

"I came here to ask my friend to call with me on my patron," said Tsang. "I little thought my patron would honour us first with a visit."

"Don't mention it!" said the magistrate.

He bowed his way to his chair, then left.

Tu Shao-ching kept Tsang, and gave him a hundred and twenty taels to settle Dr. Chang's business the following day; and Tsang took the silver home with him. The next day Magistrate Wang moved in. And the day after that Chang Chun-min gave a feast in Tu's house, to which Tsang and Ting-hsi were also invited.

"It's time for you to speak up," said Whiskers Wang to Ting-hsi in private. "According to my calculations, he'll soon reach the end of that silver; and if anyone else comes to ask for money, there'll be none left for you. You must speak this evening."

By this time all the guests had arrived, and the feast was laid in the library by the hall. The four of them went to the table; but before taking his seat Chang Chun-min offered a cup of wine to Tu Shao-ching to express his gratitude, then filled another cup and bowed his thanks to Tsang. During the meal they chatted at random. Then Ting-hsi addressed Tu.

"I have been here for half a year, sir, and seen you spend money like water," he said. "Even the tailor carried handfuls of silver away. But in my seven or eight months here I've had nothing but a little meat and wine—not a copper have I seen. Why should I carry on with this thankless job, getting nothing for my pains? I'd better wipe my eyes and go somewhere else to weep. I will take my leave of you tomorrow."

"Why didn't you mention this earlier, Mr. Pao?" asked Tu. "How could I know you had this on your mind? You should have spoken out."

Ting-hsi hastily filled a cup and passed it to him.

"My father and I both made a living by managing an opera company," he said. "Unhappily my father died, and instead of proving a credit to the old man I lost my capital. I have an old mother, yet I can't support her. I am the most miserable of men, unless the young master will give me some capital to take home so that I can provide for my mother."

"How admirable that an actor should show such filial piety!" exclaimed Tu. "Of course I will help you!"

Ting-hsi stood up.

"Thank you, sir, for your goodness!" he said.

"Sit down," replied Tu. "How much money do you need?"

Ting-hsi glanced at Whiskers Wang, who was standing at the foot of the table, and the steward stepped forward.

"You'll need a good deal of silver, Mr. Pao," he said. "It'll cost you five to six hundred taels I should think to get together a company and buy costumes. The young master doesn't have so much here. All he can do is give you a few dozen taels to take back across the river, and you can make a start with that."

"A few dozen taels is not enough," said Tu. "I'll give you a hundred taels to start training a company. When that's finished, you can come back again."

Ting-hsi knelt down and thanked him.

"I would have done more for you before letting you go," said Tu, stopping him, "but Mr. Lou is seriously ill, and I have to be ready for any emergency."

Tsang and Chang praised Tu's generosity, and soon the party broke up.

Mr. Lou's illness was becoming daily more serious.

"My friend," he said one day, when Tu was sitting at his bedside, "I hoped I might recover, but now it doesn't look as if I shall, and I want you to send me home."

"I have not been able to do all I should for you, uncle," said Tu. "How can you speak of going home?"

"Don't be foolish! I have sons and grandsons; and though I've spent my life away from home, it's natural now to want to go home to die. No one's going to accuse you of turning me out."

"In that case I won't keep you," said Tu with tears in his eyes. "I've prepared your coffin, uncle; but now you won't be needing it, and it's not easy to take. So I'll give you a few dozen taels instead with which to buy another. The clothes and bedding are all ready, and you can take them with you."

"I will take the coffin and clothes, but don't give any more silver to my sons and grandsons. I want to leave within the next three days, and since I can't sit up I'll have to be carried in a litter. Tomorrow go to your father's shrine and inform his spirit that Mr. Lou wishes to take his leave and go home. I have been with your family for thirty years, as one of your worthy father's closest friends; and since his death your treatment of me has left nothing to be desired. Your conduct and learning are unparalleled; and your son in particular is a boy of extraordinary promise—you must bring him up to be an honest man. You are not a good manager, however, and don't make the right friends; so you will soon come to the end of your property! I like to see you acting in a just and generous manner, but you must consider with whom you are dealing. The way you are going on, all your money is being tricked out of you by people who will never repay your kindness; and while we say charity expects no reward, you should distinguish between those who deserve help and those who don't. The third Mr. Tsang and Chang Chun-min, of whom you see so much, are unscrupulous characters. And recently this Pao Ting-hsi has joined them. There are no good men among players, yet you want to be his patron. As for your steward, Whiskers Wang, he's even worse! Money is of small account, and after I'm dead you and your son must imitate your noble father in everything. If you have virtue, it doesn't matter even if you go hungry. Your closest friend is your cousin Shen-ching; but though Shen-ching is brilliant you can't trust him too far. Imitate your worthy father, and you won't go wrong. Since you set no store by officials or by your own family, this is no place for you. Nanking is a great metropolis, and there you may find friends to appreciate your talent and be able to achieve something. What's left of your property won't last long! If you take my advice, I shall die happy!"

"I shall remember all your excellent advice, uncle," replied Tu with tears in his eyes.

He went out immediately and ordered his men to hire four bearers to carry Mr. Lou to Taohung by way of Nanking, then gave Mr. Lou's son over a hundred taels to take home for his father's funeral. On the third day, he saw Mr. Lou off on his journey.

Further Readings

Ichisada Miyazaki, *China's Examination Hell*, translated by Conrad Shirokauer (Tokyo and New York: John Weatherhill, 1976), and Chung-li Chang, *The Chinese Gentry: Studies on Their Role in Nineteenth-Century Chinese Society* (Seattle, WA: University of Washington Press, 1967), are useful studies of the Chinese civil-service examination system and the gentry-official system it created. Tung-tsu Ch'ü, *Local Government in China under the Ch'ing* (Stanford, CA: Stanford University Press, 1969), covers the duties of the various local officials of Ch'ing China. A strikingly different perspective on Ch'ing China is provided by Jonathan Spence, *The Death of Woman Wang* (New York: Penguin Books, 1979).

Timothy C. Wong, *Wu Ching-tzu* (Boston, MA: Twayne Publishers, 1978), provides a useful analysis of *The Scholars* as a satire, focusing on cultural and literary factors. Robert S. Hegel, *The Novel in Seventeenth-Century China* (New York: Columbia University Press, 1981), examines the influence of seventeenth-century novels—*The Scholars* and *The Dream of the Red Chamber* in particular—in shaping later Ch'ing fiction. Also helpful in understanding the development of the Chinese novel is William Theodore de Bary, Wing-tsit Chan, and Burton Watson, *Sources of Chinese Traditions* (New York: Columbia University Press, 1960). C. T. Hsia, *The Classic Chinese Novel* (New York: Columbia University Press, 1968), is a study of six major Chinese novels, including *The Scholars*.

Speeches of Minavavana and Pontiac

During the period 1756–1763, the European powers engaged in the first global conflict, the Seven Years' War. On the Continent itself, the hostile parties were Prussia on the one hand and France, Austria, and Russia on the other. Outside the continent, the main adversaries were France and England, who struggled for supremacy in the building of colonial empires. In India, the conflict was soon over, with the English defeat of the French in 1757. In North America, the other main theater of operations, the French were defeated in the battle of Quebec in 1759 and formally ceded control of Canada to the British in the Treaty of Paris in 1763. This did not end what the British called the French and Indian Wars, however, since the Indian allies of the French were inclined to continue the struggle. They fought on, although in desultory fashion, until 1765, when they were persuaded to accept the British presence in their lands.

The factors that motivated the Indians to continue this struggle were many and varied, but the speeches of two leaders of this resistance, the Chippewa chief, Minavavana, and the Ottawa chief, Pontiac, reveal two fundamental issues that were paramount to the Indians and incomprehensible to the whites: the sovereignty of the Indian nations and their right to maintain native ways of life.

In 1761, Alexander Henry, a young English trader, determined to take advantage of the elimination of his French competitors and take his trade goods deep into the western country. Even though British troops had not yet penetrated that far, he went all the way to Mackinac Island. Minavavana and a body of armed warriors soon arrived and the chief addressed Henry in a formal speech. He began by noting that the Indians were French allies and that the defeat of the French army did not mean that the alliance was ended. He then stated that the western territories were Indian, not French, lands,

From Francis Parkman, *The Conspiracy of Pontiac and the Indian Wars After the Conquest of Canada* (2 vols.: Boston, MA: Little, Brown and Co., 1898), pp. 212–215, 341–343.

and the sovereignty of these lands could not be transferred by anyone other than the Indians. He ended by remarking that the Indians were at war with the British. If the British expected peace, they should negotiate with the Indians to end that state of war. It is clear that Minavavana considered the Indian tribes to be independent and sovereign states, and claimed for his people the right to be treated as such. Throughout the long years of the Indian Wars that were to follow, this basic Indian concept was never accepted by their white opponents. As rational as it might have seemed to Minavavana, his position was perhaps unintelligible and certainly unacceptable to the British. Recognition of the Indian tribes as states would have admitted them to the community of nations and to the rights and protection afforded by the international law of the time.

The Indians were well aware that their struggle was not simply political or military. The advantages of European technology were so enticing that the Indians had already become dependent upon the Europeans for certain manufactured goods. This dependency had become painfully clear to them with the defeat of the French. Over time, they had come to rely upon firearms for hunting. Without gunpowder and flints, they feared that they could neither feed their families nor obtain furs to trade for other goods. The French had fostered this dependency by freely providing them with these necessary items. Now the Indians had to turn to the British, who proved to be much less understanding in this matter than their predecessors. Moreover, how could the Indians continue to resist the whites if their opponents could at any time deprive them of such necessities?

In 1762 a prophet appeared among the Delawares who proclaimed his vision of his journey to the Great Father. The vision spread rapidly among the western tribes, and Pontiac used it in the speech urging war upon the British that he delivered to the Indians assembled at the Escorce River near Detroit. The basic message was that the Great Father, who had given the land to the Indians and not to anyone else, wished them to abandon the ways and tools of the whites, to return to spear and bow, abandon rum and brandy, and live virtuous lives. If they did so, He would protect and sustain them. Pontiac hoped for French assistance, but he suggested to his audience that, if they returned to their native ways, they would gain Divine Grace and would be able to maintain themselves free and aloof from the white civilization that had already rendered them dependent and that gave promise of destroying them utterly. This visionary and nativist hope persisted among the Indians through the many trials that lay ahead, and would arise again in the Ghost Dances of the 1880s. Utopian fervor was not foreign to the whites, but they failed to recognize it in its Indian guise and discounted it as simple fancy and superstition.

From their speeches, it is apparent that Minavavana and Pontiac had a clear idea of the perils their peoples faced. Their tribes were caught up in political struggles wide beyond their comprehension, and their opponents refused to allow them any standing in that political game. Moreover, they were being absorbed into an economy in a way over which they would be allowed no control and which would eventually destroy their capacity for independence. They hoped that it was not yet too late to remedy this situation. This is why they advocated continued resistance to the British.

Questions

1. How does Minavavana propose that the British should make peace?

2. Do you see any contradictions in Minavavana's speech?

3. What do you think the three paths represent in Pontiac's description of the Delaware prophet's vision?

4. How do you think Pontiac may have adapted the prophet's vision to serve his own political purposes?

SPEECHES OF MINAVAVANA AND PONTIAC

The Speech of Minavavana (1761)

Englishman, it is to you that I speak, and I demand your attention.

Englishman, you know that the French King is our father. He promised to be such; and we, in return, promised to be his children. This promise we have kept.

Englishman, it is you that have made war with this our father. You are his enemy; and how, then, could you have the boldness to venture among us, his children? You know that his enemies are ours.

Englishman, we are informed that our father, the King of France, is old and infirm; and that, being fatigued with making war upon your nation, he is fallen asleep. During his sleep you have taken advantage of him, and possessed yourselves of Canada. But his nap is almost at an end. I think I hear him already stirring, and inquiring for his children, the Indians; and when he does awake, what must become of you? He will destroy you utterly.

Englishman, although you have conquered the French, you have not yet conquered us. We are not your slaves. These lakes, these woods and mountains, were left to us by our ancestors. They are our inheritance; and we will part with them to none. Your nation supposes that we, like the white people, cannot live without bread, and pork, and beef! But you ought to know that He, the

Great Spirit and Master of Life, has provided food for us in these spacious lakes, and on these woody mountains.

Englishman, our father, the King of France, employed our young men to make war upon your nation. In this warfare many of them have been killed; and it is our custom to retaliate until such time as the spirits of the slain are satisfied. But the spirits of the slain are to be satisfied in either of two ways: the first is by the spilling of the blood of the nation by which they fell; the other, by *covering the bodies of the dead,* and thus allaying the resentment of their relations. This is done by making presents.

Englishman, your king has never sent us any present, nor entered into any treaty with us; wherefore he and we are still at war; and, until he does these things, we must consider that we have no other father nor friend, among the white men, than the King of France; but for you, we have taken into consideration that you have ventured your life among us, in the expectation that we should not molest you. You do not come armed, with an intention to make war; you come in peace, to trade with us, and supply us with necessaries, of which we are in much want. We shall regard you, therefore, as a brother; and you may sleep tranquilly, without fear of the Chippewas. As a token of our friendship, we present you this pipe to smoke.

The Speech of Pontiac (1763)

After urging the assembled warriors to make war on the British, Pontiac continued his speech as follows:

A Delaware Indian . . . conceived an eager desire to learn wisdom from the Master of Life; but, being ignorant where to find him, he had recourse to fasting, dreaming, and magical incantations. By these means it was revealed to him, that, by moving forward in a straight, undeviating course, he would reach the abode of the Great Spirit. He told his purpose to no one, and having provided the equipments of a hunter,—gun, powder-horn, ammunition, and a kettle for preparing his food,—he set out on his errand. For some time he journeyed on in high hope and confidence. On the evening of the eighth day, he stopped by the side of a brook at the edge of a meadow, where he began to make ready his evening meal, when, looking up, he saw three large openings in the woods before him, and three well-beaten paths which entered them. He was much surprised; but his wonder increased, when, after it had grown dark, the three paths were more clearly visible than ever. Remembering the important object of his journey, he could neither rest nor sleep; and, leaving his fire, he crossed the meadow, and entered the largest of the three openings. He had advanced but a short distance into the forest, when a bright flame sprang out of the ground before him, and arrested his steps. In great amazement, he turned back, and entered the second path, where the same wonderful phenomenon again encountered him; and now, in terror and bewilderment, yet still resolved to persevere, he took the last of the three paths. On this he journeyed a whole day without interruption, when at length, emerging from the forest, he saw before him a vast mountain, of dazzling whiteness. So precipitous was the ascent that the Indian thought it hopeless to go farther, and looked around him in despair: at that moment, he saw, seated at some distance above, the figure of a beautiful woman arrayed in white, who arose as he looked upon her, and thus accosted him: "How can you hope, encumbered as you are, to succeed in your design? Go down to the foot of the mountain, throw away your gun, your ammunition, your provisions, and your clothing; wash yourself in the stream which flows there, and you will then be prepared to stand before the Master of Life." The Indian obeyed, and again began to ascend among the rocks, while the woman, seeing him still discouraged, laughed at his faintness of heart, and told him that, if he wished for success, he must climb by the aid of one hand and one foot only. After great toil and suffering, he at length found himself at the summit. The woman had disappeared, and he was left alone. A rich and beautiful plain lay before him, and at a little distance he saw three great villages, far superior to the squalid wigwams of the Delawares. As he approached the largest, and stood hesitating whether he should enter, a man gorgeously attired stepped forth, and, taking him by the hand, welcomed him to the celestial abode. He then conducted him into the presence of the Great Spirit, where the Indian stood confounded at the unspeakable splendor which surrounded him. The Great Spirit bade him be seated, and thus addressed him:—

"I am the Maker of heaven and earth, the trees, lakes, rivers, and all things else. I am the Maker of mankind; and because I love you, you must do my will. The land on which you live I have made for you, and not for others. Why do you suffer the white men to dwell among you? My children, you have forgotten the customs and traditions of your forefathers. Why do you not clothe yourselves in skins, as they did, and use the bows and arrows, and the stone-pointed lances, which they used? You have bought guns, knives, kettles, and blankets, from the white men, until you can no longer do without them; and, what is worse, you have drunk the poison fire-water, which turns you into fools. Fling all these things away; live as your wise forefathers lived before you. And as for these English,—these dogs dressed in red, who have come to rob you of your hunting-grounds, and drive away the game,—you must lift the hatchet against them. Wipe them from the face of the earth, and then you will win my favor back again, and once more be happy and prosperous. The children of your great father, the King of France, are not like the English. Never forget that they are your brethren. They are very dear to me, for they love the red men, and understand the true mode of worshipping me."

Further Readings

Julian S. Corbett, *England in the Seven Years' War: A Study in Combined Strategy* (2 vols.: London: Longman's, Green and Co., 1907), places British participation in the conflict in its global context. Robert Furneaux, *The Seven Years' War* (London: Hart-Davis MacGibbon, Ltd., 1973), is a well-illustrated short account of the war in North America. George Donaldson, *Battle for a Continent: Quebec, 1759* (Garden City, NY: Doubleday, 1973), presents the history of the Quebec campaign that resulted in the defeat of the French forces in Canada. Howard H. Peckham, *Pontiac and the Indian Uprising* (Princeton, NJ: Princeton University Press, 1947), is a readable and scholarly account of the wars, with particular attention to the life and activities of Pontiac. Allen W. Eckert, *The Conquerors: A Narrative* (Boston, MA: Little, Brown, 1970), is a historical-novelistic narrative covering the period 1759–1765. Although opinionated, by modern standards, Francis Parkman, *The Conspiracy of Pontiac and the Indian War Following the Conquest of Canada* (first published in 1851, many editions), is still one of the monuments of American historical writing. David Horowitz, *The First Frontier: The Indian Wars and America's Origins, 1607–1776* (New York: Simon and Schuster, 1978), reminds the reader that, for the first 200 years following the first English colonists, the American frontier was the scene of a constant warfare that presented a greater danger to the development of the nation than has any subsequent struggle.

Some excellent fiction has been set in this period. Among the classics are the works of James Fenimore Cooper, most particularly *The Deerslayer, or, The First Warpath* and *The Last of the Mohicans, a Narrative of 1757*, both of which have appeared in many editions. A more modern treatment is the excellent novel by Kenneth Roberts, *Northwest Passage* (Garden City, NY: Doubleday, 1937), that chronicles the career of Major Robert Rogers, founder and leader of Rogers' Rangers. *Northwest Passage* (1940: MGM, color) is a colorful film version of Part I of Roberts' work.

Candide

The eighteenth century marked a significant advance in the development of the Western tradition. The traditional reliance upon the past as the repository of truth was largely ended. Influenced by the triumph of Newtonian science, the leading thinkers of the time sought to apply the objectivity and methodology of science to the social, economic, political, and spiritual questions of the day. This movement, known as the Englightenment, marked a break with the past and a challenge to the existing institutions of society. The Enlightenment spread rapidly throughout Europe and an intellectual generation was born devoted to a rationalism based upon experience and observed fact rather than upon a logic based upon deduction from established axioms. If inductive reason could discover the fundamental workings of the universe, they thought, it could also discover the means to make society more sensible and humane.

Eighteenth-century literature embraced rationalism and reached out to an ever-expanding public. Although the advocates of the Enlightenment came from a wide variety of religious and political backgrounds, they shared the important characteristic of rejecting the authority of tradition in every sphere of knowledge. In seventeenth- and eighteenth-century France, this meant challenging the power and prerogatives of the established Church and questioning the privileges of the ruling aristocracy. The promotion of the principles of the Enlightenment was more than an idle intellectual exercise; it often involved attacking powerful interests and it provoked powerful enemies. Nevertheless, France produced some of the greatest figures of the Enlightenment.

The most successful and famous of these was François-Marie Arouet (1694–1778), better known by his pen name, Voltaire. The son of a middle-class Parisian lawyer, he received his early schooling

From Voltaire, *Candide*, translated by Richard Aldington, in *The Portable Voltaire*, edited by Ben Ray Redman (New York: Viking Press, Inc., 1969 pr.), pp. 229–260, 322–328.

under Jesuit teachers who sharpened his talent and appetite for argumentation. He gained a literary reputation while still in his teens and quickly came in conflict with a social establishment that showed little toleration for his satirical wit and freedom of spirit. By 1722, he had already been arrested twice for his writings and subsequently suffered imprisonment in the ancient Parisian fortress known as the Bastille. Despite his personal misfortunes, Voltaire continued to attack what he saw as society's indifference to human dignity, intellectual freedom, and individual conscience.

The final two decades of his life, from 1759 to 1778, were spent on his estate near the town of Ferney on the French–Swiss border. He established a small community there based upon principles much like those he advocates at the end of *Candide*. He produced some of his most important works during this period, distributing throughout Europe countless pamphlets printed under scores of pseudonyms. Frequently banned and confiscated by the authorities, they were nevertheless read and admired by the intellectuals of the time. He was one of the true inspirations of the French Revolution that swept away the old order after his death. In 1791, his ashes were triumphantly carried to Paris and buried by the Revolutionary government in the Pantheon, the shrine of the heroes of France.

The best known and most widely read of Voltaire's numerous works is his wickedly funny and deadly serious satirical novel, *Candide* (1759). The story line is quite simple. Candide is a naive and idealistic young man raised in the optimistic philosophical doctrine that "all things are for the best in this best of all possible worlds." In the course of an incredible series of misadventures, Candide learns the foolishness of this belief. Expelled from his home, he is forced into the army and survives a battle in which 30,000 men are killed. He then endures a shipwreck, the great Lisbon earthquake, and a ferocious flogging by the Inquisition. Candide gradually learns through these and further experiences that human beings are fundamentally cruel and foolish, and that the miserable state of the world is largely the product of human greed, pride, intolerance, and stupidity. The only recourse for a sane person is to busy himself with those things within his own competence and to avoid attempting to impose his views on others. In the concluding chapter of *Candide*, we find the hero and his companions living on a small farm trying to shut out the world's stupidities and indecencies by minding their own business and "tending their own garden."

Candide is considered a masterpiece of European literature not so much because of its style as for its portrayal of the human condition. Although displaying the elements of ridicule and humorous exaggeration typical of satire, *Candide* offers a fundamentally accurate picture of life in the period. It is a savage attack on oppression and injustice and a spirited defense of the principles of moderation and truth.

Questions

1. Many Enlightenment authors believed that the further development of civilization would usher in a new era of peace and prosperity. How do you think Voltaire would have reacted to this assertion?

2. Institutionalized religion in the eighteenth century professed to be something that brought people together. What is Voltaire's reaction to this claim?

3. What does Voltaire see as the causes of human misery?

CANDIDE

Chapter I

**HOW CANDIDE WAS BROUGHT UP
IN A NOBLE CASTLE AND HOW HE WAS EXPELLED FROM THE SAME**

In the castle of Baron Thunder-ten-tronckh[1] in Westphalia[2] there lived a youth, endowed by Nature with the most gentle character. His face was the expression of his soul. His judgment was quite honest and he was extremely simple-minded; and this was the reason, I think, that he was named Candide.[3] Old servants in the house suspected that he was the son of the Baron's sister and a decent honest gentleman of the neighborhood, whom this young lady would never marry because he could only prove seventy-one quarterings,[4] and the rest of his genealogical tree was lost, owing to the injuries of time. The Baron was one of the most powerful lords in Westphalia, for his castle possessed a door and windows. His Great Hall was even decorated with a piece of tapestry. The dogs in his stableyards formed a pack of hounds when necessary; his grooms were his huntsmen; the village curate[5] was his Grand Almoner.[6] They all called him "My Lord," and laughed heartily at his stories. The Baroness weighed about three hundred and fifty pounds, was therefore greatly respected, and did the honors of the house with a dignity which rendered her still more respectable. Her daughter

---

[1] Voltaire was contemptuous of the numerous lesser German nobles, who although often ignorant and uneducated, generally held an arrogant pride over their long, and frequently questionable, lineage.
[2] A German province stretching eastward from the location where the Rhine River crosses into Dutch territory.
[3] Meaning "glowing white," or "pure," and suggesting an innocent and honest character.
[4] Each quartering represents one generation.
[5] Priest.
[6] A high-ranking clergyman in charge of the distribution of alms.

Cunegonde,[7] aged seventeen, was rosy-cheeked, fresh, plump and tempting. The Baron's son appeared in every respect worthy of his father. The tutor Pangloss[8] was the oracle of the house, and little Candide followed his lessons with all the candor of his age and character. Pangloss taught metaphysico-theologo-cosmolonigology.[9] He proved admirably that there is no effect without a cause and that in this best of all possible worlds, My Lord the Baron's castle was the best of castles and his wife the best of all possible Baronesses. " 'Tis demonstrated," said he, "that things cannot be otherwise; for, since everything is made for an end, everything is necessarily for the best end. Observe that noses were made to wear spectacles; and so we have spectacles. Legs were visibly instituted to be breeched, and we have breeches. Stones were formed to be quarried and to build castles; and My Lord has a very noble castle; the greatest Baron in the province should have the best house; and as pigs were made to be eaten, we eat pork all the year round; consequently, those who have asserted that all is well talk nonsense; they ought to have said that all is for the best." Candide listened attentively and believed innocently; for he thought Mademoiselle Cunegonde extremely beautiful, although he was never bold enough to tell her so. He decided that after the happiness of being born Baron of Thunder-ten-tronckh, the second degree of happiness was to be Mademoiselle Cunegonde; the third, to see her every day; and the fourth to listen to Doctor Pangloss, the greatest philosopher of the province and therefore of the whole world. One day when Cunegonde was walking near the castle, in a little wood which was called The Park, she observed Doctor Pangloss in the bushes, giving a lesson in experimental physics to her mother's waiting-maid, a very pretty and docile brunette. Mademoiselle Cunegonde had a great inclination for science and watched breathlessly the reiterated experiments she witnessed; she observed clearly the Doctor's sufficient reason, the effects and the causes, and returned home very much excited, pensive, filled with the desire of learning, reflecting that she might be the sufficient reason of young Candide and that he might be hers. On her way back to the castle she met Candide and blushed; Candide also blushed. She bade him good morning in a hesitating voice; Candide replied without knowing what he was saying. Next day, when they left the table after dinner, Cunegonde and Candide found themselves behind a

[7] The name is inspired by Kunigunde, the wife of the medieval German Emperor Henry II. She reputedly "kept her virginity to her death"—thus abusing the sacrament of marriage.
[8] Literally (in Greek), "all tongue."
[9] Pangloss is employed as an instrument in Voltaire's mocking of the optimistic assumptions and statements of the English poet Alexander Pope (1688–1744), the German philosopher Gottfried Wilhelm Leibnitz (1646–1716), and Christian Wolff (1679–1754), who developed and popularized Leibnitz' philosophy.

Voltaire in his study.

screen; Cunegonde dropped her handkerchief, Candide picked it up; she innocently held his hand; the young man innocently kissed the young lady's hand with remarkable vivacity, tenderness and grace; their lips met, their eyes sparkled, their knees trembled, their hands wandered. Baron Thunder-ten-tronckh passed near the screen, and, observing this cause and effect, expelled Candide from the castle by kicking him in the backside frequently and hard. Cunegonde swooned; when she recovered her senses, the Baroness slapped her in the face; and all was in consternation in the noblest and most agreeable of all possible castles.

Chapter II

WHAT HAPPENED TO CANDIDE AMONG THE BULGARIANS[10]

Candide, expelled from the earthly paradise, wandered for a long time without knowing where he was going, turning up his eyes to Heaven, gazing back frequently at the noblest of castles which held the most beautiful of young Baronesses; he lay down to sleep supperless between two furrows in the open fields; it snowed heavily in large flakes. The next morning the shivering Candide, penniless, dying of cold and exhaustion, dragged himself toward the neighboring town, which was called Waldberghoff-trarbk-dikdorff.[11] He halted sadly at the door of an inn. Two men dressed in blue[12] noticed him. "Comrade," said one, "there's a well-built young man of the right height." They went up to Candide and very civilly invited him to dinner. "Gentlemen," said Candide with charming modesty, "you do me a great honor, but I have no money to pay my share." "Ah, sir," said one of the men in blue, "persons of your figure and merit never pay anything; are you not five feet five tall?" "Yes, gentlemen," said he, bowing, "that is my height." "Ah, sir, come to table; we will not only pay your expenses, we will never allow a man like you to be short of money; men were only made to help each other." "You are in the right," said Candide, "that is what Doctor Pangloss was always telling me, and I see that everything is for the best." They begged him to accept a few crowns,[13] he took them and wished to give them an IOU; they refused to take it and all sat down to table. "Do you not love tenderly . . ." "Oh, yes," said he. "I love Mademoiselle Cunegonde tenderly." "No," said one of the gentlemen. "We were asking if you do not tenderly love the King of the Bulgarians."[14] "Not a bit," said he, "for I have never seen him." "What! He is the most charming of Kings, and you must drink his health." "Oh, gladly, gentlemen." And he drank.[15] "That is sufficient," he was told. "You are now the support, the aid, the defender, the hero of the Bulgarians; your fortune is made and your glory assured." They immediately put irons on his legs and took him to a regiment. He was made to turn to the right and left, to raise the ramrod and return the ramrod,[16] to take aim, to fire, to double up, and he was given thirty strokes with a stick; the next day he drilled not quite so badly, and received only twenty strokes; the day after, he only had ten and was

[10] A fictitious name for the Prussians. In Voltaire's day, the states of Prussia and Austria contained the largest German-speaking populations.
[11] A reference to Voltaire's dislike of the sound of the Germanic language, which he considered to be so ugly as to be fit only for soldiers and horses.
[12] Uniforms of Prussian recruiting officers. Armies incurred substantial losses in numerous battles and Prussian recruiters were continually looking for replacements.
[13] Silver coins.
[14] Frederick II (Frederick the Great), King of Prussia from 1740 to 1786.
[15] Candide's act of drinking to the King takes the place of signing up.
[16] A rod used to force a powder charge into a gun through the muzzle.

looked on as a prodigy by his comrades. Candide was completely mystified and could not make out how he was a hero. One fine spring day he thought he would take a walk, going straight ahead, in the belief that to use his legs as he pleased was a privilege of the human species as well as of animals. He had not gone two leagues[17] when four other heroes, each six feet tall, fell upon him, bound him and dragged him back to a cell. He was asked by his judges whether he would rather be thrashed thirty-six times by the whole regiment or receive a dozen lead bullets at once in his brain. Although he protested that men's wills are free and that he wanted neither one nor the other, he had to make a choice; by virtue of that gift of God which is called *liberty*, he determined to run the gauntlet thirty-six times and actually did so twice. There were two thousand men in the regiment. That made four thousand strokes which laid bare the muscles and nerves from his neck to his backside. As they were about to proceed to a third turn, Candide, utterly exhausted, begged as a favor that they would be so kind as to smash his head; he obtained this favor; they bound his eyes and he was made to kneel down. At that moment the King of the Bulgarians came by and inquired the victim's crime; and as this King was possessed of a vast genius, he perceived from what he learned about Candide that he was a young metaphysician very ignorant in worldly matters, and therefore pardoned him with a clemency which will be praised in all newspapers and all ages. An honest surgeon healed Candide in three weeks with the ointments recommended by Dioscorides.[18] He had already regained a little skin and could walk when the King of the Bulgarians went to war with the King of the Abares.[19]

Chapter III

HOW CANDIDE ESCAPED FROM THE BULGARIANS AND WHAT BECAME OF HIM

Nothing could be smarter, more splendid, more brilliant, better drawn up than the two armies. Trumpets, fifes, hautboys,[20] drums, cannons, formed a harmony such as has never been heard even in hell. The cannons first of all laid flat about six thousand men on each side; then the musketry removed from the best of worlds some nine or ten thousand blackguards[21] who infested its surface. The bayonet also was the sufficient reason for the death of some thousands of men. The whole might amount to thirty thou-

---

[17] A unit of distance varying from 2½ to 4½ miles, depending on the country.
[18] Refers to the Greek physician Penadius Dioscorides of the first century A.D. Voltaire possessed little respect for the medical profession, because of physicians' continued use of long-since outmoded remedies and methods.
[19] The French, who in the Seven Years' War (1756–1763) were allied with the Austrians against Prussia and England.
[20] Oboes.
[21] Scoundrels.

sand souls. Candide, who trembled like a philosopher, hid himself as well as he could during this heroic butchery. At last, while the two Kings each commanded a Te Deum[22] in his camp, Candide decided to go elsewhere to reason about effects and causes. He clambered over heaps of dead and dying men and reached a neighboring village, which was in ashes; it was an Abare village which the Bulgarians had burned in accordance with international law. Here, old men dazed with blows watched the dying agonies of their murdered wives who clutched their children to their bleeding breasts; there, disemboweled girls who had been made to satisfy the natural appetites of heroes gasped their last sighs; others, half-burned, begged to be put to death. Brains were scattered on the ground among dismembered arms and legs. Candide fled to another village as fast as he could; it belonged to the Bulgarians, and Abarian heroes had treated it in the same way. Candide, stumbling over quivering limbs or across ruins, at last escaped from the theater of war, carrying a little food in his knapsack, and never forgetting Mademoiselle Cunegonde. His provisions were all gone when he reached Holland; but, having heard that everyone in that country was rich and a Christian, he had no doubt at all but that he would be as well treated as he had been in the Baron's castle before he had been expelled on account of Mademoiselle Cunegonde's pretty eyes. He asked an alms of several grave persons, who all replied that if he continued in that way he would be shut up in a house of correction to teach him how to live.[23] He then addressed himself to a man who had been discoursing on charity in a large assembly for an hour on end. This orator, glancing at him askance, said: "What are you doing here? Are you for a good cause?" "There is no effect without a cause," said Candide modestly. "Everything is necessarily linked up and arranged for the best. It was necessary that I should be expelled from the company of Mademoiselle Cunegonde, that I ran the gauntlet, and that I beg my bread until I can earn it; all this could not have happened differently." "My friend," said the orator, "do you believe that the Pope is Anti-Christ?"[24] "I had never heard so before," said Candide, "but whether he is or isn't, I am starving." "You don't deserve to eat," said the other. "Hence, rascal; hence, you wretch; and never come near me again." The orator's wife thrust her head out of the window and seeing a man who did not believe that the Pope was Anti-Christ, she poured on his head a full . . . O Heavens! To what excess religious zeal is carried by ladies! A man who had not been

---

[22] *Te Deum Laudamus* ("We Praise Thee, O God"), a Christian hymn of praise to God.
[23] Although Voltaire admired the Dutch for their concern for the unfortunate, he had also observed that they were capable of hardheartedness and greed.
[24] For years, many Protestants had considered the Pope the Antichrist (the enemy of Christ). Voltaire felt that preoccupation with such questions was often an escape from charitable actions.

baptized, an honest Anabaptist[25] named Jacques, saw the cruel and ignominious treatment of one of his brothers, a featherless two-legged creature with a soul;[26] he took him home, cleaned him up, gave him bread and beer, presented him with two florins,[27] and even offered to teach him to work at the manufacture of Persian stuffs[28] which are made in Holland. Candide threw himself at the man's feet, exclaiming: "Doctor Pangloss was right in telling me that all is for the best in this world, for I am vastly more touched by your extreme generosity than by the harshness of the gentleman in the black cloak and his good lady." The next day when he walked out he met a beggar covered with sores, dull-eyed, with the end of his nose fallen away, his mouth awry, his teeth black, who talked huskily, was tormented with a violent cough and spat out a tooth at every cough.

Chapter IV

HOW CANDIDE MET HIS OLD MASTER IN PHILOSOPHY, DOCTOR PANGLOSS, AND WHAT HAPPENED

Candide, moved even more by compassion than by horror, gave this horrible beggar the two florins he had received from the honest Anabaptist, Jacques. The phantom gazed fixedly at him, shed tears and threw its arms round his neck. Candide recoiled in terror. "Alas!" said the wretch to the other wretch, "don't you recognize your dear Pangloss?" "What do I hear? You, my dear master! You, in this horrible state! What misfortune has happened to you? Why are you no longer in the noblest of castles? What has become of Mademoiselle Cunegonde, the pearl of young ladies, the masterpiece of Nature?" "I am exhausted,"[29] said Pangloss. Candide immediately took him to the Anabaptist's stable where he gave him a little bread to eat; and when Pangloss had recovered: "Well!" said he, "Cunegonde?" "Dead," replied the other. At this word Candide swooned; his friend restored him to his senses with a little bad vinegar which happened to be in the stable. Candide opened his eyes. "Cunegonde dead! Ah! best of worlds, where are you? But what illness did she die of? Was it because she saw me kicked out of her father's noble castle?" "No," said Pangloss. "She was disemboweled by Bulgarian soldiers, after having been raped to the limit of possibility; they broke the Baron's head when he tried to defend

---

[25] A religious group that in the sixteenth century attracted many followers in southwestern Germany and Switzerland. Anabaptists rejected infant baptism and insisted upon baptism of the adult believer. Voltaire possessed great admiration for their piety, hard work, love of peace, and charity.
[26] A reference to Plato's definition of a human being.
[27] Gold coins from thirteenth-century Florence which were accepted as currency throughout Europe.
[28] Persian rugs.
[29] Pangloss claims that he is dying.

her; the Baroness was cut to pieces; my poor pupil was treated exactly like his sister; and as to the castle, there is not one stone standing on another, not a barn, not a sheep, not a duck, not a tree; but we were well avenged, for the Abares did exactly the same to a neighboring barony which belonged to a Bulgarian Lord." At this, Candide swooned again; but, having recovered and having said all that he ought to say, he inquired the cause and effect, the sufficient reason which had reduced Pangloss to so piteous a state. "Alas!" said Pangloss, " 'tis love; love, the consoler of the human race, the preserver of the universe, the soul of all tender creatures, gentle love." "Alas!" said Candide, "I am acquainted with this love, this sovereign of hearts, this soul of our soul; it has never brought me anything but one kiss and twenty kicks in the backside. How could this beautiful cause produce in you so abominable an effect?" Pangloss replied as follows: "My dear Candide! You remember Paquette,[30] the maid-servant of our august Baroness; in her arms I enjoyed the delights of Paradise which have produced the tortures of Hell by which you see I am devoured; she was infected[31] and perhaps is dead. Paquette received this present from a most learned monk, who had it from the source; for he received it from an old countess, who had it from a cavalry captain, who owed it to a marchioness,[32] who derived it from a page, who had received it from a Jesuit, who, when a novice, had it in a direct line from one of the companions of Christopher Columbus. For my part, I shall not give it to anyone, for I am dying." "O Pangloss!" exclaimed Candide, "this is a strange genealogy! Wasn't the devil at the root of it?" "Not at all," replied that great man. "It was something indispensable in this best of worlds, a necessary ingredient; for, if Columbus in an island of America had not caught this disease, which poisons the source of generation, and often indeed prevents generation, we should not have chocolate and cochineal;[33] it must also be noticed that hitherto in our continent this disease is peculiar to us, like theological disputes. The Turks, the Indians, the Persians, the Chinese, the Siamese and the Japanese are not yet familiar with it; but there is a sufficient reason why they in their turn should become familiar with it in a few centuries. Meanwhile, it has made marvelous progress among us, and especially in those large armies composed of honest, well-bred stipendiaries who decide the destiny of States; it may be asserted that when thirty thousand men fight a pitched battle against an equal number of troops, there are about twenty thousand with the pox on either side." "Admirable!" said Candide. "But you must get cured." "How can I?" said Pangloss. "I haven't a sou,[34] my friend, and in the whole extent of this globe,

---

[30] Her name comes from the French word *pâquerette*, meaning "daisy."
[31] She had contracted syphilis, a disease introduced to Europe from the Americas.
[32] The wife or widow of a marquis, a high-ranking nobleman.
[33] A red dye from Central and South America.
[34] A French coin possessing little value.

you cannot be bled or receive an enema without paying or without someone paying for you." This last speech determined Candide; he went and threw himself at the feet of his charitable Anabaptist, Jacques, and drew so touching a picture of the state to which his friend was reduced that the good easy man did not hesitate to succor Pangloss; he had him cured at his own expense. In this cure Pangloss only lost one eye and one ear. He could write well and knew arithmetic perfectly. The Anabaptist made him his bookkeeper. At the end of two months he was compelled to go to Lisbon on business and took his two philosophers on the boat with him. Pangloss explained to him how everything was for the best. Jacques was not of this opinion. "Men," said he, "must have corrupted nature a little, for they were not born wolves, and they have become wolves. God did not give them twenty-four-pounder cannons or bayonets, and they have made bayonets and cannons to destroy each other. I might bring bankruptcies into the account and Justice which seizes the goods of bankrupts in order to deprive the creditors of them." "It was all indispensable," replied the one-eyed doctor, "and private misfortunes make the public good, so that the more private misfortunes there are, the more everything is well." While he was reasoning, the air grew dark, the winds blew from the four quarters of the globe and the ship was attacked by the most horrible tempest in sight of the port of Lisbon.

Chapter V

STORM, SHIPWRECK, EARTHQUAKE, AND WHAT HAPPENED
TO DR. PANGLOSS, TO CANDIDE AND THE ANABAPTIST JACQUES

Half the enfeebled passengers, suffering from that inconceivable anguish which the rolling of a ship causes in the nerves and in all the humors of bodies shaken in contrary directions, did not retain strength enough even to trouble about the danger. The other half screamed and prayed; the sails were torn, the masts broken, the vessel leaking. Those worked who could, no one cooperated, no one commanded. The Anabaptist tried to help the crew a little; he was on the main deck; a furious sailor struck him violently and stretched him on the deck; but the blow he delivered gave him so violent a shock that he fell head-first out of the ship. He remained hanging and clinging to part of the broken mast. The good Jacques ran to his aid, helped him to climb back, and from the effort he made was flung into the sea in full view of the sailor, who allowed him to drown without condescending even to look at him. Candide came up, saw his benefactor reappear for a moment and then be engulfed for ever. He tried to throw himself after him into the sea; he was prevented by the philosopher Pangloss, who proved to him that the Lisbon roads had been expressly created for the Anabaptist to be drowned in them. While he was proving this *a priori*,[35] the vessel sank, and everyone perished except Pangloss, Candide and the brutal sailor who had drowned the virtuous Anabaptist; the blackguard swam successfully to the shore and Pangloss and Candide were carried there on a plank. When they had recovered a little, they walked toward Lisbon; they had a little money by the help of which they hoped to be saved from hunger after having escaped the storm. Weeping the death of their benefactor, they had scarcely set foot in the town when they felt the earth tremble under their feet;[36] the sea rose in foaming masses in the port and smashed the ships which rode at anchor. Whirlwinds of flame and ashes covered the streets and squares; the houses collapsed, the roofs were thrown upon the foundations, and the foundations were scattered; thirty thousand inhabitants of every age and both sexes were crushed under the ruins. Whistling and swearing, the sailor said: "There'll be something to pick up here." "What can be the sufficient reason for this phenomenon?" said Pangloss. "It is the last day!" cried Candide. The sailor immediately ran among the debris, dared death to find money, found it, seized it, got drunk, and having slept off his wine, purchased the favors of the first woman of good-will he met on the ruins of the houses and among the dead and dying. Pangloss, however, pulled him by the sleeve. "My friend," said he, "this is not well, you are disregarding universal reason, you choose the wrong time." "Blood and 'ounds!" he retorted, "I am a sailor and I was born in Batavia;[37] four times have I stamped on the crucifix during four voyages to Japan;[38] you have found the right man for your universal reason!" Candide had been hurt by some falling stones; he lay in the street covered with debris. He said to Pangloss: "Alas! Get me a little wine and oil; I am dying." "This earthquake is not a new thing," replied Pangloss. "The town of Lima felt the same shocks in America last year; similar causes produce similar effects; there must certainly be a train of sulphur underground from Lima to Lisbon." "Nothing is more probable," replied Candide; "but, for God's sake, a little oil and wine." "What do you mean, probable?" replied the philosopher; "I maintain that it is proved." Candide lost consciousness, and Pangloss brought him a little water from a neighboring fountain. Next day they found a little food as they wandered among the ruins and regained a little strength. Afterward they worked like others to help the inhabitants who had escaped death. Some citizens they had assisted gave them

---

[35] Reasoning from an accepted presumption.
[36] The Lisbon earthquake and fire took place on November 1, 1755. Much of the city was destroyed and over 30,000 people lost their lives.
[37] A Dutch colony founded on the island of Java in the East Indies during the early seventeenth century.
[38] In 1638 all European traders, except the Dutch, were expelled from Japan. In an attempt to discourage trading and to exclude Christian missionaries, Japanese authorities supposedly required the Dutch merchants to stamp on a crucifix or an image of Jesus.

as good a dinner as could be expected in such a disaster; true, it was a dreary meal; the hosts watered their bread with their tears, but Pangloss consoled them by assuring them that things could not be otherwise. "For," said he, "all this is for the best; for, if there is a volcano at Lisbon, it cannot be anywhere else; for it is impossible that things should not be where they are; for all is well." A little, dark man, a familiar[39] of the Inquisition,[40] who sat beside him, politely took up the conversation, and said: "Apparently, you do not believe in original sin; for, if everything is for the best, there was neither fall nor punishment." "I most humbly beg your excellency's pardon," replied Pangloss still more politely, "for the fall of man and the curse necessarily entered into the best of all possible worlds." "Then you do not believe in free-will?" said the familiar. "Your excellency will pardon me," said Pangloss; "free-will can exist with absolute necessity; for it was necessary that we should be free; for in short, limited will . . ." Pangloss was in the middle of his phrase when the familiar nodded to his armed attendant who was pouring out port or Oporto wine for him.

Chapter VI

HOW A SPLENDID AUTO-DA-FÉ WAS HELD TO PREVENT EARTHQUAKES, AND HOW CANDIDE WAS FLOGGED

After the earthquake which destroyed three-quarters of Lisbon, the wise men of that country could discover no more efficacious way of preventing a total ruin than by giving the people a splendid *auto-da-fé*.[41] It was decided by the university of Coimbra that the sight of several persons being slowly burned in great ceremony is an infallible secret for preventing earthquakes. Consequently they had arrested a Biscayan[42] convicted of having married his fellow-godmother,[43] and two Portuguese who, when eating a chicken, had thrown away the bacon;[44] after dinner they came and bound Dr. Pangloss and his disciple Candide, one because he had spoken and the other because he had listened with an air of approbation; they were both carried separately to extremely cool apartments, where there was never any discomfort from the sun; a week afterward each was dressed in a sanbenito[45] and their heads were

---

[39] A secret agent.
[40] The Inquisition (Congregation of the Holy Office), begun in the thirteenth century and lasting until 1834, was a Roman Catholic tribunal which sought out heresy and punished heretics.
[41] A Portuguese phrase meaning "act of faith." It refers to the public sentencing and punishment of heretics.
[42] A person residing near the Gulf of Biscay, off the northern coast of Spain.
[43] Alluding to the supposed illicit marriage of two godparents of the same child.
[44] Hence, making them suspect of being Jewish.
[45] Refers to the cape worn by individuals sentenced at the *auto-da-fé*. A yellow sanbenito with flames painted on it pointing downward indicated that the heretic's life was spared; a person to be burned wore a black sanbenito with flames pointing upward.

ornamented with paper mitres;[46] Candide's mitre and sanbenito were painted with flames upside down and with devils who had neither tails nor claws; but Pangloss's devils had claws and tails, and his flames were upright. Dressed in this manner they marched in procession and listened to a most pathetic sermon, followed by lovely plain-song music. Candide was flogged in time to the music, while the singing went on; the Biscayan and the two men who had not wanted to eat bacon were burned, and Pangloss was hanged, although this is not the custom. The very same day, the earth shook again with a terrible clamour. Candide, terrified, dumbfounded, bewildered, covered with blood, quivering from head to foot, said to himself: "If this is the best of all possible worlds, what are the others? Let it pass that I was flogged, for I was flogged by the Bulgarians, but, O my dear Pangloss! The greatest of philosophers! Must I see you hanged without knowing why! O my dear Anabaptist! The best of men! Was it necessary that you should be drowned in port! O Mademoiselle Cunegonde! The pearl of women! Was it necessary that your belly should be slit!" He was returning, scarcely able to support himself, preached at, flogged, absolved and blessed, when an old woman accosted him and said: "Courage, my son, follow me."

Chapter VII

HOW AN OLD WOMAN TOOK CARE OF CANDIDE AND HOW HE REGAINED THAT WHICH HE LOVED

Candide did not take courage, but he followed the old woman to a hovel; she gave him a pot of ointment to rub on, and left him food and drink; she pointed out a fairly clean bed; near the bed there was a suit of clothes. "Eat, drink, sleep," said she, "and may our Lady of Atocha, my Lord Saint Anthony of Padua and my Lord of Saint James of Compostella take care of you; I shall come back tomorrow." Candide, still amazed by all he had seen, by all he had suffered, and still more by the old woman's charity, tried to kiss her hand. " 'Tis not my hand you should kiss," said the old woman, "I shall come back tomorrow. Rub on the ointment, eat and sleep." In spite of all his misfortune, Candide ate and went to sleep. Next day the old woman brought him breakfast, examined his back and smeared him with another ointment; later she brought him dinner, and returned in the evening with supper. The next day she went through the same ceremony. "Who are you?" Candide kept asking her. "Who has inspired you with so much kindness? How can I thank you?" The good woman never made any reply; she returned in the evening without any supper. "Come with me," said she, "and do not speak a word." She took him by the arm and walked into the country with him for about a quarter of a

---

[46] Cone or beehive-shaped paper hats.

mile; they came to an isolated house, surrounded with gardens and canals. The old woman knocked at a little door. It was opened; she led Candide up a back stairway into a gilded apartment, left him on a brocaded sofa, shut the door, and went away. Candide thought he was dreaming, and felt that his whole life was a bad dream and the present moment an agreeable dream. The old woman soon reappeared; she was supporting with some difficulty a trembling woman of majestic stature, glittering with precious stones and covered with a veil. "Remove the veil," said the old woman to Candide. The young man advanced and lifted the veil with a timid hand. What a moment! What a surprise! He thought he saw Mademoiselle Cunegonde, in fact he was looking at her, it was she herself. His strength failed him, he could not utter a word and fell at her feet. Cunegonde fell on the sofa. The old woman dosed them with distilled waters; they recovered their senses and began to speak: at first they uttered only broken words, questions and answers at cross purposes, sighs, tears, exclamations. The old woman advised them to make less noise and left them alone. "What! Is it you?" said Candide. "You are alive, and I find you here in Portugal! Then you were not raped? Your belly was not slit, as the philosopher Pangloss assured me?" "Yes, indeed," said the fair Cunegonde; "but those two accidents are not always fatal." "But your father and mother were killed?" " 'Tis only too true," said Conegonde, weeping. "And your brother?" "My brother was killed too."[47] "And why are you in Portugal? And how did you know I was here? And by what strange adventure have you brought me to this house?" "I will tell you everything," replied the lady, "but first of all you must tell me everything that has happened to you since the innocent kiss you gave me and the kicks you received." Candide obeyed with profound respect; and, although he was bewildered, although his voice was weak and trembling, although his back was still a little painful, he related in the most natural manner all he had endured since the moment of their separation. Cunegonde raised her eyes to heaven; she shed tears at the death of the good Anabaptist and Pangloss, after which she spoke as follows to Candide, who did not miss a word and devoured her with his eyes.

Chapter VIII

CUNEGONDE'S STORY

"I was fast asleep in bed when it pleased Heaven to send the Bulgarians to our noble castle of Thunder-ten-tronckh; they murdered my father and brother and cut my mother to pieces. A large Bulgarian six feet tall, seeing that I had swooned at the spectacle, began to rape me; this brought me to, I recovered my senses, I

---

[47] They learn later that her brother also recovered from his wounds.

screamed, I struggled, I bit, I scratched, I tried to tear out the big Bulgarian's eyes, not knowing that what was happening in my father's castle was a matter of custom; the brute stabbed me with a knife in the left side where I still have the scar." "Alas! I hope I shall see it," said the naïve Candide. "You shall see it," said Cunegonde, "but let me go on." "Go on," said Candide. She took up the thread of her story as follows: "A Bulgarian captain came in, saw me covered with blood, and the soldier did not disturb himself. The captain was angry at the brute's lack of respect to him, and killed him on my body. Afterwards, he had me bandaged and took me to his billet as a prisoner of war. I washed the few shirts he had and did the cooking; I must admit he thought me very pretty; and I will not deny that he was very well built and that his skin was white and soft; otherwise he had little wit and little philosophy; it was plain that he had not been brought up by Dr. Pangloss. At the end of three months he lost all his money and got tired of me; he sold me to a Jew named Don Issachar, who traded in Holland and Portugal and had a passion for women. This Jew devoted himself to my person but he could not triumph over it; I resisted him better than the Bulgarian soldier; a lady of honor may be raped once, but it strengthens her virtue. In order to subdue me, the Jew brought me to this country house. Up till then I believed that there was nothing on earth so splendid as the castle of Thunder-ten-tronckh; I was undeceived. One day the Grand Inquisitor noticed me at Mass; he ogled me continually and sent a message that he wished to speak to me on secret affairs. I was taken to his palace; I informed him of my birth; he pointed out how much it was beneath my rank to belong to an Israelite. A proposition was made on his behalf to Don Issachar to give me up to His Lordship. Don Issachar, who is the court banker and a man of influence, would not agree. The Inquisitor threatened him with an *auto-da-fé*. At last the Jew was frightened and made a bargain whereby the house and I belong to both in common. The Jew has Mondays, Wednesdays and the Sabbath day, and the Inquisitor has the other days of the week. This arrangement has lasted for six months. It has not been without quarrels; for it has often been debated whether the night between Saturday and Sunday belonged to the old law or the new.[48] For my part, I have hitherto resisted them both; and I think that is the reason why they still love me. At last My Lord the Inquisitor was pleased to arrange an *auto-da-fé* to remove the scourge of earthquakes and to intimidate Don Issachar. He honored me with an invitation. I had an excellent seat; and refreshments were served to the ladies between the Mass and the execution. I was indeed horror-stricken when I saw the burning of the two Jews and the honest Biscayan who had married his fellow-godmother; but what was my surprise, my terror, my anguish, when I saw in a san-

---

[48] The Old Testament or the New Testament.

benito and under a mitre a face which resembled Pangloss's! I rubbed my eyes, I looked carefully, I saw him hanged; and I fainted. I had scarcely recovered my senses when I saw you stripped naked; that was the height of horror, of consternation, of grief and despair. I will frankly tell you that your skin is even whiter and of a more perfect tint than that of my Bulgarian captain. This spectacle redoubled all the feelings which crushed and devoured me. I exclaimed, I tried to say: 'Stop, Barbarians!' but my voice failed and my cries would have been useless. When you had been well flogged, I said to myself: 'How does it happen that the charming Candide and the wise Pangloss are in Lisbon, the one to receive a hundred lashes, and the other to be hanged, by order of My Lord the Inquisitor, whose darling I am? Pangloss deceived me cruelly when he said that all is for the best in the world.' I was agitated, distracted, sometimes beside myself and sometimes ready to die of faintness, and my head was filled with the massacre of my father, of my mother, of my brother, the insolence of my horrid Bulgarian soldier, the gash he gave me, my slavery, my life as a kitchen-wench, my Bulgarian captain, my horrid Don Issachar, my abominable Inquisitor, the hanging of Dr. Pangloss, that long plain-song *miserere*[49] during which you were flogged, and above all the kiss I gave you behind the screen that day when I saw you for the last time. I praised God for bringing you back to me through so many trials, I ordered my old woman to take care of you and to bring you here as soon as she could. She has carried out my commission very well; I have enjoyed the inexpressible pleasure of seeing you again, of listening to you, and of speaking to you. You must be very hungry; I have a good appetite; let us begin by having supper." Both sat down to supper; and after supper they returned to the handsome sofa we have already mentioned; they were still there when Signor Don Issachar, one of the masters of the house, arrived. It was the day of the Sabbath. He came to enjoy his rights and to express his tender love.

Chapter IX

WHAT HAPPENED TO CUNEGONDE, TO CANDIDE, TO THE GRAND INQUISITOR AND TO A JEW

This Issachar was the most choleric Hebrew who had been seen in Israel since the Babylonian captivity. "What!" said he. "Bitch of a Galilean, isn't it enough to have the Inquisitor? Must this scoundrel share with me too?" So saying, he drew a long dagger which he always carried and, thinking that his adversary was unarmed, threw himself upon Candide; but our good Westphalian

---

[49] A musical composition based upon the opening phrase of Psalm 51: "Have mercy upon me, O God." It is a plea for pardon of deadly sins.

had received an excellent sword from the old woman along with his suit of clothes. He drew his sword, and although he had a most gentle character, laid the Israelite stone-dead on the floor at the feet of the fair Cunegonde. "Holy Virgin!" she exclaimed, "what will become of us? A man killed in my house! If the police come we are lost." "If Pangloss had not been hanged," said Candide, "he would have given us good advice in this extremity, for he was a great philosopher. In default of him, let us consult the old woman." She was extremely prudent and was beginning to give her advice when another little door opened. It was an hour after midnight, and Sunday was beginning. This day belonged to My Lord the Inquisitor. He came in and saw the flogged Candide sword in hand, a corpse lying on the ground, Cunegonde in terror, and the old woman giving advice. At this moment, here is what happened in Candide's soul and the manner of his reasoning: "If this holy man calls for help, he will infallibly have me burned; he might do as much to Cunegonde; he had me pitilessly lashed; he is my rival; I am in the mood to kill, there is no room for hesitation." His reasoning was clear and swift; and, without giving the Inquisitor time to recover from his surprise, he pierced him through and through and cast him beside the Jew. "Here's another," said Cunegonde, "there is no chance of mercy; we are excommunicated, our last hour has come. How does it happen that you, who were born so mild, should kill a Jew and a prelate in two minutes?" "My dear young lady," replied Candide, "when a man is in love, jealous, and has been flogged by the Inquisition, he is beside himself." The old woman then spoke up and said: "In the stable are three Andalusian horses, with their saddles and bridles; let the brave Candide prepare them; mademoiselle has moidores[50] and diamonds; let us mount quickly, although I can only sit on one buttock, and go to Cadiz;[51] the weather is beautifully fine, and it is most pleasant to travel in the coolness of the night." Candide immediately saddled the three horses. Cunegonde, the old woman and he rode thirty miles without stopping. While they were riding away, the Holy Hermandad[52] arrived at the house; My Lord was buried in a splendid church and Issachar was thrown into a sewer. Candide, Cunegonde and the old woman had already reached the little town of Avacena in the midst of the mountains of the Sierra Morena; and they talked in their inn as follows.

---

[50] Portuguese gold coins.
[51] A maritime city in southwestern Spain.
[52] The clerical police.

Chapter X

HOW CANDIDE, CUNEGONDE AND THE OLD WOMAN ARRIVED AT CADIZ IN GREAT DISTRESS, AND HOW THEY EMBARKED

"Who can have stolen my pistoles[53] and my diamonds?" said Cunegonde, weeping. "How shall we live? What shall we do? Where shall we find Inquisitors and Jews to give me others?" "Alas!" said the old woman, "I strongly suspect a reverend Franciscan father who slept in the same inn at Badajoz[54] with us; Heaven forbid that I should judge rashly! But he twice came into our room and left long before we did." "Alas!" said Candide, "the good Pangloss often proved to me that this world's goods are common to all men and that everyone has an equal right to them. According to these principles the monk should have left us enough to continue our journey. Have you nothing left then, my fair Cunegonde?" "Not a maravedi,"[55] said she. "What are we to do?" said Candide. "Sell one of the horses," said the old woman. "I will ride postillion[56] behind Mademoiselle Cunegonde, although I can only sit on one buttock, and we will get to Cadiz." In the same hotel there was a Benedictine friar. He bought the horse very cheap. Candide, Cunegonde and the old woman passed through Lucena, Chillas, Lebrixa, and at last reached Cadiz. A fleet was there being equipped and troops were being raised to bring to reason the reverend Jesuit fathers of Paraguay, who were accused of causing the revolt of one of their tribes against the kings of Spain and Portugal near the town of Sacramento. Candide, having served with the Bulgarians, went through the Bulgarian drill before the general of the little army with so much grace, celerity, skill, pride and agility, that he was given the command of an infantry company. He was now a captain; he embarked with Mademoiselle Cunegonde, the old woman, two servants, and the two Andalusian horses which had belonged to the Grand Inquisitor of Portugal. During the voyage they had many discussions about the philosophy of poor Pangloss. "We are going to a new world," said Candide, "and no doubt it is there that everything is for the best; for it must be admitted that one might lament a little over the physical and moral happenings in our own world." "I love you with all my heart," said Cunegonde, "but my soul is still shocked by what I have seen and undergone." "All will be well," replied Candide; "the sea in this new world already is better than the seas of our Europe; it is calmer and the winds are more constant. It is certainly the new world which is the best of all possible worlds." "God grant it!" said Cunegonde, "but I have been so

---

[53] Spanish gold coins.
[54] A Spanish city near the Portuguese border.
[55] A Spanish copper coin of little value.
[56] A cushion attached behind the saddle to carry an extra rider.

horribly unhappy in mine that my heart is nearly closed to hope." "You complain," said the old woman to them. "Alas! you have not endured such misfortunes as mine." Cunegonde almost laughed and thought it most amusing of the old woman to assert that she was more unfortunate. "Alas! my dear," said she, "unless you have been raped by two Bulgarians, stabbed twice in the belly, have had two castles destroyed, two fathers and mothers murdered before your eyes, and have seen two of your lovers flogged in an *auto-da-fé*, I do not see how you can surpass me; moreover, I was born a Baroness with seventy-two quarterings and I have been a kitchen wench." "You do not know my birth," said the old woman, "and if I showed you my backside you would not talk as you do and you would suspend your judgment." This speech aroused intense curiosity in the minds of Cunegonde and Candide. And the old woman spoke as follows.

Chapter XI

THE OLD WOMAN'S STORY

"My eyes were not always bloodshot and red-rimmed; my nose did not always touch my chin and I was not always a servant. I am the daughter of Pope Urban X[57] and the Princess of Palestrina. Until I was fourteen I was brought up in a palace to which all the castles of your German Barons would not have served as stables; and one of my dresses cost more than all the magnificence of Westphalia. I increased in beauty, in grace, in talents, among pleasures, respect and hopes; already I inspired love, my breasts were forming; and what breasts! White, firm, carved like those of the Venus de' Medici. And what eyes! What eyelids! What black eyebrows! What fire shone from my two eyeballs, and dimmed the glitter of the stars, as the local poets pointed out to me. The women who dressed and undressed me fell into ecstasy when they beheld me in front and behind; and all the men would have liked to be in their place. I was betrothed to a ruling prince of Massa-Carrara.[58] What a prince! As beautiful as I was, formed of gentleness and charms, brilliantly witty and burning with love; I loved him with a first love, idolatrously and extravagantly. The marriage ceremonies were arranged with unheard-of pomp and magnificence; there were continual fêtes, revels, and comic operas; all Italy wrote sonnets for me and not a good one among them. I touched the moment of my happiness when an old marchioness who had been my prince's mistress invited him to take chocolate with her; less than two hours afterwards he died in horrible convulsions; but that is only a trifle.

---

[57] Many years after his death, the following note, left by Voltaire, was first published: "Observe the author's extreme discretion, for there has not up to the present time been any pope named Urban X. He avoids attributing a bastard daughter to a known pope. What circumspection! How delicate a conscience!"

[58] A small Italian duchy, lying northwest of Pisa.

My mother was in despair, though less distressed than I, and wished to absent herself for a time from a place so disastrous. She had a most beautiful estate near Gaeta;[59] we embarked on a galley, gilded like the altar of St. Peter's at Rome. A Salle[60] pirate swooped down and boarded us; our soldiers defended us like soldiers of the Pope; they threw down their arms, fell on their knees and asked the pirates for absolution *in articulo mortis*.[61] They were immediately stripped as naked as monkeys and my mother, our ladies of honor, and myself as well. The diligence with which these gentlemen strip people is truly admirable but I was still more surprised by their inserting a finger in a place belonging to all of us where we woman usually only allow the end of a syringe. This appeared to me a very strange ceremony; but that is how we judge everything when we leave our own country. I soon learned that it was to find out if we had hidden any diamonds there; 'tis a custom established from time immemorial among the civilized nations who roam the seas. I have learned that the religious Knights of Malta never fail in it when they capture Turks and Turkish women; this is an international law which has never been broken. I will not tell you how hard it is for a young princess to be taken with her mother as a slave to Morocco; you will also guess all we had to endure in the pirates' ship. My mother was still very beautiful; our ladies of honor, even our waiting-maids, possessed more charms than could be found in all Africa; and I was ravishing, I was beauty, grace itself, and I was a virgin; I did not remain so long; the flowers which had been reserved for the handsome prince of Massa-Carrara was ravished from me by a pirate captain; he was an abominable Negro who thought he was doing me a great honor. The Princess of Palestrina and I must indeed have been strong to bear up against all we endured before our arrival in Morocco! But let that pass; these things are so common that they are not worth mentioning. Morocco was swimming in blood when we arrived. The fifty sons of the Emperor Muley Ismael[62] had each a faction; and this produced fifty civil wars, of blacks against blacks, browns against browns, mulattoes against mulattoes. There was continual carnage throughout the whole extent of the empire. Scarcely had we landed when the blacks of a party hostile to that of my pirate arrived with the purpose of depriving him of his booty. After the diamonds and the gold, we were the most valuable possessions. I witnessed a fight such as is never seen in your European climates. The blood of the northern peoples is not sufficiently ardent; their madness for women does not reach the point which is common in Africa. The Europeans seem to have milk in their veins; but vitriol

---

[59] A coastal town near Naples.
[60] This coastal city in Morocco was well known as a stronghold for pirates.
[61] A religious rite given at the point of death.
[62] Mawlay Isma'il, sultan of Morocco from 1673 to 1727. The large number of his offspring eventually led to his country's political instability.

and fire flow in the veins of the inhabitants of Mount Atlas and the neighboring countries. They fought with the fury of the lions, tigers and serpents of the country to determine who should have us. A Moor[63] grasped my mother by the right arm, my captain's lieutenant held her by the left arm; a Moorish soldier held one leg and one of our pirates seized the other. In a moment nearly all our women were seized in the same way by four soldiers. My captain kept me hidden behind him; he had a scimitar[64] in his hand and killed everybody who opposed his fury. I saw my mother and all our Italian women torn in pieces, gashed, massacred by the monsters who disputed them. The prisoners, my companions, those who had captured them, soldiers, sailors, blacks, browns, whites, mulattoes and finally my captain were all killed and I remained expiring on a heap of corpses. As everyone knows, such scenes go on in an area of more than three hundred square leagues and yet no one ever fails to recite the five daily prayers ordered by Mohammed. With great difficulty I extricated myself from the bloody heaps of corpses and dragged myself to the foot of a large orange-tree on the bank of a stream; there I fell down with terror, weariness, horror, despair and hunger. Soon afterward, my exhausted senses fell into a sleep which was more like a swoon than repose. I was in this state of weakness and insensibility between life and death when I felt myself oppressed by something which moved on my body. I opened my eyes and saw a white man of good appearance who was sighing and muttering between his teeth: *O che sciagura d'essere senza coglioni!*[65]

Chapter XII

CONTINUATION OF THE OLD WOMAN'S MISFORTUNES

"Amazed and delighted to hear my native language, and not less surprised at the words spoken by this man, I replied that there were greater misfortunes than that of which he complained. In a few words I informed him of the horrors I had undergone and then swooned again. He carried me to a neighboring house, had me put to bed, gave me food, waited on me, consoled me, flattered me, told me he had never seen anyone so beautiful as I, and that he had never so much regretted that which no one could give back to him. 'I was born at Naples,' he said, 'and every year they make two or three thousand children there into capons;[66] some die of it, others acquire voices more beautiful than women's, and others become the governors of States. This operation was performed upon

---

[63] The Moors, the primary inhabitants of northwestern Africa, are Muslim by religion and ethnically of mixed Arab and African ancestry.
[64] A short, curved sword.
[65] Italian: "Oh, what misfortune to have no testicles!"
[66] A rooster that has been castrated for better fattening.

me with very great success and I was a musician in the chapel of the Princess of Palestrina.' 'Of my mother,' I exclaimed. 'Of your mother!' cried he, weeping. 'What! Are you that young princess I brought up to the age of six and who even then gave promise of being as beautiful as you are?' 'I am! my mother is four hundred yards from here, cut into quarters under a heap of corpses . . .' I related all that had happened to me; he also told me his adventures and informed me how he had been sent to the King of Morocco by a Christian power to make a treaty with that monarch whereby he was supplied with powder, cannons, and ships to help exterminate the commerce of other Christians. 'My mission is accomplished,' said this honest eunuch, 'I am about to embark at Ceuta[67] and I will take you back to Italy. *Ma che sciagura d'essere senza coglioni!*' I thanked him with tears of gratitude; and instead of taking me back to Italy he conducted me to Algiers and sold me to the Dey.[68] I had scarcely been sold when the plague which had gone through Africa, Asia and Europe, broke out furiously in Algiers. You have seen earthquakes; but have you ever seen the plague?" "Never," replied the Baroness. "If you had," replied the old woman, "you would admit that it is much worse than an earthquake. It is very common in Africa; I caught it. Imagine the situation of a Pope's daughter aged fifteen, who in three months had undergone poverty and slavery, had been raped nearly every day, had seen her mother cut into four pieces, had undergone hunger and war, and was now dying of the plague in Algiers. However, I did not die; but my eunuch and the Dey and almost all the seraglio[69] of Algiers perished. When the first ravages of this frightful plague were over, the Dey's slaves were sold. A merchant bought me and carried me to Tunis; he sold me to another merchant who resold me at Tripoli; from Tripoli I was resold to Alexandria, from Alexandria resold to Smyrna, from Smyrna to Constantinople. I was finally bought by an Aga[70] of the Janizaries,[71] who was soon ordered to defend Azov[72] against the Russians who were besieging it. The Aga, who was a man of great gallantry, took his whole seraglio with him, and lodged us in a little fort on the Islands of Palus-Maeotis,[73] guarded by two black eunuchs and twenty soldiers. He killed a prodigious number of Russians but they returned the compliment as well. Azov was given up to fire and blood, neither sex nor age was pardoned; only our little fort remained; and the enemy tried to reduce it by starving us. The twenty Janizaries had sworn never to surrender us. The extremities of hunger to which they were re-

---

[67] A maritime city at the northwestern tip of Africa.
[68] The title of the Turkish governor.
[69] Harem.
[70] Title of respect for a high-ranking officer or official.
[71] A unit of Turkish infantry composed of former slaves, natives, and sons of captured Christians.
[72] A city located at the mouth of the River Don in southern Russia.
[73] Latin name for the Sea of Azov.

duced forced them to eat our two eunuchs for fear of breaking their oaths. Some days later they resolved to eat the women. We had with us a most pious and compassionate Imam[74] who delivered a fine sermon to them by which he persuaded them not to kill us altogether. 'Cut,' said he, 'only one buttock from each of these ladies and you will make very good cheer; if you have to return, there will still be as much left in a few days; Heaven will be pleased at so charitable an action and you will be saved.' He was very eloquent and persuaded them. This horrible operation was performed upon us; the Imam anointed us with the same balm that is used for children who have just been circumcized; we were all at the point of death. Scarcely had the Janizaries finished the meal we had supplied when the Russians arrived in flat-bottomed boats; not a Janizary escaped. The Russians paid no attention to the state we were in. There are French doctors everywhere; one of them who was very skillful took care of us; he healed us and I shall remember all my life that, when my wounds were cured, he made propositions to me. For the rest, he told us all to cheer up; he told us that the same thing had happened in several sieges and that it was a law of war. As soon as my companions could walk they were sent to Moscow. I fell to the lot of a Boyar[75] who made me his gardener and gave me twenty lashes a day. But at the end of two years this lord was broken on the wheel with thirty other Boyars owing to some court disturbance, and I profited by this adventure; I fled; I crossed all Russia; for a long time I was servant in an inn at Riga,[76] then at Rostock, at Wismar, at Leipzig, at Cassel,[77] at Utrecht, at Leyden, at The Hague, at Rotterdam;[78] I have grown old in misery and in shame, with only half a backside, always remembering that I was the daughter of a Pope; a hundred times I wanted to kill myself but I still loved life. This ridiculous weakness is perhaps the most disastrous of our inclinations; for is there anything sillier than to desire to bear continually a burden one always wishes to throw on the ground; to look upon oneself with horror and yet to cling to oneself; in short, to caress the serpent which devours us until he has eaten our heart? In the countries it has been my fate to traverse and in the inns where I have served I have seen a prodigious number of people who hated their lives; but I have only seen twelve who voluntarily put an end to their misery: three Negroes, four Englishmen, four Genevans and a German professor named Robeck.[79] I ended up as servant to the Jew, Don Issachar; he placed me in your service, my fair young lady; I attached myself to

[74] Muslim official.
[75] Russian aristocrat.
[76] A city on the coast of Latvia.
[77] Cities in northern Germany.
[78] Cities in Holland.
[79] Johann Robe(c)k (1672–1739), who claimed that the love of life was nothing but a ridiculous idea. Having composed a treatise entitled "Exercise in Voluntary Death" in which he justified suicide, he drowned himself.

your fate and have been more occupied with your adventures than with my own. I should never even have spoken of my misfortunes, if you had not piqued me a little and if it had not been the custom on board ship to tell stories to pass the time. In short, Mademoiselle, I have had experience, I know the world; provide yourself with an entertainment, make each passenger tell you his story; and if there is one who has not often cursed his life, who has not often said to himself that he was the most unfotunate of men, throw me head-first into the sea."

◇ ◇ ◇

Upon Candide's arrival in the New World, he begins a series of misadventures which give him further reason to question his optimistic view of life. Only in the South American paradise called El Dorado does he discover a truly virtuous society exhibiting naturally gracious, charitable, and rational characteristics. His attempt to win back his precious Cunegonde, earlier lost to a Spanish noble, is thwarted and Candide decides to return to Europe. He is accompanied by Martin, a disillusioned pessimist, under whose influence Candide begins to doubt Pangloss's philosophical optimism. Martin offers the example of Candide's own misadventures as proof that the world is evil.

Back in Europe, Candide finds further testimony to Martin's views in the conduct of intellectuals, monks, prostitutes, and deposed kings they encounter. Disillusioned, they are unable to find a truly happy man. Candide's adventures come to an end in the following two chapters.

Chapter XXIX

HOW CANDIDE FOUND CUNEGONDE AND THE OLD WOMAN AGAIN

While Candide, the Baron,[80] Pangloss, Martin and Cacambo[81] were relating their adventures, reasoning upon contingent or non-contingent events of the universe, arguing about effects and causes, moral and physical evil, free will and necessity, and the consolations to be found in the Turkish galleys, they came to the house of the Transylvanian prince on the shores of Propontis.[82] The first objects which met their sight were Cunegonde and the old woman hanging out towels to dry on the line. At this sight the Baron grew pale. Candide, that tender lover, seeing his fair Cunegonde sunburned,

---

[80] The son of Baron Thunder-ten-tronckh who appeared in Chapter 1. Candide found him serving as a galley slave and obtained his freedom. He was, of course, Cunegonde's long-lost brother. Candide found in the same crew his old tutor, Pangloss, who had survived his hanging, a partial dissection, merciless floggings, and a long stint as a galley-slave.
[81] Candide's valet, brought from Cadiz.
[82] Sea of Marmara, between the Bosporus and the Dardanelles in Turkey.

blear-eyed, flat-breasted, with wrinkles round her eyes and red, chapped arms, recoiled three paces in horror, and then advanced from mere politeness. She embraced Candide and her brother. They embraced the old woman; Candide bought them both. In the neighborhood was a little farm; the old woman suggested that Candide should buy it, until some better fate befell the group. Cunegonde did not know that she had become ugly, for nobody had told her so; she reminded Candide of his promises in so peremptory a tone that the good Candide dared not refuse her. He therefore informed the Baron that he was about to marry his sister. "Never," said the Baron, "will I endure such baseness on her part and such insolence on yours; nobody shall ever reproach me with this infamy; my sister's children could never enter the chapters[83] of Germany. No, my sister shall never marry anyone but a Baron of the Empire." Cunegonde threw herself at his feet and bathed them in tears; but he was inflexible. "Madman," said Candide, "I rescued you from the galleys, I paid your ransom and your sister's; she was washing dishes here, she is ugly, I am so kind as to make her my wife, and you pretend to oppose me! I should kill you again if I listened to my anger." "You may kill me again," said the Baron, "but you shall never marry my sister while I am alive."

Chapter XXX

CONCLUSION

At the bottom of his heart Candide had not the least wish to marry Cunegonde. But the Baron's extreme impertinence determined him to complete the marriage, and Cunegonde urged it so warmly that he could not retract. He consulted Pangloss, Martin and the faithful Cacambo. Pangloss wrote an excellent memorandum by which he proved that the Baron had no rights over his sister and that by all the laws of the empire she could make a left-handed marriage[84] with Candide. Martin advised that the Baron should be thrown into the sea; Cacambo decided that he should be returned to the Levantine captain and sent back to the galleys, after which he would be returned by the first ship to the Vicar-General at Rome. This was thought to be very good advice; the old woman approved it; they said nothing to the sister; the plan was carried out with the aid of a little money and they had the pleasure of duping a Jesuit and punishing the pride of a German Baron. It would be natural to suppose that when, after so many disasters, Candide was married to his mistress, and living with the philosopher Pangloss, the philosopher Martin, the prudent Cacambo and the old woman, having brought back so many diamonds from the

---

[83] Knightly assemblies.
[84] Marriage between individuals of unequal rank.

country of the ancient Incas, he would lead the most pleasant life imaginable. But he was so cheated by the Jews that he had nothing left but his little farm; his wife, growing uglier every day, became shrewish and unendurable; the old woman was ailing and even more bad-tempered than Cunegonde. Cacambo, who worked in the garden and then went to Constantinople to sell vegetables, was overworked and cursed his fate. Pangloss was in despair because he did not shine in some German university. As for Martin, he was firmly convinced that people are equally uncomfortable everywhere; he accepted things patiently. Candide, Martin, and Pangloss sometimes argued about metaphysics and morals. From the windows of the farm they often watched the ships going by, filled with effendis,[85] pashas,[86] and cadis,[87] who were being exiled to Lemnos, to Mitylene[88] and Erzerum.[89] They saw other cadis, other pashas, and other effendis coming back to take the place of the exiles and to be exiled in their turn. They saw the neatly impaled heads which were taken to the Sublime Porte.[90] These sights redoubled their discussions; and when they were not arguing, the boredom was so excessive that one day the old woman dared to say to them: "I should like to know which is worse, to be raped a hundred times by Negro pirates, to have a buttock cut off, to run the gauntlet among the Bulgarians, to be whipped and flogged in an *auto-da-fé*, to be dissected, to row in a galley, in short, to endure all the miseries through which we have passed, or to remain here doing nothing?" " 'Tis a great question," said Candide. These remarks led to new reflections, and Martin especially concluded that man was born to live in the convulsions of distress or in the lethargy of boredom. Candide did not agree, but he asserted nothing. Pangloss confessed that he had always suffered horribly; but, having once maintained that everything was for the best, he had continued to maintain it without believing it. One thing confirmed Martin in his detestable principles, made Candide hesitate more than ever, and embarrassed Pangloss. And it was this. One day there came to their farm Paquette and Friar Giroflée,[91] who were in the most extreme misery; they had soon wasted their three thousand piastres,[92] had left each other, made it up, quarreled again, been put in prison, escaped, and finally Friar Giroflée had turned Turk. Paquette continued her occupation everywhere and now earned nothing by it. "I foresaw," said Martin to Candide, "that your gifts would soon be wasted and would only make them the more miserable. You and

---

[85] Turkish title of respect for a government official.
[86] High military or civilian official.
[87] A minor official.
[88] Islands located in the Aegean Sea.
[89] City in Northeastern Turkey.
[90] Main gate of the Sultan's palace in Constantinople. The heads of those executed were often displayed there as a deterrent to crime.
[91] A monk Candide encountered earlier in Venice. Literally (in French), "wallflower."
[92] Turkish money.

Cacambo were once bloated with millions of piastres and you are no happier than Friar Giroflée and Paquette." "Ah! Ha!" said Pangloss to Paquette, "so Heaven brings you back to us, my dear child? Do you know that you cost me the end of my nose, an eye, and an ear! What a plight you are in! Ah! What a world this is!" This new occurrence caused them to philosophize more than ever. In the neighborhood there lived a very famous Dervish,[93] who was supposed to be the best philosopher in Turkey; they went to consult him; Pangloss was the spokesman and said: "Master, we have come to beg you to tell us why so strange an animal as man was ever created." "What has it to do with you?" said the Dervish. "Is it your business?" "But, reverend father," said Candide, "there is a horrible amount of evil in the world." "What does it matter," said the Dervish, "whether there is evil or good? When his highness sends a ship to Egypt, does he worry about the comfort or discomfort of the rats in the ship?" "Then what should we do?" said Pangloss. "Hold your tongue," said the Dervish. "I flattered myself," said Pangloss, "that I should discuss with you effects and causes, this best of all possible worlds, the origin of evil, the nature of the soul and pre-established harmony." At these words the Dervish slammed the door in their faces. During this conversation the news went round that at Constantinople two viziers[94] and the mufti[95] had been strangled and several of their friends impaled. This catastrophe made a prodigious noise everywhere for several hours. As Pangloss, Candide, and Martin were returning to their little farm, they came upon an old man who was taking the air under a bower of orange-trees at his door. Pangloss, who was as curious as he was argumentative, asked him what was the name of the mufti who had just been strangled. "I do not know," replied the old man. "I have never known the name of any mufti or of any vizier. I am entirely ignorant of the occurrence you mention; I presume that in general those who meddle with public affairs sometimes perish miserably and that they deserve it; but I never inquire what is going on in Constantinople; I content myself with sending there for sale the produce of the garden I cultivate." Having spoken thus, he took the strangers into his house. His two daughters and his two sons presented them with several kinds of sherbet which they made themselves, caymac[96] flavored with candied citron peel, oranges, lemons, limes, pineapples, dates, pistachios, and Mocha coffee which had not been mixed with the bad coffee of Batavia and the Isles.[97] After which this good Mussulman's two daughters perfumed the beards of Candide, Pangloss, and Martin. "You must have a vast and magnificent estate?" said Candide to the Turk. "I

---

[93] Member of a Muslim religious order.
[94] Ministers of state.
[95] An official interpreter of Muslim law.
[96] Turkish word for cream.
[97] Probably the East Indies.

have only twenty acres," replied the Turk. "I cultivate them with my children; and work keeps at bay three great evils: boredom, vice and need." As Candide returned to his farm he reflected deeply on the Turk's remarks. He said to Pangloss and Martin: "That good old man seems to me to have chosen an existence preferable by far to that of the six kings with whom we had the honor to sup." "Exalted rank," said Pangloss, "is very dangerous, according to the testimony of all philosophers; for Eglon, King of the Moabites, was murdered by Ehud; Absalom was hanged by the hair and pierced by three darts; King Nadab, son of Jeroboam, was killed by Baasha; King Elah by Zimri; Ahaziah by Jehu; Athaliah by Jehoiada; the Kings Jehoiakim, Jeconiah, and Zedekiah[98] were made slaves. You know in what manner died Croesus, Astyages, Darius, Denys of Syracuse, Pyrrhus, Perseus, Hannibal, Jugurtha, Ariovistus, Caesar, Pompey, Nero, Otho, Vitellius, Domitian, Richard II of England, Edward II, Henry VI, Richard III, Mary Stuart, Charles I, the three Henrys of France, the Emperor Henry IV. You know . . ." "I also know," said Candide, "that we should cultivate our gardens." "You are right," said Pangloss, "for, when man was placed in the Garden of Eden, he was placed there *ut operaretur eum,* to dress it and to keep it; which proves that man was not born for idleness." "Let us work without theorizing," said Martin; " 'tis the only way to make life endurable." The whole small fraternity entered into this praiseworthy plan, and each started to make use of his talents. The little farm yielded well. Cunegonde was indeed very ugly, but she became an excellent pastrycook; Paquette embroidered; the old woman took care of the linen. Even Friar Giroflée performed some service; he was a very good carpenter and even became a man of honor; and Pangloss sometimes said to Candide: "All events are linked up in this best of all possible worlds; for, if you had not been expelled from the noble castle by hard kicks in your backside for love of Mademoiselle Cunegonde, if you had not been clapped into the Inquisition, if you had not wandered about America on foot, if you had not stuck your sword in the Baron, if you had not lost all your sheep from the land of Eldorado, you would not be eating candied citrons and pistachios here." " 'Tis well said," replied Candide, "but we must cultivate our gardens."

Further Readings

W. H. Barber, *The Age of the Enlightenment* (London: Oliver and Boyd, 1967), and Robert Anchor, *The Enlightenment Tradition* (New York: Harper and Row, 1967), are two standard works on the period. Peter Gay, *The Enlightenment: An Interpretation* (2 vols.: New York: Vintage Press, 1977), examines the complex intellectual forces of the period. The attitude of eighteenth-century intellectuals toward the masses is explored in Harry C. Payne, *The Philoso-*

---

[98] Names of victims and villains mentioned in the Old Testament.

pher and the People (New Haven, CT: Yale University Press, 1976). Ira Owen Wade, *The Structure and Form of the French Enlightenment* (2 vols.: Princeton, NJ: Princeton University Press, 1977), analyzes the influence of the previous two centuries on the Enlightenment. Henry Vyverberg, *Historical Pessimism in the French Enlightenment* (Cambridge, MA: Harvard University Press, 1958), examines the historical philosophies of the period with particular attention to the role of pessimism within the movement. Lester G. Crocker, *An Age of Crisis* (Baltimore, MD: Johns Hopkins Press, 1959), emphasizes the values and ethical systems that evolved in eighteenth-century France.

Ira Owen Wade, *Voltaire and Candide* (Port Washington, NY: Kennikat Press, 1959), explores the historical, philosophical, intellectual, and aesthetic forces behind *Candide*. Theodore Besterman, *Voltaire* (Oxford: Blackwell, 1976), is a notable biography that utilizes a topical, as well as a chronological, organization. Voltaire's political thought is skillfully analyzed by Peter Gay, *Voltaire's Politics* (Princeton, NJ: Princeton University Press, 1956). Ira Owen Wade, *The Intellectual Development of Voltaire* (Princeton, NJ: Princeton University Press, 1969), offers a thorough survey of Voltaire's intellectual life. *Voltaire: A Collection of Critical Essays,* edited by William F. Bottiglia (Englewood Cliffs, NJ: Prentice-Hall, 1968), includes an analysis of the conclusion of *Candide*. Hayden Trevor Mason, *Voltaire: A Biography* (London: P. Elik, Granada Publishers, 1981), concentrates on those periods of Voltaire's life that most revealed his character. *The Selected Letters of Voltaire,* translated and edited by Richard Brooks (New York: New York University Press, 1973), covers a wide variety of topics from various periods of the author's life. Leonard Bernstein's operatic version of *Candide* preserves much of the verve of the original in its music and staging.

The Sufferings of Young Werther

The two centuries dominated by the Scientific Revolution and the Enlightenment placed great confidence in the power of reason to solve even the most complex problems. At the beginning of the nineteenth century, however, a new literary movement arose that rejected this belief and challenged the Enlightenment's emphasis on the rational nature of humankind and the logical order of the universe. Turning from reason as the ultimate solution, many intellectuals looked to faith, intuition, and emotion as the keys to understanding the human condition. This new philosophical direction marked the beginnings of the movement that came to be called Romanticism.

The term defies precise definition, and its meaning seems to have varied from country to country and even from individual to individual. In all of its expressions, however, Romanticism represented a revolt against the rationalism and optimism of the eighteenth century. The Romantics rejected the simplicity and unity that had typified Enlightenment thought. They pointed out that the universe was not the perfect machine it had seemed since Newton, nor were human beings simply cogs in that machine. By emphasizing individuality and emotion, the Romantics offered a more complex and troubling view of the world.

One of the foremost proponents of this new view as Johann Wolfgang von Goethe (1749–1832), a German intellectual of wide-ranging abilities and great genius. Almost single-handedly, he succeeded in creating a German national literature at the very forefront of European intellectual expression. He was born into a well-to-do family of jurists and governmental administrators, and was converted to Romanticism while studying law at Strassburg. In 1775, he became political advisor to the duke of Saxe-Weimar, a small inde-

From Johann Wolfgang von Goethe, *The Sufferings of Young Werther*, translated by Harry Steinhauer (New York: W. W. Norton and Co., Inc., 1970), pp. 76–84, 88–96.

pendent German state, and remained in this post for the rest of his life. Under the patronage of his duke, Goethe was free to study, write, and travel widely. He made good use of this opportunity. His interests continued to expand throughout his life, and his intellectual growth was unceasing. It was these two qualities that set him apart from most of the other authors of his period and gained him great respect throughout the continent. He came to regard himself as a prophet of his time and an interpreter of the spiritual issues of his day. In many ways this was so; his dramas, novels, and poetry had the most profound influence upon his contemporaries. He is still widely regarded as perhaps the greatest genius Germany has ever produced.

One of the earliest and most striking examples of his Romanticism is *The Sufferings of Young Werther* (1774), a novel that recounts the extravagant sufferings of a young man driven to suicide by frustrated passion. This work was composed when Goethe was a member of *Sturm und Drang* ("Storm and Stress"), one of the most famous movements in German literary history. *Sturm und Drang* was a loose-knit group of German intellectuals who had rebelled against the Enlightenment's prevailing mood of optimism. They considered the world a far from perfect place and stressed the inevitable conflict between society and the individual. The more intense the individualism, the more tempestuous the conflict must be. Motivated by a profound sense of social responsibility, many of the group's writings were imbued with a passion for social reform.

The Sufferings of Young Werther is one of the most peculiar and magnificent products of the *Sturm and Drang* movement. It was also the work that first gained Goethe European fame. Its hero is a talented, sensitive, and gentle young man whose passions rise far above the commonplace. In the first part of the work, Werther becomes acquainted with Lotte and develops an absorbing passion for her. Lotte, however, is already engaged to Albert, and Werther decides to leave. Albert is not a man prone to jealousy, and Werther persuades himself to stay near Lotte. He is unable to control his love for her, however, and, recognizing the hopelessness of his situation begins to contemplate killing himself. The first part of the novel ends at this point.

The second part, the final section of which is excerpted here, begins with Werther away from Lotte and employed in an embassy. Regular work and his separation from the object of his passion have raised his spirits, but circumstances lead to his resignation from his post and his eventual return to Lotte. Lotte and Albert, now married, welcome Werther, who draws even closer to Lotte. Realizing that even though Lotte loves him she will remain faithful to her husband, Werther concludes that his passion is hopeless. Once again his thoughts turn to death. He visits Lotte once more and, in an emotional scene, she pushes him away from her and Werther flees the room. The next evening he takes his own life.

The novel was such a success and so appealed to the temper of the youth of the times, that many young German intellectuals sought to imitate Werther. They wore the blue frock coat and yellow waistcoat and trousers of their hero, and not a few of them carried their imitation to the extreme of committing suicide. Meanwhile, young wives pined for a lover with Werther's depths of feeling.

The Sufferings of Young Werther, however, is more than the story of a young man dying because of unrequited love. It contains profound observations on the relationship between the individual and society, the individual and nature, and the conflicts between duty and desire and good and evil. With *Werther,* Goethe explored new depths of feeling. His work not only opened up new possibilities in Western literature, but remains a moving and profound work. The fundamental issues it raises are still unresolved.

Questions

1. Love is often the victim of convention. How was Werther affected by the constraints imposed upon him by society?

2. Even if he could have won Lotte, do you think Werther could have lived a more or less normal life?

3. Was unrequited love the only reason for Werther's death?

THE SUFFERINGS OF YOUNG WERTHER

He threw himself down before Lotte in all his despair, grasped her hands, pressed them to his eyes, against his forehead, and a premonition of his terrible resolve seemed to rush through her mind. Her senses became confused, she pressed his hands, pressed them against her breast, leaned toward him with a mournful movement, and their cheeks touched. The world ceased to exist for them. He threw his arms about her, pressed her to his breast, and covered her trembling, stammering lips with violent kisses. — "Werther!" she cried in a suffocating voice, turning from him, "Werther!" and with a weak hand she pushed his body away from hers. "Werther!" she cried in the steady tone of the noblest emotion. —He did not resist, released her from his arms and threw himself before her, senseless. She jumped up, and in confusion and anxiety, quivering between love and anger, she said, "This is the last time, Werther. You shall not see me again." —And, casting a look full of love at the wretched man, she hurried into the next room and locked the door behind her. Werther extended his arms after her but did not dare to retain her. He lay on the floor, his head on the sofa, and remained in this position for more than half an hour, until a noise brought him back to his senses. It was the maid, who wanted to set the table. He paced up and down the room, and when he found himself alone again, he went to the door of the study and called in a low voice: "Lotte! Lotte! just one more word, a word of farewell." —She was silent. He waited and begged and waited; then he tore himself away and cried: "Farewell, Lotte! Farewell forever!"

He came to the city gate. The guards, who knew him, let him out without a word. A mixture of rain and snow was falling, and he did not knock at the door again till about eleven. His servant noticed that his master was without his hat when he came home. He did not venture to say anything, he helped him undress; all his clothes were wet. Later, his hat was found on a rock which overhangs the valley from the slope of the hill; it is beyond comprehension how he could have climbed this rock on a dark, wet night without falling.

He went to bed and slept long. Next morning, when he answered Werther's call and brought him his coffee, the servant found him writing. He added the following to his letter to Lotte:

For the last time, then, for the last time I open these eyes. They shall, alas, never see the sun again, for a gloomy, foggy day obscures it. Mourn then, O Nature! Your son, your friend, your lover is approaching his end. Lotte, this is an incomparable feeling, and yet it comes closest to a twilight dream to say to yourself: this is the last morning. The last! Lotte, I have no feeling for that word: last. Do I not stand here in all my strength, and tomorrow I shall lie on the ground, stretched out and limp? To die: what does that mean? Behold, we dream when we talk of death. I have seen many die; but so restricted is human nature that it has no feeling for the beginning or end of its existence. At this moment there is still mine and yours—yours, O my beloved. And in another moment—separated, parted—perhaps forever? —No, Lotte, no—How can I pass away? How can you pass away? For we exist! —Pass away—what does that mean? It is just another word, an empty sound, which does not touch my heart. —Dead, Lotte! buried in the cold ground, so confined, so dark! —I had a friend who was everything to me in my helpless youth; she died and I followed her corpse and stood at her grave when they lowered the coffin and then pulled the whirring ropes from under it and up again; then the first shovelful of earth pattered down, and the frightened box reverberated with a dull thud which grew duller and duller until at last it was completely covered. —I threw myself down beside the grave—moved, shaken, frightened, ravaged to the core; but I did not know what was happening to me—what will happen to me—Dying! Grave! I don't understand these words.

Oh forgive me, forgive me! Yesterday! It should have been the last moment of my life. Oh you angel! For the first time, for the first time without any doubt whatever, the joyful feeling glows through my innermost depths: she loves me! she loves me! The sacred fire that streamed from your lips is still burning on mine; a new, warm joy is in my heart. Forgive me! Forgive me!

Oh, I knew that you loved me, knew it from the first soulful looks, from the first handclasp, and yet, when I was away from you, when I saw Albert at your side, I despaired again in feverish doubt.

Do you remember the flowers you sent me when you could not say a word to me at that awful party and could not give me your hand? Oh, I knelt before them through half the night, and they put the seal on your love for me. But alas, these impressions passed, as the soul of the believer gradually loses the feeling of grace given him by his God with all the fullness of Heaven, with a sacred, visible symbol.

All this is transitory, but no eternity shall extinguish the glowing life which I savored yesterday on your lips, and which I feel within me now. She loves me! This arm has embraced her, these lips have trembled on hers, this mouth has stammered words on hers. She is mine! You are mine! Yes, Lotte, forever.

And what does it signify that Albert is your husband? Husband! That is something for this world—and for this world it is a sin that I love you, that I should like to snatch you out of his arms into mine. Sin? Very well! And I am punishing myself for it; I have tasted this sin in all its heavenly rapture, I have sucked the balm of life and strength into my heart. From this moment on you are mine. Mine, Lotte! I am going ahead, going to my Father, to your Father. I will bring my plaint to Him and He will comfort me until you come, and I will fly to meet you, clasp you, and remain with you before the countenance of the Infinite in an eternal embrace.

I am not dreaming, I am not delusional; so near the grave the light grows brighter for me. We shall be! We shall see each other again! To see your mother! I shall see her, shall find her, ah, and pour out my whole heart to her! Your mother, your image.

Toward eleven o'clock Werther asked his servant whether Albert had returned yet. The servant replied: yes, he had seen his horse being led home. Thereupon his master gave him an unsealed note with the following content:

Will you loan me your pistols for a journey I am planning? Farewell.

The dear woman had slept little that night; what she had feared had been realized in a way she could neither have suspected nor dreaded. Her blood, which usually flowed so pure and light, was in a feverish rebellion; a thousand different emotions ravaged her fair heart. Was it the fire of Werther's embraces she felt in her bosom? Was it displeasure at his boldness? Was it an irritating comparison between her present state and the days of perfectly natural, naive innocence and carefree confidence in herself? How was she to face her husband? How confess to him a scene that she might well confess but which she nevertheless did not dare confess? They had been silent toward each other for such a long time, was she to be the first to break the silence and make such an unexpected revelation to her husband at this inopportune time? She was afraid that the mere report of Werther's visit would make an unpleasant impression on him, how much more this unexpected catastrophe! Could she really hope that her husband would see it in its true light and accept it entirely without prejudice? Dare she wish that he might read her soul? But then again, could she dissimulate before the man toward whom she had always been open and free like glass of clear cystal, and from whom she never had, nor could have, concealed any of her feelings? Either alternative was a cause of anxiety and embarrassment to her; and always her thoughts returned to Werther, who was lost to her, whom she could not give up, yet whom she must unfortunately abandon to himself and for whom there was nothing left when he had lost her.

At that moment she could not clearly understand how heavily the estrangement that had settled over them now weighed on her. Such intelligent, such good people began to observe a silence toward each other because of certain private differences, each pondering his right and the other's wrong, and the relationship grew so entangled and so harassed that it become impossible to loosen the knot at the critical moment on which everything depended. If a happy intimacy had re-established their former closeness sooner, if their mutual love and understanding had flourished and opened their hearts, perhaps there might still have been help for our friend.

Another strange circumstance entered the situation. Werther, as we know from his letters, had never made a secret of the fact that he longed to leave this world. Albert had often challenged him on it; Lotte and her husband had sometimes discussed the subject too. Albert, who felt a decided aversion to the act, had quite often, with a sort of irritation that was wholly out of character, made it very clear that he had reason to doubt the seriousness of such an intention; he had even permitted himself to joke about the matter and had communicated his skepticism to Lotte. This, to be sure, calmed her when her thoughts presented the sad picture to her; on the other hand, it made her feel reluctant to inform her husband of the anxiety that tormented her at the moment.

Albert returned and Lotte went to meet him with an embarrassed haste. He was not in a cheerful mood; his business had not been completed and he had found in the neighboring magistrate a petty, unbending man. The bad road, too, had spoiled his temper.

He asked whether anything had happened, and she answered with excessive haste that Werther had been there the night before. He asked if any letters had come and received the reply that a letter and some packages were lying in his room. He went in and Lotte remained alone. The presence of the man whom she loved and honored had made a new impression on her heart. The memory of his noble spirit, his love, and kindness had somewhat calmed her emotions, and she felt a secret impulse to follow him; she took her sewing and went into his room, as she was accustomed to do. She found him occupied opening his packages and reading. Some of the contents did not seem to be of the most agreeable sort. She put some questions to him, which he answered curtly, and then took up his position at his desk to write.

They had been together like this for an hour and Lotte's heart was sinking lower and lower. She felt how difficult it would be for her to reveal to her husband what weighed on her mind, even if he were in the best of humors; she lapsed into a state of melancholy, which became all the more frightening to her as she sought to conceal it and to choke back her tears.

The appearance of Werther's servant threw her into the greatest embarrassment. He handed the note to Albert, who turned calmly to his wife and said: "Give him the pistols." —"I wish him a happy journey," he said to the boy. The words struck her like a thunderclap; she staggered to her feet, not knowing what she was doing. Slowly she went to the wall; she trembled as she took down the weapons, dusted them off, and hesitated, and she would have hesitated longer still if Albert had not pressed her with a questioning look. She handed the boy the dreadful weapons without being able to utter a word, and when the boy had left the house she gathered up her work and went to her room in a state of the most indescribable uncertainty. Her heart foretold her every possible terror. At one point she was on the verge of throwing herself at the feet of her husband, and disclosing everything to him: the events of the previous evening, her guilt, and her forebodings. Then, again, she saw no solution in such a course of action, least of all could she hope to persude her husband to go to Werther. The table was set; a good friend, who had merely come in to ask a question, and intended to go at once but stayed on, made the dinner conversation endurable. They forced themselves to talk, told stories and forgot themselves.

The boy brought the pistols to Werther, who took them from him with delight when he heard that Lotte had handed them to him. He had bread and wine[1] brought up, told the boy to have his dinner, and sat down to write:

They have passed through your hands, you dusted them off; I kiss them a thousand times, for you have touched them. And you, heavenly spirit, favor my resolve! And you, Lotte, hand me the instrument, you, from whose hands I wished to receive death, and, ah, receive it now. Oh, I questioned my boy. You trembled when you handed them to him, you did not say farewell. —Alas, alas, no farewell! —Can you have closed your heart to me for the sake

---

[1] Possibly an allusion to the Last Supper, in line with Werther's version of himself as a Christlike martyr.

of the moment which bound me to you forever? Lotte, not even a thousand years can efface the impression! and I feel it: you cannot hate the man who burns so passionately for you.

After dinner he ordered the boy to finish packing, tore up many papers, and went out to take care of some small debts. He came home again, then went out once more, through the town gate, heedless of the rain, into the Count's garden, wandered about in the area, returned home as night descended, and wrote:

Wilhelm, I have seen the fields and the woods and the sky for the last time. Farewell to you, too! Dear mother, forgive me. Comfort her, Wilhelm. God bless you both. All my affairs are in order. Farewell! We shall see each other again, in happier circumstances.

I have ill rewarded you, Albert, but you will forgive me. I have disturbed the peace of your home, I have brought distrust between you. Farewell; I will end it. Oh I pray that my death may restore your happiness. Albert, Albert, make the angel happy! And so may God's blessing be upon you.

That evening he continued to rummage among his papers, tore up many and threw them into the stove, and sealed some packages addressed to Wilhelm. They contained short essays and fragmentary thoughts, some of which I have seen. At ten o'clock he had the fire replenished and a bottle of wine brought in. He then sent his servant to bed, whose bedroom, like those of the other servants, was far to the rear of the house. The boy slept in his clothes so that he could be at hand early next morning; for his master had told him that the post horses would be in front of the house before six.

After 11 o'clock

Everything is so silent around me and my soul is calm too. I thank You, Lord, for giving me such warmth, such strength, in these last moments.

I go to the window, my dearest one, and I can still see individual stars in the eternal sky, through the passing storm clouds. No, you will not fall! The Eternal One bears you on His heart and me too. I see the handle of the Great Wain,[2] which I love best of all the constellations. When I went from you at night, as I left your gate, it stood facing me. With what intoxication have I often looked at it! Often, with uplifted hands, I have made it the symbol, the sacred milestone of happiness I felt; and even now—O Lotte, doesn't everything remind me of you? Do you not surround me? And haven't I, like a child, greedily snatched up every trifle your sacred hands had touched?

---

[2] Big Dipper.

Beloved silhouette! I bequeath it back to you, Lotte, and beg you to revere it. I have pressed a thousand kisses on it, waved a thousand greetings to it when I went out or came home.

I have asked your father in a note I sent him to protect my body. In the churchyard there are two linden trees, at the rear in the corner, toward the field; there I wish to rest. He can, he will do this for his friend. You ask him too. I do not expect God-fearing Christians to lay their bodies near that of a poor, unhappy man like me.[3] Ah, I wish you would bury me beside the road or in some lonely valley, so that priest and Levite might pass the stone marker and bless themselves, and the Samaritan shed a tear.[4]

See, Lotte, I do not shudder to take into my hand the cold frightful cup, from which I shall drink the ecstasy of death. You handed it to me, and I do not hesitate. All! all the wishes and hopes of my life are thus fulfilled—to knock at the brazen portals of death, so cold, so stiff.

If I could have experienced the joy of dying for you, Lotte, of sacrificing myself for you! I would die bravely, die joyfully, if I could restore to you the peace, the bliss of your life. But alas, it was granted only to a few noble souls to shed their blood for their dear ones and by their death to kindle a new life for their friends a hundredfold strong.

I wish to be buried in these clothes, Lotte. You have touched them, hallowed them; I have requested this of your father too. My soul will hover over my coffin. My pockets are not to be emptied. This pale pink ribbon which you wore at your breast when I saw you for the first time among the children—O kiss them a thousand times and tell them about the fate of their unhappy friend. The dear ones! They are crowding about me. Oh, how I clung to you! I could not leave you from the first moment. —This ribbon shall be buried with me. You gave it to me on my birthday. How eagerly I grasped it all. —Ah, I did not think that my road was to lead me to this. —Be calm, I beg you, be calm!—

They are loaded—the clock strikes twelve. So be it then! Lotte, Lotte, farewell, farewell!

A neighbor saw the flash of the powder and heard the report; but as it was followed by silence, he paid no attention to it.

At six in the morning the servant comes in with a light. He finds his master on the floor, the pistol, and blood. He cries to him, and touches him; no answer, only the death rattle. He runs for a doctor and for Albert. Lotte hears the bell and is seized with a trembling in all her limbs. She wakes her husband, they get up; the servant gives them the news, weeping and stuttering. Lotte sinks down unconscious at Albert's feet.

When the doctor came to the unhappy man, he found him on the floor beyond help, his pulse still beating but all his limbs

---

[3] Orthodox Christians refuse burial to a suicide in consecrated ground.
[4] An allusion to the parable of the Good Samaritan (Luke 10:30–37), in which a priest and a priest's assistant (Levite) ignore a man robbed, beaten, and left by the roadside, but a traveler from Samaria stops to help him.

paralyzed. He had shot himself through the head above the right eye; his brains were protruding. A vein was needlessly opened in his arm; the blood flowed, he was still breathing.

From the blood on the arm of the chair one could infer that he had done the deed as he sat before his desk, then slumped down in his chair thrashing about convulsively. He lay on his back near the window, exhausted, fully dressed, wearing his boots, his blue coat, and yellow vest.

The house, the neighbors, the whole town was in an uproar. Albert came in. Werther had been laid on the bed, his forehead bandaged; his face already touched with the look of death, he was unable to move a limb. A horrible rattle still came from his lungs, now weak, now stronger; the end was expected momentarily.

He had drunk only one glass of the wine. *Emilia Galotti* lay open on his desk.

I shall say nothing of Albert's consternation nor of Lotte's grief.

The old magistrate, upon hearing the news, came galloping over; he kissed the dying man, shedding the most passionate tears. His oldest son soon followed after him on foot; they fell down beside the bed with an expression of the most uncontrollable anguish, and kissed his hands and lips; and the oldest, whom he had always liked best, clung to his lips until he had expired; and the boy was removed by force. He died at noon. The presence of the magistrate, and the measures he had taken, prevented a disturbance. At about eleven o'clock at night he had him buried at the spot which he had selected for himself. The old man and his sons followed the body; Albert was unable to do so. Lotte's life was feared to be in danger. Workmen bore him. No clergyman was present.[5]

Further Readings

Numerous studies of Goethe and his times have been published. Some of the notable biographies are J. G. Robertson, *The Life and Work of Goethe, 1749–1832* (New York: E. P. Dutton, 1932), Albert Bielschowsky, *The Life of Goethe*, translated by William Cooper (3 vols.: New York: Haskell House Publishers, 1969), Derek Maurice van Abbe, *Goethe: New Perspectives on a Writer and His Time* (London: Allen and Unwin, 1972), and Pietro Citati, *Goethe*, translated by Raymond Rosenthal (New York: Dial Press, 1974). Richard Friedenthal's *Goethe, His Life and Times* (Cleveland, OH: World Publishing Co., 1965), provides a modern German view of the subject. *The Autobiography of Johann Wolfgang von Goethe*, translated by John Oxenford (New York: Horizon Press, 1969), and *Goethe's World as Seen in Letters and Memoirs*, edited by Berthold Bierman (New York: New Directions, 1949), provide important insights into Goethe's character and thought.

Alan P. Cottrell, *Goethe's View of Evil and the Search for a New Image of Man in*

---

[5] Burial at night was usual in the eighteenth century; also that the coffin should be borne by the members of some guild. The absence of a clergyman at the burial is explained by the fact that in the eyes of the Church, Werther was a murderer. But it also underlines Werther's religious independence.

Our Times (Edinburgh: Floris Books, 1982), and Arnold Bergsträsser, *Goethe's Image of Man and Society* (Chicago: H. Regnery and Co., 1949), are useful studies of Goethe's philosophical beliefs. Barker Fairley, *A Study of Goethe* (Oxford: Clarendon Press, 1948), and Henry C. Hatfield, *Goethe, a Critical Introduction* (Cambridge, MA: Harvard University Press, 1964), are valuable guides to interpreting Goethe's works. Ian Loram, *Goethe and His Publishers* (Lawrence: University of Kansas Press, 1963), provides a fascinating study of an important aspect of Goethe's career as an author.

Romanticism, edited by J. B. Halsted (Boston: Heath, 1965), offers a good introduction to the complexities of Romanticism. Howard Mumford Jones, *Revolution and Romanticism* (Cambridge, MA: Belknap Press of Harvard University Press, 1974), covers the period 1763–1861. Lilian R. Furst, *European Romanticism: Self Definition* (New York: Methuen, 1980), is an insightful investigation of English, French, and German literature of the late eighteenth and early nineteenth centuries. Henri Brunschwig, *Enlightenment and Romanticism in Eighteenth-Century Prussia* (Chicago: University of Chicago Press, 1974), W. H. Bruford, *Germany in the Eighteenth Century: The Social Background of the Literary Revival* (Cambridge: Cambridge University Press, 1939), and Glyn Tegai Hughes, *Romantic German Literature* (London: B. Arnold, 1979), are important studies of Romanticism in Germany. The *Sturm und Drang* movement is thoroughly covered in Bruce Kieffer, *The Storm and Stress of Language* (University Park, PA: The Pennsylvania State University Press, 1986), and Roy Pascal, *The German Sturm und Drang* (Manchester: Manchester University Press, 1953).

The Interesting Narrative of the Life of Olaudah Equiano

Shortage of labor played a large role in limiting the pace of European exploitation of the New World. The native Indian population lacked immunity to the numerous diseases introduced by the Europeans, and was severely reduced by waves of epidemics. At the same time, the region was not congenial to the Europeans, and a significant proportion of immigrants died after a short time in the Americas. Nevertheless, Europe clamored for ever-increasing supplies of American products, particularly sugar, that could only be supplied by a labor-intensive plantation system of agriculture. The enslavement of the Indians and the forced emigration of European rebels, petty criminals, debtors, and indentured servants failed to meet the constantly increasing labor needs of the new colonies. The solution to this problem lay in tapping an African slave trade that had developed over the centuries, and utilizing the labor of Africans, who were relatively resistant to the diseases that decimated both Europeans and Indians.

In the seventeenth and eighteenth centuries, millions of African slaves were integrated into the European-controlled labor force, where they played a major role in settling and developing the New World. Although most slaves went to the plantations of Brazil and the Caribbean, blacks could be found throughout the Western World, engaged in virtually every pursuit. Some few even gained their freedom and achieved respected positions. Olaudah Equiano (1745–1797) was one of these lucky individuals. Kidnapped at the age of twelve, he was one of the relatively fortunate five percent shipped to North America rather than to the Caribbean, where hard labor and the fever-ridden climate killed many slaves. He was soon put to service

From Olaudah Equiano, *The Interesting Narrative of the Life of Olaudah Equiano,* in *Three Black Writers in Eighteenth-Century England,* edited by Francis Adams and Barry Sanders (Belmont, CA: Wadsworth Publishing Co., Inc., 1971), pp. 109–117.

on a sailing ship and became a creditable seaman, serving on British warships during the war with France (1756–1763). He was allowed to earn money and eventually saved enough to buy his freedom. He continued in the naval trade, and became a leader of the free blacks resident in England. His autobiography, from which this selection is drawn, was published in 1789. It became a considerable success, with thirteen editions appearing over the next thirty years.

There were many reasons for the popularity of Equiano's account, but his portrayal of his life before being enslaved was certainly one of the more remarkable aspects of his narrative. He had been Europeanized to a degree sufficient to allow him to describe native life in a fashion intelligible to his white audience, but he was still close enough to his origins to present a far more perceptive and sympathetic picture than a European observer might have done. European audiences had long been intrigued by the concept of the "noble savage," and many authors had played with the idea that there might exist in the simple life of native cultures ethical and moral standards wanting in European life: Thomas More's *Utopia* had been based on this concept, and the land of El Dorado in Voltaire's *Candide* was a variation on this theme. Equiano's account of his homeland was thus a contribution to a popular and significant European literary tradition.

It also had an immediate political relevance. Many Europeans, particularly the English, were uncomfortable with the institution of slavery and were actively working for its abolition. Equiano's autobiography furnished such abolitionists ammunition in their struggle. His account of native life stressed its fundamental morality and goodness, and allowed the reader to discern the pernicious influence of the slave trade not only on those taken into slavery but even upon those left behind. Finally, Equiano's life was itself proof of the accomplishments of which an African was capable when allowed a decent chance. It is interesting to note that John Wesley (1703–1791), founder of Methodism and implacable foe of slavery, when on his deathbed, asked that Equiano's *Narrative* be read to him.

Questions

1. How would you evaluate the morality of Equiano's people?

2. What is the religion of his people?

3. What are the effects of the slave trade of the region upon native society?

4. In what sort of warfare do Equiano's people engage, and to what purpose?

THE NARRATIVE OF OLAUDAH EQUIANO

That part of Africa, known by the name of Guinea, to which the trade for slaves is carried on, extends along the coast above 3400 miles, from the Senegal to Angola, and includes a variety of kingdoms. Of these the most considerable is the kingdom of Benin, both as to extent and wealth, the richness and cultivation of the soil, the power of its king, and the number and warlike disposition of the inhabitants. It is situated nearly under the line,[1] and extends along the coast about 170 miles, but runs back into the interior part of Africa to a distance hitherto I believe unexplored by any traveller; and seems only terminated at length by the empire of Abyssinia, near 1500 miles from its beginning. This kingdom is divided into many provinces or districts: in one of the most remote and fertile of which, called Eboe, I was born, in the year 1745, in a charming fruitful vale, named Essaka. The distance of this province from the capital of Benin and the sea coast must be very considerable; for I had never heard of white men or Europeans, nor of the sea: and our subjection to the king of Benin was little more than nominal; for every transaction of the government, as far as my slender observation extended, was conducted by the chiefs or elders of the place. The manners and government of a people who have little commerce with other countries are generally very simple; and the history of what passes in one family or village may serve as a specimen of a nation. My father was one of those elders or chiefs I have spoken of, and was styled Embrenche; a term, as I remember, importing the highest distinction, and signifying in our language a *mark* of grandeur. This mark is conferred on the person entitled to it, by cutting the skin across at the top of the forehead, and drawing it down to the eye-brows; and while it is in this situation applying a warm hand, and rubbing it until it shrinks up into a thick *weal* across the lower part of the forehead. Most of the judges and senators were thus marked; my father had long borne it: I had seen it conferred on one of my brothers, and I was also *destined* to receive it by my parents. Those Embrenche, or chief men, decided disputes and punished crimes; for which purpose they always assembled together. The proceedings were generally short; and in most cases the law of retaliation prevailed. I remember a man was brought before my father, and the other judges, for kidnapping a boy; and, although he was the son of a chief or senator, he was condemned to make recompense by a man or woman slave. Adultery, however, was sometimes punished with slavery or death; a punishment which I believe is inflicted on it throughout most of the nations of Africa: so sacred among them is the honour of the marriage bed, and so jealous are they of the fidelity of their wives. Of this I recollect an instance:—a woman was convicted before the

[1] Equator.

judges of adultery, and delivered over, as the custom was, to her husband to be punished. Accordingly he determined to put her to death: but it being found, just before her execution, that she had an infant at her breast; and no woman being prevailed on to perform the part of a nurse, she was spared on account of the child. The men, however, do not preserve the same constancy to their wives, which they expect from them; for they indulge in a plurality, though seldom in more than two. Their mode of marriage is thus:—both parties are usually betrothed when young by their parents, (though I have known the males to betroth themselves). On this occasion a feast is prepared, and the bride and bridegroom stand up in the midst of all their friends, who are assembled for the purpose, while he declares she is thenceforth to be looked upon as his wife, and that no other person is to pay any addresses to her. This is also immediately proclaimed in the vicinity, on which the bride retires from the assembly. Some time after she is brought home to her husband, and then another feast is made, to which the relations of both parties are invited: her parents then deliver her to the bridegroom, accompanied with a number of blessings, and at the same time they tie round her waist a cotton string of the thickness of a goose-quill, which none but married women are permitted to wear: she is now considered as completely his wife; and at this time the dowry is given to the new married pair, which generally consists of portions of land, slaves, and cattle, household goods, and implements of husbandry. These are offered by the friends of both parties; besides which the parents of the bridegroom present gifts to those of the bride, whose property she is looked upon before marriage; but after it she is esteemed the sole property of her husband. The ceremony being now ended the festival begins, which is celebrated with bonfires, and loud acclamations of joy, accompanied with music and dancing.

We are almost a nation of dancers, musicians, and poets. Thus every great event, such as a triumphant return from battle, or other cause of public rejoicing is celebrated in public dances, which are accompanied with songs and music suited to the occasion. The assembly is separated into four divisions, which dance either apart or in succession, and each with a character peculiar to itself. The first division contains the married men, who in their dances frequently exhibit feats of arms, and the representation of a battle. To these succeed the married women, who dance in the second division. The young men occupy the third; and the maidens the fourth. Each represents some interesting scene of real life, such as a great achievement, domestic employment, a pathetic story, or some rural sport; and as the subject is generally founded on some recent event, it is therefore ever new. This gives our dances a spirit and a variety which I have scarcely seen elsewhere. We have many musical instruments, particularly drums of different kinds, a piece of music which resembles a guitar, and another much like a stickado.[2] These last are chiefly used by betrothed virgins, who play on them on all grand festivals.

As our manners are simple, our luxuries are few. The dress of both sexes is nearly the same. It generally consists of a long piece of callico, or muslin, wrapped loosely round the body, somewhat in the form of a highland plaid. This is usually dyed blue, which is our favourite colour. It is extracted from a berry, and is brighter and richer than any I have seen in Europe. Besides this, our women of distinction wear golden ornaments; which they dispose with some profusion on their arms and legs. When our women are not employed with the men in tillage, their usual occupation is spinning and weaving cotton, which they afterwards dye, and make it into garments. They also manufacture earthen vessels, of which we have many kinds. Among the rest tobacco pipes, made after the same fashion, and used in the same manner, as those in Turkey.

Our manner of living is entirely plain; for as yet the natives are unacquainted with those refinements in cookery which debauch the taste: bullocks, goats, and poultry, supply the greatest part of their food. These constitute likewise the principal wealth of the country, and the chief articles of its commerce. The flesh is usually stewed in a pan; to make it savoury we sometimes use also pepper, and other spices, and we have salt made of wood ashes. Our vegetables are mostly plantains, eadas, yams, beans, and Indian corn. The head of the family usually eats alone; his wives and slaves have also their separate tables. Before we taste food we always wash our hands: indeed our cleanliness on all occasions is extreme; but on this it is an indispensable ceremony. After washing, libation is made, by pouring out a small portion of the food, in a certain place, for the spirits of departed relations, which the natives suppose to preside over their conduct, and guard them from evil. They are totally unacquainted with strong or spiritous liquours; and their principal beverage is palm wine. This is gotten from a tree of that name by tapping it at the top, and fastening a large gourd to it; and sometimes one tree will yield three or four gallons in a night. When just drawn it is of a most delicious sweetness; but in a few days it acquires a tartish and more spirituous flavour: though I never saw any one intoxicated by it. The same tree also produces nuts and oil. Our principal luxury is in perfumes; one sort of these is an odoriferous wood of delicious fragrance: the other a kind of earth; a small portion of which thrown into the fire diffuses a most powerful odour. We beat this wood into powder, and mix it with palm oil; with which both men and women perfume themselves.

In our buildings we study convenience rather than ornament. Each master of a family has a large square piece of ground, surrounded with a moat or fence, or enclosed with a wall made of red

---

[2] A type of xylophone (also *sticcado*).

earth tempered; which, when dry, is as hard as brick. Within this are his houses to accommodate his family and slaves; which, if numerous, frequently present the appearance of a village. In the middle stands the principal building, appropriated to the sole use of the master, and consisting of two apartments; in one of which he sits in the day with his family, the other is left apart for the reception of his friends. He has besides these a distinct apartment in which he sleeps, together with his male children. On each side are the apartments of his wives, who have also their separate day and night houses. The habitations of the slaves and their families are distributed throughout the rest of the enclosure. These houses never exceed one story in height: they are always built of wood, or stakes driven into the ground, crossed with wattles, and neatly plastered within, and without. The roof is thatched with reeds. Our dayhouses are left open at the sides; but those in which we sleep are always covered, and plastered in the inside, with a composition mixed with cowdung, to keep off the different insects, which annoy us during the night. The walls and floors also of these are generally covered with mats. Our beds consist of a platform, raised three or four feet from the ground, on which are laid skins, and different parts of a spungy tree called plaintain. Our covering is calico or muslin, the same as our dress. The usual seats are a few logs of wood; but we have benches, which are generally perfumed, to accommodate strangers: these compose the greater part of our household furniture. Houses so constructed and furnished require but little skill to erect them. Every man is a sufficient architect for the purpose. The whole neighbourhood afford their unanimous assistance in building them and in return receive, and expect no other recompense than a feast.

As we live in a country where nature is prodigal of her favours, our wants are few and easily supplied; of course we have few manufactures. They consist for the most part of calicoes, earthen ware, ornaments, and instruments of war and husbandry. But these make no part of our commerce, the principal articles of which, as I have observed, are provisions. In such a state money is of little use; however we have some small pieces of coin, if I may call them such. They are made something like an anchor; but I do not remember either their value or denomination. We have also markets, at which I have been frequently with my mother. These are sometimes visited by stout mahogany-coloured men from the south west of us: we call them Oye-Eboe, which term signifies red men living at a distance. They generally bring us firearms, gunpowder, hats, beads, and dried fish. The last we esteemed a great rarity, as our waters were only brooks and springs. These articles they barter with us for odoriferous woods and earth, and our salt of wood ashes. They always carry slaves through our land; but the strictest account is exacted of their manner of procuring them before they are suffered to pass. Sometimes indeed we sold slaves to them, but they were only prisoners of war, or such among us as had been convicted of kidnapping, or adultery, and some other crimes, which we esteemed heinous. This practice of kidnapping induces me to think, that, notwithstanding all our strictness, their principal business among us was to trepan[3] our people. I remember too they carried great sacks along with them, which not long after I had an opportunity of fatally seeing applied to that infamous purpose.[4]

Our land is uncommonly rich and fruitful, and produces all kinds of vegetables in great abundance. We have plenty of Indian corn, and vast quantities of cotton and tobacco. Our pine apples grow without culture; they are about the size of the largest sugar-loaf, and finely flavoured. We have also spices of different kinds, particularly pepper; and a variety of delicious fruits which I have never seen in Europe; together with gums of various kinds, and honey in abundance. All our industry is exerted to improve those blessings of nature. Agriculture is our chief employment; and every one, even the children and women, are engaged in it. Thus we are all habituated to labour from our earliest years. Every one contributes something to the common stock; and as we are unacquainted with idleness, we have no beggars. The benefits of such a mode of living are obvious. The West India planters prefer the slaves of Benin or Eboe to those of any other part of Guinea, for their hardiness, intelligence, integrity, and zeal. Those benefits are felt by us in the general healthiness of the people, and in their vigour and activity; I might have added too in their comeliness. Deformity is indeed unknown amongst us, I mean that of shape. Numbers of the natives of Eboe now in London might be brought in support of this assertion: for, in regard to complexion, ideas of beauty are wholly relative. I remember while in Africa to have seen three negro children, who were tawny, and another quite white, who were universally regarded by myself, and the natives in general, as far as related to their complexions, as deformed. Our women too were in my eyes at least uncommonly graceful, alert, and modest to a degree of bashfulness; nor do I remember to have ever heard of an instance of incontinence amongst them before marriage. They are also remarkably cheerful. Indeed cheerfulness and affability are two of the leading characteristics of our nation.

Our tillage is exercised in a large plain or common, some hours walk from our dwellings, and all the neighbours resort thither in a body. They use no beasts of husbandry; and their only instruments are hoes, axes, shovels, and beaks, or pointed iron to dig with. Sometimes we are visited by locusts, which come in large clouds, so as to darken the air, and destroy our harvest. This how-

---

[3] Ensnare.
[4] Slavers used the sacks like nets to bag their victims over the head and arms and carry them off to be bound more securely.

ever happens rarely, but when it does, a famine is produced by it. I remember an instance or two wherein this happened. This common is often the theatre of war; and therefore when our people go out to till their land, they not only go in a body, but generally take their arms with them for fear of a surprise; and when they apprehend an invasion they guard the avenues to their dwellings, by driving sticks into the ground, which are so sharp at one end as to pierce the foot, and are generally dipt in poison. From what I can recollect of these battles, they appear to have been irruptions of one little state or district on the other, to obtain prisoners or booty. Perhaps they were incited to this by those traders who brought the European goods I mentioned amongst us. Such a mode of obtaining slaves in Africa is common; and I believe more are procured this way, and by kidnaping, than any other. When a trader wants slaves, he applies to a chief for them, and tempts him with his wares. It is not extraordinary, if on this occasion he yields to the temptation with as little firmness, and accepts the price of his fellow creatures' liberty with as little reluctance as the enlightened merchant. Accordingly he falls on his neighbours, and a desperate battle ensues. If he prevails and takes prisoners, he gratifies his avarice by selling them; but, if his party be vanquished, and he falls into the hands of the enemy, he is put to death: for, as he has been known to foment their quarrels, it is thought dangerous to let him survive, and no ransom can save him, though all other prisoners may be redeemed. We have fire-arms, bows and arrows, broad two-edged swords and javelins: we have shields also which cover a man from head to foot. All are taught the use of these weapons; even our women are warriors, and march boldly out to fight along with the men. Our whole district is a kind of militia: on a certain signal given, such as the firing of a gun at night, they all rise in arms and rush upon their enemy. It is perhaps something remarkable, that when our people march to the field a red flag or banner is borne before them. I was once a witness to a battle in our common. We had been all at work in it one day as usual, when our people were suddenly attacked. I climbed a tree at some distance, from which I beheld the fight. There were many women as well as men on both sides; among others my mother was there, and armed with a broad sword. After fighting for a considerable time with great fury, and after many had been killed our people obtained the victory, and took their enemy's Chief prisoner. He was carried off in great triumph, and, though he offered a large ransom for his life, he was put to death. A virgin of note among our enemies had been slain in the battle, and her arm was exposed in our market-place, where our trophies were always exhibited. The spoils were divided according to the merit of the warriors. Those prisoners which were not sold or redeemed we kept as slaves: but how different was their condition from that of the slaves in the West Indies! With us they do no more work than other members of the community, even their masters; their food, clothing and lodging were nearly the same as theirs (except that they were not permitted to eat with those who were free-born); and there was scarce any other difference between them, than a superior degree of importance which the head of a family possesses in our state, and that authority which, as such, he exercises over every part of his household. Some of these slaves have even slaves under them as their own property, and for their own use.

As to religion, the natives believe that there is one Creator of all things, and that he lives in the sun, and is girted round with a belt that he may never eat or drink; but, according to some, he smokes a pipe, which is our own favourite luxury. They believe he governs events, especially our deaths or captivity; but, as for the doctrine of eternity, I do not remember to have ever heard of it: some however believe in the transmigration of souls in a certain degree. Those spirits, which are not transmigrated, such as our dear friends or relations, they believe always attend them, and guard them from the bad spirits or their foes. For this reason they always before eating, as I have observed, put some small portion of the meat, and pour some of their drink, on the ground for them, and they often make oblations of the blood of beasts or fowls at their graves. I was very fond of my mother, and almost constantly with her. When she went to make these oblations at her mother's tomb, which was a kind of small solitary thatched house, I sometimes attended her. There she made her libations, and spent most of the night in cries and lamentations. I have been often extremely terrified on these occasions. The loneliness of the place, the darkness of the night, and the ceremony of libation, naturally awful and gloomy, were heightened by my mother's lamentations; and these, concurring with the cries of doleful birds, by which these places were frequented, gave an inexpressible terror to the scene.

We compute the year from the day on which the sun crosses the line,[5] and on its setting that evening there is a general shout throughout the land; at least I can speak from my own knowledge throughout our vicinity. The people at the same time make a great noise with rattles, not unlike the basket rattles used by children here, though much larger, and hold up their hands to heaven for a blessing. It is then the greatest offerings are made; and those children whom our wise men foretell will be fortunate are then presented to different people. I remember many used to come to see me, and I was carried about to others for that purpose. They have many offerings, particularly at full moons; generally two at harvest before the fruits are taken out of the ground: and when any young animals are killed, sometimes they offer up part of them as a sacrifice. These offerings, when made by one of the heads of a family, serve for the whole. I remember we often had them at my father's

---

[5] That is, at the spring and fall equinoxes.

and my uncle's, and their families have been present. Some of our offerings are eaten with bitter herbs. We had a saying among us to any one of a cross temper, "That if they were to be eaten, they should be eaten with bitter herbs."

We practised circumcision like the Jews, and made offerings and feasts on that occasion in the same manner, as they did. Like them also, our children were named from some event, some circumstance, or fancied foreboding at the time of their birth. I was named *Olaudah,* which, in our language, signifies vicissitude or fortune also, one favoured, and having a loud voice and well spoken. I remember we never polluted the name of the object of our adoration; on the contrary, it was always mentioned with the greatest reverence; and we were totally unacquainted with swearing, and all those terms of abuse and reproach which find their way so readily and copiously into the languages of more civilized people. The only expressions of that kind I remember were "May you rot, or may you swell, or may a beast take you."

Further Readings

The general history of the African slave trade is covered by three excellent works: Basil Davidson, *Black Mother: The Years of the African Slave Trade* (Boston: Little, Brown, 1961), Philip D. Curtin, *The Atlantic Slave Trade: A Census* (Madison, WI: University of Wisconsin Press, 1969), and Paul Bohannan and Philip D. Curtin, *Africa and Africans* (Garden City, NY: Doubleday, 1971). The relationship between the early capitalism of Great Britain and the slave trade in the sixteenth and seventeenth centuries is the theme of Eric Williams, *Capitalism and Slavery* (New York: Capricorn Books, 1966).

The literature of slavery in the New World is quite large, but, considering that half of all black slaves sent to the New World went to the Caribbean plantations, one might recommend a few relating to that area. Orlando Patterson, *The Sociology of Slavery* (Rutherford, NJ: Fairleigh Dickinson University Press, 1969), discusses conditions in the region generally and the slave revolts of the area in particular. The economic structure of the plantation economy is treated by Richard S. Dunn, *Sugar and Slaves: The Rise of the Planter Class in the English West Indies, 1624–1713* (Chapel Hill, NC: University of North Carolina Press, 1972). Edward Braithwaite, *The Development of Creole Society in Jamaica, 1770–1820* (New York: Oxford University Press, 1971), treats one of the most populous of the plantation societies.

Alex Haley, *Roots* (Garden City, NY: Doubleday, 1971), is remarkable both for its insight and readability. A runaway best-seller, it served as the basis for an acclaimed television miniseries and sparked widespread interest in family history.

The Dream of the Red Chamber

Shortly after Wu Ching-tzu completed *The Scholars,* his fellow southerner, Tsao Hsueh-ch'in (?1715–1763), was in the northern capital of Peking, composing a masterpiece of vernacular fiction that was to become the most highly acclaimed piece of writing in all of Chinese literature. Like the author of *The Scholars,* Tsao felt the need for greater realism in literature as well as for an increased reliance on personal experience. Although relatively little is known about Tsao, it is clear that he had personal knowledge of the stresses and problems of a once-affluent family, now losing status. His family had for generations held the highly lucrative post of commissioner of the imperial textile mills, first in Soochow and then in Nanking. His grandfather had been a patron of letters and a notable poet in his own right. His father was removed from his post for political reasons, however, and his property was confiscated. The family then moved to Peking, where it lived in reduced circumstances. By 1744, when he had begun writing his novel, Tsao had moved to the suburbs, where he lived for a time in dire poverty. He died in 1763, shortly after having lost his young son.

First published in 1792, *The Dream of the Red Chamber (Hung-lou meng)* was soon recognized as China's greatest and most beloved novel. A complex work, it provides a valuable and realistic portrayal of the aristocratic house of Chia, a formerly powerful clan in great favor with imperial authorities, but now in rapid decline. It focuses upon two Peking households, housing five generations of the Chia family, together with their numerous servants, retainers, relatives, and other hangers-on. The central figure is a young boy, Pao-yu, the hope of the house of Chia to restore their fortunes. He is outrageously spoiled by his female relatives, detests conventional learning, and prefers the company of his female cousins and the family maidservants.

From Tsao Hsueh-ch'in, *The Dream of the Red Chamber,* translated by Chi-chen Wang (Garden City, NY: Doubleday and Co., Inc., 1958), pp. 27–47.

He falls in love with his cousin Black Jade, a girl of delicate beauty, and the portrayal of their young affection possesses an enduring charm. As the story progresses, however, their love turns into tragedy. The desires of two members of the family have little importance when compared to the needs and aspirations of the family as a whole, and so are ignored when the time comes to arrange a marriage for Pao-yu. Phoenix, who rules the affairs of the family with a merciless efficiency and callous disregard for matters of the heart, arranges that Pao-yu should marry Precious Clasp. Stricken with grief, Black Jade dies on her lover's wedding night.

The marriage affords little happiness for Precious Clasp. Pao-yu never recovers from his bereavement. He goes off and successfully completes the examination for the imperial civil service, the achievement for which the entire family had hoped. However, instead of returning home to help raise the fortunes of the house of Chia, Pao-yu renounces the world and becomes a Buddhist monk. All that is left to Precious Clasp is the child she is expecting.

The excerpt presented here is from the novel's famous dream sequence. While visiting the neighboring family compound, Pao-yu, barely a teenager, insists on taking a nap in the bedroom of Chin-shih, the young wife of his nephew. He dreams of a celestial beauty, also named Chin-shih. Pao-yu is struck by the fact that she seems to him to combine all the charms and graces of both Black Jade and Precious Clasp. He soon enters the Great Void of Illusions Land, presided over by the Goddess of Disillusionment. At the request of his ancestors, the Goddess reprimands him for being the most lustful of men because of his potential commitment to the excessive love that afflicts the unconventional heroes of romance. She then introduces the young man to her sister for sexual initiation. Following a blissful union, Pao-yu is chased by demons and wild beasts to the brink of an impassable river. At this point, he awakes.

The dream sequence symbolizes Pao-yu's passage from childhood to adolescence, a passage in which the mysteries of love and sexuality are revealed to him, and in which the difference between love and lust are made clear. The lesson seems to have been imperfectly learned, however; that same evening Pao-yu seduces a young girl, Pervading Fragrance. The memory of pleasure has completely overcome his fear of the demons and wild beasts. The author seems to suggest that men are incorrigible once they have been exposed to the delights of sex, and that any sort of human attachment is only a source of illusion.

While *The Dream of the Red Chamber* is essentially a love story, its characters transcend time and culture. Pao-yu is not simply a spoiled and self-indulgent young man, he is a sensitive human being who does his best to conduct his life in terms of what little he knows of reality and unreality. His struggle to do so is played out in the midst of a bustling clan of dozens of people, each with his or her own individual hopes, desires, and aspirations. The author manages to people his stage in such a way as to present a profound and realistic view of the life of a noble family in eighteenth-century China, and yet to maintain such sympathy and respect for the individual suffering of the young lovers that his work remains one of the great examples of the romantic tradition in world literature.

Questions

1. Why do you think that Pao-yu was able to enjoy the trust and friendship of all the young women of the family compound?

2. What are the characters' attitudes towards religion and morality?

3. Do you think that the author is criticizing Chinese society? If so, what are his particular concerns?

4. There is a recurring contrast between love and lust in the novel. What difference does the author see between these two passions?

THE DREAM OF THE RED CHAMBER

IN WHICH BLACK JADE IS LOVINGLY WELCOMED BY HER GRANDMOTHER AND PAO-YU IS UNWITTINGLY UPSET BY HIS COUSIN

In the meantime, Black Jade was met by more servants from the Yungkuofu. She had heard a great deal of the wealth and luxury of her grandmother's family and was much impressed by the costumes of the maidservants who had been sent to escort her to the Capital, though they were ordinary servants of the second or third rank. Being a proud and sensitive child, she told herself that she must watch every step and weigh every word so as not to make any mistakes and be laughed at.

From the windows of her sedan chair, she took in the incomparable wealth and splendor of the Imperial City, which, needless to say, far surpassed that of Yangchow. Suddenly she saw on the north side of a street an imposing entrance, consisting of a great gate and a smaller one on either side. Two huge stone lions flanked the approach, and over the main gate there was a panel bearing the characters "ning kuo fu."[1] The center gate was closed, but one of the side doors was open, and under it there were more than a score of manservants lounging about on long benches. A little further to the west, there was another entrance of similar proportions,

---

[1] "Ning kuo fu" means "peace to the country mansion."

with the inscription "yung kuo fu"[2] over the main gate. Black Jade's sedan was carried through the side door to the west. After proceeding a distance of an arrow's flight, the bearers stopped and withdrew, as four well-dressed boys of about seventeen came up and took their places. The maidservants alighted from their carriages and followed the sedan on foot until they reached another gate, covered with overhanging flowers. Here the bearers stopped again and withdrew. The maids raised the curtain of the sedan for Black Jade to descend.

Inside the flower-covered gate two verandas led to a passage hall with a large marble screen in the center. Beyond, there was a large court dominated by the main hall with carved beams and painted pillars. From the rafters of the side chambers hung cages of parrots, thrushes, and other pet birds. The maids sitting on the moon terrace of the main hall rose at the approach of Black Jade. "Lao Tai-tai[3] was just asking about Ku-niang,"[4] they said. Then raising the door curtain, they announced, "Lin Ku-niang is here."

As Black Jade entered the door, a silver-haired lady rose to meet her. Concluding that it must be her grandmother, Black Jade was about to kneel before her, but her grandmother took her in her arms and began to weep, calling her many pet names. The attendants all wept at the touching sight. When the Matriarch finally stopped crying, Black Jade kowtowed and was then introduced to her aunts, Madame Hsing and Madame Wang, and to Li Huan, the wife of the late Chia Chu. Turning to the attendants, the Matriarch said, "Ask your young mistresses to come, and tell them they need not go to school today as there is a guest from far away." Presently the three young ladies entered, escorted by their own nurses and maids. Welcome Spring was inclined to plumpness and looked affable. Quest Spring was slender, strong-willed, and independent. Compassion Spring was yet a child.

After the introductions, tea was served. Black Jade answered the endless questions asked by her grandmother and aunts. When did her mother become ill? Who were the doctors called in to attend her? What sort of medicine did they prescribe? When did the funeral take place and who was there? The Matriarch was again in tears as Black Jade told of her mother's illness and death. She said, "Of all my children, I loved your mother best. Now she has preceded me to the grave. And I did not even have a chance to take a last look at her." Again she took Black Jade in her arms and wept.

Though her delicate features were lovely, it was evident that Black Jade was not strong. The Matriarch asked her what medicine she was taking and whether a careful diagnosis had been made.

---

[2] "Yung kuo fu" means "may the country mansion long endure."
[3] Honorific designation for the mother of the master of the house.
[4] Designation for unmarried young ladies.

"I have been like this ever since I can remember," she answered with a wan smile. "Some of the best-known physicians examined me and prescribed all kinds of medicine and pills, but I did not get any better. I remember that when I was about three years old, a mangy old Buddhist monk came to see my parents and asked them to give me away as a sacrifice to Buddha, saying that I would always be sick unless they let him take me away. The only other remedy, he said, was to keep me from weeping and crying and that I must never be allowed to see any of my maternal relatives. No one paid any attention, of course, to such ridiculous and farfetched talk. For the present, I am taking some ginseng pills."

"We are having some pills made," the Matriarch said, "and I will order some of yours for you."

Suddenly Black Jade heard the sound of laughter in the rear courtyard and the rather loud voice of a young woman saying, "I am late in greeting the guest from the south." Who could this be, Black Jade wondered. Everyone else was quiet and demure. This loud laughter was unsuitable to the general atmosphere of dignity and reserve. As Black Jade was thinking thus to herself, a pretty young woman came in. She was tall and slender and carried herself with grace and self-assurance. She was dressed in brighter colors than the granddaughters of the Matriarch and wore an astonishing amount of jewelry; somehow it seemed to suit her well, but there was a certain hardness about her that did not escape the careful observer.

"You wouldn't know who she is, of course," the Matriarch said to Black Jade, as the latter rose to greet the new arrival, "but she has the sharpest and cleverest tongue in this family. She is what they call a 'hot pepper' in Nanking, so you can just call her that."

One of the cousins came to Black Jade's rescue and introduced "Hot Pepper" as Phoenix, the wife of Chia Lien. Phoenix took Black Jade's hands and looked at her admiringly for a long time before returning her to the Matriarch. "What a beautiful girl!" she said. "Positively the most beautiful thing I've ever seen. No wonder Lao Tai-tai is always talking about her. But how cruel of Heaven to deprive such a lovely thing of her mother." She took out a handkerchief and began to wipe her eyes.

"Are you trying to make me cry all over again?" the Matriarch said. "Moreover, your Mei-mei[5] has just come from a long journey and she is not well. We've just succeeded in quieting her. So don't you upset her again."

"Forgive me," Phoenix said, quickly assuming a smile. "I was so overwhelmed with joy and sorrow at meeting Mei-mei that I quite forgot that Lao Tai-tai mustn't grieve too much." Again she took Black Jade's hands and asked her how old she was, whether she had had a tutor, and what medicine she was taking. She enjoined

---

[5] "Younger sister."

her not to be homesick, to feel perfectly at home, and not hesitate to ask for anything she wanted, and to report to her if any of the maids should be negligent or disrespectful. "You must remember, Mei-mei, that you are not in a stranger's house," she concluded.

Presently Madame Hsing took Black Jade to pay her respects to Chia Sheh. At the flower-covered gate they entered a carriage, which bore them out through the western side gate, east past the main entrance, and then entered a black-lacquered gate. It appeared to Black Jade that this compound must formerly have been a part of the garden of the Yungkuofu. It was built on a less pretentious scale than the Yungkuofu proper but it had its verandas, side chambers, flower plots, artificial rocks, and everything else that goes with a well-planned mansion. A number of maids came out to meet Black Jade and Madame Hsing as they entered the inner court. After they were seated in Madame Hsing's room, a maid was sent to inform Chia Sheh of Black Jade's presence. She said when she returned, "Lao-yeh says he is not feeling well and that, since the meeting will only renew their sorrow, he will not see the guest today. He wants Lin Ku-niang to feel at home and to regard her grandmother's house on her own."

Black Jade rose and listened deferentially while the maid delivered the message from her first uncle. Madame Hsing asked her to stay for dinner, but she declined, as etiquette required her to call on her second uncle without delay.

Madame Wang excused Black Jade from her call on Chia Cheng. "He is busy today," she said. "You will see him some other time. But there is something that I must warn you about. You will have no trouble with your sisters. You will all study and embroider together, and I am sure you will be considerate of one another and have no quarrels. But I have my misgivings about that scourge of mine. He is not home now but he will be back later, and you can see for yourself. You must not pay any attention to him. None of his sisters dare to encourage him in the least."

Black Jade had often heard her mother speak of this cousin of hers, how he was born with a piece of jade in his mouth,[6] how his grandmother doted on him and would not suffer his father to discipline him. Madame Wang must be referring to him now. "I have heard Mother speak of this elder brother," the girl said. "But what is there to fear? Naturally I shall be with my sisters, and he will be with the brothers."

"But he has not been brought up like other children," Madame Wang explained. "He lives with Lao Tai-tai and is a good deal with the girls and maids. He behaves tolerably well if left alone but, if any of the girls encourages him in the least, he becomes quite impossible and may say all sorts of wild things. That's why you must not pay any attention to him or take seriously anything he says."

---

[6] That is, he was wealthy.

On their way to dinner at the Matriarch's, they passed by Phoenix's compound. Madame Wang pointed it out to Black Jade and said, "You know now where to go if you want anything." When they arrived in the Matriarch's room, the maids were ready to serve the dinner. There were two chairs on either side of the Matriarch, and Black Jade was ushered by Phoenix to one on the left side nearest to the Matriarch, Black Jade refused the honor, but her grandmother said, "Your aunts and sister-in-law do not dine here. Besides, you are a guest today. So take the seat." Black Jade murmured an apology and obeyed. Madame Wang sat near the table, while Phoenix and Li Huan stood by and waited upon the Matriarch. The three Springs took their places according to age: Welcome Spring sat on the right, nearest the Matriarch; Quest Spring, second on the left; Compassion Spring, second on the right. Out in the courtyard many maids stood by to carry dishes back and forth from the kitchen. After dinner, the Matriarch dismissed Madame Wang, Li Huan, and Phoenix so that she could talk more freely with her granddaughters.

Suddenly there was a sound of footsteps in the courtyard and a maid announced, "Pao-yu has returned." Instead of the slovenly and awkward boy she expected to see, Black Jade looked upon a youth of great beauty and charm. His face was as bright as the harvest moon, his complexion as fresh as flowers of a spring dawn, his hair as neat as if sculptured with a chisel, his eyebrows as black as if painted with ink. He was gracious even in anger and amiable even when he frowned. He wore a purple hat studded with precious stones and a red coat embroidered with butterflies and flowers. His jade was suspended from his neck by a multicolored silk cord.

Black Jade was startled; so familiar were his features that she felt she must have seen him somewhere before. Pao-yu, on his part, was deeply impressed by her delicate and striking features. Her beautifully curved eyebrows seemed, and yet did not seem, knitted; her eyes seemed, and yet did not seem, pleased. Their sparkle suggested tears, and her soft quick breathing indicated how delicately constituted she was. In repose she was like a fragile flower mirrored in the water; in movement she was like a graceful willow swaying in the wind. Her heart had one more aperture than Pi Kan;[7] she was noticeably more fragile than Hsi Shih.

"It seems that I have seen this Mei-mei before," Pao-yu said, with open admiration.

"Nonsense," the Matriarch said. "How could you have seen her?"

"I may not really have seen her," Pao-yu admitted. "Nevertheless, I feel as if I were meeting a friend whom I have not heard from for years."

"I am glad to hear that," the Matriarch said, "for that ought to mean that you will be good friends."

---

[7] This is another way of saying that Black Jade was supersensitive.

Pao-yu sat by his cousin and asked her all sorts of questions about the south. "Have you any jade?" he asked finally.

"No, I do not have any," Black Jade answered. "It is rare, and not everybody has it as you do."

Pao-yu suddenly flared up with passion. "Rare indeed!" he cried. "I think it is a most stupid thing. I shall have none of it." He took the jade from his neck and dashed it to the floor. The maids rushed forward to pick it up and as the Matriarch took Pao-yu in her arms and scolded him for venting his anger on the precious object upon which his very life depended. Pao-yu said, weeping, "None of my sisters has anything like it. I am the only one who has it. Now this Mei-mei, who is as beautiful as a fairy, doesn't have any either. What do I want this stupid thing for?"

"Your Mei-mei did have a piece of jade," the Matriarch fabricated. "But your aunt was so reluctant to part with your Mei-mei that she took the jade from her as a memento. Your Mei-mei said she had none only because she did not want to appear boastful. As a matter of fact, her jade was even better than yours. Now put it back on before your mother hears of this." Pao-yu appeared to be satisfied with the explanation and made no protest when the Matriarch replaced the jade on his neck.

Black Jade was assigned rooms adjoining Pao-yu's in the Matriarch's apartment. As she had brought with her only her nurse and a very young maid named Snow Duck, the Matriarch gave her Purple Cuckoo, one of her own favorite maids. Besides these, Black Jade was given four matrons and four or five maids-of-all-work, the same as the other granddaughters of the Matriarch.

Pao-yu's nurse was called Li Ma; his handmaid was Pervading Fragrance, who had also been a favorite maid of the Matriarch's. She was a good and conscientious girl and faithful to any person to whom she was assigned. Thus when she was in the Matriarch's service, she took thought for no one else. Now that she was Pao-yu's handmaid, she was entirely devoted to him. Originally she was called Pearl, but Pao-yu, because her family name was Hua (flower), gave her a new name, derived from the line, "By the pervading fragrance of the flowers, one knows that the day is warm." She was given to chiding him for his perverse behavior and was often distressed because he would not listen to her advise.

That evening after Pao-yu and Li Ma had gone to bed, Pervading Fragrance, noticing that Black Jade and Purple Cuckoo were still up, quietly went over for a visit. "Please sit down, Chieh-chieh,"[8] Black Jade said to her, and Pervading Fragrance sat down on the edge of the bed.

"Lin Ku-niang was crying just a while ago because she had unwittingly caused Pao-yu to fly into one of his mad tantrums," Purple Cuckoo said.

---

[8] "Elder sister." Note the courtesy with which some of the more favored bondmaids are treated. The fact that Pervading Fragrance had been the Matriarch's maid adds to her status.

"Ku-niang mustn't mind him," Pervading Fragrance said to Black Jade. "You have not seen anything yet of his unpredictable ways. If you let yourself be upset by a little thing like what happened today, you will never have a moment's peace."

The next morning, after presenting herself before the Matriarch, Black Jade went to call on Madame Wang and found her talking with Phoenix and two maidservants from the house of Madame Wang's brother. Not wishing to disturb them, Black Jade joined the three Springs, who were also there for the morning presentation. From Quest Spring she learned that they were discussing what to do to help Hsueh Pan, the son of Madame Wang's sister, against whom a charge of homicide was pending in the yamen[9] of the prefect of Yingtienfu.

It should be remembered that Chia Yu-tsun had been recently appointed prefect of Yingtienfu through the good offices of Chia Cheng. Needless to say, he spared no pains in order to exonerate Hsueh Pan. It should be pointed out also that the case involved Lotus, the lost daughter of Chen Shih-yin, who was sold by her kidnaper first to a certain Feng Yuan and then to Hsueh Pan. It was in a fight over the possession of the ill-fated girl that Feng Yuan was so severely beaten by Hsueh Pan's servants that he died shortly afterward.

Now Hsueh Pan was an only son. His father had died when he was still a child, and as a consequence he was very much spoiled by his mother. He was all but illiterate, though he came from a family about which "there lingers the fragrance of books." He was arrogant and quick-tempered by nature and extravagant and dissolute in his ways. Though ostensibly a merchant and purchasing agent for the Imperial Household, he knew nothing of business and depended entirely upon his managers and trusted servants. His mother was the sister of General Wang Tzu-teng, commander of the metropolitan garrison, and of Madame Wang, the wife of Chia Cheng. She was therefore closely related to the Yungkuofu and was known among the Chias as Hsueh Yi-ma.[10] She was about forty years old and had, besides Hsueh Pan, a daughter named Precious Virtue, who was a few years younger than Hsueh Pan. She was both beautiful and well mannered. Her father had loved her dearly. He gave her a chance to study under a private tutor, and as a scholar she turned out to be ten times better than her brother. But after her father's death, she gave little thought to books; she realized how irresponsible her brother was and decided that she must share her mother's burdens and cares.

There were three reasons why the Hsuehs were going to the Capital. First, Hsueh Yi-ma wanted to present her daughter as a candidate for the honor of lady in waiting in the Imperial House-

---

[9] Headquarters of a public official or department.
[10] "Maternal aunt."

hold. Secondly, it was many years since she had seen her sister and brother. Then, Hsueh Pan wanted, ostensibly, to audit the accounts of the various family-owned stores and shops there, though his real reason was the distractions offered by the metropolis.

Shortly before the Hsuehs reached the Capital, they heard that General Wang has been appointed military inspector of nine provinces and was about to leave for his post. The news pleased Hsueh Pan, for if his mother had been able to stay with her brother as planned, he would not have been as free to do as he chose. So he suggested to his mother that they open up one of their houses in the Capital. His mother guessed his reason. "We can go to your aunt's house," she said. "I am sure she will feel offended if we do not. Besides, I have not seen her for many years and would like to be with her. If you are afraid you will not be as free as you would like, you can live by yourself, but I and your sister will stay with your aunt."

As Hsueh Yi-ma had expected, Madame Wang urged them to stay in the Yungkuofu. They were installed in Pear Fragrance Court, at the northwestern corner of the mansion. It had its own entrance from the street and was connected to Madame Wang's compound by a passageway, so that Hsueh Yi-ma and her daughter were able to visit the inner apartments of the Yungkuofu without having to go outside the gate. This they did almost every day, sometimes after lunch, sometimes in the evening. The mother would visit with the Matriarch and her own sister, while Precious Virtue visited with the three Springs or Black Jade. Nor did Hsueh Pan have any reason for regret; he soon found among the young men of the Chia clan many boon companions with whom he could carouse, gamble, or visit the courtesans' quarters. In fact, he found that he had a great deal to learn from his new friends. For though Chia Cheng was a strict disciplinarian, he could not possibly know everything that went on in his clan. Moreover, Chia Gen, the nominal head of the clan, was far from being above reproach himself. Thus, Hsueh Pan found himself quite free to follow his own devices and gave up all thought of refurbishing one of his own houses.

IN WHICH THE DIVINE STONE PAGE
DOES NOT RECOGNIZE HIS FORMER HAUNT AND THE GODDESS
OF DISILLUSIONMENT FAILS TO AWAKEN HER ERSTWHILE ATTENDANT

Ever since Black Jade had arrived in the Yungkuofu, the Matriarch had lavished on her the love and tender solicitude hitherto reserved for Pao-yu. The young girl occupied an even warmer place in the Matriarch's heart than the three Springs, her real granddaughters.[11] She and Pao-yu had also been drawn closer together,

---

[11] A daughter's child, having a different surname, is only an "outside" or pseudo grandchild.

not only because they shared the same apartment, but also because of a natural affinity which manifested itself at their first meeting. Now there suddenly appeared on the scene Precious Virtue. Though only a trifle older than Black Jade, she showed a tact and understanding far beyond her years. She was completely unspoiled, always ready to please and enter into the spirit of the occasion and always kind to the servants and bondmaids. In contrast, Black Jade was inclined to haughtiness and held herself aloof. Thus in a short time, Precious Virtue won the hearts of all, and Black Jade could not help feeling a little jealous. Precious Virtue seemed wholly unaware of the situation her presence created.

As for Pao-yu, he was so simple in nature and so completely guileless that his behavior often struck people as odd, if not mad. He treated everyone alike and never stopped to consider the nearness of kinship of one as compared with that of another. Often he would unwittingly offend Black Jade, sometimes in his very efforts to please her. On such occasions, it was always Pao-yu who made the conciliatory gesture.

One day when the plums in the garden of the Ningkuofu were in full bloom, Yu-shih, the wife of Chia Gen, took the occasion to invite the Matriarch, Madame Wang, Madame Hsing, and other members of the Yungkuofu to a plum-flower feast. Nothing of particular note occurred; it was simply one of these many seasonal family gatherings. After dinner, Pao-yu said he felt tired and wished to take a nap.

"We have a room ready for Uncle Pao," Chin-shih said to the Matriarch. "I'll take him there and see that he has a nice rest."

Now Chin-shih was Chia Jung's wife and the Matriarch's favorite great-granddaughter-in-law. She was a very beautiful young woman, possessed of a slender figure and a most gentle and amiable disposition. The Matriarch felt safe to leave Pao-yu in her hands.

The room to which Chin-shih took Pao-yu was one of the main apartments in the Ningkuofu and was luxuriously furnished, but Pao-yu took objection to the center scroll on the wall, a painting depicting the famous Han scholar Liu Hsiang receiving divine enlightenment. He took an even more violent objection to the scrolls on either side of the painting on which was inscribed the couplet:

To know through and through the ways of the world is Real Knowledge;
To conform in every detail the customs of society is True Accomplishment.

"I cannot possibly sleep in this room," he declared.

"If you do not like this room, I am afraid nothing will suit you," Chin-shih said and then added, "unless perhaps you want to use mine."

Pao-yu smiled assent, but his nurse Li Ma objected, saying, "It is hardly proper for an uncle to sleep in the bedroom of his nephew's wife."

"Don't be ridiculous," Chin-shih said, laughing. "Uncle Pao is just a boy, if he doesn't mind my saying so. Didn't you see my younger brother when he came to visit last month? He is just Uncle Pao's age but he is the taller of the two."

"Where is your brother?" Pao-yu asked, for he wanted to see what the brother of the beautiful Chin-shih was like. "Bring him and let me meet him."

"He is home, many miles from here," she answered. "You will meet him some other time."

Pao-yu detected a subtle and yet intoxicating fragrance as he entered Chin-shih's room. On the wall there was a painting by T'ang Yin, entitled "Lady Taking Nap under Begonia" and a couplet by a Sung poet:

> A gentle chill pervades her dreams because it is spring;
> The fragrance intoxicates one like that of wine.

In the center of the table was a mirror once used by Empress Wu Tse T'ien. At one side there was a golden plate on which the nimble Chao Fei-yen had danced, and on the plate there was a quince that An Lu-shan had playfully thrown at the beautiful Yang Kuei-fei. The carved bed once held the Princess Shou Yang, and the pearl curtains were made for the Princess T'ung Chang.[12]

"I like your room!" Pao-yu exclaimed with delight.

"It is fit for the immortals, if I may say so," Chin-shih said with a smile. She spread out the silk coverlet that was once washed by Hsi Shih and put in place the embroidered cushion that was once embraced by the Red Maid. Pao-yu's nurse withdrew after helping him to bed. Only his four handmaids—Pervading Fragrance, Bright Design, Autumn Sky, and Musk Moon—remained, and they were encouraged by Chin-shih to go outside and watch the kittens play under the eaves.

Pao-yu fell asleep almost as soon as he closed his eyes. In a dream he seemed to follow Chin-shih to some wondrous place where the halls and chambers were of jade and gold and the gardens were filled with exotic blooms. Pao-yu was filled with delight. He thought to himself that he would gladly spend the rest of his life here. Suddenly he heard someone singing on the far side of the hill.

> Spring dreams vanish like ever-changing clouds,
> Fallen flowers drift downstream never to return.
> And so lovers everywhere, heed my words,
> 'Tis folly to court sorrow and regret.

---

[12] All famous lovers in Chinese history and legend.

The dream of the Red Chamber.

The song still lingered in Pao-yu's ears when there appeared before him a fairy goddess whose beauty and grace were unlike anything in the mortal world. Pao-yu greeted her and said, "Sister Immortal, where have you come from and where are you going? I have lost my way. Please help me."

She replied, "I am the Goddess of Disillusionment. I inhabit the Realm of Parting Sorrow in the Ocean of Regrets. I am in charge of the plaints of unhappy maidens and sad lovers, their debts of love, and their unfulfilled desires. It is not by accident that I have encountered you. My home is not far from here. I have not much to offer you, but I have some tender tea leaves, which I gathered myself, and a few jars of my own wine. I have several singers trained in exotic dances and have just completed a series of twelve songs which I call 'Dream of the Red Chamber.' Why don't you come with me?"

Chin-shih having now disappeared, Pao-yu followed the Goddess and reached a place dominated by a huge stone arch, across which was written the inscription: "Great Void Illusion Land." On either side this couplet was inscribed:

> When the unreal is taken for the real, then the
>   real becomes unreal;
> Where non-existence is taken for existence, then
>   existence becomes non-existence.

Passing through the arch, Pao-yu found himself standing in front of the gate of a palace, above which was the inscription: "Sea of Passion and Heaven of Love." The couplet read:

> Enduring as heaven and earth—no love however
>   ancient can ever die;
> Timeless as light and shadow—no debt of breeze
>   and moonlight can ever be repaid.

Pao-yu was still too young to understand the meaning of the couplet. He had a vague notion about love but no idea at all of what breeze and moonlight might be. He was naturally curious and said to himself that he must be sure to find out before he left the place. By this innocent thought, Pao-yu became inexplicably involved with the demons of passion.

Entering the second gate, Pao-yu saw long rows of chapels with inscriptions such as "Division of Perverse Sentiments," "Division of Rival Jealousies," "Division of Morning Weeping," "Division of Evening Lament," "Division of Spring Affections," and "Division of Autumn Sorrows."

"Would it be possible for you to take me through these chapels?" Pao-yu asked.

"No," the Goddess answered. "They contain the past, present, and future of the maidens of the entire world. Mortal eyes may not look upon them." As they walked on, Pao-yu continued to importune the Goddess until she finally yielded, saying, "You may see this one." Pao-yu looked up and saw that the chapel was inscribed "Division of the Ill-Fated." There was also this couplet:

> *Sorrows of spring and sadness of autumn are all*
> *one's own doing;*
> *A face like a flower and features like the moon are*
> *all in vain in the end.*

Inside, Pao-yu saw more than ten large cabinets all sealed and labeled with the names of the different provinces. Wishing to find out about his own, he went to the cabinet marked "The Twelve Maidens of the Chinling, File No. 1."

"I have heard that Chinling is a large city. Why is it that there are only twelve maidens? Just in our own family there are several hundred of them."

"We keep records of only the more important ones," the Goddess smiled indulgently.

Pao-yu looked at the next two cabinets and noted that they were marked "The Twelve Maidens of Chinling, File No. 2" and "The Twelve Maidens of Chinling, File No. 3," respectively. He opened the last cabinet and took out a large album. The first page was completely obscured by heavy mist and dark clouds. There was no foreground whatever. Inscribed on the page were the following lines:

> *Clear days are rarely encountered,*
> *Bright clouds easily scattered.*
> *Her heart was proud as the sky,*
> *But her position was lowly on earth.*
> *Her beauty and accomplishments only invited*
> *jealousy,*
> *Her death was hastened by baseless slander.*
> *And in vain her faithful Prince mourns.*[13]

Pao-yu could make nothing of all this. On the next page there was a painting of a bunch of flowers and a broken mat, together with a poem.

> *Gentle and gracious well she may be,*
> *Like cassia and orchid indeed she is.*
> *But what are these things to the young Prince*
> *When it is the mummer that destiny has favored?*[14]

This meant even less to Pao-yu. He replaced the album and took the one in Cabinet 2. The first page was also a picture—this time a

---

[13] Picture and poem forecast the fate of Bright Design, one of Pao-yu's handmaids, who languished and died in disgrace.
[14] The picture represents Pervading Fragrance, whose family name means "flower." She eventually married an actor friend of Pao-yu.

sprig of cassia at the top and below it a withered lotus flower on a dried-up pond. The accompanying poem read:

> *O symbol of purity and innocence,*
> *Your cruel fate is least deserved.*
> *For in two fields one tree will grow*
> *And send your gentle soul to its ancient home.*

Again Pao-yu failed to see the significance of the picture or poem. He tried the album in Cabinet 1 and found the pictures and poems equally baffling. He was about to try again when the Goddess, fearing that he might succeed in penetrating the secrets of Heaven if allowed to go on, took the album from him and put it back in the cabinet, saying, "Come and see the rest of the place. What is the use of puzzling over these?"

Pao-yu was led into the inner palace, which was even more splendid than what he had already seen. Several fairies came out at the call of the Goddess, but they seemed to be disappointed when they saw Pao-yu. One of them said rudely, "We thought you were going to bring Sister Crimson. Why this common creature from the mortal world?"

While Pao-yu stood in awkward silence, the Goddess explained to her fairies that she had brought him in order to enlighten him and she begged them to help her in the task. The tea, the wine, and the food were all delicious beyond anything that Pao-yu had ever tasted. After the feast, the Goddess bade her fairies sing "Dream of the Red Chamber." She gave Pao-yu the manuscript so that he might follow it while it was sung. "For you may not understand this, as you are accustomed only to mortal music," she explained. The singing was exquisite, but Pao-yu could not understand the references and allusions in the lyrics. The Goddess sighed compassionately when she saw that Pao-yu remained unenlightened.

After a while, Pao-yu began to feel sleepy and begged to be excused. The Goddess then took him to a chamber where to his astonishment he found a girl who reminded him of Precious Virtue in graciousness of manner and of Black Jade in beauty of features. He was wondering what was going to happen next when he heard the voice of the Goddess speaking to him. "In the Red Dust,"[15] she said, "the embroidered chambers are often desecrated by licentious men and loose women. What is even more deplorable are the attempts to distinguish between love of beauty and licentiousness, forgetting that one always leads to the other. The meetings at Witches' Hill and the transports of cloud and rain invariably climax what is supposedly a pure and chaste love of beauty. I am now, of

---

[15] The world of mortals.

course, speaking of the generality of men and women. There are rare exceptions, of which you are one. Indeed, I admire you because you are the most licentious of men."

"How could you make such an accusation!" Pao-yu protested. "I have been taken to task for not applying myself to my studies and have been severely reprimanded for it by my parents, but no one has accused me of licentiousness. Besides, I am still young. I hardly know the meaning of the word."

"Do not be alarmed," the Goddess said. "Licentiousness simply means excess, and there are all kinds of excesses. The most common kind is an insatiable greed of the flesh. We are all familiar with those coarse creatures who cannot think of beautiful women except as means for gratifying their animal desires. They are a constant danger and threat to womankind. Your licentiousness, however, is of a more subtle kind, one that can only be apprehended but not described. Nevertheless, it is just as excessive and insatiable as the kind the world is familiar with, but whereas the latter constitutes a constant danger to womankind, your licentiousness makes you a most welcome companion in the maidens' chambers. But what makes you desirable in the maidens' chambers also makes you appear strange and unnatural in the eyes of the world. It is necessary for you to experience what most men experience, so that you may know its nature and limitations. I have, therefore, arranged that you should marry my sister Chien-mei.[16] This is the night for you to consummate your union. After you have seen for yourself that the pleasures of fairyland are but thus and so, you may perhaps realize their vanity and turn your mind to the teachings of Confucius and Mencius and devote your efforts to the welfare of mankind."

She whispered in Pao-yu's ears the secrets of cloud and rain and pushed him toward her sister Chien-mei. Then she left them, closing the door after her. Pao-yu followed the instructions of the Goddess and disported himself with his bride in ways that may well be imagined but may not be detailed here. The next day Pao-yu went out for a walk with his bride. Suddenly he found himself in a field overgrown with thorn and bramble and overrun with tigers and wolves. In front of him an expanse of water blocked the way of escape. As he tried desperately to think of what to do, the Goddess' voice spoke to him from behind, "Stop and turn back before it is too late!" As she spoke, a deafening roar issued from the water, and a horde of monsters rushed toward Pao-yu. Frantically he cried out, "Help me, Chien-mei! Help! Help!"

Thereupon he awoke, bathed in a cold sweat, as Pervading Fragrance and the other maids rushed to his bedside, saying, "Don't be afraid Pao-yu. We are all here with you."

---

[16] Meaning "combining the best features of both," that is, of Precious Virtue and Black Jade.

Chin-shih, who had heard Pao-yu calling Chien-mei, wondered, "How did he happen to know my child's name?"

As Pervading Fragrance helped Pao-yu to adjust his clothes, her hand came in contact with something cold and clammy. Quickly withdrawing her hand, she asked Pao-yu what it was. Pao-yu did not answer but only blushed and gave her hand a gentle squeeze. Being a clever maid and a year or two older than Pao-yu, she too blushed and said no more. Later that evening, when she was alone with him in the apartment, she brought Pao-yu a change of clothing.

"Please don't tell anyone," Pao-yu said embarrassedly. Then he confided to her his dream. When he came to what happened in the bridal chamber, the maid blushed and laughed and covered her face with her hands. Now Pao-yu had always been very fond of the maid, so he proposed to demonstrate what the Goddess had taught him. At first Pervading Fragrance refused but in the end she acquiesced, since she knew that she would eventually be Pao-yu's concubine. Thenceforward, Pao-yu treated her with more tenderness than ever, and the maid on her part ministered to the comforts of her young master even more faithfully than before.

Further Readings

Maurice Freeman, *Family and Kinship in Chinese Society* (Stanford, CA: Stanford University Press, 1970), presents an interesting look at Chinese family life. Chung-li Chang, *The Chinese Gentry: Studies on Their Role in Nineteenth-Century Chinese Society* (Seattle, WA: University of Washington Press, 1967), provides an interesting insight into China's gentry-official system. A fascinating portrayal of life in rural Ch'ing China is afforded by Jonathan Spence, *Death of Woman Wang* (New York: Penguin Books, 1979).

Klaus-Peter Koepping and Lam Lai Sing, *New Interpretation of the Dream of the Red Chamber* (Singapore: Public Press Co., Ltd., 1973), examine the historical background of the novel, its major themes, and the importance of its analysis of social problems. Jean Knoerle, *The Dream of the Red Chamber* (Bloomington, IN: Indiana University Press, 1972), concentrates on elements of structure and technique. An excellent discussion of the many textual problems surrounding the novel's authorship is found in Wu Shih-ch'ang, *On the Red Chamber Dream* (Oxford: Clarendon Press, 1961). Robert E. Hegel, *The Novel in Seventeenth-Century China* (New York: Columbia University Press, 1981) stresses the importance of seventeenth-century novels in shaping later Ch'ing fiction, including *The Dream of the Red Chamber*. C. T. Hsia, *The Classic Chinese Novel* (New York: Columbia University Press, 1968), contains a helpful study of *The Dream of the Red Chamber*.

Robespierre's Speech of 17 Pluviôse

In the summer of 1793, Revolutionary France was in dire straits. A coalition of monarchical powers had been raised against the new Republic, and foreign troops ringed it on all sides. Prussian and Austrian armies threatened its eastern and northern frontiers, where its military commander had just deserted to the enemy and its armies were in retreat. Spanish troops had crossed the Pyrenees, and the British navy had established control over the island of Corsica and the Mediterranean port of Toulon. Affairs were not much better internally. The coastal province of La Vendée was in revolt, and royalist conspirators were rousing the Rhône valley to rebel. The cost of food was skyrocketing and the value of government currency was plummeting. As yet another misfortune, Jean-Paul Marat, the most widely admired of the revolutionary leaders, was assassinated in July. Decisive steps were needed if the Republic was to survive. Accordingly, the Committee of Public Safety was formed to take over direction of the revolution; chief among its members was Maximilien François-Marie-Isidore de Robespierre (1758–1794).

Robespierre had been born of middle-class parents in the provincial capital of Arras in northern France. Deserted by the father, the family was thrown into poverty, and young Robespierre gained his education through winning scholarships. Studying Classics and Law, he was admitted to the bar in 1780. After some years of eking out a living as a lawyer, he was elected by Arras to the Estates General, a national assembly meeting in 1789. He soon became deeply involved in revolutionary politics and emerged as a leader of the radical Jacobin Club. It was as a representative of the radical faction that he took his place on the Committee of Public Safety on 27 July 1793.

From *The Ninth of Thermidor: The Fall of Robespierre,* edited by Richard Bienvenu (New York: Oxford University Press, 1968), pp. 32–41, 46–49.

He was a dry and humorless man, personally incorruptible and completely devoted to the cause of the Revolution, which he supported with an almost religious fervor. On the Committee, he asked for an end to compromises and half-way measures, demanding nothing less than complete national dedication to the tasks at hand. This approach was the key to the success of the government. A wave of patriotic fervor swept over France and made possible the implementation of the stern policies of the Committee of Public Safety. Enemy armies were driven back, revolts were crushed, and a measure of order was restored to the French economy. Robespierre then addressed himself to the task of establishing on a permanent foundation the national unity that had, for the moment at least, saved the Revolution. His solution was to establish on a more regular basis the previously sporadic execution of spies, conspirators, and "enemies of the state." His "Speech of 17 Pluviôse," delivered to the Convention (the representative assembly) in the name of the Committee of Public Safety, laid the basis of that policy.

The speech falls into two parts: a grand and passionate exposition of the meaning of the Revolution, of democracy, and of civil virtue; and a coldly logical explanation that, in time of war, the defense of so great a prize warrants the use of any means that might prove effective. The logic was accepted, and the Committee of Public Safety began to eliminate those individuals, factions, and institutions that they considered as weakening the Revolutionary Republic. In so doing, they betrayed the principles of the Revolution itself and became a tyranny as bad or worse than those they were attempting to defeat, a tyranny that came to be known as "the Reign of Terror."

As long as the danger to the state was evident and real, the iron hand of the Committee was tolerated. Once the Committee had succeeded and France was relatively safe, however, the Convention was free to act. On 28 July 1794, six thousand troops were sent to City Hall, where they arrested Robespierre and twenty-one of his colleagues. A few hours later, the prisoners were taken to the Place de la Concorde, where they were executed by the guillotine. Historians still debate what flaw of character had led such a passionate lover of democracy to a tyrant's death.

Questions

1. How do Robespierre's revolutionary sentiments compare with those of the Declaration of Independence?

2. What does he consider to have been the aim of the Revolution?

3. How does he justify the use of terror in defense of democracy?

SPEECH OF 17 PLUVIÔSE[1]

Citizen-representatives of the people.

Some time ago we set forth the principles of our foreign policy; today we come to expound the principles of our internal policy.

After having proceeded haphazardly for a long time, swept along by the movement of opposing factions, the representatives of the French people have finally demonstrated a character and a government. A sudden change in the nation's fortune announced to Europe the regeneration that had been effected in the national representation. But, up to the very moment when I am speaking, it must be agreed that we have been guided, amid such stormy circumstances, by the love of good and by the awareness of our country's needs rather than by an exact theory and by precise rules of conduct, which we did not have even leisure enough to lay out.

It is time to mark clearly the goal of the revolution, and the end we want to reach; it is time for us to take account both of the obstacles that still keep us from it, and of the means we ought to adopt to attain it: a simple and important idea which seems never to have been noticed. Eh! how could a lax and corrupt government have dared realize it? A king, a haughty senate, a Caesar, a Cromwell are obliged above all to cover their plans with a religious veil, to compromise with all the vices, to humor all the parties, to crush the party of the honest folk, to oppress or deceive the people, in order to reach the goal of their perfidious ambition. If we had not had a greater task to fulfill, if we had been concerned here only with the interests of a faction or of a new aristocracy, we could have believed, like certain writers still more ignorant than they are depraved, that the plan of the French revolution was written out in full in the books of Tacitus and Machiavelli, and we could have sought the duties of the people's representatives in the histories of Augustus, Tiberius, or Vespasian, or even in that of certain French legislators; because, except for a few nuances of perfidy or cruelty, all tyrants are alike.

For ourselves, we come today to make the world privy to your political secrets, so that all our country's friends can rally to the voice of reason and the public interest; so that the French nation and its representatives will be respected in all the countries of the world where the knowledge of their real principles can penetrate; so that the intriguers who seek always to replace other intriguers will be judged by sure and easy rules.

---

[1] 5 February (1794). To emphasize its break with with the past, the revolutionary regime in France substituted a new calendar to replace the Gregorian system. The republican calendar, in effect from 1793 through 1805, consisted of twelve thirty-day months: *Vendémiare* (the month of vintage), *Brumaire* (fog), *Frimaire* (frost), *Nivôse* (snow), *Pluviôse* (rain), *Ventôse* (wind), *Germinal* (buds), *Floréal* (flowers), *Prairial* (meadows), *Messidor* (reaping), *Thermidor* (heat), and *Fructidor* (fruit).

We must take far-sighted precautions to return the destiny of liberty into the hands of the truth, which is eternal, rather than into those of men, who are transitory, so that if the government forgets the interests of the people, or if it lapses into the hands of corrupt individuals, according to the natural course of things, the light of recognized principles will illuminate their treachery, and so that every new faction will discover death in the mere thought of crime.

Happy the people who can arrive at that point! Because, whatever new outrages are prepared against them, what resources are presented by an order of things in which the public reason is the guarantee of liberty!

What is the goal toward which we are heading? The peaceful enjoyment of liberty and equality; the reign of that eternal justice whose laws have been inscribed, not in marble and stone, but in the hearts of all men, even in that of the slave who forgets them and in that of the tyrant who denies them.

We seek an order of things in which all the base and cruel passions are enchained, all the beneficent and generous passions are awakened by the laws; where ambition becomes the desire to merit glory and to serve our country; where distinctions are born only of equality itself; where the citizen is subject to the magistrate, the magistrate to the people, and the people to justice; where our country assures the well-being of each individual, and where each individual proudly enjoys our country's prosperity and glory; where every soul grows greater through the continual flow of republican sentiments, and by the need of deserving the esteem of a great people; where the arts are the adornments of the liberty which ennobles them and commerce the source of public wealth rather than solely the monstrous opulence of a few families.

In our land we want to substitute morality for egotism, integrity for formal codes of honor, principles for customs, a sense of duty for one of mere propriety, the rule of reason for the tyranny of fashion, scorn of vice for scorn of the unlucky, self-respect for insolence, grandeur of soul for vanity, love of glory for the love of money, good people in place of good society. We wish to substitute merit for intrigue, genius for wit, truth for glamor, the charm of happiness for sensuous boredom, the greatness of man for the pettiness of the great, a people who are magnanimous, powerful, and happy, in place of a kindly, frivolous, and miserable people—which is to say all the virtues and all the miracles of the republic in place of all the vices and all the absurdities of the monarchy.

We want, in a word, to fulfill nature's desires, accomplish the destiny of humanity, keep the promises of philosophy, absolve providence from the long reign of crime and tyranny. Let France, formerly illustrious among the enslaved lands, eclipsing the glory of all the free peoples who have existed, become the model for the nations, the terror of oppressors, the consolation of the oppressed, the ornament of the world—and let us, in sealing our work with our blood, see at least the early dawn of universal bliss—that is our ambition, that is our goal.

What kind of government can realize these wonders? Only a democratic or republican government—these two words are synonyms, despite the abuses in common speech, because an aristocracy is no closer than a monarchy to being a republic. Democracy is not a state in which the people, continually meeting, regulate for themselves all public affairs, still less is it a state in which a tiny fraction of the people, acting by isolated, hasty, and contradictory measures, decide the fate of the whole society. Such a government has never existed, and it could exist only to lead the people back into despotism.

Democracy is a state in which the sovereign people, guided by laws which are of their own making, do for themselves all that they can do well, and by their delegates do all that they cannot do for themselves.

It is therefore in the principles of democratic government that you should seek the rules of your political conduct.

But, in order to lay the foundations of democracy among us and to consolidate it, in order to arrive at the peaceful reign of constitutional laws, we must finish the war of liberty against tyranny and safely cross through the storms of the revolution: that is the goal of the revolutionary system which you have put in order. You should therefore still base your conduct upon the stormy circumstances in which the republic finds itself; and the plan of your administration should be the result of the spirit of revolutionary government, combined with the general principles of democracy.

Now, what is the fundamental principle of popular or democratic government, that is to say, the essential mainspring which sustains it and makes it move? It is virtue. I speak of the public virtue which worked so many wonders in Greece and Rome and which ought to produce even more astonishing things in republican France—that virtue which is nothing other than the love of the nation and its laws.

But as the essence of the republic or of democracy is equality, it follows that love of country necessarily embraces the love of equality.

It is still true that that sublime sentiment supposes the preference of public interest to all particular interests, whence it follows that love of country implies or produces all the virtues; There is no other force, for what are they but the strength of soul which makes men capable of these sacrifices? And how, for example, can the slave of avarice or ambition be made to sacrifice his idol for the good of the country?

Not only is virtue the soul of democracy, but virtue can only exist within that form of government. Under a monarchy I know of only one individual who can love his country—and who, for this, does not even need virtue—the monarch. The reason for this is that among all the people of his state, the monarch alone has a fatherland. Is he not the sovereign, at least in fact? Does he not stand in place of the people? And what is the fatherland if it is not the land where one is a citizen and a participant in the sovereign power?

As a consequence of the same principle, within aristocratic states the word *patrie* means nothing except to the patrician families who have invaded sovereignty.

It is only under a democracy that the state is the fatherland of all the individuals who compose it and can count as many active defenders of its cause as it has citizens. There lies the source of the superiority of free peoples above all others. If Athens and Sparta triumphed over the tyrants of Asia and the Swiss over the tyrants of Spain and Austria, one can seek no other cause.

But the French are the first people of the world who have established real democracy, by calling all men to equality and full rights of citizenship; and there, in my judgment, is the true reason why all the tyrants in league against the Republic will be vanquished.

There are important consequences to be drawn immediately from the principles we have just explained.

Since the soul of the Republic is virtue, equality, and since your goal is to found, to consolidate the Republic, it follows that the first rule of your political conduct ought to be to relate all your efforts to maintaining equality and developing virtue; because the first care of the legislator ought to be to fortify the principle of the government. Thus everything that tends to excite love of country, to purify morals, to elevate souls, to direct the passions of the human heart toward the public interest, ought to be adopted or established by you. Everything which tends to concentrate them in the abjection of selfishness, to awaken enjoyment for petty things and scorn for great ones, ought to be rejected or curbed by you. Within the scheme of the French revolution, that which is immoral is impolitic, that which is corrupting is counter-revolutionary. Weakness, vice, and prejudices are the road to royalty. Dragged too often, perhaps, by the weight of our former customs, as much as by the imperceptible bent of human frailty, toward false ideas and fainthearted sentiments, we have less cause to guard ourselves against too much energy than against too much weakness. The greatest peril, perhaps, that we have to avoid is not that of zealous fervor, but rather of weariness in doing good works and of timidity in displaying our own courage. Maintain, then, the sacred power of the republican government, instead of letting it decline. I do not need to say that I have no wish here to justify any excess. The most sacred principles can indeed be abused. It is up to the wisdom of the government to pay heed to circumstances, to seize the right moments, to choose the proper means; because the manner of preparing great things is an essential part of the talent for performing them, just as wisdom is itself an element of virtue.

We do not intend to cast the French Republic in the Spartan mold; we wish to give it neither the austerity nor the corruption of a monastic cloister. We have come to present to you in all its purity the moral and political principle of popular government. Thus you have a compass which can guide you amid the storms of all the passions and the whirlwinds of intrigue which surround you. You have the touchstone by which you can test all your laws, all the proposals which are made to you. In comparing them unceasingly with that principle, you can from now on avoid the usual perils which threaten large assemblies, the danger of surprises and of hasty, incoherent, and contradictory measures. You can give to all your operations the cohesion, the unity, the wisdom and the dignity that ought to distinguish the representatives of the first people of the world.

The obvious consequences of the principle of democracy do not require detailed description; it is the simple and fruitful principle itself which deserves to be expounded.

Republican virtue can be considered as it relates to the people and as it relates to the government. It is necessary in both. When the government alone is deprived of it, there remains a resource in the virtue of the people; but when the people themselves are corrupt, liberty is already lost.

Happily virtue is natural to the people, despite aristocratic prejudices to the contrary. A nation is truly corrupt when, having gradually lost its character and its liberty, it passes from democracy to aristocracy or to monarchy; this is the death of the body politic through decrepitude. When after four hundred years of glory avarice finally drove from Sparta its morality together with the laws of Lycurgus, Agis died in vain trying to bring them back![2] Demosthenes thundered in vain against Philip of Macedon, Philip found more eloquent advocates than Demosthenes among the degenerate inhabitants of Athens. There was still as large a population in Athens as in the times of Miltiades and Aristides, but there were no longer any true Athenians.[3] And what did it matter that Brutus killed a tyrant? Tyranny still lived in every heart, and Rome existed only in Brutus.

---

[2] Agis IV, king of Sparta 244–240 B.C., tried to bring back traditional customs and the laws of Lycurgus, of several hundred years before, under which Sparta had been the austere garrison-state of so much renown. Agis also sought to temper the power of the oligarchy which dominated Sparta in his own day, but he was imprisoned and murdered.

[3] Demosthenes (384?–322 B.C.) unsuccessfully opposed the Macedonian conquest of Greece led by Philip, father of Alexander the Great. On Alexander's death he tried to raise a general Greek revolt but was forced to flee, and took poison. Miltiades was the Greek commander in the Battle of Marathon (490 B.C.); Aristides served as a general at the Battle of Salamis (480 B.C.) and was instrumental in organizing the Athenian confederacy (478 B.C.).

But, when, by prodigious efforts of courage and reason, a people breaks the chains of despotism in order to make of them trophies to liberty; when, by the force of its moral character, it leaves, as it were, the arms of death in order to recapture the vigor of youth; when it is in turn sensitive and proud, intrepid and docile—such a people can be stopped neither by impregnable ramparts nor by the countless armies of tyrants ranged against it; it halts only before the image of the law. If such a people does not move rapidly forward to the height of its destiny, it can only be the fault of those who govern it.

Moreover one could say, in a sense, that in order to love justice and equality the people have no need of a great degree of virtue; it suffices if they love themselves.

But the magistrate is obliged to sacrifice his interest to the interest of the people, and his pride in power to equality. The law must speak with authority especially to those who are its instruments. The government must weigh heavily upon its parts in order to hold them all in harmony. If there exists a representative body, a highest authority constituted by the people, it is up to it to inspect and ceaselessly control all the public functionaries. But who will curb the legislature itself, if not its own sense of virtue? The higher this source of public order is elevated in position, the purer it should be; the representative body must begin, then, by submitting all the private passions within it to the general passion for the public welfare. Fortunate are the representatives when their glory and even their interests, as much as their duties, attach them to the cause of liberty!

We deduce from all this a great truth—that the characteristic of popular government is to be trustful towards the people and severe towards itself.

Here the development of our theory would reach its limit, if you had only to steer the ship of the Republic through calm waters. But the tempest rages, and the state of the revolution in which you find yourselves imposes upon you another task.

This great purity of the French revolution's fundamental elements, the very sublimity of its objective, is precisely what creates our strength and our weakness: our strength, because it gives us the victory of truth over deception and the rights of public interest over private interests; our weakness, because it rallies against us all men who are vicious, all those who in their hearts plan to despoil the people, and all those who have despoiled them and want impunity, and those who reject liberty as a personal calamity, and those who have embraced the revolution as a livelihood and the Republic as if it were an object of prey. Hence the defection of so many ambitious or greedy men who since the beginning have abandoned us along the way, because they had not begun the voyage in order to reach the same goal. One could say that the two contrary geniuses that have been depicted competing for control of the realm of nature, are fighting in this great epoch of human history to shape irrevocably the destiny of the world, and that France is the theater of this mighty struggle. Without, all the tyrants encircle you; within, all the friends of tyranny conspire—they will conspire until crime has been robbed of hope. We must smother the internal and external enemies of the Republic or perish with them. Now, in this situation, the first maxim of your policy ought to be to lead the people by reason and the people's enemies by terror.

If the mainspring of popular government in peacetime is virtue, amid revolution it is at the same time [both] virtue and *terror*: virtue, without which terror is fatal; terror, without which virtue is impotent. Terror is nothing but prompt, severe, inflexible justice; it is therefore an emanation of virtue. It is less a special principle than a consequence of the general principle of democracy applied to our country's most pressing needs.

It has been said that terror was the mainspring of despotic government. Does your government, then, resemble a despotism? Yes, as the sword which glitters in the hands of liberty's heroes resembles the one with which tyranny's lackeys are armed. Let the despot govern his brutalized subjects by terror; he is right to do this, as a despot. Subdue liberty's enemies by terror, and you will be right, as founders of the Republic. The government of the revolution is the despotism of liberty against tyranny. Is force made only to protect crime? And is is not to strike the heads of the proud that lightning is destined?

Nature imposes upon every physical and moral being the law of providing for its own preservation. Crime slaughters innocence in order to reign, and innocence in the hands of crime fights with all its strength.

Let tyranny reign for a single day, and on the morrow not one patriot will be left. How long will the despots' fury be called justice, and the people's justice barbarism or rebellion? How tender one is to the oppressors and how inexorable against the oppressed! And how natural—whoever has no hatred for crime cannot love virtue.

Yet one or the other must succumb. Indulgence for the royalists, some people cry out. Mercy for the scoundrels! No—mercy for innocence, mercy for the weak, mercy for the unfortunate, mercy for humanity!

Social protection is due only to peaceful citizens; there are no citizens in the Republic but the republicans. The royalists, the conspirators are, in its eyes, only strangers or, rather, enemies. Is not the terrible war, which liberty sustains against tyranny, indivisible? Are not the enemies within the allies of those without? The murderers who tear our country apart internally; the intriguers who purchase the consciences of the people's agents; the traitors who sell them; the mercenary libelers subsidized to dishonor the popular cause, to kill public virtue, to stir up the fires of civil discord, and to prepare political counter-revolution by means of moral counter-revolution—are all these men less to blame or less dangerous than the tyrants whom they serve? All those who interpose their parricidal gentleness to protect the wicked from the avenging blade of national justice are like those who would throw themselves between the tyrants' henchmen and our soldiers' bayonets. All the outbursts of their false sensitivity seem to me only longing sighs for England and Austria.

Well! For whom, then, would they be moved to pity? Would it be for two hundred thousand heroes, the elite of the nation, cut down by the iron of liberty's enemies or by the daggers of royalist or federalist assassins? No, those are only plebeians, patriots; in order to be entitled to their tender interest, one must be at least the widow of a general who has betrayed our country twenty times. To obtain their indulgence, one must almost prove that he has sacrificed ten thousand Frenchmen, as a Roman general, in order to obtain his triumph, was supposed to have killed, I believe, ten thousand enemies. They listen composedly to the recital of the horrors committed by the tyrants against the defenders of liberty—our women horribly mutilated, our children murdered at their mothers' breasts, our prisoners undergoing horrible torments for their moving, sublime heroism. The too slow punishment of a few monsters who have fattened on the purest blood of our country is termed by them a horrible butchery.

They suffer patiently the misery of generous citizens who have sacrificed their brothers, children, husbands to the finest of causes, while they lavish their most generous consolations upon conspirators' wives. It is accepted that such women can seduce justice with impunity, pleading (against liberty) the cause of their near relations and their accomplices. They have been made almost a privileged corporation, creditor and pensioner of the people.

With what simple good-heartedness are we still the dupes of words! How aristocracy and moderatism still govern us by the murderous maxims they have given us!

Aristocracy defends itself better by its intrigues than patriotism does by its services. Some people would like to govern revolutions by the quibbles of the law courts and treat conspiracies against the Republic like legal proceedings against private persons. Tyranny kills; liberty argues. And the code made by the conspirators themselves is the law by which they are judged.

When it is a matter of the national safety, the testimony of the whole world cannot compensate for the proof of actual witnesses, nor obviousness itself for documentary evidence.

Slowness of judgments is equal to impunity. Uncertainty of punishment encourages all the guilty. Yet there are complaints of the severity of justice, of the detention of enemies of the Republic. Examples are sought in the history of tyrants because our enemies do not wish to select them from the history of peoples nor derive them from the spirit of threatened liberty. In Rome, when the consul discovered a plot and simultaneously smothered it by putting to death the accomplices of Catiline, he was accused of having violated the legal forms. And by whom? By the ambitious Caesar, who wanted to swell his faction with the horde of conspirators, by Piso, Clodius, and all the evil citizens who themselves feared the virtue of a true Roman and the severity of the laws.

To punish the oppressors of humanity is clemency; to pardon them is barbarity. The rigor of tyrants has only rigor for a principle; the rigor of the republican government comes from charity.

Therefore, woe to those who would dare to turn against the people the terror which ought to be felt only by its enemies! Woe to those who, confusing the inevitable errors of civic conduct with the calculated errors of perfidy, or with conspirators' criminal attempts, leave the dangerous schemer to pursue the peaceful citizen! Perish the scoundrel who ventures to abuse the sacred name of liberty, or the redoubtable arms which liberty has entrusted to him, in order to bring mourning or death into patriots' hearts! This abuse has existed, one cannot doubt it. It has been exaggerated, no doubt, by the aristocracy. But if in all the Republic there existed only one virtuous man persecuted by the enemies of liberty, the government's duty would be to seek him out vigorously and give him a dazzling revenge.

But must one conclude from these persecutions, brought upon the patriots by the hypocritical zeal of the counter-revolutionaries, that one must give freedom to the counter-revolutionaries and renounce severity? These new crimes of the aristocracy only show the need for severity. What proves the audacity of our enemies, if not the weakness with which they have been pursued? That is due, in large part, to the slack doctrine that has been preached lately in order to reassure them. If you listen to those counsels, your enemies will reach their goal and will receive from your own hands the ultimate prize of their evil crimes.

How frivolous it would be to regard a few victories achieved by patriotism as the end of all our dangers. Glance over our true situation. You will become aware that vigilance and energy are more necessary for you than ever. An unresponding ill-will everywhere opposes the operations of the government. The inevitable influence of foreign courts is no less active for being more hidden, and no less baneful. One senses that crime, frightened, has only covered its tracks with greater skill.

The internal enemies of the French people are divided into two factions, like two corps of an army. They march under the banners of different colors and by diverse routes, but they march toward the same goal. That goal is the disruption of the popular government, the ruin of the Convention—which is to say, the triumph of tyranny. One of these two factions pushes us toward weakness, the other toward excess. The one wants to change liberty into a frenzied nymph, the other into a prostitute.

The minor intriguers, and often even some good but misled citizens, are ranged in one or the other of these parties. But the chiefs belong to the cause of royalty or aristocracy and always unite against the patriots. The rascals, even when they make war upon each other, hate each other much less than they detest the well-meaning folk. Our country is their prey; they fight each other in order to divide it. But they form a league against those who are defending it.

One group has been given the name of moderates. There is perhaps more wit than accuracy in the term *ultra-revolutionaries* by which the others have been called. That name, which cannot be applied in a single case to the men of good faith whose zeal and ignorance can carry them beyond the sound policy of the revolution, does not precisely characterize the perfidious men whom tyranny hires in order, by a false and deadly digilence, to compromise the sacred principles of our revolution.

The false revolutionary is even more often, perhaps, short of rather than in excess of the revolution. He is moderate; he is insanely patriotic, according to the circumstances. What he will think tomorrow is set for him today by the committees of Prussia, England, Austria, even by those of Muscovy. He opposes energetic measures and exaggerates their import when he has been unable to impede them. He is severe toward innocence but indulgent toward crime, accusing even the guilty who are not rich enough to purchase his silence nor important enough to merit his zeal, but carefully refraining from being compromised to the point of defending slandered courage; now and then discovering plots that have already been discovered, ripping the masks off traitors who are already unmasked and even decapitated, but extolling living and still influential traitors; always eager to embrace the opinion of the moment and not less alert never to enlighten it, and above all never to clash with it; always quick to adopt bold measures, provided they have many drawbacks; slandering those who speak only of the advantages, or better, adding all the amendments which can render the measures harmful; speaking the truth sparingly, and just so much as he must in order to acquire the right to lie with impunity; exuding good drop by drop and pouring out evil in torrents; full of fire for the grand resolutions which signify nothing; worse than indifferent to those which can honor the people's cause and save our country; giving much attention to the forms of patriotism; very much attached, like the devout whose enemy he declares himself to be, to formal observances—he would prefer to wear out a hundred red caps[4] than to do one good deed.

What difference can you find between the false revolutionaries and your moderates? They are servants employed by the same master, or, if you wish, accomplices who feign a quarrel in order better

---

[4] Red caps were a common symbol of revolutionary sympathies.

to hide their crimes. Judge them not by the different words they use but by the identity of the results. He who attacks the National Convention by his senseless speeches, and he who deceives it in order to compromise it, are they not in agreement? He who, by unjust rigors forces patriotism to tremble for itself, invokes amnesty in favor of aristocracy and treason. Such a man, who was calling France to the conquest of the world, had no other goal than to call the tyrants to the conquest of France. The foreign hypocrite who for five years has been proclaiming Paris the capital of the globe only expresses, in another jargon, the anathemas of the vile federalists who dedicated Paris to destruction. To preach atheism is only a way of absolving superstition and accusing philosophy; and the war declared against divinity is only a diversion in royalty's favor.

What other method remains for combatting liberty? Will one, on the example of the first champions of the aristocracy, go about praising the delights of servitude and the benefits of the monarchy, the supernatural genius and the incomparable virtues of kings?

Will one go about proclaiming the vanity of the rights of man and the principles of eternal justice?

Will one go about exhuming the nobility and the clergy or calling for the imprescriptible rights of the high bourgeoisie to their double inheritance?

No. It is much more convenient to don the mask of patriotism in order to disfigure, by insolent parodies, the sublime drama of the revolution, in order to compromise the cause of liberty by a hypocritical moderation or by studied extravagance.

And so the aristocracy establishes itself in popular societies; counter-revolutionary pride hides its plots and its daggers beneath rags; fanaticism smashes its own altars; royalism sings victory hymns to the Republic; the nobility, overwhelmed with memories, tenderly embraces equality in order to smother it; tyranny, tainted with the blood of the defenders of liberty, scatters flowers on their tomb. If all hearts are not changed, how many countenances are masked! How many traitors meddle in our affairs only to ruin them!

Do you wish to test these people? Ask of them, in place of oaths and declamations, real services.

Is action needed? They orate. Is deliberation required? Then they clamor for action. Have the times become peaceful? They obstruct all useful change. Are times stormy? Then they speak of reforming everything, in order to throw everything into confusion. Do you want to keep sedition in check? Then they remind you of Caesar's clemency. Do you want to deliver patriots from persecution? Then they propose to you as a model the firmness of Brutus. They discover that so-and-so was a noble when he served the Republic; they no longer remember this as soon as he has betrayed it. Is peace appropriate? Then they display the rewards of victory. Has war become necessary? They praise the delights of peace. Must our territory be defended? They wish to go and punish the tyrants beyond the mountains and seas. Is it necessary to recapture our own fortresses? They want to take the churches by assault and ascend to heaven. They forget the Austrians in order to make war on the devout. Do we need the faithful support of our allies? They declaim against all the governments of the world and suggest that you put on trial the great Mogul himself. Do the people come to the capital to give thanks to the gods for their victories? They intone lugubrious chants over our previous reverses. Is it a matter of winning new victories? In our midst they sow hatreds, divisions, persecutions, and discouragement. Must we make the sovereignty of the people a reality and concentrate their strength by a strong, respected government? They discover that the principles of government injure popular sovereignty. Must we call for the rights of the people oppressed by the government? They talk only of respect for the laws and of obedience owed to constituted authority.

They have found an admirable expedient for promoting the efforts of the republican government: it is to disorganize it, to degrade it completely, to make war on the patriots who have joined in our successes.

Do you seek the means for provisioning your armies? Are you busy wresting from greed and fear the supplies of food that they have caused to be hidden away? They groan patriotically over the public misery and announce a famine. The desire to foresee evil is for them always a reason for magnifying it. In the north they have killed the hens and deprived us of eggs on the pretext that the hens eat grain. In the south it was a question of destroying the mulberry trees and the orange trees, on the pretext that silk is a luxury article and oranges are superfluous.

You could never have imagined some of the excesses committed by hypocritical counter-revolutionaries in order to blight the cause of the revolution. Would you believe that in the regions where superstition has held the greatest sway, the counter-revolutionaries are not content with burdening religious observances under all the forms that could render them odious, but have spread terror among the people by sowing the rumor that all children under ten and all old men over seventy are going to be killed? This rumor was spread particularly through the former province of Brittany and in the *départements* of the Rhine and the Moselle. It is one of the crimes imputed to [Schneider] the former public prosecutor of the criminal court of Strasbourg. That man's tyrannical follies make everything that has been said of Caligula and Heliogabalus[5] credible; one can scarcely believe it, despite the evidence. He pushed his delirium to the point of commandeering women for his own use—we are told that he even employed that

---

[5] Caligula (A.D. 12–41) and Heliogabalus (or Elagabalus; A.D. 204–222) were Roman emperors infamous for their dissolution and cruelty.

method in selecting a wife. Whence came this sudden swarm of foreigners, priests, nobles, intriguers of all kinds, which at the same instant spread over the length and breadth of the Republic, seeking to execute, in the name of philosophy, a plan of counter-revolution which has only been stopped by the force of public reason? Execrable conception, worthy of the genius of foreign courts leagued against liberty, and of the corruption of all the internal enemies of the Republic!

Thus among the continual miracles worked by the virtue of a great people, intrigue still mingles the baseness of its criminal plots, baseness directed by the tyrants and quickly incorporated into their ridiculous manifestos, in order to keep the ignorant peoples in the mire of shame and the chains of servitude.

Eh! what effects do the heinous crimes of its enemies have upon liberty? Is the sun, veiled by a passing cloud, any less the star which animates nature? Does the impure scum on the beach make the Ocean any less mighty?

In deceitful hands all the remedies for our ills turn into poisons. Everything you can do, everything you can say, they will turn against you, even the truths which we come here to present this very day.

Thus, for example, after having disseminated everywhere the germs of civil war by a violent attack against religious prejudices, these individuals will seek to fortify fanaticism and aristocracy against the very measures, in favor of freedom of religion, that sound policy has prescribed to you. If you had left free play to the conspiracy, it would have produced, sooner or later, a terrible and universal reaction; but if you stop it, they will seek to turn this to their account by urging that you protect the priests and the moderates. You must not even be surprised if the authors of this strategy are the very priests who have most boldly confessed that they were charlatans.

If the patriots, carried away by a pure but thoughtless zeal, have somewhere been made the dupes of their intrigues, they will throw all the blame upon the patriots; because the principal point of their Machiavellian doctrine is to ruin the Republic, by ruining the republicans, as one conquers a country by overthrowing the army which defends it. One can thereby appreciate one of their favorite principles, which is that one must count men as nothing—a maxim of royal origin, which means that one must abandon to them all the friends of liberty.

It is to be noticed that the destiny of men who seek only the public good is to be made the victims of those who seek to advance themselves, and this comes from two causes: first, that the intriguers attack using the vices of the old regime; second, that the patriots defend themselves only with the virtues of the new.

Such an internal situation ought to seem to you worthy of all your attention, above all if you reflect that at the same time you have the tyrants of Europe to combat, a million and two hundred thousand men under arms to maintain, and that the government is obliged continually to repair, with energy and vigilance, all the injuries which the innumerable multitude of our enemies has prepared for us during the course of five years.

What is the remedy for all these evils? We know no other than the development of that general motive force of the Republic—virtue.

Democracy perishes by two kinds of excess: either the aristocracy of those who govern, or else popular scorn for the authorities whom the people themselves have established, scorn which makes each clique, each individual take unto himself the public power and bring the people through excessive disorders, to annihilation or to the power of one man.

The double task of the moderates and the false revolutionaries is to toss us back and forth perpetually between these two perils.

But the people's representatives can avoid them both, because government is always the master at being just and wise; and, when it has that character, it is sure of the confidence of the people.

It is indeed true that the goal of all our enemies is to dissolve the Convention. It is true that the tyrant of Great Britain and his allies promise their parliament and subjects that they will deprive you of your energy and of the public confidence which you have merited; that is the first instruction for all their agents.

But it is a truth which ought to be regarded as commonplace in politics that a great body invested with the confidence of a great people can be lost only through its own failings. Your enemies know this; therefore do not doubt that they are applying themselves above all to awaken in your midst all the passions which can further their sinister designs.

What can they do against the national representation if they do not succeed in beguiling it into impolitic acts which can furnish the excuse for their criminal declamations? They are therefore necessarily obliged to desire two kinds of agents, those who seek to degrade it by their speeches, and those, in its very bosom, who do their utmost to deceive it in order to compromise its glory and the interests of the Republic.

In order to attack this Convention with success, it was useful to begin civil war against the representatives in the *départements* which had justified your confidence, and against the Committee of Public Safety; and so they have been attacked by men who seemed to be fighting among themselves.

What better could they do than to paralyze the government of the Convention and to smash its mainsprings at the moment which is to decide the destiny of the Republic and of the tyrants?

Far from us is the idea that there yet exists in our midst a single man weakling enough to wish to serve the tyrants' cause! But farther from us still is the crime, for which we would not be pardoned, of deceiving the National Convention and betraying the French people by a culpable silence! For this is the good fortune of a free people, that truth, which is the scourge of despots, is always its strength and safety. Now it is true that there still exists a danger for our liberty, perhaps the only serious danger which remains for it to undergo. That danger is a plan which has existed for rallying all the enemies of the Republic by reviving the spirit of faction; for persecuting patriots, disheartening them, ruining the faithful agents of the republican government, rendering inadequate the most essential parts of our public service. Some have wished to deceive the Convention about men and about things; they have sought to put it on the wrong track about the causes of abuses which they have at the same time exaggerated, so as to make them irremediable; they have studiously filled it with false terrors, in order to lead it astray or paralyze it; they seek to divide it, above all to divide the representatives sent out to the *départements* and the Committee of Public Safety. They have sought to influence the former to contradict the measures of the central authority, in order to bring disorder and confusion; they have sought to embitter them upon their return, in order to make them the unknowing instruments of a cabal. The foreigners profit from all private passions, even from abused patriotism.

They first decided on going straight to their goal by slandering the Committee of Public Safety; they flattered themselves aloud that it would succumb under the weight of its laborious duties. Victory and the good fortune of the French people defended it. Since that time they have decided on praising it while paralyzing it and destroying the fruit of its labors. All those vague declamations against necessary agents of the Committee; all those plans for disorganization, disguised under the name of reforms, already rejected by the Convention, and reproduced today with a strange affectation; this eagerness to extol the intriguers whom the Committee of Public Safety was obliged to remove; this terror inspired in good citizens; this indulgence with which one flatters the conspirators—this entire scheme of imposture and intrigue, whose principal author is a man [Fabre d'Églantine] whom you have driven from your bosom, is directed against the National Convention and tends to give reality to the vows of all the enemies of France.

It is since the time when this scheme was made public and made real by public actions, that aristocracy and royalism have again begun to raise their insolent heads and patriotism has again been persecuted in a part of the Republic, that the national authority has experienced resistance of a sort which the intriguers had not lately displayed. Even if these indirect attacks had served only to divide the attention and energy of those who have to carry the immense burden which is your charge, and to distract them too often from the great measures of public safety, to occupy themselves with thwarting dangerous intrigues,—even so, they could still be considered as a division useful to our enemies.

But let us reassure ourselves. Here is the sanctuary of truth; here reside the founders of the Republic, the avengers of humanity and the destroyers of tyrants.

Here, to destroy an abuse it suffices to point out its existence. It suffices for us to appeal, in the name of our country, from counsels of self-love or from the weaknesses of individuals, to the virtue and the glory of the National Convention.

We are beginning a solemn debate upon all the objects of its anxiety, and everything that can influence the progress of the revolution. We adjure it not to permit any particular hidden interest to usurp ascendancy here over the general will of the assembly and the indestructible power of reason.

We will limit ourselves today to proposing that by your formal approval you sanction the moral and political truths upon which your internal administration and the stability of the Republic ought to be founded, as you have already sanctioned the principles of your conduct toward foreign peoples. Thereby you will rally all good citizens, you will take hope away from the conspirators; you will assure your progress, and you will confound the kings' intrigues and slanders; you will honor your cause and your character in the eyes of all peoples.

Give the French people this new gage of your zeal to protect patriotism, of your inflexible justice for the guilty, and of your devotion to the people's cause. Order that the principles of political morality which we just expounded will be proclaimed, in your name, within and without the Republic.

Further Readings

Few periods have so engaged the historians' attention as the French Revolution, and there is an enormous literature on the subject. Thomas Carlyle, *The French Revolution* (1837, many editions), is a classic of English historical writing. George Lefebvre, *The Coming of the French Revolution,* translated by Elizabeth Evanson (Princeton, NJ: Princeton University Press, 1947), and Albert Soboul, *The French Revolution, 1789–1799: From the Storming of the Bastille to Napoleon,* translated by Alan Forrest and Colin Jones (London: NLB, 1974), are two of the best of the modern studies. Robert Palmer, *The World of the French Revolution* (New York: Harper and Row, 1971), presents a European view of events to 1799, while Stanley Loomis, *Paris in the Terror: June 1793–July 1794* (Philadelphia: J. B. Lippencott Company, 1964), concentrates on the murder of Marat, the execution of Georges-Jacques Danton, and the final days of Robespierre. Georges Lefebvre, *The Thermidorians and the Directory: Two Phases of the French Revolution,* translated by Robert Baldick (New York: Random House, 1964), discusses events following the fall of Robespierre.

Robespierre has been the subject of numerous bibliographical studies. Otto J. Scott, *Robespierre: The Voice of Virtue* (New York: Mason and Lipscomb, 1974), is a popular and readable account. George Rudé, *Robespierre:*

Portrait of a Revolutionary Democrat (New York: Viking, 1975), is an excellent synthesis by an active writer in the field. Rudé has also edited *Robespierre* (Englewood Cliffs, NJ: Prentice-Hall, 1967), which uses Robespierre's own words, those of his contemporaries, and those of leading historians to form an unusual three-part perspective on the man.

Revolutionary France has inspired a number of literary works, many set against the drama of the Reign of Terror. Perhaps the most famous of these is Charles Dickens, *A Tale of Two Cities* (many editions).

DISCUSSION QUESTIONS: THE EARLY MODERN WORLD

1. The search for the secret of the "good life" is a recurring theme in literature. What is the secret according to Voltaire, in *Candide,* and Robespierre, in his "Speech of 17 Pluviôse"? Olaudah Equiano, in *The Interesting Narrative,* attempts to portray his native village as the "good life." What is the secret of his people? Can you find any similarities among these examples? What do you consider to be the necessary qualities of the ideal society? Would one of them be that every individual should be sure of his or her position and function in life?

2. The decline of native cultures and traditional ways of life in the face of European expansion and growing industrialism is a common concern of modern authors. How is this problem reflected in the "Speeches of Minavavana and Pontiac" and *The Interesting Narrative of the Life of Olaudah Equiano*? How did Westernization threaten these societies—directly or through more subtle means? Do you think such forces may still be at work today, breaking down our traditional attitudes and patterns of living? What do you think people will be like a century from now, and how do you think they will live? Will there be room for the freedom and variety we enjoy today?

3. Good manners are sometimes called the cement that binds society together. In *The Dream of the Red Chamber,* how does the elaborate code of conduct act to reduce family frictions? What effect do strong-willed and direct individuals have on family harmony? What are some modern forms of good manners and proper conduct, and how do they act to reduce friction and promote harmony? Should a greater emphasis be placed on good manners in today's society? Why or why not?

4. In *The Dream of the Red Chamber,* Pao-yu is presented as a spoiled and ill-mannered youth. From what attitude of his did his lack of manners spring? We might consider his attitudes admirable, but does that excuse his lack of proper conduct? In the same work, Hsueh Pan is also presented as a spoiled and ill-mannered youth. How do his bad manners differ from those of Pao-yu, and why? Are good manners simply a social convention, or are they the necessary first step of self-discipline leading towards responsible social conduct?

5. In *The Treasury of Loyal Retainers,* how does Yuranosuke play upon the difference between "proper manners" and "proper conduct?" Is the play saying that proper manners and proper conduct are two different things, and that only individuals of great principle can appreciate this distinction? What do you think? What is the difference between manners and conduct?

6. The distinction between love and physical desire is difficult to make. In *The Dream of the Red Chamber,* the Goddess of Disillusionment attempts to teach that distinction to Pao-yu. What is that difference, according to the Goddess? Can there be such a thing as love between a man and a woman, or is the Goddess saying that the only real love is a concern for the welfare of mankind?

7. In *The Treasury of Loyal Retainers*, Yuranosuke tries to convince Heiemon that duty is the responsibility of those who are richer and more powerful. Heiemon argues that duty weighs equally upon all. Is Heiemon's position valid and, if so, how important an idea is this? Replace the word *duty* with *civic responsibility:* should civic responsibility bear equally upon all, or should the greater obligation of defending and preserving society be borne by those who have benefitted the most from society?

8. When speaking of justice, Aristotle says that different degrees of merit must be rewarded proportionately, not equally. In this sense, how is the behavior of Pao-yu, in *The Dream of the Red Chamber*, and Tu Shao-ch'ing, in *The Scholars*, unjust? If their behavior is unjust, is it not also antisocial?

9. Literary Romanticism brought with it a new view of Nature consonant with its new view of human nature and of society. Compare the role of Nature in *The Sufferings of Young Werther* and in the roughly contemporary *The Scholars*, as well as in *The Sorrows of Misfortune* in Part II. How do these views of Nature differ, and what do they suggest of the differing views of human nature and of society held by these authors and their culture? What do you think the modern view of Nature is, and how does it compare with these earlier conceptions?

10. The passionate youth struggling against society's constraints is a popular literary figure. Werther, in *The Sufferings of Young Werther*, and Pao-yu, in *The Dream of the Red Chamber*, are two examples drawn from two different cultures. Why do you think that their audiences found these two characters to be attractive? Is it possible that people resent social constraints even in a well-ordered society, and take pleasure in reading stories of revolt? To what extent is the theme of social revolt an important element in Molière's *Love's the Best Doctor* and in *The Scholars*? What social function do you think such tales play, and is the theme best suited for comedy, as in *Love's the Best Doctor*, or tragedy, as in *The Sufferings of Young Werther*?

11. A "just war" was once defined as the act of killing people for a cause worth killing people for. The problem with this definition is determining what cause is worth killing people for. What causes are advanced by Minavavana and Pontiac in the "Speeches of Minavavana and Pontiac," by Yuranosuke and Heiemon in *The Treasury of Loyal Retainers*, and by Robespierre in his "Speech of 17 Pluviôse"? Which—if any—of these causes do you find acceptable, and why? How do you think Candide might regard them? A lot of people were killed in the Thirty Years' War: for what cause did they die, according to *The Adventures of a Simpleton*? What was considered a just cause for killing among Olaudah Equiano's people?

12. In *The Dream of the Red Chamber*, the Goddess of Disillusionment seems to say that a concern for the welfare of mankind is the only real form of love. If so, is Candide's achievement of the "good life" admirable? Hasn't he simply abandoned any concern for the welfare of mankind, and said that the only way to get by in this world is to mind your own business? What is the proper balance between minding your own business and showing a concern for the welfare of others?

13. Consider Candide as a representative of the Enlightenment approach to life and Werther as an example of Romanticism. Each is confronted with unhappy and painful situations; how do their reactions differ and why? Do these differences reflect the contrasts between the views of human nature and the Universe presented by Enlightenment and Romantic thinkers? Is Candide or Werther the more admirable character, and why? How would you expect a modern young man to behave in similar circumstances, and how may Darwin, Freud, and Einstein have contributed to such different attitudes and conduct?

PART II

INDUSTRIALISM AND DEMOCRACY

1789 TO 1914

	1913	1929
EUROPE	**1913** D. H. Lawrence: SONS AND LOVERS **1914–1918** World War I **1917** Bolshevik Revolution **1922** T. S. Eliot: *The Waste Land* **1922** Mussolini's march on Rome **1924–1925** Adolf Hitler: *Mein Kampf*	**1929** Erich Marie Remarque: ALL QUIET ON THE WESTERN FRONT **1931** Frank O'Connor: GUESTS OF THE NATION **1931** Aldous Huxley: BRAVE NEW WORLD **1932** Ortega y Gasset's *Revolt of the Masses* published in English **1936–1939** Spanish Civil War **1939–1945** World War II
SOUTHWEST ASIA AND AFRICA	**b. 1914** Flavien Ranaivo: *Choice* **b. 1916** Bernard Dadie: *Dry Your Tears, Africa* **1920** Faisal proclaimed king of Syria **1923** Kermal Attaturk, president of Turkey **b. 1924** Dennis Brutus: *Nightsong: Country*	**1925–1979** Pahlavi dynasty, Iran **1926** Ali Esfandiari: *The Soldier's Family* **1932–1967** Christopher Okigbo: *Love Apart* **1935** Italian invasion of Ethiopia begins **b. 1936** Valente Malangatatna: *To the Anxious Mother* **1939** Negritude movement begins
SOUTH AND SOUTHEAST ASIA	**1915** Annie Bebant: *India A Nation* **1918** Ananda Coomaraswamy: *The Dance of Shiva* **1919–1924** Khilafai movement led by Muhammad Ali **1920–1922** Gandhi's first civil disobedience movement **1922** Gandhi's STATEMENT IN THE GREAT TRIAL OF 1922	**1927** Sukarno founds Indonesian Nationalist party **1930** Gandhi's march to the sea **1932** Constitutional government established in Siam **1935** Government of India Act grants provincial self-government **1935** Commonwealth government established in Philippines
EAST ASIA	**1914** Japanese violation of China's neutrality **1915** Ch'en Tu-hsiu founds journal *New Youth* **1919** Kita Ikki: *Outline for the Reconstruction of Japan* **1921** World tour of Crown Prince Hirohito **1922** Sino-Japanese treaty	**1929** Kobayashi Takiji: *The Cannery Boat* **1931** Japan seizes Manchuria **1931** Pa Chin: *Family* **1934** Long March of the Chinese Communists **1937–1945** Sino-Japanese War
THE AMERICAS AND THE PACIFIC	**1915** Mariano Azuela: *The Underdogs* **1917** U.S. enters World War I **1918** César Vallejo: *Los Heraldos Negros* **1919** Prohibition begins in the U.S.	**1926** Langston Hughes: *The Weary Blues* **1929** The Great Depression begins **1933** Franklin D. Roosevelt's New Deal **1934** Jorge Icaza: *The Villagers* **1938** Alfred Herbert: *Capricornia* **1939** Lillian Hellman: *The Little Foxes*

1941	1953	1973
1941–1945 Mass murder of Jews **1942** Albert Camus: *The Stranger* **1943** Jean Paul Sartre: *Being and Nothingness* **1947** Marshall Plan **1949** Germany divided **1949** NATO alliance	**1953** Death of Stalin **1954** Mario Soldati: *The Capri Letters* **1955** West Germany joins NATO **1955** Warsaw Pact **1957** European Economic Community **1960** Yuri Gagarin, first man in space	**1973** Chancellor Helmut Schmidt of West Germany **1979** Mother Teresa: THE NOBEL PRIZE ADDRESS **1980** Solidarity movement in Poland **1985** Rise of Mikhail Gorbachev **1987** INF treaty between U.S.S.R. and U.S.
1946 Peter Abrahams: *Mine Boy* **b. 1946** Odia Ofeimun: *Without You* **1948** Apartheid begins in South Africa **1949** Founding of Israel; First Arab–Israeli War	**1956** Second Arab–Israeli War **1957** Ghana becomes independent Black African nation **1957** Ahmad Shamlu: *Fresh Air* **1958** Chinua Achebe: *Things Fall Apart* **1960–1975** Independence movement sweeps Africa **1967** Third Arab–Israeli (Six Day) War	**1974** Fourth Arab–Israeli War **1979** U.S.S.R. invades Afghanistan **1979** Iranian Revolution **1980** Iran–Iraq War begins **1981** President Sadat of Egypt assassinated **1986** Desmond Tutu, first black archbishop of Cape Town
1946 Philippines gain independence **1947** M. N. Roy: *New Humanism: A Manifesto* **1947** India gains independence **1948** Gandhi assassinated **1949** Indonesia gains independence	**1954** South East Asia Treaty Organization **1955** Bandung Conference, Indonesia **1956** T. S. Pillai: *Shrimps* **1961** Increasing U.S. involvement in Vietnam **1965** India–Pakistan War **1966** Indira Gandhi becomes prime minister of India	**1971** Independence of People's Republic of Bangladesh **1973** U.S. forces withdraw from Vietnam **1975** Communists takes over Vietnam, Laos, and Cambodia **1979** ASEAN protests Vietnam's invasion of Cambodia **1984** Indira Gandhi assassinated by Sikh terrorists
1941–1945 Pacific war with Japan (THE NIGHT OF A THOUSAND SUICIDES) **1945** Atomic bombing of Hiroshima and Nagasaki **1946–1949** Civil war in China **1949** People's Republic of China established **1949** Mao Zedong: ON THE PEOPLE'S DEMOCRATIC DICTATORSHIP	**1950–1953** Korean War **1954** French defeat at Dien Bien Phu **1956** Japan admitted to United Nations **1956** Mishima Yukio: *The Temple of the Golden Pavilion* **1965–1969** The Great Proletarian Cultural Revolution, China	**1971** People's Republic of China joins U.N. **1971** Kurahashi Yumiko: *The Bridge of Dreams* **1972** President Nixon visits Beijing **1976** Death of Mao Zedong **1977** China begins liberalization under Deng Xiaoping
1941 U.S. enters World War II **1941** Ciro Alegría: *Broad and Alien is the World* **1944** Tennessee Williams: *The Glass Menagerie* **1945** United Nations organized **1947** U.N. Security Council approves U.S. trusteeship for Pacific islands **1949** Arthur Miller: *Death of a Salesman*	**1952** Ernest Hemingway: *The Old Man and the Sea* **1959** Fidel Castro's victory in Cuba **1963** President Kennedy assassinated **1967** Gabriel García Márquez: *One Hundred Years of Solitude* **1968** Martin Luther King, Jr., assassinated **1969** Neil Armstrong, first man on the moon	**1974** President Nixon resigns **1975** Helsinki Accords **1979** Civil wars begin in Nicaragua and El Salvador **1981** Beth Henley: *Crimes of the Heart* **1984** Octavio Paz: ONE EARTH

Two major developments dominated the history of Europe during this period. The Industrial Revolution, reinforced by the steady progress of scientific discovery, fostered an unprecedented growth in Western wealth and power. At the same time, the sometimes fitful advance of democratic ideals led to fundamental changes within Western society itself. By 1914, however, Europe stood at the apex of its power, and the Western powers and their way of life dominated the globe.

The era was born in conflict. The growing radicalism of the French Revolution, as exemplified by Robespierre's "Speech of 17 Pluviôse" in Part I, made way for an eventual reaction in the form of the usurpation of power by Napoleon Bonaparte and the establishment of the French Empire. In many ways, Napoleon represented the ideal of the Romantic intellectuals, the great man who would shape events by the force of his own will. Drawing upon this support, posing as the friend of democratic and liberal reform movements, and tapping the patriotic fervor roused by the French Republic, Napoleon succeeded in creating a military machine of hitherto unparalleled size and efficiency. It was not until his disastrous invasion of Russia in 1812, an episode of which is portrayed in Tolstoy's *War and Peace,* that his power was effectively challenged. Napoleon's defeat at Waterloo in 1816 at the hands of a federation of European powers finally ended the French threat.

Following their victory over the French, the allied nations agreed to attempt to maintain peace through a balance of power and to cooperate in curbing revolutionary movements within Europe. By and large, they succeeded. Europe enjoyed almost a century of relative peace and stability until the entire system collapsed in 1914 with the onset of the First World War. By this time, however, the Industrial Revolution had succeeded in changing traditional patterns of life throughout the world.

Based upon coal-, steam-, and water-powered spinning machines, looms, furnaces, forges, and other tools capable of producing vast quantities of goods, the Industrial Revolution began in Great Britain but soon spread to other countries. Coal-powered locomotives and steam-driven ships allowed the industrial powers to reach out to acquire the enormous amount of raw materials their factories consumed and to open up the vast new markets required to absorb their production. Coupled with these industrial developments were scientific advances in medicine that reduced infant mortality and extended the average life span; in physics that harnessed electricity to provide light, power, and long-distance communication; and in chemistry that produced new fuels and synthetic materials.

One of the effects of these developments was a significant increase in Europe's population. The problems of population pressure had already been noted in the eighteenth century and had been discussed by Thomas Malthus in *An Essay on the Principle of Population,* but the actual results had not been foreseen. An industrial Europe not only needed, but could support, a greatly increased population, and there were ample opportunities for any surplus population on Europe's overseas frontiers. *Democracy In America* illustrates some of the fascination, as well as some of the reservations, Europeans felt about the new societies developing in these lands, but "The Death of Beth" suggests how quickly these societies became what were, in all essential respects, European in outlook, organization, and values. This expansion of the base of Western civilization was not obtained without cost. "Wounded Knee" illustrates how indigenous cultures were often ruthlessly crushed, and "The Gaucho: Martín Fierro" is an example of how the individualism of those who bore the brunt of settling the frontiers was submerged in the more settled economies that soon evolved.

European power grew so great that non-Western cultures could no longer dictate the degree to which they would accept Western influences. Seeing the inevitability of the matter, Japan embarked upon a complete program of Westernization in 1868. In an extraordinary example of cultural adaptation and economic development, only forty years later its Western-style army and fleet were capable of defeating Russia, a major European power. China was less open to change. As "The Sorrows of Misfortune" and *The Tale of Kieu* demonstrate, traditional Chinese culture and institutions were relatively unchanged by Western influences as late as 1820. In the 1840s, however, Great Britain forced China to grant it commercial privileges and cede coastal ports. Other nations followed, and China was quickly divided up by the European powers into various zones of influence. Steam-powered gunboats carried Western influences along Chinese rivers deep into the interior, and the imperial government steadily lost power and credibility with its own people. It was not until 1912, however, that the Manchu dynasty was finally overthrown. Despite a general commitment to Westernization on the part of the revolutionaries, China began a long descent into anarchy and civil war that did not end until 1949.

In India, Great Britain extended its power steadily with the aid of river fleets and a growing rail system. In 1858, the economic domination that the British had established over the region was transformed into political authority, and India was proclaimed a part of the British Empire.

The badly divided lands of Islam were threatened on all sides by European power. The Muslim community of India passed under British control, Russia pressed against Persia and the Ottoman empire from the north, and the French extended their sovereignty over the Muslim states of Northwest Africa. There was resistance to these encroachments, as *Commentary on the Commentator* demonstrates, but such dissent had little immediate effect on the overwhelmingly richer and more powerful imperial nations of the West.

Central Africa remained the one area that continued to defy European domination, and here it was disease and terrain that were the effective obstacles. As a consequence, from the middle of the century, it was Africa that attracted European adventurers such as "Stanley and Livingstone." The development of quinine protected explorers from fever and allowed them to open up the country, and steamboats and railroads allowed the settlers that followed them to develop it. By 1914, all of Africa, with the exception of Ethiopia and Liberia, was in European hands. Thus, by the end of the period, Western dominance of the globe, either directly or indirectly, was virtually complete.

Generally speaking, the Westerners of the day, as well as many of their subject peoples, were convinced of the natural superiority of the West and its inhabitants. Although they were aware that they owed their dominance to their science and technology, many Westerners felt that science and technology, as well as freedom and stability, could flourish only within a Western way of life, replete with Western values and Western political institutions, and under a Western God. Many even believed that non-Western peoples were genetically incapable of adapting to the new way of life that the Industrial Revolution was thrusting upon the world and that, as a consequence, Westerners must lead and govern the "lesser races" of the globe for the foreseeable future. The outbreak of the First World War in the late summer of 1914 shattered that illusion.

An Essay on the Principle of Population

The Newtonian view of the universe gave the intellectuals of the Enlightenment a model for their endeavors. If reason could discover the impersonal laws that govern physical phenomena with such mathematical regularity and precision, then reason might also disclose objective principles of similar precision to describe human attitudes and actions. If this were so, human affairs could be managed on a scientific basis and—or at least so thought the thinkers of the Enlightenment—much of the world's folly and misery could be ended.

Near the close of the eighteenth century, when the rationalism of the Enlightenment was already giving way to the new intellectual orientations of Romanticism, two books within the rationalist tradition appeared that would greatly influence the governmental and social policies of the developed nations of the world and would be the source of continuing debate among policymakers. The first was Adam Smith's *The Wealth of Nations* (1776), which argued that there existed impersonal economic laws that would regulate economic activity even in the absence of governmental management, and, what is more, would do so more effectively and efficiently. *The Wealth of Nations* helped to undermine the prevailing mercantilist economic philosophy and to lay the bases of the *laissez faire* economic philosophy and free-trade policies adopted by many of the Western nations. The second work was a slim pamphlet published in 1798, and entitled, *An Essay on the Principle of Population, as it Affects the Future Improvement of Society*. Although published anonymously, it was the work of an English cleric, Thomas Robert Malthus (1766–1834).

Malthus was a child of the Enlightenment. His father, a friend and admirer of Rousseau, had his son privately educated by tutors dedicated to Enlightenment ideals. In 1784, Robert entered Jesus College, Cambridge, where he studied mathematics. He published in

From Thomas Robert Malthus, *An Essay on the Principle of Population*, edited by Philip Appleman (New York: W. W. Norton and Co., Inc., 1976), pp. 18–26, 46–53, 55–56, 62–65, 94–95, 120–123.

the field and in 1784 was elected a Fellow of the college. His father and he enjoyed intellectual discussions, and, on one occasion, his father argued that human society could be greatly improved and human happiness and prosperity could be greatly increased. Robert had fundamental reservations on the issue and wrote a refutation of his father's position. His father was so impressed by this rebuttal that he urged his son to publish it. It soon appeared as *An Essay on the Principle of Population.*

Malthus' argument was both simple and compelling. He suggested that, while the production of goods could be increased arithmetically (that is, in a sequence such as 2, 4, 6, 8 . . .), population increased geometrically (a sequence such as 2, 4, 8, 16 . . .). Thus, no matter what improvements might appear in the means of production, the increase of demand would inevitably outstrip any increase in supply. Malthus held that history demonstrated that although peoples might attempt to limit their numbers of restraint, in the last analysis, only war, starvation, disease, and poverty could check population increase. Although he later softened this position, his basic proposition remained the same.

His work created much furor. Its pessimistic tone was unpleasant, it clearly suggested that England's charitable institutions were worse than ineffective, and it was, so its critics held, unchristian. And yet its reasoning was fascinating and cogent. Malthus was made a professor of political economy, probably the first in the world, at the East India Company college at Haileybury, where he continued to teach, write, and expound his views until his death. As time passed, Malthus' dire predictions failed to materialize and his theory was ignored in favor of new, mathematical economic models.

The problem was, of course, that Malthus failed to appreciate the productive potential of the Industrial Revolution and a century of relative peace. Advances in technology allowed the developed nations of the world to increase their gross national products at a rate of about four to five percent annually through much of the nineteenth century. Population simply did not keep pace with this increase, and the "Malthusian doctrine" long seemed irrelevant to the world of reality. By the middle of the twentieth century, however, new factors began to appear that changed this situation. Medical advances, particularly in underdeveloped nations, made possible unprecedented increases in population. At the same time, it was noted that increased production was dependent upon limited resources such as oil and gas. Finally, the increase of the world's population was beginning to describe a curve approximating the geometric progression predicted in *An Essay on the Principle of Population.* A new generation of readers was introduced to Robert Malthus.

Questions

1. How does Malthus present the different rates of increase of population and production?

2. What are the various checks on population increase? What are the ultimate checks?

3. Upon what does Malthus believe the happiness of a country depends?

4. What degree of improvement in the human condition does Malthus believe to be possible?

AN ESSAY ON POPULATION

I have read some of the speculations on the perfectibility of man and of society with great pleasure. I have been warmed and delighted with the enchanting picture which they hold forth. I ardently wish for such happy improvements. But I see great, and, to my understanding, unconquerable difficulties in the way to them. These difficulties it is my present purpose to state, declaring, at the same time, that so far from exulting in them, as a cause of triumph over the friends of innovation, nothing would give me greater pleasure than to see them completely removed.

The most important argument that I shall adduce is certainly not new. The principles on which it depends have been explained in part by Hume, and more at large by Dr. Adam Smith. It has been advanced and applied to the present subject, though not with its proper weight, or in the most forcible point of view, by Mr. Wallace, and it may probably have been stated by many writers that I have never met with. I should certainly therefore not think of advancing it again, though I mean to place it in a point of view in some degree different from any that I have hitherto seen, if it had ever been fairly and satisfactorily answered.

The cause of this neglect on the part of the advocates for the perfectibility of mankind is not easily accounted for. I cannot doubt the talents of such men as Godwin and Condorcet. I am unwilling to doubt their candour. To my understanding, and probably to that of most others, the difficulty appears insurmountable. Yet these men of acknowledged ability and penetration scarcely deign to notice it, and hold on their course in such speculations, with unabated ardour and undiminished confidence. I have certainly no right to say that they purposely shut their eyes to such arguments. I ought rather to doubt the validity of them, when neglected by such men, however forcibly their truth may strike my own mind. Yet in this respect it must be acknowledged that we are all of us too prone to err. If I saw a glass of wine repeatedly presented to a man, and he took no notice of it, I should be apt to think that he was blind or uncivil. A juster philosophy might teach me rather to think that my eyes deceived me and that the offer was not really what I conceived it to be.

In entering upon the argument I must premise that I put out of the question, at present, all mere conjectures, that is, all suppositions, the probable realization of which cannot be inferred upon any just philosophical grounds. A writer may tell me that he thinks man will ultimately become an ostrich. I cannot properly contradict him. But before he can expect to bring any reasonable person over to his opinion, he ought to shew that the necks of mankind have been gradually elongating, that the lips have grown harder and more prominent, that the legs and feet are daily altering their shape, and that the hair is beginning to change into stubs of feathers. And till the probability of so wonderful a conversion can be shewn, it is surely lost time and lost eloquence to expatiate on the happiness of man in such a state; to describe his powers, both of running and flying, to paint him in a condition where all narrow luxuries would be contemned, where he would be employed only in collecting the necessaries of life, and where, consequently, each man's share of labour would be light, and his portion of leisure ample.

I think I may fairly make two postulata.

First, That food is necessary to the existence of man.

Secondly, That the passion between the sexes is necessary and will remain nearly in its present state.

These two laws, ever since we have had any knowledge of mankind, appear to have been fixed laws of our nature, and, as we have not hitherto seen any alteration in them, we have no right to conclude that they will ever cease to be what they now are, without an immediate act of power in that Being who first arranged the system of the universe, and for the advantage of his creatures, still executes, according to fixed laws, all its various operations.

I do not know that any writer has supposed that on this earth man will ultimately be able to live without food. But Mr. Godwin has conjectured that the passion between the sexes may in time be extinguished. As, however, he calls this part of his work a deviation into the land of conjecture, I will not dwell longer upon it at present than to say that the best arguments for the perfectibility of man are drawn from a contemplation of the great progress that he has already made from the savage state and the difficulty of saying where he is to stop. But towards the extinction of the passion between the sexes, no progress whatever has hitherto been made. It appears to exist in as much force at present as it did two thousand or four thousand years ago. There are individual exceptions now as there always have been. But, as these exceptions do not appear to increase in number, it would surely be a very unphilosophical mode of arguing, to infer merely from the existence of an exception, that the exception would, in time, become the rule, and the rule the exception.

Assuming then, my postulata as granted, I say that the power of population is indefinitely greater than the power in the earth to produce subsistence for man.

Population, when unchecked, increases in a geometrical ratio. Subsistence increases only in an arithmetical ratio. A slight acquaintance with numbers will shew the immensity of the first power in comparison of the second.

By that law of our nature which makes food necessary to the life of man, the effects of these two unequal powers must be kept equal.

This implies a strong and constantly operating check on population from the difficulty of subsistence. This difficulty must fall some where and must necessarily be severely felt by a large portion of mankind.

Through the animal and vegetable kingdoms, nature has scattered the seeds of life abroad with the most profuse and liberal hand. She has been comparatively sparing in the room and the nourishment necessary to rear them. The germs of existence contained in this spot of earth, with ample food and ample room to expand in, would fill millions of worlds in the course of a few thousand years. Necessity, that imperious all pervading law of nature, restrains them within the prescribed bounds. The race of plants and the race of animals shrink under this great restrictive law. And the race of man cannot, by any efforts of reason, escape from it. Among plants and animals its effects are waste of seed, sickness, and premature death. Among mankind, misery and vice. The former, misery, is an absolutely necessary consequence of it. Vice is a highly probable consequence, and we therefore see it abundantly prevail, but it ought not, perhaps, to be called an absolutely necessary consequence. The ordeal of virtue is to resist all temptation to evil.

This natural inequality of the two powers of population and of production in the earth and that great law of our nature which must constantly keep their effects equal form the great difficulty that to me appears insurmountable in the way to the perfectibility of society. All other arguments are of slight and subordinate consideration in comparison of this. I see no way by which man can escape from the weight of this law which pervades all animated nature. No fancied equality, no agrarian regulations in their utmost extent, could remove the pressure of it even for a single century. And it appears, therefore, to be decisive against the possible existence of a society, all the members of which should live in ease, happiness, and comparative leisure, and feel no anxiety about providing the means of subsistence for themselves and families.

Consequently, if the premises are just, the argument is conclusive against the perfectibility of the mass of mankind.

◇ ◇ ◇

Let us now take any spot of earth, this Island for instance, and see in what ratio the subsistence it affords can be supposed to increase. We will begin with it under its present state of cultivation.

If I allow that by the best possible policy, by breaking up more land and by great encouragements to agriculture, the produce of

Thomas Robert Malthus.

this Island may be doubled in the first twenty-five years, I think it will be allowing as much as any person can well demand.

In the next twenty-five years, it is impossible to suppose that the produce could be quadrupled. It would be contrary to all our knowledge of the qualities of land. The very utmost that we can conceive is that the increase in the second twenty-five years might equal the present produce. Let us then take this for our rule, though certainly far beyond the truth, and allow that by great exertion, the whole produce of the Island might be increased every twenty-five years, by a quantity of subsistence equal to what it at present produces. The most enthusiastic speculator cannot suppose a greater increase than this. In a few centuries it would make every acre of land in the Island like a garden.

Yet this ratio of increase is evidently arithmetical.

It may be fairly said, therefore, that the means of subsistence increase in an arithmetical ratio. Let us now bring the effects of these two ratios together.

The population of the Island is computed to be about seven millions, and we will suppose the present produce equal to the support of such a number. In the first twenty-five years the population would be fourteen millions, and the food being also doubled, the means of subsistence would be equal to this increase. In the next twenty-five years the population would be twenty-eight millions, and the means of subsistence only equal to the support of twenty-one millions. In the next period the population would be fifty-six millions, and the means of subsistence just sufficient for half that number. And at the conclusion of the first century the population would be one hundred and twelve millions and the means of subsistence only equal to the support of thirty-five millions, which would leave a population of seventy-seven millions totally unprovided for.

A great emigration necessarily implies unhappiness of some kind or other in the country that is deserted. For few persons will leave their families, connections, friends, and native land, to seek a settlement in untried foreign climes, without some strong subsisting causes of uneasiness where they are, or the hope of some great advantages in the place to which they are going.

But to make the argument more general and less interrupted by the partial views of emigration, let us take the whole earth, instead of one spot, and suppose that the restraints to population were universally removed. If the subsistence for man that the earth affords was to be increased every twenty-five years by a quantity equal to what the whole world at present produces, this would allow the power of production in the earth to be absolutely unlimited and its ratio to increase much greater than we can conceive that any possible exertions of mankind could make it.

◇ ◇ ◇

The way in which these effects are produced seems to be this.

We will suppose the means of subsistence in any country just equal to the easy support of its inhabitants. The constant effort towards population, which is found to act even in the most vicious societies, increases the number of people before the means of subsistence are increased. The food therefore which before supported seven millions must now be divided among seven millions and a half or eight millions. The poor consequently must live much worse, and many of them be reduced to severe distress. The number of labourers also being above the proportion of the work in the market, the price of labour must tend toward a decrease, while the price of provisions would at the same time tend to rise. The labourer therefore must work harder to earn the same as he did before. During this season of distress, the discouragements to marriage and the difficulty of rearing a family are so great that population is at a stand. In the mean time the cheapness of labour, the plenty of labourers, and the necessity of an increased industry amongst them, encourage cultivators to employ more labour upon their land, to turn up fresh soil, and to manure and improve more completely what is already in tillage, till ultimately the means of subsistence become in the same proportion to the population as at the period from which we set out. The situation of the labourer being then again tolerably comfortable, the restraints to population are in some degree loosened, and the same retrograde and progressive movements with respect to happiness are repeated.

This sort of oscillation will not be remarked by superficial observers, and it may be difficult even for the most penetrating mind to calculate its periods. Yet that in all old states some such vibration does exist, though from various transverse causes, in a much less marked, and in a much more irregular manner than I have described it, no reflecting man who considers the subject deeply can well doubt.

Many reasons occur why this oscillation has been less obvious, and less decidedly confirmed by experience, than might naturally be expected.

One principal reason is that the histories of mankind that we possess are histories only of the higher classes. We have but few accounts that can be depended upon of the manners and customs of that part of mankind, where these retrograde and progressive movements chiefly take place. A satisfactory history of this kind, of one people, and of one period, would require the constant and minute attention of an observing mind during a long life. Some of the objects of enquiry would be, in what proportion to the number of adults was the number of marriages, to what extent vicious customs prevailed in consequence of the restraints upon matrimony, what was the comparative mortality among the children of the most distressed part of the community and those who lived rather more at their ease, what were the variations in the real price of labour, and what were the observable differences in the state of the lower classes of society with respect to ease and happiness, at different times during a certain period.

Such a history would tend greatly to elucidate the manner in which the constant check upon population acts and would probably prove the existence of the retrograde and progressive movements that have been mentioned, though the times of their vibration must necessarily be rendered irregular, from the operation of many interrupting causes, such as the introduction or failure of certain manufactures, a greater or less prevalent spirit of agriculture enterprize, years of plenty, or years of scarcity, wars and pestilence, poor laws, the invention of processes for shortening labour without the proportional extension of the market for the commodity, and, particularly, the difference between the nominal and real price of labour, a circumstance which has perhaps more than any other contributed to conceal this oscillation from common view.

It very rarely happens that the nominal price of labour universally falls, but we well know that it frequently remains the same, while the nominal price of provisions has been gradually increasing. This is, in effect, a real fall in the price of labour, and during this period the condition of the lower orders of the community must gradually grow worse and worse. But the farmers and capitalists are growing rich from the real cheapness of labour. Their increased capitals enable them to employ a greater number of men. Work therefore may be plentiful, and the price of labour would consequently rise. But the want of freedom in the market of labour, which occurs more or less in all communities, either from parish laws, or the more general cause of the facility of combination among the rich, and its difficulty among the poor, operates to prevent the price of labour from rising at the natural period, and keeps it down some time longer; perhaps, till a year of scarcity, when the clamour is too loud, and the necessity too apparent to be resisted.

The true cause of the advance in the price of labour is thus concealed, and the rich affect to grant it as an act of compassion and favour to the poor, in consideration of a year of scarcity, and, when plenty returns, indulge themselves in the most unreasonable of all complaints, that the price does not again fall, when a little reflection would shew them that it must have risen long before but from an unjust conspiracy of their own.

But though the rich by unfair combinations contribute frequently to prolong a season of distress among the poor, yet no possible form of society could prevent the almost constant action of misery upon a great part of mankind, if in a state of inequality, and upon all, if all were equal.

The theory on which the truth of this position depends appears to me so extremely clear that I feel at a loss to conjecture what part of it can be denied.

That population cannot increase without the means of subsistence is a proposition so evident that it needs no illustration.

That population does invariably increase where there are the means of subsistence, the history of every people that have ever existed will abundantly prove.

And that the superior power of population cannot be checked without producing misery or vice, the ample portion of these too bitter ingredients in the cup of human life and the continuance of the physical causes that seem to have produced them bear too convincing a testimony.

◇ ◇ ◇

By great attention to cleanliness, the plague seems at length to be completely expelled from London. But it is not improbable that among the secondary causes that produce even sickly seasons and epidemics ought to be ranked a crowded population and unwholesome and insufficient food. I have been led to this remark, by looking over some of the tables of Mr. Susmilch, which Dr. Price has extracted in one of his notes to the postscript on the controversy respecting the population of England and Wales. They are considered as very correct, and if such tables were general, they would throw great light on the different ways by which population is repressed and prevented from increasing beyond the means of subsistence in any country. I will extract a part in the tables, with Dr. Price's remarks.

IN THE KINGDOM OF PRUSSIA, AND DUKEDOM OF LITHUANIA

Annual Average	Births	Burials	Marriages	Proportion of Births to Marriages	Proportion of Births to Burials
10 Yrs. to 1702	21963	14718	5928	37 to 10	150 to 100
5 Yrs. to 1716	21602	11984	4968	37 to 10	180 to 100
5 Yrs. to 1756	28392	19154	5599	50 to 10	148 to 100

"N. B. In 1709 and 1710, pestilence carried off 247,733 of the inhabitants of this country, and in 1736 and 1737, epidemics prevailed, which again checked its increase."

It may be remarked, that the greatest proportion of births to burials, was in the five years after the great pestilence.

DUCHY OF POMERANIA

Annual Average	Births	Burials	Marriages	Proportion of Births to Marriages	Proportion of Births to Burials
6 Yrs. to 1702	6540	4647	1810	36 to 10	140 to 100
6 Yrs. to 1708	7455	4208	1875	39 to 10	177 to 100
6 Yrs. to 1726	8432	5627	2131	39 to 10	150 to 100
4 Yrs. to 1756	12767	9281	2957	43 to 10	137 to 100

"In this instance the inhabitants appear to have been almost doubled in 56 years, no very bad epidemics having once interrupted the increase, but the three years immediately following the last period (to 1759) were years so sickly that the births were sunk to 10,229, and the burials raised to 15,068."

Is it not probable that in this case the number of inhabitants had increased faster than the food and the accommodations necessary to preserve them in health? The mass of the people would, upon this supposition, be obliged to live harder, and a greater number would be crowded together in one house, and it is not surely improbable that these were among the natural causes that produced the three sickly years. These causes may produce such an effect, though the country, absolutely considered, may not be extremely crowded and populous. In a country even thinly inhabited, if an increase of population take place before more foods is raised and more houses are built, the inhabitants must be distressed in some degree for room and subsistence. Were the marriages in England, for the next eight or ten years, to be more prolifick than usual, or even were a greater number of marriages than usual to take place, supposing the number of houses to remain the same, instead of five or six to a cottage, there must be seven or eight, and this, added to the necessity of harder living, would probably have a very unfavourable effect on the health of the common people.

NEUMARK OF BRANDENBURGH

Annual Average	Births	Burials	Marriages	Proportion of Births to Marriages	Proportion of Births to Burials
5 Yrs. to 1701	5433	3483	1436	37 to 10	155 to 100
5 Yrs. to 1726	7012	4254	1713	40 to 10	164 to 100
5 Yrs. to 1756	7978	5567	1891	42 to 10	143 to 100

"Epidemics prevailed for six years, from 1736, to 1741, which checked the increase."

DUKEDOM OF MAGDEBURGH

Annual Average	Births	Burials	Marriages	Proportion of Births to Marriages	Proportion of Births to Burials
5 Yrs. to 1702	6431	4103	1681	38 to 10	156 to 100
5 Yrs. to 1717	7590	5335	2076	36 to 10	142 to 100
5 Yrs. to 1756	8850	8069	2193	40 to 10	109 to 100

"The years 1738, 1740, 1750, and 1751, were particularly sickly."

For further information on this subject, I refer the reader to Mr. Susmilch's tables. The extracts that I have made are sufficient to shew the periodical though irregular returns of sickly seasons, and it seems highly probable that a scantiness of room and food was one of the principal causes that occasioned them.

It appears from the tables that these countries were increasing rather fast for old states, notwithstanding the occasional sickly seasons that prevailed. Cultivation must have been improving, and marriages, consequently, encouraged. For the checks to population appear to have been rather of the positive than of the preventive kind. When from a prospect of increasing plenty in any country, the weight that represses population is in some degree removed, it is highly probable that the motion will be continued beyond the operation of the cause that first impelled it. Or, to be more particular, when the increasing produce of a country, and the increasing demand for labour, so far ameliorate the condition of the labourer as greatly to encourage marriage, it is probable that the custom of early marriages will continue till the population of the country has gone beyond the increased produce, and sickly seasons appear to be the natural and necessary consequence. I should expect, therefore, that those countries where subsistence was increasing sufficiently at times to encourage population but not to answer all its demands, would be more subject to periodical epidemics than those where the population could more completely accommodate itself to the average produce.

An observation the converse of this will probably also be found true. In those countries that are subject to periodical sicknesses, the increase of population, or the excess of births above the burials, will be greater in the intervals of these periods than is usual, caeteris paribus, in the countries not so much subject to such disorders. If Turkey and Egypt have been nearly stationary in their average population for the last century, in the intervals of their periodical plagues, the births must have exceeded the burials in a greater proportion than in such countries as France and England.

The average proportion of births to burials in any country for a period of five or ten years will hence appear to be a very inadequate criterion by which to judge of its real progress in population. This proportion certainly shews the rate of increase during those five or ten years; but we can by no means thence infer what had been the increase for the twenty years before, or what would be the increase for the twenty years after. Dr. Price observes that Sweden, Norway, Russia, and the kingdom of Naples are increasing fast; but the extracts from registers that he has given are not for periods of sufficient extent to establish the fact. It is highly probable, however, that Sweden, Norway, and Russia are really increasing in their population, though not at the rate that the proportion of births to burials for the short periods that Dr. Price takes would seem to shew. For five years, ending in 1777, the proportion of births to burials in the kingdom of Naples was 144 to 100, but there is reason to suppose that this proportion would indicate an increase much greater than would be really found to have taken place in that kingdom during a period of a hundred years.

Dr. Short compared the registers of many villages and market towns in England for two periods; the first from Queen Elizabeth to the middle of the last century, and the second from different years at the end of the last century to the middle of the present. And from a comparison of these extracts, it appears that in the former period the births exceeded the burials in the proportion of 124 to 100 but in the latter, only in the proportion of 111 to 100. Dr. Price thinks that the registers in the former period are not to be depended upon, but probably in this instance they do not give incorrect proportions. At least there are many reasons for expecting to find a greater excess of births above the burials in the former period than in the latter. In the natural progress of the population of any country, more good land will, caeteris paribus, be taken into cultivation in the earlier stages of it than in the later. And a greater proportional yearly increase of produce will almost invariably be followed by a greater proportional increase of population. But besides this great cause, which would naturally give the excess of births above the burials greater at the end of Queen Elizabeth's reign than in the middle of the present century, I cannot help thinking that the occasional ravages of the plague in the former period must have had some tendency to increase this proportion. If an average of ten years had been taken in the intervals of the returns of this dreadful disorder, or if the years of plague had been rejected as accidental, the registers would certainly give the proportion of births to burials too high for the real average increase of the population. For some few years after the great plague in 1666, it is probable that there was a more than usual excess of births above burials, particularly if Dr. Price's opinion be founded, that England was more populous at the revolution (which happened only 22 years afterwards) than it is at present.

◇ ◇ ◇

I have mentioned some cases where population may permanently increase without a proportional increase in the means of subsistence. But it is evident that the variation in different States, between the food and the numbers supported by it, is restricted to a limit beyond which it cannot pass. In every country, the population of which is not absolutely decreasing, the food must be necessarily sufficient to support, and to continue, the race of labourers.

Other circumstances being the same, it may be affirmed that countries are populous according to the quantity of human food which they produce, and happy according to the liberality with which that food is divided, or the quantity which a day's labour will purchase. Corn countries are more populous than pasture countries, and rice countries more populous that corn countries. The lands in England are not suited to rice, but they would all bear potatoes; and Dr. Adam Smith observes that if potatoes were to become the favourite vegetable food of the common people, and if the same quantity of land was employed in their culture as is now employed in the culture of corn, the country would be able to support a much greater population, and would consequently in a very short time have it.

The happiness of a country does not depend absolutely upon its poverty or its riches, upon its youth or its age, upon its being thinly or fully inhabited, but upon the rapidity with which it is increasing, upon the degree in which the yearly increase of food approaches to the yearly increase of an unrestricted population. This approximation is always the nearest in new colonies, where the knowledge and industry of an old State operate on the fertile unappropriated land of a new one. In other cases, the youth or the age of a State is not in this respect of very great importance. It is probable that the food of Great Britain is divided in as great plenty to the inhabitants at the present period as it was two thousand, three thousand, or four thouand years ago. And there is reason to believe that the poor and thinly inhabited tracts of the Scotch Highlands are as much distressed by an overcharged population as the rich and populous province of Flanders.

Were a country never to be over-run by a people more advanced in arts, but left to its own natural progress in civilization; from the time that its produce might be considered as an unit, to the time that it might be considered as a million, during the lapse of many hundred years there would not be a single period when the mass of the people could be said to be free from distress, either directly or indirectly, for want of food. In every State in Europe, since we have first had accounts of it, millions and millions of human existences have been repressed from this simple cause; though perhaps in some of these States, an absolute famine has never been known.

Famine seems to be the last, the most dreadful resource of nature. The power of population is so superior to the power in the earth to produce subsistence for man, that premature death must in some shape or other visit the human race. The vices of mankind are active and able ministers of depopulation. They are the precursors in the great army of destruction, and often finish the dreadful work themselves. But should they fail in this war of extermination, sickly seasons, epidemics, pestilence, and plague, advance in terrific array and sweep off their thousands and ten thousands. Should success be still incomplete, gigantic inevitable famine stalks in the rear, and with one mighty blow, levels the population with the food of the world.

Must it not then be acknowledged by an attentive examiner of the histories of mankind, that in every age and in every State in which man has existed, or does now exist,

That the increase of population is necessarily limited by the means of subsistence.

That population does invariably increase when the means of subsistence increase. And that the superior power of population is repressed, and the actual population kept equal to the means of subsistence, by misery and vice.

◇ ◇ ◇

With regard to the duration of human life, there does not appear to have existed from the earliest ages of the world to the present moment the smallest permanent symptom or indication of increasing prolongation. The observable effects of climate, habit, diet, and other causes, on length of life have furnished the pretext for asserting its indefinite extension; and the sandy foundation on which the argument rests is that because of the limit of human life is undefined; because you cannot mark its precise term, and say so far exactly shall it go and no further; that therefore its extent may increase for ever, and be properly termed indefinite or unlimited. But the fallacy and absurdity of this argument will sufficiently appear from a slight examination of what Mr. Condorcet calls the organic perfectibility, or degeneration, of the race of plants and animals, which he says may be regarded as one of the general laws of nature.

I am told that it is a maxim among the improvers of cattle that you may breed to any degree of nicety you please, and they found this maxim upon another, which is that some of the offspring will possess the desirable qualities of the parents in a greater degree. In the famous Leicestershire breed of sheep, the object is to procure them with small heads and small legs. Proceeding upon these breeding maxims, it is evident that we might go on till the heads and legs are evanescent quantities, but this is so palpable an absurdity that we may be quite sure that the premises are not just and that there really is a limit, though we cannot see it or say exactly where it is. In this case, the point of the greatest degree of improvement, or the smallest size of the head and legs, may be said to be undefined, but this is very different from unlimited, or from indefinite, in Mr. Condorcet's acceptation of the term. Though I may not be able in the present instance to mark the limit at which further improvement will stop, I can very easily mention a point at which it will not arrive. I should not scruple to assert that were the breeding to continue for ever, the head and legs of these sheep would never be so small as the head and legs of a rat.

It cannot be true, therefore, that among animals some of the offspring will possess the desirable qualities of the parents in a greater degree, or that animals are indefinitely perfectible.

The progress of a wild plant to a beautiful garden flower is perhaps more marked and striking than any thing that takes place among animals, yet even here it would be the height of absurdity to assert that the progress was unlimited or indefinite. One of the most obvious features of the improvement is the increase of size. The flower has grown gradually larger by cultivation. If the progress were really unlimited it might be increased ad infinitum, but this is so gross an absurdity that we may be quite sure that among plants as well as among animals there is a limit to improvement, though we do not exactly know where it is. It is probable that the gardeners who contend for flower prizes have often applied stronger dressing without success. At the same time, it would be highly presumptuous in any man to say that he had seen the finest carnation or anemone that could ever be made to grow. He might however assert without the smallest chance of being contradicted by a future fact, that no carnation or anemone could ever by cultivation be increased to the size of a large cabbage; and yet there are assignable quantities much greater than a cabbage. No man can say that he has seen the largest ear of wheat or the largest oak that could ever grow; but he might easily, and with perfect certainty, name a point of magnitude, at which they would not arrive. In all these cases therefore, a careful distinction should be made, between an unlimited progress and a progress where the limit is merely undefined.

It will be said, perhaps, that the reason why plants and animals cannot increase indefinitely in size is that they would fall by their own weight. I answer, how do we know this but from experience? from experience of the degree of strength with which these bodies are formed. I know that a carnation, long before it reached the size of a cabbage, would not be supported by its stalk, but I only know this from my experience of the weakness and want of tenacity in the materials of a carnation stalk. There are many substances in nature of the same size that would support as large a head as a cabbage.

The reasons of the mortality of plants are at present perfectly unknown to us. No man can say why such a plant is annual, another biennial, and another endures for ages. The whole affair in all these cases, in plants, animals, and in the human race, is an affair of experience, and I only conclude that man is mortal because the invariable experience of all ages has proved the mortality of those materials of which his visible body is made.

What can we reason but from what we know.

Sound philosophy will not authorize me to alter this opinion of the mortality of man on earth, till it can be clearly proved that the human race has made, and is making, a decided progress towards an illimitable extent of life. And the chief reason why I adduced the two particular instances from animals and plants was to expose and illustrate, if I could, the fallacy of that argument which infers an unlimited progress, merely because some partial improvement has taken place, and that the limit of this improvement cannot be precisely ascertained.

The capacity of improvement in plants and animals, to a certain degree, no person can possibly doubt. A clear and decided progress has already been made; and yet I think it appears that it would be highly absurd to say that this progress has no limits. In human life, though there are great variations from different causes, it may be doubted whether, since the world began, any organic improvement whatever in the human frame can be clearly ascertained. The foundations therefore, on which the arguments for the organic perfectibility of man rest, are unusually weak and can only be considered as mere conjectures. It does not, however, by any means seem impossible that by an attention to breed, a certain degree of improvement similar to that among animals might take place among men. Whether intellect could be communicated may be a matter of doubt; but size, strength, beauty, complexion, and perhaps even longevity are in a degree transmissible. The error does not seem to lie in supposing a small degree of improvement possible, but in not discriminating between a small improvement, the limit of which is undefined, and an improvement really unlimited. As the human race however could not be improved in this way without condemning all the bad specimens to celibacy, it is not probable that an attention to breed should ever become general; indeed, I know of no well-directed attempts of this kind, except in the ancient family of the Bickerstaffs, who are said to have been very successful in whitening the skins and increasing the height of their race by prudent marriages, particularly by that very judicious cross with Maud, the milk-maid, by which some capital defects in the constitutions of the family were corrected.

It will not be necessary, I think, in order more completely to shew the improbability of any approach in man towards immortality on earth, to urge the very great additional weight that an increase in the duration of life would give to the argument of population.

◇   ◇   ◇

The real perfectibility of man may be illustrated, as I have mentioned before, by the perfectibility of a plant. The object of the enterprising florist is, as I conceive, to unite size, symmetry, and beauty of colour. It would surely be presumptuous in the most successful improver to affirm that he possessed a carnation in which these qualities existed in the greatest possible state of perfection. However beautiful his flower may be, other care, other soil, or other suns might produce one still more beautiful. Yet, although he may be aware of the absurdity of supposing that he has reached perfection; and though he may know by what means he attained that degree of beauty in the flower which he at present possesses, yet he cannot be sure that by pursuing similar means, rather increased in strength, he will obtain a more beautiful blossom. By endeavouring to improve one quality, he may impair the beauty of another. The richer mould which he would employ to increase the size of his plant would probably burst the calyx and destroy at once its symmetry. In a similar manner, the forcing manure used to bring about the French revolution, and to give a greater freedom and energy to the human mind, has burst the calyx of humanity, the restraining bond of all society; and however large the seprate petals have grown, however strongly or even beautifully a few of them have been marked, the whole is at present a loose, deformed, disjointed mass, without union, symmetry, or harmony of colouring.

Were it of consequence to improve pinks and carnations, though we could have no hope of raising them as large as cabbages, we might undoubtedly expect, by successive efforts, to obtain more beautiful specimens than we at present possess. No person can deny the importance of improving the happiness of the human species. Every the least advance in this respect is highly valuable. But an experiment with the human race is not like an experiment upon inanimate objects. The bursting of a flower may be a tifle. Another will soon succeed it. But the bursting of the bonds of society is such a separation of parts as cannot take place without giving the most acute pain to thousands, and a long time may elapse, and much misery may be endured, before the wound grows up again.

As the five propositions which I have been examining may be considered as the corner stones of Mr. Godwin's fanciful structure, and, indeed, as expressing the aim and bent of his whole work, however excellent much of his detached reasoning may be, he must be considered as having failed in the great object of his undertaking. Besides the difficulties arising from the compound nature of man, which he has by no means sufficiently smoothed, the principal argument against the perfectibility of man and society remains whole and unimpaired from any thing that he has advanced. And as far as I can trust my own judgment, this argument appears to be conclusive not only against the perfectibility of man, in the enlarged sense in which Mr. Godwin understands the term, but against any very marked and striking change for the better, in the form and structure of general society, by which I mean any great and decided amelioration of the condition of the lower classes of mankind, the most numerous and, consequently, in a general view of the subject, the most important part of the human race. Were I to live a thousand years, and the laws of nature to remain the same, I should little fear, or rather little hope, a contradiction from experience in asserting that no possible sacrifices or exertions of the rich, in a country which had been long inhabited, could for any time place the lower classes of the community in a situation equal, with regard to circumstances, to the situation of the common people about thirty years ago in the northern States of America.

The lower classes of people in Europe may at some future period be much better instructed than they are at present; they may be taught to employ the little spare time they have in many better ways than at the ale-house; they may live under better and more equal laws than they have ever hitherto done, perhaps, in any country; and I even conceive it possible, though not probable, that they may have more leisure; but it is not in the nature of things, that they can be awarded such a quantity of money or subsistence, as will allow them all to marry early, in the full confidence that they shall be able to provide with ease for a numerous family.

◇ ◇ ◇

As the reasons, therefore, for the constancy of the laws of nature seem, even to our understandings, obvious and striking, if we return to the principle of population and consider man as he really is, inert, sluggish, and averse from labour unless compelled by necessity (and it is surely the height of folly to talk of man, according to our crude fancies, of what he might be), we may pronounce with certainty that the world would not have been peopled but for the superiority of the power of population to the means of subsistence. Strong and constantly operative as this stimulus is on man to urge him to the cultivation of the earth, if we still see that cultivation proceeds very slowly, we may fairly conclude that a less stimulus would have been insufficient. Even under the operation of this constant excitement, savages will inhabit countries of the greatest natural fertility for a long period before they betake themselves to pasturage or agriculture. Had population and food increased in the same ratio, it is probable that man might never have emerged from the savage state. But supposing the earth once well peopled, an Alexander, a Julius Caesar, a Tamerlane, or a bloody revolution might irrecoverably thin the human race and defeat the great designs of the Creator. The ravages of a contagious disorder would be felt for ages, and an earthquake might unpeople a region for ever. The principle according to which population increases prevents the vices of mankind or the accidents of nature, the partial evils arising from general laws, from obstructing the high purpose of the creation. It keeps the inhabitants of the earth always fully up to the level of the means of subsistence, and is constantly acting upon man as a powerful stimulus, urging him to the further cultivation of the earth, and to enable it consequently to support a more extended population. But it is impossible that this law can operate and produce the effects apparently intended by the Supreme Being without occasioning partial evil. Unless the principle of population were to be altered, according to the circumstances of each separate country (which would not only be contrary to our universal experience, with regard to the laws of nature, but would contradict even our own reason, which sees the absolute necessity of general laws, for the formation of intellect), it is evident that the same principle which, seconded by industry, will people a fertile region in a few years must product distress in countries that have been long inhabited.

It seems, however, every way probable that even the acknowledged difficulties occasioned by the law of population tend rather to promote than impede the general purpose of Providence. They excite universal exertion and contribute to that infinite variety of situations, and consequently of impressions, which seems upon the whole favourable to the growth of mind. It is probable that too great or too little excitement, extreme poverty, or too great riches may be alike unfavourable in this respect. The middle regions of society seem to be best suited to intellectual improvement, but it is contrary to the analogy of all nature to expect that the whole of society can be a middle region. The temperate zones of the earth seem to be the most favourable to the mental and corporeal energies of man, but all cannot be temperate zones. A world warmed and enlightened but by one sun must from the laws of matter have some parts chilled by perpetual frosts and others scorched by perpetual heats. Every piece of matter lying on a surface must have an upper and an under side; all the particles cannot be in the middle. The most valuable parts of an oak to a timber merchant are not either the roots or the branches, but these are absolutely necessary to the existence of the middle part, or stem, which is the object in request. The timber merchant could not possibly expect to make an oak grow without roots or branches, but if he could find out a mode of cultivation which would cause more of the substance to go to stem, and less to root and branch, he would be right to exert himself in bringing such a system into general use.

In the same manner, though we cannot possibly expect to exclude riches and poverty from society, yet if we could find out a mode of government by which the numbers in the extreme regions would be lessened and the numbers in the middle regions increased, it would be undoubtedly our duty to adopt it. It is not, however, improbable that as in the oak, the roots and branches could not be diminished very greatly without weakening the vigorous circulation of the sap in the stem, so in society the extreme parts could not be diminished beyond a certain degree without lessening that animated exertion throughout the middle parts which is the very cause that they are the most favourable to the growth of intellect. If no man could hope to rise or fear to fall in society, if industry did not bring with it its reward and idleness its punishment, the middle parts would not certainly be what they now are. In reasoning upon this subject, it is evident that we ought to consider chiefly the mass of mankind and not individual instances. There are undoubtedly many minds, and there ought to be many, according to the chances, out of so great a mass that, having been vivified early by a peculiar course of excitements, would not need the constant action of narrow motives to continue them in activity. But if we were to review the various useful discoveries, the valuable writings, and other laudable exertions of mankind, I believe we should find that more were to be attributed to the narrow motives that operate upon the many than to the apparently more enlarged motives that operate upon upon the few.

Leisure is without doubt highly valuable to man, but taking man as he is, the probability seems to be that in the greater number of instances it will produce evil rather than good. It has been not unfrequently remarked that talents are more common among younger brothers than among elder brothers, but it can scarcely be imagined that younger brothers are, upon an average, born with a greater original susceptibility of parts. The difference, if there really is any observable difference, can only arise from their different situations. Exertion and activity are in general absolutely necessary in the one case and are only optional in the other.

That the difficulties of life contribute to generate talents, every days' experience must convince us. The exertions that men find it necessary to make in order to support themselves or families, frequently awaken faculties that might otherwise have lain for ever dormant, and it has been commonly remarked that new and extraordinary situations generally create minds adequate to grapple with the difficulties in which they are involved.

Further Readings

E. A. Wrigley, *Population and History* (New York: McGraw-Hill, 1969), provides an excellent introduction to the field of population study, while Grosvenor T. Griffith, *Population Problems in the Age of Malthus* (Cambridge: The University Press, 1926), considers population trends in the period in which Malthus formulated his concept. Two books from the 1960s indicate the growth of concern in the period: Cyril W. Park, *The Population Explosion* (London: Heinemann Educational Books, 1965), and George W. Zinke, *The Problem of Malthus: Must Progress End in Overpopulation?* (Boulder, CO: University of Colorado Press, 1967). The revival of popular interest in Malthusian concerns, however, may be traced to one book in particular: Paul D. Ehrlich, *The Population Bomb* (New York: Ballantine Books, 1968). This work became a runaway best seller and brought tremendous publicity to the issues it treats.

A short biography of Malthus is presented by John Maynard Keynes, one of the most influential economists of the twentieth century, in "Robert Malthus: The First of the Cambridge Economists," contained in his *Essays in Biography* (New York: Harcourt Brace, 1933). Patricia D. James, *Population Malthus: His Life and Times* (London: Routledge and Kegan Paul, 1979), and William Petersen, *Malthus* (Cambridge, MA: Harvard University Press, 1979), are two scholarly biographies that complement each other well.

The Sorrows of Misfortune

The examinations for the Imperial Civil Service play an important role in Chinese literature, as illustrated by *The Scholars* and *The Dream of the Red Chamber.* This is not surprising, for they played an important role in Chinese life. Every three years, young men attended the local examinations held throughout the land. Here they were examined on their scholarly knowledge of the traditional classics of literature and upon their ability to write gracefully and correctly. Those who received the very highest marks were allowed to proceed to the examinations held in the capital of Peking, where they competed for the two highest degrees. Success at this level qualified a young man for an appointment in the Imperial Civil Service and practically guaranteed the respect and comfort that attended high position. The prize was great, and the examinations were accordingly very competitive. It has been estimated that fewer than one out of five thousand men ever achieved the highest degrees.

This meant, of course, that there were many more failures than successes. The failures had received an expensive literary education and were, by and large, unfitted for trade. The lucky ones managed to obtain a position as a clerk in one of the district offices. These jobs were poorly paid, were viewed with little respect, and offered little security. Nevertheless, they were highly prized, because there were many competitors who found it difficult to earn a living in any other way.

Shen Fu was one of the these failures. He was born in 1763 in the city of Soochow. His father was an irascible and sometimes tyrannical figure, a clerk who hoped that his son would succeed where he had failed. This was not to be. Shen Fu took district examinations in 1778, apparently with little success. He took a job as a government

From Shen Fu, *Six Records of a Floating Life,* translated by Leonard Pratt and Chiang Su-hui (New York: Penguin Books, 1983), pp. 86–92.

clerk in 1781, but soon quit for unknown reasons. He tried going into business, working with his father, and selling his paintings. It was a hard life. He was often in debt, and more than once he was expelled from his family by his irate father. He finally found a patron and moved to Peking. In 1809, at the age of forty-six, he was writing his autobiography, *Six Records of a Floating Life*, but nothing is known of his life after this date.

The organization of the work is unusual. Rather than simply presenting a chronological account, Shen Fu discussed his life from six topical points of view. Only the first four have survived: "The Joys of the Wedding Chamber," "The Pleasures of Leisure," "The Sorrows of Misfortune," and "The Delights of Roaming Afar." Shen Fu intended to write an autobiography, but he also produced a love story of remarkable tenderness. When he was thirteen, a marriage was arranged between him and a neighbor girl, Chen Yün. The marriage was consummated four years later, in 1780. They shared their life as intellectual partners, playmates, and companions in distress until Yün's death in 1803. When Shen Fu tries to write about his life, he constantly returns to his wife. Discussing miniature gardens, he remembers one he and Yün built together and how they would dream over it. When alluding to a classic author, he repeats a comment his wife made on the work. In short, she was so much a part of his life that he cannot write his autobiography without dwelling on her.

He was not a good husband in many ways. He fell into a drunken stupor and slept through their wedding night. He never provided her with much material comfort. When she was dying and needed medicines, and they lacked money to buy them, all he could think of to do was to try to sell paintings; the thought of getting any kind of work possible seems never to have crossed his mind. And yet, he remembers all of the times they laughed together, even when times were hard, and how witty, sensitive, and caring she was. Rarely has married love been so tenderly and candidly portrayed.

The selection is taken from "The Sorrows of Misfortune" and narrates Yün's death and its aftermath. Shen Fu is utterly bereft after the loss of his best companion of twenty-three years. On the day that the Chinese believe that the spirits of the dead return, and try to avoid them, Shen Fu seeks out the room where she died, hoping to catch one last glimpse of her, but is disappointed. He continues to try to earn a living, but spends much time at her grave remembering the good times, when they were together.

It is unknown whether Shen Fu was writing for publication or simply to comfort his own spirit, but there is no evidence that *Six Records of a Floating Life* was published during his lifetime. A partial manuscript of the work was discoverd in the 1870s, and it has been published many times since then. It is a great favorite with the Chinese public and, with its tragic but tender tale of love, it deserves an even wider audience.

Questions

1. Why does Yün believe she is dying?

2. How do you account for the belief of Shen Fu and Yün that too much affection between husband and wife makes for a short marriage?

3. What are Yün's concerns before her death?

4. How did Shen Fu's family support him in his grief?

THE SORROWS OF MISFORTUNE

I returned to find Yün moaning and weeping, looking as if something awful had happened. As soon as she saw me she burst out, 'Did you know that yesterday noon Ah Shuang stole all our things and ran away? I have asked people to search everywhere, but they still have not found him. Losing our things is a small matter, but what of our relationship with our friends? As we were leaving, his mother told me over and over again to take good care of him. I'm terribly worried he's running back home and will have to cross the Great River. And what will we do if his parents have hidden him to blackmail us? How can I face my sworn sister again?'

'Please calm down,' I said. 'You've been worrying about it too much. You can only blackmail someone who has money; with you and me, it's all our four shoulders can do to support our two mouths. Besides, in the half year the boy has been with us, we have given him clothing and shared our food with him. Our neighbours all know we have never once beaten him or scolded him. What's really happened is that the wretched child has ignored his conscience and taken advantage of our problems to run away with our belongings. Your sworn sister at the Huas' gave us a thief. How can you say you cannot face her? It is she who should not be able to face you. What we should do now is report this case to the magistrate, so as to avoid any questions being raised about it in the future.'

After Yün heard me speak, her mind seemed somewhat eased, but from then on she began frequently to talk in her sleep, calling out, 'Ah Shuang has run away!' or 'How could Han-yüan turn her back on me?' Her illness worsened daily.

Finally I was about to call a doctor to treat her, but she stopped me. 'My illness began because of my terribly deep grief over my brother's running away and my mother's death,' said Yün. 'It continued because of my affections, and now it has returned because of my indignation. I have always worried too much about things, and while I have tried my best to be a good daughter-in-law, I have failed.

'These are the reasons why I have come down with dizziness and palpitations of the heart. The disease has already entered my vitals, and there is nothing a doctor can do about it. Please do not spend money on something that cannot help.

'I have been happy as your wife these twenty-three years. You have loved me and sympathized with me in everything, and never rejected me despite my faults. Having had for my husband an intimate friend like you, I have no regrets over this life. I have had warm cotton clothes, enough to eat, and a pleasant home. I have strolled among streams and rocks, at places like the Pavilion of the Waves and the Villa of Serenity. In the midst of life, I have been just like an Immortal. But a true Immortal must go through many incarnations before reaching enlightenment. Who could dare hope to become an Immortal in only one lifetime? In our eagerness for immortality, we have only incurred the wrath of the Creator, and brought on our troubles with our passion. Because you have loved me too much, I have had a short life!'

Later she sobbed and spoke again. 'Even someone who lives a hundred years must still die one day. I am only sorry at having to leave you so suddenly and for so long, halfway through our journey. I will not be able to serve you for all your life, or to see Feng-sen's wedding with my own eyes.' When she finished, she wept great tears.

I forced myself to be strong and comforted her saying, 'You have been ill for eight years, and it has seemed critical many times. Why do you suddenly say such heartbreaking things now?'

'I have been dreaming every night that my parents have sent a boat to fetch me,' said Yün. 'When I shut my eyes it feels as if I'm floating, as if I were walking in the mist. Is my spirit leaving me, while only my body remains?'

'That is only because you are upset,' I said. 'If you will relax, drink some medicine, and take care of yourself, you will get better.'

Yün only sobbed again and said, 'If I thought I had the slightest thread of life left in me I would never dare alarm you by talking to you like this. But the road to the next world is near, and if I do not speak to you now there will never be a day when I can.

'It is all because of me that you have lost the affection of your parents and drifted apart from them. Do not worry, for after I die you will be able to regain their hearts. Your parents' springs and autumns are many, and when I die you should return to them quickly. If you cannot take my bones home, it does not matter if you leave my coffin here for a while until you can come for it. I also want you to find someone who is attractive and capable, to serve our parents and bring up my children. If you will do this for me, I can die in peace.'

When she had said this a great sad moan forced itself from her, as if she was in an agony of heartbreak.

'If you part from me half way I would never want to take another wife,' I said. 'You know the saying, "One who has seen the ocean cannot desire a stream, and compared with Wu Mountain there are no clouds anywhere."'

Yün then took my hand and it seemed there was something else she wanted to say, but she could only brokenly repeat the two words 'next life'. Suddenly she fell silent and began to pant, her eyes staring into the distance. I called her name a thousand times, but she could not speak. Two streams of agonized tears flowed from her eyes in torrents, until finally her panting grew shallow and her tears dried up. Her spirit vanished in the mist and she began her long journey. This was on the 30th day of the third month in the 7th year of the reign of the Emperor Chia Ching.[1] When it happened there was a solitary lamp burning in the room. I looked up but saw nothing, there was nothing for my two hands to hold, and my heart felt as if it would shatter. How can there be anything greater than my everlasting grief?

My friend Hu Ken-tang loaned me ten golds, and by selling every single thing remaining in the house I put together enough money to give my beloved a proper burial.

Alas! Yün came to this world a woman, but she had the feelings and abilities of a man. After she entered the gate of my home in marriage, I had to rush about daily to earn our clothing and food, there was never enough, but she never once complained. When I was living at home, all we had for entertainment was talk about literature. What a pity that she should have died in poverty and after long illness. And whose fault was it that she did? It was my fault, what else can I say? I would advise all the husbands and wives in the world not to hate one another, certainly, but also not to love too deeply. As it is said, 'An affectionate couple cannot grow old together.' My example should serve as a warning to others.

The Time the Spirits Return is, according to custom, the day on which the ghosts of the recently deceased return for a visit to this world. Everything in the house must be arranged the way it was while they were alive, and, particularly, the old clothes they wore must be put on the bed and their old shoes must be put under it, so the ghost can return and see them. Around Soochow, people call this 'the closing of the eyes'. Some would engage a Taoist priest to perform a ceremony in which the spirit would first be called to the bed and then sent away, and this was called 'welcoming the ghost'. The custom in Hanchiang, however, was to set out wine and food in the room of the deceased, after which everyone would leave the house; this was called 'avoiding the ghost'. Some people had even had things stolen while they were out of the house avoiding the ghost.

My landlord was living with me when the time came for Yün's

---

[1] Spring, 1803.

spirit to return, and he left so as to avoid it. Neighbours told me I should set out food and then go away too, but because I was hoping to catch a glimpse of her spirit when it returned, I gave them only vague answers. Chang Yü-men, who was from my home county, warned me about this: 'People have been possessed after toying with the supernatural. You should accept the existence of spirits and not try this.'

'I am staying in the house precisely because I do believe in them,' I said.

'It is dangerous to risk offending a ghost when it returns. Even if your wife's spirit does come home, there will still be a gulf between the dead and the living, so her spirit may not take shape to accept your welcome in any case. All things considered, you should avoid the ghost rather than risk running foul of it.'

I was, however, beside myself with longing for Yün, and paid him no attention. 'It is fate that determines life and death,' I said firmly. 'If you are that concerned about me, why not keep me company?'

'I will stand guard outside the door,' Chang said. 'If you see anything strange, I can come in as soon as you shout.'

I took a lantern and went into the house. I saw to it that everything was arranged the same way as before, but with the sight and sound of Yün gone I could at first not keep myself from weeping sadly. Yet I was afraid that tears would blur my vision and keep me from seeing what I wished to see, so I forced them back, opened my eyes, and sat down on the bed to wait. I touched Yün's old clothes and smelled the fragrance of her that still lingered in them. It was more than I could bear, and I felt my heart was breaking; stupefied, I began to faint away. But then I thought, how could I suddenly fall asleep while waiting for her spirit?

I opened my eyes, looked all around, and noticed that the glimmering blue flames of the pair of candles on the mat had shrunk to the size of beans. I was frightened, and seized with a cold trembling. Rubbing my hands and forehead, I gazed steadily at the candles; as I watched, both their flames gradually lengthened and grew more than a foot tall, until they scorched the paper pasted over the framework on the ceiling. Just as I was taking advantage of this light to look around, the flames suddenly shrank to their previous size.

By now, my heart was pounding and my knees were trembling, and I wanted to call in my guardian. But then I thought of Yün's gentle and impressionable spirit, and feared she might be repelled by having another man in the room. Instead I just called her name softly and prayed to her, but the room remained silent and there was nothing to be seen. The candle flames then grew bright again, but did not rise up as before. I went out to tell Yü-men what had happened; he thought me very brave, not realizing that in fact I was merely transported with love the whole time.

After I lost Yün, remembering how the poet Lin Ho-ching wrote that 'the plum tree is my wife and the crane my son', I called myself 'he who has lost the plum tree'. For the time being I buried Yün at Chinkuei Hill outside the West Gate at Yangchou, at a place usually called the Precious Pagoda of the Ho Family. I bought a plot for one coffin and left her there temporarily, in accordance with her wishes. Then I took her tablet[2] home, where my mother also grieved for her. Ching-chün and Feng-sen returned home, wept bitterly, and went into mourning with me.

While I was home Chi-tang approached me and said, 'Father is still angry with you, so I think you should go back to Yangchou. After father returns I will explain things and then write and let you know you may come home.'

So I took leave of my mother and said goodbye to my son and daughter, bitterly weeping the while. I returned to Yangchou, where I began to sell paintings for a living. There I often wept at Yün's grave, utterly alone and in deepest mourning. If I happened to pass by our old house, I found the sight so painful I could hardly bear it. By the time of the Double Ninth Festival, the grass on all the neighbouring graves had turned yellow, while that on Yün's grave alone remained green. The grave-keeper told me hers was a good place for a grave, because the earth spirits there were powerful.

Further Readings

The organization of Ch'ing China is thoroughly discussed in Albert Feurwerker, *State and Society in Eighteenth-Century China: The Ch'ing Empire in its Glory* (Ann Arbor, MI: University of Michigan Press, 1976). T'ung-tou Ch'ü, *Local Government under the Ch'ing* (Cambridge, MA: Harvard University Press, 1962), describes the office of the district magistrate and the work of the lesser government clerks. Ichisada Miyazaki, *China's Examination Hell*, translated by Conrad Shirokauer (Tokyo and New York: John Weatherhill, 1976), describes the Civil Service examination system. Chung-li Chang, *The Chinese Gentry: Studies on Their Role in Nineteeenth-Century Chinese Society* (Seattle, WA: University of Washington Press, 1967), discusses the scholar-gentry class created by the examination system and its influence on Chinese society.

Shou-yi Ch'en, *Chinese Literature: A Historical Introduction* (New York: Ronald Press, 1961), and Herbert A. Giles, *History of Chinese Literature* (New York: F. Ungar, 1967), provide general introductions to Chinese literature.

Robert Hans van Gulik, *Sexual Life in Ancient China: A Preliminary Survey of Chinese Sex and Society from ca. 1500 B.C. to A.D. 1644* (Atlantic Highlands, NJ: Humanities Press, 1974), provides much useful background on the role of women in Chinese society, while Jonathan Spence, *The Death of Woman Wang* (New York: Penguin Books, 1979), provides a chilling account of the place of women at a still lower level of Chinese society than that of Shen Fu and Chen Yün. *The Face of China as Seen by Photographers and Travellers*, with historical commentary by Nigel Cameron (Millerton, NY: Aperture, 1978), offers some early photographs of traditional Chinese life that record conditions probably very close to those in which Shen Fu and Chen Yün lived.

---

[2] A memorial plaque placed in the home.

The Tale of Kieu

The country of Vietnam was ruled by China for some nine hundred years, gaining its independence in 939. During this period, Chinese influence in the region was sufficient to draw Vietnam permanently into the tradition of classical Chinese civilization. Much as British and Americans find their aesthetic models and intellectual roots in the classical world of Graeco–Roman civilization, so the Vietnamese regard the traditions of Han China as their cultural heritage. Even after independence, the proximity of her powerful northern neighbor ensured that Chinese institutions and attitudes would continue to exert a great influence on Vietnam's development. The Le dynasty gained power in 1427 and, from their base of power in the North, maintained their power until 1788. The Le rulers quickly became tributaries of the Chinese emperors and were guaranteed by them protection from both external and internal threats. It is not surprising, therefore, to observe that the political administration of eighteenth-century Vietnam was in many ways an imitation of that of the Ch'ing dynasty of China (1644–1911). The administration of the country was entrusted to men who had proven their worth by mastering Confucian philosophy and the Chinese literary classics. Vietnam did not possess sufficient resources to support as complete a civil-service system as Ch'ing China, but her administrators rivalled those of China in their adherence to the scholarly tradition and loyalty to the ruling dynasty.

Nguyen Du (1765–1820) was born to a Northern Vietnamese family that had produced generations of scholar-administrators and he was trained to follow that career. It was his misfortune, however,

From Nguyên Du, *The Tale of Kiêu*, translated by Huynh Sanh Thông, (bilingual edition: New Haven and London: Yale University Press, 1983, 1987 pr.), pp. 141, 143, 145, 147, 149, 151, 153, 155, 157, 159, 161, 163, 165, and 167.

to be born during the waning years of the Le dynasty. In 1771, the popular uprising known as the Tay-son Revolution broke out in the southern part of the country. Under the leadership of the charismatic Nguyen Hue, and espousing ideals of social justice, the movement swept over Vietnam. The Chinese sent a large army in 1788 to defend the interests of the Le ruler, but they were decisively defeated and the Le dynasty was overthrown. No sooner had Nguyen Du and his fellow scholar-officials adapted to the necessity of transferring their loyalty to a new monarch than the Tay-son movement was defeated. The victorious Nguyen emperor, Gia-long (1802–1820), established a new capital, Hué, in central Vietnam, and the scholar-officials faced the task of transferring their loyalty once again. The task was made harder in that the new dynasty was from the South, and were for this reason held in some contempt by the Northerners.

Nguyen Du served the Nguyen emperor for the rest of his life in a series of minor posts and poorly endowed sinecures. He continued to cultivate the Chinese classics, and wrote a verse novel entitled *The Tale of Kieu (Kim Van Kieu Tan Truyen)*. It was circulated among his friends and published only shortly after his death. It was immediately recognized as the greatest work of Vietnamese literature ever produced and has continued to be so regarded.

As is to be expected from a scholar steeped in the Chinese classics, the work is based on a Chinese model, a novel of the Ming dynasty (1368–1644), and is rich with literary allusions. It is not a pedantic work, however, but a very human tale that raises basic moral issues of universal significance. The tangled plot revolves around a beautiful, talented, and virtuous girl named Thuy Kieu. Kieu and Kim Trong, a young scholar, fall in love at first sight, but he is called away by the death of his father. Kieu finds her family arrested on some vague charge, and sells herself into prostitution to get money to save them. She is rescued from the brothel by a young man who marries her. He has another wife, however, a member of a powerful family, who has Kieu kidnapped and made a slave in her household. Kieu flees her constant humiliation and is taken up by the warrior Tu Hai. After five years as his wife, Kieu is again forced to flee when Tu Hai is treacherously murdered. Kieu seeks refuge in a Buddhist convent. In the excerpt presented here, the action shifts to Kieu's first love, Kim. He returns to her home to find her gone and is persuaded to marry her sister, but cannot forget Kieu. He achieves the highest grade in the Imperial Civil Service examinations and enters the imperial service. As time passes, he hears of Kieu's continuing misfortunes and degradations. Finally, by accident, he and Kieu's family discover Kieu in her convent. Kim marries her, thus restoring her honor, but Kieu cannot make love to him. Because of her past, she says, she would feel only shame. He replies that true lovers need not share a bed. As friends and companions, they contrive to make a full and prosperous life based on mutual respect and the deepest friendship.

The key concepts in the story are personal degradation and undeserved punishment. Kieu has done nothing to deserve what happens to her, and her only sin is to submit to what she cannot avoid. Those about her use her body, but she retains control of her inner self. She will not give Kim her body, because this has been sullied, but she does share with him her untarnished spirit. This distinction between the inner and outer self is a critical one, and explains much about the character of the Vietnamese people. It is not surprising that *The Tale of Kieu* is a treasured part of their national heritage.

Questions

1. How does her family convince Kieu to abandon the life of a Buddhist nun?

2. What objections does Kieu raise to marrying Kim? How does Kim reply to them?

3. Why does Kieu refuse to share Kim's bed?

4. What does their eventual agreement to sleep in separate beds disclose about their love?

THE TALE OF KIEU

As Kiêu shook off the filth of all past woes,
how could her erstwhile love know she lived here?

    If Kiêu had shouldered her full load of griefs,
young Kim himself had suffered much the while.
For mourning rites he'd made that far-flung trip
and from Liao-yang came back in half a year.
    He hurried toward his dear Kingfisher's nest
and took one startled look—the scene had changed.
The garden was a patch of weeds and reeds.
Hushed, moon-lit windows, weather-beaten walls.
Not one lone soul—peach blossoms of last year
were smiling, flirting yet with their east wind.[1]
Swallows were rustling through the vacant house.
Grass clad the ground, moss hid all marks of shoes.
At the wall's end, a clump of thorns and briers:
this pathway both had walked a year ago.
A silent chill was brooding over all—
who could relieve the anguish of his heart?
    A neighbor happened by—approaching him,

---

[1] The east wind blows in the spring and therefore favors love.

Kim asked some questions he discreetly phrased.
Old Vuong? He'd somehow tangled with the law.
And Kiêu? She'd sold herself to ransom him.
The family? All had moved a long way off.
And what about young Vuong and young Thúy Vân?
The two had fallen on hard days of need:
he scribed, she sewed—both lived from hand to mouth.
    It was a firebolt striking from mid-sky:
Kim heard the news, was staggered by it all.
He asked and learned where all those folks had moved—
he slowly found his way to their new home.
A tattered hut, a roof of thatch, mud walls;
reed blinds in rags, bamboo screens punched with holes;
a rain-soaked yard where nothing grew but weeds:
the sight distressed and shocked him all the more.
    Still, making bold, he called outside the wall.
Young Vuong, on hearing him, rushed out at once—
he took him by the hand, led him inside.
From their back room the parents soon appeared.
    They wept and wailed as they retold their woes:
"Young man, you know what happened to us all?
Our daughter Kiêu is cursed by evil fate:
she failed her word to you, her solemn troth.
Disaster struck our family, forcing her
to sell herself and save her father's life.
How torn and wrenched she was when she left home!
Grief-bowed, she told us time and time again:
since she had sworn to you a sacred oath,
she begged her sister Vân to take her place
and in some way redeem her pledge to you.
But her own sorrow will forever last.
In this existence she broke faith with you—
she'll make it up to you when she's reborn.
These were the words she said and said again:
we graved them in our souls before she left.
O daughter Kiêu, why does fate hurt you so?
Your Kim is back with us, but where are you?"
    The more they spoke of Kiêu, the more they grieved—
the more Kim heard them speak, the more he ached.
He writhed in agony, he sorely wept,
his face tear-drowned and sorrow-crazed his mind.
It hurt him so he fainted many times
and, coming to, he shed more bitter tears.
    When he saw Kim so desolate, old Vuong
curbed his own grief and sought to comfort him:
"The plank's now nailed and fastened to the boat.[2]

---

[2] This proverb expresses resigned acceptance of an irreversible situation.

Ill-starred and doomed, she can't requite your love.
Although you care so much for her you've lost,
must you throw off a life as good as gold?"
    To soothe his pain, they tried a hundred ways—
grief, smothered, flared and burned more fiercely yet.
They showed him those gold bracelets from the past
and other keepsakes: incense, that old lute.
The sight of them rekindled his despair—
it roused his sorrow, rent his heart again.
"Because I had to go away," he cried,
"I let the fern, the flower float downstream.
We two did take and swear our vows of troth,
vows firm as bronze or stone, not idle words.
Though we have shared no bed, we're man and wife:
how could I ever cast her from my heart?
Whatever it may cost in gold, in time,
I shall not quit until I see her face."
    He suffered more than all the words could say—
stifling his sobs, he bade goodbye and left.
He hurried home, arranged a garden lodge,
then he went back to fetch Kiêu's parents there.
He saw to their well-being day and night
like their own son, in their lost daughter's stead.
    With ink and tears he wrote away for news—
agents he sent and missives he dispatched.
Who knows how much he spent on things, on men,
and several times he trekked to far Lin-ch'ing.
He would search here while she was staying there.
Where should he look between the sky and sea?
He yearned and pined—he seemed to have his soul
inside a kiln, his heart beneath a plow.
The silkworm, spinning, wasted day by day;
the gaunt cicada, bit by frost, shrank more.
He languished, half alive, half dead—he'd weep
real tears of blood, but lose his soul to dreams.
    His parents took alarm because they feared
what, gone too far, his grief might lead him to.
In haste they readied things and chose a date:
an early marriage tied young Kim and Vân.
A graceful girl, a brilliant scholar wed,
uniting charms and gifts in their full flush.
Though he found joy in matrimonial life,
how could this happiness outweigh that grief?
They lived together—as he came to care
for his new union, surged his love of old.
Whenever he remembered Kiêu's ordeal,
he wept and felt a tightened knot inside.
    At times, in his hushed study, he would light

the incense burner, play the lute of yore.
Silk strings would sigh sweet moans while scentwood smoke
spread fragrant wisps and breezes stirred the blinds.
Then, from the steps beneath the roof, he'd hear
a girl's faint voice—he'd glimpse what seemed a skirt.
Because he'd etched his love in stone and bronze,
he'd dream of her and think she had come back.

    His days and nights were steeped in dismal gloom
while spring and autumn wheeled and wheeled about.
For learned men a contest now took place:
young Vuong and Kim attained the honor roll.[3]
Heaven's broad gate swung open—flowers hailed them
in His Majesty's park, fame reached their heaths.
    Young Vuong still kept in mind those days long past:
he called on Chung to settle his great debt.
He paid it off in full, then took to wife
Chung's daughter, thus allying their two clans.
    As Kim stepped briskly on amidst blue clouds,[4]
he thought of Kiêu and sorrowed all the more.
With whom had he exchanged those vows of troth?
With whom was he now sharing jade and gold?
Poor fern afloat down in the troughs of waves—
with honors blessed, he mourned her wandering life.
    Then he was sent to serve in far Lin-tzu:
with loved ones he trekked over hill and dale.
Now, in his yamen,[5] he lived leisured days
amidst the lute's sweet sounds, the crane's soft cries.[6]
    On a spring night, in her peach-curtained room,
asleep Vân dreamed and saw her sister Kiêu.
When she awoke, she told her spouse at once.
He wondered, torn between mistrust and hope:
"Lin-ch'ing, Lin-tzu—they differ by one word:[7]
they may have been mistaken each for each.
Two sisters, kindred souls, met in a dream—
perchance, we shall receive good tidings here."
    Now, working in his office, he inquired.
Old Dô, one of his clerks, gave this report:
"It all began more than ten years ago—
I knew them all quite well, each name, each face.
Dame Tú and Scholar Mã went to Peking—

---

[3] Examinations for the *chin-shih* or highest degree, the equivalent of a doctorate.
[4] An official career for *chin-shih* graduates.
[5] Official residence.
[6] Under the Sung Dynasty, Chao Pien (Trieu Bien) was an honest official with a simple way of life. When he was sent as governor to Shu (modern Szechwan) he took nothing with him but a lute and a crane.
[7] Kim had heard reports that Kieu was in Lin-ch'ing. He now begins to suspect that the reports were confused and that Kieu is in Lin-tzu, where Kim is now stationed.

they purchased Kiêu and brought her back with them.
In looks and gifts she stood without a peer.
She played the lute and wrote both prose and verse.
She wished to save her virtue, fiercely fought,
and tried to kill herself, so they used tricks.
She had to live in mud till she turned numb,
then marriage ties attached her to young Thúc.
But his first wife laid cruel hands on her
and held her in Wu-hsi to nip the flower.
When she betook herself from there and fled,
bad luck would have her fall among the Bacs.
No sooner caught than she was sold once more:
a cloud, a fern, she drifted here and there.
She happened on a man: he beat the world
in wit and grit, shook heaven by sheer might.
Leading a hundred thousand seasoned troops,
he came and stationed them throughout Lin-tzu.
Here Kiêu cleared off all scores from her sad past:
she rendered good for good or ill for ill.
She proved her loyal heart, her kindly soul—
she paid all debts, won praise from near and far.
I did not get to know the hero's name—
for this detail please query Scholar Thúc."
    After he heard old Dô's clear-drawn account,
Kim sent his card and bade Thúc visit him.
He asked his guest to settle dubious points:
"Where is Kiêu's husband now? And what's his name?"
    Thúc answered: "Caught in those wild times of strife,
I probed and asked some questions while at camp.
The chieftain's name was Hai, his surname Tù—
he won all battles, overwhelmed all foes.
He chanced to meet her while he was in T'ai—
genius and beauty wed, a natural course.
For many years he stormed about the world:
his thunder made earth quake and heaven quail!
He garrisoned his army in the East—
since then, all signs and clues of him are lost."
    Kim heard and knew the story root and branch—
anguish and dread played havoc with his heart:
"Alas for my poor leaf, a toy of winds!
When could she ever shake the world's foul dust?
As flows the stream, the flower's swept along—
I grieve her wave-tossed life, detached from mine.
From all our broken pledges I still keep
a bit of incense there, and here this lute.
Its soul has fled the strings—will incense there
give us its fire and fragrance in this life?
While she's now wandering, rootless, far from home,

how can I wallow in soft ease and wealth?"
His seal of office he'd as soon resign—
then he could cross all streams and scale all heights,
then he would venture onto fields of war
and risk his life to look for his lost love.
But heaven showed no track, the sea no trail—
where could he seek the bird or find the fish?
   While he was pausing, waiting for some news,
who knows how often cycled sun and rain?
Now from the throne, on rainbow-tinted sheets,
arrived decrees that clearly ordered thus:
Kim should assume new office in Nan-ping,
Vuong was transferred to functions at Fu-yang.
In haste they purchased horse and carriage, then
both families left together for their posts.
The news broke out: The rebels had been crushed—
waves stilled, fires quenched in Fukien and Chekiang.
Informed, Kim thereupon requested Vuong
to help him look for Kiêu along the way.
When they both reached Hang-chow, they could obtain
precise and proven facts about her fate.
This they were told: "One day, the fight was joined.
Tù, ambushed, fell a martyr on the field.
Kiêu's signal service earned her no reward:
by force they made her wed a tribal chief.
She drowned that body fine as jade, as pearl:
the Ch'ien-t'ang river has become her grave."
   Ah, torn asunder not to meet again!
They all were thriving—she had died foul death.

   To rest her soul, they set her tablet up,
installed an altar on the riverbank.
The tide cast wave on silver-crested wave:
gazing, all pictured how the bird had dropped.[8]
Deep love, a sea of griefs—so strange a fate!
Where had it strayed, the bird's disconsolate soul?[9]
   How queerly fortune's wheel will turn and spin!
Giác Duyên now somehow happened by the spot.
She saw the tablet, read the written name.
She cried, astonished: "Who are you, my friends?
Are you perchance some kith or kin of hers?
But she's alive! Why all these mourning rites?"
   They heard the news and nearly fell with shock.
All mobbed her, talked away, asked this and that:

---

[8] The fall of a wild goose is used as a metaphor for a quick, often heroic, death.
[9] According to Chinese mythology, after the daughter of Emperor Yen drowned at sea, her unhappy soul turned into a little bird that has tried ever since to fill up the deep with twigs and pebbles.

"Her husband here, her parents over there,
and there her sister, brother, and his wife.
From truthful sources we heard of her death,
but now you tell us this amazing news!"
   "Karma drew us together," said the nun,
"first at Lin-tzu, and next by the Ch'ien-t'ang.
When she would drown her beauteous body there,
I stood at hand and brought her safe to shore.
She's made her home within the Bodhi gate—
our grass-roofed cloister's not too far from here.
At Buddha's feet calm days go round and round,
but her mind's eye still fastens on her home."
   At what was heard all faces glowed and beamed:
could any bliss on earth exceed this joy?
The leaf had left its grove—since that dark day,
they'd vainly searched all streams and scanned all clouds.
The rose had fallen, its sweet scent had failed:
they might see her in afterworlds, not here.
She's gone the way of night, they dwelt with day—
now, back from those Nine Springs,[10] she walked on earth!
   All knelt and bowed their thanks to old Giác Duyên,
then in a group they followed on her heels.
They cut and cleared their way through reed and rush,
their loving hearts half doubting yet her word.
By twists and turns they edged along the shore,
pushed past that jungle, reached the Buddha's shrine.
In a loud voice, the nun Giác Duyên called Kiêu,
and from an inner room she hurried out.
   She glanced and saw her folks—they all were here:
Father looked still quite strong, and Mother spry;
both sister Vân and brother Quan grown up;
and over there was Kim, her love of yore.
Could she believe this moment, what it seemed?
Was she now dreaming open-eyed, awake?
Tear-pearls dropped one by one and damped her smock—
she felt such joy and grief, such grief and joy.
   She cast herself upon her mother's knees
and, weeping, told of all she had endured:
"Since I set out to wander through strange lands,
a wave-tossed fern, some fifteen years have passed.
I sought to end it in the river's mud—
who could have hoped to see you all on earth?"
   The parents held her hands, admired her face:
that face had not much changed since she left home.
The moon, the flower, lashed by wind and rain
for all that time, had lost some of its glow.

---

[10] The nether world or the world of the dead.

What scale could ever weigh their happiness?
Present and past, so much they talked about!
The two young ones kept asking this or that
while Kim looked on, his sorrow turned to joy.
Before the Buddha's altar all knelt down
and for Kiêu's resurrection offered thanks.
 At once they ordered sedans decked with flowers—
old Vuong bade Kiêu be carried home with them.
"I'm nothing but a fallen flower," she said.
"I drank of gall and wormwood half my life.
I thought to die on waves beneath the clouds—
how could my heart nurse hopes to see this day?
Yet I've survived and met you all again,
and slaked the thirst that long has parched my soul.
This cloister's now my refuge in the wilds—
to live with grass and trees befits my age.
I'm used to salt and greens in Dhyana fare;
I've grown to love the drab of Dhyana garb.
Within my heart the fire of lust is quenched—
why should I roll again in worldly dust?
What good is that, a purpose half achieved?
To nunhood vowed, I'll stay here till the end.
I owe to her who saved me sea-deep debts—
how can I cut my bonds with her and leave?"
 Old Vuong exclaimed: "Other times, other tides![11]
Even a saint must bow to circumstance.
You worship gods and Buddhas—who'll discharge
a daughter's duties, keep a lover's vows?
High Heaven saved your life—we'll build a shrine
and have our Reverend come, live there near us."
Heeding her father's word, Kiêu had to yield:
she took her leave of cloister and old nun.
 The group returned to Kim's own yamen where,
for their reunion, they all held a feast.
After mum wine instilled a mellow mood,
Vân rose and begged to air a thought or two;
"It's Heaven's own design that lovers meet,
so Kim and Kiêu did meet and swear their troth.
Then, over peaceful earth wild billows swept,
and in my sister's place I wedded him.
Amber and mustard seed, lodestone and pin![12]
Besides, 'when blood is spilt, the gut turns soft.'[13]
Day after day, we hoped and prayed for Kiêu

---

[11] Now is now, and then was then.
[12] Predestined, people are drawn together in love and marriage just as a mustard seed is attracted by amber and an iron pin or needle by lodestone.
[13] A proverb about family solidarity: When a relative gets hurt, the other members of the family cannot remain unconcerned about his or her troubles.

with so much love and grief these fifteen years.
But now the mirror cracked is whole again.
Wise Heaven's put her back where she belongs.
She still loves him and, luckily, still has him—
still shines the same old moon both once swore by.
The tree still bears some three or seven plums,[14]
the peach stays fresh[15]—it's time to tie the knot!"
    Kiêu brushed her sister's speech aside and said:
"Why now retell a tale of long ago?
We once did pledge our troth, but since those days,
my life has been exposed to wind and rain.
I'd die of shame discussing what's now past—
let those things flow downstream and out to sea!"
    "A curious way to put it!" Kim cut in.
"Whatever you may feel, your oath remains.
A vow of troth is witnessed by the world,
by earth below and heaven far above.
Though things may change and stars may shift their course,
sworn pledges must be kept in life or death.
Does fate, which brought you back, oppose our love?
We two are one—why split us in two halves?"
    "A home where love and concord reign," Kiêu said,
"whose heart won't yearn for it? But I believe
that to her man a bride should bring the scent
of a close bud, the shape of a full moon.
It's priceless, chastity—by nuptial torch,
am I to blush for what I'll offer you?
Misfortune struck me—since that day the flower
fell prey to bees and butterflies, ate shame.
For so long lashed by rain and swept by wind,
a flower's bound to fade, a moon to wane.
My cheeks were once two roses—what's now left?
My life is done—how can it be remade?
How dare I, boldfaced, soil with worldly filth
the homespun costume of a virtuous wife?[16]
You bear a constant love for me, I know—
but where to hide my shame by bridal light?
From this day on I'll shut my chamber door:
though I will take no vows, I'll live a nun.
If you still care for what we both once felt,
let's turn it into friendship—let's be friends.

---

[14] Van implies that Kieu is not yet too old for marriage by alluding to a courtship song.
[15] The young, fresh peach tree is the image of a beautiful bride according to a wedding song.
[16] The phrase "a skirt of coarse cloth and a thorn for a hairpin" stands for virtuous wifehood according to Confucian ethics.

Why speak of marriage with its red silk thread?[17]
It pains my heart and further stains my life."
    "How skilled you are in spinning words!" Kim said.
"You have your reasons—others have their own.
Among those duties falling to her lot,
a woman's chastity means many things.
For there are times of ease and times of stress:
in crisis, must one rigid rule apply?
True daughter, you upheld a woman's role:
what dust or dirt could ever sully you?
Heaven grants us this hour: now from our gate
all mists have cleared; on high, clouds roll away.
The faded flower's blooming forth afresh,
the waning moon shines more than at its full.
What is there left to doubt? Why treat me like
another Hsiao, a passerby ignored?"[18]
    He argued, pleaded, begged—she heard him through.
Her parents also settled on his plans.
Outtalked, she could no longer disagree:
she hung her head and yielded, stifling sighs.
    They held a wedding-feast—bright candles lit
all flowers, set aglow the red silk rug.
Before their elders groom and bride bowed low—
all rites observed, they now were man and wife.
    In their own room they traded toasts, still shy
of their new bond, yet moved by their old love.
Since he, a lotus sprout,[19] first met with her,
a fresh peach bud, fifteen full years had fled.
To fall in love, to part, to reunite—
both felt mixed grief and joy as rose the moon.
    The hour was late—the curtain dropped its fringe:
under the light gleamed her peach-blossom cheeks.
Two lovers met again—out of the past,
a bee, a flower constant in their love.
    "I've made my peace with my own fate," she said.
"What can this cast-off body be good for?
I thought of your devotion to our past—
to please you, I went through those wedding rites.
But how ashamed I felt in my own heart,
lending a brazen front to all that show!

---

[17] A crimson or red silk thread spun by the Marriage God bound a man and a woman together in wedlock.

[18] Under the T'ang dynasty, young Hsiao had a beautiful wife named Lu-chu. She was abducted and offered as a concubine to the powerful general Kuo Tzu-i. After that time, she no longer recognized her former husband and looked away when she saw him in the street.

[19] The lotus is long associated with love.

Don't go beyond the outward marks of love—
perhaps, I might then look you in the face.
But if you want to get what they all want,
glean scent from dirt, or pluck a wilting flower,
then we'll flaunt filth, put on a foul display,
and only hate, not love, will then remain.
When you make love and I feel only shame,
then rank betrayal's better than such love.
If you must give your clan a rightful heir,
you have my sister—there's no need for me.
What little chastity I may have saved,
am I to fling it under trampling feet?
More tender feelings pour from both our hearts—
why toy and crumple up a faded flower?"
    "An oath bound us together," he replied.
"We split, like fish to sea and bird to sky.
Through your long exile how I grieved for you!
Breaking your troth, you must have suffered so.
We loved each other, risked our lives, braved death—
now we two meet again, still deep in love.
The willow in mid-spring still has green leaves—
I thought you still attached to human love.
But no more dust stains your clear mirror now:
your vow can't but increase my high regard.
If I long searched the sea for my lost pin,[20]
it was true love, not lust, that urged me on.
We're back together now, beneath one roof:
to live in concord, need two share one bed?"
    Kiêu pinned her hair and straightened up her gown,
then knelt to touch her head in gratitude:
"If ever my soiled body's cleansed of stains,
I'll thank a gentleman, a noble soul.
The words you spoke came from a kindred heart:
no truer empathy between two souls.
A home, a refuge—what won't you give me?
My honor lives again as of tonight."
    Their hands unclasped, then clasped and clasped again—
now he esteemed her, loved her all the more.
They lit another candle up, refilled
the incense urn, then drank to their new joy.
His old desire for her came flooding back—
he softly asked about her luting skill.
"Those strings of silk entangled me," she said,
"in sundry woes which haven't ceased till now.

---

[20] "To grope for a pin on the bottom of the sea" is the Vietnamese equivalent of "to look for a needle in a haystack."

Alas, what's done regrets cannot undo—
but I'll obey your wish just one more time."
    Her elfin fingers danced and swept the strings—
sweet strains made waves with curls of scentwood smoke.
Who sang this hymn to life and peace on earth?
Was it a butterfly or Master Chuang?[21]
And who poured forth this rhapsody of love?
The king of Shu or just a cuckoo-bird?[22]
Clear notes like pearls dropped in a moon-lit bay.
Warm notes like crystals of new Lan-t'ien jade.[23]
    His ears drank in all five tones of the scale—
all sounds which stirred his heart and thrilled his soul.
"Whose hand is playing that old tune?" he asked.
"What sounded once so sad now sounds so gay!
It's from within that joy or sorrow comes—
have bitter days now set and sweet ones dawned?"
"This pleasant little pastime," answered she,
"once earned me grief and woe for many years.
For you my lute just sang its one last song—
henceforth, I'll roll its strings and play no more."
    The secrets of their hearts were flowing still
when cocks crowed up the morning in the east.
Kim spoke, told all about their private pact.
All marveled at her wish and lauded her—
a woman of high mind, not some coquette
who'd with her favors skip from man to man.
    Of love and friendship they fulfilled both claims—
they shared no bed but joys of lute and verse.
Now they sipped wine, now played a game of chess,
admiring flowers, waiting for the moon.
Their wishes all came true since fate so willed,
and of two lovers marriage made two friends.
    As pledged, they built a temple on the hill,
then sent a trusted man to fetch the nun.
When he got there, he found doors shut and barred—
he saw a weed-grown rooftop, moss-filled cracks.
She'd gone to gather simples,[24] he was told:

---

[21] A well-known passage in the *Chuang-tzu*, a Taoist classic, reads: "Chuang Chou once dreamed that he was a butterfly, fluttering to and fro and enjoying itself. Suddenly he woke up and was Chuang Chou again. But he did not know whether he was Chuang Chou who had dreamed that he was a butterfly, or whether he was a butterfly dreaming that it was Chuang Chou."

[22] Emperor Wang ruled Shu (in modern Szechwan) as an exemplary sovereign until he fell in love with his minister's wife and had an affair with her. Discovered, he yielded the throne to the offended husband and fled into shamed seclusion in the mountains. He died there and turned into the cuckoo (or nightjar), whose mournful cry bemoans the double loss of his realm and his love.

[23] A mountain in Shensi renowned for its jade.

[24] Medicinal plants.

the cloud had flown, the crane had fled—but where?
For old times' sake, Kiêu kept the temple lit,
its incense candles burning night and day.
   The twice-blessed home enjoyed both weal and wealth.
Kim climbed the office ladder year by year.
Vân gave him many heirs: a stooping tree,[25]
a yardful of sophoras and cassia shrubs.[26]
In rank or riches who could rival them?
Their garden throve, won glory for all times.

   This we have learned: with Heaven rest all things.
Heaven appoints each human to a place.
If doomed to roll in dust, we'll roll in dust;
we'll sit on high when destined for high seats.
Does Heaven ever favor anyone,
bestowing both rare talent and good luck?
In talent take no overweening pride,
for talent and disaster form a pair.
Our karma we must carry as our lot—
let's stop decrying Heaven's whims and quirks.
Inside ourselves there lies the root of good:
the heart outweighs all talents on this earth.

Further Readings

Studies in English of Vietnam before the Vietnam Conflict are relatively sparse. Joseph Buttinger, *A Dragon Defiant: A Short History of Vietnam* (New York: Praeger, 1972), is a short survey concentrating on the twentieth century. The foundation of an independent Vietnam is the subject of Keith W. Taylor, *The Birth of Vietnam* (Berkeley, CA: University of California Press, 1983). Chinese influences on Vietnamese institutional development are considered in Alexander B. Woodside, *Vietnam and the Chinese Model* (Cambridge, MA: Harvard University Press, 1971), and *Historical Interaction of China and Vietnam: Institutional and Cultural Themes*, compiled by Edgar Wickberg (Lawrence, KS: Center for East Asian Studies, University of Kansas, 1969). *Traditional Vietnam: Some Historical Stages*, edited by Nguyen Khac Vien (Hanoi: Xunhasaba, 1965), is an interesting survey of Vietnamese history,

---

[25] A tree with down-curving branches around which cling many vines. Originally, it must have referred to a lord, who shelters and supports many dependents and retainers. In Vietnamese literary tradition, it has mainly stood for a first-rank wife as the protector of her husband's concubines. In this line, while the "stooping tree" clearly designates Van as Kim's chief spouse, it can also be broadly interpreted to mean a mother who takes good care of her numerous brood of children, a tree that casts its shade over "a yardful of sophoras and cassia shrubs."

[26] Under the Sung dynasty, Tou Yü-chün was blessed with five brilliant sons: they all took the highest honors at literary examinations. The poet Feng Tao celebrated them in a poem as the Five Cassias. Again, under the Sung Dynasty, Wang Hu who had three sons, planted in his front yard three sophora trees in symbolic hope that they all would grow up to become ministers of state. Therefore, a yardful of sophoras means one's children, especially one's sons, for whom one entertains great expectations.

with good coverage of the end of the Le dynasty and the Tay-son movement, written from a Marxist and patriotic point of view.

Maurice Durand and Nguyen Tran Huan, *A History of Vietnamese Literature*, translated by D. M. Hawke (New York: Columbia University Press, 1985), is an excellent French study newly translated into English. Some excellent examples of Vietnamese poetry are found in *The Heritage of Vietnamese Poetry*, edited and translated by Huynh Sanh Thong (New Haven, CT: Yale University Press, 1979).

Democracy in America

In July 1830, a popular uprising in France ended the reactionary regime of Charles X (1824–1830) and initiated a period of conflict between liberals and conservatives that would persist until the establishment of the Second Empire (1851–1870). Many of the liberals felt their position to be precarious, even apart from present political considerations. During the French Revolution of 1789, a similar attempt to establish a moderate liberal government had slid steadily toward mob rule, radicalism, and finally to the seizure of power by Napoleon Bonaparte. It was clear that the concept of liberalism, embodying the tenets of individual liberty and responsive government, and that of democracy, advocating a greater popular participation in political power, could not be separated. It was not clear, however, that these two concepts were compatible, that a democracy could provide the basis for a stable, liberal state. There was only one place in the world in 1830 where this seemed to be happening, the United States of North America. Here the Americans had preserved a constitutional government embodying the basic principles of liberalism without serious difficulties for over forty years.

It was against this background that a young French magistrate, Count Alexis de Tocqueville (1805–1859), obtained a commission from the government to visit the United States. Ostensibly studying American prisons and prison reform, his real interest was in observing the great American experiment in liberal republicanism and ascertaining the effect democratizing tendencies were having in American society. He arrived in May 1831 and returned to France in February 1832, after a stay of only nine months. He had spent his time well, however. His study of the United States, entitled *Democracy*

From Alexis de Tocqueville, *Democracy in America*, edited by Richard D. Heffner (New York: New American Library, 1956), pp. 26, 29, 32–34, 36, 112–119, 189–192, 306–307, and 309–314.

in America, was published in 1835 and immediately caught the attention of liberal leaders in both France and Great Britain. De Tocqueville had made available for the first time a reasoned analysis of American government and society and, in so doing, he had defined some of the basic philosophical issues and conflicts with which liberal and democratic governments would have to contend.

Upon his arrival in America, he found a nation that was, in many ways, a liberal utopia. It was free of the oppressive established institutions and entrenched privileged classes that characterized European society. Its Constitution, particularly its Bill of Rights, guaranteed and protected those individual rights and liberties that liberal thinkers held to be fundamental to a truly just society. Moreover, the open frontier and abundant natural resources had largely eliminated any poor or disadvantaged classes. Widely spread wealth and universally held liberties, with the obvious anomaly of the slave economy of the South, gave America every chance of establishing and maintaining a free society in which the individual would be allowed the fullest opportunity of personal growth and achievement.

De Tocqueville had arrived in America at a time when democratizing tendencies were ascendant. The extension of suffrage, the restriction of indirect elections, the disappearance of property qualifications for voting and holding office, the perfection of the system of popular political parties, and the spread of the idea of equality were changing the face of American society and politics. And yet, de Tocqueville saw problems in America's future. With the triumph of Jacksonian democracy and what some American historians have called the "rise of the common man," the educated elite that had shaped the foundation of the Republic was being supplanted by a new, less-educated, and often less-discerning generation of leaders.

De Tocqueville was troubled also by what he perceived as fundamental conflicts raised by the spread of democracy within America. He feared that the emphasis on the will of the popular majority could erode the rights and liberties of the few and make a mockery of American freedom. He questioned whether the ideal of equality might not obscure true merit and swamp quality with quantity. He asked whether the rule of the popular majority and the concept of equality might not in time reduce Americans to a general conformity that would destroy that very individualism that the founders of the Republic had set out to secure. This is not to say, however, he was willing to sacrifice the concept of popular rule to preserve individual liberty or vice versa. He concluded that these two principles did conflict and that, if a liberal democracy were to survive, it would be necessary to maintain a balance between the two tendencies.

De Tocqueville attempted to put his ideas into practice as a member of the French government, but with little success. A *coup d'état* in 1851 ended the liberal regime and inaugurated the Second Empire under Napoleon III. De Tocqueville was imprisoned for a short time. Having regained his freedom, he published his second great work, *The Old Regime,* in 1855. He died in 1859 in the South of France, but his study of *Democracy in America* has continued to be the inspiration of discussion and debate. Enlightenment intellectuals, inspired by Newton's view of a universe moving in perfect order in conformance with its own internal laws, had assumed that the basic principles of a perfect society would be harmonious and that the state would therefore be stable. De Tocqueville suggested that liberal democracy is not inherently stable and that its preservation depends upon its citizens maintaining a balance between the various dynamic elements of their government and society. For this reason, *Democracy in America* has sometimes been called "a school for citizenship."

Questions

1. What does de Tocqueville consider to be the social and political effects of the concept of equality?

2. Where does the power of the majority manifest itself?

3. How does equality endanger liberty?

4. How can liberty be protected from equality and the tyranny of the majority?

DEMOCRACY IN AMERICA

Amongst the novel objects that attracted my attention during my stay in the United States, nothing struck me more forcibly than the general equality of condition among the people. I readily discovered the prodigious influence which this primary fact exercises on the whole course of society; it gives a peculiar direction to public opinion, and a peculiar tenor to the laws; it imparts new maxims to the governing authorities, and peculiar habits to the governed.

I soon perceived that the influence of this fact extends far beyond the political character and the laws of the country, and that it has no less empire over civil society than over the government; it creates opinions, gives birth to new sentiments, founds novel customs, and modifies whatever it does not produce. The more I advanced in the study of American society, the more I perceived that this equality of condition is the fundamental fact from which all others seem to be derived, and the central point at which all my observations constantly terminated.

I then turned my thoughts to our own hemisphere, and thought that I discerned there something analogous to the spectacle which the New World presented to me. I observed that equality of condition, though it has not there reached the extreme limit which it seems to have attained in the United States, is constantly approaching it; and that the democracy which governs the American communities appears to be rapidly rising into power in Europe. Hence I conceived the idea of the book which is now before the reader.

◇ ◇ ◇

Nor is this peculiar to France. Whithersoever we turn our eyes, we perceive the same revolution going on throughout the Christian world. The various occurrences of national existence have everywhere turned to the advantage of democracy: all men have aided it by their exertions, both those who have intentionally labored in its cause, and those who have served it unwittingly; those who have fought for it, and those who have declared themselves its opponents, have all been driven along in the same track, have all labored to one end; some ignorantly and some unwillingly, all have been blind instruments in the hands of God.

The gradual development of the principle of equality is, therefore, a Providential fact. It has all the chief characteristics of such a fact: it is universal, it is durable, it constantly eludes all human interference, and all events as well as all men contribute to its progress.

Would it, then, be wise to imagine that a social movement, the causes of which lie so far back, can be checked by the efforts of one generation? Can it be believed that the democracy which has overthrown the feudal system, and vanquished kings, will retreat before tradesmen and capitalists? Will it stop now that it has grown so strong, and its adversaries so weak? Whither, then, are we tending? No one can say, for terms of comparison already fail us. The conditions of men are more equal in Christian countries at the present day than they have been at any previous time, or in any part of the world; so that the magnitude of what already has been done prevents us from foreseeing what is yet to be accomplished.

The whole book which is here offered to the public has been written under the impression of a kind of religious terror produced in the author's mind by the view of that irresistible revolution which has advanced for centuries in spite of every obstacle, and which is still advancing in the midst of the ruins it has caused.

◇ ◇ ◇

But the scene is now changed. Gradually the distinctions of rank are done away; the barriers which once severed mankind are falling down; property is divided, power is shared by many, the light of intelligence spreads, and the capacities of all classes are equally cultivated. The State becomes democratic, and the empire of democracy is slowly and peaceably introduced into the institutions and the manners of the nation.

I can conceive of a society in which all men would feel an equal love and respect for the laws of which they consider themselves as the authors; in which the authority of the government would be respected as necessary, though not as divine; and in which the loyalty of the subject to the chief magistrate would not be a passion, but a quiet and rational persuasion. Every individual being in the possession of rights which he is sure to retain, a kind of manly confidence and reciprocal courtesy would arise between all classes, alike removed from pride and servility. The people, well acquainted with their own true interests, would understand that, in order to profit by the advantages of society, it is necessary to satisfy its requisitions. The voluntary association of the citizens might then take the place of the individual exertions of the nobles, and the community would be alike protected from anarchy and from oppression.

I admit that, in a democratic state thus constituted, society would not be stationary. But the impulses of the social body might there be regulated and made progressive. If there were less splendor than in the midst of an aristocracy, the contrast of misery would also be less frequent; the pleasures of enjoyment might be less excessive, but those of comfort would be more general; the sciences might be less perfectly cultivated, but ignorance would be less common; the impetuosity of the feelings would be repressed, and the habits of the nation softened; there would be more vices and fewer great crimes.

In the absence of enthusiasm and an ardent faith, great sacrifices may be obtained from the members of a commonwealth by an appeal to their understandings and their experience; each individual will feel the same necessity of union with his fellows to protect his own weakness; and as he knows that he can obtain their help only on condition of helping them, he will readily perceive that his personal interest is identified with the interests of the whole community. The nation, taken as a whole, will be less brilliant, less glorious, and perhaps less strong; but the majority of the citizens will enjoy a greater degree of prosperity, and the people will remain quiet, not because they despair of a change for the better, but because they are conscious that they are well off already. If all the consequences of this state of things were not good or useful, society would at least have appropriated all such as were useful and good; and having once and for ever renounced the social advantages of aristocracy, mankind would enter into possession of all the benefits which democracy can afford.

But here it may be asked what we have adopted in the place of those institutions, those ideas, and those customs of our forefathers which we have abandoned. The spell of royalty is broken, but it has not been succeeded by the majesty of the laws. The people have learned to despise all authority, but they still fear it; and fear now extorts more than was formerly paid from reverence and love. I perceive that we have destroyed those individual powers which were able, single-handed, to cope with tyranny; but it is the government that has inherited the privileges of which families, corporations, and individuals have been deprived; to the power of a small number of persons—which, if it was sometimes oppressive, was often conservative—has succeeded the weakness of the whole community.

The division of property has lessened the distance which separated the rich from the poor; but it would seem that the nearer they draw to each other, the greater is their mutual hatred, and the more vehement the envy and the dread with which they resist each other's claims to power; the idea of Right does not exist for either party, and Force affords to both the only argument for the present, and the only guaranty for the future.

The poor man retains the prejudices of his forefathers without their faith, and their ignorance without their virtues; he has adopted the doctrine of self-interest as the rule of his actions, without understanding the science which puts it to use; and his selfishness is no less blind than was formerly his devotedness to others. If society is tranquil, it is not because it is conscious of its strength and its well-being, but because it fears its weakness and its infirmities; a single effort may cost it its life. Everybody feels the evil, but no one has courage or energy enough to seek the cure. The desires, the repinings, the sorrows, and the joys of the present time lead to no visible or permanent result, like the passions of old men, which terminate in impotence.

We have, then, abandoned whatever advantages the old state of things afforded, without receiving any compensation from our present condition; we have destroyed an aristocracy, and we seem inclined to survey its ruins with complacency, and to fix our abode in the midst of them.

◇ ◇ ◇

There is a country in the world where the great social revolution which I am speaking of seems to have nearly reached its natural limits. It has been effected with ease and quietness; say rather that this country is reaping the fruits of the democratic revolution which we are undergoing, without having had the revolution itself.

The emigrants who colonized the shores of America in the beginning of the seventeenth century somehow separated the democratic principle from all the principles which it had to contend with in the old communities of Europe, and transplanted it alone to the New World. It has there been able to spread in perfect freedom, and peaceably to determine the character of the laws by influencing the manners of the country.

It appears to me beyond a doubt that, sooner or later, we shall arrive, like the Americans, at an almost complete equality of condition. But I do not conclude from this, that we shall ever be necessarily led to draw the same political consequences which the Americans have derived from a similar social organization. I am far from supposing that they have chosen the only form of government which a democracy may adopt; but as the generative cause of laws and manners in the two countries is the same, it is of immense interest for us to know what it has produced in each of them.

It is not, then, merely to satisfy a legitimate curiosity that I have examined America; my wish has been to find there instruction by which we may ourselves profit. Whoever should imagine that I have intended to write a panegyric would be strangely mistaken, and on reading this book, he will perceive that such was not my design: nor has it been my object to advocate any form of government in particular, for I am of opinion that absolute excellence is rarely to be found in any system of laws. I have not even pretended to judge whether the social revolution, which I believe to be irresistible, is advantageous or prejudicial to mankind. I have acknowledged this revolution as a fact already accomplished, or on the eve of its accomplishment; and I have selected the nation, from amongst those which have undergone it, in which its development has been the most peaceful and the most complete, in order to discern its natural consequences, and to find out, if possible, the means of rendering it profitable to mankind. I confess that, in America, I saw more than America; I sought there the image of democracy itself, with its inclinations, its character, its prejudices, and its passions, in order to learn what we have to fear or to hope from its progress.

◇ ◇ ◇

Unlimited Power of the Majority in the United States and Its Consequences

The very essence of democratic government consists in the absolute sovereignty of the majority; for there is nothing in democratic states which is capable of resisting it. Most of the American constitutions have sought to increase this natural strength of the majority by artificial means.

The legislature is, of all political institutions, the one which is most easily swayed by the will of the majority. The Americans determined that the members of the legislature should be elected by the people *directly*, and for a *very brief term*, in order to subject them, not only to the general convictions, but even to the daily passions, of their constituents. The members of both houses are taken from the same classes in society, and nominated in the same manner; so that the movements of the legislative bodies are almost as rapid, and quite as irresistible, as those of a single assembly. It is to a legislature thus constituted, that almost all the authority of the government has been intrusted.

At the same time that the law increased the strength of those authorities which of themselves were strong, it enfeebled more and more those which were naturally weak. It deprived the representatives of the executive power of all stability and independence; and, by subjecting them completely to the caprices of the legislature, it robbed them of the slender influence which the nature of a democratic government might have allowed them to exercise. In several States, the judicial power was also submitted to the election of the majority; and in all of them, its existence was made to depend on the pleasure of the legislative authority, since the representatives were empowered annually to regulate the stipend of the judges.

Custom has done even more than law. A proceeding is becoming more and more general in the United States, which will, in the end, do away with the guaranties of representative government: it frequently happens that the voters, in electing a delegate, point out a certain line of conduct to him, and impose upon him certain positive obligations which he is pledged to fulfil. With the exception of the tumult, this comes to the same thing as if the majority itself held its deliberations in the market-place.

Several other circumstances concur to render the power of the majority in America not only preponderant, but irresistible. The moral authority of the majority is partly based upon the notion, that there is more intelligence and wisdom in a number of men united than in a single individual, and that the number of the legislators is more important than their quality. The theory of equality is thus applied to the intellects of men; and human pride is thus assailed in its last retreat by a doctrine which the minority hesitate to admit, and to which they will but slowly assent. Like all other powers, and perhaps more than any other, the authority of the many requires the sanction of time in order to appear legitimate. At first, it enforces obedience by constraint; and its laws are not *respected* until they have been long maintained.

The right of governing society, which the majority supposes itself to derive from its superior intelligence, was introduced into the United States by the first settlers; and this idea, which of itself would be sufficient to create a free nation, has now been amalgamated with the manners of the people and the minor incidents of social life.

The French, under the old monarchy, held it for a maxim that the king could do no wrong; and if he did do wrong, the blame was imputed to his advisers. This notion made obedience very easy; it enabled the subject to complain of the law, without ceasing to love and honor the lawgiver. The Americans entertain the same opinion with respect to the majority.

The moral power of the majority is founded upon yet another principle, which is, that the interests of the many are to be preferred to those of the few. It will readily be perceived that the respect here professed for the rights of the greater number must naturally increase or diminish according to the state of parties. When a nation is divided into several great irreconcilable interests, the privilege of the majority is often overlooked, because it is intolerable to comply with its demands.

If there existed in America a class of citizens whom the legislating majority sought to deprive of exclusive privileges which they had possessed for ages, and to bring down from an elevated station to the level of the multitude, it is probable that the minority would be less ready to submit to its laws. But as the United States were colonized by men holding equal rank, there is as yet no natural or permanent disagreement between the interests of its different inhabitants.

There are communities in which the members of the minority can never hope to draw over the majority to their side, because they must then give up the very point which is at issue between them. Thus, an aristocracy can never become a majority whilst it retains its exclusive privileges, and it cannot cede its privileges without ceasing to be an aristocracy.

In the United States, political questions cannot be taken up in so general and absolute a manner; and all parties are willing to recognize the rights of the majority, because they all hope at some time to be able to exercise them to their own advantage. The majority, therefore, in that country, exercise a prodigious actual authority, and a power of opinion which is nearly as great; no obstacles exist which can impede or even retard its progress, so as to make it heed the complaints of those whom it crushes upon its path. This state of things is harmful in itself, and dangerous for the future.

◇ ◇ ◇

Tyranny of the Majority

I hold it to be an impious and detestable maxim, that, politically speaking, the people have a right to do anything; and yet I have asserted that all authority originates in the will of the majority. Am I, then, in contradiction with myself?

A general law, which bears the name of justice, has been made and sanctioned, not only by a majority of this or that people, but by a majority of mankind. The rights of every people are therefore confined within the limits of what is just. A nation may be considered as a jury which is empowered to represent society at large, and to apply justice, which is its law. Ought such a jury, which represents society, to have more power than the society itself, whose laws it executes?

When I refuse to obey an unjust law, I do not contest the right of the majority to command, but I simply appeal from the sovereignty of the people to the sovereignty of mankind. Some have not feared to assert that a people can never outstep the boundaries of justice and reason in those affairs which are peculiarly its own; and that consequently full power may be given to the majority by which they are represented. But this is the language of a slave.

A majority taken collectively is only an individual, whose opinions, and frequently whose interests, are opposed to those of another individual, who is styled a minority. If it be admitted that a man possessing absolute power may misuse that power by wronging his adversaries, why should not a majority be liable to the same reproach? Men do not change their characters by uniting with each other; nor does their patience in the presence of obstacles increase with their strength. For my own part, I cannot believe it; the power to do everything, which I should refuse to one of my equals, I will never grant to any number of them.

I do not think, for the sake of preserving liberty, it is possible to combine several principles in the same government so as really to oppose them to one another. The form of government which is usually termed *mixed* has always appeared to me a mere chimera. Accurately speaking, there is no such thing as a *mixed government,* in the sense usually given to that word, because, in all communities, some one principle of action may be discovered which preponderates over the others. England, in the last century,—which has been especially cited as an example of this sort of government,—was essentially an aristocratic state, although it comprised some great elements of democracy; for the laws and customs of the country were such that the aristocracy could not but preponderate in the long run, and direct public affairs according to its own will. The error arose from seeing the interests of the nobles perpetually contending with those of the people, without considering the issue of the contest, which was really the important point. When a community actually has a mixed government,—that is to say, when it is equally divided between adverse principles,—it must either experience a revolution, or fall into anarchy.

I am therefore of opinion, that social power superior to all others must always be placed somewhere; but I think that liberty is endangered when this power finds no obstacle which can retard its course, and give it time to moderate its own vehemence.

Unlimited power is in itself a bad and dangerous thing. Human beings are not competent to exercise it with discretion. God alone can be omnipotent, because his wisdom and his justice are always equal to his power. There is no power on earth so worthy of honor in itself, or clothed with rights so sacred, that I would admit its uncontrolled and all-predominant authority. When I see that the right and the means of absolute command are conferred on any power whatever, be it called a people or a king, an aristocracy or a democracy, a monarchy or a republic, I say there is the germ of tyranny, and I seek to live elsewhere, under other laws.

In my opinion, the main evil of the present democratic institutions of the United States does not arise, as is often asserted in Europe, from their weakness, but from their irresistible strength. I am not so much alarmed at the excessive liberty which reigns in that country, as at the inadequate securities which one finds there against tyranny.

When an individual or a party is wronged in the United States, to whom can he apply for redress? If to public opinion, public opinion constitutes the majority; if to the legislature, it represents the majority, and implicitly obeys it; if to the executive power, it is appointed by the majority, and serves as a passive tool in its hands. The public force consists of the majority under arms; the jury is the majority invested with the right of hearing judicial cases; and in certain States, even the judges are elected by the majority. However iniquitous or absurd the measure of which you complain, you must submit to it as well as you can.

If, on the other hand, a legislative power could be so constituted as to represent the majority without necessarily being the slave of its passions, an executive so as to retain a proper share of authority, and a judiciary so as to remain independent of the other two powers, a government would be formed which would still be democratic, without incurring hardly any risk of tyranny.

I do not say that there is a frequent use of tyranny in America, at the present day; but I maintain that there is no sure barrier against it, and that the causes which mitigate the government there are to be found in the circumstances and the manners of the country, more than in its laws.

◇ ◇ ◇

Power Exercised by the Majority in America upon Opinion

It is in the examination of the exercise of thought in the United States, that we clearly perceive how far the power of the majority surpasses all the powers with which we are acquainted in Europe. Thought is an invisible and subtle power, that mocks all the efforts of tyranny. At the present time, the most absolute monarchs in Europe cannot prevent certain opinions hostile to their authority from circulating in secret through their dominions, and even in their courts. It is not so in America; as long as the majority is still undecided, discussion is carried on; but as soon as its decision is irrevocably pronounced, every one is silent, and the friends as well as the opponents of the measure unite in assenting to its propriety. The reason of this is perfectly clear: no monarch is so absolute as to combine all the powers of society in his own hands, and to conquer all opposition, as a majority is able to do, which has the right both of making and of executing the laws.

The authority of a king is physical, and controls the actions of men without subduing their will. But the majority possesses a power which is physical and moral at the same time, which acts upon the will as much as upon the actions, and represses not only all contest, but all controversy.

I know of no country in which there is so little independence of mind and real freedom of discussion as in America. In any constitutional state in Europe, every sort of religious and political theory may be freely preached and disseminated; for there is no country in Europe so subdued by any single authority, as not to protect the man who raises his voice in the cause of truth from the consequences of his hardihood. If he is unfortunate enough to live under an absolute government, the people are often upon his side; if he inhabits a free country, he can, if necessary, find a shelter behind the throne. The aristocratic part of society supports him in some countries, and the democracy in others. But in a nation where democratic institutions exist, organized like those of the United States, there is but one authority, one element of strength and success, with nothing beyond it.

In America, the majority raises formidable barriers around the liberty of opinion: within these barriers, an author may write what he pleases; but woe to him if he goes beyond them. Not that he is in danger of an *auto-da-fé*,[1] but he is exposed to continued obloquy and persecution. His political career is closed forever, since he has offended the only authority which is able to open it. Every sort of compensation, even that of celebrity, is refused to him. Before publishing his opinions, he imagined that he held them in common with others; but no sooner has he declared them, than he is loudly censured by his opponents, whilst those who think like him, without having the courage to speak out, abandon him in silence. He yields at length, overcome by the daily effort which he has to make, and subsides into silence, as if he felt remorse for having spoken the truth.

Fetters and headsmen were the coarse instruments which tyranny formerly employed; but the civilization of our age has perfected despotism itself, though it seemed to have nothing to learn. Monarchs had, so to speak, materialized oppression: the democratic republics of the present day have rendered it as entirely an affair of the mind, as the will which it is intended to coerce. Under the absolute sway of one man, the body was attacked in order to subdue the soul; but the soul escaped the blows which were directed

---
[1] Inquisitorial judgment and punishment.

against it, and rose proudly superior. Such is not the course adopted by tyranny in democratic republics; there the body is left free, and the soul is enslaved. The master no longer says, "You shall think as I do, or you shall die"; but he says, "You are free to think differently from me, and to retain your life, your property, and all that you possess; but you are henceforth a stranger among your people. You may retain your civil rights, but they will be useless to you, for you will never be chosen by your fellow-citizens, if you solicit their votes; and they will affect to scorn you, if you ask for their esteem. You will remain among men, but you will be deprived of the rights of mankind. Your fellow-creatures will shun you like an impure being; and even those who believe in your innocence will abandon you, lest they should be shunned in their turn. Go in peace! I have given you your life, but it is an existence worse than death."

Absolute monarchies had dishonored despotism; let us beware lest democratic republics should reinstate it, and render it less odious and degrading in the eyes of the many, by making it still more onerous to the few.

Works have been published in the proudest nations of the Old World, expressly intended to censure the vices and the follies of the times: Labruyère inhabited the palace of Louis XIV, when he composed his chapter upon the Great, and Molière criticised the courtiers in the pieces which were acted before the court. But the ruling power in the United States is not to be made game of. The smallest reproach irritates its sensibility, and the slightest joke which has any foundation in truth renders it indignant; from the forms of its language up to the solid virtues of its character, everything must be made the subject of encomium. No writer, whatever be his eminence, can escape paying this tribute of adulation to his fellow-citizens. The majority lives in the perpetual utterance of self-applause; and there are certain truths which the Americans can only learn from strangers or from experience.

If America has not as yet had any great writers, the reason is given in these facts; there can be no literary genius without freedom of opinion, and freedom of opinion does not exist in America. The Inquisition has never been able to prevent a vast number of anti-religious books from circulating in Spain. The empire of the majority succeeds much better in the United States, since it actually removes any wish to publish them. Unbelievers are to be met with in America, but there is no public organ of infidelity. Attempts have been made by some governments to protect morality by prohibiting licentious books. In the United States, no one is punished for this sort of books, but no one is induced to write them; not because all the citizens are immaculate in conduct, but because the majority of the community is decent and orderly.

In this case the use of the power is unquestionably good; and I am discussing the nature of the power itself. This irresistible authority is a constant fact, and its judicious exercise is only an accident.

◇ ◇ ◇

Why Democratic Nations Show a More Ardent and Enduring Love of Equality Than of Liberty

The first and most intense passion which is produced by equality of condition is, I need hardly say, the love of that equality. My readers will therefore not be surprised that I speak of this feeling before all others.

Everybody has remarked that, in our time, and especially in France, this passion for equality is every day gaining ground in the human heart. It has been said a hundred times, that our contemporaries are far more ardently and tenaciously attached to equality than to freedom; but, as I do not find that the causes of the fact have been sufficiently analyzed, I shall endeavor to point them out.

It is possible to imagine an extreme point at which freedom and equality would meet and be confounded together. Let us suppose that all the people take a part in the government, and that each one of them has an equal right to take a part in it. As no one is different from his fellows, none can exercise a tyrannical power; men will be perfectly free, because they are all entirely equal; and they will all be perfectly equal, because they are entirely free. To this ideal state democratic nations tend. This is the only complete form that equality can assume upon earth; but there are a thousand others which, without being equally perfect, are not less cherished by those nations.

The principle of equality may be established in civil society, without prevailing in the political world. Equal rights may exist of indulging in the same pleasures, of entering the same professions, of frequenting the same places; in a word, of living in the same manner and seeking wealth by the same means,—although all men do not take an equal share in the government. A kind of equality may even be established in the political world, though there should be no political freedom there. A man may be the equal of all his countrymen save one, who is the master of all without distinction, and who selects equally from among them all the agents of his power. Several other combinations might be easily imagined, by which very great equality would be united to institutions more or less free, or even to institutions wholly without freedom.

Although men cannot become absolutely equal unless they are entirely free; and consequently equality, pushed to its furthest extent, may be confounded with freedom, yet there is good reason for distinguishing the one from the other. The taste which men have for liberty, and that which they feel for equality, are, in fact, two different things; and I am not afraid to add, that, amongst democratic nations, they are two unequal things.

Upon close inspection, it will be seen that there is in every age some peculiar and preponderating fact with which all others are connected; this fact almost always gives birth to some pregnant idea or some ruling passion, which attracts to itself and bears away in its course all the feelings and opinions of the time: it is like a great stream, towards which each of the neighboring rivulets seems to flow.

Freedom has appeared in the world at different times and under various forms; it has not been exclusively bound to any social condition, and it is not confined to democracies. Freedom cannot, therefore, form the distinguishing characteristic of democratic ages. The peculiar and preponderating fact which marks those ages as its own is the equality of condition; the ruling passion of men in those periods is the love of this equality. Ask not what singular charm the men of democratic ages find in being equal, or what special reasons they may have for clinging so tenaciously to equality rather than to the other advantages which society holds out to them: equality is the distinguishing characteristic of the age they live in; that, of itself, is enough to explain that they prefer it to all the rest.

But independently of this reason, there are several others, which will at all times habitually lead men to prefer equality to freedom.

If a people could ever succeed in destroying, or even in diminishing, the equality which prevails in its own body, they could do so only by long and laborious efforts. Their social condition must be modified, their laws abolished, their opinions superseded, their habits changed, their manners corrupted. But political liberty is more easily lost; to neglect to hold it fast, is to allow it to escape. Men therefore cling to equality not only because it is dear to them; they also adhere to it because they think it will last forever.

That political freedom may compromise in its excesses the tranquillity, the property, the lives of individuals, is obvious even to narrow and unthinking minds. On the contrary, none but attentive and clear-sighted men perceive the perils with which equality threaten us, and they commonly avoid pointing them out. They know that the calamities they apprehend are remote, and flatter themselves that they will only fall upon future generations, for which the present generation takes but little thought. The evils which freedom sometimes brings with it are immediate; they are apparent to all, and all are more or less affected by them. The evils which extreme equality may produce are slowly disclosed; they creep gradually into the social frame; they are seen only at intervals; and at the moment at which they become more violent, habit already causes them to be no longer felt.

The advantages which freedom brings are only shown by the lapse of time; and it is always easy to mistake the cause in which they originate. The advantages of equality are immediate, and they may always be traced from their source.

Political liberty bestows exalted pleasures, from time to time, upon a certain number of citizens. Equality every day confers a number of small enjoyments on every man. The charms of equality are every instant felt, and are within the reach of all; the noblest hearts are not insensible to them, and the most vulgar souls exult in them. The passion which equality creates must therefore be at once strong and general. Men cannot enjoy political liberty unpurchased by some sacrifices, and they never obtain it without great exertions. But the pleasures of equality are self-proffered: each of the petty incidents of life seems to occasion them; and in order to taste them, nothing is required but to live.

Democratic nations are at all times fond of equality, but there are certain epochs at which the passion they entertain for it swells to the height of fury. This occurs at the moment when the old social system, long menaced, is overthrown after a severe intestine struggle, and the barriers of rank are at length thrown down. At such times, men pounce upon equality as their booty, and they cling to it as to some precious treasure which they fear to lose. The passion for equality penetrates on every side into men's hearts, expands there, and fills them entirely. Tell them not that, by this blind surrender of themselves to an exclusive passion, they risk their dearest interests: they are deaf. Show them not freedom escaping from their grasp, whilst they are looking another way: they are blind, or, rather, they can discern but one object to be desired in the universe.

What I have said is applicable to all democratic nations; what I am about to say concerns the French alone. Amongst most modern nations, and especially amongst all those of the continent of Europe, the taste and the idea of freedom only began to exist and to be developed at the time when social conditions were tending to equality, and as a consequence of that very equality. Absolute kings were the most efficient levellers of ranks amongst their subjects. Amongst these nations, equality preceded freedom: equality was therefore a fact of some standing when freedom was still a novelty; the one had already created customs, opinions, and laws belonging to it, when the other, alone and for the first time, came into actual existence. Thus the latter was still only an affair of opinion and of taste, whilst the former had already crept into the habits of the people, possessed itself of their manners, and given a particular turn to the smallest actions in their lives. Can it be wondered at that the men of our own time prefer the one to the other?

I think that democratic communities have a natural taste for freedom: left to themselves, they will seek it, cherish it, and view any privation of it with regret. But for equality, their passion is ardent, insatiable, incessant, invincible: they call for equality in freedom; and if they cannot obtain that, they still call for equality in slavery. They will endure poverty, servitude, barbarism; but they will not endure aristocracy.

This is true at all times, and especially in our own day. All men and all powers seeking to cope with this irresistible passion will be overthrown and destroyed by it. In our age, freedom cannot be established without it, and despotism itself cannot reign without its support.

◇ ◇ ◇

I believe that it is easier to establish an absolute and despotic government amongst a people in which the conditions of society are equal, than amongst any other; and I think that, if such a government were once established amongst such a people, it would not only oppress men, but would eventually strip each of them of several of the highest qualities of humanity. Despotism, therefore, appears to me peculiarly to be dreaded in democratic times. I should have loved freedom, I believe, at all times, but in the time in which we live I am ready to worship it.

On the other hand, I am persuaded that all who shall attempt, in the ages upon which we are entering, to base freedom upon aristocratic privilege, will fail; that all who shall attempt to draw and to retain authority within a single class, will fail. At the present day, no ruler is skilful or strong enough to found a despotism by re-establishing permanent distinctions of rank amongst his subjects: no legislator is wise or powerful enough to preserve free institutions, if he does not take equality for his first principle and his watchword. All of our contemporaries who would establish or secure the independence and the dignity of their fellow-men, must show themselves the friends of equality; and the only worthy means of showing themselves as such is to be so: upon this depends the success of their holy enterprise. Thus, the question is not how to reconstruct aristocratic society, but how to make liberty proceed out of that democratic state of society in which God has placed us.

These two truths appear to me simple, clear, and fertile in consequences; and they naturally lead me to consider what kind of free government can be established amongst a people in which social conditions are equal.

It results, from the very constitution of democratic nations and from their necessities, that the power of government amongst them must be more uniform, more centralized, more extensive, more searching, and more efficient than in other countries. Society at large is naturally stronger and more active, the individual more subordinate and weak; the former does more, the latter less; and this is inevitably the case.

It is not, therefore, to be expected that the range of private independence will ever be as extensive in democratic as in aristocratic countries;—nor is this to be desired; for amongst aristocratic nations, the mass is often sacrificed to the individual, and the prosperity of the greater number to the greatness of the few. It is both necessary and desirable that the government of a democratic people should be active and powerful: and our object should not be to render it weak or indolent, but solely to prevent it from abusing its aptitude and its strength.

◇ ◇ ◇

I think that men living in aristocracies may, strictly speaking, do without the liberty of the press: but such is not the case with those who live in democratic countries. To protect their personal independence I trust not to great political assemblies, to parliamentary privilege, or to the assertion of popular sovereignty. All these things may, to a certain extent, be reconciled with personal servitude. But that servitude cannot be complete if the press is free: the press is the chief democratic instrument of freedom.

Something analogous may be said of the judicial power. It is a part of the essence of judicial power to attend to private interests, and to fix itself with predilection on minute objects submitted to its observation: another essential quality of judicial power is never to volunteer its assistance to the oppressed, but always to be at the disposal of the humblest of those who solicit it; their complaint, however feeble they may themselves be, will force itself upon the ear of justice and claim redress, for this is inherent in the very constitution of courts of justice.

A power of this kind is therefore peculiarly adapted to the wants of freedom, at a time when the eye and finger of the government are constantly intruding into the minutest details of human actions, and when private persons are at once too weak to protect themselves, and too much isolated for them to reckon upon the assistance of their fellows. The strength of the courts of law has even been the greatest security which can be offered to personal independence; but this is more especially the case in democratic ages: private rights and interests are in constant danger, if the judicial power does not grow more extensive and more strong to keep pace with the growing equality of conditions.

Equality awakens in men several propensities extremely dangerous to freedom, to which the attention of the legislator ought constantly to be directed. I shall only remind the reader of the most important amongst them.

Men living in democratic ages do not readily comprehend the utility of forms: they feel an instinctive contempt for them,—I have elsewhere shown for what reasons. Forms excite their contempt, and often their hatred; as they commonly aspire to none but easy and present gratifications, they rush onwards to the object of their desires, and the slightest delay exasperates them. This same temper, carried with them into political life, renders them hostile to forms, which perpetually retard or arrest them in some of their projects.

Yet this objection, which the men of democracies make to forms, is the very thing which renders forms so useful to freedom; for their chief merit is to serve as a barrier between the strong and the weak, the ruler and the people, to retard the one, and give the other time to look about him. Forms become more necessary in proportion as the government becomes more active and more powerful, whilst private persons are becoming more indolent and more feeble. Thus democratic nations naturally stand more in need of forms than other nations, and they naturally respect them less. This deserves most serious attention.

Nothing is more pitiful than the arrogant disdain of most of our contemporaries for questions of form; for the smallest questions of form have acquired in our time an importance which they never had before: many of the greatest interests of mankind depend upon them. I think, that, if the statesmen of aristocratic ages could sometimes contemn froms with impunity, and frequently rise above them, the statesmen to whom the government of nations is now confided ought to treat the very least among them with respect, and not neglect them without imperious necessity. In aristocracies, the observance of forms was superstitious; amongst us, they ought to be kept up with a deliberate and enlightened deference.

Another tendency, which is extremely natural to democratic nations and extremely dangerous, is that which leads them to despise and undervalue the rights of private persons. The attachment which men feel to a right, and the respect which they display for it, is generally proportioned to its importance, or to the length of time during which they have enjoyed it. The rights of private persons amongst democratic nations are commonly of small importance, of recent growth, and extremely precarious; the consequence is, that they are often sacrificed without regret, and almost always violated without remorse.

But it happens that, at the same period and amongst the same nations in which men conceive a natural contempt for the rights of private persons, the rights of society at large are naturally extended and consolidated: in other words, men become less attached to private rights just when it is most necessary to retain and defend what little remains of them. It is therefore most especially in the present democratic times, that the true friends of the liberty and the greatness of man ought constantly to be on the alert, to prevent the power of government from lightly sacrificing the private rights of individuals to the general execution of its designs. At such times, no citizen is so obscure that it is not very dangerous to allow him to be oppressed; no private rights are so unimportant that they can be surrendered with impunity to the caprices of a government. The reason is plain:—if the private right of an individual is violated at a time when the human mind is fully impressed with the importance and the sanctity of such rights, the injury done is confined to the individual whose right is infringed; but to violate a right at the present day is deeply to corrupt the manners of the nation, and to put the whole community in jeopardy, because the very notion of this kind of right constantly tends amongst us to be impaired and lost.

◇ ◇ ◇

I shall conclude by one general idea, which comprises not only all the particular ideas which have been expressed in the present chapter, but also most of those which it is the object of this book to treat of. In the ages of aristocracy which preceded our own, there were private persons of great power, and a social authority of extreme weakness. The outline of society itself was not easily discernible, and constantly confounded with the different powers by which the community was ruled. The principal efforts of the men of those times were required to strengthen, aggrandize, and secure the supreme power; and, on the other hand, to circumscribe individual independence within narrower limits, and to subject private interests to the interests of the public. Other perils and other cares await the men of our age. Amongst the greater part of modern nations, the government, whatever may be its origin, its constitution, or its name, has become almost omnipotent, and private persons are falling, more and more, into the lowest stage of weakness and dependence.

In olden society, everything was different; unity and uniformity were nowhere to be met with. In modern society, everything threatens to become so much alike, that the peculiar characteristics of each individual will soon be entirely lost in the general aspect of the world. Our forefathers were ever prone to make an improper use of the notion that private rights ought to be respected; and we are naturally prone, on the other hand, to exaggerate the idea that the interest of a private individual ought always to bend to the interest of the many.

The political world is metamorphosed: new remedies must henceforth be sought for new disorders. To lay down extensive but distinct and settled limits to the action of the government; to confer certain rights on private persons, and to secure to them the undisputed enjoyment of those rights; to enable individual man to maintain whatever independence, strength, and original power he still possesses; to raise him by the side of society at large, and uphold him in that position,—these appear to me the main objects of legislators in the ages upon which we are now entering.

It would seem as if the rulers of our time sought only to use men in order to make things great; I wish that they would try a little more to make great men; that they would set less value on the work, and more upon the workman; that they would never forget that a nation cannot long remain strong when every man belonging to it is individually weak; and that no form or combination of social polity has yet been devised to make an energetic people out of a community of pusillanimous and enfeebled citizens.

I trace amongst our contemporaries two contrary notions which are equally injurious. One set of men can perceive nothing in the principle of equality but the anarchical tendencies which it engenders: they dread their own free agency, they fear themselves. Other thinkers, less numerous but more enlightened, take a different view: beside that track which starts from the principle of equality to terminate in anarchy, they have at last discovered the road which seems to lead man to inevitable servitude. They shape their souls beforehand to this necessary condition; and, despairing of remaining free, they already do obeisance in their hearts to the master who is soon to appear. The former abandon freedom because they think it dangerous; the latter, because they hold it to be impossible.

If I had entertained the latter conviction, I should not have written this book, but I should have confined myself to deploring in secret the destiny of mankind. I have sought to point out the dangers to which the principle of equality exposes the independence of man, because I firmly believe that these dangers are the most formidable, as well as the least foreseen, of all those which futurity holds in store; but I do not think that they are insurmountable.

The men who live in the democratic ages upon which we are entering have naturally a taste for independence; they are naturally impatient of regulation, and they are wearied by the permanence even of the condition they themselves prefer. They are fond of power; but they are prone to despise and hate those who wield it, and they easily elude its grasp by their own mobility and insignificance.

These propensities will always manifest themselves, because they originate in the groundwork of society, which will undergo no change: for a long time they will prevent the establishment of any despotism, and they will furnish fresh weapons to each succeeding generation which shall struggle in favor of the liberty of mankind. Let us, then, look forward to the future with that salutary fear which makes men keep watch and ward for freedom, not with that faint and idle terror which depresses and enervates the heart.

Further Readings

The historical literature of the period is extensive, but two works are outstanding for their perception and readability. George Dangerfield, *The Era of Good Feelings* (New York: Harcourt, Brace, 1952), discusses the period 1817–1825, while Arthur M. Schlesinger, Jr., *The Age of Jackson* (Boston, MA: Little, Brown and Co., 1945), narrates the rise of Jacksonian Democracy. Walter Hugins, *Jacksonian Democracy and the Working Class: A Study of the New York Workingmen's Movement, 1829–1837* (Stanford, CA: Stanford University Press, 1967), emphasizes the strength of Jacksonianism among the urban workers, and Robert McCormack, *The Second American Party System: Party Formation in the Jacksonian Era* (Chapel Hill, NC: University of North Carolina Press, 1966), examines the growth of the political party system as an expression of popular will. F. O. Matthiessen, *American Renaissance: Art and Expression in the Age of Emerson and Thoreau* (London: Oxford University Press, 1962), discusses the burst of American artistic genius that suggests that de Tocqueville's concern about the deleterious effect of democracy upon American culture may have been unfounded.

Other foreign travellers visited and described America in the period. Excerpts from the writings of some of these may be found in *American Social History as Recorded by British Travellers*, edited by Allen Nevins (New York: H. Holt and Co., 1931). The views of the prolific and outspoken Harriet Martineau may be found in her *Society in America* (3 vols.: London: 1837). First published in 1839, Frederick Marryat, *A Diary in America, With Remarks on its Institutions*, edited by Sydney Jackson (Westport, CT: Greenwood Press, 1973), has many interesting observations.

The best study of de Tocqueville's visit is found in George W. Pierson, *Tocqueville and Beaumont in America* (New York: Oxford University Press, 1938). Details of that visit, drawn from the notebooks he kept, are presented in Alexis de Tocqueville, *Journey to America*, translated by George Lawrence and edited by J. P. Mayer (London: Faber and Faber, 1959). De Tocqueville's other great work, *The Old Regime and the French Revolution*, has been translated by Stuart Gilbert (Garden City, NY: Doubleday, 1955).

War and Peace

In 1812, Napoleon was at the height of his power. His French empire and its allies comprehended all of Western Europe with the exception of Spain and Portugal, where the inhabitants, with British assistance, were waging a tenacious and brutal guerrilla war. There were only two European powers remaining to dispute his supremacy. One, Great Britain, was an island power that controlled the sea and was secure from attack by Napoleon's magnificent army. The other was Russia, an empire controlling a vast extent of land and ruled by the young and volatile Tsar Alexander I. Some historians argue that conflict with Russia was inevitable. Be that as it may, Napoleon massed his Grand Army of some 500,000 men along the river Vistula and, without any formal declaration of war, invaded Russia 24 June 1812.

Napoleon's strategy depended on meeting the Russian army in a decisive battle, defeating them, and forcing Alexander to sue for terms. Except for Spain, this strategy had always been successful for Napoleon before, and there was no reason to believe that it would fail him now. The French leader was thus frustrated as the Russian army would not confront him outright but continued to withdraw, and he attempted with every means in his power to draw them into a battle. The French capture of the strategic center of Smolensk in August did occasion Russian resistance, but the Russians again withdrew before a decisive encounter could be forced, and left Smolensk a blazing ruin. In that same month, Marshal Kutuzof, an old and experienced general, was given command of the Russian armies, and continued the policy of slow withdrawal.

In September, Kutuzof decided to offer battle at Borodino, if only for the purpose of weakening the French. He was successful in

From Leo Tolstoy, *War and Peace*, translated by Ann Dunnigan (New York: New American Library, 1968), pp. 925–934, 947–959, and 967–975.

this, but at a terrible cost. The French lost 30,000 men, but Kutuzof lost as many as 43,000, a third of his army. He was forced to continue his retreat to Moscow. At this point, Napoleon appears to have decided that the capture of Moscow would be the decisive stroke for which he was searching. Knowing that no French leader could survive the loss of Paris, he supposed that neither could Tsar Alexander survive the loss of Moscow. Napoleon rode into Moscow unopposed on 15 September, expecting the surrender of the populace. He found the city virtually empty instead. Almost immediately, fires broke out throughout the city and, after four days, three-quarters of Moscow lay destroyed. Napoleon's messages to Alexander suggesting a surrender went unanswered, and it became clear to Napoleon that his army was isolated deep in Russia in a ruined base of operations, with an enemy still ready to fight and the severe Russian winter coming on.

On 19 October, he led the Grand Army out of Moscow, heading home. The retreat turned into a nightmare for Napoleon's forces. Early winter blizzards soon impeded the army's progress, and Russian cavalry hounded them incessantly. Hunger, cold, and exhaustion took their toll, and when the Grand Army finally fought its way across the Berezina River at the end of November, it numbered only 50,000 effective troops. The campaign was over. It has been estimated that Napoleon lost almost half a million men in his six months' campaign. His armies never recovered from this loss, and the days of his power were numbered.

Russian losses were severe, but the magnitude and finality of their victory was awesome. It was a source of pride and wonder, and many Russian authors and artists have celebrated the accomplishment. One of the greatest of these monuments is Leo Tolstoy's (1828–1910) great novel, *War and Peace*. Born a member of the Russian landed aristocracy, Tolstoy entered the army in 1851, and served in the siege of Sevastopol during the Crimean War of 1854–1855. He gave up the army, and returned to his estate to write. Between 1863 and 1869, he wrote *War and Peace*.

It was Tolstoy's view that events are not shaped by individuals. Although the moral responsibility for an act belongs to the individual in authority, the physical responsibility belongs to each of those who accept that leader's authority. Even a great leader cannot prevail against a mass of individuals who oppose him. *War and Peace* was written to exemplify this view. To accomplish this, Tolstoy had to show how *individuals* played their role in these great events. As a consequence, *War and Peace* is a sprawling work, populated by hundreds of characters, all realistically drawn. It is generally conceded that Prince Andrei, a proud and honorable man hungering for great deeds, and Pierre, a somewhat bumbling intellectual searching for the proper way to live, are the main characters, each representing a side of the author's own personality.

The excerpts presented below present the battle of Borodino, in which Prince Andrei is mortally wounded, and in which Pierre, a civilian, learns what warfare is *really* like. It is a great artistic achievement that Tolstoy is able to portray the sweep of this action in terms of the experiences of a few individuals. When reading these passages, it is important to remember that they form only a part of a large book that is essentially a celebration of life. Through the carnage of war, both Andrei and Pierre learn more about life and about themselves. So too, Tolstoy implies, Russia had learned more about itself.

In the course of time, Tolstoy put into practice many of the ideas in *War and Peace*. He gave up his personal wealth and attempted to live a simple life among his peasants. He preached a revolutionary philosophy to those who were willing to listen: that the individual should refuse to participate in any form of violence against others, even to the point of refusing military conscription and jury service. Without popular support, states could not oppress either their own people or others. During the last ten or fifteen years of his life, Tolstoy was probably one of the most beloved men in the world, and his idealistic teachings influenced many intellectuals, including Mahatma Gandhi of India.

Questions

1. How does Prince Andrei characterize war when speaking to Pierre before the battle?

2. What is Andrei's opinion of chivalry and the rules of war?

3. What does Pierre learn about warfare?

4. What does Andrei learn about warfare?

WAR AND PEACE

On that bright evening of August twenty-fifth, Prince Andrei lay propped on his elbow in a tumbledown shed in the village of Knyazkovo, at the far end of his regiment's encampment. Through a gap in the broken wall he was looking along the fence at a row of thirty-year-old birches with their lower branches lopped off, at a field on which shocks of oats were standing, and at the bushes near which rose the smoke of campfires—the soldiers' field kitchens.

Narrow and useless and burdensome as his life now seemed to him, Prince Andrei nevertheless felt as agitated and irritable on the eve of battle as he had felt seven years before at Austerlitz.

He had received and issued orders for the next day's battle. He had nothing to do. But his thoughts, which were of the simplest, clearest, and therefore most dreadful sort, would give him no peace. He knew that tomorrow's battle would be the most terrible of all he had ever taken part in, and for the first time in his life the possibility of death presented itself to him—not in relation to his earthly life or to any consideration of the effect of his death on others, but simply in relation to himself, to his own soul—plainly, vividly, horrifically, and almost as a certainty. And from the height of this perception, all that had previously tormented and preoccupied him was suddenly illumined by a cold, white light, without shadows, without perspective, without distinction of outline. All life appeared to him like magic-lantern pictures at which he had long been gazing through a glass by artificial light. Now he suddenly saw those badly daubed pictures in clear daylight and without the glass. "Yes, yes, there they are, those false images which agitated, enthralled, and tormented me," he said to himself, passing in review the principal pictures of the magic lantern of life and looking at them now in the cold, white daylight of his clear perception of death. "There they are, those crudely painted figures that once seemed splendid and mysterious. Glory, the commonweal, love for a woman, the fatherland itself—how grand those pictures appeared to me, and with what profound meaning they seemed to be filled! And it is all so simple, colorless and crude in the cold, white light of the morning that I feel is dawning for me." The three great sorrows of his life particularly held his attention: his love for a woman, the death of his father, and the invasion by the French, which had made inroads upon half of Russia. "Love! . . . That young girl who seemed to me brimming with mystic forces! How I loved her! I made romantic plans of love and happiness with her. Oh, what a nice little boy I was!" he bitterly exclaimed aloud. "To be sure! I believed in some sort of ideal love that was to keep her faithful to me for the entire year of my absence! Like the gentle dove of the fable, she was to pine away parted from me. But it was all so very much simpler. . . . So horribly simple, and revolting!

"My father too built Bald Hills, and thought it was his place, his land, his air, his peasants. But Napoleon came and swept him aside, unaware of his existence, as he might brush a chip from his path. And his Bald Hills and his whole life fell to pieces. Princess Marya says it is a trial sent from above. What is this trial for when he is no longer here and never will be? Never! He is no more! For whom then is this trial? The fatherland, the destruction of Moscow! And tomorrow I shall be killed—perhaps not even by a Frenchman but by one of our own men, like the soldier who fired his gun close to my ear yesterday—and the French will come along and take me by the head and heels and pitch me into a hole that I may not stink under their noses, and new conditions of life will arise, which will seem quite ordinary to others, and I shall not know about them, for I shall not exist."

He gazed at the row of birches with their motionless green and yellow foliage and white bark gleaming in the sun. "To die, to be killed tomorrow, to be no more . . . That all this should still exist, and I not be . . ."

He pictured the world without himself. The birches with their light and shade, the fleecy clouds, the smoke of the campfires—everything around him underwent a sudden transformation and seemed to him sinister and menacing. A cold shiver ran down his spine. He quickly rose, went out, and began walking up and down.

When he returned to the shed he heard a voice outside.

"Who's there?" Prince Andrei called.

The red-nosed Captain Timokhin, formerly Dolokhov's company commander and now, from a lack of officers, battalion commander, shyly entered the shed, followed by an adjutant and the regimental paymaster.

Prince Andrei quickly stood up, listened to the business they had come about, gave some further orders, and was about to dismiss them, when he heard a familiar, lisping voice outside the shed.

"*Que diable!*" said the voice of a man stumbling over something.

Prince Andrei looked out of the shed and saw Pierre, who had tripped over a stake lying on the ground and had almost fallen. Prince Andrei generally disliked seeing people from his own circle, and especially Pierre, who reminded him of all the painful moments he had endured on his last visit to Moscow.

"Well, what a surprise!" he said. "What brings you here? I never expected to see you here!"

As he said this, his eyes and the whole expression of his face was more than cold—it was positively hostile, as Pierre instantly noticed. He had approached the shed with the greatest eagerness, but when he saw Prince Andrei's face, he felt constrained and ill at east.

"I came— Well, you know—I came— It interested me . . ." said Pierre, who had senselessly repeated the word "interesting" so many times that day. "I wanted to see the battle."

"Oh, yes, and what do your brother Masons say about the war? How would they prevent it?" said Prince Andrei sarcastically. "Well, and how is Moscow? And my people? Have they reached Moscow at last?" he asked seriously.

"Yes, they have. Julie Drubetskaya told me they had arrived. I went to call, but missed them. They have gone to your estate near Moscow."

◇ ◇ ◇

The officers were about to retire, but Prince Andrei, apparently reluctant to be left alone with his friend, asked them to stay and have tea. Benches were set out and tea was brought in. The officers, not without a certain astonishment, stared at Pierre's huge, stout figure as they listened to his talk of Moscow and the disposition of our forces, around which he had succeeded in making a tour. Prince Andrei remained silent, and his expression was so forbidding that Pierre addressed himself more to Timokhin, the good-natured battalion commander, than to Bolkonsky.

"So you understand the whole disposition of our troops?" Prince Andrei interrupted him.

"Yes, that is—how do you mean?" asked Pierre. "Not being a military man, I can't say I do entirely, but at least I understand the general plan."

"Well, then you know more than anyone else," observed Prince Andrei in French.

"Oh!" said Pierre, looking over his spectacles in perplexity at Prince Andrei. "Well, and what do you think of Kutuzov's appointment?" he asked.

"I welcomed his appointment—more than that I cannot say," replied Prince Andrei.

"And tell me, what is your opinion of Barclay de Tolly? In Moscow they are saying heaven knows what about him. What do you think of him?"

"Ask them," replied Prince Andrei, indicating the officers.

Pierre looked at Timokhin with the quizzical, condescending smile with which everyone involuntarily addressed him.

"It was a gleam of *serene* light in the darkness, Your Excellency, when His Serene Highness took over," said Timokhin, continually darting shy glances at his colonel.

"Why is that?" asked Pierre.

"Well, to speak only of firewood and fodder—let me tell you. Why, when we were retreating from Swieciani we didn't dare to touch a stick of wood, a wisp of hay, or anything. And, you see, with us leaving, *he* would get it all—isn't that right, Your Excellency?" he said, turning again to his prince. "We didn't dare! Two of our officers were court-martialed for that kind of thing. Well, since His Serene Highness took command, everything became quite simple as far as this is concerned. Now we see light . . ."

"Then why had it been forbidden?"

Timokhin looked about in confusion, at a loss to know how to answer such a question. Pierre put the same question to Prince Andrei.

"Why, so as not to lay waste the country we were abandoning to the enemy," said Prince Andrei with venomous sarcasm. "That is very sound: one cannot allow pillage and accustom the troops to marauding. At Smolensk too he very correctly judged that the French might outflank us and that they had larger forces. But he could not understand this," cried Prince Andrei in a shrill voice that seemed beyond his control, "he could not understand that there, for the first time, we were fighting for Russian soil, that there was a spirit in the men such as I have never seen before, that for two consecutive days we had repulsed the French, and that this success had increased our strength tenfold. He ordered us to retreat, and all our efforts and losses went for nothing. He had no thought of betraying us, he was doing the best he could and had thought out everything beforehand, but that is exactly why he is unsuited. He is unsuited now just because he considers everything very thoroughly and precisely, as every German is bound to do. How can I explain? . . . Well, say your father has a German valet, and he's an excellent valet and satisfies all your father's requirements better than you could, and all's well and good. But if your father is mortally ill, you'll send away the valet and attend to your father with your own clumsy, unpracticed hands, and you will be more comfort to him than a skilled man who is a stranger could be. So it has been with Barclay. While Russia was well, a foreigner could serve her and be an excellent minister, but as soon as she is in danger, she needs one of her own kin. But in your Club they make him out a traitor! The only result of vilifying him now as a traitor will be that later on, ashamed of their false accusations, they will suddenly make him out a hero or a genius, which will be still more unjust. He is an honest and very punctilious German."

"They do say he is a skilled commander."

"I don't know what is meant by 'a skilled commander,'" retorted Prince Andrei derisively.

"A skilled commander," began Pierre, "well, . . . it's one who foresees all contingencies and . . . well, divines the enemy's intentions."

"But that is impossible," said Prince Andrei, as if it were a matter that had been settled long ago.

Pierre looked at him in surprise.

"And yet, isn't it said that war is like a game of chess?"

"Yes," replied Prince Andrei, "but with the slight difference that in chess you can think over each move as long as you please, unrestricted by conditions of time, and with the further difference that a knight is always stronger than a pawn, and two pawns are always stronger than one, while in war a battalion is sometimes stronger than a division, and sometimes weaker than a company. No one can ever be certain of the relative strength of armies. You may be sure," he continued, "that if things depended on arrangements made by the staff, I should be there, making those arrangements, instead of which I have the honor of serving here in the regiment with these gentlemen, and I consider that tomorrow's battle, in fact, will depend on us rather than on them. . . . Success never has and never will depend on position or equipment, or even on numbers—least of all on position."

"On what then?"

"On the feeling that is in me and in him," he pointed to Timokhin, "and in every soldier."

Prince Andrei glanced at Timokhin, who was staring at his commander in bewilderment and dismay. In contrast to his former reticence and taciturnity, Prince Andrei now seemed excited. Apparently he could not refrain from expressing the thoughts that had suddenly occurred to him.

"A battle is won by the side that has firmly resolved to win it. Why did we lose the battle of Austerlitz? The French losses were almost equal to ours, but very early in the day we said to ourselves that we were losing the battle—so we lost it. And we said so because there we had nothing to fight for: we simply wanted to quit the battlefield as soon as possible. 'We've lost—let's run!' And we ran. If we had not said that till evening, God knows what might have happened. But tomorrow we shan't say it. You talk about our position: the left flank weak, the right flank extended," he went on. "That's all nonsense, doesn't mean a thing. But what we are facing tomorrow? A hundred million diverse chances, which will be decided on the instant by whether we run or they run, whether this man or that man is killed. But all that's being done at this moment is mere pastime. The fact is that those men with whom you rode around inspecting the position not only do not help matters, but hinder them. They are only concerned with their own petty interests."

"At such a moment?" said Pierre in a tone of disapprobation.

"*At such a moment*," Prince Andrei repeated. "For them it is only a moment to undermine a rival and get an extra cross or ribbon. For me what tomorrow means is this: a hundred thousand French troops and a hundred thousand Russian troops have come together to fight, and the fact is that these two hundred thousand men will fight, and the side that fights more fiercely and spares itself least will conquer. And, if you like, I can tell you that whatever happens, and whatever mess those at the top may make, we shall win tomorrow's battle. Tomorrow, happen what may, we shall win the battle!"

"You're right, Your Excellency, absolutely right!" declared Timokhin. "Who would spare himself now? The soldiers in my battalion, believe me, wouldn't touch their vodka! 'This is not the time for it,' they say."

All were silent.

The officers rose. Prince Andrei went out of the shed with them, giving the adjutant his final orders. After the officers had gone, Pierre moved nearer to Prince Andrei and was about to start a conversation when they heard the hoofbeats of three horses on the road not far from the shed, and looking in that direction Prince Andrei recognized Wolzogen and Clausewitz, accompanied by a Cossack. As they rode by, Pierre and Prince Andrei could not help overhearing a fragment of their conversation.

"The war must be extended over a broader area. That is a view which I cannot recommend too highly," one of them was saying in German.

"Most certainly!" replied the other.

"Since the aim is to weaken the enemy, one cannot, of course, take into account loss of civilian lives."

"Certainly not!"

"Extended over a broader area!" repeated Prince Andrei with an angry snort, when they had ridden by. "In that 'broader area' I had a father and a son and a sister at Bald Hills. But it's all the same to him. That's what I was just saying to you—those German gentlemen won't win the battle tomorrow but will only make a filthy mess of it, insofar as they can, because they have nothing in their German heads but theories, which are not worth a straw, and their hearts lack the one thing needed for tomorrow—what Timokhin has. They have yielded up all Europe to him, and now have come to teach us. Fine teachers!" And again his voice grew shrill.

"So you think that tomorrow's battle will be won by us?" asked Pierre.

"Yes, yes," replied Prince Andrei absently. "One thing I would establish if I had the power," he began again. "I would not take prisoners. Why take prisoners? That's chivalry. The French have destroyed my home and are on their way to destroy Moscow; they have outraged and continue to outrage me every instant. They are my enemies. In my opinion they are all criminals. And that's exactly what Timokhin and the entire army think. They should be executed. Since they are my enemies they cannot be my friends, whatever may have been said at Tilsit."

"Yes, yes," murmured Pierre, gazing at Prince Andrei with shining eyes. "I absolutely agree with you, absolutely!"

The question that had troubled Pierre on the Mozhaisk hill and all that day now seemed to him quite clear and fully solved. Now he understood the whole meaning and importance of this war and of the impending battle. All he had seen that day, all the significant, stern expressions on the faces he had glimpsed in passing, appeared to him in a new light. He understood that suppressed (latent, as they say in physics) heat of patriotism in all those men he had seen, and it explained to him the composure and ostensible lightheartedness with which they faced death.

"Not to take prisoners," Prince Andrei continued, "that alone would change the whole war and make it less cruel. As it is we have been playing at war—that is what's so vile—acting chivalrous, and all the rest of it. Such magnanimity and sensibility are like that of the lady who faints at the sight of a slaughtered calf; she is so kindhearted she can't bear the sight of blood, but she eats the fricasseed veal with gusto. They're forever harping on the rules of warfare, on chivalry, on flags of truce, on mercy to the victims, and so on. It's all rubbish. I saw chivalry and flags of truce in 1805; they gulled us and we gulled them. . . . They plunder people's homes, issue counterfeit money, and worst of all they kill our children and our fathers, and then they talk of the rules of war, and of magnanimity to the foe. No prisoners, I say: kill and be killed! Anyone who has arrived at this through the same sufferings as I have . . ."

Prince Andrei, who had thought it was a matter of indifference to him whether or not they took Moscow as they had taken Smolensk, was suddenly checked by a contraction of the throat. He paced up and down several times in silence, but his eyes glittered feverishly and his lips quivered when he began to speak again.

"If there were none of this chivalry in war, we should go to war only when it was worth going to certain death, as now. Then there would not be wars merely because Pavel Ivanych had insulted Mikhail Ivanych. And if there was a war like this one, it would be a war! And the intensity of the troops would be quite different. Then all these Westphalians and Hessians Napoleon is leading against us would not have followed him to Russia, nor should we have gone to fight in Austria and Prussia without knowing why. War is not a polite recreation, but the vilest thing in life, and we ought to realize this and not make a game of it. We ought to take this terrible necessity soberly and seriously. It all comes to this: eliminate the humbug, and let war be war, not a game. As it is now, it's the favorite pastime of the idle and the frivolous. . . .

"The military class is the most highly honored. And what is war, what is required for success in warfare, what are the moral standards of the military world? The aim of war is murder; the implements of warfare—espionage, treachery, and the inducements thereto, the ruination of a country's inhabitants by ravage and robbery to provision the army, the trickery and deceit known as military stratagems; the ethics of the military class—lack of freedom, in other words, discipline, idleness, ignorance, cruelty, debauchery, and drunkenness. Yet in spite of all this, it is the highest class, respected by all. Every sovereign, except the Chinese, wears a military uniform and bestows the greatest rewards on those who kill the most people.

"They meet, as we shall meet tomorrow, to murder one another; they kill and maim tens of thousands of men, and then hold thanksgiving services for having slaughtered so many (they even exaggerate the number) and proclaim a victory, assuming that the greater the slaughter the greater the merit. How God can look down and hear them!" cried Prince Andrei in a shrill, piercing voice. "Ah, my friend, life has become a burden for me of late. I see that I have begun to understand too much. It does not do for a man to eat of the tree of the knowledge of good and evil. . . . Ah, well, it's not for long!" he added. "However, you're sleepy, and it's time for me to turn in. Go back to Gorky," said Prince Andrei suddenly.

"Oh, no!" responded Pierre, looking at Prince Andrei with eyes full of compassion and dismay.

"Yes, you must go: before a battle one needs to get a good night's sleep," said Prince Andrei.

He quickly went up to Pierre and embraced and kissed him.

"Good-bye, go now!" he cried. "Whether we shall meet again or not . . ." and hastily turning away, he went into the shed.

It was now dark, and Pierre could not make out whether the expression on Prince Andrei's face was angry or tender.

For some time he stood in silence, wondering whether to follow him or go away. "No, he does not want that," Pierre decided. "But I know this is our last meeting." He heaved a deep sigh and rode back to Gorky.

In the shed Prince Andrei lay down on a rug, but he could not sleep.

He closed his eyes. One set of images followed another in his imagination. On one of them he dwelt long and happily. He vividly recalled a certain evening in Petersburg. Natasha, with a vivacious, excited expression, was telling him about how she had gone to hunt for mushrooms the previous summer and had lost her way in the great forest. Incoherently describing to him the dense forest, her sensations, her talk with a beekeeper she met, she continually interrupted her story to say: "No, I can't, I'm not telling it properly . . . No, you don't understand . . ." although Prince Andrei tried to reassure her by telling her that he did understand, and he suddenly had understood everything she was trying to tell him. But Natasha had been dissatisfied with her own words: she felt that they did not convey the passionately poetic feeling she had experienced that day, which she wanted to re-create. "He was such a charming old man . . . and it was so dark in the forest . . . and he had such a kind . . . No, I can't describe it," she had said, flushed with emotion. Prince Andrei smiled now the same happy smile as then, when he had looked into her eyes. "I understood her," he thought. "I not only understood her, but it was just that spiritual force, that sincerity, that openheartedness, that soul of hers which seemed inseparable from her body—it was that soul I loved in her . . . loved so intensely, so happily . . ." And suddenly he recalled what it was that had put an end to his love. "*He* cared nothing for all that. *He* neither saw nor understood anything of the sort. All he saw was a pretty, *fresh* young girl . . . with whom he did not deign to link his destiny. And I? . . . And he is still alive and enjoying life."

Prince Andrei jumped up as though he had been scalded, and commenced pacing up and down in front of the shed.

◇ ◇ ◇

On returning to Gorky after having seen Prince Andrei, Pierre ordered his groom to get the horses ready and to call him early in the morning; then he immediately fell asleep behind a screen in a corner Boris had let him have.

By the time he was fully awake the next morning, everyone had left the hut. The panes were rattling in the little windows, and his groom was standing at his side shaking him.

"Your Excellency! Your Excellency! Your Excellency!" the groom persistently repeated, shaking Pierre by the shoulder without looking at him, as if having lost hope of rousing him.

"What? Has it begun? Is it time?" Pierre mumbled sleepily.

"If you please, sir, listen to the firing!" said the groom, a discharged soldier. "The other gentlemen have already gone. His Serene Highness himself rode past long ago."

Pierre hastily dressed and ran out to the porch. Outside it was fresh and dewy, a bright, clear day. The sun had just burst forth from behind a cloud that had obscured it, and its rays refracted through rifts in the clouds, splashed over the roofs and walls of the houses opposite, over the dew-flecked dust of the road, the fence palings, and Pierre's horses standing in front of the hut. The boom of cannons sounded more distinct outside. An adjutant accompanied by a Cossack rode by at a trot.

"It's time, Count! It's time!" cried the adjutant.

Telling his groom to follow with a horse, Pierre walked along the street to the knoll from which he had surveyed the battlefield the day before. A crowd of officers had assembled there, and Pierre heard the members of the staff talking in French, saw Kutuzov's gray head in a white cap with a red band, saw his gray nape sunk between his shoulders. He was peering through a field glass at the highway.

Looking before him as he mounted the steps of the approach to the knoll, Pierre was spellbound by the beauty of the scene. It was the same panorama he had admired the day before, but now the entire region was covered with troops and clouds of smoke from the guns, and in the clear morning air the slanting rays of the bright sun, which was rising slightly to the left behind Pierre, suffused it with a rosy, golden light streaked with long dark shadows. The distant forests that enclosed the panorama seemed carved out of some precious stone of a yellowish-green color; its undulating contour, silhouetted against the horizon, was intersected beyond Valuyevo by the Smolensk highway, now crowded with troops. In the foreground shimmered golden fields and thickets. Everywhere—in front and to the right and left—there were troops. The whole scene was vivid, majestic, and astounding, but what impressed Pierre most was the view of the battlefield itself, of Borodino, and the ravines on either side of the Kolocha.

Over the river, over Borodino and on both sides of it—especially to the left where the Voyna flowed through marshy land and fell into the Kolocha—hung a mist that spread, dissolved, and grew translucent in the brilliant sunlight, magically tinting and outlining everything seen through it. The smoke of the guns mingled with this mist, and everywhere glints of morning light sparkled through it, now on the water, now on the dew, now on the bayonets of the soldiers crowded along the riverbanks and in Borodino. A white church could be seen through the mist, here and there a cottage roof, dense masses of troops, green caissons, cannons. And all was in motion, or appeared to move, as the smoke and mist drifted over the whole landscape. Just as in the mist-covered hollows near Borodino, so along the entire line beyond and above it, and especially to the left, in woods and meadows, over valleys and on ridges, clouds of cannon smoke seemed to materialize out of nothing, now singly, now several at a time, now sparse, now dense, expanding, billowing, merging, swirling over the whole expanse.

These puffs of smoke and, strange to say, the reports that accompanied them, produced the chief beauty of the spectacle.

Poof! suddenly a round, dense ball of smoke was seen turning from violet to gray to a milky white, and *boom!* came the report a second later.

Poof-poof! two clouds of smoke rose, colliding and merging with one another; *boom-boom!* came the sounds confirming what the eye had seen.

Pierre looked back at the first puff of smoke, which an instant before had been a round, compact ball, and in its place he saw balloons of smoke drifting away to one side, and *poof!* . . . a pause . . . three more, then four appeared, each one answered at identical intervals by a firm, precise, majestic *boom!* . . . *boom-boom!* At one moment the smoke clouds seemed to scud across the sky, at the next, to remain fixed while the woods and fields and glittering bayonets sped past them. From the left, over fields and bushes, these great balls of smoke were continually appearing, followed by their solemn reverberations, while nearer still, in the woods and hollows, burst little puffs of musket smoke that hardly formed into balls, but in the same way had their tiny reports. *Trak-ta-ta-tak!* came the rapid, uneven crack of musketry, which sounded feeble in comparison with the rhythmic roar of the cannons.

Pierre wanted to be there, in the midst of that smoke and sound and movement, where all those gleaming bayonets and cannons were. He looked around at Kutuzov and his suite, to compare his impressions with those of others. They too were all looking at the battlefield and, as it seemed to him, with the same feelings. Every face shone with that *latent heat* of emotion Pierre had noticed the day before, and which he fully understood after his talk with Prince Andrei.

"Go, my dear fellow, go, and Christ be with you," Kutuzov was saying to the general standing beside him, his eyes still fixed on the battlefield.

The general who received the order passed Pierre on his way down the knoll.

"To the crossing," replied the general in a cold, austere tone to the staff officer who asked where he was going.

"I too, I'll go there too!" thought Pierre, and followed him.

The general mounted the horse a Cossack led up to him. Pierre went to the groom who was holding his horses. After ascertaining which of them was the most docile, he mounted, and, clutching the horse's mane, turned out his toes and pressed his heels into the horse's belly. He felt that his spectacles were slipping off, but was unable to let go of the mane or the reins and galloped after the general, eliciting smiles of amusement from the staff officers who were watching him.

◇ ◇ ◇

When he reached the bottom of the hill, the general turned sharply to the left, and Pierre, losing sight of him, plunged into the ranks of an infantry battalion marching in front of him. He tried to extricate himself, turning to the right and to the left, but there were soldiers everywhere, all with the same preoccupied expression, intent on some unseen but patently important task. They all directed the same questioning look of annoyance at this stout man in the white hat, who for some reason threatened to trample them under his horse's hoofs.

"Why ride into the middle of a battalion?" one of them shouted at him.

Another prodded his horse with the butt end of a musket, and Pierre, bending over his saddlebow and hardly able to hold in his horse, galloped ahead of the soldiers to where there was an open space.

On a bridge ahead of him there were soldiers firing. Pierre rode up to them. Though unaware of it, he had come to the bridge over the Kolocha, between Gorky and Borodino, which the French (having taken Borodino) were attacking in the first action of the battle. Pierre saw the bridge, saw that there were soldiers doing something in the smoke on both sides of it and in the meadow among the rows of new-mown hay that he had noticed the day before, but despite the incessant firing going on there, it never occurred to him that this was the actual field of battle. He did not hear the bullets whistling on all sides, or the projectiles flying overhead, nor did he see the enemy on the other side of the river, and for a long time failed to notice the dead and wounded, though many fell near him. He looked around him with a smile that never left his face.

"What's he doing in front of the line?" someone shouted.

"To the left! . . . Go to the right!" the men shouted to him.

Pierre went to the right and unexpectedly encountered one of General Rayevsky's adjutants. The adjutant glanced furiously at him, and he too was about to shout, then recognized him and nodded.

"How did you get here?" he said, and galloped on.

Feeling out of place and useless, and afraid of getting in someone's way again, Pierre galloped after the adjutant.

"What's happening here? May I come with you?" he asked.

"Just a moment, just a moment," replied the adjutant, and, riding up to a stout colonel who was standing in the meadow, gave him a message, then turned to Pierre.

"What bring you here, Count?" he asked with a smile. "Still curious?"

"Yes, yes," replied Pierre.

But the adjutant wheeled about and started to ride on.

"It's not so bad here," he said, "but on the left flank, with Bagration, they're getting it hot!"

"Really?" said Pierre. "Where is that?"

"Come along with me to our knoll. We can get a view from there. It's still not too bad at our battery," said the adjutant. "Will you come?"

"Yes, I'll come with you," said Pierre, looking around, trying to see his groom.

It was only now, for the first time, that Pierre noticed the wounded men, frantically staggering along or being carried on stretchers. On the very meadow he had ridden over the day before, a soldier lay athwart the rows of sweet-scented hay, his head awkwardly thrown back, his shako[1] off.

"Why haven't they picked him up?" Pierre was about to ask, but seeing the adjutant's stern face turned in the same direction, he checked himself.

Pierre did not find his groom, and rode about the hollow with the adjutant toward Rayevsky's Redoubt. His horse trailed behind the adjutant and jolted him at every step.

"You don't seem to be accustomed to riding, Count," remarked the adjutant.

"No, it's not that, but her action is somewhat jerky," said Pierre in a puzzled tone.

"Why, she's wounded!" exclaimed the adjutant. "The off foreleg above the knee. A bullet, no doubt. I congratulate you, Count, on your baptism of fire."

Having ridden through the smoke past the 6th Corps, behind the artillery which had been moved forward and was keeping up a deafening cannonade, they came to a small wood. There it was cool and quiet, with a scent of autumn.

"Is the general here?" asked the adjutant, on reaching the redoubt.

---

[1] A high-crowned and plumed military hat.

"He was here a minute ago—he went that way," someone answered, pointing to the right.

The adjutant looked at Pierre as if not knowing what to do with him.

"Don't bother about me," said Pierre. "I'll go up on the knoll, if I may."

"Yes, do. You'll see everything from here, and it's less dangerous. I'll come for you."

Pierre went to the battery and the adjutant rode on. They did not meet again, and only much later did Pierre learn that the adjutant had lost an arm that day.

The knoll to which Pierre ascended was that famous one (afterward known to the Russians as the Knoll Battery or Rayevsky's Redoubt, and to the French as *la grande redoute, la fatale redoute, la redoute du centre*) around which tens of thousands fell, and which the French regarded as the key position.

This redoubt consisted of a knoll, on three sides of which trenches were dug. Within the entrenchment stood ten guns that were firing through the embrasures of the breastworks.

In line with the knoll on both sides were other cannons that were also firing. A little behind the guns stood infantry. When he ascended this knoll Pierre had no notion that this spot, on which some not very large trenches had been dug and from which a few guns were firing, was the most important point of the battle. On the contrary, he thought it one of the least significant places simply because he happened to be there.

When he reached the knoll, Pierre sat down at the end of the trench that enclosed the battery and gazed at what was going on around him with an unconsciously happy smile. From time to time he stood up and walked about the battery, still with the same smile, trying not to get in the way of the soldiers who were continually running past him with powder pouches and charges, loading and returning the guns to battery position. The guns of that battery were being fired one after another without interruption, creating a deafening roar and enveloping the whole vicinity in smoke.

In contrast to the dread felt by the infantrymen of the covering force, here in the battery, where there was a small number of men, separated from the rest by a trench and busy with their jobs, there was a general feeling of excitement, a family feeling as it were, shared by all.

The apparition of Pierre's unmilitary figure and white hat made an unfavorable impression at first. The soldiers cast sidelong glances of surprise and even alarm as they passed him. The senior artillery officer, a tall, long-legged man with a pockmarked face, on the pretense of inspecting the action of the end gun, walked over to Pierre and looked at him with curiosity.

A young, round-faced little officer, still a mere boy and apparently just out of the Cadet Corps, who was diligently commanding the two guns entrusted to him, addressed Pierre sternly.

"Sir, permit me to ask you to stand aside," he said. "You cannot remain here."

The soldiers shook their heads disapprovingly as they looked at Pierre. But when they were convinced that this man in the white hat was not only doing no harm as he sat quietly on the slope of the trench or, with a shy, courteous smile made way for the soldiers, but that he walked about the battery under fire as calmly as if he were strolling on a boulevard, their feeling of hostile perplexity gradually changed to a friendly, playful sodality, such as soldiers have with the dogs, cocks, goats, and other animals that share the fortunes of the regiment. And before long Pierre was tacitly accepted as one of the family; they adopted him, nicknamed him "our gentleman," and made good-natured fun of him among themselves.

A shell tore up the earth a couple of paces from Pierre. Brushing off the earth that had been scattered over his clothes, he looked about him with a smile.

"How is it you're not afraid, sir? Really, now!" a red-faced, broad-shouldered soldier asked Pierre, with a grin that disclosed a sound set of white teeth.

"Are you afraid, then?" asked Pierre.

"Of course, what do you expect?" replied the soldier. "That one's merciless, you know. She smashes into you—your guts fly out. You can't help being afraid," he said, laughing.

Several of the men stopped beside Pierre with amused, friendly faces. For some reason they had not expected him to talk like anybody else, and seemed delighted to discover that he did.

"It's our job—we're soldiers. But for a gentleman, it's amazing! Now, there's a real gentleman for you!"

"Resume stations!" shouted the young officer to the men gathered around Pierre.

It was evidently the first or second time this young officer had been on duty, and consequently he was scrupulously correct and formal in his behavior both to the soldiers and his superior officer. The booming cannonade and the rattle of musketry was intensifying over the whole field, especially to the left at Bagration's *flèches*,[2] but from where Pierre stood hardly anything could be seen for the smoke. In any case, his whole attention was absorbed in watching the little family circle of men shut off from all the rest. His first unconscious delight in the sights and sounds of the battlefield had given place to another feeling, especially since he had seen that solitary figure lying on the meadow. Now, seated on the slope of the trench, he observed the faces of those around him.

---

[2] Projecting sections of a fortification.

By ten o'clock some twenty men had been borne away, two guns were disabled, shells were falling more and more frequently on the battery, and bullets hummed and whistled through the air. But the men in the battery appeared not to notice all this, and their cheerful voices and their quips rang out on all sides.

"Little pineapple!" cried a soldier, as a grenade came whistling through the air toward them.

"Not here—over to the infantry!" added another, with a boisterous laugh, seeing the missile fly past and fall into the ranks of the covering forces.

"Friend of yours?" remarked a third soldier, laughing at a peasant who ducked as a cannonball flew over.

Several soldiers gathered at the bulwark, trying to make out what had happened in front.

"They've withdrawn the front line. Look, they've moved back!" they were saying, pointing over the bulwark.

"Mind your own business!" an old sergeant shouted at them. "If they've moved back it's because the action is there."

And taking one of the men by the shoulder, he gave him a shove with his knee. There was a burst of laughter.

"Fifth gun—in battery position!" rang out the command from one side.

"Now then, all together, like bargemen!" rose the merry voices of the men wheeling up the cannon.

"Ay! That one nearly picked off our gentleman's hat!" cried the red-faced wag, grinning at Pierre. "Ah, you're a bungler!" he added reproachfully to a shell that struck a cannon wheel and tore off a man's leg.

"Now then, you foxes!" another said with a laugh to some militiamen, who, stooping low, entered the battery to carry away the wounded man.

"Don't much care for our diet, do you? Oh, you crows! That gave 'em a turn!" they shouted at the militiamen hesitating before the soldier whose leg had been torn off.

"Come on, fellows!" they taunted the peasants. "They can't take it."

Pierre noticed that after every cannonball that hit the redoubt and after every man that fell, the general exhilaration was heightened. Lightning flashes of a hidden, blazing fire, like those of an approaching thunder cloud, flamed in the faces of the men (as if to counteract what was happening) with increasing brightness and frequency. Pierre did not look out at the battlefield, and was not concerned to know what was going on there; he was wholly absorbed in contemplating this fire that burned ever more brightly, and which he felt was burning in his own soul too.

At ten o'clock the infantry that had been in the thicket and along the Kamenka River retreated. They could be seen running back past the battery, bearing their wounded on their muskets. A general with his suite came up onto the knoll, spoke to the colonel, looked angrily at Pierre, and having ordered the infantry covering forces behind the battery to lie down so as to be less exposed to fire, went away again. After this, from amid the ranks of the infantry to the right of the battery came the sound of a drum and shouts of command, and from the battery they could see the infantry ranks move forward.

Looking over the earthworks, Pierre was particularly struck by one pale young officer who, letting his sword hang down and glancing uneasily about him, was walking backward.

The infantry disappeared in the smoke, but their prolonged cheers and rapid musket fire could still be heard. A few minutes later, crowds of wounded men and stretcher-bearers came from that direction. Shells were beginning to fall on the battery with greater and greater frequency. Several men had been left lying there. The soldiers around the cannons moved with still more alacrity and dispatch. They no longer paid any attention to Pierre. Once or twice he was furiously shouted at for being in the way. The colonel quickly strode from one gun to another, a scowl on his face. The young officer, his cheeks deeply flushed, was increasingly punctilious in giving his commands. The soldiers serving the guns turned, loaded, and bounded about as if on strings, performing their tasks with strained alertness.

The thunder cloud had come upon them, and the fire that Pierre had seen kindling now flamed in every face. He was standing beside the colonel when the young officer, his hand to his shako, ran up to his superior officer.

"I have the honor to report, sir, that there are only eight rounds left. Are we to continue firing?" he asked.

"Grapeshot!" cried the senior officer, who was looking over the wall of the trench and ignored the question.

All at once something happened: the young officer gasped, bent double, and sank to the ground like a bird shot on the wing. Everything blurred before Pierre's eyes, seemed murky and uncanny.

Cannonball after cannonball whistled past, striking the earthworks, a soldier, a gun. Pierre, who had scarcely heard these sounds before, now heard nothing else. On the right of the battery, soldiers shouting "Hurrah!" were running, not forward, it seemed to Pierre, but back.

"All with grapeshot!" shouted the officer.

The sergeant ran up to him and in a terrified whisper (like a butler informing the host at a dinner party that there is no more of the wine he asked for) said that they were out of charges.

"Cutthroats! What are they doing!" cried the officer, turning toward Pierre.

The officer's face was flushed and perspiring, and his eyes glittered under his lowering brows.

"Run to the reserves—bring up the ammunition chests!" he yelled, his furious glance passing over Pierre to one of his men.

"I'll go!" said Pierre.

The colonel, without answering, strode across to the other side.

"Cease fire! . . . Wait!" he roared.

The soldier who had been ordered to go for ammunition collided with Pierre.

"Ah, sir, this is no place for you," he said, and ran down the slope.

Pierre ran after him, avoiding the place where the young officer had slumped to the ground and was left in a sitting position.

One cannonball, a second, a third, flew over him, falling in front, behind, and beside him. Pierre continued to run down the slope. "Where am I going?" he suddenly asked himself, as he neared the green powder wagons. He stopped, uncertain whether to return or go on. All at once a violent concussion flung him backward to the ground. At the same instant there was a blinding flash and a deafening, resounding whistle and detonation.

When he came to himself he was sitting on the ground leaning on his hands. The powder wagon that had been beside him was gone—only a few charred green boards and some rags littered the scorched grass, and a horse, dragging fragments of its shafts after it, galloped by, while another horse lay, like Pierre, on the ground, and uttered prolonged, piercing shrieks.

◇ ◇ ◇

Beside himself with terror, Pierre jumped up and ran back to the battery, as to the only refuge from the horrors surrounding him.

On entering the trench he noticed that there was no sound of firing from the battery, but that there were men doing something there. He had no time to grasp who these men were. He caught sight of the colonel lying across the breastwork, his back to him, as though examining something below, and saw a soldier he had noticed earlier, who kept shouting "Brothers!" as he struggled to free himself from some men who were holding him by the arms. And he saw something else that was strange.

But he had not had time to realize that the colonel had been killed, that the man shouting "Brothers!" was taken prisoner, and that another man had been bayoneted in the back right before his eyes; for hardly had he come running into the redoubt when a thin, sallow-faced, perspiring man in blue uniform rushed at him, sword in hand and shouting. Instinctively guarding himself against the shock, as they were running full tilt against each other, he put out his hands and clutched the man (a French officer) by the shoulder and the throat. The officer dropped his sword and seized Pierre by the collar. For several seconds they gazed in consternation at one another's unfamiliar faces, both confounded by what they had done, and wondering what to do next. "Am I taken prisoner, or have I taken him prisoner?" each was thinking. But the French officer was evidently more inclined to think he had been captured, for Pierre's hand, in an instinctive reaction to terror, was tightening its grip on his throat. The Frenchman was attempting to say something, when just over their heads a cannonball whistled terrifyingly low, and it seemed to Pierre that the Frenchman's head had been torn off, so swiftly had he ducked.

Pierre too bent his head and let his hands fall. Without further thought as to who had taken whom prisoner, the Frenchman ran back to the battery and Pierre ran down the slope, stumbling over the dead and wounded, who, it seemed to him, were catching at his feet. But before he had reached the foot of the knoll he was met by a dense crowd of Russian soldiers, stumbling, foundering, shouting in wild elation as they ran into the battery. (This was the attack for which Yermolov claimed the credit, declaring that it was only his bravery and good fortune that made such a feat possible, the attack in which he incited his men by flinging onto the redoubt a handful of St. George crosses which he had in his pocket.)

The French who had taken the battery fled. Our troops, shouting "Hurrah!' pursued them so far beyond the battery that it was difficult to stop them.

The prisoners were brought down from the battery, among them a wounded French general, whom the officers surrounded. Crowds of wounded, both French and Russian—several of whom Pierre recognized—their faces distorted by suffering, walked, crawled, or were carried on stretchers from the battery. Pierre went up on the knoll, where he had spent over an hour, and of that little family circle that had accepted him as one of themselves not one was left. There were many among the dead whom he did not know, but some he recognized. At the end of the trench the young officer, still slumped over, sat in a pool of blood. The red-faced soldier was still twitching, but they did not carry him away.

Pierre ran down the slope.

"Surely now they must stop, now they will be horrified at what they have done!" he thought, aimlessly following the crowd of stretcher-bearers that was leaving the battery.

But behind the veil of smoke the sun was still high, and in front, especially on the left around Smolensk, there was a seething turmoil in the smoke; the roar of cannons and musketry, far from abating, had increased furiously, like a man exerting himself to the utmost to put forth one final, desperate cry.

◇ ◇ ◇

Kutuzov sat on the rug-covered bench where Pierre had seen him in the morning, his head drooping, his heavy body relaxed. He issued no commands, but simply gave or withheld his assent whenever anything was suggested to him.

"Yes, yes, do that," he replied to various proposals. "Yes, yes, go, my dear boy, go and have a look," he would say to one or another of his entourage; or, "No, don't, we'd better wait." He heard the reports that were brought to him, gave an order when his subordinates required it of him, but when listening to the reports he appeared to be interested not so much in the words that were spoken to him as in the expression or tone of voice of the man reporting to him.

Long years of military experience had taught him, and the wisdom of old age had convinced him, that it is impossible for one man to direct hundreds of thousands of men struggling with death, and he knew that the fate of a battle is decided not by the dispositions of a commander in chief, nor by where the troops are stationed, nor by the number of cannons or of men killed, but by that intangible force called the spirit of the army, and he took cognizance of that force and guided it insofar as it lay in his power.

Kutuzov's general expression was one of calm, concentrated attention, and of strain, as though he were hard put to master the fatigue of his weak and aging body.

At eleven o'clock the news was brought to him that the *flèches* captured by the French had been retaken, but that Prince Bagration was wounded. Kutuzov groaned and wagged his head.

"Ride over to Prince Pyotr Ivanovich and find out the details," he said to one of his adjutants, and turning to the Prince of Württemberg, who was standing behind him, said:

"Will Your Highness please take command of the First Army?"

Soon after the Prince's departure—so soon, in fact, that he could not have reached Semyonovsk—his adjutant came back to report that the Prince requested more troops.

Kutuzov frowned and sent an order to Dokhturov to take command of the First Army, and he asked that the Prince—whom he said that he could not spare at such a critical time—return to him.

When they brought him the news that Murat had been taken prisoner, Kutuzov smiled.

"Wait, gentlemen," he said. "The battle is won, and there is nothing extraordinary in the capture of Murat. Still, it is better to wait a bit before rejoicing."

Nevertheless, he sent an adjutant to take the news to the troops.

When Shcherbinin came galloping from the left flank with news that the French had captured the *flèches* and the village of Semyonovsk, Kutuzov, inferring from the sounds of battle and the look on Shcherbinin's face, that the news was bad, got up as though to stretch his legs, and taking Shcherbinin by the arm, led him aside.

"Go, my dear fellow," he said to Yermolov, "and see whether something can't be done."

Kutuzov was in Gorky, the center of the Russian position. The attack directed by Napoleon against our left flank had been several times repulsed. In the center the French had not got beyond Borodino, and on their left flank Uvarov's cavalry had put the French to flight.

Toward three o'clock the French attacks ceased. On the faces of all who came from the battlefield and of those who stood around him, Kutuzov noticed an expression of extreme tension. He was satisfied with the day's success, which had exceeded his expectations. But the old man's strength was failing. Several times his head drooped as though falling, and he sank into a doze. Dinner was brought to him.

Adjutant General Wolzogen, the man whom Prince Andrei had overheard saying: "The war must be extended over a broader area," and whom Bagration so detested, rode up while Kutuzov was at dinner. Wolzogen had come from Barclay de Tolly to report on the progress of the battle on the left flank. The perspicacious Barclay de Tolly, seeing crowds of wounded men running back and the rear of the army in disorder, weighed all the circumstances, concluded that the battle was lost, and sent his favorite officer to the Commander in Chief with this news.

Kutuzov, who was chewing on a piece of roast chicken with some difficulty, glanced at Wolzogen with eyes that narrowed with amusement.

Wolzogen nonchalantly stretched his legs and approached Kutuzov with a half-contemptuous smile, barely touching the peak of his cap. He treated His Serene Highness with a certain affectation of indifference, the aim of which was to show that, as a highly trained military man, he left it to the Russians to make an idol of this useless old man, but that he knew whom he was dealing with. *"Der alte Herr"* (as the Germans referred to him among themselves) "is making himself quite comfortable," thought Wolzogen, and with a stern glance at the dishes in front of Kutuzov, proceeded to report to "the old gentleman" the state of affairs on the left flank, according to Barclay's orders and as he himself saw it.

"All points of our position are in the hands of the enemy, and they cannot be driven back because we haven't the troops to do it; the men are running away and it is impossible to stop them," he announced.

Kutuzov stopped chewing and stared at Wolzogen in amazement, as if not comprehending what was said to him. Wolzogen, noticing "the old gentleman's" agitation, said with a smile:

"I did not consider myself justified in keeping from Your Highness what I have seen. The troops are in complete disorder—"

"What have you— What you have seen?" shouted Kutuzov,

and glowering at Wolzogen, he hastily rose and walked up to him. "How—how dare you!" he cried in a choked voice, raising his trembling arms in a threatening gesture. "How dare you, sir, say that to *me?* You know nothing about it. Tell General Barclay from me that his information is incorrect, and that the actual course of the battle is better known to me, the Commander in Chief, than to him."

Wolzogen was about to make a rejoinder, but Kutuzov interrupted him.

"The enemy has been repulsed on the left, and defeated on the right flank. If you were unable to see well, sir, then do not permit yourself to speak of what you don't know. Be so good as to return to General Barclay and inform him of my firm intention to attack the enemy tomorrow," said Kutuzov.

All were silent, and the only sound to be heard was the heavy breathing of the old general.

"They have been repulsed at all points, for which I thank God and our brave army. The enemy is defeated, and tomorrow we shall drive him from the sacred soil of Russia," said Kutuzov, crossing himself and suddenly uttering a sob as his eyes filled with tears.

Wolzogen shrugged his shoulders and his lip curled as he walked away in silence, marveling at "the old gentleman's" obsession.

"Ah, here he is, my hero," said Kutuzov to a portly, handsome, black-haired general, who at this moment was ascending the hill.

It was Rayevsky, who had been the whole day at the most critical point of the Borodino field.

Rayevsky reported that the men were steadfastly standing their ground, and that the French were not risking a further attack.

After hearing him, Kutuzov said in French:

"Then you do not think, *like some others,* that we are compelled to retreat?"

"On the contrary, Your Highness, in an indecisive engagement, it is always the most tenacious side that emerges victorious," replied Rayevsky, "and in my opinion . . ."

"Kaisarov!" Kutuzov called his adjutant. "Sit down and write out the order of the day for tomorrow. And you," he turned to another adjutant, "ride along the line and announce that tomorrow we attack."

While Kutuzov was talking to Rayevsky and dictating the order of the day, Wolzogen returned from Barclay and said that General Barclay de Tolly wished to have written confirmation of the order that the Field Marshal had given him.

Kutuzov, without looking at Wolzogen, directed that the order be written out, which the former Commander in Chief so prudently required in order to avoid all personal responsibility.

And by means of that mysterious, indefinable bond that maintains throughout entire armies an identical temper known as the spirit of the army, and which constitutes the chief sinew of war,

Kutuzov's order for the battle the next day was instantaneously communicated to every part of the army.

The words, the exact form of the order, were by no means the same when they reached the farthest links of that chain. The accounts passing from mouth to mouth in the various units did not even resemble what Kutuzov had said, but the sense of his words spread from one end of the army to the other, because what he said was not the result of shrewd calculation but of a feeling that lay deep in the soul of the Commander in Chief, as it did in that of every Russian.

And when they learned that tomorrow they were to attack the enemy, and received from the highest quarters of the army confirmation of what they wanted to believe, the exhausted, unnerved men took comfort and courage.

◇ ◇ ◇

Prince Andrei's regiment was among the reserves which till after one o'clock were stationed behind Semyonovsk, inactive and under heavy artillery fire. Toward two o'clock, the regiment, which by then had lost over two hundred men, was moved forward into a trampled oat field in the gap between Semyonovsk and the Knoll Battery, where thousands of men perished that day, and on which, between one and two o'clock, an intensely concentrated fire from several hundred enemy guns was directed.

There, without moving from the spot or firing a single shot, the regiment lost another third of its men. In front, especially on the right, the guns boomed incessantly, and out of that mysterious region perpetually shrouded in smoke came the swift hiss of flying cannonballs and the more slowly whistling grenades. Now and then, as if to allow the men a respite, a quarter of an hour would pass during which the missiles flew past them, but at other times, several men would be torn from the regiment within a minute, and the dead were continually being dragged away and the wounded carried off.

With each fresh hit, the chances of survival diminished for these who were left. The regiment was drawn up in line of battalions, three hundred paces apart; nevertheless the same mood prevailed throughout the regiment. All alike were taciturn and morose. Talk was rarely heard in the ranks and ceased altogether at every direct hit and the cry of "Stretchers!"

Most of the time, by command of their officers, the men sat on the ground. One, taking off his shako, carefully loosened the lining and tightened it again; another crumbled some clay between his palms and polished his bayonet; another shifted the strap and tightened the buckle of his bandolier; while still another smoothed and rewound his leg wrappings and pulled on his boots again. Some built little houses of the tufts in the plowed field, or plaited straws of stubble. All of them appeared to be completely absorbed in these pursuits. When men were killed or wounded, when rows of stretchers were carried by, when some of our troops returned, or when great masses of the enemy came into view through the smoke, no one took any notice. But if our artillery or cavalry advanced, or the infantry was seen moving up, words of approval were heard on all sides. The liveliest attention, however, was attracted by quite extraneous incidents having nothing to do with the battle, as if these men, whose morale was depleted, found relief in ordinary, everyday occurrences.

An artillery battery passed in front of the regiment and a horse drawing one of the powder wagons put its leg over a trace. "Hey, look at the trace horse! . . . Get her leg out! She'll fall! . . . Hey, they don't see it! . . ." were the comments shouted all along the line.

Another time general attention was attracted by a small brown dog—which had appeared from heaven knows where—busily trotting along in front of the regiment with its tail erect, till suddenly a cannonball fell close by and it darted off with a yelp, its tail between its legs. Howls and shrieks of laughter rose from the whole regiment. But distractions of this kind lasted only a few minutes, and the pale and sullen faces of these men, who for eight hours had been inactive, without food, and in constant fear of death, kept growing paler and more sullen.

Prince Andrei, pale and depressed like everyone else in the regiment, paced up and down from one border to another in the meadow next to the oat field, his head bowed, his hands clasped behind his back. There were no orders to be given, nothing for him to do. Everything happened of itself. The dead were dragged back from the front, the wounded carried away, and again the ranks closed up. If any soldier ran to the rear, he made haste to return at once. At first Prince Andrei, considering it his duty to keep up the spirits of his men and to set them an example, had walked about among the ranks, but he was soon convinced that this served no purpose, that there was nothing they could learn from him. All the powers of his soul, like those of every soldier there, were unconsciously directed to keeping his mind off the horrors of their situation. He walked along the meadow, dragging his feet, rustling the grass, and contemplating the dust that covered his boots; then he took long strides, trying to step on the tracks left by the mowers; then counted his steps, calculating how many times he would have to walk from one border to another to make a verst;[3] then stripped the flowers from the wormwood growing along the edge of the field, rubbed them between his palms and inhaled their pungent, bittersweet aroma. Nothing remained of the previous

---

[3] About two-thirds of a mile.

day's thoughts. He was thinking of nothing at all. He listened with ears that had grown weary of the same sounds, distinguishing the hiss of flying projectiles and cannon reports, and glanced at the tiresomely familiar faces of the men in the first battalion. . . .

"Here it comes . . . this one's for us!" he thought, hearing the approaching whistle of something flying out of that smoke-filled region. "One! Another! Still another! . . . A hit . . ." he stopped and looked along the ranks. "No, it's gone over. . . . But that one hit!" And he resumed his pacing up and down, trying to take long strides to reach the border in sixteen paces.

A hiss and a thud! Five paces from him a cannonball tore up the dry earth and vanished. A chill ran down his spine. Again he glanced at the ranks. Probably many had been blown up; a large crowd had gathered near the second battalion.

"Adjutant!" he shouted. "Order them not to crowd together."

The adjutant, having obeyed the order, approached Prince Andrei. The battalion commander rode up from the other side.

"Look out!" cried a soldier in a terrified voice, and like a bird in swift flight coming to earth with a whirr of wings, a shell landed almost noiselessly two paces from Prince Andrei.

The horse, not having to question whether it was right or wrong to show fear, was the first to react, snorting, rearing, and almost throwing the major as it sprang to one side. The horse's terror was communicated to the men.

"Lie down!" shouted the adjutant, throwing himself to the ground.

Prince Andrei hesitated. The smoking shell, which had fallen near a clump of wormwood on the border of the plowed field and the meadow, spun like a top between him and the prostrate adjutant.

"Can this be death?" thought Prince Andrei, looking with unwonted yearning at the grass, the wormwood, and then at the wisp of smoke curling up from the rotating black ball. "I can't die, I don't want to die. I love life—love this grass, this earth, this air . . ."

Even while he was thinking these thoughts, he remembered that people were looking at him.

"It's shameful, sir!" he said to the adjutant. "What kind of—"

He did not finish. There was the sound of an explosion, like the splintering of a window frame being ripped out, and at the same moment, a suffocating smell of powder, and Prince Andrei was hurled to one side, and flinging up his arm fell face downward.

Several officers ran up to him. Blood poured from the right side of his abdomen, making a great stain on the grass.

The militiamen with stretchers, who had been summoned, stood behind the officers. Prince Andrei lay flat on his chest, his face in the grass, breathing in hoarse gasps.

"Well, what are you waiting for? Come along!"

The peasants took Prince Andrei by the legs and shoulders, but he moaned piteously, and the men exchanged glances and set him down again.

"Pick him up, get him on there anyhow!" someone shouted.

Once more they lifted him by the shoulders and laid him on the stretcher.

"Oh, my God, my God! . . . What is it? . . . In the belly? . . . He's done for . . . Oh, my God!" the officers were heard exclaiming.

"It whizzed right past my ear—just grazed it!" said the adjutant.

The peasants, adjusting the stretcher to their shoulders, hastily set off along the path they had trodden to the dressing station.

"Keep in step! . . . Ah, these peasants!" cried an officer, putting his hand on the shoulder of one of the men to check the uneven pace that was jolting the stretcher.

"Keep in step, Fyodor! Hey, Fyodor!" said the foremost peasant.

"That's it, I've got it now," said the one behind, delighted that he had fallen into step.

"Your Excellency! Ah! Prince!" said Timokhin in a trembling voice, having run up and looked down at the stretcher.

Prince Andrei opened his eyes and looked up at the speaker from the depths of the stretcher into which his head was sunk, and his eyelids drooped again.

The militiamen carried Prince Andrei to a dressing station near a wood. The dressing station consisted of three tents with their flaps tied back, which had been pitched at the edge of a birch wood. The horses and berlins[4] stood among the trees. The horses were feeding, and sparrows flew down to pick up the grains that fell from their feed bags. The crows, scenting blood, were flying about in the trees, cawing clamorously. Over an area of more than five versts around the tents, bloodstained men, variously attired, stood, sat, or lay. Crowds of stretcher-bearers, whom the officers maintaining order tried in vain to disperse, stood about, dolefully gazing at them. Paying no heed to the officers, these men leaned on their stretchers, staring intently before them, as if trying to grasp the perplexing significance of the spectacle they were witnessing. From the tents came loud frantic cries mingled with plaintive moans. At intervals, a doctor's assistant ran out for water or to point out those who were to be brought in next. The wounded men, awaiting their turn outside the tents, cried out in raucous voices, groaned, wept, screamed, swore, begged for vodka. Some were delirious.

Prince Andrei's bearers, stepping over the wounded who had not yet been attended to, carried him, as a regimental commander,

---

[4] Covered carriages.

close to one of the tents, where they stopped and waited for instructions. Prince Andrei opened his eyes, but for a long time was unable to make out what was going on around him. He remembered the meadow, the clump of wormwood, the plowed field, the whirling black ball, and his sudden, passionate surge of love for life.

A couple of paces from him, leaning on the branch of a tree and attracting general attention with his loud talk, stood a tall, handsome, black-haired noncommissioned officer with a bandaged head. He had bullet wounds in both his head and his leg. A crowd of wounded men and stretcher-bearers were gathered around him, eagerly listening to what he said.

"We battered away at him till he chucked everything—we caught the king himself," he said, looking about with black eyes that glittered feverishly. "If only the reserves had come up just then, believe me, lads, there wouldn't have been nothing left of him."

Like all the others near the speaker, Prince Andrei looked at him with shining eyes, feeling a sense of comfort.

"But isn't it all the same now?" he thought. "And what will it be like there . . . and what has it been here? Why was I so reluctant to relinquish life? There was something about this life that I did not and do not now understand."

Further Readings

The Horizon Book of the Age of Napoleon (New York: American Heritage, 1963) is a profusely illustrated survey of Napoleon's France. Hugh Seton Watson, *The Russian Empire, 1801–1917* (Oxford: Clarendon Press, 1967), is a scholarly survey, part of the Oxford History of Modern Europe series, and has a chapter devoted to the events of 1812. Curtis Cate, *The War of the Two Emperors: The Duel between Napoleon and Alexander: Russia, 1812* (New York: Random House, 1985), is a popularly written but detailed account of the conflict. That of Allen W. Palmer, *Napoleon in Russia* (New York: Simon and Schuster, 1967), focuses on military action. Ronald Delderfield, *The Retreat from Moscow* (New York: Atheneum Publishers, 1967), is an excellent narrative of the French retreat drawn largely from journals and other accounts of participants.

Aylmer Maude, *The Life of Tolstoy* (2 vols.: London: Oxford University Press, 1930), is the standard biography of Tolstoy in English. William W. Rowe, *Leo Tolstoy* (Boston: Twayne Publishers, 1986), provides a brief biography of the author and an analysis of his major works. R. F. Christian, *Tolstoy's "War and Peace": A Study* (Oxford: Clarendon Press, 1962), provides a full analysis of the structure of the work. Tolstoy's political and historical theories are the subject of Isaiah Berlin, *The Hedgehog and the Fox: An Essay on Tolstoy's View of History* (New York: Simon and Schuster, 1953). An interesting comparison of two remarkable men may be found in Martin Green, *Tolstoy and Gandhi: Men of Peace* (New York: Basic Books, 1983).

Two massive films have been made of *War and Peace*. The Italian–American version (1956: Paramount) is generally conceded to have the superior entertainment value, but the six-hour Russian version (1968: Mosfilm) presents some truly spectacular battle scenes.

Little Women

In the years following the Civil War (1861–1865), the United States underwent profound changes. The government debts incurred during the war had created a great pool of liquid capital with which eastern bankers funded great projects: railroad and telegraph lines soon spanned the continent, the factory system expanded, and massive new industrial complexes sprang up. Entire new fields of activity, such as the petrochemical and electrical industries, were established, and new technology began to change the face of the nation. Immigration and the Homestead Act began to fill up the empty spaces in the country; in 1890 the United States Census Bureau declared that the frontier had been closed.

As is the case with most periods of rapid progress, however, it was an era of turmoil. Economic exploitation was widespread and traditional social institutions were being supplanted. The beginnings of the American labor and women's suffrage movements were only two indications of extensive dissatisfaction. Literature and the arts also suffered during this period. Although there were ample funds to support intellectual endeavors, there seemed to be little appreciation of native excellence. The era is sometimes denigrated as "the Gilded Age," and some commentators have gone so far as to suggest that there was a complete disappearance of good taste on the American scene.

This could not be said of the village of Concord, a few miles outside of Boston, Massachusetts. Concord's most famous citizen, the philosopher and author Ralph Waldo Emerson, drew about him an impressive collection of American intellectuals, including Henry David Thoreau and Nathaniel Hawthorne. One of the lesser lights of this group was Bronson Alcott, a man of high and unshakable ideals,

From Louisa May Alcott, *Little Women* (New York: Bantam Books, 1983), pp. 348–352, and 387–392.

deeply interested in educational reform. Alcott was a philosopher and refused to compromise his life of the mind with the mundane concerns of a workaday world. Although this attitude earned him the respect of New England intellectuals, it worked considerable hardship on his wife and four daughters. Since Alcott seemed incapable of earning a living, his family always lived near the edge of poverty and his wife and children were forced to provide for the family's needs in an era when few paying careers were open to women.

Bronson Alcott's second daughter, Louisa May, turned to writing at a young age, turning out numbers of the Gothic potboilers that were so popular at the time, particularly among the female audience. She always wrote for money, and her earnings were an important addition to the family's income. In 1868, when she was thirty-five years old, she began work on *Little Women*, the book that was to bring her both fame and fortune, and that was to become the most popular girl's book ever written in the United States.

Little Women is an autobiographical work, although somewhat idealized. It portrays the life of the March family, a mother and four daughters living in near poverty while the father is away at war, and lovingly traces each girl's progress towards maturity and self-realization. Headstrong Jo, with her fierce drive to become a successful writer, is the author herself and the central figure of the narrative. Although Alcott's intent was to portray family affection and the cultivation of Christian virtue in the warmest possible light, the autobiographical basis of the work kept *Little Women* from becoming facile. This is nowhere more evident than in the account of the death of Jo's younger sister, Beth.

The account is based upon actual events. In the spring of 1856, Louisa May's younger sister Elizabeth contracted scarlet fever while engaged in charity work. It was a protracted and painful illness, and Elizabeth was glad to die when the time came in January of 1857. Louisa was deeply distressed by the loss. It not only lessened the family circle, but it raised in very real and personal terms the troubling question of why God permits the innocent to suffer. Louisa was also disturbed by her own feelings. She had had to nurse Beth during the last stages of her illness, and her journals show that she sometimes harbored hostile feelings towards the invalid.

In her account of the death of Beth, Louisa attempts to exorcise her doubts and ambivalences, and presents a deep and moving portrayal of a family coping with death and dying. Like the rest of *Little Women*, this selection presents an idealized picture, but a sympathetic reading will reveal that at heart it is a real story about real people as seen through loving eyes. This, perhaps, accounts for its lasting popularity.

Questions

1. How has Beth come to terms with the fact that she is dying?

2. How does the family come to terms with the fact that Beth is dying?

3. How does Jo picture death in her poem?

4. How does the author "sanitize" the process of Beth's dying?

THE DEATH OF BETH

Beth's Secret

When Jo came home that spring, she had been struck with the change in Beth. No one spoke of it or seemed aware of it, for it had come too gradually to startle those who saw her daily, but to eyes sharpened by absence, it was very plain and a heavy weight fell on Jo's heart as she saw her sister's face. It was no paler and but little thinner than in the autumn, yet there was a strange, transparent look about it, as if the mortal was being slowly refined away, and the immortal shining through the frail flesh with an indescribably pathetic beauty. Jo saw and felt it, but said nothing at the time, and soon the first impression lost much of its power, for Beth seemed happy, no one appeared to doubt that she was better, and presently in other cares Jo for a time forgot her fear.

But when Laurie was gone, and peace prevailed again, the vague anxiety returned and haunted her. She had confessed her sins and been forgiven, but when she showed her savings and proposed the mountain trip, Beth had thanked her heartily, but begged not to go so far away from home. Another little visit to the seashore would suit her better, and as Grandma could not be prevailed upon to leave the babies, Jo took Beth down to the quiet place, where she could live much in the open air, and let the fresh sea breezes blow a little color into her pale cheeks.

It was not a fashionable place, but even among the pleasant people there, the girls made few friends, preferring to live for one another. Beth was too shy to enjoy society, and Jo too wrapped up in her to care for anyone else; so they were all in all to each other, and came and went, quite unconscious of the interest they excited in those about them, who watched with sympathetic eyes the strong sister and the feeble one, always together, as if they felt instinctively that a long separation was not far away.

They did feel it, yet neither spoke of it; for often between ourselves and those nearest and dearest to us there exists a reserve which it is very hard to overcome. Jo felt as if a veil had fallen between her heart and Beth's, but when she put out her hand to lift it up, there seemed something sacred in the silence, and she waited for Beth to speak. She wondered, and was thankful also, that her parents did not seem to see what she saw, and during the quiet weeks when the shadows grew so plain to her, she said nothing of it to those at home, believing that it would tell itself when Beth came back no better. She wondered still more if her sister really guessed the hard truth, and what thoughts were passing through her mind during the long hours when she lay on the warm rocks with her head in Jo's lap, while the winds blew healthfully over her and the sea made music at her feet.

One day Beth told her. Jo thought she was asleep, she lay so still, and putting down her book, sat looking at her with wistful eyes, trying to see signs of hope in the faint color on Beth's cheeks. But she could not find enough to satisfy her, for the cheeks were very thin, and the hands seemed too feeble to hold even the rosy little shells they had been gathering. It came to her then more bitterly than ever that Beth was slowly drifting away from her, and her arms instinctively tightened their hold upon the dearest treasure she possessed. For a minute her eyes were too dim for seeing, and, when they cleared, Beth was looking up at her so tenderly that there was hardly any need for her to say, "Jo, dear, I'm glad you know it. I've tried to tell you, but I couldn't."

There was no answer except her sister's cheek against her own, not even tears, for when most deeply moved, Jo did not cry. She was the weaker then, and Beth tried to comfort and sustain her, with her arms about her and the soothing words she whispered in her ear.

"I've known it for a good while, dear, and, now I'm used to it, it isn't hard to think of or to bear. Try to see it so, and don't be troubled about me, because it's best; indeed it is."

"Is this what made you so unhappy in the autumn, Beth? You did not feel it then, and keep it to yourself so long, did you?" asked Jo, refusing to see or say that it *was* best, but glad to know that Laurie had no part in Beth's trouble.

"Yes, I gave up hoping then, but I didn't like to own it. I tried to think it was a sick fancy, and would not let it trouble anyone. But when I saw you all so well and strong and full of happy plans, it was hard to feel that I could never be like you, and then I was miserable, Jo."

"Oh, Beth, and you didn't tell me, didn't let me comfort and help you! How could you shut me out, and bear it all alone?"

Jo's voice was full of tender reproach, and her heart ached to think of the solitary struggle that must have gone on while Beth learned to say good-by to health, love, and life, and take up her cross so cheerfully.

"Perhaps it was wrong, but I tried to do right. I wasn't sure, no one said anything, and I hoped I was mistaken. It would have been selfish to frighten you all when Marmee was so anxious about Meg, and Amy away, and you so happy with Laurie—at least, I thought so then."

"And I thought that you loved him, Beth, and I went away because I couldn't," cried Jo, glad to say all the truth.

Beth looked so amazed at the idea that Jo smiled in spite of her pain, and added softly, "Then you didn't, deary? I was afraid it was so, and imagined your poor little heart full of lovelornity all that while."

"Why, Jo, how could I, when he was so fond of you?" asked Beth, as innocently as a child. "I do love him dearly; he is so good to me, how can I help it? But he never could be anything to me but my brother. I hope he truly will be, sometime."

"Not through me," said Jo decidedly. "Amy is left for him, and they would suit excellently, but I have no heart for such things, now. I don't care what becomes of anybody but you, Beth. You *must* get well."

"I want to, oh, so much! I try, but every day I lose a little, and feel more sure that I shall never gain it back. It's like the tide, Jo, when it turns, it goes slowly, but it can't be stopped."

"It *shall* be stopped, your tide must not turn so soon, nineteen is too young. Beth, I can't let you go. I'll work and pray and fight against it. I'll keep you in spite of everything; there must be ways, it can't be too late. God won't be so cruel as to take you from me," cried poor Jo rebelliously, for her spirit was far less piously submissive than Beth's.

Simple, sincere people seldom speak much of their piety; it shows itself in acts rather than in words, and has more influence than homilies or protestations. Beth could not reason upon or explain the faith that gave her courage and patience to give up life, and cheerfully wait for death. Like a confiding child, she asked no questions, but left everything to God and nature, Father and mother of us all, feeling sure that they, and they only, could teach and strengthen heart and spirit for this life and the life to come. She did not rebuke Jo with saintly speeches, only loved her better for her passionate affection, and clung more closely to the dear human love, from which our Father never means us to be weaned, but through which He draws us closer to Himself. She could not say, "I'm glad to go," for life was very sweet to her; she could only sob out, "I try to be willing," while she held fast to Jo, as the first bitter wave of this great sorrow broke over them together.

By and by Beth said, with recovered serenity, "You'll tell them this when we go home?"

"I think they will see it without words," sighed Jo, for now it seemed to her that Beth changed every day.

"Perhaps not, I've heard that the people who love best are often blindest to such things. If they don't see it, you will tell them for me. I don't want any secrets, and it's kinder to prepare them.

Meg has John and the babies to comfort her, but you must stand by Father and Mother, won't you, Jo?"

"If I can. But, Beth, I don't give up yet. I'm going to believe that it *is* a sick fancy, and not let you think it's true," said Jo, trying to speak cheerfully.

Beth lay a minute thinking, and then said in her quiet way, "I don't know how to express myself, and shouldn't try to anyone but you, because I can't speak out except to my Jo. I only mean to say that I have a feeling that it never was intended I should live long. I'm not like the rest of you; I never made any plans about what I'd do when I grew up; I never thought of being married, as you all did. I couldn't seem to imagine myself anything but stupid little Beth, trotting about at home, of no use anywhere but there. I never wanted to go away, and the hard part now is the leaving you all. I'm not afraid, but it seems as if I should be homesick for you even in heaven."

Jo could not speak, and for several minutes there was no sound but the sigh of the wind and the lapping of the tide. A white-winged gull flew by, with the flash of sunshine on its silvery breast; Beth watched it till it vanished, and her eyes were full of sadness. A little gray-coated sand bird came tripping over the beach, "peeping" softly to itself, as if enjoying the sun and sea; it came quite close to Beth, looked at her with a friendly eye and sat upon a warm stone, dressing its wet feathers, quite at home. Beth smiled and felt comforted, for the tiny thing seemed to offer its small friendship and remind her that a pleasant world was still to be enjoyed.

"Dear little bird! See, Jo, how tame it is. I like peeps better than the gulls: they are not so wild and handsome, but they seem happy, confiding little things. I used to call them my birds last summer, and Mother said they reminded her of me—busy, quaker-colored creatures, always near the shore, and always chirping that contented little song of theirs. You are the gull, Jo, strong and wild, fond of the storm and the wind, flying far out to sea, and happy all alone. Meg is the turtledove, and Amy is like the lark she writes about, trying to get up among the clouds, but always dropping down into its nest again. Dear little girl! She's so ambitious, but her heart is good and tender, and no matter how high she flies, she never will forget home. I hope I shall see her again, but she seems *so* far away."

"She is coming in the spring, and I mean that you shall be all ready to see and enjoy her. I'm going to have you well and rosy by that time," began Jo, feeling that of all the changes in Beth, the talking change was the greatest, for it seemed to cost no effort now, and she thought aloud in a way quite unlike bashful Beth.

"Jo, dear, don't hope any more. It won't do any good, I'm sure of that. We won't be miserable, but enjoy being together while we wait. We'll have happy times, for I don't suffer much, and I think the tide will go out easily, if you help me."

Jo leaned down to kiss the tranquil face, and with that silent kiss, she dedicated herself soul and body to Beth.

She was right: there was no need of any words when they got home, for Father and Mother saw plainly now what they had prayed to be saved from seeing. Tired with her short journey, Beth went at once to bed, saying how glad she was to be home, and when Jo went down, she found that she would be spared the hard task of telling Beth's secret. Her father stood leaning his head on the mantelpiece, and did not turn as she came in; but her mother stretched out her arms as if for help, and Jo went to comfort her without a word.

The Valley of the Shadow

When the first bitterness was over, the family accepted the inevitable, and tried to bear it cheerfully, helping one another by the increased affection which comes to bind households tenderly together in times of trouble. They put away their grief, and each did his or her part toward making that last year a happy one.

The pleasantest room in the house was set apart for Beth, and in it was gathered everything that she most loved—flowers, pictures, her piano, the little worktable, and the beloved pussies. Father's best books found their way there, Mother's easy chair, Jo's desk, Amy's finest sketches, and every day Meg brought her babies on a loving pilgrimage, to make sunshine for Aunty Beth. John quietly set apart a little sum, that he might enjoy the pleasure of keeping the invalid supplied with the fruit she loved and longed for; old Hannah never wearied of concocting dainty dishes to tempt a capricious appetite, dropping tears as she worked; and from across the sea came little gifts and cheerful letters, seeming to bring breaths of warmth and fragrance from lands that know no winter.

Here, cherished like a household saint in its shrine, sat Beth, tranquil and busy as ever, for nothing could change the sweet, unselfish nature, and even while preparing to leave life, she tried to make it happier for those who should remain behind. The feeble fingers were never idle, and one of her pleasures was to make little things for the schoolchildren daily passing to and fro—to drop a pair of mittens from her window for a pair of purple hands, a needlebook for some small mother of many dolls, penwipers for young penmen toiling through forests of pothooks,[1] scrapbooks for picture-loving eyes, and all manner of pleasant devices, till the reluctant climbers up the ladder of learning found their way strewn

---

[1] Written characters, so-called for their fancied resemblance to the S-shaped hooks for hanging pots and kettles over a fire.

with flowers, as it were, and came to regard the gentle giver as a sort of fairy godmother, who sat above there, and showered down gifts miraculously suited to their tastes and needs. If Beth had wanted any reward, she found it in the bright little faces always turned up to her window, with nods and smiles, and the droll little letters which came to her, full of blots and gratitude.

The first few months were very happy ones, and Beth often used to look round, and say "How beautiful this is!" as they all sat together in her sunny room, the babies kicking and crowing on the floor, mother and sisters working near, and father reading, in his pleasant voice, from the wise old books which seemed rich in good and comfortable words, as applicable now as when written centuries ago; a little chapel, where a paternal priest taught his flock the hard lessons all must learn, trying to show them that hope can comfort love, and faith make resignation possible. Simple sermons, that went straight to the souls of those who listened, for the father's heart was in the minister's religion, and the frequent falter in the voice gave a double eloquence to the words he spoke or read.

It was well for all that this peaceful time was given them as preparation for the sad hours to come; for, by-and-by, Beth said the needle was "so heavy," and put it down forever; talking wearied her, faces troubled her, pain claimed her for its own, and her tranquil spirit was sorrowfully perturbed by the ills that vexed her feeble flesh. Ah me! Such heavy days, such long, long nights, such aching hearts and imploring prayers, when those who loved her best were forced to see the thin hands stretched out to them beseechingly, to hear the bitter cry, "Help me, help me!" and to feel that there was no help. A sad eclipse of the serene soul, a sharp struggle of the young life with death, but both were mercifully brief, and then, the natural rebellion over, the old peace returned more beautiful than ever. With the wreck of her frail body, Beth's soul grew strong, and though she said little, those about her felt that she was ready, saw that the first pilgrim called was likewise the fittest, and waited with her on the shore, trying to see the Shining Ones coming to receive her when she crossed the river.

Jo never left her for an hour since Beth had said, "I feel stronger when you are here." She slept on a couch in the room, walking often to renew the fire, to feed, lift, or wait upon the patient creature who seldom asked for anything, and "tried not to be a trouble." All day she haunted the room, jealous of any other nurse, and prouder of being chosen then than of any honor her life ever brought her. Precious and helpful hours to Jo, for now her heart received the teaching that it needed: lessons in patience were so sweetly taught her that she could not fail to learn them; charity for all, the lovely spirit that can forgive and truly forget unkindness, the loyalty to duty that makes the hardest easy, and the sincere faith that fears nothing, but trusts undoubtingly.

Often when she woke Jo found Beth reading in her well-worn

little book, heard her singing softly, to beguile the sleepless night, or saw her lean her face upon her hands, while slow tears dropped through the transparent fingers; and Jo would lie watching her with thoughts too deep for tears, feeling that Beth, in her simple, unselfish way, was trying to wean herself from the dear old life, and fit herself for the life to come, by sacred words of comfort, quiet prayers, and the music she loved so well.

Seeing this did more for Jo than the wisest sermons, the saintliest hymns, the most fervent prayers that any voice could utter; for, with eyes made clear by many tears, and a heart softened by the tenderest sorrow, she recognized the beauty of her sister's life—uneventful, unambitious, yet full of the genuine virtues which "smell sweet, and blossom in the dust," the self-forgetfulness that makes the humblest on earth remembered soonest in heaven, the true success which is possible to all.

One night when Beth looked among the books upon her table, to find something to make her forget the mortal weariness that was almost as hard to bear as pain, as she turned the leaves of her old favorite, *Pilgrim's Progress*, she found a little paper, scribbled over in Jo's hand. The name caught her eye and the blurred look of the lines made her sure that tears had fallen on it.

"Poor Jo! She's fast asleep, so I won't wake her to ask leave; she shows me all her things, and I don't think she'll mind if I look at this," thought Beth, with a glance at her sister, who lay on the rug, with the tongs beside her, ready to wake up the minute the log fell apart.

MY BETH

Sitting patient in the shadow
  Till the blessed light shall come,
A serene and saintly presence
  Sanctifies our troubled home.
Earthly joys and hopes and sorrows
  Break like ripples on the strand
Of the deep and solemn river
  Where her willing feet now stand.
O my sister, passing from me,
  Out of human care and strife,
Leave me, as a gift, those virtues
  Which have beautified your life.
Dear, bequeath me that great patience
  Which has power to sustain
A cheerful, uncomplaining spirit
  In its prison-house of pain.

Give me, for I need it sorely,
  Of that courage, wise and sweet,

> *Which has made the path of duty*
>   *Green beneath your willing feet.*
> *Give me that unselfish nature,*
>   *That with charity divine*
> *Can pardon wrong for love's dear sake—*
>   *Meek heart, forgive me mine!*
>
> *Thus our parting daily loseth*
>   *Something of its bitter pain,*
> *And while learning this hard lesson,*
>   *My great loss becomes my gain.*
> *For the touch of grief will render*
>   *My wild nature more serene,*
> *Give to life new aspirations,*
>   *A new trust in the unseen.*
>
> *Henceforth, safe across the river,*
>   *I shall see forevermore*
> *A beloved, household spirit*
>   *Waiting for me on the shore.*
> *Hope and faith, born of my sorrow,*
>   *Guardian angels shall become,*
> *And the sister gone before me*
>   *By their hands shall lead me home.*

Blurred and blotted, faulty and feeble as the lines were, they brought a look of inexpressible comfort to Beth's face, for her one regret had been that she had done so little, and this seemed to assure her that her life had not been useless, that her death would not bring the despair she feared. As she sat with the paper folded between her hands, the charred log fell asunder. Jo started up, revived the blaze, and crept to the bedside, hoping Beth slept.

"Not asleep, but so happy, dear. See, I found this and read it. I knew you wouldn't care. Have I been all that to you, Jo?" she asked, with wistful, humble earnestness.

"Oh, Beth, so much, so much!" And Jo's head went down upon the pillow beside her sister's.

"Then I don't feel as if I'd wasted my life. I'm not so good as you make me, but I *have* tried to do right; and now, when it's too late to begin even to do better, it's such a comfort to know that someone loves me so much, and feels as if I'd helped them."

"More than any one in the world, Beth. I used to think I couldn't let you go, but I'm learning to feel that I don't lose you, that you'll be more to me than ever, and death can't part us, though it seems to."

"I know it cannot, and I don't fear it any longer, for I'm sure I shall be your Beth still, to love and help you more than ever. You must take my place, Jo, and be everything to Father and Mother when I'm gone. They will turn to you, don't fail them; and if it's hard to work alone, remember that I don't forget you, and that you'll be happier in doing that than writing splendid books or seeing all the world; for love is the only thing that we can carry with us when we go, and it makes the end so easy."

"I'll try, Beth." And then and there Jo renounced her old ambition, pledged herself to a new and better one, acknowledging the poverty of other desires, and feeling the blessed solace of a belief in the immortality of love.

So the spring days came and went, the sky grew clearer, the earth greener, the flowers were up fair and early, and the birds came back in time to say good-by to Beth, who, like a tired but trustful child, clung to the hands that had led her all her life, as Father and Mother guided her tenderly through the Valley of the Shadow, and gave her up to God.

Seldom except in books do the dying utter memorable words, see visions, or depart with beatified countenances, and those who have sped many parting souls know that to most the end comes as naturally and simply as sleep. As Beth had hoped, the "tide went out easily," and in the dark hour before the dawn, on the bosom where she had drawn her first breath, she quietly drew her last, with no farewell but one loving look, one little sigh.

With tears and prayers and tender hands, Mother and sisters made her ready for the long sleep that pain would never mar again, seeing with grateful eyes the beautiful serenity that soon replaced the pathetic patience that had wrung their hearts so long, and feeling with reverent joy that to their darling death was a benignant angel, not a phantom full of dread.

When morning came, for the first time in many months the fire was out, Jo's place was empty, and the room was very still. But a bird sang blithely on a budding bough, close by, the snowdrops blossomed freshly at the window, and the spring sunshine streamed in like a benediction over the placid face upon the pillow—a face so full of painless peace that those who loved it best smiled through their tears, and thanked God that Beth was well at last.

Further Readings

The later nineteenth century has received considerable attention from historians. H. Wayne Morgan, *The Gilded Age: A Reappraisal* (Syracuse, NY: University of Syracuse Press, 1963), attempts to balance the generally unfavorable views presented of the period. *The Gilded Age*, edited by H. Wayne Morgan (Syracuse, NY: Syracuse University Press, 1970), presents a collection of articles by various authors discussing several aspects of American life during the period. The close of the Gilded Age is discussed in Lanzer Ziff, *The American 1890's: Life and Times of a Lost Generation* (London: Chatto and Windus, 1967). Vernon L. Parrington, *Main Currents in American Thought* (3 volumes in 1: New York: Harcourt Brace and Co., n.d.), is a standard of American intellectual history, and places the Alcott's Concord within the broader perspective of American intellectual development. Van Wyck Brooks, *New England: Indian Summer* (New York: E. P. Dutton and Co., Inc., 1965), is a well-written and affectionate literary history of New England between the Civil War and the First World War.

Numerous biographies of the Alcotts have appeared. The family as a whole is treated in Madelon Bedell, *The Alcotts: Biography of a Family* (New York: C. W. Potter, distributed by Crown Publishers, 1980). Honoré W. Morrow, *The Father of Little Women* (Boston, MA: Little, Brown, 1927), and Franklin B. Sanborn and William T. Harris, *A. Bronson Alcott: His Life and Philosophy* (New York: Biblo and Tannen, 1965), cover the father, while Sanford Sayler, *Marmee, The Mother of Little Women* (Norman, OK: University of Oklahoma Press, 1949), discusses the mother, one of the first American professional social workers. Louisa's younger sister May, who became a recognized artist, is the subject of Caroline Ticknor, *May Alcott: A Memoir* (Boston: Little, Brown, 1928). Louisa herself exerts a never-ending attraction to biographers. Some of the more prominent are Katherine S. Anthony, *Louisa May Alcott* (New York: A. A. Knopf, 1938); Catherine O. Peare, *Louisa May Alcott: Her Life* (New York: Holt, 1954); Madeline B. Sterne, *Louisa May Alcott* (Norman, OK: University of Oklahoma Press, 1950); Marjorie M. Worthington, *Miss Alcott of Concord: A Biography* (Garden City, NY: Doubleday, 1958); and Martha Saxton, *A Modern Biography of Louisa May Alcott* (Boston, MA: Houghton Mifflin, 1977). An analysis of her literary works may be found in Ruth K. MacDonald, *Louisa May Alcott* (Boston, MA: Twayne Publishers, 1982).

Social historians have also applied themselves to Louisa's works. Charles Strickland, *Victorian Domesticity: Families in the Life and Art of Louisa May Alcott* (University, AL: University of Alabama Press, 1985), and Joy A. Marsella, *The Promise of Destiny: Children and Women in the Short Stories of Louisa May Alcott* (Westport, CT: Greenwood Press, 1983), are two of the more recent. Helen Rosen, *Unspoken Grief: Coping with Childhood Sibling Loss* (Lexington, MA: Lexington Books, 1986), can provide some useful insights into "The Death of Beth."

Two film versions of *Little Women* have been produced, a black-and-white version in 1933 by RKO, and a color version by MGM in 1949. Although both depart from the book to a certain degree, they manage to capture much of the flavor of the text.

Commentary on the Commentator

Under the stimulus of the Industrial Revolution, the pace of European technological progress increased throughout the nineteenth century. Although Western superiority over non-Western civilizations in 1800 had been relatively slight—except in the critical areas of weaponry, metallurgy, and transportation—by 1900 that superiority extended to virtually all aspects of material culture. Developments in medicine, chemistry, engineering, and physics had markedly increased the disparity between the Western and the non-Western cultures of the world. What is more, the European powers used this new strength to extend their economic and political authority to areas that had hitherto been successful in resisting them. This often led to confusion on the part of the peoples who fell under Western domination. Members of traditional societies hated their new masters, but were fascinated by their technological superiority as well as by the wealth and power that that technology made possible. It was obvious that traditional societies would have to progress technologically if they were to survive, much less prosper. The question that plagued many was whether Western technology was compatible with the patterns of traditional culture. This was one of the major problems that confronted the leaders that began to arise in opposition to European domination. The questions of nationalism and scientific progress were inextricably interwoven.

Providing one answer to this question was the great contribution of the remarkable figure, Jamal ed-Din (1838–1897), known as al-Afghani ("the Afghan"). Although he claimed to be an Afghan, he

From Afghânî, *An Islamic Response to Imperialism; Political and Religious Writings of Sayyid Jamâl Dîn "al-Afghânî*," edited and translated by Nikki R. Keddie (Berkeley, CA: University of California Press, 1983), pp. 123–129.

was born in Persia and received a traditional Shi'ite religious education. In about 1855, he travelled to India and probably was there during the Indian Mutiny of 1857. He appears to have been shocked by his experiences in India, having experienced for the first time Western rule over a Muslim population. He became a Muslim nationalist and, in particular, an opponent of British imperialism. Muslim countries were in state of ferment at the time, since Great Britain, France, and Russia were all encroaching upon Islamic lands. Nationalists and anti-imperialists found welcome and support in many countries, and al-Afghani travelled widely. In 1866–1868, he was a political advisor in Afghanistan before being expelled as a troublemaker. He was expelled from Istanbul in 1870 on the charge of being irreligious. He was in Cairo from 1871 to 1879, again ending up by being expelled. He travelled to India once again (1880–1881), and then to London, Paris, Russia, and back to Iran. He spent his final years (1891–1897) in Istanbul, where the government closely monitored his activities and worked to limit his political influence. The cancer that finally ended his life appears to have affected his faculties; his last writings lost focus and effectiveness, just as he himself seems to have lost touch with political reality.

After his death, however, his memory was rehabilitated, and he was praised as one of the founders of Arab nationalism. There is something to be said for this view. Many Muslim leaders of the time were convinced that the only way to compete with the Europeans was to imitate them, even to the extent of abandoning or modifying some basic aspects of the Muslim faith. Al-Afghani led the way in opposing this policy, arguing persuasively that Islam was dynamic and that all necessary reforms could be accommodated within the structure of the faith. Moreover, he carried the battle to his Muslim opponents, challenging not only their willingness to modify and weaken the faith, but also their tendency to admire and work with the imperial forces that were oppressing their co-religionists. At a time when many Muslim leaders were either retreating into reactionary resistance to new ideas or were indiscriminately embracing Western culture along with Western science, al-Afghani championed a middle way. Most modern leaders of Muslim lands have followed this path.

In 1880–1882, al-Afghani was in India. The most prominent of the Indian Muslims at the time was Sir Sayyid Ahmad Khan, who was a leader in cooperating with the British and who promoted a rationalist and materialist philosophy at total variance with Muslim theology. Ahmad Khan had written a rationalist *Commentary on the Koran,* that was seen by many as casting doubt upon the Koran as absolute truth and the word of God. Al-Afghani wrote the *Commentary on the Commentator* as a refutation of Ahmad Khan's views on this fundamental issue. Not only does al-Afghani point out that religious belief and material progress historically have had no necessary connection, but he also observes that this needless challenge to Muslim

COMMENTARY ON THE COMMENTATOR

belief in the interest of advancing material progress simply serves to confuse and divide the Muslim community, thus making them more vulnerable to Western domination. His message to his Muslim readers was that it was inevitable that their societies would advance into the modern world, but that it was important that they do so without abandoning those beliefs and practices that gave them their unique identity.

Questions

1. According to al-Afghani, what shapes human societies?

2. What is his view of the nature of man?

3. How does he use history to argue his point?

4. What does he believe to have been the goal of the Commentator?

COMMENTARY ON THE COMMENTATOR

Man is man because of education. None of the peoples of mankind, not even the savage, is completely deprived of education. If one considers man at the time of his birth, one sees that his existence without education is impossible. Even if we assumed that his existence were possible without education, his life would in that state be more repulsive and vile than the life of animals. Education consists of a struggle with nature, and overcoming her, whether the education be in plants, animals, or men.

Education, if it is good, produces perfection from imperfection, and nobility from baseness. If it is not good it changes the basic state of nature and becomes the cause of decline and decadence. This appears clearly among agriculturalists, cattle raisers, teachers, civil rulers, and religious leaders. In general, good education in these three kingdoms [human, animal, and plant] is the cause of all perfections and virtues. Bad education is the source of all defects and evils.

When this is understood, one must realize that if a people receives a good education, all of its classes and ranks, in accord with the natural law of relationships, will flourish simultaneously and will progress. Each class and group among that people, according to its rank and degree, tries to acquire the perfections that are appropriate to it, and does obtain them. The classes of that people, according to their rank, will always be in a state of balance and equilibrium with each other. This means that just as great rulers will appear among such a people because of their good education, so there will also come into existence excellent philosophers, erudite scholars, skilled craftsmen, able agriculturalists, wealthy merchants, and other professions. If that people because of its good education reaches such a level that its rulers are distinguished beyond the rulers of other peoples, one can be certain that all its classes will be distinguished above the classes of other countries. This is because perfect progress in each class depends on the progress of the other classes. This is the general rule, the law of nature, and the divine practice.

When, however, corruption finds its way into that people's education, weakness will occur in all its classes in proportion to their rank and to the extent of the corruption. That is, if weakness appears in the ruling circles, this weakness will surely overtake the class of philosophers, scholars, craftsmen, agriculturalists, merchants, and the other professions. For their perfection is the effect of a good education. When weakness, disorder, and corruption are introduced into a good education, which is the causative factor, inevitably the same weakness, disorder, and corruption will enter into the effects of that education. When corruption enters a nation's education it sometimes happens that, because of the increase of corruption in education and the ruin of manners and customs, the various classes, which are the cause of stability, and especially the noble classes, are gradually destroyed. The individuals of that nation, after removing their former clothes and changing their name, become part of another nation and appear with new adornments. This happened to the Chaldeans, the Phoenicians, the Copts, and similar people.

Sometimes Eternal Grace aids that people, and some men of high intelligence and pure souls appear among them and bring about a new life. They remove that corruption which was the cause of decline and destruction, and rescue souls and minds from the terrible malady of bad education. And through their own basic luster and brightness they return the good education and give back life once more to their people. They restore to them greatness, honor, and the progress of classes.

This is why every people who enter into decline, and whose classes are overtaken by weakness, are always, because of their expectation of Eternal Grace, waiting to see if perhaps there is to be found among them a wise renewer, experienced in policy, who can enlighten their minds and purify their souls through his wise management and fine efforts, and do away with the corrupt education. By the policies of that sage they could return to their former condition.

There is no doubt that in the present age, distress, misfortune, and weakness besiege all classes of Muslims from every side. Therefore every Muslim keeps his eyes and ears open in expectation—to the East, West, North, and South—to see from what corner of the earth the sage and renewer will appear and will reform the minds and souls of the Muslims, repel the unforeseen corruption, and again educate them with a virtuous education. Perhaps through that good education they may return to their former joyful condition.

Since I am certain that the Absolute Truth (*haqq-i mutlaq*) will not destroy this true religion and right *shari'a*,[1] I more than others expect that the minds and souls of the Muslims will very soon be enlightened and rectified by the wisdom of a sage. For this reason I always want to keep abreast of the articles and treatises that are now appearing from the pens of Muslims, and be thoroughly acquainted with the views of their authors. I hope that in these readings I may discover the elevated ideas of a sage who could be the cause of good education, virtue, and prosperity for the Muslims. I would then hope, to the extent of my ability, to assist him in his elevated ideas and become a helper and associate in the reform of my people.

In the course of discussions and investigations about the ideas of the Muslims, I heard of one of them who, mature in years and rich in experience, took a trip to European countries. After much labor and effort he wrote a Commentary on the Koran in order to improve the Muslims. I said to myself, "Here is just what you wanted."

And as is customary with those who hear new things, I let my imagination wander, and formed various conceptions of that commentator and that commentary. I believed that this commentator, after all the commentaries written by Traditionists, jurists, orators, philosophers, Sufis, authors, grammarians, and heretics like Ibn Râwandî[2] and others, would have done justice to that subject, unveiled the truth and achieved the precise goal. For he had followed the ideas of both Easterners and Westerners. I thought that this commentator would have explained in the introduction to his commentary, as wisdom requires, the truth and essence of religion for the improvement of his people. That he would have demonstrated the necessity of religion in the human world by rational proofs, and that he would have set up a general rule, satisfying the intellect, to distinguish between true and false religions. I imagined that this commentator had undoubtedly explained the influence of each of the prior, untrue religions on civilization and the social order and on men's souls and minds. I thought he would have explained in a philosophical way the reason for the divergence of religions on some matters, along with their agreement on many precepts, and the reason for the special relation of each age to a particular religion and prophet.

Since he claims to have written this commentary for the improvement of the community, I was certain he had in the introduc-

---

[1] Law.
[2] Ninth-century heretic who criticized prophecy in general and Muhammad's prophecy in particular.

tion of his book described and explained in a new manner, with the light of wisdom, those divine policies and Koranic ethics that were the cause of the superiority and expansion of the Arabs in every human excellence. I was sure he had included in his introduction those precepts that were the cause of the unity of the Arabs, the transformation of their ideas, the enlightenment of their minds, and the purification of their souls; and all that when they were in the extremity of discord, savagery, and hardship.[3]

When I read the commentary I saw that this commentator in no way raised a word about these matters or about divine policy. In no manner are Koranic ethics explained. He has not mentioned any of those great precepts that were the cause of the enlightenment of the minds and purification of the souls of the Arabs. He has left without commentary those verses that relate to divine policy, support the promulgation of virtuous ethics and good habits, rectify domestic and civil intercourse, and cause the enlightenment of minds. Only at the beginning of his commentary does he pronounce a few words on the meaning of "sura," "verse," and the separate letters at the beginning of the suras. After that all his effort is devoted to taking every verse in which there is mention of angels, or *jinns*,[4] or the faithful spirit [Gabriel], revelation, paradise, hell, or the miracles of the prophets, and, lifting these verses from their external meaning, interpreting them according to the specious allegorical interpretations of the heretics of past Muslim centuries.

The difference is that the heretics of past Muslim centuries were scholars, whereas this unfortunate commentary is very ignorant. Therefore he cannot grasp their words correctly. Taking the subject of man's *nature* as a subject of discourse, he pronounces some vague and meaningless words, without rational demonstrations or natural proofs. He apparently does not know that man is man through education, and all his virtues and habits are acquired. The man who is nearest to his nature is the one who is the farthest from civilization and from acquired virtues and habits. If men abandoned the legal and intellectual virtues they have acquired with the greatest difficulty and effort, and gave over control to the hands of nature, undoubtedly they would become lower than animals.

Even stranger is the fact that this commentator has lowered the divine, holy rank of prophecy and placed it on the level of the *reformer*. He has considered the prophets to be men like Washington, Napoleon, Palmerston, Garibaldi, Mister Gladstone, and Monsieur Gambetta.

When I saw the commentary to be of this kind, amazement overtook me, and I began to ask myself what was the purpose of

---

[3] Afghani believed in the Muslim religion as a basis for political unity among Muslims of his day.
[4] Spirits. (The English word *genie* derives from the Arabic *jinni*.)

this commentator in writing such a commentary. If the goal of this commentator is, as he says, the improvement of his community, then why does he try to end the belief of Muslims in the Islamic religion, especially in these times when other religions have opened their mouths to swallow this religion?

Does he not understand that if the Muslims, in their current state of weakness and misery, did not believe in miracles and hellfire, and considered the Prophet to be like Gladstone, they undoubtedly would soon abandon their own weak and conquered camp, and attach themselves to a powerful conqueror? For in that event there would no longer remain anything to prevent this, nor any fear or anxiety. And from another standpoint the prerequisites for changing religion now exist, since being like the conqueror, and having the same religion as he, is attractive to everyone.

After these ideas and reflections, it first occurred to me that this commentator certainly believes that the cause of the decline of the Muslims and of their distressed condition is their religion itself, and that if they abandoned their beliefs they would restore their former greatness and honor. Therefore, he is trying to remove these beliefs, and because of his motivation he could be forgiven.

Having reflected further, however, I said to myself that the Jews, thanks to these same beliefs, rescued themselves from the humiliation of slavery to the pharoahs and rubbed in the dust the pride of the tyrants of Palestine. Has not the commentator heard of this.

And the Arabs, thanks to these same beliefs, came up from the desert lands of the Arabian peninsula, and became masters of the whole world in power, civilization, knowledge, manufacture, agriculture, and trade. The Europeans in their speeches referred aloud to those believing Arabs as their masters. Has not this fact reached the ears of this commentator? Of course it has.

After considering the great effects of these true beliefs and their followers, I looked at the followers of false beliefs. I saw that the Hindus at the same time that they made progress in the laws of civilization, and in science, knowledge, and the various crafts, believed in thousands of gods and idols. This commentator is not ignorant of this. The Egyptians at the times when they laid the foundations of civilization, science, and manufactures, and were the masters of the Greeks, believed in idols, cows, dogs, and cats. This commentator undoubtedly knows this. The Chaldeans, at the time that they founded observatories, manufactured astronomical instruments, built high castles, and composed books on agricultural science, were worshippers of the stars. This is not hidden from the commentator. The Phoenicians, in the age that they made manufacture and commerce on land and sea flourish, and colonized the lands of Britain, Spain, and Greece, presented their own children as sacrifices to idols. This is clear to the commentator.

The Greeks, in that century that they were rulers of the world, and at the time that great sages and revered philosophers appeared among them, believed in hundreds of gods and thousands of superstitions. This is known to the commentator. The Persians, at the time when they ruled from the regions of Kashgar to the frontiers of Istanbul, and were considered incomparable in civilization, had hundreds of absurdities engraved in their hearts. Of course the commentator remembers this. The modern Christians, at the same time as they acknowledged the Trinity, the cross, resurrection, baptism, purgatory, confession, and transubstantiation, assured their domination; progressed in the spheres of science, knowledge, and industry; and reached the summit of civilization. Most of them still, with all their science and knowledge, follow the same beliefs. The commentator knows this well.

When I considered these matters I realized that the commentator never was of the opinion that faith in these true beliefs caused the decline of the Muslims. For religious beliefs, whether true or false, are in no way incompatible with civilization and worldly progress unless they forbid the acquisition of science, the earning of a livelihood, and progress in sound civilization. I do not believe that there is a religion in the world that forbids these things, as appears clearly from what has been said above. Rather I can say that the lack of faith results only in disorder and corruption in civil life, and in insecurity. Reflect—this is *Nihilism!*

If the lack of faith brought about the progress of peoples, then the Arabs of the Age of Ignorance would have had to have precedence in civilization. For they were mostly followers of the materialist path, and for this reason they used to say aloud: "Wombs push us forth, the earth swallows us up, and only time destroys us." They also always used to say: "Who can revive bones after they have decomposed?" This despite the fact that they lived in the utmost ignorance, like wild animals.

After all these various thoughts and considerations, I understood well that this commentators is not a reformer, nor was his commentary written for the improvement and education of the Muslims. Rather this commentator and this commentary are for the Islamic community at the present time like those terrible and dangerous illnesses that strike man when he is weak and decrepit. The aim of his modifications has been demonstrated above.

The goal of this commentator from this effort to remove the beliefs of the Muslims is to serve others and to prepare the way for conversion to their religion.

These few lines have been written hastily. Later, by the power of God, I will write in detail about this commentary and the aims of the commentator.

Further Readings

George Antonius, *The Arab Awakening: The Story of the Arab National Movement* (London: H. Hamilton, 1938), and Raphael Patai, *The Arab Mind* (New York: Scribner's, 1973), are indispensable for the study of the origins of Arab nationalism. *Arab Nationalism: An Anthology,* selected and edited by Sylvia G. Haim (Berkeley, CA: University of California Press, 1962), presents a number of relevant readings.

The origins of the national movements of various countries are available from diverse authors. Mangol Bayat, *Mysticism and Dissent: Socio-Religious Thought in Qajar Iran* (Syracuse, NY: Syracuse University Press, 1982), Guity Nashat, *The Origins of Modern Reform in Iran, 1870–1880* (Urbana, IL: University of Illinois Press), and Edward G. Browne, *The Persian Revolution of 1905–1909* (Cambridge: The University Press, 1910), together provide an account of nationalist stirrings in Iran. Nikki R. Keddie, *Religion and Rebellion in Iran: The Tobacco Protest of 1891–1892* (London: Cass, 1966), discusses a protest movement in which al-Afghani played a leading role. Charles C. Adams, *Islam and Modernism in Egypt: A Study of the Reform Movement Inaugurated by Muhammad 'Abduh* (London: Oxford University Press, 1933), focuses on the activities of al-Afghani's most famous disciple. The situation in India is discussed in Wilfrid S. Blunt, *India under Ripon* (London: Unwin, 1909).

Nikki R. Keddie, *Sayyid Jamal ed-Din "al-Afghani": A Political Biography* (Berkeley, CA: University of California Press, 1972), is the standard biography of al-Afghani, written by the recognized expert on the subject. The same author's *An Islamic Response to Imperialism: Political and Religious Writings of Sayyid Jamal ad-Din "al-Afghani"* (Berkeley, CA: University of California, 1968), provides a brief biography of al-Afghani but concentrates upon his writings. Finally, Elie Kedourie, *Afghani and 'Abduh: An Essay on Religious Unbelief and Political Activism in Modern Iran* (London: Cass, 1966), is a perceptive analysis on al-Afghani's religious and political thought by an authority on modern Iran.

Stanley and Livingstone

The nineteenth century marked a second golden age of European exploration. During the first, extending from the sixteenth through the eighteenth centuries, Europeans opened up and dominated the world's sea-lanes; during the second, they travelled into the interiors of the great continental land masses, surveying and mapping as they went. This activity did not spring simply from a love of adventure, however. Such explorers discovered natural resources for European economic interests, they established claims of sovereignty for European political powers, and they built the bases from which the natives could be introduced to the benefits of European civilization and religion. Europe had embraced the concept of the "White Man's burden," the belief that Europeans had a divine mission to rule and, insofar as possible, to improve the lot of the lesser, childlike races of the globe. Explorers and geographers were at the vanguard of that mission and often became national heroes. Moreover, through their books and lectures, they could also amass fortunes. It is no wonder that a number of extraordinary men and women devoted their lives to the hazardous enterprise of exploration. The following selection is about two such individuals and recounts a story that was well known to every school child in the country only a generation ago.

David Livingstone (1813–1873) was born in Scotland of poor parents and went to work in the local cotton mill at the age of ten. He studied in the little spare time available to him, saved his money, and was able to enter college at the age of twenty-three. Four years later, he obtained a medical degree and committed himself to the life of a missionary. He was sent to Africa and soon reached the

From *The Autobiography of Sir Henry Morton Stanley*, edited by Dorothy Stanley (New York: Houghton Mifflin Co., 1909), pp. 251–252, 255–256, 263–267, 279–280, and 281–284.

conclusion that a few missionaries alone could do little to better the lot of the inhabitants; it was necessary to open up the continent to European settlement and development. He began to pioneer, moving his medical-missionary stations ever further into the bush and conducting explorations of the country from these bases. He soon saw that the slave trade of the interior was a major source of misery for the inhabitants of the regions. His accounts of his travels and the conditions he had discovered gained him great popularity in England, and funds were provided for him to continue his explorations, particularly to find the source of the Nile river. He left Zanzibar in 1866 and departed for the interior, finally setting up a station at Ujiji, in what is now the nation of Zaire. The reports he sent back failed to reach his friends and backers, and the conviction soon spread that this popular figure was most probably dead.

At this point, Gordon Bennett, publisher of the *New York Herald*, decided that an expedition to find Livingstone would provide his newspaper with a great deal of welcome publicity. He called upon Henry Morton Stanley (1841–1904), his star foreign reporter, to undertake the venture. Stanley was every bit as remarkable an individual as the man whom he set out to find. Born in Wales of an impoverished family, he was sent to the local workhouse at the age of seven. At the age of sixteen he had matured sufficiently to realize his life's ambition of beating up the tyrannical and cruel director of the establishment. He then fled, eventually making his way to New Orleans, where he joined the Confederate army and was captured at the battle of Shiloh (April 1862). He made his way back to England, went to sea, finally joining the United States Navy, in which he served until the end of the Civil War. He undertook the career of a journalist, where he served as correspondent for the *Missouri Democrat* covering the Indian wars. He was then commissioned by the *New York Herald* to cover the British invasion of Abyssinia (Ethiopia). It was after this experience that he was asked by the *Herald* to undertake the search for Livingstone.

Stanley left Zanzibar on 21 March 1871, leading his expedition through immense difficulties. The following selection recounts how, after almost eight months, he arrived at Ujiji and greeted Livingstone with the memorable phrase, "Doctor Livingstone, I presume?" They spent a relatively short time together, but recognized in each other kindred souls. When Stanley returned to England with the news, he gained great popular acclaim. He went on to explore widely in Central Africa, tracing the course of the Congo, and opening up the region for settlement. He died in 1904, having been knighted for his efforts, and was mourned by the nation. Livingstone's later career was much briefer than Stanley's, but no less glorious in the eyes of his contemporaries. Using the supplies Stanley had left with him, Livingstone embarked once more in a search for the sources of the Nile. Fever finally caught up with him deep in the jungle, and he died 1 May 1873. His native bearers carried his sun-dried body to Zanzibar, whence it was transported to London. On 18 April 1874, his body was laid to rest in Westminster Abbey among Britain's other national heroes.

Questions

1. How would you characterize Stanley's attitude toward the native Africans?

2. How does Stanley's attitude compare with Livingstone's?

3. What character traits does Stanley particularly value?

4. Characterize the manners and speech of both Stanley and Livingstone. Do they seem incongruous in the setting? Why do the two behave in this peculiar fashion?

STANLEY AND LIVINGSTONE

Though fifteen months had elapsed since I had received my commission, no news of Livingstone had been heard by any mortal at Zanzibar. According to one, he was dead; and, according to another, he was lost; while still another hazarded the conviction that he had attached himself to an African princess, and had, in fact, settled down. There was no letter for me from Mr. Bennett, confirming his verbal order to go and search for the traveller; and no one at Zanzibar was prepared to advance thousands of dollars to one whom nobody knew; in my pocket I had about eighty dollars in gold left, after my fifteen months' journey!

Many people since have professed to disbelieve that I discovered the lost traveller in Africa! Had they known the circumstances of my arrival at Zanzibar, they would have had greater reason for their unbelief than they had. To me it looked for a time as though it would be an impossibility for me even to put foot on the mainland, though it was only twenty-five miles off. But, thanks to Captain Webb, the American consul, I succeeded in raising a sum of money amply sufficient, for the time being, for my purpose.

The 'sinews of war' having been obtained, the formation of the expedition was proceeded with. On the 21st of March, 1871, it stood a compact little force of three whites, thirty-one armed freemen of Zanzibar, as escort, one hundred and fifty-three porters, and twenty-seven pack-animals, for a transport corps, besides two riding-horses, on the outskirts of the coast-town of Bagamoyo; equipped with every needful article for a long journey that the experience of many Arabs had suggested, and that my own ideas of necessaries for comfort or convenience, in illness or health, had provided. Its very composition betrayed its character. There was nothing aggressive in it. Its many bales of cloth, and loads of beads and wire, with its assorted packages of provisions and medicine, indicated a peaceful caravan about to penetrate among African tribes accustomed to barter and chaffer; while its few guns showed a sufficient defensive power against bands of native banditti, though offensive measures were utterly out of the question.

I passed my apprenticeship in African travel while traversing the maritime region—a bitter school—amid rank jungles, fetid swamps, and fly-infested grass-lands, during which I encountered nothing that appeared to favour my journey. My pack and riding-animals died, my porters deserted, sickness of a very grievous nature thinned my numbers; but, despite the severe loss I sustained, I struggled through my troubles.

◇ ◇ ◇

My mission to find Livingstone was very simple, and was a clear and definite aim. All I had to do was to free my mind from all else, and relieve it of every earthly desire but the finding of the man whom I was sent to seek. To think of self, friends, banking-account, life-insurance, or any worldly interest but the one sole purpose of reaching the spot where Livingstone might happen to rest, could only tend to weaken resolution. Intense application to my task assisted me to forget all I had left behind, and all that might lie ahead in the future.

In some ways, it produced a delightful tranquillity which was foreign to me while in Europe. To be indifferent to the obituaries the papers may publish to-morrow, that never even a thought should glance across the mind of law-courts, jails, tombstones; not to care what may disturb a Parliament, or a Congress, or the state of the Funds, or the nerves excited about earthquakes, floods, wars, and other national evils, is a felicity few educated men in Britain know; and it compensated me in a great measure for the distress from heat, meagreness of diet, malaria, and other ills, to which I became subject soon after entering Africa.

Every day added something to my experience. I saw that exciting adventures could not happen so often as I had anticipated, that the fevers in Africa were less frequent than in some parts of the Mississippi Valley, that game was not visible on every acre, and that the ambushed savage was rare. There were quite as many bright pictures to be met with as there were dark. Troubles taught patience, and with the exercise of patience came greater self-control and experience. My ideas respecting my Zanzibari and Unyamwezi followers were modified after a few weeks' observation and trials of them. Certain vices and follies, which clung to their uneducated natures, were the source of great trouble; though there were brave virtues in most of them, which atoned for much that appeared incorrigible.

Wellington is reported to have said that he never knew a good-tempered man in India; and Sydney Smith thought that sweetness of temper was impossible in a very cold or a very hot climate. With such authorities it is somewhat bold, perhaps, to disagree; but after experiences of Livingstone, Pocock, Swinburne, Surgeon Parke, and other white men, one must not take these remarks too literally. As for my black followers, no quality was so conspicuous and unvarying as good-temper; and I think that, since I had more occasion to praise my black followers than blame them, even I must surely take credit for being more often good-tempered than bad; and besides, I felt great compassion for them. How often the verse in the Psalms recurred to me: 'Like as a father pitieth his own children'!

◇ ◇ ◇

Stanley's expedition continued to search for news of Livingstone. Finally, on 10 November 1871, after almost eight months on the march, they reached the village of Ujiji.

The column continued on its way, beset on either flank by a vehemently-enthusiastic and noisily-rejoicing mob, which bawled a jangling chorus of 'Yambos' to every mother's son of us, and maintained an inharmonious orchestral music of drums and horns. I was indebted for this loud ovation to the cheerful relief the people felt that we were not Mirambo's bandits, and to their joy at the happy rupture of the long silence that had perforce existed between the two trading colonies of Unyanyembe and Ujiji, and because we brought news which concerned every householder and freeman of this lake port.

After a few minutes we came to a halt. The guides in the van had reached the market-place, which was the central point of interest. For there the great Arabs, chiefs, and respectabilities of Ujiji, had gathered in a group to await events; thither also they had brought with them the venerable European traveller who was at that time resting among them. The caravan pressed up to them, divided itself into two lines on either side of the road, and, as it did so, disclosed to me the prominent figure of an elderly white man clad in a red flannel blouse, grey trousers, and a blue cloth, gold-banded cap.

Up to this moment my mind had verged upon non-belief in his existence, and now a nagging doubt intruded itself into my mind that this white man could not be the object of my quest, or if he were, he would somehow contrive to disappear before my eyes would be satisfied with a view of him.

Consequently, though the expedition was organized for this supreme moment, and every movement of it had been confidently ordered with the view of discovering him, yet when the moment of

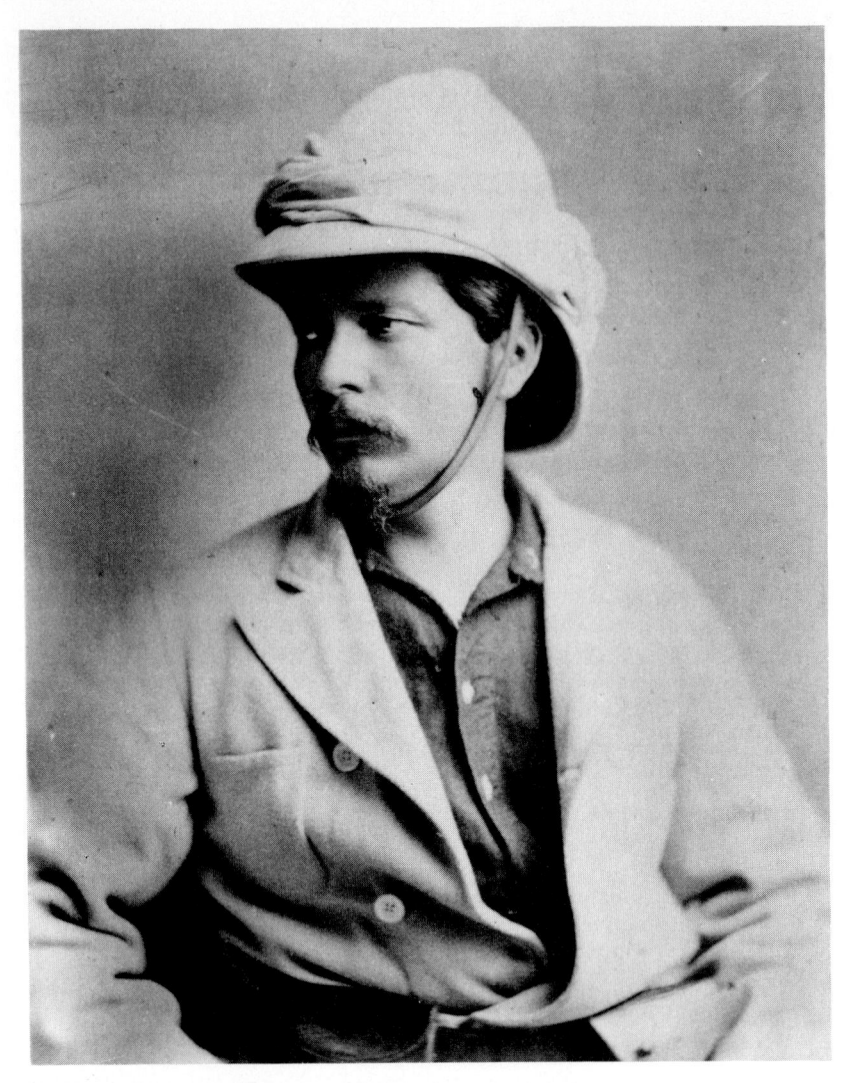

Sir Henry Morton Stanley.

discovery came, and the man himself stood revealed before me, this constantly recurring doubt contributed not a little to make me unprepared for it. 'It may not be Livingstone after all,' doubt suggested. If this is he, what shall I say to him? My imagination had not taken this question into consideration before. All around me was the immense crowd, hushed and expectant, and wondering how the scene would develop itself.

Under all these circumstances I could do no more than exercise some restraint and reserve, so I walked up to him, and, doffing my helmet, bowed and said in an inquiring tone,—

'Dr. Livingstone, I presume?'

Smiling cordially, he lifted his cap, and answered briefly, 'Yes.'

This ending all scepticism on my part, my face betrayed the earnestness of my satisfaction as I extended my hand and added,—

'I thank God, Doctor, that I have been permitted to see you.'

In the warm grasp he gave my hand, and the heartiness of his voice, I felt that he also was sincere and earnest as he replied,—

'I feel most thankful that I am here to welcome you.'

The principal Arabs now advanced, and I was presented by the Doctor to Sayed bin Majid, a relative of the Prince of Zanzibar; to Mahommed bin Sali, the Governor of Ujiji; to Abed bin Suliman, a rich merchant; to Mahommed bin Gharib, a constant good friend; and to many other notable friends and neighbours.

Then, remarking that the sun was very hot, the Doctor led the way to the verandah of his house, which was close by and fronted the market-place. The vast crowd moved with us.

After the Arab chiefs had been told the latest news of the war of their friends with Mirambo, with salaams, greetings, and warm hand-shakings, and comforting words to their old friend David (Livingstone), they retired from the verandah, and a large portion of the crowd followed them.

Then Livingstone caught sight of my people still standing in the hot sunshine by their packs, and extending his hand, said to me,—

'I am afraid I have been very remiss, too. Let me ask you now to share my house with me. It is not a very fine house, but it is rain-proof and cool, and there are enough spare rooms to lodge you and your goods. Indeed, one room is far too large for my use.'

I expressed my gratification at his kind offer in suitable terms, and accordingly gave directions to the chiefs of the caravan about the storing of the goods and the purchase of rations; and Livingstone charged his three servants, Susi, Chuma, and Hamoyda, to assist them. Relieved thus happily and comfortably from all further trouble about my men, I introduced the subject of breakfast, and asked permission of the Doctor to give a few directions to my cook.

The Doctor became all at once anxious on that score. Was my cook a good one? Could he prepare a really satisfactory breakfast? If not, he had a gem of a female cook—and here he laughed, and continued, 'She is the oddest, most eccentric woman I have ever seen. She is quite a character, but I must give her due credit for her skill in cooking. She is exceedingly faithful, clean, and deft at all sorts of cooking fit for a toothless old man like myself. But, perhaps, the two combined would be still better able to satisfy you?'

Halima, a stout, buxom woman of thirty, was brought at once to our presence, grinning, but evidently nervous and shy. She was not uninteresting by any means, and as she opened her capacious mouth, two complete and perfect rows of teeth were revealed.

'Halima,' began Livingstone, in kind, grave tones, 'my young brother has travelled far, and is hungry. Do you think you and Ferajji, his cook, can manage to give us something nice to eat? What have you?'

'I can have some dampers,[1] and kid kabobs, and tea or coffee ready immediately, master, if you like; and by sending to the market for something, we can do better.'

'Well, Halima, we will leave it to you and Ferajji; only do your best, for this is a great day for us all in Ujiji.'

'Yes, master. Sure to do that.'

I now thought of Livingstone's letters, and calling Kaif-Halek, the bearer of them, I delivered into the Doctor's hands a long-delayed letter-bag that I had discovered at Unyanyembe, the cover of which was dated November 1st, 1870.

A gleam of joy lighted up his face, but he made no remark, as he stepped on to the verandah and resumed his seat. Resting the letter-bag on his knees, he presently, after a minute's abstraction in thought, lifted his face to me and said, 'Now sit down by my side, and tell me the news.'

'But what about your letters, Doctor? You will find the news, I dare say, in them. I am sure you must be impatient to read your letters after such a long silence.'

'Ah!' he replied, with a sigh, 'I have waited years for letters; and the lesson of patience I have well learned!—I can surely wait a few hours longer! I would rather hear the general news, so pray tell me how the old world outside of Africa is getting along.'

Consenting, I sat down, and began to give a résumé of the exciting events that had transpired since he had disappeared in Africa, in March, 1866.

When I had ended the story of triumphs and reverses which had taken place between 1866 and 1871, my tent-boys advanced to spread a crimson table-cloth, and arrange the dishes and smoking platters heaped up profusely with hot dampers, white rice, maize porridge, kid kabobs, fricasseed chicken, and stewed goat-meat. There were also a number of things giving variety to the meal, such as honey from Ukawendi, forest plums, and wild-fruit jam, besides sweet milk and clabber,[2] and then a silver tea-pot full of 'best tea,' and beautiful china cups and saucers to drink it from. Before we could commence this already magnificent breakfast, the servants of Sayed bin Majid, Mohammed bin Sali, and Muini Kheri brought three great trays loaded with cakes, curries, hashes, and stews, and three separate hillocks of white rice, and we looked at one another with a smile of wonder at this Ujiji banquet.

We drew near to it, and the Doctor uttered the grace: 'For what we are going to receive, make us, O Lord, sincerely thankful.'

---

[1] Broad, flat cakes of unleavened bread.
[2] Curdled sour milk.

◇ ◇ ◇

March 13, 1872. This is the last day of my stay with dear old Livingstone; the last night we shall be together is present, and I cannot evade the morrow. I feel as though I should like to rebel against the necessity of departure. The minutes beat fast, and grow into hours. Our door to-night is closed, and we both think our own thoughts. What his are, I know not—mine are sad. My days seem to have been spent far too happily, for, now that the last day is almost gone, I bitterly regret the approach of the parting hour. I now forget the successive fevers, and their agonies, and the semi-madness into which they often plunged me. The regret I feel now is greater than any pains I have endured. But I cannot resist the sure advance of time, which is flying to-night far too fast. What must be, must be! I have often parted with friends before, and remember how I lingered and wished to put it off, but the inevitable was not to be prevented. Fate came, and, at the appointed hour, stood between us. To-night I feel the same aching pain, but in a greater degree; and the farewell I fear may be for ever. For ever? and 'For ever' echo the reverberations of a woeful whisper!

I have received the thanks that he had repressed all these months in the secrecy of his heart, uttered with no mincing phrases, but poured out, as it were, at the last moment, until I was so affected that I sobbed, as one only can in uncommon grief. The hour of night and the crisis,—and oh! as some dreadful doubts suggested the eternal parting,—his sudden outburst of gratitude, with that kind of praise that steals into one and touches the softer parts of the ever-veiled nature,—all had their influence; and, for a time, I was as a sensitive child of eight or so, and yielded to such bursts of tears that only such a scene as this could have forced.

I think it only needed this softening to secure me as his obedient and devoted servitor in the future, should there ever be an occasion where I could prove my zeal.

On the 14th March, my expedition left Unyanyembe, he accompanying me for a few miles. We reached the slope of a ridge overlooking the valley, in the middle of which our house where we had lived together looked very small in the distance. I then turned to him and said,—

'My dear Doctor, you must go no further. You have come far enough. See, our house is a good distance now, and the sun is very hot. Let me beg of you to turn back.'

'Well," he replied, 'I will say this to you: you have done what few men could do. And for what you have done for me, I am most grateful. God guide you safe home and bless you, my friend!'

'And may God bring you safe back to us all, my dear friend! Farewell!'

'Farewell!' he repeated.

We wrung each other's hands, our faces flushed with emotion, tears rushing up, and blinding the eyes. We turned resolutely away from each other; but his faithful followers, by rushing up to give their parting words, protracted the painful scene.

'Good-bye, all! Good-bye, Doctor, dear friend!'

'Good-bye!'

At the moment of parting, the old man's noble face slightly paled, which I knew to be from suppressed emotion, while, when I looked into his eyes, I saw there a kind of warning, to look well at him as a friend looks for the last time; but the effort well-nigh unmanned me,—a little longer, and I should have utterly collapsed. We both, however, preferred dry eyes, and outward calm.

From the crest of the ridge I turned to take a last long look at him, to impress his form on my mind; then, waving a last parting signal, we descended the opposite slope on the home road.

◇ ◇ ◇

From an unpublished Memorial to Livingstone by Stanley, the following passages are taken:

He preached no sermon, by word of mouth, while I was in company with him; but each day of my companionship with him witnessed a sermon acted. The Divine instructions, given of old on the Sacred Mount, were closely followed, day by day, whether he rested in the jungle-camp, or bided in the traders' town, or savage hamlet. Lowly of spirit, meek in speech, merciful of heart, pure in mind, and peaceful in act, suspected by the Arabs to be an informer, and therefore calumniated, often offended at evils committed by his own servants, but ever forgiving, often robbed and thwarted, yet bearing no ill-will, cursed by the marauders, yet physicking their infirmities, most despitefully used, yet praying daily for all manner and condition of men! Narrow, indeed, was the way of eternal life that he elected to follow, and few are those who choose it.

Though friends became indifferent to his fate, associates neglectful, and his servants mocked and betrayed him, though suitable substance was denied to him, and though the rain descended in torrents on him in his wanderings, and the tropic tempests beat him sore, and sickened him with their rigours, he toiled on, and laboured ever in the Divine service he had chosen, unyielding and unresting, for the Christian man's faith was firm that 'all would come right at last.'

Had my soul been of brass, and my heart of spelter,[3] the powers of my head had surely compelled me to recognise, with due

---

[3] Zinc.

honour, the Spirit of Goodness which manifested itself in him. Had there been anything of the Pharisee or the hypocrite in him, or had I but traced a grain of meanness or guile in him, I had surely turned away a sceptic. But my every-day study of him, during health or sickness, deepened my reverence and increased my esteem. He was, in short, consistently noble, upright, pious, and manly, all the days of my companionship with him.

He professed to be a Liberal Presbyterian. Presbyterianism I have heard of, and have read much about it; but Liberal Presbyterianism,—whence is it? What special country throughout the British Isles is its birthplace? Are there any more disciples of that particular creed, or was Livingstone the last? Read by the light of this good man's conduct and single-mindedness, its tenets would seem to be a compound of religious and practical precepts.

'Whatever thy right hand findeth to do, do it with all thy might.'

'By the sweat of thy brow thou shalt eat bread.'

'For every idle word thou shalt be held accountable.'

'Thou shalt worship the Lord thy God, and Him only shalt thou serve.'

'Thou shalt not kill.'

'Swear not at all.'

'Be not slothful in business, but be fervent in spirit, and serve the Lord.'

'Mind not high things, but condescend to men of low estate.'

'Live peaceably with all men.'

'We count those happy who endure.'

'Remember them that are in bonds, and them which suffer adversity.'

'Watch thou, in all things; endure afflictions; do the work of an evangelist; make full proof of thy ministry.'

'Whatsoever ye do, do it heartily.'

'Set your affections on things above, not on things of the earth.'

'Be kind to one another, tender-hearted, and forgiving.'

'Preach the gospel in the regions beyond you, and boast not in another man's line, of things made ready to your hand.'

I never discovered that there was any printed code of religious laws or moral precepts issued by his church, wherein these were specially alluded to; but it grew evident during our acquaintance that he erred not against any of them. Greater might he could not have shown in this interminable exploration set him by Sir Roderick Murchison, because the work performed by him was beyond all proportion to his means and physical strength. What bread he ate was insufficient for his bodily nourishment, after the appalling fatigues of a march in a tropical land.

His conversation was serious, his demeanour grave and earnest. Morn and eve he worshipped, and, at the end of every march, he thanked the Lord for His watchful Providence. On Sundays he conducted Divine Service, and praised the glory of the Creator, the True God, to his dark followers. His hand was clear of the stain of blood-guiltiness. Profanity was an abomination to him. He was not indolent either in his Master's service, or in the cause to which he was sacrificing himself. His life was an evidence that he served God with all his heart.

Nothing in the scale of humanity can be conceived lower than the tribes of Manyuema with whom he daily conversed as a friend. Regardless of such honours as his country generally pays to exceeding merit, he continued his journeyings, bearing messages of peace wherever he went; and when he rested, chief and peasant among the long-neglected tribes ministered to his limited wants. Contented with performing his duty according as he was enabled to, such happiness as can be derived from righteous doings, pure thoughts, and a clear conscience, was undoubtedly his. His earnest labours for the sake of those in bonds, and the unhappy people who were a prey to the Arab kidnapper and land pirate, few will forget. The number of his appeals, the constant recurrence to the dismal topic, and the long lines of his travels, may be accepted as proofs of his heartiness and industry.

He was the first to penetrate to those lands in the Chambezi and the Lualaba valleys; his was the first voice heard speaking in the hamlets of Eastern Sunda of the beauties of the Christian religion; and he was the first preacher who dared denounce the red-handed Arab for his wickedly aggressive acts. In regions beyond ken of the most learned geographers of Europe, he imitated the humility of the Founder of his religion, and spoke in fervent strains of the Heavenly message of peace and good-will.

Should I ever return to the scenes that we knew together, my mind would instantaneously revert to the good man whom I shall never see more. Be it a rock he sat upon, a tree upon which he rested, ground that he walked upon, or a house that he dwelt in, my first thought would naturally be that it was associated with him. But my belief is that they would flush my mind with the goodness and nobleness of his expression, appealing to me, though so silently, to remember, and consider, and strive.

I remember well when I gazed at Ujiji, five years later, from the same hill as where I had announced the coming of my caravan: I had not been thinking much of him until that moment, when, all at once, above the palm grove of Ujiji, and the long broad stretch of blue water of the lake beyond, loomed the form of Livingstone, in the well-remembered blue-grey coat of his marching costume, and the blue naval cap, gold-banded, regarding me with eyes so trustful, and face so grave and sad.

It is the expression of him that so follows and clings to me, and, indeed, is ever present when I think of him, though it is difficult to communicate to others the expression that I first studied and that most attracted me. There was an earnest gravity in it; life long ago shorn of much of its beauty—I may say of all its vulgar beauty and coarser pleasures, a mind long abstracted from petty discontents, by preference feeding on itself, almost glorifying in itself as all-sufficient to produce content; therefore a composure settled, calm, and trustful.

Even my presence was impotent to break him from his habit of abstraction. I might have taken a book to read, and was silent. If I looked up a few minutes later, I discovered him deeply involved in his own meditations, right forefinger bent, timing his thoughts, his eyes gazing far away into indefinite distance, brows puckered closely—face set, and resolute, now and then lips moving, silently framing words.

'What can he be thinking about?' I used to wonder, and once I ventured to break the silence with,—

'A penny for your thoughts, Doctor.'

'They are not worth it, my young friend, and let me suggest that, if I had any, possibly, I should wish to keep them!'

After which I invariably let him alone when in this mood. Sometimes these thoughts were humorous, and, his face wearing a smile, he would impart the reason with some comic story or adventure.

I have met few so quickly responsive to gaiety and the lighter moods, none who was more sociable, genial, tolerant, and humorous. You must think of him as a contented soul, who had yielded himself with an entire and loving submission, and who laboured to the best of his means and ability, awakening to the toil of the day, and resigning himself, without the least misgiving, to the rest of the night; believing that the effect of his self-renunciation would not be altogether barren.

If you can comprehend such a character, you will understand Livingstone's motive principle.

Further Readings

The best work covering the history of East Africa, the base of Central African exploration during the mid-nineteenth century, is provided by Kenneth Ingham, *A History of East Africa* (3rd ed.: London: Longmans, 1965). The explorations of David Livingstone did much to open up modern Uganda, the history of which is discussed in Kenneth Ingham, *The Making of Modern Uganda* (London: Allen and Unwin, 1958). Stanley's later activities concentrated on the basin of the Congo River. The exploration of this region is covered in Roger Anstey, *Britain and the Congo in the Nineteenth Century* (Oxford: Clarendon Press, 1962), and the colonial period is the subject of Roger Anstey, *King Leopold's Legacy: The Congo under Belgian Rule, 1908–1960* (London: Oxford University Press, 1966). Joseph Conrad's powerful novel, *Heart of Darkness* (1902, many editions), is set in the Congo during the early years of Belgian exploitation of the area. Something of the attraction of Africa for nineteenth-century Europeans is conveyed in Ronald Robinson and John Gallagher, with Alice Denny, *Africa and the Victorians: The Climax of Imperialism* Garden City, NY: Doubleday, 1968).

David Livingstone has received the attention of a number of authors. Some of the more significant of these works are Ian Anstruther, *Dr. Livingstone, I Presume?* (New York: Dutton, 1956), Frank Debenham, *The Way to Ilala: David Livingstone's Pilgrimage* (London: Longmans, Green, 1955), Oliver Ransford, *David Livingstone: The Dark Interior* (London: J. Murray, 1978), and Dorothy O. Helly, *Livingstone's Legacy: Horace Walker and Victorian Mythmaking* (Athens, OH: Ohio University Press, 1987).

The film *Stanley and Livingstone* (1939: Fox, black and white) is rather romanticized and suffers from technical imperfections, but well illustrates the degree to which Stanley and Livingstone continued to appeal to the popular imagination.

The Gaucho: Martín Fierro

Stretching for hundreds of miles west and south of Buenos Aires, capital of the Argentine Republic, lies an extraordinary region known as the Pampas. Now dotted with farms and ranches, up to little more than a century ago it was a vast expanse of level grasslands, without trees or roads, through which travellers guided themselves by the stars and kept always on the alert for attack by Indians. Despite its lack of economic development, the Pampas were Argentina's greatest economic resource: hundreds of thousands of cattle raised on the Pampas provided the meat and hides that were the nation's main export. The Pampas were also the home of the gauchos, people as extraordinary as the region in which they lived.

The gauchos were horsemen who herded cattle, fought Indians, and bitterly resisted any attempt to limit their freedom to roam the plains at will. The gaucho's dress was simple: boots, leather trousers, a woolen cloak and a broad hat. His drink was *maté*, a bitter herb tea that he drank with a straw from a gourd that he always carried with him. He ate fresh beef, which was cooked over an open fire and eaten with the long knife that served the gaucho as both eating utensil and weapon. When fighting Indians or herding cattle, he used a long, light wooden lance, a braided horsehair lasso, and the *bola*, a few stones tied to braided string and used to entangle the legs of his quarry. He drank whatever alcoholic beverages were available whenever he could get them, sang songs accompanied by the guitar, worked when he felt like it, and was generally untroubled by formal education, any sense of civic responsibility, or refined sensibilities.

The gaucho was much admired, at least in the abstract, by the city-dwellers of Argentina and by foreign visitors. The gaucho's life represented for them a freedom from responsibility and from the

From José Hernández, *Martín Fierro*, translated by C. E. Ward (Albany, NY: State University of New York, 1967), pp. 9–21 and 167–173.

growing complexities of nineteenth-century life. Their romanticization of the gaucho was affected by the knowledge that he was a dying breed. Wire fences were beginning to set ever-narrowing boundaries to the free range; railroads were driven across the grasslands and towns sprang up at the railheads; and the sod was being broken for the great wheat fields that now dominate the region. Civilization reached out into the Pampas and left little room for the freedom that characterized the gaucho's way of life. New technology, oppressive government, corrupt public officials, and the inescapable march of progress were combining to doom the gaucho.

This way of life, and its decline, were captured by José Hernández (1834–1886) in his poem, *Martín Fierro*. Published in 1872, it quickly caught the imagination of the public and has become the Argentine national epic. Hernández was born near Buenos Aires of a well-established family and was reared on the Pampas. He became involved, as an opponent of strong central government, in the fierce political struggles that racked Argentina. In 1871, he joined a rebellion against the further extension of the power of the central government into local affairs. When the uprising was defeated, he went into exile. A short time later and without a pardon, he returned to Bueno Aires and shut himself up in a hotel room. When he emerged, it was to publish the poem that made him famous.

Martín Fierro is a gaucho who once lived the ideal gaucho life, and the poem is his account of his misfortunes. Drafted into the frontier militia, he was impoverished in the service. He stole a horse and deserted, but when he returned home, he found that the district in which he once lived was now deserted and his family had disappeared. He turned bandit, defeated the police sent to capture him, and escaped to live a free life among the Indians. He returned to civilization, killed two ruffians in "a fair fight," and finally became the wandering minstrel who sings the story of his life of misfortune. In the following section, Martín describes what it means to be a gaucho and the joys of life when the gauchos were left alone. He then explains to his companion, Cruz, by what right he has defied government and society, and calls to his friend to escape with him to a land where they can once again live free.

Martín is a realistic figure and the life he describes is an accurate reflection of actual conditions. He also represents the gaucho in the abstract, and the recitation of his misfortunes portrays the forces that were working to end the gaucho way of life. Finally, in his dogged fight to remain free, Martín Fierro serves to remind us of the inevitable struggle between personal liberty and social constraint.

Questions

1. How free of social constraints is the good life that Martín describes?

2. How does a society as individualistic as Martín describes continue to function?

3. How does Martín justify his defiance of law and order?

4. What flaws do you see in Martín's attitudes and actions?

MARTÍN FIERRO

I am a gaucho, and take this from me
as my tongue explains to you:
for me the earth is a small place
and it could well be bigger—
the snake does not bite me
nor the sun burn my brow.

I was born as a fish is born
at the bottom of the sea;
no one can take from me
what I was given by God—
what I brought into the world
I shall take from the world with me.

It is my glory to live as free
as a bird in the sky:
I make no nest on this ground
where there's so much to be suffered,
and no one will follow me
when I take to flight again.

In love I have no one
to come to me with quarrels—
like those beautiful birds
that go hopping from branch to branch,
I make my bed in the clover
and the stars cover me.

Let whoever may be listening
to the tale of my sorrows—
know that I never fight nor kill
except when it has to be done,
and that only injustice threw me
into so much adversity.

And listen to the story told
by a gaucho who's hunted by the law;
who's been a father and husband
hard-working and willing—
and in spite of that, people take him
to be a criminal.

ii

No one speak of sorrows to me
because I live sorrowing:
and nobody give himself airs
even though he's got a foot in the stirrup—
as even the gaucho with most sense
often finds himself left on foot.

You gather experience in life,
enough to lend and give away,
if you have to go through it
between tears and suffering—
because nothing teaches you so much
as to suffer and cry.

Man comes blind into the world
with hope tugging him on,
and within a few steps, misfortunes
have caught him and beat him up. . . .
La pucha[1]—the hard lessons
Time with its changes brings!

I have known this land
when the working-man lived in it
and had his little cabin
and his children and his wife. . . .
It was a delight to see
the way he spent his days.

Then . . . when the morning star
was shining in the blessed sky,
and the crowing of the cocks
told us that day was near,
a gaucho would make his way
to the kitchen . . . it was a joy.

And sitting beside the fire
waiting for day to come,
he'd suck at the bitter maté[2]
till he was glowing warm,
while his girl[3] was sleeping
tucked up in his poncho.

---

[1] Euphemism for *puta* (whore).
[2] A bitter herb commonly drunk as tea. The gaucho preferred his maté unsweetened, considering sugared maté the drink of women and city folk.
[3] Legal marriages were the exception among the gauchos.

And as soon as the dawn
started to turn red
and the birds to sing
and the hens came down off their perch,
it was time to get going
each man to his work.

One would be tying on his spurs,
another go out singing;
one choose a supple sheepskin,
one a lasso, someone else a whip—
and the whinnying horses
would be calling them from the hitching-rail.

The one whose job was horse-breaking
headed for the corral
where the beast was waiting,
snorting fit to burst—
wild and wicked as they come
and tearing itself to bits.

And there the skilful gaucho,
as soon as he'd got a rein on the colt,
would settle the leathers on his back
and mount him straight away. . . .
A man shows, in this life,
the craft God gave to him.

And plunging round the clearing,
the nag would tear itself up
while the man was playing him
with the round spurs, on his shoulders—
and he'd rush out squirming
with the leathers squeaking loud.

Ah, those times! . . . you felt proud
to see how a man could ride.
When a gaucho really knew his job,
even if the colt went over backwards,
not one of them wouldn't land on his feet
with the halter-rein in his hand.

And while some were breaking-in,
others went out on the land
and rounded up the cattle
and got together the horse-herds—
and like that, without noticing,
they'd pass the day, enjoying themselves.

And as night fell, you'd see them
together again in the kitchen,
with the fire well alight
and hundreds of things to talk over—
they'd be quite happy, chatting
till after the evening meal.

And with your belly well filled
it was a fine thing
to go to sleep the way things ought to be
in the arms of love—
and so to next day, to begin
the work from the day before.

I remember—ah, that was good!
how the gauchos went around,
always cheerful and well mounted
and willing to work. . . .
But these days—curse it!
you don't see them, they're so beaten down.

Even the poorest gaucho
had a string of matching horses;
he could always afford some amusement,
and people were ready for anything. . . .
Looking out across the land
you'd see nothing but cattle and sky.

When the branding-time came round
that was work to warm you up!
What a crowd! lassoing the running steers
and keen to hold and throw them. . . .
What a time that was! in those days surely
there were champions to be seen.

You couldn't call that work,
it was more like a party—
and after a good throw
when you'd managed it skilfully,
the boss used to call you over
for a swig of raw liquor.

Because the great jug of booze
always lived under the cart,
and anyone who wasn't shy,
when he saw the open spout
would take a hold on it fearlessly
as an orphan calf to the teat.

And the games that would get going
when we were all of us together!
We were always ready for them,
as at times like those
a lot of neighbors would turn up
to help out the regular hands.[4]

For the womenfolk, those were days
full of hurry and bustling
to get the cooking done
and serve the people properly . . .
and so like this, we gauchos
always lived in grand style.

In would come meat roasted in the skin
and the tasty stew,
cooked cornmeal well ground,
pies and wine of the best. . . .
But it has been the will of fate
that all these things should come to an end.

A gaucho'd live in his home country
as safe as anything,
but now—it's a crime!
things have got to be so twisted
that a poor man wears out his life
running from the authorities.

Because if you set foot in your house
and if the mayor finds out about it,
he'll hunt you like a beast
even if it makes your wife miscarry. . . .
There's no time that won't come to an end
nor a rope that won't break sometime.

And you can give yourself up for dead
right away, if the mayor catches you,
because he'll come down on you
there and then, with a flogging—
and then if a gaucho puts up a fight
they call him a hard case.

After many misfortunes, Martín kills two men in a knife fight and is forced to flee into the Pampas. He makes an acquaintance by the name of Cruz and explains his situation to him.

---

[4] Neighbors would turn up not so much to help as to enjoy the festivities that generally were associated with important work projects.

I can see we're both of us
chips off the same block.
I'm known as an outlaw
and you're in the same situation—
And as for me, to make an end of it all
I'm off to the Indians.

I ask my God to forgive me
as he's been so good to me,
but since it has to be
that I go and live with heathens,
I'll be cruel where others are cruel—
that's how my fate has willed it.

God created the flowers, as pretty
and delicate as they are,
he made them perfect in every way
as much as he knew how—
but he gave something more to man
when he gave him a heart.

He gave light its clearness
and strength to the wind in its course,
he gave out life and motion
from the eagle to the worm—
but he gave more to Christian men
when he gave them intelligence.

And even though he gave the birds
(besides other things I don't know of)
their little golden beaks
and feathers bright as paint—
he gave a greater treasure to man
when he gave him a speaking tongue.

And since he gave to the wild beasts
such great fierce strength
that no power can overcome them
and nothing can frighten them—
what less could he give to man
than courage to defend himself?

But I suspect that when he gave him
so many good things at once,
he was thinking to himself
that man was going to need them—
because he balanced the good things
with the sorrows he gave him.

And it's forced by my sorrows
that I want to leave this hell.
I'm no longer a young fledgling,
and I know how to handle a spear—
and the powers of the Government
don't reach to the Indians.

I know that the chiefs over there
will give shelter to Christians
and they treat them as "brothers"
when they go of their own accord. . . .
Why keep on going through these alarms?
Let's clear out of here and go.

I'm not afraid of thirst, either,
I can bear it quite cheerfully—
I can find water sniffing the wind,
and while I'm still sound of limb
I can dig and reach it right away
anywhere there's a white-peach tree.

We'll find safety over there
since we can't have it here—
we'll have less troubles to bear,
and there'll be a happy time to come
the day we light upon
one of the Indians' camps.

We'll fashion ourselves a tent
out of a few horse-hides
as so many others do—
It'll be our kitchen and living-room—
maybe there'll be an Indian girl
who'll come and be kind to us.

Over there, there's no need to work,
you live like a lord—
going on a raid from time to time,
and if you get out alive from that
you live lying belly-up
watching the sun go round.[5]

And now that Fate has beaten us
and left us high and dry,
maybe we'll see light, over there,

---

[5] The Indians left all domestic and field chores to the women, who would cook, sow
and harvest crops, butcher livestock, and even tame colts.

and our sorrows will come to an end. . . .
Any land will do for us—
let's go, Cruz, my friend.

Further Readings

There is not a wide variety of books available in English on Argentine history and life. Ysabel F. Rennie, *The Argentine Republic* (New York: Macmillan, 1945), is a standard history. Robert J. Alexander, *An Introduction to Argentina* (New York: Praeger, 1969), and Arthur P. Whitaker, *Argentina* (Englewood Cliffs, NJ: Prentice-Hall, 1964), are good brief surveys. David Rock, *Argentina, 1516–1982: From Spanish Colonization to the Falklands War* (Berkeley, CA: University of California Press, 1985), is an excellent recent treatment of the subject.

Walter Lorden, *Estancia Life: Agricultural, Economic, and Cultural Aspects of Argentine Farming* (London: Unwin, 1911; reprinted Detroit: B. Etheridge Books, 1974), is a good account of the organization and operation of the great Argentine ranches. One of the best accounts in English of gaucho life and the Pampas can be found in Charles Darwin, *The Voyage of the Beagle* (1845, many editions). Darwin travelled on the Pampas in 1833 and described life on the Pampas before the encroachments of civilization. The Argentine writer W. H. Hudson has published a collection of short stories in English, entitled *Tales of the Pampas* (New York: Knopf, 1939), that is well worth the reader's attention.

There is no substantial biography of José Hernández in English, but the student who can read Spanish will find Horacio Zorraquín Becú, *Tiempo y vida de José Hernández, 1834–1886* (Buenos Aires: Emecé Editores, 1972), to be an excellent and thorough account of his life and thought.

A film version of Ulises Petit de Murat's novel, *Pampa Barbara*, was made under the title *Savage Pampas* (1967: Samuel Bronston, color). Filmed on location on the Pampas, it gives a good picture of army life on the Indian frontier in the mid-1800s, approximately the period in which Martín Fierro was drafted into the frontier militia.

Wounded Knee

The last real opportunity for a united Indian resistance to white encroachment ended with the death of Tecumseh during the War of 1812. The years that followed saw the steady westward expansion of the whites, and the development of the practice of restricting the Indian population to specific tracts of land set aside for that purpose. This policy required that some groups move great distances from their homelands, often with great suffering. Although the lands alloted to Indian relocation were at first quite extensive, increasing white land-hunger and the frequent discovery of natural resources on reservation lands led to almost constant attempts to reduce the Indians' allotted lands. This was accompanied by a policy of reservation management designed to ensure that the Indians would remain dependent upon government subsidies, unable to develop any real economic strength themselves. Although a few voices were raised in protest, white relations with the Indians were generally characterized by faithlessness and a basic lack of concern for Indian interests.

Various tribal leaders arose from time to time who struggled against the increasing restriction and impoverishment of their people. Chieftains such as Black Hawk, Cochise, and Geronimo could and did cause the government considerable concern and expense, but they did little more than delay their tribes' eventual fate. In the final stages of the process of "taming" the Indians in the years following the Civil War (1861–1865), the government encountered its greatest difficulties in its relations with the Indians of the Great Plains. Here the Dakota (or Lakota) Indians were united in a loose confederation often called by the whites the Sioux Nation. Relatively numerous, capable of cooperative action, and excellent horsemen, the Dakotas were formidable adversaries. The high tide of Indian for-

From John G. Neihardt, *Black Elk Speaks* (Lincoln, NE: University of Nebraska Press, 1961), pp. 257–276.

tunes came in 1876, when some three or four thousand warriors surrounded a U.S. cavalry regiment under the command of General George Custer at the Little Big Horn River and destroyed it utterly.

They gained no real advantage from this victory, however, and surrendered the next year. Much of their land was taken from them. By 1890, they were concentrated on the Great Sioux Reservation, with the tribes dispersed to impede united action on their part and to make it easier for speculators to acquire land from them. Morale was low, and tribal leaders saw no hope for the future.

It was at this time that news came from the West. Wovoka, of the Paiute tribe in Nevada, had had a vision that had an electrifying effect. According to the vision, in the spring of 1891 new soil would settle on the earth and bury all the whites and their works. The game would return, and the Indian dead would arise to join their rejuvenated peoples. The Indians would reclaim their land and live in peace and plenty forever. All that was necessary was to dance the new Dance of the Ghosts and to sing the new songs that Wovoka taught the people. Wearing a ghost shirt, the Indian could not be harmed by bullets and need not fear the whites.

The Ghost Dance spread rapidly throughout the Indians of the West during the fall and winter of 1890. Although their frenzy was fueled by misery and a hatred of the whites, the Ghost Dancers posed no real threat to their white neighbors. Convinced of their imminent deliverance by the Great Father, the Dancers saw no need to resort to violence. They only needed to dance and wait.

The whites did not see it that way and were apprehensive about the entire affair. They could not understand the Ghost Dance for what it was and they were fearful that the solidarity and energy the Indians were showing were portents of a widespread armed uprising. Militia and troops were assembled, and, after some hesitation, the decision was made that the Ghost Dances must be stopped and "fomenters of unrest" be made prisoner. During these arrests, Sitting Bull, the most respected of the Dakota chiefs, was killed. The Indians were thrown into turmoil. This was the state of affairs on 28 December 1890, when Big Foot, an old and sick Minneconjou chief whose arrest had been ordered, attempted to lead his tribe, numbering about 450 men, women, and children, to the supposed safety of the Pine Ridge Reservation.

This selection provides an eyewitness account of subsequent events. The narrator is Black Elk, a holy man of the Oglala Sioux. Born in 1863, he was sixty-seven in 1930, when he recounted his story to the author. There is great poignancy in his words even apart from the tragic events themselves. When a child, Black Elk had experienced a great vision that embraced all the universe and the place of the Indians in it. The vision had given him holy powers to help his people. Looking back upon his life, he realizes that his vision had foretold the sorry fate of his people and that, even with his powers, he had been unable to do anything to prevent it. In this, he epitomizes all those Indians who had believed in the superiority of their way of life and had seen the direction in which events were moving but who, though they resisted as best they could, had been powerless to impede the constant encroachment of the whites upon their lands and liberties.

Questions

1. How important was magic to Black Elk, and how did he use it?

2. What is his immediate reaction to the massacre? What does he do?

3. What does the massacre finally mean to him?

WOUNDED KNEE

It was about this time that bad news came to us from the north. We heard that some policemen from Standing Rock had gone to arrest Sitting Bull on Grand River, and that he would not let them take him; so there was a fight, and they killed him.

It was now near the end of the Moon of Popping Trees, and I was twenty-seven years old (December, 1890). We heard that Big Foot was coming down from the Badlands with nearly four hundred people. Some of these were from Sitting Bull's band. They had run away when Sitting Bull was killed, and joined Big Foot on Good River. There were only about a hundred warriors in this band, and all the others were women and children and some old men. They were all starving and freezing, and Big Foot was so sick that they had to bring him along in a pony drag.[1] They had all run away to hide in the Badlands, and they were coming in now because they were starving and freezing. When they crossed Smoky Earth River, they followed up Medicine Root Creek to its head. Soldiers were over there looking for them. The soldiers had everything and were not freezing and starving. Near Porcupine Butte the soldiers came up to the Big Foots, and they surrendered and went along with the soldiers to Wounded Knee Creek where the Brenan store is now.

It was in the evening when we heard that the Big Foots were camped over there with the soldiers, about fifteen miles by the old road from where we were. It was the next morning (December 29, 1890) that something terrible happened.

That evening before it happened, I went in to Pine Ridge and heard these things, and while I was there, soldiers started for

---

[1] He was very ill with pneumonia.

where the Big Foots were. These made about five hundred soldiers that were there next morning. When I saw them starting I felt that something terrible was going to happen. That night I could hardly sleep at all. I walked around most of the night.

In the morning I went out after my horses, and while I was out I heard shooting off toward the east, and I knew from the sound that it must be wagon-guns (cannon) going off. The sounds went right through my body, and I felt that something terrible would happen.

When I reached camp with the horses, a man rode up to me and said: "Hey-hey-hey! The people that are coming are fired on! I know it!"

I saddled up my buckskin and put on my sacred shirt. It was one I had made to be worn by no one but myself. It had a spotted eagle outstretched on the back of it, and the daybreak star was on the left shoulder, because when facing south that shoulder is toward the east. Across the breast, from the left shoulder to the right hip, was the flaming rainbow, and there was another rainbow around the neck, like a necklace, with a star at the bottom. At each shoulder, elbow, and wrist was an eagle feather; and over the whole shirt were red streaks of lightning. You will see that this was from my great vision, and you will know how it protected me that day.

I painted my face all red, and in my hair I put one eagle feather for the One Above.

It did not take me long to get ready, for I could still hear the shooting over there.

Battle of Wounded Knee.

I started out alone on the old road that ran across the hills to Wounded Knee. I had no gun. I carried only the sacred bow of the west that I had seen in my great vision. I had gone only a little way when a band of young men came galloping after me. The first two who came up were Loves War and Iron Wasichu. I asked what they were going to do, and they said they were just going to see where the shooting was. Then others were coming up, and some older men.

We rode fast, and there were about twenty of us now. The shooting was getting louder. A horseback from over there came galloping very fast toward us, and he said: "Hey-hey-hey! They have murdered them!" Then he whipped his horse and rode away faster toward Pine Ridge.

In a little while we had come to the top of the ridge where, looking to the east, you can see for the first time the monument and the burying ground on the little hill where the church is. That is where the terrible thing started. Just south of the burying ground on the little hill a deep dry gulch runs about east and west, very crooked, and it rises westward to nearly the top of the ridge where we were. It had no name, but the Wasichus[2] sometimes call it Battle Creek now. We stopped on the ridge not far from the head of the dry gulch. Wagon guns were still going off over there on the little hill, and they were going off again where they hit along the gulch. There was much shooting down yonder, and there were many cries, and we could see cavalrymen scattered over the hills ahead of us. Cavalrymen were riding along the gulch and shooting into it, where the women and children were running away and trying to hide in the gullies and the stunted pines.

A little way ahead of us, just below the head of the dry gulch, there were some women and children who were huddled under a clay bank, and some cavalrymen were there pointing guns at them.

We stopped back behind the ridge, and I said to the others: "Take courage. These are our relatives. We will try to get them back." Then we all sang a song which went like this:

"*A thunder being nation I am, I have said.*
A thunder being nation I am, I have said.
You shall live.
You shall live.
You shall live.
You shall live."

Then I rode over the ridge and the others after me, and we were crying: "Take courage! It is time to fight!" The soldiers who were guarding our relatives shot at us and then ran away fast, and some more cavalrymen on the other side of the gulch did too. We got our relatives and sent them across the ridge to the northwest where they would be safe.

---

[2] Whites, though blacks were also called Wasichus.

I had no gun, and when we were charging, I just held the sacred bow out in front of me with my right hand. The bullets did not hit us at all.

We found a little baby lying all alone near the head of the gulch. I could not pick her up just then, but I got her later and some of my people adopted her. I just wrapped her up tighter in a shawl that was around her and left her there. It was a safe place, and I had other work to do.

The soldiers had run eastward over the hills where there were some more soldiers, and they were off their horses and lying down. I told the others to stay back, and I charged upon them holding the sacred bow out toward them with my right hand. They all shot at me, and I could hear bullets all around me, but I ran my horse right close to them, and then swung around. Some soldiers across the gulch began shooting at me too, but I got back to the others and was not hurt at all.

By now many other Lakotas, who had heard the shooting, were coming up from Pine Ridge, and we all charged on the soldiers. They ran eastward toward where the trouble began. We followed down along the dry gulch, and what we saw was terrible. Dead and wounded women and children and little babies were scattered all along there where they had been trying to run away. The soldiers had followed along the gulch, as they ran, and murdered them in there. Sometimes they were in heaps because they had huddled together, and some were scattered all along. Sometimes bunches of them had been killed and torn to pieces where the wagon guns hit them. I saw a little baby trying to suck its mother, but she was bloody and dead.

There were two little boys at one place in this gulch. They had guns and they had been killing soldiers all by themselves. We could see the soldiers they had killed. They boys were all alone there, and they were not hurt. These were very brave little boys.

When we drove the soldiers back, they dug themselves in, and we were not enough people to drive them out from there. In the evening they marched off up Wounded Knee Creek, and then we saw all that they had done there.

Men and women and children were heaped and scattered all over the flat at the bottom of the little hill where the soldiers had their wagon-guns, and westward up the dry gulch all the way to the high ridge, the dead women and children and babies were scattered.

When I saw this I wished that I had died too, but I was not sorry for the women and children. It was better for them to be happy in the other world, and I wanted to be there too. But before I went there I wanted to have revenge. I thought there might be a day, and we should have revenge.

After the soldiers marched away, I heard from my friend, Dog Chief, how the trouble started, and he was right there by Yellow Bird when it happened. This is the way it was:

In the morning the soldiers began to take all the guns away from the Big Foots, who were camped in the flat below the little hill where the monument and burying ground are now. The people had stacked most of their guns, and even their knives, by the tepee where Big Foot was lying sick. Soldiers were on the little hill and all around, and there were soldiers across the dry gulch to the south and over east along Wounded Knee Creek too. The people were nearly surrounded, and the wagon-guns were pointing at them.

Some had not yet given up their guns, and so the soldiers were searching all the tepees, throwing things around and poking into everything. There was a man called Yellow Bird, and he and another man were standing in front of the tepee where Big Foot was lying sick. They had white sheets around and over them, with eye-holes to look through, and they had guns under these. An officer came to search them. He took the other man's gun, and then started to take Yellow Bird's. But Yellow Bird would not let go. He wrestled with the officer, and while they were wrestling, the gun went off and killed the officer. Wasichus and some others have said he meant to do this, but Dog Chief was standing right there, and he told me it was not so. As soon as the gun went off, Dog Chief told me, an officer shot and killed Big Foot who was lying sick inside the tepee.

Then suddenly nobody knew what was happening, except that the soldiers were all shooting and the wagon-guns began going off right in among the people.

Many were shot down right there. The women and children ran into the gulch and up west, dropping all the time, for the soldiers shot them as they ran. There were only about a hundred warriors and there were nearly five hundred soldiers. The warriors rushed to where they had piled their guns and knives. They fought soldiers with only their hands until they got their guns.

Dog Chief saw Yellow Bird run into a tepee with his gun, and from there he killed soldiers until the tepee caught fire. Then he died full of bullets.

It was a good winter day when all this happened. The sun was shining. But after the soldiers marched away from their dirty work, a heavy snow began to fall. The wind came up in the night. There was a big blizzard, and it grew very cold. The snow drifted deep in the crooked gulch, and it was one long grave of butchered women and children and babies, who had never done any harm and were only trying to run away.

After the soldiers marched away, Red Crow and I started back toward Pine Ridge together, and I took the little baby that I told you about. Red Crow had one too.

We were going back to Pine Ridge, because we thought there was peace back home; but it was not so. While we were gone, there was a fight around the Agency, and our people had all gone away.

They had gone away so fast that they left all the tepees standing.

It was nearly dark when we passed north of Pine Ridge where the hospital is now, and some soldiers shot at us, but did not hit us. We rode into the camp, and it was all empty. We were very hungry because we had not eaten anything since early morning, so we peeped into the tepees until we saw where there was a pot with papa (dried meat) cooked in it. We sat down in there and began to eat. While we were doing this, the soldiers shot at the tepee, and a bullet struck right between Red Crow and me. It threw dust in the soup, but we kept right on eating until we had our fill. Then we took the babies and got on our horses and rode away. If that bullet had only killed me, then I could have died with papa in my mouth.

The people had fled down Clay Creek, and we followed their trial. It was dark now, and late in the night we came to where they were camped without any tepees. They were just sitting by little fires, and the snow was beginning to blow. We rode in among them and I heard my mother's voice. She was singing a death song for me, because she felt sure I had died over there. She was so glad to see me that she cried and cried.

Women who had milk fed the little babies that Red Crow and I brought with us.

I think nobody but the little children slept any that night. The snow blew and we had no tepees.

When it was getting light, a war party went out and I went along; but this time I took a gun with me. When I started out the day before to Wounded Knee, I took only my sacred bow, which was not made to shoot with; because I was a little in doubt about the Wanekia religion[3] at that time, and I did not really want to kill anybody because of it.

But I did not feel like that any more. After what I had seen over there, I wanted revenge; I wanted to kill.

We crossed White Clay Creek and followed it up, keeping on the west side. Soon we could hear many guns going off. So we struck west, following a ridge to where the fight was. It was close to the Mission, and there are many bullets in the Mission yet.

From this ridge we could see that the Lakotas were on both sides of the creek and were shooting at soldiers who were coming down the creek. As we looked down, we saw a little ravine, and across this was a big hill. We crossed and rode up the hillside.

They were fighting right there, and a Lakota cried to me: "Black Elk, this is the kind of a day in which to do something great!" I answered: "How!"[4]

Then I got off my horse and rubbed earth on myself, to show the Powers that I was nothing without their help. Then I took my rifle, got on my horse and galloped up to the top of the hill. Right

---

[3] The Ghost Dance religion.
[4] Signifying assent.

below me the soldiers were shooting, and my people called out to me not to go down there; that there were some good shots among the soldiers and I should get killed for nothing.

But I remembered my great vision, the part where the geese of the north appeared. I depended upon their power. Stretching out my arms with my gun in the right hand, like a goose soaring when it flies low to turn in a change of weather, I made the sound the geese make—br-r-r-p, br-r-r-p, br-r-r-p; and, doing this, I charged. The soldiers saw, and began shooting fast at me. I kept right on with my buckskin running, shot in their faces when I was near, then swung wide and rode back up the hill.

All this time the bullets were buzzing around me and I was not touched. I was not even afraid. It was like being in a dream about shooting. But just as I had reached the very top of the hill, suddenly it was like waking up, and I was afraid. I dropped my arms and quit making the goose cry. Just as I did this, I felt something strike my belt as though some one had hit me there with the back of an ax. I nearly fell out of my saddle, but I managed to hold on, and rode over the hill.

An old man by the name of Protector was there, and he ran up and held me, for now I was falling off my horse. I will show you where the bullet struck me sidewise across the belly here (showing a long deep scar on the abdomen). My insides were coming out. Protector tore up a blanket in strips and bound it around me so that my insides would stay in. By now I was crazy to kill, and I said to Protector: "Help me on my horse! Let me go over there. It is a good day to die, so I will go over there!" But Protector said: "No, young nephew! You must not die to-day. That would be foolish. Your people need you. There may be a better day to die." He lifted me into my saddle and led my horse away down hill. Then I began to feel very sick.

By now it looked as though the soldiers would be wiped out, and the Lakotas were fighting harder; but I heard that, after I left, the black Wasichu soldiers came, and the Lakotas had to retreat.

There were many of our children in the Mission, and the sisters and priests were taking care of them. I heard there were sisters and priests right in the battle helping wounded people and praying.

There was a man by the name of Little Soldier who took charge of me and brought me to where our people were camped. While we were over at the Mission Fight, they had fled to the O-ona-gazhee[5] and were camped on top of it where the women and children would be safe from soldiers. Old Hollow Horn was there. He was a very powerful bear medicine man, and he came

---

[5] Sheltering place, an elevated plateau in the Badlands, with precipitous sides, and inaccessible save by one narrow neck of land easily defended.

over to heal my wound. In three days I could walk, but I kept a piece of blanket tied around my belly.

It was now nearly the middle of the Moon of Frost in the Tepee (January). We heard that soldiers were on Smoky Earth River and were coming to attack us in the O-ona-gazhee. They were near Black Feather's place. So a party of about sixty of us started on the war-path to find them. My mother tried to keep me at home, because, although I could walk and ride a horse, my wound was not all healed yet. But I would not stay; for, after what I had seen at Wounded Knee, I wanted a chance to kill soldiers.

We rode down Grass Creek to Smoky Earth, and crossed, riding down stream. Soon from the top of a little hill we saw wagons and cavalry guarding them. The soldiers were making a corral of their wagons and getting ready to fight. We got off our horses and went behind some hills to a little knoll, where we crept up to look at the camp. Some soldiers were bringing harnessed horses down to a little creek to water, and I said to the others: "If you will stay here and shoot at the soldiers, I will charge over there and get some good horses." They knew of my power, so they did this, and I charged on my buckskin while the others kept shooting. I got seven of the horses; but when I started back with these, all the soldiers saw me and began shooting. They killed two of my horses, but I brought five back safe and was not hit. When I was out of range, I caught up a fine bald-faced bay and turned my buckskin loose. Then I drove the others back to our party.

By now more cavalry were coming up the river, a big bunch of them, and there was some hard fighting for a while, because there were not enough of us. We were fighting and retreating, and all at once I saw Red Willow on foot running. He called to me: "Cousin, my horse is killed!" So I caught up a soldier's horse that was dragging a rope and brought it to Red Willow while the soldiers were shooting fast at me. Just then, for a little while, I was a wanekia[6] myself. In this fight Long Bear and another man, whose name I have forgotten, were badly wounded; but we saved them and carried them along with us. The soldiers did not follow us far into the Badlands, and when it was night we rode back with our wounded to the On-ona-gazhee.

We wanted a much bigger war-party so that we could meet the soldiers and get revenge. But this was hard, because the people were not all of the same mind, and they were hungry and cold. We had a meeting there, and were all ready to go out with more warriors, when Afraid-of-His-Horses came over from Pine Ridge to make peace with Red Cloud, who was with us there.

Our party wanted to go out and fight anyway, but Red Cloud made a speech to us something like this: "Brothers, this is a very hard winter. The women and children are starving and freezing. If

---

[6] A "make-live," savior.

this were summer, I would say to keep on fighting to the end. But we cannot do this. We must think of the women and children and that it is very bad for them. So we must make peace, and I will see that nobody is hurt by the soldiers."

The people agreed to this, for it was true. So we broke camp next day and went down from the O-ona-gazhee to Pine Ridge, and many, many Lakotas were already there. Also, there were many, many soldiers. They stood in two lines with their guns held in front of them as we went through to where we camped.

And so it was all over.

I did not know then how much was ended. When I look back now from this high hill of my old age, I can still see the butchered women and children lying heaped and scattered all along the crooked gulch as plain as when I saw them with eyes still young. And I can see that something else died there in the bloody mud, and was buried in the blizzard. A people's dream died there. It was a beautiful dream.

And I, to whom so great a vision was given in my youth,—you see me now a pitiful old man who has done nothing, for the nation's hoop is broken and scattered. There is no center any longer, and the sacred tree is dead.

Further Readings

The reader's attention is directed to *The Civilization of the American Indian*, a series published by the University of Oklahoma Press, running well over a hundred titles that cover many aspects of Indian life. Doane Robinson, *A History of the Dakota or Sioux Indians* (Minneapolis, MN: Ross and Haines, Inc., 1974), is a detailed history written in 1904 and generally presents contemporary white views. The Dakota way of life is discussed in J. R. Walker, *Lakota Society* (Lincoln, NE: University of Nebraska Press, 1982). The events leading up to Wounded Knee are compellingly presented in Dee A. Brown, *Bury My Heart at Wounded Knee* (New York: Holt, Rinehart and Winston, 1970). The life of Sitting Bull (1831–1890), the paramount Dakota chief, is portrayed in Stanley Vestal, *Sitting Bull, Champion of the Sioux: A Biography* (Norman, OK: University of Oklahoma Press, 1957). *The Great Chiefs*, text by Benjamin Capps (Alexandria, VA: Time–Life Books, 1975), is a profusely illustrated account of the Indian Wars. The last chapter contains some chilling photographs of the aftermath of the events at Wounded Knee.

Numerous scholars have helped to preserve a record of the Indian view of events by interviewing surviving participants. *Black Elk Speaks* is an excellent example of such endeavors. Other worthwhile accounts are those of two Dakota chiefs: White Bull (1849–1947), published in Stanley Vestal, *Warpath: The True Story of the Fighting Sioux Told in a Biography of Chief White Bull* (Lincoln, NE: University of Oklahoma Press, 1894), and Flying Hawk (1852–1931), presented in Major Israel McCreight, *Firewater and Forked Tongues: A Sioux Chief Interprets U.S. History* (Pasadena, CA: Trail's End Publishing Co., 1947).

DISCUSSION QUESTIONS: INDUSTRIALISM AND DEMOCRACY

1. Martín Fierro considers himself a free man. How much of that freedom is due to the fact that he seems to feel no sense of obligation to others, even his wife and children? Does society have the duty to protect the freedom of someone who refuses to recognize that he himself has duties to society?

2. Both Malthus and de Tocqueville are Enlightenment thinkers insofar as they seek objective laws governing human affairs. After considering their writings, do you think that individual human beings really have control over their destinies? Based upon his view of battle in *War and Peace*, Tolstoy obviously feels that individuals are not in control of events. Does he feel that objective laws govern their behavior? If not, what force does he believe shapes human actions and human destinies?

3. Consider the account of the death of Beth by Louisa May Alcott and that of the death of Chen in Shen Fu's "The Sorrows of Misfortune." In what ways are they similar? What is the most significant difference? What do the differences tell us about the Western view of death in modern times?

4. The Greek dramatist Aeschylus said that "man learns through suffering." Martín Fierro in "The Gaucho," Kieu in *The Tale of Kieu*, and Shen Fu in "The Sorrows of Misfortune" have all undergone suffering. What have they learned from their misfortunes? Do you believe the cliché that suffering makes one a better person? If so, why do you think that this should be true? If not, why do people keep saying that it does?

5. One of the recurring themes in literature and life is the desire of the individual "to die well." What does "dying well" consist of for Beth, in "The Death of Beth," and for Chen, in "The Sorrows of Misfortune"? Do you think that dying well makes any real difference to the individual? If not, why is so much concern shown about it?

6. Al-Afghani, in *Commentary on the Commentator*, and Hernández, in "The Gaucho: Martín Fierro," present their views of the "good life." What sort of good life do they envision, and how is it achieved? Malthus, in *An Essay on the Principle of Population*, seems to believe that substantial human progress—and thus the achievement of the "good life"—is impossible. Why does he believe so? What is your opinion? Is the good life attainable? If so, by what means can it be achieved and of what should it consist?

7. Compare the figure of Livingstone in "Stanley and Livingstone" with that of Beth in "The Death of Beth." Both are portrayals of virtuous individuals. What does your comparison tell you about the relative role of men and women in late nineteenth-century Western society? Louisa May Alcott, who wrote "The Death of Beth," was an early feminist. Does her ideal of female virtue give any indication of this? Compare the character of Livingstone with that of Martín Fierro, in "The Gaucho: Martín Fierro." What does this comparison tell you about conflict-

ing attitudes towards masculine virtue in the nineteenth-century Western world? Do such conflicting tendencies still exist?

8. How do the events of "Wounded Knee" fulfill the vision of the Delaware presented by Pontiac, in "Speeches by Minavavana and Pontiac" in Part I? Why do you think the soldiers massacred the Indians at Wounded Knee? Why do you think that Black Elk thought it was the end of the dream? What dream was he talking about?

9. One aspect of the Western way of preparing for death would appear to be the stripping away of "life's illusions," as can be seen most clearly in *Everyman* in Volume I, Part III. Consider how Prince Andrei in *War and Peace* and Beth in "The Death of Beth" go through this process. What function does ridding oneself of "life's illusions" play in the process of dying? If it is an important activity, do you think that it is proper to shield a person from the knowledge that he or she is dying? What about the use of drugs that impede the dying person's ability to think?

10. In *The Tale of Kieu* and "The Sorrows of Misfortune," we have two portrayals of a happy married life, although each are marred by misfortune—the inability of Kieu to offer physical love and the death of Chen. What are the qualities that make these unions happy? What do the husband and wife offer each other? Are the same things equally important in a modern Western marriage? Could young Werther, in *The Sorrows of Young Werther* in Part I, have offered Lotte the things necessary for a loving and lasting marriage? If not, why did she feel that she was in love with him?

11. The massacre at Wounded Knee represented, for Black Elk as well as for white observers at the time, the end of any hope that the Indians could retain any political or cultural independence. Why were the Indians unable to resist the whites successfully? What did they offer to oppose the superior technology of the whites? What advice might al-Afghani, author of *Commentary on the Commentator,* have had to offer if he had ever had the opportunity to discuss affairs with Black Elk? How might Black Elk have replied to al-Afghani's suggestions?

12. Black Elk said that the Wounded Knee massacre was the end of a dream, but was this true? There is a modern renaissance of Indian culture and political power in the native American movement, as well as the cultivation of African arts and traditions by blacks in America. Do you think that these developments represent the resurgence of native traditions and spirituality that could not be submerged by the Western tradition, or are they primarily the revival of old customs by a wealthier and better-educated generation attempting to create an ethnic identity for themselves? If the latter, do you think that this ability to reshape traditional approaches to life provides hope that people can resist the dehumanizing forces of modern industrial society? If so, how should they go about it?

DISCUSSION QUESTIONS: INDUSTRIALISM AND DEMOCRACY

PART III

THE TWENTIETH CENTURY

1914 TO THE PRESENT

	1790	
EUROPE	**1790** Edmund Burke: *Reflections on the Revolution in France* **1790** Alexander Radishchev: *A Journey from St. Petersburg to Moscow* **1795–1821** John Keats, English poet **1798** Thomas Malthus: AN ESSAY ON THE PRINCIPLE OF POPULATION **1804–1814** Napoleonic Empire **1811** Luddite movement	**1815** Congress of Vienna **1821–1830** Greek War of Independence **1825** Decembrist Revolt, Russia **1832** Britain's Great Reform Bill **1837** Hegel: *Reason in History* **1848** Karl Marx: *Communist Manifesto* **1848–1870** Napoleon III
SOUTHWEST ASIA AND AFRICA	**1796–1925** Quajar dynasty, Iran **1799** Sierra Leone becomes separate British colony **1805–1848** Mohammed Ali founds dynasty in Egypt **r. 1806–1856** Arab Sultan Seyyid Said of Zanzibar **1806** British control Cape Colony **1807** Slavery abolished in British Empire	**1818–1828** King Shaka of the Zulus **1820–1822** Egypt conquers Sudan **1822** Liberia founded as colony for freed American slaves **1835–1839** Dost Mohammed founds Bora Kzai dynasty, Afghanistan **1836** Boers' Great Trek begins **1839–1842** First Afghan War
SOUTH AND SOUTHEAST ASIA	**1796** British conquer Ceylon **1798–1805** Lord Mornington, Governor General of India **1802–1945** Nguyen dynasty, Vietnam **1813–1823** Lord Moira, Governor General of India	**1818** End of effective Indian resistance to British rule **1820** Nguyen Du: THE TALE OF KIEU **1825–1917** Dadabhai Nagoroji, architect of Indian nationalism **1835** English system of education introduced to India **1848–1925** Surendranath Banerjea, leader of Indian National Congress
EAST ASIA	**1796–1804** White Lotus Rebellion, China **1798** Motoori Norinaga: *Kojikiden* **1805** Christian literature proscribed in China **1809** Shen Fu: THE SORROWS OF MISFORTUNE **1809–1813** Shikitei Samba: *The World at the Bath-House*	**1818–1891** Kuo Sung-tao, first Chinese representative to Western country (minister to England) **1827** Ho Chang-lin: *A Compilation of Essays on Statecraft* **1830** Kyoku Sanjin: *The Greater Learning for Women* **1835–1908** Dowager Empress Tzu Hsi of China **1839–1842** Opium War
THE AMERICAS AND THE PACIFIC	**1792** Esteban de Terralla y Landa (Simón Ayanque): *Lima por Dentro y Fuera* **1803** Louisiana Purchase **1806–1872** Benito Juárez, President of Mexico **1807–1830** Latin American wars of independence	**1816** Fernández de Lizardi: *El Periquillo Sarniento* (first Spanish-American novel) **1820** Great immigration into United States **1823** Monroe Doctrine **1835** Alexis de Tocqueville: DEMOCRACY IN AMERICA **1846–1848** Mexican War

	1850		1870	
EUROPE	1854–1856 Crimean War 1856–1939 Sigmund Freud 1859 Charles Darwin: *Origin of Species* 1860 Turgenev: *Fathers and Children* 1861–1871 Unification of Germany 1869 Tolstoy: WAR AND PEACE	1870–1871 Franco-Prussian War 1880 Dostoevsky: *The Brothers Karamazov* 1882–1941 James Joyce 1887 Nietzsche: *Genealogy of Morals* 1890 Henrik Ibsen: *Hedda Gabler* 1894 Russo-French Alliance	1904 Anton Chekhov: *The Cherry Orchard* 1905 Russian Revolution begins 1905 Einstein's Theory of Relativity 1907–1973 W. H. Auden 1912–1913 Balkan Wars
SOUTHWEST ASIA AND AFRICA	1856–1918 Carl Peters, founder of German East Africa 1860 French expansion in West Africa 1860–1864 Sir Samuel Baker explores Nile region 1864 First telegraph in Persia 1869 Suez Canal	1873 STANLEY AND LIVINGSTONE 1874–1926 Iraj Mirza, Persian poet 1885 The Madhi takes Khartum 1886 Gold discovered in southern Africa 1889 Rhodesia colonized 1899–1902 Boer War	1903–1951 Sadeq Hedayat, Persian writer 1905 Persian Revolution begins 1906–1907 Suppression of Zulu Rebellion b. 1906 Leopold Sedor Senghor: *Relentlessly She Drives Me* 1910 Union of South Africa formed
SOUTH AND SOUTHEAST ASIA	r. 1851–1868 King Mongkut of Thailand 1856–1920 Bal Gangadhar Tilak, Indian militant leader 1857–1858 Indian Mutiny 1859 French seize Saigon 1861–1896 José Rizal, Philippines nationalist 1869 Nazir Ahmad: *The Bride's Mirror*	1877 Romesh Chunder Dutt: *The Literature of Bengal* 1879 G. Subvamanya Iyer founds the journal *New India* ca. 1882 al-Afghani: COMMENTARY ON THE COMMENTATOR 1886 India's First National Congress 1893 France acquires protectorate over Laos	1901 Bipin Chandra Pal founds the journal *New India* 1905 Partition of Bengal arouses nationalist agitation 1906 Muslim League founded 1913 Rabindranath Tagore awarded Nobel Prize
EAST ASIA	1850–1864 Taiping Rebellion 1854 Perry opens U.S. trade with Japan 1854 Yung Wing, first Chinese to graduate from an American university (Yale) 1859–1935 Tsubouchi Shoyo: *The Essence of the Novel* 1866–1925 Sun Yat-sen	1881–1936 Lu Hsun, Chinese writer 1886–1942 Hagiwara Sakutaro, Japanese poet 1887–1889 Futabatei Shimei: *Drifting Cloud* 1893–1976 Mao Zedong 1894–1895 Sino-Japanese War	1900 Boxer Rebellion 1904–1905 Russo-Japanese War 1906 Shimazaki Toson: *Broken Commandment* 1911 Chinese Revolution 1912–1949 Chinese Republic 1914 Natsume Soseki: *Kokoro*
THE AMERICAS AND THE PACIFIC	1854 Henry David Thoreau: *Walden* 1861–1865 American Civil War 1867 Russia sells Alaska to the U.S. 1867 British North America Act 1869 Louisa May Alcott: LITTLE WOMEN	1871 MARTÍN FIERRO: THE GAUCHO 1879–1883 War of the Pacific 1889 First Pan-American Conference 1890 Battle of Wounded Knee (BLACK ELK SPEAKS) 1898 Spanish-American War	1903 Ada Cambridge: *Thirty Years in Australia* 1906 Upton Sinclair: *The Jungle* 1910 Mexican Revolution begins 1911 Edith Wharton: *Ethan Frome* 1913 Willa Cather: *O Pioneers!* 1914 Panama Canal

If one regards the European domination of the globe to be the main theme of modern world history, then 1914 can be legitimately considered the most important date since the end of the middle ages. In 1914, Western powers dominated most of the world, and Europe dominated the Western nations. European technology, science, and organization were clearly superior to those of any other culture, and most of the non-Western cultures of the world were attempting to find ways to emulate the Europeans in these areas. Although capable of introspective doubts, as exemplified in *Sons and Lovers,* European society was generally confident of its own preeminence. A hundred years of relative peace and almost unbroken progress had convinced Europeans of not only their material superiority but their moral superiority also. As a consequence, they had no hesitation in forcing their will upon subject peoples and in proclaiming all religions other than their own to be false and all non-European cultures to be primitive and backward. Moreover, they seemed convinced of the stability of the institutions of their society, and expected a steady continuation into the foreseeable future of the progress they had enjoyed in the past. They were quite unprepared for what was to ensue.

To maintain the balance of political power on the continent, the European states had established a series of interlocking alliances that effectively divided them into two blocs, one dominated by Germany and Austria-Hungary, and the other consisting of Great Britain, France, and Russia. When a conflict did break out, this system, designed to prevent a major war, succeeded in dragging all of the various allies into the conflict. By the summer of 1914, most of Europe was at war. What is more, once having gotten their countries into war, the political leaders seemed unable to extricate them. Technological improvements in weaponry, particularly barbed wire and the machine gun, ensured that the war could not be won by traditional means. Meanwhile, the superior organization of the modern state assured that entire nations would be geared for war, and that no one would escape the pain and sacrifice that war entailed.

The war bogged down into the static trench warfare described in *All Quiet on the Western Front,* as each side attempted to secure victory through simple attrition. Some ten million men and women were killed in the fighting, and, when the United States entered the war, the Germans lacked sufficient manpower to hold their lines any longer. The fighting stopped in 1918 with the European economy totally disrupted, the contending powers virtually exhausted, and nothing significant having been accomplished.

The repercussions were extensive. Their faith shaken, many Europeans were ready to reject their discredited governments and political philosophies. Ireland threw off British domination in a struggle reflected in *Guests of the Nation.* Austria-Hungary ceased to exist as a unified empire, and the reigning monarchies of Germany and Russia were overthrown. New political philosophies, such as Russian communism and Italian fascism, were embraced by many throughout the continent. In 1929, a world-wide economic depression not only caused severe distress for many, but cast as much doubt upon the validity of Europe's traditional economic organization as the war had cast upon its traditional political structures. Throughout the 1930s, European society suffered a general malaise. Europeans were no longer assured of the effectiveness, much less the superiority, of any of their institutions. Some felt, as did Aldous Huxley in *Brave New World*, that scientific and technological progress was leading Europe away from the moral strength possessed by native cultures.

All of this was not lost on the non-Western peoples of the world. Many non-Western leaders had seen that the European way of life was far from perfect and were more than ever determined to recover their independence and to protect their traditional cultures. With Europe weakened and hesitant, anti-Western movements achieved a power and solidity that would never have been possible before 1914. Mohandas Gandhi's "Statement in the Great Trial of 1922" is but one example of the rising tide of opposition to European political control of the world's destinies.

The situation was aggravated by the resumption of European hostilities in 1939–1945. Victory was achieved this time through the virtually complete destruction of the war-making industrial capacities of Germany and her allies. The conflict was characterized by an almost scientific savagery. The discovery of the Nazi death camps in Germany, the land of Goethe and Beethoven, was yet another factor in causing widespread doubts of the moral superiority of Western culture. Although the Japanese were defeated in their challenge to Western domination of the Pacific, their early victories and stubborn unwillingness to accept defeat, documented in *The Night of a Thousand Suicides,* demonstrated to many that the supposed inferiority of non-Western peoples was a myth.

The aftermath of the war saw the redistribution of power within the world. Only the Soviet Union and the United States of America had emerged from the conflict with sufficient ideological and economic strength to continue hostilities, and soon both possessed the nuclear weaponry that had ended the world war and made its resumption difficult to contemplate. These two powers were soon engaged in the Cold War, a continuing international conflict carried on at levels generally below that of actual warfare. Europe, meanwhile, had neither the resources nor the will to overcome native resistance to their continued political domination. The 1950s and 1960s saw the dissolution of the great colonial empires.

Despite continuing international tensions, the general trend of affairs in recent years has increasingly been towards a global community. Western technology, science, and even culture are no longer the exclusive possession of the old Western powers. Non-Western peoples are now able to create their own blend of traditional culture and Western ways. The "Fifteen Poems Out of Africa" demonstrate how tribal forms contribute to a new and significant poetry that constitutes an enrichment of the Western tradition. "On the People's Democratic Dictatorship," on the other hand, illustrates how the basically European tenets of revolutionary communism were adapted to the peculiar circumstances of China. In recent years, the global tendency has been towards cultural convergence. The demands of international cooperation and the requirements of a modern industrial economy have dictated that nations and cultures share more and hence that they grow more similar.

One of the forces shaping this tendency has been the growth of serious problems of global scope, problems that simply cannot be solved by local action. One of the most prominent is that of peace. An increasing number of nations possess the nuclear capability to cause immense destruction. Many more possess the nonnuclear but nonetheless powerful weapons to inflict great suffering upon their neighbors. Octavio Paz' *One Earth* is a noteworthy attempt to address this problem. Yet another challenge is that caused by a swiftly increasing world population in the face of the very uneven distribution of the world's limited resources. "The Nobel Prize Address" of Mother Teresa of Calcutta illustrates the urgency of this problem.

Still other challenges face the peoples of the world. Nuclear accidents, ozone depletion, acid rains, epidemic diseases, species extinction, oil spills, atmospheric pollution, commercial dumping, and the like are more than simply the afflictions of modern life; they are problems that require global cooperation to be solved. As such cooperation increases, so too will the various nations and cultures of this world tend to merge into a greater whole. The challenge of the future is whether this can be accomplished without eliminating the rich variety of human life by reducing all the participants in the world community to a faceless common denominator.

Sons and Lovers

Sons and Lovers, the autobiographical novel by the frequently controversial British author David Herbert Lawrence (1885–1930), is generally considered to be one of his finest works. Lawrence was prolific and versatile, writing in various literary genres, but his novels and short stories were decidedly his most significant and interesting efforts. He was born in 1885 in Eastwood, a small mining town near Nottingham, England. His father was an uncouth miner, and his mother, a woman of some education and great ambition, made no secret of her feelings of superiority to her husband. This unhappy relationship was aggravated by his father's drinking and the family's poverty.

Fond of reading and drawing, Lawrence showed early promise and excelled in school. Following the death of his older brother, his dissatisfied mother concentrated her affections and ambitions on Lawrence, and an unusually strong bond was forged between the two. After completing his primary education, he worked for a short time in a local warehouse, enjoyed two years' education at Nottingham University on scholarship, and turned to teaching. The death of his mother, however, coupled with the publication of his first literary work, convinced him to devote himself entirely to writing.

His third major publication, and the first of his novels with any claim to greatness, was *Sons and Lovers,* which appeared in 1913 when Lawrence was twenty-eight. In writing it, he drew heavily upon his early experiences to produce a superior work of self-analysis. The novel traces the lives of the Morel family: the three sons, William, Paul (Lawrence himself), and Arthur, their sister Annie, and their parents, Gertrude and Walter. The focus is upon Paul's uncritical adulation of his mother, and her stultifying love for him. Smothered

---

From D. H. Lawrence, *Sons and Lovers* (New York: Penguin Books, 1983), pp. 240–246 and 249–252.

by his mother's love, Paul finds it increasingly difficult to adjust to the demands of an adult life and to form mature and responsible relationships with others. In his account of the intense and excessive love between Paul and his mother, Lawrence provides a gripping examination of how parental love can affect the child's development.

Paul's struggle into maturity is chronicled through his changing relationships with three women: his mother; his platonic love, Miriam Leivers; and Clara Dawes, his first sexual partner. His efforts to comprehend and deal with the complexities of these relationships comprise the central theme of the narrative. Lawrence considers the demands made upon him by these three women as having restricted his ability to mature and achieve self-realization.

Sons and Lovers focuses upon the relationship between a mother and her son, but places it within a well-defined social context. Lawrence was one of the few outstanding Victorian writers to come from a lower-class background and he vividly describes the society and economy of the small mining town of his youth. Thus *Sons and Lovers* affords the reader a valuable glimpse at the tensions and conflicts of that class of English society most deeply affected by the changes introduced by the Industrial Revolution.

The first excerpt in the following selection recounts an excursion taken by Paul and his mother to the city of Lincoln. Although it is a happy occasion for the two, the outing takes on a tragic tone with Paul's realization that his mother is much older than he and that she will one day die and leave him alone. He reacts by vowing that he will not marry, but will stay with her until death separates them. The second excerpt graphically depicts the frustration of Paul's relationship with Miriam and his inability to establish any meaningful relationship with her. This marks the end of Paul's first love affair and the beginning of his search for a physical relationship.

Questions

1. Paul remarks that "God doesn't *know* things, He *is* things." What does he mean by this statement?

2. Paul seems incapable of establishing satisfying relationships with women. Is Paul at fault? If not, who is?

3. Individual sacrifice is a common theme in this novel. What sacrifices occur in these excerpts? What motivates these individuals to make these sacrifices?

SONS AND LOVERS

At this time Paul took his mother to Lincoln. She was bright and enthusiastic as ever, but as he sat opposite her in the railway carriage, she seemed to look frail. He had a momentary sensation as if she were slipping away from him. Then he wanted to get hold of her, to fasten her, almost to chain her. He felt he must keep hold of her with his hand.

They drew near to the city. Both were at the window looking for the cathedral.

"There she is, mother!" he cried.

They saw the great cathedral lying couchant above the plain.

"Ah!" she exclaimed. "So she is!"

He looked at his mother. Her blue eyes were watching the cathedral quietly. She seemed again to be beyond him. Something in the eternal repose of the uplifted cathedral, blue and noble against the sky, was reflected in her, something of the fatality. What was, *was*. With all his young will he could not alter it. He saw her face, the skin still fresh and pink and downy, but crow's-feet near her eyes, her eyelids steady, sinking a little, her mouth always closed with disillusion; and there was on her the same eternal look, as if she knew fate at last. He beat against it with all the strength of his soul.

"Look, mother, how big she is above the town! Think, there are streets and streets below her! She looks bigger than the city altogether."

"So she does!" exclaimed his mother, breaking bright into life again. But he had seen her sitting, looking steady out of the window at the cathedral, her face and eyes fixed, reflecting the relentlessness of life. And the crow's-feet near her eyes, and her mouth shut so hard, made him feel he would go mad.

They ate a meal that she considered wildly extravagant.

"Don't imagine I like it," she said, as she ate her cutlet. "I *don't* like it, I really don't! Just *think* of your money wasted!"

"You never mind my money," he said. "You forget I'm a fellow taking his girl for an outing."

And he bought her some blue violets.

"Stop it at once, sir!" she commanded. "How can I do it?"

"You've got nothing to do. Stand still!"

And in the middle of High Street he stuck the flowers in her coat.

"An old thing like me!" she said, sniffing.

"You see," he said, "I want people to think we're awful swells. So look ikey."

"I'll jowl your head," she laughed.

"Strut!" he commanded. "Be a fantail pigeon."

It took him an hour to get her through the street. She stood above Glory Hole, she stood before Stone Bow, she stood everywhere, and exclaimed.

A man came up, took off his hat, and bowed to her.

"Can I show you the town, madam?"

"No, thank you," she answered. "I've got my son."

Then Paul was cross with her for not answering with more dignity.

"You go away with you!" she exclaimed. "Ha! that's the Jew's House. Now, do you remember that lecture, Paul—?"

But she could scarcely climb the cathedral hill. He did not notice. Then suddenly he found her unable to speak. He took her into a little public-house, where she rested.

"It's nothing," she said. "My heart is only a bit old; one must expect it."

He did not answer, but looked at her. Again his heart was crushed in a hot grip. He wanted to cry, he wanted to smash things in fury.

They set off again, pace by pace, so slowly. And every step seemed like a weight on his chest. He felt as if his heart would burst. At last they came to the top. She stood enchanted, looking at the castle gate, looking at the cathedral front. She had quite forgotten herself.

"Now *this* is better than I thought it could be!" she cried.

But he hated it. Everywhere he followed her, brooding. They sat together in the cathedral. They attended a little service in the choir. She was timid.

"I suppose it is open to anybody?" she asked him.

"Yes," he replied. "Do you think they'd have the damned cheek to send us away?"

"Well, I'm sure," she exclaimed, "they would if they heard your language."

Her face seemed to shine again with joy and peace during the service. And all the time he was wanting to rage and smash things and cry.

Afterwards, when they were leaning over the wall, looking at the town below, he blurted suddenly:

"Why can't a man have a *young* mother? What is she old for?"

"Well," his mother laughed, "she can scarcely help it."

"And why wasn't I the oldest son? Look—they say the young ones have the advantage—but look, *they* had the young mother. You should have had me for your eldest son."

"*I* didn't arrange it," she remonstrated. "Come to consider, you're as much to blame as me."

He turned on her, white, his eyes furious.

"What are you old for!" he said, mad with his impotence. "*Why* can't you walk? *Why* can't you come with me to places?"

"At one time," she replied, "I could have run up that hill a good deal better than you."

"What's the good of that to *me?*" he cried, hitting his fist on the wall. Then he became plaintive. "It's too bad of you to be ill, Little, it is—"

"Ill!" she cried. "I'm a bit old, and you'll have to put up with it, that's all."

They were quiet. But it was as much as they could bear. They got jolly again over tea. As they sat by Brayford, watching the boats, he told her about Clara. His mother asked him innumerable questions.

"Then who does she live with?"

"With her mother, on Bluebell Hill."

"And have they enough to keep them?"

"I don't think so. I think they do lace work."

"And wherein lies her charm, my boy?"

"I don't know that she's charming, mother. But she's nice. And she seems straight, you know—not a bit deep, not a bit."

"But she's a good deal older than you."

"She's thirty, I'm going of twenty-three."

"You haven't told me what you like her for."

"Because I don't know—a sort of defiant way she's got—a sort of angry way."

Mrs. Morel considered. She would have been glad now for her son to fall in love with some woman who would—she did not know what. But he fretted so, got so furious suddenly, and again was melancholic. She wished he knew some nice woman—She did not know what she wished, but left it vague. At any rate, she was not hostile to the idea of Clara.

Annie, too, was getting married. Leonard had gone away to work in Birmingham. One week-end when he was home she had said to him:

"You don't look very well, my lad."

"I dunno," he said. "I feel anyhow or nohow, ma."

He called her "ma" already in his boyish fashion.

"Are you sure they're good lodgings?" she asked.

"Yes—yes. Only—it's a winder when you have to pour your own tea out—an' nobody to grouse if you team it in your saucer and sup it up. It somehow takes a' the taste out of it."

Mrs. Morel laughed.

"And so it knocks you up?" she said.

"I dunno. I want to get married," he blurted, twisting his fingers and looking down at his boots. There was a silence.

"But," she exclaimed, "I thought you said you'd wait another year."

"Yes, I did say so," he replied stubbornly.

Again she considered.

"And you know," she said, "Annie's a bit of a spend-thrift. She's saved no more than eleven pounds. And I know, lad, you haven't had much chance."

He coloured up to the ears.

"I've got thirty-three quid," he said.

"It doesn't go far," she answered.

He said nothing, but twisted his fingers.

"And you know," she said, "I've nothing—"

D. H. Lawrence.

"I didn't want, ma!" he cried, very red, suffering and remonstrating.

"No, my lad, I know. I was only wishing I had. And take away five pounds for the wedding and things—it leaves twenty-nine pounds. You won't do much on that."

He twisted still, impotent, stubborn, not looking up.

"But do you really want to get married?" she asked. "Do you feel as if you ought?"

He gave her one straight look from his blue eyes.

"Yes," he said.

"Then," she replied, "we must all do the best we can for it, lad."

The next time he looked up there were tears in his eyes.

"I don't want Annie to feel handicapped," he said, struggling.

"My lad," she said, "you're steady—you've got a decent place. If a man had *needed* me I'd have married him on his last week's wages. She may find it a bit hard to start humbly. Young girls *are* like that. They look forward to the fine home they think they'll have. But *I* had expensive furniture. It's not everything."

So the wedding took place almost immediately. Arthur came home, and was splendid in uniform. Annie looked nice in a dove-grey dress that she could take for Sundays. Morel called her a fool for getting married, and was cool with his son-in-law. Mrs. Morel had white tips in her bonnet, and some white on her blouse, and was teased by both her sons for fancying herself so grand. Leonard was jolly and cordial, and felt a fearful fool. Paul could not quite see what Annie wanted to get married for. He was fond of her, and she of him. Still, he hoped rather lugubriously that it would turn out all right. Arthur was astonishingly handsome in his scarlet and yellow, and he knew it well, but was secretly ashamed of the uniform. Annie cried her eyes up in the kitchen, on leaving her mother. Mrs. Morel cried a little, then patted her on the back and said:

"But don't cry, child, he'll be good to you."

Morel stamped and said she was a fool to go and tie herself up. Leonard looked white and overwrought. Mrs. Morel said to him:

"I s'll trust her to you, my lad, and hold you responsible for her."

"You can," he said, nearly dead with the ordeal. And it was all over.

When Morel and Arthur were in bed, Paul sat talking, as he often did, with his mother.

"You're not sorry she's married, mother, are you?" he asked.

"I'm not sorry she's married—but—it seems strange that she should go from me. It even seems to me hard that she can prefer to go with her Leonard. That's how mothers are—I know it's silly."

"And shall you be miserable about her?"

"When I think of my own wedding day," his mother answered, "I can only hope her life will be different."

"But you can trust him to be good to her?"

"Yes, yes. They say he's not good enough for her. But I say if a man is *genuine,* as he is, and a girl is fond of him—then—it should be all right. He's as good as she."

"So you don't mind?"

"I would *never* have let a daughter of mine marry a man I didn't *feel* to be genuine through and through. And yet, there's a gap now she's gone."

They were both miserable, and wanted her back again. It seemed to Paul his mother looked lonely, in her new black silk blouse with its bit of white trimming.

"At any rate, mother, I s'll never marry," he said.

"Ay, they all say that, my lad. You've not met the one yet. Only wait a year or two."

"But I shan't marry, mother. I shall live with you, and we'll have a servant."

"Ay, my lad, it's easy to talk. We'll see when the time comes."

"What time? I'm nearly twenty-three."

"Yes, you're not one that would marry young. But in three years' time—"

"I shall be with you just the same."

"We'll see, my boy, we'll see."

"But you don't want me to marry?"

"I shouldn't like to think of you going through your life without anybody to care for you and do—no."

"And you think I ought to marry?"

"Sooner or later every man ought."

"But you'd rather it were later."

"It would be hard—and very hard. It's as they say:

" 'A son's my son till he takes him a wife,
But my daughter's my daughter the whole of her life.' "

"And you think I'd let a wife take me from you?"

"Well, you wouldn't ask her to marry your mother as well as you," Mrs. Morel smiled.

"She could do what she liked; she wouldn't have to interfere."

"She wouldn't—till she'd got you—and then you'd see."

"I never will see. I'll never marry while I've got you—I won't."

"But I shouldn't like to leave you with nobody, my boy," she cried.

"You're not going to leave me. What are you? Fifty-three! I'll give you till seventy-five. There you are, I'm fat and forty-four. Then I'll marry a staid body. See!"

His mother sat and laughed.

"Go to bed," she said—"go to bed."

"And we'll have a pretty house, you and me, and a servant, and it'll be just all right. I s'll perhaps be rich with my painting."

"Will you go to bed!"

"And then you s'll have a pony-carriage. See yourself—a little Queen Victoria trotting round."

"I tell you to go to bed," she laughed.

He kissed her and went. His plans for the future were always the same.

◇ ◇ ◇

Paul felt life changing around him. The conditions of youth were gone. Now it was a home of grown-up people. Annie was a married woman, Arthur was following his own pleasure in a way unknown to his folk. For so long they had all lived at home, and gone out to pass their time. But now, for Annie and Arthur, life lay outside their mother's house. They came home for holiday and for rest. So there was that strange, half-empty feeling about the house, as if the birds had flown. Paul became more and more unsettled. Annie and Arthur had gone. He was restless to follow. Yet home was for him beside his mother. And still there was something else, something outside, something he wanted.

He grew more and more restless. Miriam did not satisfy him. His old mad desire to be with her grew weaker. Sometimes he met Clara in Nottingham, sometimes he went to meetings with her, sometimes he saw her at Willey Farm. But on these last occasions the situation became strained. There was a triangle of antagonism between Paul and Clara and Miriam. With Clara he took on a smart, worldly, mocking tone very antagonistic to Miriam. It did not matter what went before. She might be intimate and sad with him. Then as soon as Clara appeared, it all vanished, and he played to the newcomer.

Miriam had one beautiful evening with him in the hay. He had been on the horse-rake, and having finished, came to help her to put the hay in cocks. Then he talked to her of his hopes and despairs, and his whole soul seemed to lie bare before her. She felt as if she watched the very quivering stuff of life in him. The moon came out: they walked home together: he seemed to have come to her because he needed her so badly, and she listened to him, gave him all her love and her faith. It seemed to her he brought her the best of himself to keep, and that she would guard it all her life. Nay, the sky did not cherish the stars more surely and eternally than she would guard the good in the soul of Paul Morel. She went on home alone, feeling exalted, glad in her faith.

And then, the next day, Clara came. They were to have tea in the hayfield. Miriam watched the evening drawing to gold and shadow. And all the time Paul was sporting with Clara. He made higher and higher heaps of hay that they were jumping over. Miriam did not care for the game, and stood aside. Edgar and Geoffrey and Maurice and Clara and Paul jumped. Paul won, because he was light. Clara's blood was roused. She could run like an Amazon. Paul loved the determined way she rushed at the haycock and leaped, landed on the other side, her breasts shaken, her thick hair come undone.

"You touched!" he cried. "You touched!"

"No!" she flashed, turning to Edgar. "I didn't touch, did I? Wasn't I clear?"

"I couldn't say," laughed Edgar.

None of them could say.

"But you touched," said Paul. "You're beaten."

"I did *not* touch!" she cried.

"As plain as anything," said Paul.

"Box his ears for me!" she cried to Edgar.

"Nay," Edgar laughed. "I daren't. You must do it yourself."

"And nothing can alter the fact that you touched," laughed Paul.

She was furious with him. Her little triumph before these lads and men was gone. She had forgotten herself in the game. Now he was to humble her.

"I think you are despicable!" she said.

And again he laughed, in a way that tortured Miriam.

"And I *knew* you couldn't jump that heap," he teased.

She turned her back on him. Yet everybody could see that the only person she listened to, or was conscious of, was he, and he of her. It pleased the men to see this battle between them. But Miriam was tortured.

Paul could choose the lesser in place of the higher, she saw. He could be unfaithful to himself, unfaithful to the real, deep Paul Morel. There was a danger of his becoming frivolous, of his running after his satisfaction like any Arthur, or like his father. It made Miriam bitter to think that he should throw away his soul for this flippant traffic of triviality with Clara. She walked in bitterness and silence, while the other two rallied each other, and Paul sported.

And afterwards, he would not own it, but he was rather ashamed of himself, and prostrated himself before Miriam. Then again he rebelled.

"It's not religious to be religious," he said. "I reckon a crow is religious when it sails across the sky. But it only does it because it feels itself carried to where it's going, not because it thinks it is being eternal."

But Miriam knew that one should be religious in everything, have God, whatever God might be, present in everything.

"I don't believe God knows such a lot about Himself," he cried. "God doesn't *know* things, He *is* things. And I'm sure He's not soulful."

And then it seemed to her that Paul was arguing God on to his own side, because he wanted his own way and his own pleasure. There was a long battle between him and her. He was utterly unfaithful to her even in her own presence; then he was ashamed, then repentant; then he hated her, and went off again. Those were the ever-recurring conditions.

She fretted him to the bottom of her soul. There she remained—sad, pensive, a worshipper. And he caused her sorrow. Half the time he grieved for her, half the time he hated her. She was his conscience; and he felt, somehow, he had got a conscience that was too much for him. He could not leave her, because in one way she did hold the best of him. He could not stay with her because she did not take the rest of him, which was three-quarters. So he chafed himself into rawness over her.

When she was twenty-one he wrote her a letter which could only have been written to her.

"May I speak of our old, worn love, this last time. It, too, is changing, is it not? Say, has not the body of that love died, and left you its invulnerable soul? You see, I can give you a spirit love, I have given it you this long, long time; but not embodied passion. See, you are a nun. I have given you what I would give a holy nun—as a mystic monk to a mystic nun. Surely you esteem it best. Yet you regret—no, have regretted—the other. In all our relations no body enters. I do not talk to you through the senses—rather through the spirit. That is why we cannot love in the common sense. Ours is not an everyday affection. As yet we are mortal, and to live side by side with one another would be dreadful, for somehow with you I cannot long be trivial, and, you know, to be always beyond this mortal state would be to lose it. If people marry, they must live together as affectionate humans, who may be commonplace with each other without feeling awkward—not as two souls. So I feel it.

"Ought I to send this letter?—I doubt it. But there—it is best to understand. *Au revoir.*"

Miriam read this letter twice, after which she sealed it up. A year later she broke the seal to show her mother the letter.

"You are a nun—you are a nun." The words went into her heart again and again. Nothing he ever had said had gone into her so deeply, fixedly, like a mortal wound.

She answered him two days after the party.

" 'Our intimacy would have been all-beautiful but for one little mistake,' " she quoted. "Was the mistake mine?"

Almost immediately he replied to her from Nottingham, sending her at the same time a little "Omar Khayyám."

"I am glad you answered; you are so calm and natural you put me to shame. What a ranter I am! We are often out of sympathy. But in fundamentals we may always be together I think.

"I must thank you for your sympathy with my painting and drawing. Many a sketch is dedicated to you. I do look forward to your criticisms, which, to my shame and glory, are always grand appreciations. It is a lovely joke, that. *Au revoir.*"

This was the end of the first phase of Paul's love affair. He was now about twenty-three years old, and, though still virgin, the sex instinct that Miriam had over-refined for so long now grew particularly strong. Often, as he talked to Clara Dawes, came that thickening and quickening of his blood, that peculiar concentration in the breast, as if something were alive there, a new self or a new centre of consciousness, warning him that sooner or later he would have to ask one woman or another. But he belonged to Miriam. Of that she was so fixedly sure that he allowed her right.

Further Readings

There are numerous biographies of Lawrence. Edward Nehls, *D. H. Lawrence: A Composite Biography* (3 vols.: Madison, WI: University of Wisconsin Press, 1959), is a comprehensive study. Three less-extensive studies are Philip

Callow, *Son and Lover: The Young Lawrence* (London: The Bodley Head, 1975), Richard Aldington, *D. H. Lawrence* (New York: Collier Books, 1953), and Geoffrey Trease, *D. H. Lawrence: The Phoenix and the Flame* (London: Macmillan, 1973). There are several bibliographies that are useful in sifting through the mass of material dealing with Lawrence. Chief among these are *A D. H. Lawrence Handbook*, edited by Keith Sagar (New York: Barnes and Noble, 1982); Warren Roberts, *A Bibliography of D. H. Lawrence* (London: Cambridge University Press, 1963); and *D. H. Lawrence: An Annotated Bibliography*, edited by James C. Cowan (De Kalb, IL: Northern Illinois University Press, 1985). The *D. H. Lawrence Review* was founded by Cowan at the University of Arkansas in 1968. Published three times yearly, it has become an important source for material on Lawrence.

Critical studies of Lawrence and his works exist in abundance. J. Moynahan, *The Deed of Life: The Novels and Tales of D. H. Lawrence* (Princeton, NJ: Princeton University Press, 1933), provides a study of Lawrence's major works of fiction. An examination of Lawrence's better-known works, including *Sons and Lovers*, is available in George J. Becker, *D. H. Lawrence* (New York: Frederick Ungar Publishing Co., 1980). Valuable collections of essays discussing aspects of the major works of Lawrence are contained in *D. H. Lawrence: A Critical Study of the Major Novels and Other Writings*, edited by A. H. Gomme (New York: Barnes and Noble, 1978); *D. H. Lawrence: A Centenary Consideration*, edited by Peter Balbert and Phillip L. Marcus (Ithaca, NY: Cornell University Press, 1985); and Harry T. Moore, *A D. H. Lawrence Miscellany* (Carbondale, IL: Southern Illinois University Press, 1959). Stephen J. Miko, *Toward Women in Love* (New Haven, CT: Yale University Press, 1971), provides a critical look at some of Lawrence's better-known novels, including *Sons and Lovers*. Peter Scheckner, *Class, Politics and the Individual* (London: Associated University Presses, 1985), focuses on Lawrence's social and political background, while Gavriel Ben-Ephraim, *The Moon's Dominion* (London: Associated University Presses, 1985), considers male–female relationships and the theme of female dominance in Lawrence's first five novels. *D. H. Lawrence and Tradition*, edited by Jeffrey Meyes (Amherst, MA: University of Massachusetts Press, 1985), looks at Lawrence's relationship to tradition and his receptivity to its influence.

D. H. Lawrence published voluminously, in many different genres. A number of his works have been made available by Penguin Books, including: *The Virgin and the Gypsy* (1970), *Women in Love* (1976), *Kangaroo* (1960), *Lady Chatterly's Lover* (1969), *Aaron's Rod* (1976), *The Plumed Serpent* (1970), *The Rainbow* (1976), *The White Peacock* (1950), and *Sons and Lovers* (1977). Two excellent collections containing Lawrence's short stories are *The Complete Short Stories of D. H Lawrence* (3 vols.: New York: Penguin, 1976), and *The Portable D. H. Lawrence* (New York: Penguin, 1977). *The Complete Poems of D. H. Lawrence*, edited by Vivian da Sola Pinto and Warren Roberts (New York: Viking, 1964), covers his poetry well. His collected correspondence is presented in *The Letters of D. H. Lawrence*, edited by James T. Boulton (3 vols.: Cambridge: Cambridge University Press, 1979), and *The Collected Letters of D. H. Lawrence*, edited by Harry T. Moore (2 vols.: New York: Viking, 1962).

Six of Lawrence's more famous works have been made into films: *The Rocking Horse Winner* (1949: Two Cities Films, black and white), *L'Amant de Lady Chatterly* (1956: Columbia, black and white, in French), *Sons and Lovers* (1960: Twentieth Century-Fox, black and white), *The Fox* (1968: Claridge Pictures, color), *Women in Love* (1970: United Artists, color), and *The Virgin and the Gypsy* (1970: London Screenplays, color).

Statement in the Great Trial of 1922

The British presence in the Indian subcontinent was longstanding. The Company of Merchants of London Trading into the East Indies, generally known as the East India Company, was founded by Queen Elizabeth in 1600. These British merchants, along with French and Dutch traders, broke the monopoly of the Indian trade enjoyed by the Portuguese since 1500. The Company established trading stations along the coast, chief among them being Bombay, Madras, and Calcutta, and shared the Indian trade with the Dutch and French for some time. During the Seven Years' War (1757–1763), however, Company forces defeated their competitors and established British commercial supremacy in the region. During the next century, this commercial corporation acted almost as an independent government in India, administering all British affairs there, annexing territory, forming its own army and navy, and establishing protectorates over native princes.

The downfall of the Company was indirectly the result of the Industrial Revolution. Throughout most of its history, the Company worked with native merchants and rulers, brought prosperity to its partners, and had little effect upon the traditional life and culture of the land. With the advent of steam-driven ships and the opening of China to trade, however, the Company adopted a free-trade policy that effectively eliminated its Indian partners. Better weaponry allowed it to adopt a less conciliatory policy with native rulers. Finally, the railroads that it began to build and the telegraph wires that it began to string led the Indians to believe that it was the Company's

From Mohandas K. Gandhi, *The Selected Works of Mahatma Gandhi: Volume VI*, edited by Shriman Narayan (Ahmedabad-14, India: Navajivan Printing House, 1968), pp. 16–24.

ultimate aim to replace Indian culture with British civilization. For these and other, more immediate reasons, the Company's native troops mutinied in 1857–1858. As a result, the administration of the Company was taken over by the British government, which also assumed political control over India. With this act, India became an integral part of the British Empire.

British rule in India was, by most colonial standards, remarkably efficient and, in the word the British administrators themselves preferred, benign. Peace was maintained, health and hygiene improved, a remarkably efficient transportation and communication system built, and education greatly expanded. And yet there were drawbacks. India was prized by the British as a source of raw materials and as a vast market for their own manufactured goods. British policy was directed at keeping India economically dependent and politically quiet. Moreover, British racism, coupled with their apprehension at the great numerical superiority of the natives, led them to hold themselves aloof from the Indian population and often to subject individual Indians to slight but very real personal humiliations. It was not surprising that the Indians, particularly the educated class that the British themselves fostered, felt resentment at British rule. These educated Indians were so imbued with British culture as to make it difficult for them to consider using violence against their imperial masters. With the British unwilling to grant the Indians any real power and the Indians unwilling to fight for it, the situation appeared at an impasse until an Indian leader emerged to show his countrymen a way to drive out the British without violence.

Mohandas K. Gandhi (1869–1948), often called Mahatma ("Great Soul"), was born in the native state of Porbadar, in western India. His parents were Hindu, and his father and grandfather had served as prime ministers to the native prince of the region. It was decided that Gandhi should pursue law, and he was sent to London in 1888 for his legal studies. During his three years in an alien culture, he became more aware of his Indian roots and was led by his study of the *Bhagavad Gita* to a greater appreciation of the concept of selfless service. Having completed his law degree, he accepted a position in South Africa. Here he was made personally aware that, although Indians might be subjects of the same queen as whites, they possessed few of the rights of their fellow subjects. Gandhi became the leader and spokesman for the Indian community in South Africa and, from 1893 to 1914, he worked fearlessly and effectively to gain his countrymen rights and protection under the law. Influenced in part by the ideas of Leo Tolstoy, he developed the policy he called *satyagraha*, commonly translated as "passive resistance." Generally speaking, *satyagraha* meant that one should neither obey an unjust law nor cooperate in its enforcement, even at the cost of personal punishment. His application of that principle led to his imprisonment, but it also led the British government in South Africa to accord the Indian population there a somewhat greater respect.

News of Gandhi's efforts had reached India, and when he returned home in 1915, he found himself a popular hero and much sought-after by Indian political leaders. He undertook a year's travel about India to acquaint himself with local conditions and to begin to spread among the masses his philosophy of *satyagraha*. He took pains to identify himself with the Indian people in dress, speech, and way of life, and encouraged other Indian leaders to follow his lead. In this way, the Indian educated class began to be drawn away from its dependence on the British. He also actively courted the cooperation of Muslim leaders, who were apprehensive of being dominated by a Hindu majority in any all-India movement. By 1921, he felt sufficiently strong to call for a massive demonstration of *satyagraha*. All Indians were to cease buying foreign cloth, to picket foreign liquor stores, and to participate in a policy of noncooperation with the British government. If these policies were followed, Gandhi declared, India would achieve self-rule in a year.

These pronouncements caused a sensation throughout India, but it soon became clear that the mass of Indians were insufficiently prepared for the self-discipline required for nonviolent action. Sporadic violence broke out everywhere. After a particularly brutal incident in which a crowd beat to death and burned a number of policemen, Gandhi realized that he had misjudged the situation and cancelled the campaign of noncooperation. In March 1922, he was arrested on the charge of having written seditious newspaper articles. This selection is the answer he gave in court to this charge. Though he was sentenced to six years' imprisonment, he had rescued his moral ascendancy. By condemning the entire British imperial administration of India, he had placed himself above politicians with limited aims and expedient policies. He had established himself as the moral leader of the Indian independence movement.

Questions

1. According to Gandhi, how has British rule weakened India?

2. How just does Gandhi consider the law under which he is being tried?

3. How does Gandhi describe noncooperation?

4. According to Gandhi, what is the highest duty of the citizen?

STATEMENT IN THE GREAT TRIAL OF 1922

I owe it perhaps to the Indian public and to the public in England, to placate which this prosecution is mainly taken up, that I should explain why, from a staunch loyalist and co-operator, I have become an uncompromising disaffectionist and non-co-operator. To the Court, too, I should say why I plead guilty to the charge of promoting disaffection towards the Government established by law in India.

My public life began in 1893 in South Africa in troubled weather. My first contact with British authority in that country was not of a happy character. I discovered that as a man and an Indian I had no rights. More correctly, I discovered that I had no rights as a man because I was a Indian.

But I was not baffled. I thought that this treatment of Indians was an excrescence upon a system that was intrinsically and mainly good. I gave the Government my voluntary and hearty co-operation, criticizing it freely where I felt it was faulty, but never wishing its destruction. Consequently, when the existence of the Empire was threatened in 1899 by the Boer challenge, I offered my services to it, raised a volunteer ambulance corps and served at several actions that took place for the relief of Ladysmith. Similarly in 1906, at the time of the Zulu revolt, I raised a stretcher-bearer party and served till the end of the rebellion. On both these occasions I received medals and was even mentioned in despatches. For my work in South Africa I was given by Lord Hardinge a Kaiser-i-Hind Gold Medal. When the War broke out in 1914 between England and Germany, I raised a volunteer ambulance corps in London consisting of the then resident Indians in London, chiefly students. Its work was acknowledged by the authorities to be valuable. Lastly, in India, when a special appeal was made at the War Conference in Delhi in 1918 by Lord Chelmsford for recruits, I struggled at the cost of my health to raise a corps in Kheda and the response was being made when the hostilities ceased and orders were received that no more recruits were wanted. In all these efforts at service, I was actuated by the belief that it was possible by such services to gain a status of full equality in the Empire for my countrymen.

The first shock came in the shape of the Rowlatt Act, a law designed to rob the people of all real freedom. I felt called upon to lead an intensive agitation against it. Then followed the Punjab horrors beginning with the massacre at Jallianwala Bagh and culminating in crawling orders,[1] public floggings and other indescribable humiliations. I discovered, too, that the plighted word of the Prime Minister to the Mussalmans of India regarding the integrity of Turkey and the holy places of Islam was not likely to be fulfilled. But, in spite of the forebodings and the grave warnings of friends, at the Amritsar Congress in 1919, I fought for co-operation and working the Montagu-Chelmsford reforms, hoping that the Prime Minister would redeem his promise to the Indian Mussalmans, that

---

[1] An order that Indians were to crawl on their hands and knees in the presence of Europeans.

the Punjab wound would be healed and that the reforms, inadequate and unsatisfactory though they were, marked a new era of hope in the life of India.

But all that hope was shattered. The Khilafat promise was not to be redeemed. The Punjab crime was white-washed and most culprits went not only unpunished, but remained in service and some continued to draw pensions from the Indian revenue, and in some cases were even rewarded. I saw, too, that not only did the reforms not mark a change of heart, but they were only a method of further draining India of her wealth and of prolonging her servitude.

I came reluctantly to the conclusion that the British connection had made India more helpless than she ever was before, politically and economically. A disarmed India has no power of resistance against any aggressor if she wanted to engage in an armed conflict with him. So much is this the case that some of our best men consider that India must take generations before she can achieve the Dominion status. She has become so poor that she has little power of resisting famines. Before the British advent, India spun and wove in her millions of cottages just the supplement she needed for adding to her meagre agricultural resources. This cottage industry, so vital for India's existence, has been ruined by incredibly heartless and inhuman processes as described by English witnesses. Little do town-dwellers know how the semi-starved masses of India are slowly sinking to lifelessness. Little do they know that their miserable comfort represents the brokerage they get for the work they do for the foreign exploiter, that the profits and the brokerage are sucked from the masses. Little do they realize that the Government established by law in British India is carried on for this exploitation of the masses. No sophistry, no jugglery in figures can explain away the evidence that the skeletons in many villages present to the naked eye. I have no doubt whatsoever that both England and the town-dwellers of India will have to answer, if there is a God above, for this crime against humanity which is perhaps unequalled in history. The law itself in this country has been used to serve the foreign exploiter. My unbiassed examination of the Punjab Martial Law cases has led me to believe that at least ninety-five per cent of convictions were wholly bad. My experience of political cases in India leads one to the conclusion that in nine out of every ten cases the condemned men were totally innocent. Their crime consisted in the love of their country. In ninety-nine cases out of hundred, justice has been denied to Indians as against Europeans in the Courts of India. This is not an exaggerated picture. It is the experience of almost every Indian who has had anything to do with such cases. In my opinion, the administration of the law is thus prostituted consciously or unconsciously for the benefit of the exploiter.

The greatest misfortune is that Englishmen and their Indian associates in the administration of the country do not know that they are engaged in the crime I have attempted to describe. I am

Mahatma Gandhi.

satisfied that many English and Indian officials honestly believe that they are administering one of the best systems devised in the world and that India is making steady though slow progress. They do not know that a subtle but effective system of terrorism and an organized display of force on the one hand, and the deprivation of all powers of retaliation or self-defence on the other, have emasculated the people and induced in them the habit of simulation. This awful habit has added to the ignorance and the self-deception of the administrators. Section 124 A under which I am happily charged is perhaps the prince among the political sections of the Indian Penal Code designed to suppress the liberty of the citizen. Affection cannot be manufactured or regulated by law. If one has no affection for a person or system, one should be free to give the fullest expression to his disaffection, so long as he does not contemplate, promote or incite to violence. But the section under which Mr. Banker and I are charged is one under which mere promotion of disaffection is a crime. I have studied some of the cases tried under it, and I know that some of the most loved of India's patriots have been convicted under it. I consider it a privilege, therefore, to be charged under it. I have endeavoured to give in their briefest outline the reasons for my disaffection. I have no personal ill will against any single administrator, much less can I have any disaffection towards the King's person. But I hold it to be a virtue to be disaffected towards a Government which in its totality has done more harm to India than any previous system. India is less manly under the British rule than she ever was before. Holding such a belief, I consider it to be a sin to have affection for the system. And it has been a precious privilege for me to be able to write what I have in the various articles tendered in evidence against me.

In fact, I believe that I have rendered a service to India and England by showing in non-co-operation the way out of the unnatural state in which both are living. In my humble opinion, non-co-operation with evil is as much a duty as is co-operation with good. But, in the past, non-co-operation has been deliberately expressed in violence to the evil-doer. I am endeavouring to show to my countrymen that violent non-co-operation only multiplies evil and that, as evil can only be sustained by violence, withdrawal of support of evil requires complete abstention from violence. Non-violence implies voluntary submission to the penalty for non-co-operation with evil. I am here, therefore, to invite and submit cheerfully to the highest penalty that can be inflicted upon me for what in law is a deliberate crime and what appears to me to be the highest duty of a citizen. The only course open to you, the Judge, is either to resign your post and thus dissociate yourself from evil, if you feel that the law you are called upon to administer is an evil and that in reality I am innocent; or to inflict on me the severest penalty if you believe that the system and the law you are assisting to administer are good for the people of this country and that my activity is, therefore, injurious to the public weal.

Further Readings

Thomas G. F. Spear, *The Oxford History of Modern India* (Delhi: Oxford University Press, 1978), is a standard survey of recent Indian history, while Durga Das, *India from Curzon to Nehru and After* (New York: John Day Co., 1969), provides a political history of India from 1900 to 1969 written by an eminent Indian journalist. A richly illustrated social history of British India is provided by Geoffrey Moorhouse, *India Britannica* (New York: Harper and Row, 1983). Rudyard Kipling's novel *Kim* (many editions) is more than a rousing adventure, it is a celebration of the excitement and diversity of Indian life. Edward Morgan Forster, *A Passage to India* (many editions) is a novel that studies how strained the relations between individual British and Indians could become, and suggests some of the factors that turned many Indian intellectuals against the British.

There are numerous biographies of Gandhi. Louis Fischer, *The Life of Mahatma Gandhi* (New York: Harper, 1950), is an admiring account written shortly after Gandhi's death. Gerald Gould, *Gandhi: A Pictorial Biography* (New York: Newmarket Press, 1983), offers a wealth of illustrations. Gandhi was himself a prolific author. *An Autobiography: The Story of My Experiments with the Truth,* translated by Mahadev Desai (Boston: Beacon Press, 1957), was written over a period of years and is unusually intimate.

Among the various works on Gandhi's thought, William Borman, *Gandhi and Non-violence* (Albany, NY: State University of New York Press, 1986), and Martin B. Green, *The Origins of Non-violence: Tolstoy and Gandhi in Their Historical Settings* (University Park, PA: Pennsylvania State University Press, 1986), are of particular interest.

All Quiet on the Western Front

For almost a century, the European states attempted to avoid general conflict by maintaining a balance of power on the continent. The limited fighting that had occurred had been aimed at adjusting that balance. In 1870, Germany's victory in the Franco–Prussian war had disrupted that balance. The European powers sought to reestablish a secure system by concluding military alliances with each other. Far from restoring security, this expedient promoted disunity. By 1914, Europe consisted of two great power blocs: Germany and Austria-Hungary on the one hand, and France, England, and Russia on the other. Other states were either protected by one or the other of the alliances, or maintained a precarious neutrality. The major powers had each established a massive military machine capable of organizing millions of fully armed and equipped troops within a matter of days. What had been envisioned as a means of avoiding conflict had become a system for assuring that, if war were to come, it would be a major conflict.

On 28 June 1914, a young Serbian nationalist assassinated the Archduke Francis Ferdinand, heir to the throne of Austria-Hungary. Austria-Hungary sought assurances of assistance from Germany and began mobilizing its troops against Serbia. Germany was faced with the prospect of having to fight the Russians (protectors of Serbia) on the east and the French on the west, and had developed the plan of launching a massive attack upon France before French mobilization could be completed. Germany therefore declared war on Russia and France in early August, and attacked through neutral Belgium, thus forcing Britain to declare war on Germany. Eventually much of the

From Erich Maria Remarque, *All Quiet on the Western Front,* translated by A. W. Wheen (New York: Ballantine Books, 1984), pp. 91–111.

world was in a state of war. By September, Germany's sweeping attack on France had ground to a halt.

All of the combatants had been relatively sure of victory in a short time. Given the masses of men and material assembled, it had been unthinkable to them that the war could be a prolonged affair. And yet, it became so. The invention of barbed wire had made traditional battles of manoeuver impossible, and the development of the machine gun allowed one man to withstand the attack of hundreds. The balance of power was clearly in the hands of the defending forces, and yet wars cannot be won by defense. The contending generals thus continued hopeless infantry attacks even as their casualties mounted into the hundreds of thousands. Technological improvements, such as poison gas, aerial bombing, and armored attack vehicles were made on both sides, and largely tended to cancel each other out. Conditions in the trenches were unspeakable; the death rate so high that an individual's chance of survival for any length of time was small. Unable to gain victories, the opposing generals turned to attrition, each side accepting great losses in the hope of reducing the enemy by an even greater number. These tactics, too, largely cancelled each other out. Each side sustained tremendous casualties without gaining an advantage. One can only wonder why millions of men were willing, even eager, to expend themselves in such a fashion.

In 1917, the United States entered the war, and the manpower it supplied finally turned the balance in favor of the French and British. Their numbers reduced and their equipment worn by four years of war, the Germans began to retreat in the summer of 1918. On 11 November 1918, an armistice was declared. None of the opposing powers had achieved their war aims, because none had any clear purpose in entering the conflict in the first place. Ten million men and women had died in the fighting, and about twice that number had been maimed or wounded.

Patriotism had sustained them while the war was actually underway, but a somber mood settled on Europe when the cost of the conflict began to sink in. A number of combatants began to look back on their experiences and to question what had happened and to what purpose. In 1929, a book appeared that seemed to put into words what many veterans felt. *All Quiet on the Western Front* (*Im Westen nichts Neues*) was the product of a young German writer, Erich Maria Remarque (1898–1970), himself a wounded veteran of trench warfare. Its acceptance was immediate. A million copies were sold in Germany in one year and a quarter-million copies of its English translation in the first six weeks after publication, and an Academy Award Hollywood movie was completed within a year.

The hero of the story is young Paul Bäumer, one of a group of schoolboys led by their respected schoolmaster to volunteer for the army. Without much of a past, he is taken into a world in which there is not much of future. Neither he nor his fellows really know why they are fighting, except perhaps to protect each other. He visits home and finds that his war experiences are such that he can no longer respond to family, home town, or indeed anything other than his comrades and to the urgent reality of trying to stay alive. Returning to the front, he continues what he believes to be a losing fight. One by one, the war swallows up his comrades until he alone is left. He is finally killed on a spring day, and the high command reports "Nothing new on the Western Front."

Millions of readers who were in a position to know declared that *All Quiet on the Western Front* had finally explained what it had really been like. Not all agreed with that assessment, however, particularly in Germany. Many Germans were already preparing themselves for the resumption of the struggle and objected to the antiwar tone of the book. The Nazis, in particular, condemned Remarque for betraying the memory of the German soldiers and for corrupting the youth of the nation. He was forced to flee the country in 1931, and eventually became an American citizen. *All Quiet on the Western Front* was prominently included in the great Nazi book-burning in 1933, but this did not satisfy the revulsion the Nazis felt toward the work. In 1943, largely because she was Erich's sister, Elfriede Scholz was beheaded by a Nazi executioner.

Questions

1. What do Paul and his comrades do to try to withstand the effects of the barrage?

2. What factors have reduced the soldiers to acting almost automatically, without sensitivity and without fear?

3. What has separated Paul and his friends from their memories of childhood?

4. What sort of men have Paul and his friends become, and what has made them so?

ALL QUIET ON THE WESTERN FRONT

There are rumours of an offensive. We go up to the front two days earlier than usual. On the way we pass a shelled school-house. Stacked up against its longer side is a high double wall of yellow, unpolished, brand-new coffins. They still smell of resin, and pine, and the forest. There are at least a hundred.

"That's a good preparation for the offensive," says Müller astonished.

"They're for us," growls Detering.

"Don't talk rot," says Kat to him angrily.

"You be thankful if you get so much as a coffin," grins Tjaden, "they'll slip you a waterproof sheet for your old Aunt Sally of a carcase."

The others jest too, unpleasant jests, but what else can a man do?—The coffins are really for us. The organization surpasses itself in that kind of thing.

Ahead of us everything is shimmering. The first night we try to get our bearings. When it is fairly quiet we can hear the transports behind the enemy lines rolling ceaselessly until dawn. Kat says that they do not go back but are bringing up troops—troops, munitions, and guns.

The English artillery has been strengthened, that we can detect at once. There are at least four more batteries of nine-inch guns to the right of the farm, and behind the poplars they have put in trench-mortars. Besides these they have brought up a number of those little French beasts with instantaneous fuses.

We are now in low spirits. After we have been in the dug-outs two hours our own shells begin to fall in the trench. This is the third time in four weeks. If it were simply a mistake in aim no one would say anything, but the truth is that the barrels are worn out. The shots are often so uncertain that they land within our own lines. To-night two of our men were wounded by them.

The front is a cage in which we must await fearfully whatever may happen. We lie under the net-work of arching shells and live in a suspense of uncertainty. Over us Chance hovers. If a shot comes, we can duck, that is all; we neither know nor can determine where it will fall.

It is this Chance that makes us indifferent. A few months ago I was sitting in a dug-out playing skat;[1] after a while I stood up and went to visit some friends in another dug-out. On my return nothing more was to be seen of the first one, it had been blown to pieces by a direct hit. I went back to the second and arrived just in time to lend a hand digging it out. In the interval it had been buried.

It is just as much a matter of chance that I am still alive as that I might have been hit. In a bomb-proof dug-out I may be smashed to atoms and in the open may survive ten hours' bombardment unscathed. No soldier outlives a thousand chances. But every soldier believes in Chance and trusts his luck.

We must look out for our bread. The rats have become much more numerous lately because the trenches are no longer in good condition. Detering says it is a sure sign of a coming bombardment.

The rats here are particularly repulsive, they are so fat—the

---

[1] A card game.

kind we all call corpse-rats. They have shocking, evil, naked faces, and it is nauseating to see their long, nude tails.

They seem to be mighty hungry. Almost every man has had his bread gnawed. Kropp wrapped his in his waterproof sheet and put it under his head, but he cannot sleep because they run over his face to get at it. Detering meant to outwit them: he fastened a thin wire to the roof and suspended his bread from it. During the night when he switched on his pocket-torch he saw the wire swing to and fro. On the bread was riding a fat rat.

At last we put a stop to it. We cannot afford to throw the bread away, because then we should have nothing left to eat in the morning, so we carefully cut off the bits of bread that the animals have gnawed.

The slices we cut off are heaped together in the middle of the floor. Each man takes out his spade and lies down prepared to strike. Detering, Kropp, and Kat hold their pocket-torches ready.

After a few minutes we hear the first shuffling and tugging. It grows, now it is the sound of many little feet. Then the torches switch on and every man strikes at the heap, which scatters with a rush. The result is good. We toss the bits of rat over the parapet and again lie in wait.

Several times we repeat the process. At last the beasts get wise to it, or perhaps they have scented the blood. They return no more. Nevertheless, before morning the remainder of the bread on the floor has been carried off.

In the adjoining sector they attacked two large cats and a dog, bit them to death and devoured them.

Next day there was an issue of Edamer cheese. Each man gets almost a quarter of a cheese. In one way that is all to the good, for Edamer is tasty—but in another way it is vile, because the fat red balls have long been a sign of a bad time coming. Our forebodings increase as rum is served out. We drink it of course; but are not greatly comforted.

During the day we loaf about and make war on the rats. Ammunition and hand-grenades become more plentiful. We overhaul the bayonets—that is to say, the ones that have a saw on the blunt edge. If the fellows over there catch a man with one of those he's killed at sight. In the next sector some of our men were found whose noses were cut off and their eyes poked out with their own sawbayonets. Their mouths and noses were stuffed with sawdust so that they suffocated.

Some of the recruits have bayonets of this sort; we take them away and give them the ordinary kind.

But the bayonet has practically lost its importance. It is usually the fashion now to charge with bombs and spades only. The sharpened spade is a more handy and many-sided weapon; not only can it be used for jabbing a man under the chin, but it is much better for striking with because of its greater weight; and if one hits between the neck and shoulder it easily cleaves as far down as the chest. The bayonet frequently jams on the thrust and then a man has to kick hard on the other fellow's belly to pull it out again; and in the interval he may easily get one himself. And what's more the blade often gets broken off.

At night they send over gas. We expect the attack to follow and lie with our masks on, ready to tear them off as soon as the first shadow appears.

Dawn approaches without anything happening—only the everlasting, nerve-wracking roll behind the enemy lines, trains, trains, lorries, lorries; but what are they concentrating? Our artillery fires on it continually, but still it does not cease.

We have tired faces and avoid each other's eyes. "It will be like the Somme," says Kat gloomily. "There we were shelled steadily for seven days and nights." Kat has lost all his fun since we have been here, which is bad, for Kat is an old front-hog, and can smell what is coming. Only Tjaden seems pleased with the good rations and the rum; he thinks we might even go back to rest without anything happening at all.

It almost looks like it. Day after day passes. At night I squat in the listening-post. Above me the rockets and parachute-lights shoot up and float down again. I am cautious and tense, my heart thumps. My eyes turn again and again to the luminous dial of my watch; the hands will not budge. Sleep hangs on my eyelids, I work my toes in my boots in order to keep awake. Nothing happens till I am relieved;—only the everlasting rolling over there. Gradually we grow calmer and play skat and poker continually. Perhaps we will be lucky.

All day the sky is hung with observation balloons. There is a rumour that the enemy are going to put tanks over and use low-flying planes for the attack. But that interests us less than what we hear of the new flame-throwers.

We wake up in the middle of the night. The earth booms. Heavy fire is falling on us. We crouch into corners. We distinguish shells of every calibre.

Each man lays hold of his things and looks again every minute to reassure himself that they are still there. The dug-out heaves, the night roars and flashes. We look at each other in the momentary flashes of light, and with pale faces and pressed lips shake our heads.

Every man is aware of the heavy shells tearing down the parapet, rooting up the embankment and demolishing the upper layers of concrete. When a shell lands in the trench we note how the hollow, furious blast is like a blow from the paw of a raging beast of prey. Already by morning a few of the recruits are green and vomiting. They are too inexperienced.

Slowly the grey light trickles into the post and pales the flashes of the shells. Morning is come. The explosion of mines mingles with the gun-fire. That is the most dementing convulsion of all. The whole region where they go up becomes one grave.

The reliefs go out, the observers stagger in, covered with dirt, and trembling. One lies down in silence in the corner and eats, the other, an older man of the new draft, sobs; twice he has been flung over the parapet by the blast of the explosions without getting any more than shell-shock.

The recruits are eyeing him. We must watch them, these things are catching, already some lips begin to quiver. It is good that it is growing day-light; perhaps the attack will come before noon.

The bombardment does not diminish. It is falling in the rear too. As far as one can see spout fountains of mud and iron. A wide belt is being raked.

The attack does not come, but the bombardment continues. We are gradually benumbed. Hardly a man speaks. We cannot make ourselves understood.

Our trench is almost gone. At many places it is only eighteen inches high, it is broken by holes, and craters, and mountains of earth. A shell lands square in front of our post. At once it is dark. We are buried and must dig ourselves out. After an hour the entrance is clear again, and we are calmer because we have had something to do.

Our Company Commander scrambles in and reports that two dug-outs are gone. The recruits calm themselves when they see him. He says that an attempt will be made to bring up food this evening.

That sounds reassuring. No one had thought of it except Tjaden. Now the outside world seems to draw a little nearer: if food can be brought up, think the recruits, then it can't really be so bad.

We do not disabuse them; we know that food is as important as ammunition and only for that reason must be brought up.

But it miscarries. A second party goes out, and it also turns back. Finally Kat tries, and even he reappears without accomplishing anything. No one gets through, not even a fly is small enough to get through such a barrage.

We pull in our belts tighter and chew every mouthful three times as long. Still the food does not last out; we are damnably hungry. I take out a scrap of bread, eat the white and put the crust back in my knapsack; from time to time I nibble at it.

The night is unbearable. We cannot sleep, but stare ahead of us and doze. Tjaden regrets that we wasted the gnawed pieces of bread on the rats. We would gladly have them again to eat now. We are short of water, too, but not seriously yet.

Towards morning, while it is still dark, there is some excitement. Through the entrance rushes in a swarm of fleeing rats that try to storm the walls. Torches light up the confusion. Everyone yells and curses and slaughters. The madness and despair of many hours unloads itself in this outburst. Faces are distorted, arms strike out, the beasts scream; we just stop in time to avoid attacking one another.

The onslaught has exhausted us. We lie down to wait again. It is a marvel that our post has had no casualties so far. It is one of the less deep dug-outs.

A corporal creeps in; he has a loaf of bread with him. Three people have had the luck to get through during the night and bring some provisions. They say the bombardment extends undiminished as far as the artillery lines. It is a mystery where the enemy gets all his shells.

We wait and wait. By midday what I expected happens. One of the recruits has a fit. I have been watching him for a long time, grinding his teeth and opening and shutting his fists. These hunted, protruding eyes, we know them too well. During the last few hours he has had merely the appearance of calm. He had collapsed like a rotten tree.

Now he stands up, stealthily creeps across the floor, hesitates a moment and then glides towards the door. I intercept him and say: "Where are you going?"

"I'll be back in a minute," says he, and tries to push past me.

"Wait a bit, the shelling will stop soon."

He listens for a moment and his eyes become clear. Then again he has the glowering eyes of a mad dog, he is silent, he shoves me aside.

"One minute, lad," I say. Kat notices. Just as the recruit shakes me off Kat jumps in and we hold him.

Then he begins to rave: "Leave me alone, let me go out, I will go out!"

He won't listen to anything and hits out, his mouth is wet and pours out words, half choked, meaningless words. It is a case of claustrophobia, he feels as though he is suffocating here and wants to get out at any price. If we let him go he would run about everywhere regardless of cover. He is not the first.

Though he raves and his eyes roll, it can't be helped, we have to give him a hiding to bring him to his senses. We do it quickly and mercilessly, and at last he sits down quietly. The others have turned pale; let's hope it deters them. This bombardment is too much for the poor devils, they have been sent straight from a recruiting-depot into a barrage that is enough to turn an old soldier's hair grey.

After this affair the sticky, close atmosphere works more than ever on our nerves. We sit as if in our graves waiting only to be closed in.

Suddenly it howls and flashes terrifically, the dug-out cracks in all its joints under a direct hit, fortunately only a light one that the concrete blocks are able to withstand. It rings metallically, the walls reel, rifles, helmets, earth, mud, and dust fly everywhere. Sulphur fumes pour in.

If we were in one of those light dug-outs that they have been building lately instead of this deeper one, none of us would be alive.

But the effect is bad enough even so. The recruit starts to rave again and two others follow suit. One jumps up and rushes out, we have trouble with the other two. I start after the one who escapes and wonder whether to shoot him in the leg—then it shrieks again, I fling myself down and when I stand up the wall of the trench is plastered with smoking splinters, lumps of flesh, and bits of uniform. I scramble back.

The first recruit seems actually to have gone insane. He butts his head against the wall like a goat. We must try to-night to take him to the rear. Meanwhile we bind him, but in such a way that in case of attack he can be released at once.

Kat suggests a game of skat: it is easier when a man has something to do. But is no use, we listen for every explosion that comes close, miscount the tricks, and fail to follow suit. We have to give it up. We sit as though in a boiler that is being belaboured from without on all sides.

Night again. We are deadened by the strain—a deadly tension that scrapes along one's spine like a gapped knife. Our legs refuse to move, our hands tremble, our bodies are a thin skin stretched painfully over repressed madness, over an almost irresistible, bursting roar. We have neither flesh nor muscles any longer, we dare not look at one another for fear of some incalculable thing. So we shut our teeth—it will end—it will end—perhaps we will come through.

Suddenly the nearer explosions cease. The shelling continues but it has lifted and falls behind us, our trench is free. We seize the hand-grenades, pitch them out in front of the dug-out and jump after them. The bombardment has stopped and a heavy barrage now falls behind us. The attack has come.

No one would believe that in this howling waste there could still be men; but steel helmets now appear on all sides out of the trench, and fifty yards from us a machine-gun is already in position and barking.

The wire entanglements are torn to pieces. Yet they offer some obstacle. We see the storm-troops coming. Our artillery opens fire. Machine-guns rattle, rifles crack. The charge works its way across. Haie and Kropp begin with the hand-grenades. They throw as fast as they can, others pass them, the handles with the strings already pulled. Haie throws seventy-five yards, Kropp sixty, it has been measured, the distance is important. The enemy as they run cannot do much before they are within forty yards.

We recognize the smooth distorted faces, the helmets: they are

French. They have already suffered heavily when they reach the remnants of the barbed wire entanglements. A whole line has gone down before our machine-guns; then we have a lot of stoppages and they come nearer.

I see one of them, his face upturned, fall into a wire cradle.[2] His body collapses, his hands remain suspended as though he were praying. Then his body drops clean away and only his hands with the stumps of his arms, shot off, now hang in the wire.

The moment we are about to retreat three faces rise up from the ground in front of us. Under one of the helmets a dark pointed beard and two eyes that are fastened on me. I raise my hand, but I cannot throw into those strange eyes; for one mad moment the whole slaughter whirls like a circus round me, and these two eyes alone are motionless; then the head rises up, a hand, a movement, and my hand-grenade flies through the air and into him.

We make for the rear, pull wire cradles into the trench and leave bombs behind us with the strings pulled, which ensures us a fiery retreat. The machine-guns are already firing from the next position.

We have become wild beasts. We do not fight, we defend ourselves against annihilation. It is not against men that we fling our bombs, what do we know of men in this moment when Death is hunting us down—now, for the first time in three days we can see his face, now for the first time in three days we can oppose him; we feel a mad anger. No longer do we lie helpless, waiting on the scaffold, we can destroy and kill, to save ourselves, to save ourselves and to be revenged.

We crouch behind every corner, behind every barrier of barbed wire, and hurl heaps of explosives at the feet of the advancing enemy before we run. The blast of the hand-grenades impinges powerfully on our arms and legs; crouching like cats we run on, overwhelmed by this wave that bears us along, that fills us with ferocity, turns us into thugs, into murderers, into God only knows what devils; this wave that multiplies our strength with fear and madness and greed of life, seeking and fighting for nothing but our deliverance. If your own father came over with them you would not hesitate to fling a bomb at him.

The forward trenches have been abandoned. Are they still trenches? They are blown to pieces, annihilated—there are only broken bits of trenches, holes linked by cracks, nests of craters, that is all. But the enemy's casualties increase. They did not count on so much resistance.

It is nearly noon. The sun blazes hotly, the sweat stings in our eyes, we wipe it off on our sleeves and often blood with it. At last

---

[2] A battlefield obstacle made of barbed wire wound round a wooden framework.

we reach a trench that is in a somewhat better condition. It is manned and ready for the counter-attack, it receives us. Our guns open in full blast and cut off the enemy attack.

The lines behind us stop. They can advance no farther. The attack is crushed by our artillery. We watch. The fire lifts a hundred yards and we break forward. Beside me a lance-corporal has his head torn off. He runs a few steps more while the blood spouts from his neck like a fountain.

It does not come quite to hand-to-hand fighting; they are driven back. We arrive once again at our shattered trench and pass on beyond it.

Oh, this turning back again! We reach the shelter of the reserves and yearn to creep in and disappear;—but instead we must turn round and plunge again into the horror. If we were not automata at that moment we would continue lying there, exhausted, and without will. But we are swept forward again, powerless, madly savage and raging; we will kill, for they are still our mortal enemies, their rifles and bombs are aimed against us, and if we don't destroy them, they will destroy us.

The brown earth, the torn, blasted earth, with a greasy shine under the sun's rays; the earth is the background of this restless, gloomy world of automatons, our gasping is the scratching of a quill, our lips are dry, our heads are debauched with stupor—thus we stagger forward, and into our pierced and shattered souls bores the torturing image of the brown earth with the greasy sun and the convulsed and dead soldiers, who lie there—it can't be helped—who cry and clutch at our legs as we spring away over them.

We have lost all feeling for one another. We can hardly control ourselves when our glance lights on the form of some other man. We are insensible, dead men, who through some trick, some dreadful magic, are still able to run and to kill.

A young Frenchman lags behind, he is overtaken, he puts up his hands, in one he still holds his revolver—does he mean to shoot or to give himself!—a blow from a spade cleaves through his face. A second sees it and tries to run farther; a bayonet jabs into his back. He leaps in the air, his arms thrown wide, his mouth wide open, yelling; he staggers, in his back the bayonet quivers. A third throws away his rifle, cowers down with his hands before his eyes. He is left behind with a few other prisoners to carry off the wounded.

Suddenly in the pursuit we reach the enemy line.

We are so close on the heels of our retreating enemies that we reach it almost at the same time as they. In this way we suffer few casualties. A machine-gun barks, but is silenced with a bomb. Nevertheless, the couple of seconds has sufficed to give us five stomach wounds. With the butt of his rifle Kat smashes to pulp the face of one of the unwounded machine-gunners. We bayonet the others before they have time to get out their bombs. Then thirstily we drink the water they have for cooling the gun.

Everywhere wire-cutters are snapping, planks are thrown across the entanglements, we jump through the narrow entrances into the trenches. Haie strikes his spade into the neck of a gigantic Frenchman and throws the first hand-grenade; we duck behind a breastwork for a few seconds, then the straight bit of trench ahead of us is empty. The next throw whizzes obliquely over the corner and clears a passage; as we run past we toss handfuls down into the dug-outs, the earth shudders, it crashes, smokes and groans, we stumble over slippery lumps of flesh, over yielding bodies; I fall into an open belly on which lies a clean, new officer's cap.

The fight ceases. We lose touch with the enemy. We cannot stay here long but must retire under cover of our artillery to our own position. No sooner do we know this than we dive into the nearest dug-outs, and with the utmost haste seize on whatever provisions we can see, especially the tins of corned beef and butter, before we clear out.

We get back pretty well. There is no further attack by the enemy. We lie for an hour panting and resting before anyone speaks. We are so completely played out that in spite of our great hunger we do not think of the provisions. Then gradually we become something like men again.

The corned beef over there is famous along the whole front. Occasionally it has been the chief reason for a flying raid on our part, for our nourishment is generally very bad; we have a constant hunger.

We bagged five tins altogether. The fellows over there are well looked after; they fare magnificently, as against us, poor starving wretches, with our turnip jam; they can get all the meat they want. Haie has scored a thin loaf of white French bread, and stuck it in behind his belt like a spade. It is a bit bloody at one corner, but that can be cut off.

It is a good thing we have something decent to eat at last; we still have a use for all our strength. Enough to eat is just as valuable as a good dug-out; it can save our lives; that is the reason we are so greedy for it.

Tjaden has captured two water-bottles full of cognac. We pass them round.

The evening benediction begins. Night comes, out of the craters rise the mists. It looks as though the holes were full of ghostly secrets. The white vapour creeps painfully round before it ventures to steal away over the edge. Then long streaks stretch from crater to crater.

It is chilly. I am on sentry and stare into the darkness. My strength is exhausted as always after an attack, and so it is hard for me to be alone with my thoughts. They are not properly thoughts;

they are memories which in my weakness haunt me and strangely move me.

The parachute-lights soar upwards—and I see a picture, a summer evening, I am in the cathedral cloister and look at the tall rose trees that bloom in the middle of the little cloister garden where the monks lie buried. Around the walls are the stone carvings of the Stations of the Cross. No one is there. A great quietness rules in this blossoming quadrangle, the sun lies warm on the heavy grey stones, I place my hand upon them and feel the warmth. At the right-hand corner the green cathedral spire ascends into the pale blue sky of the evening. Between the glowing columns of the cloister is the cool darkness that only churches have, and I stand there and wonder whether, when I am twenty, I shall have experienced the bewildering emotions of love.

The image is alarmingly near; it touches me before it dissolves in the light of the next star-shell.

I lay hold of my rifle to see that it is in trim. The barrel is wet, I take it in my hands and rub off the moisture with my fingers.

Between the meadows behind our town there stands a line of old poplars by a stream. They were visible from a great distance, and although they grew on one bank only, we called them the poplar avenue. Even as children we had a great love for them, they drew us vaguely thither, we played truant the whole day by them and listened to their rustling. We sat beneath them on the bank of the stream and let our feet hang in the bright, swift waters. The pure fragrance of the water and the melody of the wind in the poplars held our fancies. We loved them dearly, and the image of those days still makes my heart pause in its beating.

It is strange that all the memories that come have these two qualities. They are always completely calm, that is predominant in them; and even if they are not really calm, they become so. They are soundless apparitions that speak to me, with looks and gestures silently, without any word—and it is the alarm of their silence that forces me to lay hold of my sleeve and my rifle lest I should abandon myself to the liberation and allurement in which my body would dilate and gently pass away into the still forces that lie behind these things.

They are quiet in this way, because quietness is so unattainable for us now. At the front there is no quietness and the curse of the front reaches so far that we never pass beyond it. Even in the remote depots and rest-areas the droning and the muffled noise of shelling is always in our ears. We are never so far off that it is no more to be heard. But these last few days it has been unbearable.

Their stillness is the reason why these memories of former times do not awaken desire so much as sorrow—a vast, inapprehensible melancholy. Once we had such desires—but they return not. They are past, they belong to another world that is gone from us. In the barracks they called forth a rebellious, wild craving for their return; for then they were still bound to us, we belonged to them and they to us, even though we were already absent from them. They appeared in the soldiers' songs which we sang as we marched between the glow of the dawn and the black silhouettes of the forests to drill on the moor, they were a powerful remembrance that was in us and came from us.

But here in the trenches they are completely lost to us. They arise no more; we are dead and they stand remote on the horizon, they are a mysterious reflection, an apparition, that haunts us, that we fear and love without hope. They are strong and our desire is strong—but they are unattainable, and we know it.

And even if these scenes of our youth were given back to us we would hardly know what to do. The tender, secret influence that passed from them into us could not rise again. We might be amongst them and move in them; we might remember and love them and be stirred by the sight of them. But it would be like gazing at the photograph of a dead comrade; those are his features, it is his face, and the days we spent together take on a mournful life in the memory; but the man himself it is not.

We could never regain the old intimacy with those scenes. It was not any recognition of their beauty and their significance that attracted us, but the communion, the feeling of a comradeship with the things and events of our existence, which cut us off and made the world of our parents a thing incomprehensible to us—for then we surrendered ourselves to events and were lost in them, and the least little thing was enough to carry us down the stream of eternity. Perhaps it was only the privilege of our youth, but as yet we recognized no limits and saw nowhere an end. We had that thrill of expectation in the blood which united us with the course of our days.

To-day we would pass through the scenes of our youth like travellers. We are burnt up by hard facts; like tradesmen we understand distinctions, and like butchers, necessities. We are no longer untroubled—we are indifferent. We might exist there; but should we really live there?

We are forlorn like children, and experienced like old men, we are crude and sorrowful and superficial—I believe we are lost.

Further Readings

There are numerous histories of the First World War. A. J. P. Taylor, *Illustrated History of the First World War* (London: Putnam, 1963), is a richly illustrated account written by an authority on modern European history. Barbara W. Tuchman, *The Proud Tower: A Portrait of Europe before the War, 1890–1914* (New York: Macmillan, 1966), is a brilliant evocation of the dynamic and confident European society that was transformed by the war. The same author portrays the onset of the war and the failure of the German onslaught against France in *The Guns of August* (New York: Macmillan, 1962). Leon Wolff, *In Flanders Fields: The 1917 Campaign* (New York: Viking Press,

1958), is a well-written account of one of the war's bloodiest campaigns. Some sense of how totally the warring nations committed themselves to the struggle is conveyed in John Williams, *The Other Battleground: The Homefronts: Britain, France, and Germany, 1914–1918* (London: Constable, 1972). There are numerous published journals and diaries of participants in the fighting, a good representative being Frank Hawkings, *From Ypres to Cambrai: The Diary of an Infantryman, 1914–1919,* edited by Arthur Taylor (Morley, UK: The Elmfield Press, 1974).

The standard biography of Remarque is Christine R. Barker and R. W. Last, *Erich Maria Remarque* (New York: Barnes and Noble, 1979). Two of Remarque's later novels deal with the attempts of young men 88 adjust to life after the war: *The Road Back*, translated by A. W. Wheen (Boston, MA: Little, Brown and Co., 1931), and *Three Comrades*, translated by A. W. Wheen (Boston, MA: Little, Brown and Co., 1937).

The movie version of the book, *All Quiet on the Western Front* (1930: Universal, black and white), is generally considered the best movie made on the war. Three silent films contain portrayals of trench life and warfare prepared by men who had participated in the conflict and are well worth seeing: *The Big Parade* (1925: MGM, black and white), *What Price Glory?* (1926: Fox, black and white), and *Wings* (1927: Paramount, black and white).

Brave New World

The First World War (1914–1918) and its aftermath had a deep impact upon European ideals and attitudes, an impact that was spread by European artists and writers throughout the Western world. The assured and confident society of prewar Europe had been swept away by the war. Millions of men went to the fighting, and the death toll among them represented the greatest mortality among Europeans since the Black Death of the fourteenth century. Hundreds of thousands returned home maimed and crippled, and even among the untouched the emotional scars ran deep. Nor were the combatants the only sufferers. Families had sacrificed for the war effort, had suffered privations, and there were few who had not lost loved ones in the struggle. There were mixed emotions among those who returned home to begin to reconstruct their thoroughly disrupted lives.

In England, the 1920s were a frenetic and pleasure-seeking era. Some regarded the frivolous temper of the times as a reaction to the bleak and harrowing war years, but the general relaxation of social conventions and delight in excess betrayed a deeper social malaise. Among the upper classes and intellectuals, such pursuits as sexual promiscuity, cocaine addiction, wild parties, and generally outrageous conduct were something more than simple self-indulgence. There seemed to be a widespread contempt for tradition and convention among the younger generation. To a certain extent, tradition represented for them the generation who had led the nation into war with such high hopes and had been unable to extricate it without appalling losses. As the patriotic fervor of the war years waned, and people began to ask themselves what had actually been gained, this feeling of alienation even increased.

Among some intellectuals, however, the contempt for tradition was simply a manifestation of a rejection of belief in historical con-

From Aldous Huxley, *Brave New World* (New York: Harper and Row, 1969), pp. 134–163.

tinuity. The prewar generation, imbued with the evolutionary ideas of Darwin, had been confident that history demonstrated the steady progress of mankind and that there was no reason to believe that this progress would not continue into the foreseeable future. The belief of the younger generation had been severely shaken by the experience of the war. For them, progress that could lead to such horrors and waste was no progress at all. The pace of technological development had increased rapidly in response to war needs, but what had been developed were more effective ways of killing. It was clear to many that technological progress had had little or no effect on the the moral and ethical character of humankind.

One of the best-known proponents of the doctrine of scientific progress was the popular author H. G. Wells, whose optimistic *Outline of History*, published in 1920, had implied that human progress would proceed forever. In the light of the events of the immediately preceding years, many failed to share this confident view and doubted that history was any longer a valid guide to an uncertain future. A number of writers produced works best termed "anti-utopias," which portrayed material progress leading, not to an ideal society, but to repelling consequences. One of the most trenchant and popular of this genre was Aldous Huxley's *Brave New World*, published in 1932.

Aldous Huxley (1894–1963) was the youngest son of a talented and well-educated family devoted to literature and education. Educated at Eton and Oxford, the brilliant young Huxley began his career in teaching and then moved into literary journalism. Comfortable among the upper classes and intellectuals of the day, by 1931 he had already established his reputation as a witty and perceptive novelist of the contemporary scene. Beginning with the idea of writing a parody of one of Well's utopian works, in six months he had created *Brave New World*, a novel which he said had taken on a life of its own.

Brave New World opens in the year A.F. (After Ford) 600. Human beings are now conceived in test tubes and nurtured in bottles, all with full quality control. Genetic engineering has created several distinct types, from the Alphas, who perform administrative and managerial functions, to the semimoronic Epsilons, who are common laborers. Through psychological conditioning, each group is made perfectly happy with its lot. Though sexual relations are entirely promiscuous, contraception ensures that natural birth does not occur. For the bored, there is *soma*, a super cocaine, with no side- or aftereffects. Everything is managed, and managed well. There is no war, want, or disease. A young man, John, called the Savage, is found on a Indian reservation. John is the result of an accident by a lady tourist some years earlier who had become lost on the reservation and had given birth to him. Reared on Shakespeare and Indian spirituality, John cannot adjust to this perfect society. He is attracted by its sensual delights, but repelled by its lack of aspiration, individual integrity, and any moral sense. He tries to live as a recluse, but becomes instead a tourist attraction. After being swept into a sadomasochistic orgy by curious visitors, he realizes that there is no place for him in the society and takes his own life.

Brave New World is in many ways a biting satire on upper-class English life in the Roaring 20s. It is a world in which young people enjoy their drugs, sex, travels, and partying without inhibition or fear of the future. It is also a world in which there is really nothing else to do. Its inhabitants are shallow, thoughtless, and self-absorbed, and the reader is left to wonder whether such people are capable of an emotion such as real happiness or of a thought worth recording.

The work has a message, however, that transcends its immediate social context. There is no reason to assume that moral perfection will necessarily accompany material progress. Quite the reverse, material progress that caters to bodily comfort and panders to sensual appetites erodes spiritual and intellectual aspirations and leaves the control of human affairs to an ambitious few. The question is whether the management techniques of the perfect industrial society will reduce its members to a least common denominator, creatures lacking any real sense of what it means to be a human being. In *Brave New World*, a gloomy Huxley answers that it will.

Questions

1. Why does the Savage become enraged at the death of his mother?

2. What role do the constant allusions to Shakespeare play in the selection?

3. Why has the society of *Brave New World* abandoned science?

4. Why has it abandoned religion?

BRAVE NEW WORLD

The Park Lane Hospital for the Dying was a sixty-story tower of primrose tiles. As the Savage stepped out of his taxicopter a convoy of gaily-coloured aerial hearses rose whirring from the roof and darted away across the Park, westwards, bound for the Slough Crematorium. At the lift gates the presiding porter gave him the information he required, and he dropped down to Ward 81 (a Galloping Senility ward, the porter explained) on the seventeenth floor.

It was a large room bright with sunshine and yellow paint, and containing twenty beds, all occupied. Linda[1] was dying in com-

---
[1] The Savage's mother.

pany—in company and with all the modern conveniences. The air was continuously alive with gay synthetic melodies. At the foot of every bed, confronting its moribund occupant, was a television box. Television was left on, a running tap, from morning till night. Every quarter of an hour the prevailing perfume of the room was automatically changed. "We try," explained the nurse, who had taken charge of the Savage at the door, "we try to create a thoroughly pleasant atmosphere here—something between a first-class hotel and a feely-palace, if you take my meaning."

"Where is she?" asked the Savage, ignoring these polite explanations.

The nurse was offended. "You *are* in a hurry," she said.

"Is there any hope?" he asked.

"You mean, of her not dying?" (He nodded.) "No, of course there isn't. When somebody's sent here, there's no . . ." Startled by the expression of distress on his pale face, she suddenly broke off. "Why, whatever is the matter?" she asked. She was not accustomed to this kind of thing in visitors. (Not that there were many visitors anyhow: or any reason why there should be many visitors.) "You're not feeling ill, are you?"

He shook his head. "She's my mother," he said in a scarcely audible voice.

The nurse glanced at him with startled, horrified eyes; then quickly looked away. From throat to temple she was all one hot blush.

"Take me to her," said the Savage, making an effort to speak in an ordinary tone.

Still blushing, she led the way down the ward. Faces still fresh and unwithered (for senility galloped so hard that it had no time to age the cheeks—only the heart and brain) turned as they passed. Their progress was followed by the blank, incurious eyes of second infancy. The Savage shuddered as he looked.

Linda was lying in the last of the long row of beds, next to the wall. Propped up on pillows, she was watching the Semi-finals of the South American Reimann-Surface Tennis Championship, which were being played in silent and diminished reproduction on the screen of the television box at the foot of the bed. Hither and thither across their square of illuminated glass the little figures noiselessly darted, like fish in an aquarium—the silent but agitated inhabitants of another world.

Linda looked on, vaguely and uncomprehendingly smiling. Her pale, bloated face wore an expression of imbecile happiness. Every now and then her eyelids closed, and for a few seconds she seemed to be dozing. Then with a little start she would wake up again—wake up to the aquarium antics of the Tennis Champions, to the Super-Vox-Wurlitzeriana rendering of "Hug me till you drug me, honey," to the warm draught of verbena that came blowing through the ventilator above her head—would wake to these things, or rather to a dream of which these things, transformed and embellished by the *soma* in her blood, were the marvellous constituents, and smile once more her broken and discoloured smile of infantile contentment.

"Well, I must go," said the nurse. "I've got my batch of children coming. Besides, there's Number 3." She pointed up the ward. "Might go off any minute now. Well, make yourself comfortable." She walked briskly away.

The Savage sat down beside the bed.

"Linda," he whispered, taking her hand.

At the sound of her name, she turned. Her vague eyes brightened with recognition. She squeezed his hand, she smiled, her lips moved, then quite suddenly her head fell forward. She was asleep. He sat watching her—seeking through the tired flesh, seeking and finding that young, bright face which had stooped over his childhood in Malpais, remembering (and he closed his eyes) her voice, her movements, all the events of their life together. "Streptocock-Gee to Banbury T . . ." How beautiful her singing had been! And those childish rhymes, how magically strange and mysterious!

> *A, B, C, vitamin D:*
> *The fat's in the liver, the cod's in the sea.*

He felt the hot tears welling up behind his eyelids as he recalled the words and Linda's voice as she repeated them. And then the reading lessons: The tot is in the pot, the cat is on the mat; and the Elementary Instructions for Beta Workers in the Embryo Store. And long evenings by the fire or, in summertime, on the roof of the little house, when she told him those stories about the Other Place, outside the Reservation: that beautiful, beautiful Other Place, whose memory, as of a heaven, a paradise of goodness and loveliness, he still kept whole and intact, undefiled by contact with the reality of this real London, these actual civilized men and women.

A sudden noise of shrill voices made him open his eyes and, after hastily brushing away the tears, look round. What seemed an interminable stream of identical eight-year-old male twins was pouring into the room. Twin after twin, twin after twin, they came—a nightmare. Their faces, their repeated face—for there was only one between the lot of them—puggishly stared, all nostrils and pale goggling eyes. Their uniform was khaki. All their mouths hung open. Squealing and chattering they entered. In a moment, it seemed, the ward was maggoty with them. They swarmed between the beds, clambered over, crawled under, peeped into the television boxes, made faces at the patients.

Linda astonished and rather alarmed them. A group stood clustered at the foot of her bed, staring with the frightened and stupid curiosity of animals suddenly confronted by the unknown.

"Oh, look, look!" They spoke in low, scared voices. "Whatever is the matter with her? Why is she so fat?"

They had never seen a face like hers before—had never seen a face that was not youthful and taut-skinned, a body that had ceased to be slim and upright. All these moribund sexagenarians had the appearance of childish girls. At forty-four, Linda seemed, by contrast, a monster of flaccid and distorted senility.

"Isn't she awful?" came the whispered comments. "Look at her teeth!"

Suddenly from under the bed a pug-faced twin popped up between John's chair and the wall, and began peering into Linda's sleeping face.

"I say . . ." he began; but the sentence ended prematurely in a squeal. The Savage had seized him by the collar, lifted him clear over the chair and, with a smart box on the ears, sent him howling away.

His yells brought the Head Nurse hurrying to the rescue.

"What have you been doing to him?" she demanded fiercely. "I won't have you striking the children."

"Well then, keep them away from this bed." The Savage's voice was trembling with indignation. "What are these filthy little brats doing here at all? It's disgraceful!"

"Disgraceful? But what do you mean? They're being death-conditioned. And I tell you," she warned him truculently, "if I have any more of your interference with their conditioning, I'll send for the porters and have you thrown out."

The Savage rose to his feet and took a couple of steps towards her. His movements and the expression on his face were so menacing that the nurse fell back in terror. With a great effort he checked himself and, without speaking, turned away and sat down again by the bed.

Reassured, but with a dignity that was a trifle shrill and uncertain, "I've warned you," said the nurse, "so mind." Still, she led the too inquisitive twins away and made them join in the game of hunt-the-zipper, which had been organized by one of her colleagues at the other end of the room.

"Run along now and have your cup of caffeine solution, dear," she said to the other nurse. The exercise of authority restored her confidence, made her feel better. "Now children!" she called.

Linda had stirred uneasily, had opened her eyes for a moment, looked vaguely around, and then once more dropped off to sleep. Sitting beside her, the Savage tried hard to recapture his mood of a few minutes before. "A, B, C, vitamin D," he repeated to himself, as though the words were a spell that would restore the dead past to life. But the spell was ineffective. Obstinately the beautiful memories refused to rise; there was only a hateful resurrection of jealousies and uglinesses and miseries. Popé with the blood trickling

Aldous Huxley.

down from his cut shoulder; and Linda hideously asleep, and the flies buzzing round the spilt *mescal* on the floor beside the bed; and the boys calling those names as she passed. . . . Ah, no, no! He shut his eyes, he shook his head in strenuous denial of these memories. "A, B, C, vitamin D . . ." He tried to think of those times when he sat on her knees and she put her arms about him and sang, over and over again, rocking him, rocking him to sleep. "A, B, C, vitamin D, vitamin D, vitamin D . . ."

The Super-Vox-Wurlitzeriana had risen to a sobbing crescendo; and suddenly the verbena gave place, in the scent-circulating system, to an intense patchouli. Linda stirred, woke up, stared for a few seconds bewilderly at the Semi-finalists, then, lifting her face, sniffed once or twice at the newly perfumed air and suddenly smiled—a smile of childish ectasy.

"Popé!" she murmured, and closed her eyes. "Oh, I do so like it, I do . . ." She sighed and let herself sink back into the pillows.

"But, Linda!" The Savage spoke imploringly, "Don't you know me?" He had tried so hard, had done his very best; why wouldn't she allow him to forget? He squeezed her limp hand almost with violence, as though he would force her to come back from this dream of ignoble pleasures, from these base and hateful memories—back into the present, back into reality: the appalling present, the awful reality—but sublime, but significant, but desperately important precisely because of the imminence of that which made them so fearful. "Don't you know me, Linda?"

He felt the faint answering pressure of her hand. The tears started into his eyes. He bent over her and kissed her.

Her lips moved. "Popé!" she whispered again, and it was as though he had had a pailful of ordure thrown in his face.

Anger suddenly boiled up in him. Balked for the second time, the passion of his grief had found another outlet, was transformed into a passion of agonized rage.

"But I'm John!" he shouted. "I'm John!" And in his furious misery he actually caught her by the shoulder and shook her.

Linda's eyes fluttered open; she saw him, knew him—"John!"—but situated the real face, the real and violent hands, in an imaginary world—among the inward and private equivalents of patchouli and the Super-Wurlitzer, among the transfigured memories and the strangely transposed sensations that constituted the universe of her dream. She knew him for John, her son, but fancied him an intruder into that paradisal Malpais where she had been spending her *soma*-holiday with Popé. He was angry because she liked Popé, he was shaking her because Popé was there in the bed—as though there were something wrong, as though all civilized people didn't do the same. "Every one belongs to every . . ." Her voice suddenly died into an almost inaudible breathless croaking. Her mouth fell open: she made a desperate effort to fill her lungs with air. But it was as though she had forgotten how to breathe.

She tried to cry out—but no sound came; only the terror of her staring eyes revealed what she was suffering. Her hands went to her throat, then clawed at the air—the air she could no longer breathe, the air that, for her, had ceased to exist.

The Savage was on his feet, bent over her. "What is it, Linda? What is it?" His voice was imploring; it was as though he was begging to be reassured.

The look she gave him was charged with an unspeakable terror—with terror and, it seemed to him, reproach. She tried to raise herself in bed, but fell back on to the pillows. Her face was horribly distorted, her lips blue.

The Savage turned and ran up the ward.

"Quick, quick!" he shouted. "Quick!"

Standing in the centre of a ring of zipper-hunting twins, the Head Nurse looked round. The first moment's astonishment gave place almost instantly to disapproval. "Don't shout! Think of the little ones," she said, frowning. "You might decondition . . . But what are you doing?" He had broken through the ring. "Be careful!" A child was yelling.

"Quick, quick!" He caught her by the sleeve, dragged her after him. "Quick! Something's happened. I've killed her."

By the time they were back at the end of the ward Linda was dead.

The Savage stood for a moment in frozen silence, then fell on his knees beside the bed and, covering his face with his hands, sobbed uncontrollably.

The nurse stood irresolute, looking now at the kneeling figure by the bed (the scandalous exhibition!) and now (poor children!) at the twins who had stopped their hunting of the zipper and were staring from the other end of the ward, staring with all their eyes and nostrils at the shocking scene that was being enacted round Bed 20. Should she speak to him? try to bring him back to a sense of decency? remind him of where he was? of what fatal mischief he might do to these poor innocents? Undoing all their wholesome death-conditioning with this disgusting outcry—as thought death were something terrible, as though any one mattered as much as all that! It might give them the most disastrous ideas about the subject, might upset them into reacting in the entirely wrong, the utterly anti-social way.

She stepped forward, she touched him on the shoulder. "Can't you behave?" she said in a low, angry voice. But, looking around, she saw that half a dozen twins were already on their feet and advancing down the ward. The circle was distintegrating. In another moment . . . No, the risk was too great; the whole Group might be put back six or seven months in its conditioning. She hurried back towards her menaced charges.

"Now, who wants a chocolate éclair?" she asked in a loud, cheerful tone.

"Me!" yelled the entire Bokanovsky Group in chorus. Bed 20 was completely forgotten.

"Oh, God, God, God . . ." the Savage kept repeating to himself. In the chaos of grief and remorse that filled his mind it was the one articulate word. "God!" he whispered it aloud. "God . . ."

"Whatever *is* he saying?" said a voice, very near, distinct and shrill through the warblings of the Super-Wurlitzer.

The Savage violently started and, uncovering his face, looked round. Five khaki twins, each with the stump of a long éclair in his right hand, and their identical faces variously smeared with liquid chocolate, were standing in a row, puggily goggling at him.

They met his eyes and simultaneously grinned. One of them pointed with his éclair butt.

"Is she dead?" he asked.

The Savage stared at them for a moment in silence. Then in silence he rose to his feet, in silence slowly walked towards the door.

"Is she dead?" repeated the inquisitive twin trotting at his side.

The Savage looked down at him and still without speaking pushed him away. The twin fell on the floor and at once began to howl. The Savage did not even look round.

The menial staff of the Park Lane Hospital for the Dying consisted of one hundred and sixty-two Deltas divided into two Bokanovsky Groups of eighty-four red-headed female and seventy-eight dark dolychocephalic male twins, respectively. At six, when their working day was over, the two Groups assembled in the vestibule of the Hospital and were served by the Deputy Sub-Bursar with their *soma* ration.

From the lift the Savage stepped out into the midst of them. But his mind was elsewhere—with death, with his grief, and his remorse; mechanically, without consciousness of what he was doing, he began to shoulder his way through the crowd.

"Who are you pushing? Where do you think you're going?"

High, low, from a multitude of separate throats, only two voices squeaked or growled. Repeated indefinitely, as though by a train of mirrors, two faces, one a hairless and freckled moon haloed in orange, the other a thin, beaked bird-mask, stubbly with two days' beard, turned angrily towards him. Their words and, in his ribs, the sharp nudging of elbows, broke through his unawareness. He woke once more to external reality, looked round him, knew what he saw—knew it, with a sinking sense of horror and disgust, for the recurrent delirium of his days and nights, the nightmare of swarming indistinguishable sameness. Twins, twins. . . . Like maggots they had swarmed defilingly over the mystery of Linda's death. Maggots again, but larger, full grown, they now crawled across his grief and his repentance. He halted and, with bewildered and horrified eyes, stared round him at the khaki mob, in the midst of which, overtopping it by a full head, he stood. "How many goodly creatures are there here!" The singing words mocked him derisively. "How beauteous mankind is! O brave new world . . ."

"*Soma* distribution!" shouted a loud voice. "In good order, please. Hurry up there."

A door had been opened, a table and chair carried into the vestibule. The voice was that of a jaunty young Alpha, who had entered carrying a black iron cash-box. A murmur of satisfaction went up from the expectant twins. They forgot all about the Savage. Their attention was now focused on the black cash-box, which the young man had placed on the table, and was now in process of unlocking. The lid was lifted.

"Oo-oh!" said all the hundred and sixty-two simultaneously, as though they were looking at fireworks.

The young man took out a handful of tiny pill-boxes. "Now," he said peremptorily, "step forward, please. One at a time, and no shoving."

One at a time, with no shoving, the twins stepped forward. First two males, then a female, then another male, then three females, then . . .

The Savage stood looking on. "O brave new world, O brave new world . . ." In his mind the singing words seemed to change their tone. They had mocked him through his misery and remorse, mocked him with how hideous a note of cynical derision! Fiendishly laughing, they had insisted on the low squalor, the nauseous ugliness of the nightmare. Now, suddenly, they trumpeted a call to arms. "O brave new world!" Miranda was proclaiming the possibility of loveliness, the possibility of transforming even the nightmare into something fine and noble. "O brave new world!" It was a challenge, a command.

"No shoving there now!" shouted the Deputy Sub-Bursar in a fury. He slammed down the lid of his cash-box. "I shall stop the distribution unless I have good behaviour."

The Deltas muttered, jostled one another a little, and then were still. The threat had been effective. Deprivation of *soma*—appalling thought!

"That's better," said the young man, and reopened his cash-box.

Linda had been a slave, Linda had died; others should live in freedom, and the world be made beautiful. A reparation, a duty. And suddenly it was luminously clear to the Savage what he must do; it was as though a shutter had been opened, a curtain drawn back.

"Now," said the Deputy Sub-Bursar.

Another khaki female stepped forward.

"Stop!" called the Savage in a loud and ringing voice. "Stop!"

He pushed his way to the table; the Deltas stared at him with astonishment.

"Ford!" said the Deputy Sub-Bursar, below his breath. "It's the Savage." He felt scared.

"Listen, I beg of you," cried the Savage earnestly. "Lend me your ears . . ." He had never spoken in public before, and found it very difficult to express what he wanted to say. "Don't take that horrible stuff. It's poison, it's poison."

"I say, Mr. Savage," said the Deputy Sub-Bursar, smiling propitiatingly. "Would you mind letting me . . ."

"Poison to soul as well as body."

"Yes, but let me get on with my distribution, won't you? There's a good fellow." With the cautious tenderness of one who strokes a notoriously vicious animal, he patted the Savage's arm. "Just let me . . ."

"Never!" cried the Savage.

"But look here, old man . . ."

"Throw it all away, that horrible poison."

The words "Throw it all away" pierced through the enfolding layers of incomprehension to the quick of the Delta's consciousness. An angry murmur went up from the crowd.

"I come to bring you freedom," said the Savage, turning back towards the twins. "I come . . ."

The Deputy Sub-Bursar heard no more; he had slipped out of the vestibule and was looking up a number in the telephone book.

"Not in his own rooms," Bernard summed up. "Not in mine, not in yours. Not at the Aphroditæum; not at the Centre or the College. Where can he have got to?"

Helmholtz shrugged his shoulders. They had come back from their work expecting to find the Savage waiting for them at one or other of the usual meeting-places, and there was no sign of the fellow. Which was annoying, as they had meant to nip across to Biarritz in Helmholtz's four-seater sporticopter. They'd be late for dinner if he didn't come soon.

"We'll give him five more minutes, said Helmholtz. "If he doesn't turn up by then we'll . . .

The ringing of the telephone bell interrupted him. He picked up the receiver. "Hullo. Speaking." Then, after a long interval of listening, "Ford in Flivver!" he swore. "I'll come at once."

"What is it?" Bernard asked.

"A fellow I know at the Park Lane Hospital," said Helmholtz. "The Savage is there. Seems to have gone mad. Anyhow, it's urgent. Will you come with me?"

Together they hurried along the corridor to the lifts.

"But do you like being slaves?" the Savage was saying as they entered the Hospital. His face was flushed, his eyes bright with ardour and indignation. "Do you like being babies? Yes, babies. Mewling and puking," he added, exasperated by their bestial stupidity into throwing insults at those he had come to save. The insults bounced off their carapace of thick stupidity; they stared at him with a blank expression of dull and sullen resentment in their eyes. "Yes, puking!" he fairly shouted. Grief and remorse, compassion and duty—all were forgotten now and, as it were, absorbed into an intense overpowering hatred of these less than human monsters. "Don't you want to be free and men? Don't you even understand what manhood and freedom are?" Rage was making him fluent; the words came easily, in a rush. "Don't you?" he repeated, but got no answer to his question. "Very well then," he went on grimly. "I'll teach you; I'll *make* you be free whether you want to or not." And pushing open a window that looked on to the inner court of the Hospital, he began to throw the little pill-boxes of *soma* tablets in handfuls out into the area.

For a moment the khaki mob was silent, petrified, at the spectacle of this wanton sacrilege, with amazement and horror.

"He's mad," whispered Bernard, staring with wide open eyes. "They'll kill him. They'll . . ." A great shout suddenly went up from the mob; a wave of movement drove it menacingly towards the Savage. "Ford help him!" said Bernard, and averted his eyes.

"Ford helps those who help themselves." And with a laugh, actually a laugh of exultation, Helmholtz Watson pushed his way through the crowd.

"Free, free!" the Savage shouted, and with one hand continued to throw the *soma* into the area while, with the other, he punched the indistinguishable faces of his assailants. "Free!" And suddenly there was Helmholtz at his side—"Good old Helmholtz!"—also punching—"Men at last!"—and in the interval also throwing the poison out by handfuls through the open window. "Yes, men! men!" and there was no more poison left. He picked up the cash-box and showed them its black emptiness. "You're free!"

Howling, the Deltas charged with a redoubled fury.

Hesitant on the fringes of the battle. "They're done for," said Bernard and, urged by a sudden impulse, ran forward to help them; then thought better of it and halted; then, ashamed, stepped forward again; then again thought better of it, and was standing in an agony of humiliated indecision—thinking that *they* might be killed if he didn't help them, and that *he* might be killed if he did—when (Ford be praised!), goggle-eyed and swine-snouted in their gas-masks, in ran the police.

Bernard dashed to meet them. He waved his arms; and it was action, he was doing something. He shouted "Help!" several times, more and more loudly so as to give himself the illusion of helping. "Help! *Help*! Help!"

The policemen pushed him out of the way and got on with their work. Three men with spraying machines buckled to their shoulders pumped thick clouds of *soma* vapour into the air. Two more were busy round the portable Synthetic Music Box. Carrying water pistols charged with a powerful anæsthetic, four others had pushed their way into the crowd and were methodically laying out, squirt by squirt, the more ferocious of the fighters.

"Quick, quick!" yelled Bernard. "They'll be killed if you don't hurry. They'll . . . Oh!" Annoyed by his chatter, one of the policemen had given him a shot from his water pistol. Bernard stood for a second or two wambling unsteadily on legs that seemed to have lost their bones, their tendons, their muscles, to have become mere sticks of jelly, and at last not even jelly—water: he tumbled in a heap on the floor.

Suddenly, from out of the Synthetic Music Box a Voice began to speak. The Voice of Reason, the voice of Good Feeling. The sound-track roll was unwinding itself in Synthetic Anti-Riot Speech Number Two (Medium Strength). Straight from the depths of a non-existent heart, "My friends, my friends!" said the Voice so pathetically, with a note of such infinitely tender reproach that, behind their gas masks, even the policemen's eyes were momentarily dimmed with tears, "what is the meaning of this? Why aren't you all being happy and good together? Happy and good," the Voice repeated. "At peace, at peace." It trembled, sank into a whisper and momentarily expired. "Oh, I do want you to be happy," it began, with a yearning earnestness. "I do so want you to be good! Please, please be good and . . ."

Two minutes later the Voice and the *soma* vapour had produced their effect. In tears, the Deltas were kissing and hugging one another—half a dozen twins at a time in a comprehensive embrace. Even Helmholtz and the Savage were almost crying. A fresh supply of pill-boxes was brought in from the Bursary; a new distribution was hastily made and, to the sound of the Voice's richly affectionate, baritone valedictions, the twins dispersed, blubbering as though their hearts would break. "Good-bye, my dearest, dearest friends, Ford keep you! Good-bye, my dearest, dearest friends, Ford keep you. Good-bye my dearest, dearest . . ."

When the last of the Deltas had gone the policeman switched off the current. The angelic Voice fell silent.

"Will you come quietly?" asked the Sergeant, "or must we anæsthetize?" He pointed his water pistol menacingly.

"Oh, we'll come quietly," the Savage answered, dabbing alternately a cut lip, a scratched neck, and a bitten left hand.

Still keeping his handkerchief to his bleeding nose Helmholtz nodded in confirmation.

Awake and having recovered the use of his legs, Bernard had chosen this moment to move as inconspicuously as he could towards the door.

"Hi, you there," called the Sergeant, and a swine-masked policeman hurried across the room and laid a hand on the young man's shoulder.

Bernard turned with an expression of indignant innocence.

Escaping? He hadn't dreamed of such a thing. "Though what on earth you want *me* for," he said to the Sergeant, "I really can't imagine."

"You're a friend of the prisoner's, aren't you?"

"Well . . ." said Bernard, and hesitated. No, he really couldn't deny it. "Why shouldn't I be?" he asked.

"Come on then," said the Sergeant, and led the way towards the door and the waiting police car.

The room into which the three were ushered was the Controller's study.

"His fordship will be down in a moment." The Gamma butler left them to themselves.

Helmholtz laughed aloud.

"It's more like a caffeine-solution party than a trial," he said, and let himself fall into the most luxurious of the pneumatic armchairs. "Cheer up, Bernard," he added, catching sight of his friend's green unhappy face. But Bernard would not be cheered; without answering, without even looking at Helmholtz, he went and sat down on the most uncomfortable chair in the room, carefully chosen in the obscure hope of somehow deprecating the wrath of the higher powers.

The Savage meanwhile wandered restlessly round the room, peering with a vague superficial inquisitiveness at the books in the shelves, at the sound-track rolls and reading machine bobbins in their numbered pigeon-holes. On the table under the window lay a massive volume bound in limp black leather-surrogate, and stamped with large golden T's. He picked it up and opened it. MY LIFE AND WORK, BY OUR FORD. The book had been published at Detroit by the Society for the Propagation of Fordian Knowledge. Idly he turned the pages, read a sentence here, a paragraph there, and had just come to the conclusion that the book didn't interest him, when the door opened, and the Resident World Controller for Western Europe walked briskly into the room.

Mustapha Mond shook hands with all three of them; but it was to the Savage that he addressed himself. "So you don't much like civilization, Mr. Savage," he said.

The Savage looked at him. He had been prepared to lie, to bluster, to remain sullenly unresponsive; but, reassured by the good-humoured intelligence of the Controller's face, he decided to tell the truth, straightforwardly. "No." He shook his head.

Bernard started and looked horrified. What would the Controller think? To be labelled as the friend of a man who said that he didn't like civilization—said it openly and, of all people, to the Controller—it was terrible. "But, John," he began. A look from Mustapha Mond reduced him to an abject silence.

"Of course," the Savage went on to admit, "there are some very nice things. All that music in the air, for instance . . ."

"Sometimes a thousand twangling instruments will hum about my ears and sometimes voices."

The Savage's face lit up with a sudden pleasure. "Have you read it too?" he asked. "I thought nobody knew about that book here, in England."

"Almost nobody. I'm one of the very few. It's prohibited, you see. But as I make the laws here, I can also break them. With impunity, Mr. Marx," he added, turning to Bernard. "Which I'm afraid you *can't* do."

Bernard sank into a yet more hopeless misery.

"But why is it prohibited?" asked the Savage. In the excitement of meeting a man who had read Shakespeare he had momentarily forgotten everything else.

The Controller shrugged his shoulders. "Because it's old; that's the chief reason. We haven't any use for old things here."

"Even when they're beautiful?"

"Particularly when they're beautiful. Beauty's attractive, and we don't want people to be attracted by old things. We want them to like the new ones."

"But the new ones are so stupid and horrible. Those plays, where there's nothing but helicopters flying about and you *feel* the people kissing." He made a grimace. "Goats and monkeys!" Only in Othello's word could he find an adequate vehicle for his contempt and hatred.

"Nice tame animals, anyhow," the Controller murmured parenthetically.

"Why don't you let them see *Othello* instead?"

"I've told you; it's old. Besides, they couldn't understand it."

Yes, that was true. He remembered how Helmholtz had laughed at *Romeo and Juliet*. "Well then," he said, after a pause, "something new that's like *Othello*, and that they could understand."

"That's what we've all been wanting to write," said Helmholtz, breaking a long silence.

"And it's what you never will write," said the Controller. "Because, if it were really like *Othello* nobody could understand it, however new it might be. And if were new, it couldn't possibly be like *Othello*."

"Why not?"

"Yes, why not?" Helmholtz repeated. He too was forgetting the unpleasant realities of the situation. Green with anxiety and apprehension, only Bernard remembered them; the others ignored him. "Why not?"

"Because our world is not the same as Othello's world. You can't make flivvers without steel—and you can't make tragedies without social instability. The world's stable now. People are happy; they get what they want, and they never want what they can't get. They're well off; they're safe; they're never ill; they're not afraid of death; they're blissfully ignorant of passion and old age; they're plagued with no mothers or fathers; they've got no wives, or children, or lovers to feel strongly about; they're so conditioned that they practically can't help behaving as they ought to behave. And if anything should go wrong, there's *soma*. Which you go and chuck out of the window in the name of liberty. Mr. Savage. *Liberty!*" He laughed. "Expecting Deltas to know what liberty is! And now expecting them to understand *Othello!* My good boy!"

The Savage was silent for a little. "All the same," he insisted obstinately, "*Othello's* good, *Othello's* better than those feelies."

"Of course it is," the Controller agreed. "But that's the price we have to pay for stability. You've got to choose between happiness and what people used to call high art. We've sacrificed the high art. We have the feelies and the scent organ instead."

"But they don't mean anything."

"They mean themselves; they mean a lot of agreeable sensations to the audience."

"But they're . . . they're told by an idiot."

The Controller laughed. "You're not being very polite to your friend, Mr. Watson. One of our most distinguished Emotional Engineers . . ."

"But he's right," said Helmholtz gloomily. "Because it *is* idiotic. Writing when there's nothing to say . . ."

"Precisely. But that require the most enormous ingenuity. You're making flivvers out of the absolute minimum of steel—works of art out of practically nothing but pure sensation."

The Savage shook his head. "It all seems to me quite horrible."

"Of course it does. Actual happiness always looks pretty squalid in comparison with the over-compensations for misery. And, of course, stability isn't nearly so spectacular as instability. And being contented has none of the glamour of a good fight against misfortune, none of the picturesqueness of a struggle with temptation, or a fatal overthrow by passion or doubt. Happiness is never grand."

"I suppose not," said the Savage after a silence. "But need it be quite so bad as those twins?" He passed his hand over his eyes as though he were trying to wipe away the remembered image of those long rows of identical midgets at the assembling tables, those queued-up twin-herds at the entrance to the Brentford monorail station, those human maggots swarming round Linda's bed of death, the endlessly repeated face of his assailants. He looked at his bandaged left hand and shuddered. "Horrible!"

"But how useful! I see you don't like our Bokanovsky Groups; but, I assure you, they're the foundation on which everything else is built. They're the gyroscope that stabilizes the rocket plane of state on its unswerving course." The deep voice thrillingly vibrated; the gesticulating hand implied all space and the onrush of the irresistible machine. Mustapha Mond's oratory was almost up to synthetic standards.

"I was wondering," said the Savage, "why you had them at

all—seeing that you can get whatever you want out of those bottles. Why don't you make everybody an Alpha Double Plus while you're about it?"

Mustapha Mond laughed. "Because we have no wish to have our throats cut," he answered. "We believe in happiness and stability. A society of Alphas couldn't fail to be unstable and miserable. Imagine a factory staffed by Alphas—that is to say by separate and unrelated individuals of good heredity and conditioned so as to be capable (within limits) of making a free choice and assuming responsibilities. Imagine it!" he repeated.

The Savage tried to imagine it, not very successfully.

"It's an absurdity. An Alpha-decanted, Alpha-conditioned man would go mad if he had to do Epsilon Semi-Moron work—go mad, or start smashing things up. Alphas can be completely socialized—but only on condition that you make them do Alpha work. Only an Epsilon can be expected to make Epsilon sacrifices, for the good reason that for him they aren't sacrifices; they're the line of least resistance. His conditioning has laid down rails along which he's got to run. He can't help himself; he's foredoomed. Even after decanting, he's still inside a bottle—an invisible bottle of infantile and embryonic fixations. Each one of us, of course," the Controller meditatively continued, "goes through life inside a bottle. But if we happen to be Alphas, our bottles are, relatively speaking, enormous. We should suffer acutely if we were confined in a narrower space. You cannot pour upper-caste champagne-surrogate into lower-caste bottles. It's obvious theoretically. But it has also been proved in actual practice. The result of the Cyprus experiment was convincing."

"What was that?" asked the Savage.

Mustapha Mond smiled. "Well, you can call it an experiment in rebottling if you like. It began in A.F. 473. The Controllers had the island of Cyprus cleared of all its existing inhabitants and re-colonized with a specially prepared batch of twenty-two thousand Alphas. All agricultural and industrial equipment was handed over to them and they were left to manage their own affairs. The result exactly fulfilled all the theoretical predictions. The land wasn't properly worked; there were strikes in all the factories; the laws were set at naught, orders disobeyed; all the people detailed for a spell of low-grade work were perpetually intriguing for high-grade jobs, and all the people with high-grade jobs were counter-intriguing at all costs to stay where they were. Within six years they were having a first-class civil war. When nineteen out of the twenty-two thousand had been killed, the survivors unanimously petitioned the World Controllers to resume the government of the island. Which they did. And that was the end of the only society of Alphas that the world has ever seen."

The Savage sighed, profoundly.

"The optimum population," said Mustapha Mond, "is modelled

on the iceberg—eight-ninths below the water line, one-ninth above."

"And they're happy below the water line?"

"Happier than above it. Happier than your friend here, for example." He pointed.

"In spite of that awful work?"

"Awful? *They* don't find it so. On the contrary, they like it. It's light, it's childishly simple. No strain on the mind or the muscles. Seven and a half hours of mild, unexhausting labour, and then the *soma* ration and games and unrestricted copulation and the feelies. What more can they ask for? True," he added, "they might ask for shorter hours. And of course we could give them shorter hours. Technically, it would be perfectly simple to reduce all lower-caste working hours to three or four a day. But would they be any the happier for that? No, they wouldn't. The experiment was tried, more than a century and a half ago. The whole of Ireland was put on to the four-hour day. What was the result? Unrest and a large increase in the consumption of *soma;* that was all. Those three and a half hours of extra leisure were so far from being a source of happiness, that people felt constrained to take a holiday from them. The Inventions Office is stuffed with plans for labour-saving processes. Thousands of them." Mustapha Mond made a lavish gesture. "And why don't we put them into execution? For the sake of the labourers; it would be sheer cruelty to afflict them with excessive leisure. It's the same with agriculture. We could synthesize every morsel of food, if we wanted to. But we don't. We prefer to keep a third of the population on the land. For their own sakes—because it takes *longer* to get food out of the land than out of a factory. Besides, we have our stability to think of. We don't want to change. Every change is a menace to stability. That's another reason why we're so chary of applying new inventions. Every discovery in pure science is potentially subversive; even science must sometimes be treated as a possible enemy. Yes, even science."

Science? The Savage frowned. He knew the word. But what it exactly signified he could not say. Shakespeare and the old men of the pueblo had never mentioned science, and from Linda he had only gathered the vaguest hints: science was something you made helicopters with, something that caused you to laugh at the Corn Dances, something that prevented you from being wrinkled and losing your teeth. He made a desperate effort to take the Controller's meaning.

"Yes," Mustapha Mond was saying, "that's another item in the cost of stability. It isn't only art that's incompatible with happiness; it's also science. Science is dangerous; we have to keep it most carefully chained and muzzled."

"What?" said Helmholtz, in astonishment. "But we're always saying that science is everything. It's a hypnopædic platitude."

"Three times a week between thirteen and seventeen," put in Bernard.

"And all the science propaganda we do at the College . . ."

"Yes; but what sort of science?" asked Mustapha Mond sarcastically. "You've had no scientific training, so you can't judge. I was a pretty good physicist in my time. Too good—good enough to realize that all our science is just a cookery book, with an orthodox theory of cooking that nobody's allowed to question, and a list of recipes that mustn't be added to except by special permission from the head cook. I'm the head cook now. But I was an inquisitive young scullion once. I started doing a bit of cooking on my own. Unorthodox cooking, illicit cooking. A bit of real science, in fact." He was silent.

"What happened?" asked Helmholtz Watson.

The Controller sighed. "Very nearly what's going to happen to you young men. I was on the point of being sent to an island."

The words galvanized Bernard into violent and unseemly activity. "Send *me* to an island?" He jumped up, ran across the room, and stood gesticulating in front of the Controller. "You can't send *me*. I haven't done anything. It was the others. I swear it was the others." He pointed accusingly to Helmholtz and the Savage. "Oh, please don't send me to Iceland. I promise I'll do what I ought to do. Give me another chance. Please give me another chance." The tears began to flow. "I tell you, it's their fault," he sobbed. "And not to Iceland. Oh please, your fordship, please . . ." And in a paroxysm of abjection he threw himself on his knees before the Controller. Mustapha Mond tried to make him get up; but Bernard persisted in his grovelling; the stream of words poured out inexhaustibly. In the end the Controller had to ring for his fourth secretary.

"Bring three men," he ordered, and take Mr. Marx into a bedroom. Give him a good *soma* vaporization and then put him to bed and leave him."

The fourth secretary went out and returned with three green-uniformed twin footmen. Still shouting and sobbing, Bernard was carried out.

"One would think he was going to have his throat cut," said the Controller, as the door closed. "Whereas, if he had the smallest sense, he'd understand that his punishment is really a reward. He's being sent to an island. That's to say, he's being sent to a place where he'll meet the most interesting set of men and women to be found anywhere in the world. All the people who, for one reason or another, have got too self-consciously individual to fit into community-life. All the people who aren't satisfied with orthodoxy, who've got independent ideas of their own. Every one, in a word, who's any one. I almost envy you, Mr. Watson."

Helmholtz laughed. "Then why aren't you on an island yourself?"

"Because, finally, I preferred this," the Controller answered. "I was given the choice: to be sent to an island, where I could have got on with my pure science, or to be taken on to the Controllers' Council with the prospect of succeeding in due course to an actual Controllership. I chose this and let the science go." After a little silence, "Sometimes," he added, "I rather regret the science. Happiness is a hard master—particularly other people's happiness. A much harder master, if one isn't conditioned to accept it unquestioningly, than truth." He sighed, fell silent again, then continued in a brisker tone, "Well, duty's duty. One can't consult one's own preference. I'm interested in truth, I like science. But truth's a menace, science is a public danger. As dangerous as it's been beneficent. It has given us the stablest equilibrium in history. China's was hopelessly insecure by comparison; even the primitive matriarchies weren't steadier than we are. Thanks, I repeat, to science. But we can't allow science to undo its own good work. That's why we so carefully limit the scope of its researches—that's why I almost got sent to an island. We don't allow it to deal with any but the most immediate problems of the moment. All other enquires are most sedulously discouraged. It's curious," he went on after a little pause, "to read what people in the time of Our Ford used to write about scientific progress. They seemed to have imagined that it could be allowed to go on indefinitely, regardless of everything else. Knowledge was the highest good, truth the supreme value; all the rest was secondary and subordinate. True, ideas were beginning to change even then. Our Ford himself did a great deal to shift the emphasis from truth and beauty to comfort and happiness. Mass production demanded the shift. Universal happiness keeps the wheels steadily turning; truth and beauty can't. And, of course, whenever the masses seized political power, then it was happiness rather than truth and beauty that mattered. Still, in spite of everything, unrestricted scientific research was still permitted. People still went on talking about truth and beauty as though they were the sovereign goods. Right up to the time of the Nine Years' War. *That* made them change their tune all right. What's the point of truth or beauty or knowledge when the anthrax bombs are popping all around you? That was when science first began to be controlled—after the Nine Years' War. People were ready to have even their appetites controlled then. Anything for a quiet life. We've gone on controlling ever since. It hasn't been very good for truth, of course. But it's been very good for happiness. One can't have something for nothing. Happiness has got to be paid for. You're paying for it, Mr. Watson—paying because you happen to be too much interested in beauty. I was too much interested in truth; I paid too."

"But *you* didn't go to an island," said the Savage, breaking a long silence.

The Controller smiled. "That's how I paid. By choosing to serve happiness. Other people's—not mine. It's lucky," he added, after a pause, "that there are such a lot of islands in the world. I don't know what we should do without them. Put you all in the lethal chamber, I suppose. By the way, Mr. Watson, would you like a tropical climate? The Marquesas, for example; or Samoa? Or something rather more bracing?"

Helmholtz rose from his pneumatic chair. "I should like a thoroughly bad climate," he answered. "I believe one would write better if the climate were bad. If there were a lot of wind and storms, for example . . ."

The Controller nodded his approbation. "I like your spirit, Mr. Watson. I like it very much indeed. As much as I officially disapprove of it." He smiled. "What about the Falkland Islands?"

"Yes, I think that will do," Helmholtz answered. "And now, if you don't mind, I'll go and see how poor Bernard's getting on."

Art, science—you seem to have paid a fairly high price for your happiness," said the Savage, when they were alone. "Anything else?"

"Well, religion, of course," replied the Controller. "There used to be something called God—before the Nine Years' War. But I was forgetting; you know all about God, I suppose."

"Well . . ." The Savage hesitated. He would have liked to say something about solitude, about night, about the mesa lying pale under the moon, about the precipice, the plunge into shadowy darkness, about death. He would have liked to speak; but there were no words. Not even in Shakespeare.

The Controller, meanwhile, had crossed to the other side of the room and was unlocking a large safe set into the wall between the bookshelves. The heavy door swung open. Rummaging in the darkness within, "It's a subject," he said, "that has always had a great interest for me." He pulled out a thick black volume. "You've never read this, for example."

The Savage took it. *"The Holy Bible, containing the Old and New Testaments,"* he read aloud from the title-page.

"Nor this." It was a small book and had lost its cover.

"The Imitation of Christ."

"Nor this." He handed out another volume.

"The Varieties of Religious Experience. by William James."

"And I've got plenty more," Mustapha Mond continued, resuming his seat. "A whole collection of pornographic old books. God in the safe and Ford on the shelves." He pointed with a laugh to his avowed library—to the shelves of books, the rack full of reading-machine bobbins and sound-track rolls.

"But if you know about God, why don't you tell them?" asked the Savage indignantly. "Why don't you give them these books about God?"

"For the same reason as we don't give them *Othello:* they're old; they're about God hundreds of years ago. Not about God now."

"But God doesn't change."

"Men do, though."

"What difference does that make?"

"All the difference in the world," said Mustapha Mond. He got up again and walked to the safe. "There was a man called Cardinal Newman," he said. "A cardinal," he exclaimed parenthetically, "was a kind of Arch-Community-Songster."

" 'I Pandulph, of fair Milan, cardinal.' I've read about them in Shakespeare."

"Of course you have. Well, as I was saying, there was a man called Cardinal Newman. Ah, here's the book." He pulled it out. "And while I'm about it I'll take this one too. It's by a man called Maine de Biran. He was a philosopher, if you know what that was."

"A man who dreams of fewer things than there are in heaven and earth," said the Savage promptly.

"Quite so. I'll read you one of the things he *did* dream of in a moment. Meanwhile, listen to what this old Arch-Community-Songster said." He opened the book at the place marked by a slip of paper and began to read. " 'We are not our own any more than what we possess is our own. We did not make ourselves, we cannot be supreme over ourselves. We are not our own masters. We are God's property. Is it not our happiness thus to view the matter? Is it any happiness or any comfort, to consider that we *are* our own? It may be thought so by the young and prosperous. These may think it a great thing to have everything, as they suppose, their own way—to depend on no one—to have to think of nothing out of sight, to be without the irksomeness of continual acknowledgment, continual prayer, continual reference of what they do to the will of another. But as time goes on, they, as all men, will find that independence was not made for man—that it is an unnatural state—will do for a while, but will not carry us on safely to the end . . .' " Mustapha Mond paused, put down the first book and, picking up the other, turned over the pages. "Take this, for example," he said, and in his deep voice once more began to read: " 'A man grows old; he feels in himself that radical sense of weakness, of listlessness, of discomfort, which accompanies the advance of age; and, feeling thus, imagines himself merely sick, lulling his fears with the notion that this distressing condition is due to some particular cause, from which, as from an illness, he hopes to recover. Vain imaginings! That sickness is old age; and a horrible disease it is. They say that it is the fear of death and of what comes after death that makes men turn to religion as they advance in years. But my own experience has given me the conviction that, quite apart from any such terrors or imaginings, the religious sentiment tends to develop as we grow older; to develop because, as the passions grow calm, as the fancy and sensibilities are less excited and less excitable, our reason becomes less troubled in its working, less obscured by the images, desires and distractions, in which it used to be absorbed; whereupon God emerges as from behind a cloud; our soul feels, sees, turns towards the source of all light; turns naturally and inevitably; for now that all that gave to the world of sensations its life and charms has begun to leak away from us, now that phenomenal existence is no more bolstered up by impressions from within or from without, we feel the need to lean on something that abides, something that will never play us a false—a reality, an absolute and everlasting truth. Yes, we inevitably turn to God; for this religious sentiment is of its nature so pure, so delightful to the soul that experiences it, that it makes up to us for all our other losses.'" Mustapha Mond shut the book and leaned back in his chair. "One of the numerous things in heaven and earth that these philosophers didn't dream about was this" (he waved his hand), "us, the modern world. 'You can only be independent of God while you've got youth and prosperity; independence won't take you safely to the end.' Well, we've now got youth and prosperity right up to the end. What follows? Evidently, that we can be independent of God. 'The religious sentiment will compensate us for all our losses.' But there aren't any losses for us to compensate; religious sentiment is superfluous. And why should we go hunting for a substitute for youthful desires, when youthful desires never fail? A substitute for distractions, when we go on enjoying all the old fooleries to the very last? What need have we of repose when our minds and bodies continue to delight in activity? of consolation, when we have *soma*? of something immovable, when there is the social order?"

"Then you think there is no God?"

"No, I think there quite probably is one."

"Then why? . . ."

Mustapha Mond checked him. "But he manifests himself in different ways to different men. In premodern times he manifested himself as the being that's described in these books. Now . . ."

"How does he manifest himself now?" asked the Savage.

"Well, he manifests himself as an absence; as though he weren't there at all."

"That's your fault."

"Call it the fault of civilization. God isn't compatible with machinery and scientific medicine and universal happiness. You must make your choice. Our civilization has chosen machinery and medicine and happiness. That's why I have to keep these books locked up in the safe. They're smut. People would be shocked if . . ."

The Savage interrupted him. "But isn't it *natural* to feel there's a God?"

"You might as well ask if it's natural to do up one's trousers with zippers," said the Controller sarcastically. "You remind me of another of those old fellows called Bradley. He defined philosophy as the finding of bad reason for what one believes by instinct. As if one believed anything by instinct! One believes things because one has been conditioned to believe them. Finding bad reasons for what one believes for other bad reasons—that's philosophy. People believe in God because they've been conditioned to believe in God."

"But all the same," insisted the Savage, "it is natural to believe in God when you're alone—quite alone, in the night, thinking about death . . ."

"But people never are alone now," said Mustapha Mond. "We make them hate solitude; and we arrange their lives so that it's almost impossible for them ever to have it."

The Savage nodded gloomily. At Malpais he had suffered because they had shut him out from the communal activities of the pueblo, in civilized London he was suffering because he could never escape from those communal activities, never be quietly alone.

"Do you remember that bit in *King Lear?*" said the Savage at last. " 'The gods are just and of our pleasant vices make instruments to plague us; the dark and vicious place where thee he got cost him his eyes,' and Edmund answers—you remember, he's wounded, he's dying—'Thou hast spoken right; 'tis true. The wheel has come full circle; I am here.' What about that now? Doesn't there seem to be a God managing things, punishing, rewarding?"

"Well, does there?" questioned the Controller in his turn. "You can indulge in any number of pleasant vices with a freemartin and run no risks of having your eyes put out by your son's mistress. 'The wheel has come full circle; I am here.' But where would Edmund be nowadays? Sitting in a pneumatic chair, with his arm round a girl's waist, sucking away at his sex-hormone chewing-gum and looking at the feelies. The gods are just. No doubt. But their code of law is dictated, in the last resort, by the people who organize society; Providence takes its cue from men."

"Are you sure?" asked the Savage. "Are you quite sure that the Edmund in that pneumatic chair hasn't been just as heavily punished as the Edmund who's wounded and bleeding to death? The gods are just. Haven't they used his pleasant vices as an instrument to degrade him?"

"Degrade him from what position? As a happy, hard-working, goods-consuming citizen he's perfect. Of course, if you choose some other standard than ours, then perhaps you might say he was degraded. But you've got to stick to one set of postulates. You can't play Electro-magnetic Golf according to the rules of Centrifugal Bumble-puppy."

"But value dwells not in particular will," said the Savage. "It holds his estimate and dignity as well wherein 'tis precious of itself as in the prizer."

"Come, come," protested Mustapha Mond, "that's going rather far, isn't it?"

"If you allowed yourselves to think of God, you wouldn't allow yourselves to be degraded by pleasant vices. You'd have a reason for bearing things patiently, for doing things with courage. I've seen it with the Indians."

"I'm sure you have," said Mustapha Mond. "But then we aren't Indians. There isn't any need for a civilized man to bear anything that's seriously unpleasant. And as for doing things—Ford forbid that he should get the idea into his head. It would upset the whole social order if men started doing things on their own."

"What about self-denial, then? If you had a God, you'd have a reason for self-denial."

"But industrial civilization is only possible when there's no self-denial. Self-indulgence up to the very limits imposed by hygiene and economics. Otherwise the wheels stop turning."

"You'd have a reason for chastity!" said the Savage, blushing a little as he spoke the words.

"But chastity means passion, chastity means neurasthenia. And passion and neurasthenia mean instability. And instability means the end of civilization. You can't have a lasting civilization without plenty of pleasant vices."

"But God's the reason for everything noble and fine and heroic. If you had a God . . ."

"My dear young friend," said Mustapha Mond, "civilization has absolutely no need of nobility or heroism. These things are symptoms of political inefficiency. In a properly organized society like ours, nobody has any opportunities for being noble or heroic. Conditions have got to be thoroughly unstable before the occasion can arise. Where there are wars, where there are divided allegiances, where there are temptations to be resisted, objects of love to be fought for or defended—there, obviously, nobility and heroism have some sense. But there aren't any wars nowadays. The greatest care is taken to prevent you from loving any one too much. There's no such thing as a divided allegiance; you're so conditioned that you can't help doing what you ought to do. And what you ought to do is on the whole so pleasant, so many of the natural impulses are allowed free play, that there really aren't any temptations to resist. And if ever, by some unlucky chance, anything unpleasant should somehow happen, why, there's always *soma* to give you a holiday from the facts. And there's always *soma* to calm your anger, to reconcile you to your enemies, to make you patient and long-suffering. In the past you could only accomplish these things by making a great effort and after years of hard moral training. Now, you swallow two or three half-gramme tablets, and there you are. Anybody can be virtuous now. You can carry at least half your mortality about in a bottle. Christianity without tears—that's what *soma* is."

"But the tears are necessary. Don't you remember what Othello said? 'If after every tempest came such calms, may the winds blow till they have wakened death.' There's a story one of the old Indians used to tell us, about the Girl of Mátaski. The young men who wanted to marry her had to do a morning's hoeing in her garden. It seemed easy; but there were flies and mosquitoes, magic ones.

Most of the young men simply couldn't stand the biting and stinging. But the one that could—he got the girl."

"Charming! But in civilized countries," said the Controller, "you can have girls without hoeing for them; and there aren't any flies or mosquitoes to sting you. We got rid of them all centuries ago."

The Savage nodded, frowning. "You got rid of them. Yes, that's just like you. Getting rid of everything unpleasant instead of learning to put up with it. Whether 'tis better in the mind to suffer the slings and arrows of outrageous fortune, or to take arms against a sea of troubles and by opposing end them . . . But you don't do either. Neither suffer nor oppose. You just abolish the slings and arrows. It's too easy."

He was suddenly silent, thinking of his mother. In her room on the thirty-seventh floor, Linda had floated in a sea of singing lights and perfumed caresses—floated away, out of space, out of time, out of the prison of her memories, her habits, her aged and bloated body. And Tomakin, ex-Director of Hatcheries and Conditioning, Tomakin was still on holiday—on holiday from humiliation and pain, in a world where he could not hear those words, that derisive laughter, could not see that hideous face, feel those moist and flabby arms round his neck, in a beautiful world . . .

"What you need," the Savage went on, "is something *with* tears for a change. Nothing costs enough here."

("Twelve and a half million dollars," Henry Foster had protested when the Savage told him that. "Twelve and a half million—that's what the new Conditioning Centre cost. Not a cent less.")

"Exposing what is mortal and unsure to all that fortune, death and danger dare, even for an eggshell. Isn't there something in that?" he asked, looking up at Mustapha Mond. "Quite apart from God—though of course God would be a reason for it. Isn't there something in living dangerously?"

"There's a great deal in it," the Controller replied. "Men and women must have their adrenals stimulated from time to time."

"What?" questioned the Savage, uncomprehending.

"It's one of the conditions of perfect health. That's why we've made the V.P.S. treatments compulsory."

"V.P.S.?"

"Violent Passion Surrogate. Regularly once a month. We flood the whole system with adrenin. It's the complete physiological equivalent of fear and rage. All the tonic effects of murdering Desdemona and being murdered by Othello, without any of the inconveniences."

"But I like the inconveniences."

"We don't," said the Controller. "We prefer to do things comfortably."

"But I don't want comfort. I want God, I want poetry, I want real danger, I want freedom, I want goodness. I want sin."

"In fact," said Mustapha Mond, "you're claiming the right to be unhappy."

"All right then," said the Savage defiantly, "I'm claiming the right to be unhappy."

"Not to mention the right to grow old and ugly and impotent; the right to have syphilis and cancer; the right to have too little to eat; the right to be lousy; the right to live in constant apprehension of what may happen tomorrow; the right to catch typhoid; the right to be tortured by unspeakable pains of every kind." There was a long silence.

"I claim them all," said the Savage at last.

Mustapha Mond shrugged his shoulders. "You're welcome," he said.

Further Readings

A. J. P. Taylor, *English History, 1914–1945* (Oxford: Oxford University Press, 1965), is a thorough and perceptive treatment of the period by an outstanding modern British historian. *Fit for Heroes: A Scrapbook of Britain between the Wars*, compiled by Lionel Jackson (Glasgow: Blackie, 1975), provides numerous excellent illustrations of British life during the period, while Alan Jenkins, *The Twenties* (New York: Universe Books, 1974), offers a series of sketches of life in America and Britain written by an excellent social historian. Stella Margetson, *The Long Party: High Society in the Twenties and Thirties* (Westmead, Farnborough, UK: Saxon House, 1974), is a richly illustrated account of the life of the British upper class and intellectuals of the period.

Sybille Beford, *Aldous Huxley: A Biography* (New York: Knopf, 1974), and Jocelyn Brooke, *Aldous Huxley* (London: Longmans, Green, 1958), are excellent studies of the subject. Harold H. Watts, *Aldous Huxley* (New York: Twayne Publishers, 1969), provides a biographical sketch of the author and an extended consideration of his works. The general subject of anti-utopias is studied by Krishan Kumar, *Utopia and Anti-Utopia in Modern Times* (Oxford: Blackwell, 1987). The reaction to H. G. Wells is the subject of Mark R. Hillegas, *The Future as Nightmare: H. G. Wells and the Anti-Utopians* (New York: Oxford University Press, 1967). Peter E. Firchow, *The End of Utopia: A Study of Aldous Huxley's Brave New World* (Lewisburg, PA: Bucknell University Press, 1984), concentrates upon *Brave New World*, while Robert S. Baker, *The Dark Historic Page: Social Satire and Historicism in the Novels of Aldous Huxley, 1921–1939* (Madison, WI: University of Wisconsin Press, 1982), considers the main body of Huxley's work.

Huxley had second thoughts, which he published in *Brave New World Revisited* (New York: Harper, 1958), and published a more optimistic utopian novel just before his death, *Island* (New York: Harper, 1962). One might also wish to read the other great English anti-utopia, written by a one-time student of Huxley's, George Orwell, *1984* (New York: Harcourt, Brace, 1949).

Guests of the Nation

Written in 1931 by the young Irish author Frank O'Connor (1903–1966), "Guests of the Nation" is the title piece of a collection of short stories set in the Irish Revolt from Great Britain (1916–1921) and the ensuing Irish Civil War (1922–1924). O'Connor was a prolific author in a number of genres, but his talents were best realized in his short stories, of which "Guests of the Nation" is perhaps his greatest achievement. He was born Michael John O'Donovan in a poor district of Cork, the largest city of southwestern Ireland. The only child of an orphaned charwoman and an itinerant day laborer, O'Donovan was a frail youth who was often ridiculed by the neighborhood children. Frequently lonely and often terrorized by his alcoholic father, he depended upon his mother for love and care. Like many other young Irishmen of the period, he was an ardent nationalist and yearned for the island's independence from Britain. In 1918, he joined the First Brigade of the Irish Republican Army and for six years was immersed in a war that was to have a profound effect on his subsequent life and writing.

The Irish Revolution was one of the most successful rebellions of the twentieth century. Led by a group of patriotic individuals who waged a bloody guerrilla war against the British, the Irish in 1921 successfully effected a separation from the powerful neighbor that had been its ruler for almost eight hundred years. A time of troubles was to follow, however. The Irish peacemakers had made a serious concession to the British; they had agreed to the partitioning of the island into a northern, British-dominated section in exchange for the establishment of an Irish Free State in the south. Many Irish protested what they regarded as the betrayal of their aspirations for a free and united Ireland, and civil war quickly broke out in 1922

From Frank O'Connor, "Guests of the Nation," in *Frank O'Connor: Collected Stories* (New York: Alfred A. Knopf, 1981), pp. 3–12.

between the Free State army and the Irish Republican troops. Donovan chose the Republican side and in 1923 was captured by Free State troops and imprisoned for a year. The brutality and violence he had witnessed appalled him, and he wrote of his experiences in *The Guests of the Nation,* the collected stories that he published in 1931 under the pseudonym of Frank O'Connor.

The title story of the collection, included here in its entirety, is a stark and powerful condemnation of wartime atrocities committed in the name of honor and duty. The "guests" of the story are two British soldiers, Belcher and Hawkins, who are being held hostage against the impending execution of some Irish rebel prisoners. Their Irish guards, Donovan, Noble, and Bonaparte, the narrator of the story, quickly develop a friendship with the two likeable lads. Noble and Bonaparte, in particular, frequently engage them in friendly conversation and card-playing, while Donovan, the leader of the tiny rebel contingent, stands aloof. When the Irish prisoners are shot by the British, Donovan brings word that Hawkins and Belcher must be killed in reprisal. Noble and Bonaparte are like innocents, completely overwhelmed at this news. Captors and captives gather at a nearby bog for the execution, and Donovan tells his prisoners, "It's not so much our doing. It's our duty, so to speak." The killings are carried out, and the story concludes with Noble and Bonaparte burying the still-warm bodies in the bog, stunned by the horror of what has happened and trying to come to terms with its reality. "Guests of the Nation," in its simplicity, must certainly rank as one of the most elegant commentaries on war's inhumanity.

Questions

1. What motivated the Irish to kill men with whom they had developed such an intimate relationship? Do you see sufficient justification for their actions?

2. "Guest of the Nations" says much about the relationship between public and private commitment. Describe the conflict between these two positions in the story. What moral issues are raised by the dilemma faced by Bonaparte and Noble?

3. What do you think are the author's feelings about the place of honor, fair play, and decency in war?

GUESTS OF THE NATION

At dusk the big Englishman Belcher would shift his long legs out of the ashes and ask, "Well, chums, what about it?" and Noble or me would say, "As you please, chum" (for we had picked up some of their curious expressions), and the little Englishman 'Awkins would light the lamp and produce the cards. Sometimes Jeremiah Donovan would come up of an evening and supervise the play, and grow excited over 'Awkins's cards (which he always played badly), and shout at him as if he was one of our own, "Ach, you divil you, why didn't you play the tray?" But, ordinarily, Jeremiah was a sober and contented poor devil like the big Englishman Belcher, and was looked up to at all only because he was a fair hand at documents, though slow enough at these, I vow. He wore a small cloth hat and big gaiters over his long pants, and seldom did I perceive his hands outside the pockets of that pants. He reddened when you talked to him, tilting from toe to heel and back and looking down all the while at his big farmer's feet. His uncommon broad accent was a great source of jest to me, I being from the town as you may recognize.

I couldn't at the time see the point of me and Noble being with Belcher and 'Awkins at all, for it was and is my fixed belief you could have planted that pair in any untended spot from this to Claregalway and they'd have stayed put and flourished like a native weed. I never seen in my short experience two men that took to the country as they did.

They were handed on to us by the Second Battalion to keep when the search for them became too hot, and Noble and myself, being young, took charge with a natural feeling of responsibility. But little 'Awkins made us look right fools when he displayed he knew the countryside as well as we did and something more. "You're the bloke they calls Bonaparte?" he said to me. "Well, Bonaparte, Mary Brigid Ho'Connell was arskin abaout you and said 'ow you'd a pair of socks belonging to 'er young brother." For it seemed, as they explained it, that the Second used to have little evenings of their own, and some of the girls of the neighborhood would turn in, and seeing they were such decent fellows, our lads couldn't well ignore the two Englishmen, but invited them in and were hail-fellow-well-met with them. 'Awkins told me he learned to dance "The Walls of Limerick" and "The Siege of Ennis" and "The Waves of Tory" in a night or two, though naturally he could not return the compliment, because our lads at that time did not dance foreign dances on principle.

So whatever privileges and favors Belcher and 'Awkins had with the Second they duly took with us, and after the first evening we gave up all pretense of keeping a close eye on their behavior. Not that they could have got far, for they had a notable accent and wore khaki tunics and overcoats with civilian pants and boots. But it's my belief they never had an idea of escaping and were quite contented with their lot.

Now, it was a treat to see how Belcher got off with the old woman of the house we were staying in. She was a great warrant to scold, and crotchety even with us, but before ever she had a chance of giving our guests, as I may call them, a lick of her tongue, Belcher had made her his friend for life. She was breaking sticks at the time, and Belcher, who hadn't been in the house for more than ten minutes, jumped up out of his seat and went across to her.

"Allow me, madam," he says, smiling his queer little smile; "please allow me," and takes the hatchet from her hand. She was struck too parlatic to speak, and ever after Belcher would be at her heels carrying a bucket, or basket, or load of turf, as the case might be. As Noble wittily remarked, he got into looking before she leapt, and hot water or any little thing she wanted Belcher would have it ready for her. For such a huge man (and though I am five foot ten myself I had to look up to him) he had an uncommon shortness—or should I say lack—of speech. It took us some time to get used to him walking in and out like a ghost, without a syllable out of him. Especially because 'Awkins talked enough for a platoon, it was strange to hear big Belcher with his toes in the ashes come out with a solitary "Excuse me, chum," or "That's right, chum." His one and only abiding passion was cards, and I will say for him he was a good card-player. He could have fleeced me and Noble many a time; only if we lost to him, 'Awkins lost to us, and 'Awkins played with the money Belcher gave him.

'Awkins lost to us because he talked too much, and I think now we lost to Belcher for the same reason. 'Awkins and Noble would spit at one another about religion into the early hours of the morning; the little Englishman as you could see worrying the soul out of young Noble (whose brother was a priest) with a string of questions that would puzzle a cardinal. And to make it worse, even in treating of these holy subjects, 'Awkins had a deplorable tongue; I never in all my career struck across a man who could mix such a variety of cursing and bad language into the simplest topic. Oh, a terrible man was little 'Awkins, and a fright to argue! He never did a stroke of work, and when he had no one else to talk to he fixed his claws into the old woman.

I am glad to say that in her he met his match, for one day when he tried to get her to complain profanely of the drought she gave him a great comedown by blaming the drought upon Jupiter Pluvius (a deity neither 'Awkins nor I had ever even heard of, though Noble said among the pagans he was held to have something to do with rain). And another day the same 'Awkins was swearing at the capitalists for starting the German war, when the old dame laid down her iron, puckered up her little crab's mouth and said, "Mr. 'Awkins, you can say what you please about the war, thinking to deceive me because I'm an ignorant old woman, but I know well what started the war. It was that Italian count that stole the heathen divinity out of the temple in Japan, for believe me, Mr. 'Awkins, nothing but sorrow and want follows them that disturbs the hidden powers!" Oh, a queer old dame, as you remark!

So one evening we had our tea together, and 'Awkins lit the lamp and we all sat in to cards. Jeremiah Donovan came in too, and sat down and watched us for a while. Though he was a shy man and didn't speak much, it was easy to see he had no great love for the two Englishmen, and I was surprised it hadn't struck me so clearly before. Well, like that in the story, a terrible dispute blew up late in the evening between 'Awkins and Noble, about capitalists and priests and love for your own country.

"The capitalists," says 'Awkins, with an angry gulp, "the capitalists pays the priests to tell you all abaout the next world, so's you won't notice what they do in this!"

"Nonsense, man," says Noble, losing his temper, "before ever a capitalist was thought of people believed in the next world."

'Awkins stood up as if he was preaching a sermon. "Oh, they did, did they?" he says with a sneer. "They believed all the things you believe, that's what you mean? And you believe that God created Hadam and Hadam created Shem and Shem created Jehoshophat? You believe all the silly hold fairy-tale abaout Heve and Heden and the happle? Well, listen to me, chum. If you're entitled to 'old to a silly belief like that, I'm entitled to 'old to my own silly belief—which is, that the fust thing your God created was a bleedin' capitalist with mirality and Rolls Royce complete. Am I right, chum?" he says then to Belcher.

"You're right, chum," says Belcher, with his queer smile, and get up from the table to stretch his long legs into the fire and stroke his mustache. So, seeing that Jeremiah Donovan was going, and there was no knowing when the conversation about religion would be over, I took my hat and went out with him. We strolled down towards the village together, and then he suddenly stopped, and blushing and mumbling, and shifting, as his way was, from toe to heel, he said I ought to be behind keeping guard on the prisoners. And I, having it put to me so suddenly, asked him what the hell he wanted a guard on the prisoners at all for, and said that so far Noble and me were concerned we had talked it over and would rather be out with a column. "What use is that pair to us?" I asked him.

He looked at me for a spell and said, "I thought you knew we were keeping them as hostages." "Hostages—?" says I, not quite understanding. "The enemy," he says in his heavy way, "have prisoners belong' to us, and now they talk of shooting them. If they shoot our prisoners we'll shoot theirs, and serve them right." "Shoot them?" said I, the possibility just beginning to dawn on me. "Shoot them exactly," said he. "Now," said I, "wasn't it very unforeseen of you not to tell me and Noble that?" "How so?" he asks. "Seeing that we were acting as guards upon them, of course." "And hadn't you reason enough to guess that much?" "We had not, Jeremiah Donovan, we had not. How were we to know when the men were on our hands so long?" "And what differnce does it make?

The enemy have our prisoners as long or longer, haven't they?" "It makes a great difference," said I. "How so?" said he sharply; but I couldn't tell him the difference it made, for I was struck too silly to speak. "And when may we expect to be released from this anyway?" said I. "You may expect it tonight," says he. "Or tomorrow or the next day at latest. So if it's hanging round here that worries you, you'll be free soon enough."

I cannot explain it even now, how sad I felt, but I went back to the cottage, a miserable man. When I arrived the discussion was still on, 'Awkins holding forth to all and sundry that there was no next world at all and Noble answering in his best canonical style that there was. But I saw 'Awkins was after having the best of it. "Do you know what, chum?" he was saying, with his saucy smile. "I think you're jest as big a bleedin' hunbeliever as I am. You say you believe in the next world and you know jest as much abaout the next world as I do, which is sweet damn-all. What's 'Eaven? You dunno. Where's 'Eaven? You dunno. Who's in 'Eaven? You dunno. You know sweet damn-all! I arsk you again, do they wear wings?"

"Very well then," says Noble, "they do; is that enough for you? They do wear wings." "Where do they get them then? Who makes them? 'Ave they a fact'ry for wings? 'Ave they a sort of store where you 'ands in your chit and tikes your bleedin' wings? Answer me that."

"Oh, you're an impossible man to argue with," says Noble. "Now listen to me—" And off the pair of them went again.

It was long after midnight when we locked up the Englishmen and went to bed ourselves. As I blew out the candle I told Noble what Jeremiah Donovan had told me. Noble took it very quietly. After we had been in bed about an hour he asked me did I think we ought to tell the Englishmen. I having thought of the same thing myself (among many others) said no, because it was more than likely the English wouldn't shoot our men, and anyhow it wasn't to be supposed the Brigade who were always up and down with the Second Battalion and knew the Englishmen well would be likely to want them bumped off. "I think so," says Noble. "It would be sort of cruelty to put the wind up them now." "It was very unforeseen of Jeremiah Donovan anyhow," says I, and by Noble's silence I realized he took my meaning.

So I lay there half the night, and thought and thought, and picturing myself and young Noble trying to prevent the Brigade from shooting 'Awkins and Belcher sent a cold sweat out through me. Because there were men on the Brigade you daren't let nor hinder without a gun in your hand, and at any rate, in those days disunion between brothers seemed to me an awful crime. I knew better after.

It was next morning we found it so hard to face Belcher and 'Awkins with a smile. We went about the house all day scarcely saying a word. Belcher didn't mind us much; he was stretched into the ashes as usual with his usual look of waiting in quietness for something unforeseen to happen, but little 'Awkins gave us a bad time with his audacious gibing and questioning. He was disgusted at Noble's not answering him back. "Why can't you tike your beating like a man, chum?" he says. "You with your Hadam and Heve! I'm a Communist—or an Anarchist. An Anarchist, that's what I am." And for hours after he went around the house, mumbling when the fit took him "Hadam and Heve! Hadam and Heve!"

I don't know clearly how we got over that day, but get over it we did, and a great relief it was when the tea things were cleared away and Belcher said in his peaceable manner, "Well, chums, what about it?" So we all sat round the table and 'Awkins produced the cards, and at that moment I heard Jeremiah Donovan's footsteps up the path, and a dark presentiment crossed my mind. I rose quietly from the table and laid my hand on him before he reached the door. "What do you want?" I asked him. "I want those two soldier friends of yours," he says reddening. "Is that the way it is, Jeremiah Donovan?" I ask. "That's the way. There were four of our lads went west this morning, one of them a boy of sixteen." "That's bad, Jeremiah," says I.

At that moment Noble came out, and we walked down the path together talking in whispers. Feeney, the local intelligence officer, was standing by the gate. "What are you going to do about it?" I asked Jeremiah Donovan. "I want you and Noble to bring them out: you can tell them they're being shifted again; that'll be the quietest way." "Leave me out of that," says Noble suddenly. Jeremiah Donovan looked at him hard for a minute or two. "All right so," he said peaceably. "You and Feeney collect a few tools from the shed and dig a hole by the far end of the bog. Bonaparte and I'll be after you in about twenty minutes. But whatever else you do, don't let anyone see you with the tools. No one must know but the four of ourselves."

We saw Feeney and Noble go round to the houseen[1] where the tools were kept, and sidled in. Everything if I can so express myself was tottering before my eyes, and I left Jeremiah Donovan to do the explaining as best he could, while I took a seat and said nothing. He told them they were to go back to the Second. 'Awkins let a mouthful of curses out of him at that, and it was plain that Belcher, though he said nothing, was duly perturbed. The old woman was for having them stay in spite of us, and she did not shut her mouth until Jeremiah Donovan lost his temper and said some nasty things to her. Within the house by this time it was pitch dark, but no one thought of lighting the lamp, and in the darkness the two Englishmen fetched their khaki topcoats and said good-bye

---

[1] Shed.

to the woman of the house. "Just as a man mikes a 'ome of a bleedin' place," mumbles 'Awkins, shaking her by the hand, "some bastard at Headquarters thinks you're too cushy and shunts you off." Belcher shakes her hand very hearty. "A thousand thanks, madam," he says, "a thousand thanks for everything . . ." as though he'd made it all up.

We go round to the back of the house and down towards the fatal bog. Then Jeremiah Donovan comes out with what is in his mind. "There were four of our lads shot by your fellows this morning so now you're to be bumped off." "Cut that stuff out," says 'Awkins, flaring up. "It's bad enough to be mucked about such as we are without you plying at soldiers." "It's true," says Jeremiah Donovan, "I'm sorry, 'Awkins, but 'tis true," and comes out with the usual rigmarole about doing our duty and obeying our superiors. "Cut it out," says 'Awkins irritably. "Cut it out!"

Then when Donovan sees he is not being believed he turns to me, "Ask Bonaparte here," he says. "I don't need to arsk Bonaparte. Me and Bonaparte are chums." "Isn't it true, Bonaparte?" says Jeremiah Donovan solemnly to me. "It is," I say sadly, "it is." 'Awkins stops. "Now, for Christ's sike. . . ." "I mean it, chum," I say. "You daon't saound as if you mean it. You knaow well you don't mean it." Well, if he don't I do," says Jeremiah Donovan. "Why the 'ell sh'd you want to shoot me, Jeremiah Donovan?" "Why the hell should your people take out four prisoners and shoot them in cold blood upon a barrack square?" I perceive Jeremiah Donovan is trying to encourage himself with hot words.

Anyway, he took little 'Awkins by the arm and dragged him on, but it was impossible to make him understand that we were in earnest. From which you will perceive how difficult it was for me, as I kept feeling my Smith and Wesson and thinking what I would do if they happened to put up a fight or ran for it, and wishing in my heart they would. I knew if only they ran I would never fire on them. "Was Noble in this?" 'Awkins wanted to know, and we said yes. He laughed. But why should Noble want to shoot him? Why should we want to shoot him? What had he done to us? Weren't we chums (the word lingers painfully in my memory)? Weren't we? Didn't we understand him and didn't he understand us? Did either of us imagine for an instant that he'd shoot us for all the so-and-so brigadiers in the so-and-so British Army? By this time I began to perceive in the dusk the desolate edges of the bog that was to be their last earthly bed, and, so great a sadness overtook my mind, I could not answer him. We walked along the edge of it in the darkness, and every now and then 'Awkins would call a halt and begin again, just as if he was wound up, about us being chums, and I was in despair that nothing but the cold and open grave made ready for his presence would convince him that we meant it all. But all the same, if you can understand, I didn't want him to be bumped off.

At last we saw the unsteady glint of a lantern in the distance and made toward it. Noble was carrying it, and Feeney stood somewhere in the darkness behind, and somehow the picture of the two of them so silent in the boglands was like the pain of death in my heart. Belcher, on recognizing Noble, said " 'Allo, chum" in his usual peaceable way, but 'Awkins flew at the poor boy immediately, and the dispute began all over again, only that Noble hadn't a word to say for himself, and stood there with the swaying lantern between his gaitered legs.

It was Jeremiah Donovan who did the answering. 'Awkins asked for the twentieth time (for it seemed to haunt his mind) if anybody thought he'd shoot Noble. "You would," says Jeremiah Donovan shortly. "I wouldn't, damn you!" "You would if you knew you'd be shot for not doing it." "I wouldn't, not if I was to be shot twenty times over; he's my chum. And Belcher wouldn't—isn't that right, Belcher?" "That's right, chum," says Belcher peaceably. "Damned if I would. Anyway, who says Noble'd be shot if I wasn't bumped off? What d'you think I'd do if I was in Noble's place and were out in the middle of a blasted bog?" "What would you do?" "I'd go with him wherever he was going. I'd share my last bob with him and stick by 'im through thick and thin."

"We've had enough of this," says Jeremiah Donovan, cocking his revolver. "Is there any message you want to send before I fire?" "No, there isn't, but . . ." "Do you want to say your prayers?" 'Awkins came out with a cold-blooded remark that shocked even me and turned to Noble again. "Listen to me, Noble," he said. "You and me are chums. You won't come over to my side, so I'll come over to your side. Is that fair? Just you give me a rifle and I'll go with you wherever you want."

Nobody answered him.

"Do you understand?" he said. "I'm through with it all. I'm a deserter or anything else you like, but from this on I'm one of you. Does that prove to you that I mean what I say?" Noble raised his head, but as Donovan began to speak he lowered it again without answering. "For the last time have you any messages to send?" says Donovan in a cold and excited voice.

"Ah, shut up, you, Donovan; you don't understand me, but these fellows do. They're my chums; they stand by me and I stand by them. We're not the capitalist tools you seem to think us."

I alone of the crowd saw Donovan raise his Webley to the back of 'Awkins neck, and as he did so I shut my eyes and tried to say a prayer. 'Awkins had begun to say something else when Donovan let fly, and, as I opened my eyes at the bang, I saw him stagger at the knees and lie out flat at Noble's feet, slowly, and as quiet as a child, with the lantern light falling sadly upon his lean legs and bright farmer's boots. We all stood very still for a while watching him settle out in the last agony.

Then Belcher quietly takes out a handkerchief, and begins to tie it about his own eyes (for in our excitement we had forgotten to offer the same to 'Awkins), and, seeing it is not big enough, turns and asks for a loan of mine. I give it to him and as he knots the two together he points with his foot at 'Awkins. " 'E's not quite dead," he says, "better give 'im another." Sure enough 'Awkins's left knee as we see it under the lantern is rising again. I bend down and put my gun to his ear; then, recollecting myself and the company of Belcher, I stand up again with a few hasty words. Belcher understands what is in my mind. "Give 'im 'is first," he says. "I don't mind. Poor bastard, we dunno what's 'appening to 'im now." As by this time I am beyond all feeling I kneel down again and skilfully give 'Awkins the last shot so as to put him forever out of pain.

Belcher who is fumbling a bit awkwardly with the handkerchiefs comes out with a laugh when he hears the shot. It is the first time I have heard him laugh, and it sends a shiver down my spine, coming as it does so inappropriately upon the tragic death of his old friend. "Poor blighter," he says quietly, "and last night he was so curious abaout it all. It's very queer, chums, I always think. Naow, 'e knows as much abaout it as they'll ever let 'im know, and last night 'e was all in the dark."

Donovan helps him to tie the handkerchiefs about his eyes. "Thanks, chum," he says. Donovan asks him if there are any messages he would like to send. "Naow, chum," he says, "none for me. If any of you likes to write to 'Awkins's mother you'll find a letter from 'er in 'is pocket. But my missus left me eight years ago. Went away with another fellow and took the kid with her. I likes the feelin' of a 'ome (as you may 'ave noticed) but I couldn't start again after that."

We stand around like fools now that he can no longer see us. Donovan looks at Noble and Noble shakes his head. Then Donovan raises his Webley again and just at that moment Belcher laughs his queer nervous laugh again. He must think we are talking of him; anyway, Donovan lowers his gun. " 'Scuse me, chums," says Belcher, "I feel I'm talking the 'ell of a lot . . . and so silly . . . abaout me being so 'andy abaout a 'ouse. But this thing come on me so sudden. You'll forgive me, I'm sure." "You don't want to say a prayer?" asks Jeremiah Donovan. "No, chum," he replies, "I don't think that'd 'elp. I'm ready if you want to get it over." "You understand," says Jeremiah Donovan, "it's not so much our doing. It's our duty, so to speak." Belcher's head is raised like a real blind man's, so that you can only see his nose and chin in the lamplight. "I never could make out what duty was myself," he said, "but I think you're all good lads, if that's what you mean. I'm not complaining." Noble, with a look of desperation, signals to Donovan, and in a flash Donovan raises his gun and fires. The big man goes over like a sack of meal, and this time there is no need of a second shot.

I don't remember much about the burying, but that it was worse than all the rest, because we had to carry the warm corpses a few yards before we sunk them in the windy bog. It was all mad lonely, with only a bit of lantern between ourselves and the pitch blackness, and birds hooting and screeching all round disturbed by the guns. Noble had to search 'Awkins first to get the letter from his mother. Then having smoothed all signs of the grave away, Noble and I collected our tools, said good-bye to the others, and went back along the desolate edge of the treacherous bog without a word. We put the tools in the houseen and went into the house. The kitchen was pitch black and cold, just as we had left it, and the old woman was sitting over the hearth telling her beads. We walked past her into the room, and Noble struck a match to light the lamp. Just then she rose quietly and came to the doorway, being not at all so bold or crabbed as usual.

"What did ye do with them?" she says in a sort of whisper, and Noble took such a mortal start the match quenched in his trembling hand. "What's that?" he asks without turning round. "I heard ye," she said. "What did you hear?" asks Noble, but sure he wouldn't deceive a child the way he said it. "I heard ye. Do you think I wasn't listening to ye putting the things back in the houseen?" Noble struck another match and this time the lamp lit for him. "Was that what ye did with them?" she said, and Noble said nothing—after all what could he say?

So then, by God, she fell on her two knees by the door, and began telling her beads, and after a minute or two Noble went on his knees by the fireplace, so I pushed my way out past her, and stood at the door, watching the stars and listening to the damned shrieking of the birds. It is so strange what you feel at such moments, and not to be written afterwards. Noble says he felt he seen everything ten times as big, perceiving nothing around him but the little patch of black bog with the two Englishmen stiffening into it; but with me it was the other way, as though the patch of bog where the two Englishmen were was a thousand miles away from me, and even Noble mumbling just behind me and the old woman and the birds and the bloody stars were all far away, and I was somehow very small and very lonely. And anything that ever happened me after I never felt the same about again.

Further Readings

Notable among the works on Ireland's revolt against Britain and the Irish Civil War that followed are Desmond Williams, *The Irish Struggle, 1916–1926* (London: Routledge and Kegan Paul, 1966), and Sheila Lawlor, *Britain and Ireland: 1914–1923* (Totowa, NJ: Barnes and Noble Books, 1983). George Dangerfield, *The Damnable Question* (Boston, MA: Little, Brown and Co., 1976), examines the events leading up to and including the Irish Revolution, while Calton Younger, *Ireland's Civil War* (London: Frederick Muller, Ltd., 1968), is an informative account of the internal struggle. D. G. Boyce, *Englishmen and Irish Troubles* (Cambridge, MA: MIT Press, 1972), provides an interesting analysis of the period of "Irish Troubles" (1918–1922) in English public opinion. The Easter Rising was the most dramatic event in modern Irish history. Two works particularly useful for understanding its causes and effects are Alan J. Ward, *The Easter Rising: Revolution and Irish Nationalism* (Arlington Heights, IL: AHM Publishing Corp., 1980), and *1916: The Easter Rising*, edited by O. Dudley Edwards and Fergus Pyle (Longon: Macgibbon and Kee, 1968). A history of the Irish Republican Army is available in J. Bowyer Bell, *Secret Army: The IRA, 1916–1979* (Cambridge, MA: MIT Press, 1980). Margery Forester, *Michael Collins: The Lost Leader* (London: Sidgewick and Jackson, 1971), is a valuable biography of an Irish revolutionary leader and hero.

James Matthews, *Voices: A Life of Frank O'Connor* (New York: Atheneum, 1983), is a comprehensive examination of the author's life. William M. Tomory, *Frank O'Connor* (Boston, MA: Twayne Publishers, 1980), focuses upon O'Connor as a short-story writer and contains a useful bibliography. Maurice Wohlgelernter, *Frank O'Connor: An Introduction* (New York: Columbia University Press, 1977), concentrates on O'Connor's thoughts relating to the political and intellectual developments of his time. *Michael/Frank: Studies on Frank O'Connor,* edited by Maurice Sheehy (New York: Alfred Knopf, 1969), provides an excellent collection of nineteen elegiac essays by O'Connor's friends and colleagues, revealing much about his personality and character. O'Connor's two-volume autobiography also affords much insight into the man: *An Only Child* (New York: Alfred Knopf, 1961), covers his youth, and *My Father's Son* (New York: Alfred Knopf, 1969), chronicles his later years. Among the many collections of O'Connor's fiction are *Guests of the Nation* (New York: Macmillan, 1931), *The Stories of Frank O'Connor* (New York: Alfred Knopf, 1952), *Collected Stories* (New York: Alfred Knopf, 1981), and *My Oedipus Complex and Other Stories* (London: Penguin, 1969). O'Connor wrote a number of works of literary criticism in addition to his fiction. Among them are *Shakespeare's Progress* (Cleveland, OH: World, 1948), *The Mirror in the Roadway* (New York: Alfred Knopf, 1956), *The Lonely Voice* (Cleveland, OH: World, 1963), *A Short History of Irish Literature* (New York: Capricorn, 1967), and *Towards an Appreciation of Literature* (Port Washington, NY: Kennikat Press, 1945). A good example of his dramatic writing is Frank O'Connor and Hugh Hunt, *Moses' Rock: A Play in Seven Scenes,* edited by Ruth Sherry (Washington, DC: The Catholic University of America Press, 1983).

The Night of a Thousand Suicides

The Night of a Thousand Suicides is a moving account of an actual incident at the Cowra prisoner-of-war camp in Australia during the Second World War. Approximately one thousand Japanese prisoners, armed only with knives, forks, and baseball bats, made a futile attempt at mass escape. These Japanese troops fully realized that their action would almost certainly result in their death. Nevertheless, shamed by their imprisonment, they decided to attack their Australian guards in the hope of regaining not only their freedom, but also their honor. Their effort proved almost suicidal; hundreds were killed or wounded by machine-gun fire, and not one Japanese succeeded in escaping.

The Japanese philosophical approach to death differs significantly from that of the Westerner. The Japanese have always possessed a grim consciousness of death existing beneath the surface of their daily lives. But the Japanese concept of death is precise and clear, and is in stark contrast to the fear and reluctance with which the Westerner often approaches the inevitable end of life. The willingness of the Japanese to accept death more or less freely, or even to embrace it by committing suicide to advance a worthy cause, is an attitude generally alien to Western thought. The Japanese philosophy on the matter is deeply imbedded in the Japanese mind and, in times of difficulty, has sometimes influenced the thinking of the entire country.

These distinctive views of life and death are clearly expounded in the *Hagakure*, a seventeenth-century classic describing the moral values and responsibilities of the samurai warrior. According to this manual, "one who chooses to go on living having failed in one's mis-

From Teruhiko Asada, *The Night of a Thousand Suicides*, translated by Ray Cowan (New York: St. Martin's Press, 1972), pp. 84–100.

sion will be despised as a coward and a bungler." During the nationalistic passion that animated Japan in the 1930s, this treatise was republished and praised as embodying "the unique spirit of the Japanese." Military leaders propounded this doctrine in the training of their troops. The ideals of the *Hagakure* were reiterated in the Japanese military code, which expressly forbade soldiers from being taken alive to bear the shame of captivity. The excerpt from *The Night of a Thousand Suicides* presented here demonstrates the degree to which the Japanese common soldier accepted these samurai attitudes.

Teruhiko Asada, born in 1915, was stationed at Rabaul during the war. He wrote the following account of the tragic events at the Cowra camp in the form of a novel, but based it upon the firsthand experience of an acquaintance of his. The anguish and despair that led the Japanese prisoners at Cowra to embrace what amounted to mass suicide is vividly presented. This rush of unarmed men against machine guns presents the choice between life and death as both an individual and a group decision. The adherence of these soldiers to the Japanese military code created a fanatic patriotism in which suffering shame was literally a fate worse than death. It is easy enough for the Western reader to consider the terrible conflict that drove these men to their deaths simply as a peculiarity of the Japanese personality and to view the Cowra incident as a tragic and useless waste of life. When read with a sympathetic eye, however, the account raises fundamental and disturbing issues. Most readers would probably hold that, if there is anything worth dying for, it is individual integrity and honor. And yet, it is also clear that the individual's concepts of integrity and honor are not really personal truths, but are created and inculcated by society. If this is so, then the individual cannot win, and the distinction between gallant heroism and blind fanaticism cannot really be drawn.

Questions

1. After reading the account of the Cowra riot, do you consider the attempted escape an honorable action? Do the actions of the Japanese prisoners show a difference between Japanese attitudes towards death and those of Westerners? If so, what are these differences?

2. What motivated the prisoners to risk almost certain death? What role did group pressure play in their decision?

3. To what extent did the prisoners delude themselves by regarding their plan as an "attack"? Did they really believe that it might succeed?

THE NIGHT OF A THOUSAND SUICIDES

Gradually, as I listened to the stories of the survivors, the details of that tragic night became clear in my mind. Having received the order concerning the movement of prisoners at our interview with Major Ramsay, Sergeant-major Kajima called a section leaders' meeting immediately on returning to the Japanese compound. The move was set down for the following day and it was imperative to decide at once whether to obey or disobey. Negotiation was now out of the question.

There was considerable stir created in the camp. Such a snap action on the part of the Australian authorities had not been expected.

All had been busy getting ready for a concert to be held the next day. Technicians were decorating the stage and making costumes while Matchan (Cpl Matsuoka), the entertainment group leader, and Miyasan (Private First Class Tsuruoka) were rehearsing lines from "Kirare Yosaburo". Home-made samisen, flute and drum were to make it a really professional performance complete with the correct musical accompaniment and all were looking forward eagerly to the occasion. Cooking too was in progress, with a few old hands battling along covered in flour, baking cakes to be distributed to everyone after the concert.

In the midst of all this suddenly came the news of the move order, and chief cook Sgt Kikuchi, with flour all over his face, and Matchan, still wearing the Yosaburo costume, raced into the section leaders' meeting.

Knowing the determination of Major Ramsay, none put forward a very positive opinion, but simply allowed time to be taken up with grumblings and criticism of the injustice of the Australian order. To a man they wanted to reject the order, but every mouth was stopped when asked point blank if disobedience of the order could be maintained at the point of a bayonet. Unless considerable unity of purpose were achieved, they could be carted off in ones and twos until none were left. To disobey meant that a man had to be ready to offer his life.

The camp leader closed the meeting with the request that the section leaders report again as soon as a decision had been reached in the sections. However, the situation was the same in each section—simply that the order for the move was distasteful in the extreme but there was an unwillingness to go to the point of risking death in disobeying it.

At the second meeting of section leaders Section Leader Ishikawa reported that his section had decided that no matter how much the order was resented, the only course left open was to obey. Most of the section leaders silently indicated agreement and all appeared to have been waiting for such a proposal. Ishikawa went on to continue putting the case with some feeling:

"This is not purely and simply because of a fear of death. There is the intention to bear before the world the responsibility for having become prisoners but I don't think that time is now."

The order for the move, he added, seemed the logical step for the Australian Army to take in the circumstances.

"Shut up, you old fool!" Cpl Hotei was on his feet as he shouted the words, his face flushed from drinking.

"There's not one single coward of that kind in my section. We're all ready to die defying any such order. That's the fighting spirit of Japan!"

Flight-sergeant Tobé was the next up, also full of "jungle juice."

"There are no cowards in my section, either. Dying or living they're going to stick by me, they said. Are you going to tell men like that to pack off to Hay? Before the men are 'done' like that, how about an attack? There will never be another chance. Now is the time. We will die together like the falling blossoms."

"Hear, hear!" came from outside the window where more than a dozen quite crazy drunk men belonging to the extremists had gathered to peer in and note the trend of the meeting.

The atmosphere of the meeting changed radically.

"Have you forgotten the Field Service Code?"

"The way of the samurai is the way of death."

Met with these cries, none could demur.

After getting the men away from the immediate vicinity, the camp leader said, "It's all very well to talk of an attack, but we don't have a single weapon."

Before he could go on, Cpl Hotei stuck out a huge fist and asserted, "We do have weapons—these! We're going to fight with our bare hands. We'll beat the Australians to death and take their weapons!"

The delirium was contagious.

"We've got the baseball bats and knives and forks. If each one kills one we can account for a thousand of the enemy," put in another section leader. "How about it?"

"All right then, let's get going."

The meeting was in a ferment.

"Hold on now." W. O. Ishikawa was on his feet. "The members of my section are certainly not a bunch of cowards and if all really agreed with the sentiments just expressed my men would naturally follow the will of the majority in spite of their own misgivings. But I think we have to be sure if this is really the will of the whole body after all. I don't think it ought to be decided at a section leaders' meeting only but that every man in the compound should take part in a secret ballot on the matter and that a simple majority so obtained should be decisive."

The camp leader adopted this plan. There was to be another recess, the next meeting to take place when results of the secret ballot were known.

The matter of voting was by no means simple. It involved a

decision on a general attack—in effect, death for honour or, to put it another way, mass suicide. All were continually thinking of death, but now when faced with the challenge to get ready to die, they tended to waver. Only a very small minority had definite opinions. Most were ready to follow the lead of the majority, but it was not easy to make out just what majority opinion was after all.

Violent arguments broke out in every section, so that it was difficult to obtain a decision by which all would abide. Night fell but it wasn't possible to enjoy the evening meal. Now with shrill voices they continued the debate.

The extremists had the most to say, keen to remove the shame of imprisonment by carrying out an unarmed attack, a valiant, appealing concept.

By contrast, the case that the moderates put forward seemed so lacking in life that they were liable to be regarded as miserable and cowardly. It took considerable courage to be a spokesman for such a cause. It was necessary to have a well grounded and thought-out argument that would withstand the barbs of, "Have you forgotten the Field Service Code?" or, "Call yourself a Japanese soldier?"

Logic is not the strong point of the Japanese. They are inclined to be carried away with an atmosphere and also to submit their wills to that of a superior. In the case of the section leaders of the moderate persuasion the voices against the attack were the stronger. For all that, there was an increasing tendency for the majority in the compound to favour carrying out the attack. As the night wore on, an abnormal excitement seemed to take over, resulting in a desire to take part in vengeful acts of destruction.

For the third time the section leaders met and the votes from all the sections were totalled up. Over half were in favour of the attack, and the die was cast.

There was room for doubt that this was a true representation of the will of the entire body of prisoners. It looked very much as though they had been carried away with the admonitions of the extremists. No ballot was carried out in the sections led by Flight-sergeant Tobé and Cpl Hotei. They maintained that voices expressing a willingness to leave the decision to the section leader constituted a vote in favour of the attack. By contrast, a proper secret ballot was carried out in W. O. Ishikawa's section and the count showed two-thirds against the charge. It was quite likely that, if strict secret ballots had been carried out in all sections, those against might have been in the majority. All feared death, but feared the name coward even more. They wanted to appear patriotic, loyal soldiers before the world and they could not have it said that they would suffer any shame in order to preserve their lives.

The majority decision to take part in the attack was thus announced in a crazed atmosphere. It was already after lights out but nothing was further from the men's minds than the thought of sleep. The section leaders' meeting was discussing what form the attack should take. No matter how it was carried out it could have little effect against machinegun bullets. They would all die together and the time was now only a few hours away.

All the home brew was brought out and consumed, the cakes made for the occasion of the concert were eaten freely, and enough cigarettes smoked to make the head spin. Knives and forks were sharpened on cement-rendered surfaces; and bats, iron pipes, motor vehicle springs and the like were kept at hand for use as weapons. An atmosphere of near frenzy was maintained; a readiness to go just as soon as the camp leader's order came.

There were, however, some who were not carried away with this mood, going through torture of soul because they lacked the resolve to take action to avoid the death now facing them. They walked about the compound with arms folded debating within themselves the meaning of this death—a violent conflict going on within the heart of every man.

The searchlights were turned on them. It seemed that the Australians found evidence of disquiet in the fact that although it was now past lights out the prisoners had not turned their lights off and there was continual moving to and fro by many of them. It was, of course, possible to put it down partly to preparations for the move to take place the following morning. No doubt the possibility of an attack by unarmed men was not even considered.[1]

It had been decided that a bugle call at midnight would signal the start of the attack. Sections 1 to 10 were to get through the front gate and escape in a northerly direction; sections 11 to 20 to surmount the barricades on the north-east; sections 21 to 27 were to escape from the south-west corner of the Japanese compound and into the wide road through the centre of the greater camp area ("Broadway") and head south. Sections 27 to 36 would escape to the south-east. In this way prisoners would head in four different directions for the attack. The sick and those wounded who could not be expected to scale the barricades were not forced to take part. Civilian employees of the Japanese forces among the prisoners were not judged to be as guilty as soldiers taken prisoner and each was allowed to make up his own mind about taking part.

Huts were to be burned down at the time of the attack as a sign of the determination of the prisoners never to return to the place. Each man was to take one blanket to be used in protecting the body from barbed wire when climbing over the barricades. Further protection was afforded by wearing baseball gloves or by wrap-

---

[1] "Information was received at Group headquarters early in August that the Japanese were planning a mass outbreak. . . . That night the guards were alert and tense." (*Australia in the War of 1939–45: The Final Campaigns.*)

ping the hands in pieces of blankets. A small amount of food, including biscuits, was also to be carried. Attention was paid to a number of details of this kind in preparing for the attack.

But as to what was to be done once the men had escaped across the barricades, nothing was yet definitely decided. The attack was to be like a mass suicide but there was no way of estimating exactly the strength of Australian firepower likely to be encountered so that it was not possible to say that none of the prisoners would succeed in getting through; and some indication of what should then be done must be given. But there was no longer enough time to attend to such details of planning. It was decided simply that any who got out alive should gather in a suitable place, choose a leader, and attempt to attack Australian camps and airfields; and since none could really expect to get out alive, planning for that eventuality did not occupy the mind very much.

The section leaders passed to their men these instructions from the camp leader. Despite the fact that the men had made up their minds to take part in the attack, when the time finally came there was a certain amount of disorder and confusion. The decision had been reached by a majority vote and differed quite a deal from a military command. While it was a general attack, exemptions were to be permitted and the will of the individual respected, with the result that it was difficult to get orderly conduct. So much time was consumed in preparations for the battle, farewelling comrades, and in prevailing on those opposed to the plan to change their minds, that zero hour came and went without the sounding of the bugle. The officers had been contacted about the planned attack but had not answered to say whether they were for or against. Because I had not been there, the N.C.Os and men had not taken the officers into account in their deliberations except to pass on news of the decision reached and to leave the officers to make up their own minds.

It seemed that Lt Kimura had turned up during the deliberations, probably noting the air of unrest and desiring to persuade the men to act more sanely, but the extremists outside the window refused to let him go inside and turned him back with, "Beat it!" and, "Chicken-hearted officer!"

A full two hours after the set time, all sections were at last ready, with mattresses piled up in the fireplaces ready to set on fire and it was then that Camp Leader Kajima gave the order to blow the bugle.

Choking tension prevailed while waiting for its sound. Every face was pale and none could remain still. There was a rush on the toilets and when they became full quite a large number of men defecated by the huts.

"Buck up, men."

"See you at the Yasukuni Shrine."

As comrades gripped each other's hands and exchanged words of farewell, tears welled up in their eyes spontaneously. It has been said that a person facing death sees, as in a kaleidoscope, a recapitulation of events dating back to his infancy, and so it was here; many felt a constricting of the chest as though it were held in a tight band, and a sudden emptiness of the mind—a vacuum, and an unaccountable loss of the power to think clearly. The atmosphere of frenzy created by a crowd of a thousand men prompted all to run about and shout wildly.

The state of those wounded and sick who were unable to join the attack and must later find another way to die was pathetic. It was their desire to choose a glorious end like this. Delirious malaria cases and men with artificial limbs begged to be taken along and it wasn't easy for Section Leader Ishikawa and the others to pacify them. They ordered not only these wounded but also the civilians to remain behind and even allowed servicemen to make up their minds individually concerning participation. But, in an atmosphere of this kind, it took a lot of courage to express such an opinion, if it conflicted with the feeling of the majority. Section Leader Tobé refused to acknowledge the right to such freedom.

"We're all joining the attack and will go down fighting. The sick are to offer themselves nobly at this time and if they lack the guts to die of their own accord then I'll kill them with my own hands." Now drunk to the point being quite crazed, Tobé had been all for the idea of the attack from the beginning but was actually without previous battle experience and had never been face to face with death before, so that despite his brave talk his heart was in a state of agitation.

"We apologize for our inability to join you. We shall go ahead of you to the Yasukuni Shrine." So saying, three of the sick faced the north, gave three cheers of "Banzai" for the Emperor, and suicided by cutting their carotid arteries with razor blades.

In Cpl Hotei's section was one man who, though fit, said, "I agree with the plan to die but I am against the attack. I don't want to kill anyone, but just die on my own." A number agreed with these sentiments and before the huts were set alight they lined up beneath a beam and hanged themselves from ropes tied to it, their final request to their comrades being that, since some had opposed the idea of bodies being left hanging, they should be cut down and burned. As each one prepared to go he was encouraged by the others assuring him that they would soon follow.

Suicides took place in the other sections also, most of the physically incapacitated men choosing this way out. They died ahead of the others because they regretted not being fit enough to take part in the attack and were convinced that life as survivors would be meaningless for them. As many as twenty belonged to this group.

The compound office was the first to blaze up and on seeing this the men in the other huts immediately set fire to the blankets they had piled up. Oil that had been poured over the mattresses gave off black smoke as flames filled the huts in a matter of moments and came through the windows.

Shouts from the guards on the towers showed that they were aware of trouble in the compound and the light of searchlights directed onto the compound from all directions showed the seriousness of the incident. The alarm siren roared as machineguns were trained on the compound and the forms of Australian soldiers on the point of firing could be seen.

The trumpet sounded the charge, but what should have been a rhythmical call was faltering and broken, more like a shriek than anything else. In battle normally there would be the order, "Charge!" answered by the war cry of the men, but here there was neither, just the tumult created by animal-like gasps wrung from the bodies of a thousand men, a sound that shook the night air.

The men charged in four directions as planned, caught in the beams of the searchlights as they made for the barricades.

They split up and ran at a half crouch, or almost crawling, fast along the ground. Firing broke out from the towers and all instinctively dropped to the ground and remained motionless. The fear experienced when exposed to machinegun fire was greater than anticipated. Even those who had raged and boasted that they would kill two or three of the enemy before going down to Australian bullets now found that their legs were suddenly unwilling to carry them forward and they flattened themselves on the ground with their eyes closed. When the firing ceased they were relieved to find that they were free from pain or sign of injury. But it wasn't possible to remain flat on the ground indefinitely, and, aiming to revive each other's shaken wills with shouts of, "Let us go!" and "Let us die!", a number began to race forward again but, as soon as heavy firing recommenced, no amount of self-respect was able to prevent them from flattening to the ground once more.

The absence of casualties up to this point was explained by the fact that the Australians were not aiming to hit the prisoners but merely sending warning shots whistling over their heads. Strangely enough the discovery of this seemed to anger the escapees who now shouted defiantly in the direction of the gunners, challenging them to shoot to kill. Wave after wave now rushed the barricades, threw the blankets, and clambered over. At this the firing grew more intense and now was directed at the prisoners. The whistling sound changed to a thudding and splashing as frost columns and mud were kicked up by the bullets, and men on the barricades were hit in rapid succession, sending up curses and cries as they were struck. With their last breath they called on Emperor or mother or repeated the name of a friend over and over.

The attack had been momentarily checked and all the remaining men could do was to remain flattened on the ground and wait.

Some who had succeeded in getting to the other side of the barricades turned to berate their fellows for their tardiness. This only increased the feeling of impotence.

The threat of being regarded as timid was enough to get the men on the move once again.

Since the firing was mostly concentrated on the front gate of the compound, casualties were heaviest here. Camp Leader Kajima's and W. O. Ishikawa's sections were in this area. They had climbed over the inner barricade but, stopped at the outer, had now taken shelter in the stormwater drain at the foot of the barricade to avoid being cut down by an impassable curtain of fire coming in from both left and right.

Half the escaping prisoners were by now dead or wounded and most of the living were covered in scratches caused by contact with the barbed wire.

During a break in the firing, W. O. Ishikawa raised himself up from the drain to see about a dozen or more Australian soldiers feverishly erecting a machinegun emplacement. The Australians' cry of "Come on, you Japs!" was answered by shouts of "Bakayaro!" [fools!] from this side.

Suddenly flares turned night into day and once more heavy firing began. The only thing to do was crouch, breathless, in the drain, with a blanket for covering. To move meant to receive a bullet.

The sections in the south-east corner including those led by Deputy Camp Leader Tobé and by Cpl Matsuoka faced less concentrated fire and succeeded in breaking out into the wide road between compounds to find themselves on a thirty-yard-wide asphalt strip with no place to hide and where they all came under fire together. The end result of a rash charge in the direction of the Australian positions was annihilation.

Seeing this from the other side of the barricade, W. O. Ishikawa found himself unable to remain immobile in his place of safety, and, calling on the men of his section to follow the example of those who had just offered themselves, started to clamber up the barricade, only to be dragged off the wire and pinned to the ground by a young airman, Imanishi.

Although he was in Ishikawa's section, this Imanishi had been a member of the extremist group and a most intractable character. That one so strongly in favour of the general attack and a last-ditch stand should now restrain Ishikawa was indeed an unexpected development. The warrant officer no longer felt capable of breaking free from Imanishi and climbing the barricade, and remained where he was clenching his teeth in vexation. He had come thus far only to have his spirit broken as he witnessed the fall of his comrades. The availability of the stormwater drain in which to take refuge had been the means to turn him into a miserable coward. "A man's no good as long as he's got something to cling to for

Burial of Japanese prisoners who died in the outbreak.

support, even if he has made up his mind to die. His reason can't be trusted."

It was some time later that he asked Imanishi the reason for his action.

"I can't tell you, really. Just overwhelming fear, I suppose. Fear that you'd be killed and a desire to keep you alive with us." Here was one who had called on his comrades to die, making an about-face at the last moment and calling on those same men to live.

As with a would-be suicide who shuns the idea of a second attempt, to live through the mad moments of the attack took away the desire to die and W. O. Ishikawa and his men made no further attempt to scale the barricades, but lay on the ground still as death. "No need to face the bullets now. We'll die before a firing squad anyway."

The eastern sky brightened and the sun came up as though to signal the end of an episode.

The Australian interpreter was making an announcement. "Listen carefully, you Japanese prisoners who have just rioted. As soldiers we respect the bravery you have shown in the attack but most of you have fallen. Further resistance is useless. Those of you remaining are to throw away your weapons, raise both your hands in the air and make your way back inside the compound. No man who has his hands raised will be fired on. The commandant has given his word that none will be punished. Go back into the compound immediately."

"They're telling us to go back into the compound. Better go, then, I suppose." They slowly got up and made their way into the compound, moving like puppets without a will of their own. Fatigue and cold seemed to make both spirit and body seem remote. Nothing remained but an overwhelming desire to lie down and go to sleep. Tears flowed at the thought of how shameful the men looked marching back into the compound with their hands raised above their heads.

The most spectacular fight was put up by those at the northeast corner of the compound.[2] Sgt Kikuchi and Aoyama took part in this attack. The usually quiet Sgt Kikuchi was right in the lead going over the barricades and headed for the watchtower. Because they broke out so early they avoided coming under fire almost altogether, being at a dead angle to the guns. He called together about fifteen men and climbed a tower, whereupon the four guards, taken by surprise, tried to get away but were beaten to death with pieces of iron pipe. With a shout the prisoners took the machine-gun, only to find it inoperative because the Australians had removed vital working parts on retreating.

Guards in the nearby towers had no sooner taken in the situation than they directed a withering fire at the captured tower, mowing the captors down in quick succession. The members of this group who had not fallen, now made off up a hill towards the east, on the slopes of which gum-trees grew here and there. The men ran from tree to tree for cover. Since the trunks of the trees were of such a size that an adult could barely encircle them with both arms, four or five men found cover by huddling close together and, for that very reason, became special targets.

A civilian, Shinagawa, lay writhing in agony on the ground after receiving a bullet in the abdomen, a pool of blood around him. Sgt Kikuchi could bear to look at it no longer and ordered a soldier named Kameda, nearby, to put the wounded man at ease. Kameda failed to get the meaning of the statement.

"Choke him!" the sergeant bawled at the youngster.

Kameda didn't make a move but looked terrified. Kikuchi didn't coerce the lad further and couldn't bring himself to put an end to Shinagawa. Leaving him as he was, Kikuchi and the others ran on up the hill until they reached a place where they were no longer followed by the bullets.

The escapees instinctively made their way to low ground between the hills. There were over twenty men in all, and, following the orders given by the camp leader, they were to select a leader

---

[2] "The strongest group of Japanese—about 400—broke through the wire on the north-west. Here Privates Hardy and Jones punched their way through the prisoners, manned a Vickers gun and fired it until they were knifed and clubbed to death. The Japanese swung the gun round to fire on the Australians' huts but it jammed, and its Japanese crew was killed. . . . Including those who killed themselves, 234 Japanese died and 108 were wounded. Thirty-one killed themselves and 12 were burnt to death in huts set on fire by Japanese. Sixteen of the wounded showed signs of attempted suicide. The 22nd Garrison Battalion lost 3 killed and 3 wounded." (*Australia in the War of 1939–45: The Final Campaigns*)

and attempt to attack Australian camps and airfields. But they lacked the energy for that kind of operation. They were limp and weak from the effects of fatigue, cold and hunger. The nightmare of coming out under the hail of bullets had taken so much out of them that they had absolutely no inclination to repeat that kind of action but now gathered together in almost an apathetic way. Those who, a short time ago, had professed themselves ready to make a brave last-ditch stand, had in fact suffered a rout and now indulged in the luxury of this place of rest out of the reach of the bullets.

The men crouched on the ground shivering in the extreme pre-dawn cold.

"I can't stand this cold. Let's light a fire." The one who made the suggestion found himself unopposed. A fire would be sure to reveal their position to the Australians but they no longer cared and anyway they looked like perishing with the cold. A stockman on a white horse appeared over the hill just above them and, on seeing the group of Japanese around the fire, hurriedly wheeled his horse about and made off.

"We've been spotted."

"Can't waste any more time here."

It wasn't really possible to do much at this stage however. To move away from their present location they would have to travel across land where there was scarcely a tree in sight which they could use to take cover.

"What will we do when the enemy comes? Each man try to account for one of them? Or just surrender?" When Sgt Kikuchi put this to them there wasn't a single answer; a sign that they were in favour of surrender.

An hour later jeeps carrying Australian troops converged on the place from three sides. A truck fitted with wire panels, prison van style, was standing ready and the prisoners were forced, at bayonet-point, to board it.

"What, prisoners again!"

"What did we break out for after all?"

"We don't deserve to be called Japanese soldiers."

"We're a miserable bunch when we compare ourselves with those who died."

Every man was on the point of making such an outburst, but, knowing that such charges would apply also to the speaker, faces were turned aside from each other.

As the truck descended the hill toward the camp, one of the prisoners clambered up the side of the truck and jumped onto the road, not out of a desire to escape but in order to commit suicide. The body bounced two or three times on the frozen surface and was still. It was Sgt Kikuchi. Nobody had a chance to stop him, the incident having taken place too quickly.

Further Readings

Two useful surveys of the War in the Pacific are Edwin P. Hoyt, *Japan's War: The Great Pacific Conflict* (New York: McGraw-Hill, 1986), and Ronald Spector, *Eagle Against the Sun: The American War with Japan* (New York: Free Press, 1985). Informative accounts of the immediate events leading up to Japan's surrender may be found in Robert J. C. Butow, *Japan's Decision to Surrender.* (Stanford, CA: Stanford University Press, 1954), and Lester Brooks, *Behind Japan's Surrender. (New York: McGraw-Hill, 1968). Both provide valuable insights into the Japanese views upon surrender. Maruyama Masao is the author of a number of perceptive essays on Japanese ultranationalism published as Thought and Behavior in Japanese Politics,* edited by Ivan Morris (New York: Oxford University Press, 1963). Japanese nationalism between the two world wars is discussed by Richard Story, *The Double Patriots: A Study of Japanese Nationalism* (Boston, MA: Houghton Mifflin, 1957). Ben-Ami Shillony, *Politics and Culture in Wartime Japan* (New York: Oxford University Press, 1981), examines the political and cultural character of wartime Japan.

Hak-won Sonu, *Japanese Militarism, Past and Present* (Chicago, IL: Nelson-Hall, 1975), traces the history of Japanese militarism, from the Meiji period to the present day. *Japan, 1931–1945: Militarism, Fascism, Japanism?*, edited by Ivan Morris (Boston, MA: Heath, Problems in Asian Civilization Series, 1963), and Ernst L. Presseisen, *Before Aggression* (Tuscon, AZ: University of Arizona Press, 1965), focus upon the development of Japanese militarism prior to the beginning of the Second World War. Tsuetomo Yamamoto, *Hagakure: The Book of the Samurai*, translated by William S. Wilson (Tokyo: Kodansha, 1979), is one of the best-known classics on the "way of the samurai." Although written in the seventeenth century, many of its moral values and standards were emphasized in the ideals of Japanese militarism in the twentieth century.

On the People's Democratic Dictatorship

Although China had been faced with increasing pressure from the Western powers since the middle of the eighteenth century, and had had to contend with destructive internal uprisings, its established political institutions and traditional cultural patterns were maintained with relatively little change until 1894. In that year, however, Japan went to war with China. China was decisively defeated and forced to yield important territories, special commercial privileges, and a crushing war indemnity to the victor. European powers quickly forced other concessions from the virtually helpless Chinese. China was thrown into turmoil, with various groups contending for power to direct the course of the nation. While some groups demanded immediate Westernization, others insisted upon a return to traditional Chinese values and the expulsion of the foreigners and their ways. In 1900, the popular uprising against the Europeans known as the Boxer Rebellion occurred. The Western powers sent in an expeditionary force, capturing Peking and driving the Chinese government from its capital. It had become clear to the Chinese that they could not simply expel the foreigners, and a massive and often ill-directed program of Westernization began.

In 1902, a Western-style educational system was adopted, and in 1905, the system of imperial civil service examinations was abolished. This was a dramatic break with a long-established cultural and administrative system, and signalled the widespread conclusion on the part of the Chinese that their traditional political institutions were inadequate to deal with new conditions. Seven years later, the imperial government itself fell, and the Ch'ing dynasty (1644–1912)

From Mao Tse-tung, *Selected Works of Mao Tse-tung* (5 vols.: Peking: Foreign Language Press, 1969), 4: 411–423.

had come to an end. With the constant interference of the Western powers, with various contending schools of thought, and without the unifying influence that the scholar–administrator class had once provided, there was no force capable of overcoming the rise to power of independent local leaders. Central government disappeared, and China entered the period known as the "era of the warlords."

In 1926, a new national force did emerge, the Kuomintang, a party espousing the ideals of the democratic revolutionary, Sun Yat-sen (1866–1925). Under the leadership of Ch'iang Kai-shek (1887–1975), the Kuomintang armies began eliminating the warlords and unifying the country. In the process, they found that their greatest adversary lay in the Communist Party that had been established in China with Russian encouragement in 1921. Driven from the cities, the Communists established control over extensive sections of the countryside. In 1930, Ch'iang Kai-shek undertook a series of campaigns to eradicate these areas of Communist power. By 1934, he was ready to begin the encirclement of a large zone established by Mao Tse-tung (1893–1976).

Mao was born in a small village in the province of Hunan, the son of a prosperous farmer. He graduated from the province's Western-style teacher's college in 1918, already a political radical. He took up the life of a schoolmaster, but continued his political agitation and, in 1921, was one of the founding members of the Chinese Communist Party. Mao travelled extensively in the countryside and established particular rapport with the peasant class. Communist doctrine at this time taught that the revolution could come only from an urban, industrial proletariat (working class), and Mao's work with the rural peasants struck his colleagues as of little worth and limited his power among the party leadership. Peasant support was essential in 1927, however, when Mao established a Communist zone in the mountains of his native province. When Chiang began his encirclement, Mao's zone contained over three million people. His army was no match for the massive Nationalist forces, however, and so he determined to break out and join another Communist group far to the north.

This was the famous Long March, in which 100,000 men, women, and children fought their way for over six thousand miles before a small portion of them reached their final objective. Ch'iang's attempt to pursue them even here was halted in 1937 by the Japanese invasion of China. The Nationalists withdrew to the Southwest, while the Communists fought on against the Japanese in the North, gathering strength and extending their territorial control in the process. At Japan's defeat in 1945, the Red Army numbered over three million men and continued to grow during the civil war that broke out almost immediately with the Nationalists. In savage fighting, the Nationalists finally were driven to the island of Taiwan, and, in 1949, Mao declared the establishment of the People's Republic of China on the mainland.

Some months before, on the twenty-eighth anniversary of the founding of the Chinese Communist Party, Mao had given a speech on "The People's Democratic Dictatorship," in which he outlined the sort of government that would follow victory. This speech, provided here in full, attempts to answer questions and criticisms levelled against Mao's policies. One of the most serious was voiced by those who had believed Communist promises that victory would bring freedom and equality. Communist doctrine promises that the power of the state will be abolished, but only after a period of "consolidation" and "re-education" known as the "dictatorship of the proletariat." Using logic strikingly similar to that of Robespierre in his "Speech of 17 Pluviôse," Mao explains how the Communist struggle would continue even after victory over the Nationalists.

This speech presents the Communist ideal of the dictatorship of the proletariat; the dictatorship was far less benign in practice. Tens of millions of Chinese died under Mao's leadership, many because of simple mismanagement, and many more in the name of "uniting the people and advancing steadily towards our goal." The goal of the stateless society, in which all the means of repression, exploitation, and constraint have disappeared in a universal association of free men and women, is the ideal towards which all Communist states aspire. Needless to say, none has yet reached that goal.

Questions

1. Why had China failed to learn from the West when Japan was able to do so?

2. What have the Chinese people learned since 1900?

3. Why must there be a people's dictatorship?

4. What will the people's dictatorship accomplish?

ON THE PEOPLE'S DEMOCRATIC DICTATORSHIP

The first of July 1949 marks the fact that the Communist Party of China has already lived through twenty-eight years. Like a man, a political party has its childhood, youth, manhood and old age. The Communist Party of China is no longer a child or a lad in his teens but has become an adult. When a man reaches old age, he will die; the same is true of a party. When classes disappear, all instruments of class struggle—parties and the state machinery—will lose their function, cease to be necessary, therefore gradually wither away and end their historical mission; and human society will move to a higher stage. We are the opposite of the political parties of the bourgeoisie.¹ They are afraid to speak of the extinction of classes, state power and parties. We, on the contrary, declare openly that we are striving hard to create the very conditions which will bring about their extinction. The leadership of the Communist Party and the state power of the people's dictatorship are such conditions. Anyone who does not recognize this truth is no communist. Young comrades who have not studied Marxism–Leninism and have only recently joined the Party may not yet understand this truth. They must understand it—only then can they have a correct world outlook. They must understand that the road to the abolition of classes, to the abolition of state power and to the abolition of parties is the road all mankind must take; it is only a question of time and conditions. Communists the world over are wiser than the bourgeoisie, they understand the laws governing the existence and development of things, they understand dialectics and they can see farther. The bourgeoisie does not welcome this truth because it does not want to be overthrown. To be overthrown is painful and is unbearable to contemplate for those overthrown, for example, for the Kuomintang reactionaries whom we are now overthrowing and for Japanese imperialism which we together with other peoples overthrew some time ago. But for the working class, the labouring people and the Communist Party the question is not one of being overthrown, but of working hard to create the conditions in which classes, state power and political parties will die out very naturally and mankind will enter the realm of Great Harmony.² We have mentioned in passing the long-range perspective of human progress in order to explain clearly the problems we are about to discuss.

As everyone knows, our Party passed through these twenty-eight years not in peace but amid hardships, for we had to fight enemies, both foreign and domestic, both inside and outside the Party. We thank Marx, Engels, Lenin and Stalin for giving us a weapon. This weapon is not a machine-gun, but Marxism–Leninism.

In his book "*Left-wing*" *Communism, an Infantile Disorder* written in 1920, Lenin described the quest of he Russians for revolutionary theory. Only after several decades of hardship and suffering did the Russians find Marxism. Many things in China were the same as, or similar to, those in Russia before the October Revolution. There was the same feudal oppression. There was similar economic and cultural backwardness. Both countries were backward, China even more so. In both countries alike, for the sake of national regeneration progressives braved hard and bitter struggles in their quest for revolutionary truth.

---
¹ Capitalist classes.
² A society based on public ownership, free from class exploitation and oppression—a lofty ideal long cherished by the Chinese people. Here the realm of Great Harmony means a communist society.

From the time of China's defeat in the Opium War of 1840,[3] Chinese progressives went through untold hardships in their quest for truth from the Western countries. Hung Hsiu-chuan,[4] Kang Yu-wei,[5] Yen Fu[6] and Sun Yat-sen were representative of those who had looked to the West for truth before the Communist Party of China was born. Chinese who then sought progress would read any book containing the new knowledge from the West. The number of students sent to Japan, Britain, the United States, France and Germany was amazing. At home, the imperial examinations were abolished and modern schools sprang up like bamboo shoots after a spring rain; every effort was made to learn from the West. In my youth, I too engaged in such studies. They represented the culture of Western bourgeois democracy, including the social theories and natural sciences of that period, and they were called "the new learning" in contrast to Chinese feudal culture, which was called "the old learning." For quite a long time, those who had acquired the new learning felt confident that it would save China, and very few of them had any doubts on this score, as the adherents of the old learning had. Only modernization could save China, only learning from foreign countries could modernize China. Among the foreign countries, only the Western capitalist countries were then progressive, as they had successfully built modern bourgeois states. The Japanese had been successful in learning from the West, and the Chinese also wished to learn from the Japanese. The Chinese in those days regarded Russia as backward, and few wanted to learn from her. That was how the Chinese tried to learn from foreign countries in the period from the 1840s to the beginning of the 20th century.

Imperialist aggression shattered the fond dreams of the Chinese about learning from the West. It was very odd—why were the teachers always committing aggression against their pupil? The Chinese learned a good deal from the West, but they could not make it work and were never able to realize their ideals. Their repeated struggles, including such a country-wide movement as the Revolution of 1911,[7] all ended in a failure. Day by day, conditions in the country got worse, and life was made impossible. Doubts arose, increased and deepened. World War I shook the whole globe. The Russians made the October Revolution and created the world's first socialist state. Under the leadership of Lenin and Stalin, the revolutionary energy of the great proletariat and labouring

---

[3] Faced with the opposition of the Chinese people to her traffic in opium, Britain sent forces in 1840–42 to invade Kwangtung and other coastal regions of China under the pretext of protecting trade. The troops in Kwangtung, led by Lin Tse-hsu, fought a war of resistance.
[4] Leader of a peasant revolutionary war in the middle of the nineteenth century.
[5] Leader of a reform movement to establish a constitutional monarchy in the late nineteenth and early twentieth centuries.
[6] Another reformer advocating a constitutional rather than an autocratic monarchy.
[7] The Revolution of 1911 overthrew the Ching Dynasty.

people of Russia, hitherto latent and unseen by foreigners, suddenly erupted like a volcano, and the Chinese and all mankind began to see the Russians in a new light. Then, and only then, did the Chinese enter an entirely new era in their thinking and their life. They found Marxism–Leninism, the universally applicable truth, and the face of China began to change.

It was through the Russians that the Chinese found Marxism. Before the October Revolution, the Chinese were not only ignorant of Lenin and Stalin, they did not even know of Marx and Engels. The salvoes of the October Revolution brought us Marxism–Leninism. The October Revolution helped progressives in China, as throughout the world, to adopt the proletarian world outlook as the instrument for studying a nation's destiny and considering anew their own problems. Follow the path of the Russians—that was their conclusion. In 1919, the May 4th Movement took place in China. In 1921, the Communist Party of China was founded. Sun Yat-sen, in the depths of despair, came across the October Revolution and the Communist Party of China. He welcomed the October Revolution, welcomed Russian help to the Chinese and welcomed co-operation of the Communist Party of China. Then Sun Yat-sen died and Chiang Kai-shek rose to power. Over a long period of twenty-two years, Chiang Kai-shek dragged China into ever more hopeless straits. In this period, during the anti-fascist Second World War in which the Soviet Union was the main force, three big imperialist powers were knocked out, while two others were weakened. In the whole world only one big imperialist power, the United States of America, remained uninjured. But the United States faced a grave domestic crisis. It wanted to enslave the whole world; it supplied arms to help Chiang Kai-shek slaughter several million Chinese. Under the leadership of the Communist Party of China, the Chinese people, after driving out Japanese imperialism, waged the People's War of Liberation for three years and have basically won victory.

Thus Western bourgeois civilization, bourgeois democracy and the plan for a bourgeois republic have all gone bankrupt in the eyes of the Chinese people. Bourgeois democracy has given way to people's democracy under the leadership of the working class and the bourgeois republic to the people's republic. This has made it possible to achieve socialism and communism through the people's republic, to abolish classes and enter a world of Great Harmony. Kang Yu-wei wrote *Ta Tung Shu,* or the *Book of Great Harmony,* but he did not and could not find the way to achieve Great Harmony. There are bourgeois republics in foreign lands, but China cannot have a bourgeois republic because she is a country suffering under imperialist oppression. The only way is through a people's republic led by the working class.

All other ways have been tried and failed. Of the people who hankered after those ways, some have fallen, some have awakened and some are changing their ideas. Events are developing so swiftly that many feel the abruptness of the change and the need to learn anew. This state of mind is understandable and we welcome this worthy desire to learn anew.

The vanguard of the Chinese proletariat learned Marxism–Leninism after the October Revolution and founded the Communist Party of China. It entered at once into political struggles and only now, after a tortuous course of twenty-eight years, has it won basic victory. From our twenty-eight years' experience we have drawn a conclusion similar to the one Sun Yat-sen drew in his testament from his "experience of forty years"; that is, we are deeply convinced that to win victory, "we must arouse the masses of the people and unite in a common struggle with those nations of the world which treat us as equals". Sun Yat-sen had a world outlook different from ours and started from a different class standpoint in studying and tackling problems; yet, in the 1920s he reached a conclusion basically the same as ours on the question of how to struggle against imperialism.

Twenty-four years have passed since Sun Yat-sen's death, and the Chinese revolution, led by the Communist Party of China, has made tremendous advances both in theory and practice and has radically changed the face of China. Up to now the principal and fundamental experience the Chinese people have gained is twofold:

(1) Internally, arouse the masses of the people. That is, unite the working class, the peasantry, the urban petty bourgeoisie and the national bourgeoisie, form a domestic united front under the leadership of the working class, and advance from this to the establishment of a state which is a people's democratic dictatorship under the leadership of the working class and based on the alliance of workers and peasants.

(2) Externally, unite in a common struggle with those nations of the world which treat us as equals and unite with the peoples of all countries. That is, ally ourselves with the Soviet Union, with the People's Democracies and with the proletariat and the broad masses of the people in all other countries, and form an international united front.

"You are leaning to one side." Exactly. The forty years' experience of Sun Yat-sen and the twenty-eight years' experience of the Communist Party have taught us to lean to one side, and we are firmly convinced that in order to win victory and consolidate it we must lean to one side. In the light of the experiences accumulated in these forty years and these twenty-eight years, all Chinese without exception must lean either to the side of imperialism or to the side of socialism. Sitting on the fence will not do, nor is there a third road. We oppose the Chiang Kai-shek reactionaries who lean

Mao Tse-tung.

to the side of imperialism, and we also oppose the illusions about a third road.

"You are too irritating." We are talking about how to deal with domestic and foreign reactionaries, the imperialists and their running dogs, not about how to deal with anyone else. With regard to such reactionaries, the question of irritating them or not does not arise. Irritated or not irritated, they will remain the same because they are reactionaries. Only if we draw a clear line between reactionaries and revolutionaries, expose the intrigues and plots of the reactionaries, arouse the vigilance and attention of the revolutionary ranks, heighten our will to fight and crush the enemy's arrogance can we isolate the reactionaries, vanquish them or supersede them. We must not show the slightest timidity before a wild beast. We must learn from Wu Sung[8] on the Chingyang Ridge. As Wu Sung saw it, the tiger on Chingyang Ridge was a man-eater,

[8] A hero in the novel, *Shui Hu Chuan* (*Heroes of the Marshes*), who killed a tiger with his bare hands on the Chingyang Ridge. This is one of the most popular episodes in that famous novel.

whether irritated or not. Either kill the tiger or be eaten by him—one or the other.

"We want to do business." Quite right, business will be done. We are against no one except the domestic and foreign reactionaries who hinder us from doing business. Everybody should know that it is none other than the imperialists and their running dogs, the Chiang Kai-shek reactionaries, who hinder us from doing business and also from establishing diplomatic relations with foreign countries. When we have beaten the internal and external reactionaries by uniting all domestic and international forces, we shall be able to do business and establish diplomatic relations with all foreign countries on the basis of equality, mutual benefit and mutual respect for territorial integrity and sovereignty.

"Victory is possible even without international help." This is a mistaken idea. In the epoch in which imperialism exists, it is impossible for a genuine people's revolution to win victory in any country without various forms of help from the international revolutionary forces, and even if victory were won, it could not be consolidated. This was the case with the victory and consolidation of the great October Revolution, as Lenin and Stalin told us long ago. This was also the case with the overthrow of the three imperialist powers in World War II and the establishment of the People's Democracies. And this is also the case with the present and the future of People's China. Just imagine! If the Soviet Union had not existed, if there had been no victory in the anti-fascist Second World War, if Japanese imperialism had not been defeated, if the People's Democracies had not come into being, if the oppressed nations of the East were not rising in struggle and if there were no struggle of the masses of the people against their reactionary rulers in the United States, Britain, France, Germany, Italy, Japan and other capitalist countries—if not for all these in combination, the international reactionary forces bearing down upon us would certainly be many times greater than now. In such circumstances, could we have won victory? Obviously not. And even with victory, there could be no consolidation. The Chinese people have had more than enough experience of this kind. This experience was reflected long ago in Sun Yat-sen's death-bed statement on the necessity of uniting with the international revolutionary forces.

"We need help from the British and U.S. governments." This, too, is a naive idea in these times. Would the present rulers of Britain and the United States, who are imperialists, help a people's state? Why do these countries do business with us and, supposing they might be willing to lend us money on terms of mutual benefit in the future, why would they do so? Because their capitalists want to make money and their bankers want to earn interest to extricate themselves from their own crisis—it is not a matter of helping the Chinese people. The Communist Parties and progressive groups in these countries are urging their governments to establish trade and even diplomatic relations with us. This is goodwill, this is help, this cannot be mentioned in the same breath with the conduct of the bourgeoisie in the same countries. Throughout his life, Sun Yat-sen appealed countless times to the capitalist countries for help and got nothing but heartless rebuffs. Only once in his whole life did Sun Yat-sen receive foreign help, and that was Soviet help. Let readers refer to Dr. Sun Yat-sen's testament; his earnest advice was not to look for help from the imperialist countries but to "unite with those nations of the world which treat us as equals." Dr. Sun had experience; he had suffered, he had been deceived. We should remember his words and not allow ourselves to be deceived again. Internationally, we belong to the side of the anti-imperialist front headed by the Soviet Union, and so we can turn only to this side for genuine and friendly help, not to the side of the imperialist front.

"You are dictatorial." My dear sirs, you are right, that is just what we are. All the experience that Chinese people have accumulated through several decades teaches us to enforce the people's democratic dictatorship, that is, to deprive the reactionaries of the right to speak and let the people alone have that right.

Who are the people? At the present stage in China, they are the working class, the peasantry, the urban petty bourgeoisie and the national bourgeoisie. These classes, led by the working class and the Communist Party, unite to form their own state and elect their own government; they enforce their dictatorship over the running dogs of imperialism—the landlord class and bureaucrat-bourgeoisie, as well as the representatives of those classes, the Kuomintang reactionaries and their accomplices—suppress them, allow them only to behave themselves and not to be unruly in word or deed. If they speak or act in an unruly way, they will be promptly stopped and punished. Democracy is practised within the ranks of the people, who enjoy the rights of freedom of speech, assembly, association and so on. The right to vote belongs only to the people, not to the reactionaries. The combination of these two aspects, democracy for the people and dictatorship over the reactionaries, is the people's democratic dictatorship.

Why must things be done this way? The reason is quite clear to everybody. If things were not done this way, the revolution would fail, the people would suffer, the country would be conquered.

"Don't you want to abolish state power?" Yes, we do, but not right now; we cannot do it yet. Why? Because imperialism still exists, because domestic reaction still exists, because classes still exist in our country. Our present task is to strengthen the people's state apparatus—mainly the people's army, the people's police and the people's courts—in order to consolidate national defence and protect the people's interests. Given this condition, China can develop steadily, under the leadership of the working class and the Communist Party, from an agricultural into an industrial country and from a new-democratic into a socialist and communist society, can abolish classes and realize the Great Harmony. The state apparatus, including the army, the police and the courts, is the instrument by which one class oppresses another. It is an instrument for the oppression of antagonistic classes; it is violence and not "benevolence." "You are not benevolent!" Quite so. We definitely do not apply a policy of benevolence to the reactionaries and towards the reactionary activities of the reactionary classes. Our policy of benevolence is applied only within the ranks of the people, not beyond them to the reactionaries or to the reactionary activities of reactionary classes.

The people's state protects the people. Only when the people have such a state can they educate and remould themselves by democratic methods on a country-wide scale, with everyone taking part, and shake off the influence of domestic and foreign reactionaries (which is still very strong, will survive for a long time and cannot be quickly destroyed), rid themselves of the bad habits and ideas acquired in the old society, not allow themselves to be led astray by the reactionaries, and continue to advance—to advance towards a socialist and communist society.

Here, the method we employ is democratic, the method of persuasion, not of compulsion. When anyone among the people breaks the law, he too should be punished, imprisoned or even sentenced to death; but this is a matter of a few individual cases, and it differs in principle from the dictatorship exercised over the reactionaries as a class.

As for the members of the reactionary classes and individual reactionaries, so long as they do not rebel, sabotage or create trouble after their political power has been overthrown, land and work will be given to them as well in order to allow them to live and remould themselves through labour into new people. If they are not willing to work, the people's state will compel them to work. Propaganda and educational work will be done among them too and will be done, moreover, with as much care and thoroughness as among the captured army officers in the past. This, too, may be called a "policy of benevolence" if you like, but it is imposed by us on the members of the enemy classes and cannot be mentioned in the same breath with the work of self-education which we carry on within the ranks of the revolutionary people.

Such remoulding of members of the reactionary classes can be accomplished only by a state of the people's democratic dictatorship under the leadership of the Communist Party. When it is well done, China's major exploiting classes, the landlord class and the bureaucrat-bourgeoisie (the monopoly capitalist class), will be eliminated for good. There remain the national bourgeoisie; at the present stage, we can already do a good deal of suitable educational work with many of them. When the time comes to realize socialism, that is, to nationalize private enterprise, we shall carry the work of educating and remoulding them a step further. The people have a powerful state apparatus in their hands—there is no need to fear rebellion by the national bourgeoisie.

The serious problem is the education of the peasantry. The peasant economy is scattered, and the socialization of agriculture, judging by the Soviet Union's experience, will require a long time and painstaking work. Without socialization of agriculture, there can be no complete, consolidated socialism. The steps to socialize agriculture must be co-ordinated with the development of a powerful industry having state enterprise as its backbone. The state of the people's democratic dictatorship must systematically solve the problems of industrialization. Since it is not proposed to discuss economic problems in detail in this article, I shall not go into them further.

In 1924 a famous manifesto was adopted at the Kuomintang's First National Congress, which Sun Yat-sen himself led and in which Communists participated. The manifesto stated:

> *The so-called democratic system in modern states is usually monopolized by the bourgeoisie and has become simply an instrument for oppressing the common people. On the other hand, the Kuomintang's Principle of Democracy means a democratic system shared by all the common people and not privately owned by the few.*

Apart from the question of who leads whom, the Principle of Democracy stated above corresponds as a general political programme to what we call People's Democracy or New Democracy. A state system which is shared only by the common people and which the bourgeoisie is not allowed to own privately—add to this the leadership of the working class, and we have the state system of the people's democratic dictatorship.

Chiang Kai-shek betrayed Sun Yat-sen and used the dictatorship of the bureaucrat-bourgeoisie and the landlord class as an instrument for oppressing the common people of China. This counter-revolutionary dictatorship was enforced for twenty-two years and has only now been overthrown by the common people of China under our leadership.

The foreign reactionaries who accuse us of practising "dictatorship" or "totalitarianism" are the very persons who practise it. They practice the dictatorship or totalitarianism of one class, the bourgeoisie, over the proletariat and the rest of the people. They are the very persons Sun Yat-sen spoke of as the bourgeoisie of modern states who oppress the common people. And it is from these reactionary scoundrels that Chiang Kai-shek learned his counter-revolutionary dictatorship.

Chu Hsi, a philosopher of the Sung Dynasty, wrote many books and made many remarks which are now forgotten, but one remark is still remembered, "Deal with a man as he deals with you." This is just what we do; we deal with the imperialists and their running dogs, the Chiang Kai-shek reactionaries, as they deal with us. That is all there is to it!

Revolutionary dictatorship and counter-revolutionary dictatorship are by nature opposites, but the former was learned from the latter. Such learning is very important. If the revolutionary people do not master this method of ruling over the counter-revolutionary classes, they will not be able to maintain their state power, domestic and foreign reaction will overthrow that power and restore its own rule over China, and disaster will befall the revolutionary people.

The people's democratic dictatorship is based on the alliance of the working class, the peasantry and the urban petty bourgeoisie, and mainly on the alliance of the workers and the peasants, because these two classes comprise 80 to 90 per cent of China's population. These two classes are the main force in overthrowing imperialism and the Kuomintang reactionaries. The transition from New Democracy to socialism also depends mainly upon their alliance.

The people's democratic dictatorship needs the leadership of the working class. For it is only the working class that is most far-sighted, most selfless and most thoroughly revolutionary. The entire history of revolution proves that without the leadership of the working class revolution fails and that with the leadership of the working class revolution triumphs. In the epoch of imperialism, in no country can any other class lead any genuine revolution to victory. This is clearly proved by the fact that the many revolutions led by China's petty bourgeoisie and national bourgeoisie all failed.

The national bourgeoisie at the present stage is of great importance. Imperialism, a most ferocious enemy, is still standing alongside us. China's modern industry still forms a very small proportion of the national economy. No reliable statistics are available, but it is estimated, on the basis of certain data, that before the War of Resistance Against Japan the value of output of modern industry constituted only about 10 per cent of the total value of output of the national economy. To counter imperialist oppression and to raise her backward economy to a higher level, China must utilize all the factors of urban and rural capitalism that are beneficial and not harmful to the national economy and the people's livelihood; and we must unite with the national bourgeoisie in common struggle. Our present policy is to regulate capitalism, not to destroy it. But the national bourgeoisie cannot be the leader of the revolution, nor should it have the chief role in state power. The reason it cannot be the leader of the revolution and should not have the chief role in state power is that the social and economic position of the national bourgeoisie determines its weakness; it lacks foresight and sufficient courage and many of its members are afraid of the masses.

Sun Yat-sen advocated "arousing the masses of the people" or "giving assistance to the peasants and workers". But who is to "arouse" them or "give assistance" to them? Sun Yat-sen had the petty bourgeoisie and the national bourgeoisie in mind. As a matter of fact, they cannot do so. Why did forty years of revolution under Sun Yat-sen end in failure? Because in the epoch of imperialism the petty bourgeoisie and the national bourgeoisie cannot lead any genuine revolution to victory.

Our twenty-eight years have been quite different. We have had much valuable experience. A well-disciplined Party armed with the theory of Marxism–Leninism, using the method of self-criticism and linked with the masses of the people; an army under the leadership of such a Party; a united front of all revolutionary classes and all revolutionary groups under the leadership of such a Party—these are the three main weapons with which we have defeated the enemy. They distinguish us from our predecessors. Relying on them, we have won basic victory. We have travelled a tortuous road. We have struggled against opportunist deviations in our Party, both Right and "Left." Whenever we made serious mistakes on these three matters, the revolution suffered setbacks. Taught by mistakes and setbacks, we have become wiser and handle our affairs better. It is hard for any political party or person to avoid mistakes, but we should make as few as possible. Once a mistake is made, we should correct it, and the more quickly and thoroughly the better.

To sum up our experience and concentrate it into one point, it is: the people's democratic dictatorship under the leadership of the working class (through the Communist Party) and based upon the alliance of workers and peasants. This dictatorship must unite as one with the international revolutionary forces. This is our formula, our principal experience, our main programme.

Twenty-eight years of our Party are a long period, in which we have accomplished only one thing—we have won basic victory in the revolutionary war. This calls for celebration, because it is the people's victory, because it is a victory in a country as large as China. But we still have much work to do; to use the analogy of a journey, our past work is only the first step in a long march of ten thousand *li*.[9] Remnants of the enemy have yet to be wiped out. The serious task of economic construction lies before us. We shall soon put aside some of the things we know well and be compelled to do things we don't know well. This means difficulties. The imperialists reckon that we will not be able to manage our economy; they are standing by and looking on, awaiting our failure.

We must overcome difficulties, we must learn what we do not know. We must learn to do economic work from all who know how, no matter who they are. We must esteem them as teachers, learning from them respectfully and conscientiously. We must not pretend to know when we do not know. We must not put on bu-

---

[9] A *li* is about ⅓ mile.

reaucratic airs. If we dig into a subject for several months, for a year or two, for three or five years, we shall eventually master it. At first some of the Soviet Communists also were not very good at handling economic matters and the imperialists awaited their failure too. But the Communist Party of the Soviet Union emerged victorious and, under the leadership of Lenin and Stalin, it learned not only how to make the revolution but also how to carry on construction. It has built a great and splendid socialist state. The Communist Party of the Soviet Union is our best teacher and we must learn from it. The situation both at home and abroad is in our favour, we can rely fully on the weapon of the people's democratic dictatorship, unite the people throughout the country, the reactionaries excepted, and advance steadily to our goal.

Further Readings

The history of China's reaction to the challenges of modernization and Western influences is perceptively discussed in John K. Fairbank, *The Great Chinese Revolution, 1800–1985* (New York: Harper and Row, 1986). Ross Terrill, *Mao: A Biography* (New York: Harper and Row, 1980), is a substantial treatment by a prolific author on modern Chinese topics. Ed Hammon, *To Embrace the Moon: An Illustrated Biography of Mao Zedong* (Berkeley, CA: Lancaster Miller. Asian Humanities Press, 1980), provides a well-illustrated but uncritical and anecdotal portrait of the subject. The most substantial recent biography is the two-volume work of Han Suyin, the first volume of which, *The Morning Deluge: Mao Tsetung and the Chinese Revolution, 1893–1954* (Boston, MA: Little, Brown Co., 1972), is a detailed account of the Chinese leader's youth and career up to 1954, while the second volume, *Wind in the Tower* (Boston, Little, Brown Co., 1976), carries the account to Mao's death.

The Long March is the subject of Harrison E. Salisbury, *The Long March: The Untold Story* (New York: Harper and Row, 1985), particularly interesting because the author retraced much of the route. Edgar Snow, *Red Star Over China* (1938, many editions), not only provides a biographical sketch of Mao's career to 1937, but offers an admiring eyewitness description of the Communist base in Yanan at the beginning of the struggle with the Japanese. The history of Mao's rule in China after the Communist victory in the civil war is the subject of Maurice J. Meisner, *Mao's China: A History of the People's Republic* (New York: Free Press, 1977), while a selection of Mao's public pronouncements during that period is provided by *The Writings of Mao Zedong, 1949–1976*, edited by Michael Y. M. Kau and John Long (Armonk, NY: M. E. Sharpe, 1986).

Fifteen Poems Out of Africa

The world has been slow to recognize either the quality or quantity of literary works produced by twentieth-century African writers. Over the last three decades, however, as Africa has increasingly become the subject of international attention for political and economic reasons, the merits of its cultural accomplishments have also become better known. Conditions in Africa during the twentieth century have generally been difficult, and this is reflected in African writers, who have become the voice of African consciousness and protest. Although best known for their prose, African writers have produced an astonishing amount of good poetry that vividly reveals the changes the century has brought to the continent.

Contemporary African poets are generally concerned with the African present, but they view that present through the prism of tradition. Poetry has always been an important aspect of African creativity, and traditional tribal life is rich in poetic expression. Songs and chants are central to ceremonial and festive occasions, and are used to accompany the tasks of the day. The nonliterate tribal societies of the recent past had no written literature, but poets and singers held a respected position and contributed to a rich and vibrant oral culture. This situation changed with the coming of the Europeans and the spread of literacy among the Africans in the late nineteenth and early twentieth centuries.

The transition from an oral, tribal tradition to a modern, written culture began with the poetry written by African youths educated in European schools. Particularly among those who were trained abroad, the dominant themes were an intense protest against colonialism and against that system's abuse of the dignity of the black African. In 1939, the formalization of the Negritude movement pro-

From *The Heritage of African Poetry*, edited by Isidore Okpewho (Essex, UK: Longman Group, Ltd., 1985), pp. 39–52.

vided a focus for those dedicated to projecting the black personality and culture. Members of this movement glorified African customs, landscape, and traditions, while continuing to condemn colonial mistreatment of the Africans themselves.

The emancipation of a large number of African nations from colonial rule in the 1950s and 1960s ushered in a new literary era. Contemporary African poetry still glorifies traditional ways of life and often condemns European culture, but modern writers have moved from a preoccupation with the problems created by colonialism to those posed by political independence. Thematic approaches have multiplied to include all aspects of African life and culture. By this process, African literature has increasingly come to display sentiments and perceptions that transcend specific political and social concerns.

Love is a frequent theme in both traditional and contemporary African poetry, and demonstrates this universality of appeal. Love exists in many forms, of which three, love between a man and woman, love between a mother and child, and love of country or people, are considered in the fifteen African poems presented here. The first five are tribal songs typical of traditional oral poetry. The remaining ten are modern.

1. *Where Has My Love Blown His Horn?* A rural love song from the Acholi tribe of Uganda. The theme concerns a young woman's search for her shepherd lover, who has wandered away, blowing his horn, in search of cattle, perhaps to use as a bride-price for the woman.

2. *What a Fool He Is!* This song from the Amhara tribe of Ethiopia tells of the deteriorating relationship between lovers. The woman's frustrations and disappointment is apparent as she journeys from town to town until learning that her lover has crossed the sea (Indian Ocean). The story concludes with her alienation from and dismissal of the man.

3. *I Will Satisfy My Desire.* The emotions of a young woman preparing herself to meet her lover are colorfully described in this song from the Bagirmi of Nigeria.

4. *Nyagumbe! Nyagumbe!* In this song from the Chopi tribe of Mozambique, a young man named Nyagumbe finds the girl he wishes to marry. When the girl refuses to return his love, he refuses to eat the food she prepares for him. Her mother advises her to love Nyagumbe, and, as the poem progresses, Nyagumbe's plan for winning the girl unfolds.

5. *A Mother to Her First-Born.* The joy and love of a mother for her first-born child is vividly portrayed in this beautiful song of the Lango tribe of Uganda.

6. *Nightsong: Country.* By identifying himself with the vitality of the rural landscape, the South African Dennis Brutus (b. 1924), portrays with the deepest sensitivity the need of the South African

black to draw strength from the land in response to the repressive practices of the nation's apartheid government.

7. *Dry Your Tears, Africa!* The author, Bernard Dadié (b. 1916), is notable among the Negritude poets. The poem depicts Africa in the person of a woman who is being comforted by her sons, who had abandoned her and gone on a journey. A poem of filial love, it also conveys the sentiments of racial loyalty.

8. *For Melba.* One of South Africa's outstanding poets, Keorapetse Kgositsile (b. 1940) was exiled in 1962 and currently resides in the United States. Although his poetry most frequently displays the sentiment of anger, he has also written a number of poems such as *For Melba* that are notable for their tenderness.

9. *To The Anxious Mother* is Valente Malangatana's (b. 1936) tender tribute of love and appreciation to his mother. The poem describes his birth, focusing on the general scene surrounding his delivery.

10. *I Will Cling To Your Garment*, by the Tanzanian Eric Sikujua Ng'Maryo, tells the story of a young man who passionately professes his love to a girl who apparently has not yet offered him any encouragement.

11. *Without You.* The poems of Odia Ofeimun (b. 1946) generally deal with political and social injustices in his native country of Nigeria. *Without You* is one of his few nonradical works. Ofeimun here pays a simple tribute to a woman whose love has brightened his life.

12. *Love Apart*, by the Nigerian Christopher Okigbo (1932–1967), is one of the most moving portraits of a dying love affair ever to be rendered in African poetry. The lovers are here compared to pines whose life has left them because the love that nurtured them has gone.

13. *Choice* is a charming poem by Flavien Ranaivo (b. 1914) extolling the virtues of honesty and simplicity in love over frivolous and materialist concerns. The young man in the poem intends to win his women, one rich (a chief's daughter) and the other poor (the sister of a poor widow), with material attractions. The poem concludes by pointing out that material favors might not be as appealing as the simple personal warmth of friendship.

14. *I Came With You* was written by one of the most famous of Africa's Negritude poets, Léopold Sédar Senghor (b. 1906). A frequent theme of his work is an emphasis on the beauty of the African world or culture as reflected in the African woman, and vice versa.

15. *Relentlessly She Drives Me*, like Senghor's previous poem, presents a vivid picture of the African world. It appears that the poet met a woman in France who constantly reminded him of African women back home and of the African surroundings from which he had been absent so long.

Questions

1. African poetry often provides insights into traditional tribal society. What aspects of tribal society are apparent in the first five works?

2. The need to reassert the lost pride of the African people is a frequent theme of Negritude poets. What obvious comparisons between European and African culture exist in these poems, and what function do these comparisons perform?

1 Where Has My Love Blown His Horn?
Acholi, Uganda

> Where has my love blown his horn?
> The tune of his horn is well known.
> Young men of my clan,
> Have you heard the horn of my love?
>
> 5 The long distance has ruined me, oh!
> The distance between me and my companion.
> Youths of my clan,
> Have you heard the horn of my love?
>
> The shortage of cattle has ruined my man!
> 10 The poverty of my love.
> Young men of my clan,
> Listen to the horn of my love.
>
> Where has my love blown his horn?
> The tune of his horn is well known.
> 15 Young men of my clan,
> Listen to the horn of my love.

line 1 Shepherd boys usually play horns or other musical instruments to relieve the boredom of long hours of watching over their cattle.
lines 9–10 In cattle-raising societies, a man's wealth is frequently measured in terms of the size of his herd; payments for services and other forms of social exchange (such as marriage) are also frequently made in cattle.

2 What a Fool He Is!
Amhara, Ethiopia

> When I asked for him at Entoto, he was towards Akaki,
> So they told me;
> When I asked for him at Akaki, he was towards Jarer,
> So they told me;
> 5 When I asked for him at Jarer, he was at Mendar,

　　　　So they told me;
　　　　When I asked for him at Mendar, he was towards Awash,
　　　　So they told me;
　　　　When I asked for him at Awash, he was towards Chercher,
10　　So they told me;
　　　　When I asked for him at Chercher, he was towards Harar,
　　　　So they told me;
　　　　When I asked for him at Harar, he was towards Djibouti,
　　　　So they told me;
15　　When I asked for him at Djibouti, he had crossed the sea,
　　　　Or so they said:
　　　　I sent to find him a hundred times,
　　　　But I never found him.
　　　　I sit by the fire and weep:
20　　What a fool he is
　　　　To hope he will ever find anyone to equal me.

3　I Will Satisfy My Desire

Bagirmi, Nigeria

　　　　I painted my eyes with black antimony
　　　　I girded myself with amulets.

　　　　I will satisfy my desire,
　　　　you my slender boy.
 5　　I walk behind the wall.
　　　　I have covered my bosom.
　　　　I shall knead coloured clay
　　　　I shall paint the house of my friend,
　　　　O my slender boy.
10　　I shall take my piece of silver
　　　　I will buy silk.
　　　　I will gird myself with amulets
　　　　I will satisfy my desire
　　　　the horn of antimony in my hand,
15　　Oh my slender boy!

line 1 antimony a dark, powdery substance often used as cosmetic.
line 10 piece of silver money.

4　Nyagumbe! Nyagumbe!

Chopi, Mozambique

　　BRIDE:　　　　Nyagumbe! Nyagumbe!
　　　　　　　　　　Why do you refuse?
　　BRIDEGROOM:　I am refusing.

	5	In my heart
		is the love
		of refusing.
	BRIDE:	I will go
		to the band of men.
		Father! Father!
	10	Nyagumbe refuses.
	FATHER:	Why does he refuse?
	BRIDE:	He is refusing.
		In his heart
		is the love
	15	of refusing.
		I will go
		to the hearth.
		Mother! Mother!
		Nyagumbe refuses.
	20 MOTHER:	Why does he refuse?
	BRIDE:	He is refusing.
		In his heart
		is the love
		of refusing.
	25 MOTHER:	Go to the bin!
		Procure beans!
		Cook! Cook!
		Serve! Serve!
	BRIDE:	I will go
	30	to the boys' hut.
		Nyagumbe! Nyagumbe!
		Here are beans.
		Why do you refuse?
		I will go
	35	to the band of men.
		Father! Father!
		Nyagumbe refuses.
	FATHER:	Why does he refuse?
	BRIDE:	He is refusing
	40	in his heart.
		I will go
		to the hearth.
		Mother! Mother!
		Nyagumbe is refusing.
	45 MOTHER:	Why does he refuse?

line 8 The group of mature men who gather together and chat near a fire or under a tree.
line 17 Fireplace in the women's hut where women sit in the evening and tell stories.
line 30 Hut where only young men and boys congregrate.

| | BRIDE: | He is refusing
in his heart. |
| --- | --- | --- |
| | MOTHER: | Go to the fowl-run!
Catch a cock! |
| 50 | | Kill! Kill!
Cook! Cook! |
| | BRIDE: | I will go
to the boys' hut.
Nyagumbe! Nyagumbe! |
55	BRIDEGROOM:	What is the meat?
	BRIDE:	The meat is a cock.
	BRIDEGROOM:	What is the cock?
	BRIDE:	The cock is a cockerel.
Why do you refuse?
60	BRIDEGROOM:	I am refusing.
In my heart
is the love
of refusing.
	BRIDE:	I will go
65		to the band of men.
Father! Father!
Nyagumbe refuses.
	FATHER:	Why does he refuse?
	BRIDE:	He is refusing.
70		I will go
to the hearth.
Mother! Mother!
Nyagumbe refuses.
	MOTHER:	Why does he refuse?
75	BRIDE:	He is refusing
in his heart.
	MOTHER:	My child! My child!
Love him! Love him!
	BRIDE:	I will go
80		to the boys' hut.
Nyagumbe! Nyagumbe!
I did love you!
He is laughing!
Why are you laughing?
85	BRIDEGROOM:	I am laughing
In my heart
is the love
of laughing!

line 58 A cock not old enough to crow; considered a delicacy.

5 A Mother to Her First-Born
Lango, Uganda

Speak to me, child of my heart.
Speak to me with your eyes, your round, laughing eyes,
Wet and shining as Lupeyo's bull-calf.

Speak to me, little one,
5 Clutching my breast with your hand,
So strong and firm for all its littleness.
It will be the hand of a warrior, my son,
A hand that will gladden your father.
See how eagerly it fastens on me:
10 It thinks already of a spear:
It quivers as at the throwing of a spear.
Oh son, you will have a warrior's name and be a leader
    of men.
And your sons, and your son's sons, will remember you long
    after you have slipped into the darkness.
But I, I shall always remember your hand clutching me so.
15 I shall recall how you lay in my arms,
And looked at me so, and so,
And how your tiny hands played with my bosom.
And when they name you great warrior, then will my eyes be
    wet with remembering.
And how shall we name you, little warrior?
20 See, let us play at naming.
It will not be a name of despisal, for you are my first-born.
Not as Nawal's son is named will you be named.
Our gods will be kinder to you than theirs.
Must we call you 'Insolence' or 'Worthless One'?
25 Shall you be named, like a child of ill fortune, after the dung
    of cattle?
Our gods need no cheating, my child:
They wish you no ill.
They have washed your body and clothed it with beauty.
They have set a fire in your eyes.
30 And the little, puckering ridges of your brow—
Are they not the seal of their finger-prints when they fash-
    ioned you?
They have given you beauty and strength, child of my heart,
And wisdom is already shining in your eyes,
And laughter.
35 So how shall we name you, little one?
Are you your father's father, or his brother, or yet another?
Whose spirit is it that is in you, little warrior?
Whose spear-hand tightens round my breast?

Who lives in you and quickens to life, like last year's
    melon seed?
40 Are you silent, then?
But your eyes are thinking, thinking, and glowing like the eyes
    of a leopard in a thicket.
Well, let be.
At the day of naming you will tell us.

O my child, now indeed I am happy.
45 Now indeed I am a wife!—
No more a bride, but a Mother-of-one.
Be splendid and magnificent, child of desire.
Be proud, as I am proud.
Be happy, as I am happy.
50 Be loved, as now I am loved.
Child, child, child, love I have had from my man.
But now, only now, have I the fullness of love.
Now, only now, am I his wife and the mother of his first-born.
His soul is safe in your keeping, my child, and it was I, I, I,
    who have made you.
55 Therefore am I loved.
Therefore am I happy.
Therefore am I a wife.
Therefore have I great honour.

You will tend his shrine when he is gone.
60 With sacrifice and oblation you will recall his name year
    by year.
He will live in your prayers, my child,
And there will be no more death for him, but everlasting life
    springing from your loins.
You are his shield and spear, his hope and redemption from
    the dead.
Through you he will be reborn, as the saplings in the Spring.
65 And I, I am the mother of his first-born.
Sleep, child of beauty and courage and fulfilment, sleep.
I am content.

6 Nightsong: Country

Dennis Brutus

All of this undulant earth
heaves up to me;

line 59 A *shrine* was often set up in a traditional African household in honour of its ancestors. Sacrifices of food would occasionally be made to it and appeals and prayers (for the welfare of living members of the family) addressed to it.
Country (part of the title) Brutus plays here upon the dual meaning of 'countryside' and 'fatherland.'
lines 2–3 heave and *distend* indicate sighing and stretching of the body.

          soft curves in the dark distend
          voluptuous-submissively;
    5   primal and rank
          the pungent exudation
          of fecund growth ascends
          sibilant clamorously:
          voice of the night-land
    10   rising, shimmering,
          mixing most intimately
          with my own murmuring—
          we merge, embrace and cling:
          who now gives shelter, who begs sheltering?

line 5 primal ancient; *rank* strong-smelling.
line 6 pungent exudation sharp odour.
line 8 sibilant clamorously hissing loudly.
line 14 Because the poet and the land are now one and inseparable, it is difficult to tell which of the two of them gives or receives protection.

7 Dry Your Tears, Africa!
Bernard Dadié

          Dry your tears, Africa!
          Your children come back to you
          Out of the storms and squalls of fruitless journeys.

          Through the crest of the wave and the babbling of the breeze
    5   Over the gold of the east
          and the purple of the setting sun,
          the peaks of proud mountains
          and the grasslands drenched with light
          They return to you
    10   out of the storms and squalls of fruitless journeys.
          Dry your tears Africa!
          We have drunk
          From all the springs
             of ill fortune
    15   and of glory

          And our senses are now opened
             to the splendour of your beauty
             to the smell of your forests

line 3 The *storm and squalls* may refer to the black man's involvement in the Second World War which ended in 1945 (two years before Dadié's return to the Ivory Coast). The experience with the white man would then be seen as a *fruitless journey* in the sense that it has done the black man more harm than good.
lines 4–8 Over the seas and across all parts of the continent–east, west, and everywhere. The *proud mountains* are a reference to such heights as Kilimanjaro in east Africa and Futa Jalon in the west; the *grasslands* are for the savannah regions of western and southern Africa.

        to the charms of your waters
20   to the clearness of your skies
        to the caress of your sun
And to the charm of your foliage pearled by the dew.

Dry your tears, Africa!
Your children come back to you
25   their hands full of playthings
and their hearts full of love.
They return to clothe you
in their dreams and their hopes.

8 For Melba

Keorapetse Kgositsile

Morning smiles
In your eye
Like a coy moment
Captured by an eternal
5   Noon and from yesterdays
I emerge naked
Like a Kimberley diamond
Full like Limpopo after rain
Singing your unnumbered charms.

line 5 from yesterdays Melba is a girl the poet met in America. To be able to portray his deepest feelings for her, he tries to cast his mind back to scenes from the South African homeland which he left years ago.
line 7 Kimberley an area in South Africa where precious stones are mined.
line 8 Limpopo a river in South Africa.

9 To the Anxious Mother

Valente Malangatana

Into your arms I came
when you bore me, very anxious
you, who were so alarmed
at that monstrous moment
5   fearing that God might take me.
Everyone watched in silence
to see if the birth was going well
everyone washed their hands
to be able to receive the one who came from Heaven
10   and all the women were still and afraid.
But when I emerged
from the place where you sheltered me so long

> at once I drew my first breath
> at once you cried out with joy
> 15 the first kiss was my grandmother's.
> And she took me at once to the place
> where they kept me, hidden away
> everyone was forbidden to enter my room
> because everyone smelt bad
> 20 and I all fresh, fresh
> breathed gently, wrapped in my napkins.
> But grandmother, who seemed like a madwoman,
> always looking and looking again
> because the flies came at me
> 25 and the mosquitoes harried me
> God who also watched over me
> was my old granny's friend.

10 I Will Cling To Your Garment
Eric S. Ng'maryo

> I will cling to your garment like a wild grass seed:
> I will needle your flesh
> And pray
> That my insistent call for you
> 5 Be not met with
> A jerky
> Removal
> From your garment,
> And a throw into the fire,
> 10 But that
> You will drop me on to the fertile ground of
> Your favour.

11 Without You
Odia Ofeimun

> In your absence
> my life is all a stammer
> hunted down
> by a non-existent tomorrow
> 5 I feel guilty
> of sins I have not committed
> borne on the wings
> of incessant fears

line 7 wings The endless fears within him are seen as putting him constantly in flight and so denying him peace of mind.

         Without you.
10   my earth suffers a demise of colours
         as when a ghost leaves a house
         at night
         the light goes out

line 10 my earth suffers a demise of colours the world around me loses all brilliance and beauty. The brightness of the sun illuminates the world, revealing a variety of objects whose different colours make the world so lively and lovely. The lady is here likened to the sun, and in the next line to a ghost especially because ghosts are said to appear sometimes in shining white forms.

12 Love Apart
Christopher Okigbo

         The moon has ascended between us
         Between two pines
         That bow to each other

         Love with the moon has ascended
5   Has fed on our solitary pines

         And we are now shadows
         That cling to each other
         But kiss the air only.

13 Choice
Flavien Ranaivo

         Who is that making her steps clatter on the firm earth?
         —She is the daughter of the new chief-over-a-thousand.
         —If she is the daughter of the chief-over-a-thousand,
         Tell her night will soon be falling
5   And I would trade all the coral-red loves
         For a hint of her friendship.

         —Who is she coming from the north?
         —It is the sister of the widow scented with rose-apples.
         —Tell her to come inside at once,
10   I will make her a fine dinner.
         —She will not touch it I know:

line 5 coral-red loves women with rosy-red cheeks. The phrase suggests something that enjoys high social standing or at least a high estimation in the eyes of the man.
line 8 rose-apples a reference to very cheap cosmetics. The widow cannot afford the sophisticated scents sold in the shops, and so takes her adornment from ordinary nature. The poverty of the girl is also suggested by the young man's offer to cook her a dinner, which implies that she may be hungry (or *thirsty*, line 13).

She will take a little rice-water
Not because she is thirsty
But because it is her whim to please you.

14 I Came With You
Léopold Sédar Senghor

[For Khalam]

I came with you as far as the village of grain-huts, to the gates of Night
I had no words before the golden riddle of your smile.
A brief twilight fell on your face, freak of the divine fancy.
From the top of the hill where the light takes refuge, I saw the brightness of your cloth go out
5 And your crest like a sun dropped beneath the shadow of the ricefields
When the anxieties came against me, ancestral fears more treacherous than panthers
—The mind cannot push them back across the day's horizons.
Is it then night for ever, parting never to meet again?
I shall weep in the darkness, in the motherly hollow of the Earth
10 I will sleep in the silence of my tears
Until my forehead is touched by the milky dawning of your mouth.

khalam a small three-stringed guitar.
  line 1 grain-huts cylindrical mud huts in which grain like millet or rice is stored; *gates of Night* is a metaphor for twilight, the entrance from the final moments of daylight to the early period of darkness.
  line 2 golden riddle the faint light of the sun played on her smile, so that it was not clear whether she was smiling out of friendliness or not.
  line 3 freak of the divine fancy a wonder created (or conceived) by the mind of God.
  line 5 crest her head or headwear.
  line 6 ancestral fears more treacherous than panthers The fears—as to what the future holds—are called ancestral (ancient) because fears about the unknown have always afflicted man since time immemorial. They are compared here to panthers which lurk secretly for some time before striking their victims.
  line 9 motherly hollow of the Earth Because it is the natural source of food or nourishment, the Earth is often pictured in traditionally agricultural societies as a mother nourishing her children (mankind). *Hollow* suggests a mother's womb, deep and inexhaustible (like the earth) in its sympathy and tenderness.
  line 11 the milky dawning of your mouth Your mouth, tender as milk, as it kisses me awake in the morning.

15 Relentlessly She Drives Me
Léopold Sédar Senghor

[For two balafongs]

Relentlessly she drives me through the thickets of Time.
My black blood hounds me through the crowd to the clearing where the white night sleeps.

Sometimes I turn round in the street and see again the palm tree smiling under the breeze.
Her voice brushes me like the soft lisping sweep of a wing and I say
5 'Yes it is Signare!' I have seen the sun set in the blue eyes of a fair negress.
At Sevres-Babylone or Balangar, amber and *gongo*, her scent was near and spoke to me.
Yesterday in church at the Angelus, her eyes shone like candles burnishing
Her skin with bronze. My God, my God, why do you tear my pagan senses shrieking out of me?
I cannot sing your plain chant that has no swing to it, I cannot dance it.
10 Sometimes a cloud, a butterfly, raindrops on my boredom's window-pane.
Relentlessly she drives me across the great spaces of Time.
My black blood hounds me, to the solitary heart of the night.

balafong a traditional xylophone.
line 1 thickets of Time crowded images of past experience.
line 2 the clearing where white night sleeps the moonlit village in the midst of the tropical forest.
line 4 lisping sweep of a wing gentle brush of the wing of a butterfly or a bird. The rather thin and tender touch is compared to a similar effect of the tongue on the teeth of someone who lisps.
line 5 Signare (a word borrowed from the Portuguese) means a high-class lady. Such ladies were previously kept as mistresses by Portuguese settlers in Senegal. There are today many fair-skinned women in Senegal who are products and descendants of that association, and they enjoy a high social standing there. In the second sentence of this line, Senghor seems to be striving to reassert the African element (the tropical sun) against the European (blue eyes) in the woman.
line 6 Sevres-Babylone and *Balangar* are Senegalese towns. *Gongo* is a perfume which emits rather strong scent.
line 7 Angelus At certain hours of the day, especially at noon, every Roman Catholic church rings its bell, inviting the faithful to offer a prayer in memory of the act of the Angel Gabriel in announcing to the Virgin Mary that she would be the mother of Jesus. *Angelus* (meaning Angel) is the first word of this commemorative prayer.
line 9 plain chant Gregorian chant; chant performed during Christian rites.
line 10 Sometimes, in my boredom, I imagine a cloud or a butterfly falling on my window-pane like a drop of rain.
line 12 solitary heat of the night unperturbed village in the heart of the continent. *Night* here recalls the moonlight night of line 2; but in some of his other writing Senghor has been known to use the word (in terms of the darkness) as a colour symbol for Africa.

Further Readings

The Heritage of African Poetry, edited by Isidore Okpewho (London: Longman, 1985), is a thematically arranged anthology containing a useful analysis of oral and written poetry. Two exceptional anthologies of black African poetry are *Poems from Black Africa,* edited by Langston Hughes (Bloomington, IN: University of Indiana Press, 1968), and *Modern Poetry from Africa,* edited by Gerald Moore and Ulli Beier (Baltimore, MD: Penguin Books, 1963).

The *African Literature Today* series, edited by Eldred Durosimi Jones (14 vols.: New York: Africana Publishing Co., 1972–1985), contains scholarly articles on both African literature and individual writers. Of particular interest is volume 6 (1973), which concentrates on poetry. *Introduction to African Literature,* edited by Ulli Beier (London: Longman, 1967), is a collection of essays including a section on the oral tradition in African poetry. R. N. Egudu, *Modern African Poetry and the African Predicament* (London: Macmillan, 1978), is a study of the effect of life in colonial and postcolonial Africa on modern African poetry. David Cook, *African Literature* (London: Longman, 1977), presents a series of perceptive essays.

K. L. Goodwin, *Understanding African Poetry* (London: Heinemann, 1982), is a study of ten noteworthy African poets, including Dennis Brutus and Christopher Okigbo. *African Literature in the 20th Century,* edited by Leonard S. Klein (New York: Ungar Publishing Co., 1986), presents an overview of the literature of the different regions of Africa. O. R. Dathorne, *African Literature in the Twentieth Century* (Minneapolis, MN: University of Minnesota Press, 1975), considers writings in various African and European languages, and provides an excellent bibliography.

Three useful examinations of economic, political, and social changes in twentieth-century Africa are provided by Kofi Abrefa Busia, *The African Consciousness: Continuity and Change in Africa* (New York: American–African Affairs, 1968); Mokurigo Okoye, *African Responses* (Ifracombe, UK: A. H. Stockwell, 1964); and Ali Al'Amin Muzrui, *World Culture and the Black Experience* (Seattle, WA: University of Washington Press, 1974). The colonial experience in Africa is the subject of Norman R. Bennett, *Africa and Europe* (New York: Africana Publishing Co., 1984), and A. J. Christopher, *Colonial Africa* (Totowa, NJ: Barnes and Noble, 1984). The psychological impact of colonialism is considered in Jock McCulloch, *Black Soul, White Artifact* (New York: Cambridge University Press, 1983).

The Nobel Prize Address of Mother Teresa of Calcutta

The awarding of the Nobel Peace Prize in 1979 to Mother Teresa of Calcutta focused the attention of the world on a truly remarkable woman and provided her with universal acclaim. That this prestigious honor, normally bestowed on statesmen, scientists, and activists in the cause of human rights, should have been presented to a Catholic nun whose piety and orthodoxy might seem unfashionable to many is testimony to the magnitude of her accomplishments. Media exposure, combined with numerous awards, has given her international recognition. She has met with kings and princes, heads of state, and the pope. Nevertheless, she remains a simple and pious individual, seeking to avoid fame and to devote her time to her special vocation, the love and care of India's hungry, sick, and destitute.

For approximately forty years, Mother Teresa has lived and worked amid the squalor of Calcutta's slums, attending tirelessly to the sick and the dying. Possessing only a sari and a bucket for washing herself, she lives in a shelter whose doors are always open, in a room furnished only with a small bed and a simple wooden table. Her special message of love and compassion has provided hope and dignity to countless thousands, and the order that she founded and continues to direct, the Missionaries of Charity, has grown to over two hundred houses in twenty countries. Her utterly sincere response when she first learned of the Nobel Prize awarded her was characteristic: "I am unworthy. I accept in the name of the poor, because I believe that by giving me the prize, they've recognized the presence of the poor in the world."

Born Gonxha Bojaxhiu on 27 August 1910 in the Yugoslavian

From Robert Serrou, *Teresa of Calcutta* (New York: McGraw-Hill Book Company, 1980), pp. 109–114.

town of Skopje, she was influenced early by her deeply religious mother, who maintained a strict Roman Catholic discipline in the home. By the age of twelve, Gonxha had decided to devote herself to the care of the poor. Intrigued by accounts of conditions in Bengal related to her by returning missionaries, she determined to work in India as a missionary. At eighteen, she joined the Irish Loreto Order, which operated a mission station in Calcutta. She arrived in India in 1929 and, after two years as a novice, on 24 May 1931 took her first vows, adopting the name Teresa in memory of St. Theresa of Avila. From 1929 to 1946, she taught history and geography at St. Mary's School for Girls, run by the Loreto sisters in Calcutta.

She learned both the native language and the city, discovering for herself the terrible poverty and squalor of Calcutta's slums. In 1946, she received what she would later describe as her "second calling," " a call within my vocation." This led her to leave her students at St. Mary's School and go out into the streets to work among the poor in the slums. It was among the hungry, the diseased, the old, and the ill—often abandoned in the streets to die alone—and among the thousands of orphans of the city that she resolved to spend the rest of her life. In 1946, she applied to the archbishop of Calcutta for permission to pursue her new vocation and, in 1948, she received permission to exchange the habit of the Loreto Order for the traditional Indian sari. Joined by a number of former students and other young women, her community was recognized as a separate order, the Missionaries of Charity. In addition to the customary vows of poverty, chastity, and obedience, her followers accepted a fourth: "to give wholehearted service to the very poorest."

The year 1952 marked the opening of the first Home for the Dying, where, regardless of race or religion, those dying destitute and alone are brought so that they may spend their last hours with care and love. It is estimated that between thirty and sixty thousand have died there, under the sisters' care. By 1957, Teresa had extended her work to the care of lepers, of whom there are more than fifty thousand in the area of Calcutta alone.

Beginning with only ten members, the congregation has undergone phenomenal expansion. More and more women, both Indian and others, have joined the order. Its activities have proliferated and now include slum schools, orphanages, mobile clinics, leprosy treatment centers, hostels for the dying, food kitchens, vocational training, and much else. Although the emphasis is still on India and neighboring Bangladesh, the order has now become international.

For over two decades, Mother Teresa's work attracted little attention outside India. In 1965, however, her order was recognized as a papal congregation under the protection of the Vatican, and in 1967 she was the subject of a BBC television program that received a tremendous popular response. Recognition soon came in the form of numerous international awards, culminating in the Nobel Peace Prize in 1979. Although Mother Teresa's work is firmly rooted in

Roman Catholicism, she has transcended the barriers of race, creed, and culture. On learning that she was to receive the Nobel Prize, the *New Guardian* of London wrote, "for thirty years she has made a hell on earth a somewhat more endurable place in which to live and die for God knows how many thousands, possibly millions now."

Questions

1. To what significant problems facing contemporary society does Mother Teresa refer? Does she offer any solutions? If so, what?

2. What does she consider to be the major cause of poverty in the world?

3. She refers to abortion as the greatest destroyer of peace. What alternatives does she advocate?

THE NOBEL PRIZE ADDRESS

As we have gathered here together to thank God for the Nobel Peace Prize I think it will be beautiful that we pray the prayer of St. Francis of Assisi which always surprises me very much—we pray this prayer every day after Holy Communion, because it is very fitting for each one of us, and I always wonder that so many hundreds of years ago as St. Francis of Assisi composed this prayer that they had the same difficulties that we have today, as we recite this prayer that fits very nicely for us also. I think some of you already have got it—so we will pray together. . . .

Let us thank God for the opportunity that we all have together today, for this gift of peace that reminds us that we have been created to live that peace, and Jesus became man to bring that good news to the poor. He being God became man in all things like us except sin, and he proclaimed very clearly that he had come to give the good news. The news was peace to all of good will and this is something that we all want—the peace of heart—and God loved the world so much that he gave his son—it was a giving—it is as much as if to say it hurt God to give, because he loved the world so much that he gave his son, and he gave him to Virgin Mary, and what did she do with him?

As soon as he came in her life—immediately she went in haste to give that good news, and as she came into the house of her cousin, the child—the unborn child—the child in the womb of Elizabeth, lit with joy. He, that little unborn child, was the first messenger of peace. He recognized the Prince of Peace, he recognized that Christ has come to bring the good news for you and for me. And as if that was not enough—it was not enough to become a man—he died on the cross to show that greater love, and he died for you and for me and for that leper and for that man dying of hunger and that naked person lying in the street not only of Calcutta, but of Africa, and New York, and London, and Oslo—and insisted that we love one another as he loves each one of us. And we read that in the Gospel very clearly—love as I have loved you—as I love you—as the Father has loved me, I love you—and the harder the Father loved him, he gave him to us, and how much we love one another, we, too, must give to each other until it hurts. It is not enough for us to say: I love God, but I do not love my neighbor. St. John says you are a liar if you say you love God and you don't love your neighbor. How can you love God whom you do not see, if you do not love your neighbor whom you see, whom you touch, with whom you live. And so this is very important for us to realize that love, to be true, has to hurt. It hurt Jesus to love us, it hurt him. And to make sure we remember his great love he made himself bread of life to satisfy our hunger for his love. Our hunger for God, because we have been created for that love. We have been created in his image. We have been created to love and be loved, and then he has become man to make it possible for us to love as he loved us. He makes himself the hungry one—the naked one—the homeless one—the sick one—the one in prison—the lonely one—the unwanted one—and he says: You did it to me. Hungry for our love, and this is the hunger of our poor people. This is the hunger that you and I must find, it may be in our own home.

    I never forget an opportunity I had in visiting a home where they had all these old parents of sons and daughters who had just put them in an institution and forgotten maybe. And I went there, and I saw in that home they had everything, beautiful things, but everybody was looking towards the door. And I did not see a single one with their smile on their face. And I turned to the sister and I asked: How is that? How is it that the people they have everything here, why are they all looking towards the door, why are they not smiling? I am so used to see the smile on our people, even the dying ones smile, and she said: This is nearly every day, they are expecting, they are hoping that a son or daughter will come to visit them. They are hurt because they are forgotten, and see—this is where love comes. That poverty comes right there in our own home, even neglect to love. Maybe in our own family we have somebody who is feeling lonely, who is feeling sick, who is feeling worried, and these are difficult days for everybody. Are we there, are we there to receive them, is the mother there to receive the child?

    I was surprised in the waste to see so many young boys and girls given into drugs, and I tried to find out why—why is it like that, and the answer was: Because there is no one in the family to receive them. Father and mother are so busy they have no time. Young parents are in some institution and the child takes back to the street and gets involved in something.

We are talking of peace. These are things that break peace, but I feel the greatest destroyer of peace today is abortion, because it is a direct war, a direct killing—direct murder by the mother herself. And we read in the Scripture, for God says very clearly: Even if a mother could forget her child—I will not forget you—I have curved you in the palm of my hand. We are curved in the palm of His hand, so close to Him that unborn child has been curved in the hand of God. And that is what strikes me most, the beginning of that sentence, that even if a mother *could* forget, something impossible—but even if she could forget—I will not forget you. And today the greatest means—the greatest destroyer of Peace is abortion. And we who are standing here—our parents wanted us. We would not be here if our parents would do that to us. Our children, we want them, we love them, but what of the millions? Many people are very, very concerned with the children in India, with the children of Africa where quite a number die, maybe of malnutrition, of hunger and so on, but millions are dying deliberately by the will of the mother. And this is what is the greatest destroyer of peace today. Because if a mother can kill her own child—what is left for me to kill you and you to kill me—there is nothing between. And this I appeal in India, I appeal everywhere: Let us bring the child back, and this year being the child's year: What have we done for the child?

At the beginning of the year I told, I spoke everywhere and I said: Let us make this year that we make every single child born, and unborn, wanted. And today is the end of the year, have we really made the children wanted? I will give you something terrifying. We are fighting abortion by adoption, we have saved thousands of lives, we have sent words to all the clinics, to the hospitals, police stations—please don't destroy the child, we will take the child. So every hour of the day and night it is always somebody, we have quite a number of unwedded mothers—tell them come, we will take care of you, we will take the child from you, and we will get a home for the child. And we have a tremendous demand for families who have no children, that is the blessing of God for us.

And also, we are doing another thing which is very beautiful—we are teaching our beggars, our leprosy patients, our slum dwellers, our people of the street, natural family planning. And in Calcutta alone in six years—it is all in Calcutta—we have had 61,273 babies less from the families who would have had, but because they practise this natural way of abstaining, of self-control, out of love for each other. We teach them the temperature meter[1] which is very beautiful, very simple, and our poor people understand. And you know what they have told me? Our family is healthy, our family is united, and we can have a baby whenever we want. So clear—those people in the street, those beggars—and I think that if our

---

[1] For determining when conception is most likely to occur.

Mother Teresa.

people can do like that how much more you and all the others who can know the ways and means without destroying the life that God has created in us. The poor people are very great people. They can teach us so many beautiful things. The other day one of them came to thank us and said: You people who have evolved chastity you are the best people to teach us family planning. Because it is nothing more than self-control out of love for each other. And I think they said a beautiful sentence. And these are people who maybe have nothing to eat, maybe they have not a home where to live, but they are great people. The poor are very wonderful people. One evening we went out and we picked up four people from the street. And one of them was in a most terrible condition—and I told the sisters: You take care of the other three, I take this one that looked worse.

So I did for her all that my love can do, I put her in bed, and there was such a beautiful smile on her face. She took hold of my hand, said one word: Thank you—and died.

I could not help but examine my conscience before her, and I asked what would I say if I was in her place. And my answer was very simple. I would have tried to draw a little attention to myself, I would have said I am hungry, that I am dying, I am cold, I am in pain, or something, but she gave me much more—she gave me her grateful love. And she died with a smile on her face. As that man said whom we picked up from the drain, half eaten with worms, and we brought him to the home: I have lived like an animal in the street, but I am going to die like an angel, loved and cared for. And it was so wonderful to see the greatness of that man who could speak like that, who could die like that without blaming anybody, without cursing anybody, without comparing anything. Like an angel—this is the greatness of our people. And that is why we believe what Jesus has said: I was hungry—I was naked—I was homeless—I was unwanted, unloved, uncared for—and you did it to me. I believe that we are not real social workers. We may be doing social work in the eyes of the people, but we are really contemplatives in the heart of the world. For we are touching the body of Christ 24 hours. We have 24 hours in this presence, and so you and I. You too try to bring that presence of God in your family, for the family that prays together stays together. And I think that we in our family, we don't need bombs and guns, to destroy to bring peace—just get together, love one another, bring that peace, that joy, that strength of presence of each other in the home. And we will be able to overcome all the evil that is in the world. There is so much suffering, so much hatred, so much misery, and we with our prayer, with our sacrifice are beginning at home.

Love begins at home, and it is not how much we do, but how much love we put in the action that we do. It is to God Almighty—how much we do it does not matter, because He is infinite, but how much love we put in that action. How much we do to Him in the person that we are serving. Some time ago in Calcutta we had great difficulty in getting sugar, and I don't know how the word got around to the children, and a little boy of four years old, Hindu boy, went home and told his parents: I will not eat sugar for three days, I will give my sugar to Mother Teresa for her children. After three days his father and mother brought him to our house. I had never met them before, and this little one could scarcely pronounce my name, but he knew exactly what he had come to do. He knew that he wanted to share his love. And this is why I have received such a lot of love from you all. From the time that I have come here I have simply been surrounded with love, and with real, real understanding love. It could feel as if everyone in India, everyone in Africa is somebody very special to you. And I felt quite at home I was telling Sister today. I feel in the Convent with the Sisters as if I am in Calcutta with my own Sisters. So completely at home here, right here. And so here I am talking with you—I want you to find the poor here, right in your own home first. And begin love there. Be that good news to your own people. And find out about your nextdoor neighbors—do you know who they are?

I had the most extraordinary experience with a Hindu family who had eight children. A gentleman came to our house and said:

Mother Teresa, there is a family with eight children, they had not eaten for so long—do something. So I took some rice and I went there immediately. And I saw the children—their eyes shining with hunger—I don't know if you have ever seen hunger. But I have seen it very often. And she took the rice, she divided the rice, and she went out. When she came back I asked her—where did you go, what did you do? And she gave me a very simple answer: They are hungry also. What struck me most was that she knew—and who are they, a Muslim family—and she knew. I didn't bring more rice that evening because I wanted them to enjoy the joy of sharing. But there were those children, radiating joy, sharing the joy with their mother because she had the love to give. And you see this is where love begins—at home, and I want you—and I am very grateful for what I have received. It has been a tremendous experience and I go back to India—I will be back by next week, the 15th I hope—and I will be able to bring your love.

And I know well that you have not given from your abundance, but you have given until it has hurt you. Today the little children they gave—I was so surprised—there is so much joy for the children that are hungry. That the children like themselves will need love and care and tenderness, like they get so much from their parents. So let us thank God that we have had this opportunity to come to know each other, and this knowledge of each other has brought us very close. And we will be able to help not only the children of India and Africa, but will be able to help the children of the whole world, because as you know our Sisters are all over the world.

And with this Prize that I have received as a Prize of Peace, I am going to try to make the home for many people that have no home. Because I believe that love begins at home, and if we can create a home for the poor—I think that more and more love will spread. And we will be able through this understanding love to bring peace, be the good news to the poor. The poor in our own family first, in our country and in the world. To be able to do this, our Sisters, our lives have to be woven with prayer. They have to be woven with Christ to be able to understand, to be able to share. Because today there is so much suffering—and I feel that the passion of Christ is being relived all over again—are we there to share that passion, to share that suffering of people. Around the world, not only in the poor countries, but I found the poverty of the West so much more difficult to remove. When I pick up a person from the street, hungry, I give him a plate of rice, a piece of bread, I have satisfied. I have removed that hunger. But a person that is shut out, that feels unwanted, unloved, terrified, the person that has been thrown out from society—that poverty is so hurtable and so much, and I find that very difficult. Our Sisters are working amongst that kind of people in the West. So you must pray for us that we may be able to be that good news, but we cannot do that without you, you have to do that here in your country. You must come to know the poor, maybe our people here have material things, everything, but I think that if we all look into our own homes, how difficult we find it sometimes to smile at each other, and that the smile is the beginning of love. And so let us always meet each other with a smile, for the smile is the beginning of love, and once we begin to love each other naturally we want to do something.

So you pray for our Sisters and for me and for our Brothers, and for our co-workers that are around the world. That we may remain faithful to the gift of God, to love Him and serve Him in the poor together with you. What we have done we would not have been able to do if you did not share with your prayers, with your gifts, this continual giving. But I don't want you to give me from your abundance, I want that you give me until it hurts. The other day I received 15 dollars from a man who has been on his back for twenty years, and the only part that he can move is his right hand. And the only companion that he enjoys is smoking. And he said to me: I do not smoke for one week, and I send you this money. It must have been a terrible sacrifice for him, but see how beautiful, how he shared, and with that money I bought bread and I gave to those who are hungry with a joy on both sides, he was giving and the poor were receiving. This is something that you and I—it is a gift of God to us to be able to share our love with others. And let it be as it was for Jesus. Let us love one another as he loved us. Let us love Him with undivided love. And the joy of loving Him and each other—let us give now—that Christmas is coming so close. Let us keep that joy of loving Jesus in our hearts. And share that joy with all that we come to touch with. And that radiating joy is real, for we have no reason not to be happy because we have Christ with us. Christ in our hearts, Christ in the poor that we meet, Christ in the smile that we give and the smile that we receive. Let us make that one point: That no child will be unwanted, and also that we meet each other always with a smile, especially when it is difficult to smile.

I never forget some time ago about 14 professors came from the United States from different universities. And they came to Calcutta to our house. Then we were talking about that they had been to the home for the dying. We have a home for the dying in Calcutta, where we have picked up more than 36,000 people only from the streets of Calcutta, and out of that big number more than 18,000 have died a beautiful death. They have just gone home to God; and they came to our house and we talked of love, of compassion, and then one of them asked me: Say, Mother, please tell us something that we will remember, and I said to them: Smile at each other, make time for each other in your family. Smile at each other.

And then another one asked me: Are you married, and I said: Yes, and I find it sometimes very difficult to smile at Jesus because he can be very demanding sometimes. This is really something true, and there is where love comes—when it is demanding, and yet we can give it to Him with joy. Just as I have said today, I have said that if I don't go to Heaven for anything else I will be going to Heaven for all the publicity because it has purified me and sacrified me and made me really something ready to go to Heaven. I think that this is something, that we must live life beautifully, we have Jesus with us and He loves us. If we could only remember that God loves me, and I have an opportunity to love others as he loves me, not in big things, but in small things with great love, then Norway becomes a nest of love. And how beautiful it will be that from here a centre for peace has been given. That from here the joy of life of the unborn child comes out. If you become a burning light in the world of peace, then really the Nobel Prize is a gift of the Norwegian people. God bless you!

Further Readings

Robert Cassen, *India: Population, Economy, Society* (London: Macmillan, 1978), and Bernard Cohn, *India: The Social Anthropology of Civilization* (Englewood Cliffs, NJ: Prentice-Hall, 1971), provide two standard introductions to Indian social and economic conditions. A useful collection of addresses, essays, and lectures dealing with aspects of the problems created by India's growing population is provided by *Responses to Population Growth in India: Changes in Social, Political, and Economic Behavior,* edited by Marcus F. Franda (New York: Praeger, 1975). Paul D. Wiebe, *Social Life in an Indian Slum* (New Delhi: Vikas Publishing House, 1975), offers a glimpse of actual conditions in an Indian urban setting.

P. C. Chatterji, *Secular Views for Secular India* (New Delhi: Lola Chatterji, 1984), and Creighton Lacy, *The Conscience of India: Moral Traditions in the Modern World* (New York: Holt, Rinehart, and Winston, 1965), consider ethical and moral factors in modern Indian society. India's population problem are confronted directly in Sripati Chandrasekhar, *Abortion in a Crowded World: The Problem of Abortion with Special Reference to India* (London: George Allen and Unwin, 1974), and Gyan Chand, *Population in Perspective: Study of Population Crisis in India* (New Delhi: Orient Longman, 1972).

Desmond Doig, *Mother Teresa, Her People and Her Work* (New York: Harper and Row, 1976), is a well-known biography prepared by a journalist employed by *The Statesman,* India's major newspaper. Doig is uniquely familiar with Mother Teresa's work, having followed her activities for a considerable time and written about her frequently. Three other thorough and helpful studies are Malcolm Muggeridge, *Something Beautiful for God: Mother Teresa of Calcutta* (London: Collins, 1971); Edward LeJolly, S.J., *Mother Teresa and Calcutta* (San Francisco, CA: Harper and Row, 1985); and Eileen Egan, *Such a Vision of the Street: Mother Teresa—The Spirit and the Work* (Garden City, NY: Doubleday and Co., 1985). Kathryn Spink's biography, *The Miracle of Love: Mother Teresa of Calcutta* (San Francisco: Harper and Row, 1981), is particularly useful for its coverage of the Missionaries of Charity, the Missionary Brothers of Charity, and the Co-Workers. Robert Serrou, *Teresa of Calcutta* (New York: McGraw-Hill, 1980), provides an illustrated biography. *My Life for the Poor,* edited by José Luís González and Janet N. Playfoot (San Francisco: Harper and Row, 1985), provides a collection of short letters, addresses, and interviews with Mother Teresa that afford valuable insights into her thought and motivation.

One Earth

The Mexican poet Octavio Paz occupies a prominent place among Latin American authors of this century. His literary and intellectual reputation, long recognized in the Hispanic world, has now won international recognition. Much of his fame rests upon the startling quantity and variety of his literary achievements. He is much admired not only as a poet but also as an essayist and literary critic. In addition to over twenty books of poetry, he has published some twenty-five other works on subjects ranging from literature to anthropology, from art to politics, and from Eastern philosophy to the Mexican character. He possesses a passionate interest in politics, and his many years in the Mexican diplomatic service have provided him with extensive firsthand knowledge of both national and international affairs. Firmly based on his personal responses to the world about him, Paz' literary works have captured the spirit of the age and made him a leading figure among Latin American intellectuals.

He was born in March 1914 in Mixcoac, Mexico, of Indian and Spanish descent. His father was an eminent lawyer who had defended Emiliano Zapata, the peasant revolutionary leader. His childhood was spent in the family impoverishment that followed the Mexican revolution, living a somewhat isolated life in a crumbling mansion while attending a nearby French religious school. Access to his grandfather's library afforded him an introduction to a wide variety of literary works that included not only the classics but also popular Spanish authors from the turn of the century. He attended university, but never received a degree. At nineteen, he embarked upon his literary career with the publication of his first book of poetry, *Luna Silvestre* (1933).

From Octavio Paz, *One Earth, Four or Five Worlds: Reflections on Contemporary History,* translated by Helen R. Lane (New York: Harcourt Brace Jovanovich, Inc., 1985), pp. 202–213.

As his reputation grew, he received an invitation to attend a congress of antifascist writers in Spain in 1937. Here, at the height of the Spanish Civil War, he met some of the most famous Spanish and Spanish-American authors of the period and returned home with a sense of leftist solidarity that was to have a profound effect on his writing over the next few years. In 1950, he attracted international attention with his brilliant essay on the Mexican character entitled, *El laberinto de la soledad (The Labyrinth of Solitude)*. The period 1951–1968 was particularly productive, with the publication of eight books of poetry and seven of essays. His political career flourished, culminating in his appointment as head of the Mexican embassy in India. In both his life and work, he had become a truly international figure.

Enraged at the government-approved massacre of university-student demonstrators at Tlatelolco in 1968, he resigned from the diplomatic service in protest. He accepted several visiting appointments at universities in the United States, including Pittsburgh, Texas, and Harvard, and received a regular appointment as Professor of Comparative Literature at the latter. He retired in 1980, and was recognized by the university with an honorary degree.

On 7 October 1984, Paz was awarded the prestigious Peace Prize of the Association of German publishers and Booksellers during the Frankfort Book Fair. His acceptance speech, included here in its entirety, begins with a general consideration of the nature of war and peace and of the role of the state in their propagation. His analysis stresses, as do many of his literary works, the importance of history in understanding society. He concludes with an examination of contemporary Latin America, particularly Nicaragua, emphasizing the damage caused by foreign intervention in the affairs of the region. He advocates for Nicaragua a government based upon free elections with universal suffrage and a secret ballot. According to Paz, only in a democracy can there exist conditions conducive to the open discussion of public concerns such as war and peace. For Paz, the preservation of peace is inextricably connected to the defense of democracy.

Questions

1. How does Paz view the concept of a universal state? What ramifications of this type of organization does he see?

2. What are the functions of the state according to Paz?

3. What does he advocate as the best means of bringing peace to Nicaragua?

ONE EARTH

When my friend Siegfried Unseld announced to me that I was to be given the Peace Prize awarded each year by the Association of Publishers and Booksellers during the Frankfurt Book Fair, my first reaction was one of mingled gratitude and disbelief: why should they have thought of me? Not because of the dubious merits of my writing but, perhaps, because of my stubborn love of literature. For all of the writers of my generation (I was born in the fateful year 1914), war has been a constant and terrible presence. I began writing, that most silent of processes, in the face of and against the noisy disputes and quarrels of our century. I wrote—and I write today—because I conceive of literature as a dialogue with the world, with the reader, and with myself, and dialogue is the opposite of the noise that denies us and the silence that ignores us. I have always thought that the poet is not one who speaks but one who hears.

My disbelief is, as I said, mingled with a very real and deep feeling of gratitude. Both have grown as I listened to the President of the Federal Republic of Germany, Dr. Richard von Weizsäcker, speak about me and my writings. It is very difficult for me to express all these emotions without seeming to be fulsome or affected. You have been very generous. I am truly moved and I can only say to you that I will try, for the rest of my life, to be worthy of your words.

The first historical narrative, properly speaking, in our religious tradition is the account of Cain's slaying of Abel. With this terrible event our earthly existence begins; what happened in Eden happened before history. With the Fall the two offspring of sin and death made their appearance: work and war. Our condemnation began then; history began. In other religious traditions there are accounts whose meaning is comparable. War in particular has always been viewed with horror, even among peoples who consider it to be the expression of the battle between supernatural powers or between cosmic principles. To escape it is to escape our condition, to go beyond ourselves—or, rather, to what we were before the Fall. Thus tradition offers us another image, the radiant reverse of this black vision of man and his destiny: in the bosom of reconciled nature, beneath a kindly sun and sympathetic stars, men and women live in leisure, peace, and concord. The natural harmony between all living beings—plants, animals, men—is the visible image of spiritual harmony. The true name of this cosmic concord is "love"; its most immediate manifestation is innocence: men and women go about naked. They have nothing to hide; they are not enemies, nor do they fear each other: concord is universal transparency. Peace was a dimension of the innocence of the beginning, before history. The end of history will be the beginning of peace: the kingdom of innocence regained.

This religious vision has inspired many philosophical and political utopias. If men before history were equal, free, and peaceful, when and how did evil come to be? Although it is impossible to know, it is not impossible to presume that an act of violence unleashed the blind movement that we call history. Men ceased to be free and equal when they submitted to a leader. If the beginning of inequality, oppression, and war was the domination of the many by the few, how can we not see in authority the origin and the cause of the iniquities of history? Not in the authority of this or that prince, this one benevolent and that one tyrannical, but in the very principle of authority and in the institution that incarnates it: the State. Only its abolition could end the servitude of men and war among nations. Revolution would be the great rebellion of history, or, in religious terms, the return of primordial times: the return to the innocence of the beginning, amid which individual freedoms are united in social concord.

The power of attraction of this idea—conjoining the purest moral principles and the most generous dream—has been tremendous. Two factors, however, keep me from sharing this optimistic hypothesis. The first: we are here confronted with an unverified— and, I fear, unverifiable—assumption. The second: the birth of the State, very probably, did not mean the beginning but the end of the perpetual war that afflicted primitive communities. In the view of Marshall Sahlin, Pierre Clastres, and other contemporary anthropologists, men lived as free and relatively equal beings. The basis of this freedom was the strength of each man's own two arms and the abundance of goods: the society of primitive peoples was a society of free and self-sufficient warriors. It was also an egalitarian society: the perishable nature of material goods prevented their accumulation. In these simple and isolated communities, social ties were extremely fragile and discord was a permanent reality: the war of all against all. As far back as the dawn of the Modern Age, Spanish Neo-Thomist theologians had maintained that, in the beginning, men were free and equal—*status naturae*—but that because they lacked political organization (the State) they lived in isolation, defenseless and exposed to violence, injustice, and dispersion. The *status naturae* was not a synonym for innocence: like us, the earliest men were *fallen nature*. Hobbes went further and saw in the state of nature the image, not of concord and freedom, but of injustice and violence. The State was born to defend men from men.

If the abolition of the State would cause us to regress to a state of perpetual civil discord, how to avoid war? From the moment they appear on this earth, States fight one another. It is not surprising, then, that the aspiration after universal peace has at times been confused with the dream of a universal State without rivals. This is as impossible a dream as that of the suppression of the State, and a remedy that is perhaps even more dangerous. The peace that would result from the imposition of the same will on all nations, even if it were the will of impersonal law, would soon degenerate into uniformity and repetition, masks of sterility. Whereas doing away with the State would doom us to perpetual war among factions and individuals, establishing a single State would result in universal servitude and the death of the spirit. Fortunately, historical experience has repeatedly banished this chimera. There are no examples of a historical society without a State; there *are* examples, indeed many of them, of great empires that have sought universal domination. The fate of all great empires warns us that this dream is not only unrealizable but also, and above all, fatal. The beginning of empires is similar: conquest and plunder. Their end as well is similar: disintegration, dismemberment. Empires are doomed to fall apart, just as orthodoxies and ideologies are doomed to split apart into schisms and sects.

The function of the State is twofold and contradictory: it keeps peace and unleashes war. This ambiguity is in us as human beings. Individuals, groups, classes, nations, and governments, all of them, all of us, are doomed to divergence, dispute, dissension; we are also doomed to dialogue and negotiation. There is a difference, nonetheless, between civil society, composed of individuals and groups, and the international society of States. In the former, controversies are resolved by the mutual will of the parties involved or by the authority of the law and the government; in the latter, the only thing that really counts is the will of governments. The very nature of international society stands in the way of the existence of an effective super-State authority. Neither the United Nations nor the other international agencies have strong enough means available to them to keep the peace or punish aggressors. They are deliberative assemblies, useful for negotiating, but having the defect of being easily turned into a theater for propagandists and demagogues.

The power of making war or peace lies essentially with governments. It is, naturally, not an absolute power: even tyrannies must take opinion and popular sentiment into account to a greater or lesser degree before engaging in war. In open and democratic societies, in which governments must periodically account for their acts and a legal opposition exists, it is more difficult to pursue a policy that is bound to lead to war. Kant said that monarchies are more inclined toward war than republics, since in monarchies the sovereign considers the State to be his property. It goes without saying that in and of itself a democratic regime is no guarantee of peace, as is proved by the case, among others, of Periclean Athens and revolutionary France. Like other political systems, democracy is exposed to the deadly influence of nationalisms and other violent ideologies. Nonetheless, the superiority of democracy in this respect, as in so many others, seems to me undeniable: war and peace are subjects on which all of us have not just the right but the duty to render our opinion.

I have mentioned the adverse influence of nationalist ideologies, intolerant and exclusivist as they are on the question of peace. These ideologies become all the more baleful when they cease to be a belief of a sect or a party and become a pillar in the doctrine of a Church or State. Aspiring to the absolute—forever unattainable—is a sublime passion, but believing ourselves to be the possessors of absolute truth degrades us: we regard every person whose way of thinking is different from ours as a monster and a threat and by so doing turn our own selves into monsters and threats to our fellows. If our belief becomes the dogma of a Church or a State, those whose beliefs differ become abominable exceptions: they are outsiders, alien, *others,* the heterodox who must be either converted or exterminated. Finally, if there is a fusion of Church and State, as happened in other eras, or if a State, by self-proclamation, grants itself exclusive title to science and history, as has happened in the twentieth century, the notions of crusade, holy war, and its modern equivalents—revolutionary war, for instance—immediately make their appearance. Ideological States are bellicose by nature—doubly so, by virtue of the intolerance of their doctrines and the military discipline of their elites and cadres. The marriage, contrary to nature, of the cloister and the barracks.

Proselytism, almost always a concomitant of military conquest, has been a characteristic feature of ideological States from antiquity to our own times. Following World War II, through conjoined political and military means, the incorporation of the peoples of so-called Eastern Europe (a misnomer) within the totalitarian system became a *fait accompli.* The nations of Western Europe appeared to be condemned to the same fate. This has not happened: they have resisted. But, at the same time, they have been immobilized: their unparalleled material prosperity has been followed neither by a moral and cultural renaissance nor by political action at once imaginative and energetic, generous and effective. To speak frankly: the great democratic nations of Western Europe have ceased to be the model and the inspiration for the elites and the minorities of other peoples. The loss has been enormous—for the entire world and for the nations of Latin America in particular; nothing on the historical horizon of these last years of the century has been able to replace the fecund influence that European culture has, since the eighteenth century, exercised on the thought, the sensibility, and the imagination of our best writers, artists, and social and political reformers.

Immobility is a disturbing symptom that becomes acute once it is recognized that its cause is the nuclear balance of power. Peace is a reflection not of the accord between powers but of their mutual terror. The countries of the West and the East would seem to be doomed to immobility or to annihilation. Thus far, terror has saved us from holocaust. But if we have escaped Armageddon we have not escaped war: since 1945 not a single day has passed without fighting in Asia or in Africa, in Latin America or in the Near and

Middle East. War has become a nomad. Though it is not my concern here to discuss any of these conflicts, I must make an exception and speak of the case of Central America, which is close to my heart, and heartbreaking; what is more, it is a matter of urgent necessity to put an end to Manichaean Greeks-versus-Trojans simplifications. The first such simplification is the tendency to see the problem as merely another episode in the rivalry between the two superpowers; the second is its reduction to a local skirmish that has no international ramifications. It is evident that the United States is backing armed groups fighting the Managua regime; it is evident that the Soviet Union and Cuba are sending arms and military advisers to the Sandinistas; it is also evident that the roots of the conflict lie deep within the past of Central America.

The independence of Hispanic America (Brazil is another case entirely) precipitated the fragmentation of the former Spanish Empire. This was a phenomenon whose meaning was quite different from that of the attainment of independence by the former English colonies of North America. We Hispanic Americans are still suffering the consequences of this breakdown: within our countries, chaotic democratic regimes followed by dictatorship; without, weakness. These ills were exacerbated in Central America, a number of tiny countries without any clear national identity (what distinguishes a Salvadoran from a Honduran or a Nicaraguan?), with little economic viability and exposed to foreign ambitions. Although the five countries (Panama was invented later) chose republican regimes, none of them, with the exemplary exception of Costa Rica, succeeded in instituting an authentic and enduring democracy. The peoples of Central America very soon fell prey to the endemic evil of our part of the world: the rule of military *caudillos*. The influence of the United States began to be felt in the middle of the last century and soon became a hegemony. The initial fragmentation, the oligarchies, the dictators at once buffoons and bloodthirsty despots were not the creation of the United States, but that country took advantage of the situation, backed tyrannical regimes, and played a decisive role in the corruption of Central American political life. Its responsibility in the face of history is unquestionable, and its present difficulties in this region are the direct consequence of its policy.

Within the shadow of Washington, a hereditary dictatorship was born and thrived in Nicaragua. After many years, the conjunction of a number of circumstances—general exasperation, the birth of a new, educated middle class, the influence of a rejuvenated Catholic Church, the internal dissension of the oligarchy, and, finally, the withdrawal of U.S. aid—culminated in a popular uprising. It was national in scope and overthrew the dictatorship. Shortly after this triumph, the case of Cuba was repeated: the revolution was taken over by an elite of revolutionary cadres. Almost all of them came from the native-born oligarchy, and the majority of them have either turned from Catholicism to Marxism–Leninism or come up with a curious mixture of both doctrines. From the outset, the Sandinista leaders sought inspiration in Cuba and have been the recipients of military and technical aid from the Soviet Union and its allies. The acts of the Sandinista regime are proof of its determination to set up in Nicaragua a bureaucratic-military dictatorship modeled on the one in Havana. The original meaning of the revolutionary movement has thus been perverted.

The opposition is not homogeneous. It has a great many supporters in the interior, but no means of expressing itself (in Nicaragua there is just one independent daily paper: *La Prensa*). Another important segment of the opposition is entirely cut off from the others, living as it does in remote, desolate regions: the indigenous minority, who do not speak Spanish, who see their culture and their ways of life being threatened, who have suffered depradations and outrages under the Sandinista regime. Nor is the armed opposition homogeneous: some of those who make up this group are conservatives (their numbers include former supporters of Somoza); others are democratic dissidents who broke with the Sandinistas *after* the overthrow of Somoza (they include such former Sandinistas as Commandant Pastora, Juan Robelo, Arturo Cruz, and many others who left the movement and the government as the nature of the regime became more and more clear); still others belong to the indigenous minority. None of these groups is fighting to restore dictatorship. The U.S. government provides them with military and technical aid, although, as is common knowledge, this aid is coming under increasingly heavy fire in the Senate and in many sectors of public opinion in the United States.

I must mention, finally, the diplomatic activity of the four countries comprising the so-called Contadora group: Mexico, Venezuela, Colombia, and Panama. This group is the only one to have formulated a rational policy genuinely aimed at bringing peace by peaceful means. The efforts of the four countries are directed toward creating the conditions necessary for an end to intervention by foreign powers, an armistice between the contending forces and factions, and the beginning of peaceful negotiations. This is the first and most difficult step. It is also indispensable. The other solution—military victory by one faction or another—would merely sow the explosive seeds of another, more terrifying conflict. I point out, lastly, that the pacification of this entire region cannot be brought about until it is possible for the people of Nicaragua to express their opinion in truly free elections in which all parties participate. Such elections would pave the way for the establishment of a national government. But elections, while they are essential, are not everything. In our time the legitimacy of a government is based on the free, universal, and secret vote of the people; nonetheless, to be called "democratic" a regime must fulfill other requirements, such as the preservation of human rights and basic freedoms, pluralism, and, above all, respect for the individual and for minorities. This last condition is vital for such a country as Nicaragua, which has suffered long periods of tyranny and which harbors different racial, religious, cultural, and linguistic minorities.

There are many who will dismiss this program as an impossible dream, but it is no such thing: in the midst of a bloody civil war, El Salvador held elections. Despite the terrorist methods of the guerrillas, who did their best to scare people away from the voting booths, the overwhelming majority of the populace peacefully cast its vote. This is the second time that El Salvador has voted (the first was in 1982), and on both occasions the very high percentage of the people that voted has been an admirable example of the deep-seated democratic spirit of this people and of their civic courage. The elections in El Salvador have been a condemnation of the two-fold violence that afflicts the Central American nations: that of the groups on the far right and that of the guerrillas on the far left. It is no longer possible to claim that this country is not ready for democracy. If political freedom is not a luxury for El Salvador but a vital concern of its people, why is it not an *equally* vital concern of the people of Nicaragua? Have the writers who sign manifestoes on behalf of the Sandinistas asked themselves this question? How can they approve the imposition in Nicaragua of a system that they would find intolerable in their own countries? Why can they judge admirable *there* something that would be hideous *here*?

This digression by way of Central America—perhaps too lengthy a one: kindly excuse me—confirms that the defense of peace bears a close relationship to the preservation of democracy. I emphasize again that I do not see any direct cause-and-effect relationship between democracy and peace: democracies have more than once been aggressors. But it is my belief that democratic rule creates an open space favorable to the discussion of matters of public concern and hence of questions of war and peace. The great nonviolent movements of the recent past—Gandhi and Martin Luther King are the outstanding examples—were born and developed within democratic societies. The peace demonstrations in Western Europe and in the United States would be unthinkable, impossible in totalitarian countries. Hence it is a logical and political error, as well as a moral failing, to dissociate peace and democracy.

All these reflections can be summed up in a few words: in its simplest and most essential expression, democracy is dialogue, and that dialogue paves the way for peace. We will be in a position to preserve peace only if we defend democracy. From this principle, in my opinion, three others follow. The first is to pursue unremittingly any and every possibility for dialogue with the adversary; this dialogue requires, at one and the same time, firmness and flexibility, giving ground and refusing to do so. The second is not to yield to either the temptation of nihilism or the intimidation of terror. Freedom is not merely a precondition of peace but a consequence:

the two are indissoluble. To separate them is to yield to terrorist blackmail and in the end to lose both. The third principle is to recognize that the defense of democracy in our own country is inseparable from solidarity with those who are fighting for it in totalitarian countries or under the tyrannies and military dictatorships of Latin America and other continents. By fighting for democracy, dissidents are fighting for peace—fighting for all of us.

In one of the drafts of Hölderlin's hymn to peace on which Heidegger wrote a famous commentary, the poet says what we humans learned to name the divine and the secret powers of the universe for the reason that, and from the moment that, we realized we are a dialogue and can hear each other. Hölderlin sees history as dialogue. Yet time and time again this dialogue has been broken off, drowned out by the din of violence or interrupted by the monologue of ranting leaders. Violence exacerbates differences and keeps both parties from speaking and hearing; monologue denies the existence of the other; dialogue allows differences to remain yet at the same time creates an area in which the voices of otherness coexist and interweave. Since dialogue excludes the ultimate, it is a denial of absolutes and their despotic pretensions to totality: we are relative, and what we say and hear is relative. But this relativism is not a surrender: in order for there to be dialogue, we must affirm what we are and at the same time recognize the other in all his irreducible difference. Dialogue keeps us from denying ourselves and from denying the humanity of our adversary.

Marcus Aurelius spend a great part of his life on horseback, waging war against the enemies of Rome. He accepted armed struggle, but not hatred, and left us these words, which we ought never to cease to ponder: "The moment dawn breaks, one ought to say to oneself: I shall today meet a man who is imprudent, one who is ungrateful, one who is treacherous, one who is violent. . . . I am intimately acquainted with him; he is one of my kind, not through blood or family, but because both of us partake in reason and both of us are particles of divinity. We were born to work together, as do feet and hands, eyes and eyelids, upper teeth and lower." Dialogue is but one of the forms, perhaps the highest, of cosmic sympathy.

Further Readings

Central America's economic, political, and social difficulties are the subject of an abundant and constantly growing bibliography. *Central America: Crisis and Adaptation*, edited by Steve C. Ropp and James A. Morris (Albuquerque, NM: University of New Mexico Press, 1984), provides a good introduction to the subject and contains an excellent bibliography. Lester Langley, *Central America: The Real Stakes* (New York: Crown Publishers, 1985), examines the politics, cultures, and conflicts of Central America. *Conflict in Central America: Approaches to Peace and Security*, edited by Jack Child (London: International Peace Academy for Hurst, 1986), also addresses the major issues of conflict, peace, and security in the region. Notable among the works examining relations between the United States and its southern neighbors are Noam Chomsky, *Turning the Tide* (Boston: South End Press, 1985); Lloyd S. Etheridge, *Can Government Learn? American Foreign Policy and Central American Revolutions* (New York: Pergamon Press, 1985); *The Politics of Intervention: The United States in Central America*, edited by Roger Burbach and Patricia Flynn (New York: Monthly Review Press, 1984); and *Central America: Human Rights and U.S. Foreign Policy*, edited by Dermott Keogh (Cork, Ireland: Cork University Press, 1985).

Many of Octavio Paz' literary works are now available in English translation. A good representation of his poetry is provided by *Configurations*, translated by G. Aroul (New York: New Directions Publishing Corp., 1971); *Eagle or Sun*, translated by Eliot Weinberger (New York: October House, 1970); *Renga: A Chain of Poems*, translated by Charles Tomlinson (New York: G. Braziller, 1972); and *Early Poems, 1935–1955*, translated by Muriel Rukeyser (Bloomington, IN: Indiana University Press, 1973). Three excellent selections of his prose works are *Alternating Current*, translated by Helen R. Lane (New York: Viking Press, 1973); *The Bow and the Lyre*, translated by Ruth Simms (Austin, TX: University of Texas Press, 1973); and *The Labyrinth of Solitude: Life and Thought in Mexico*, translated by Lysander Kemp (New York: Grove Press, 1961).

John M. Fein, *Toward Octavio Paz: A Reading of His Major Poems, 1957–1976* (Lexington, KT: University of Kentucky Press, 1986), analyzes seven of Paz' major works. *The Perpetual Present: The Poetry and Prose of Octavio Paz*, edited by Ivar Ivask (Norman, OK: University of Oklahoma Press, 1973), is a collection of essays that includes an excellent bibliography. Various aspects of Paz' poetry are considered in Rachel Phillips, *The Poetic Modes of Octavio Paz* (London: Oxford University Press, 1972). Jason Wilson, *Octavio Paz: A Study of His Poetics* (Cambridge, UK: Cambridge University Press, 1979), focuses on his philosophy as reflected in his poetry.

DISCUSSION QUESTIONS: THE TWENTIETH CENTURY

1. One of the previous discussion questions considered the apparent importance of "dying well." How important does Mother Teresa consider this, and what does she believe to be the most important human element in a good death? What role did the desire to die well have in *The Night of a Thousand Suicides*?

2. Both Mahatma Gandhi and Mother Teresa share the distinction of being regarded by many as saints during their own lifetimes. Would you consider them heroic figures? Try to imagine them transported to Huxley's *Brave New World*. How well would they fit in with their surroundings? What do you imagine that they might do? Does this tell us anything about why they are so admired?

3. Both Mao Tse-tung, in "On The People's Democratic Dictatorship," and Aldous Huxley, in *Brave New World*, present images of the "good life." What has become of the nineteenth-century ideals of liberty, equality, and democracy in these utopias? Has the rise of ideology and technology made people think that these ideals are either unimportant or unattainable? Is Mother Teresa interested in these goals? Why, or why not?

4. What drives men to face almost certain death? Compare *All Quiet on the Western Front* and *The Night of a Thousand Suicides*. What similar factors do you find—belief in luck, conviction that it is a matter of kill or be killed, devotion to the "cause," the dictates of "the system," fear of the opinion of one's fellows? Does *War and Peace* in Part II offer any additional light on the subject? Is it easy to lead people to kill and be killed? If so, what do you think this tells us about human nature? How can you reconcile this with the reverence for life championed by Mother Teresa?

5. In *The Night of a Thousand Suicides*, it would appear that many of the Japanese died to avoid being thought a coward by the others. How powerful a force is peer pressure to the Japanese? Consider *The Treasury of Loyal Retainers* in Part I in making your evaluation. Is peer pressure and popular opinion more or less of an influence upon Americans than upon Japanese? If your answer is "less," what factors in our culture do you think tend to diminish the force of peer pressure upon us?

6. We have noted before the importance placed in all cultures and ages upon "dying well." How did the soldiers in *All Quiet on the Western Front* react to a situation that required most of them to die badly? Do you think that the demise of Linda in *Brave New World* is an example of dying well? How has the concept of dying well changed in modern times? How do you envision dying well?

7. We have mentioned the literary figure of the passionate youth struggling against social constraints, using Werther in *The Sorrows of Young Werther*. To this could be added Martín Fierro, in "The Gaucho: Martín Fierro." The two young men portrayed in Part III are Paul Bäumer, in *All Quiet on the Western Front*, and Paul Morel, in *Sons and Lovers*.

How do they compare with the earlier figures? Would you consider either of the modern figures heroic? Why or why not? What do the characters of their protagonists tell about the authors' attitudes towards twentieth-century society? How does the Savage in *Brave New World* fit into this picture?

8. Compare the image of American Indian culture presented in "Speeches by Minavavana and Pontiac" in Part I, "Wounded Knee" in Part II, and *Brave New World.* Do you feel that the advance of Western culture and industrialization are crushing individual integrity, spirituality, and virtue? If so, what examples of this process can you present? Or do you think that the material plenty of the modern era has made it possible for the world to reach new heights of human dignity? If so, present some examples.

9. Huxley wrote *Brave New World* many years ago. How accurate has his vision of the future proven to be? Is our society becoming more like that of the Brave New World? What tendencies do you see leading in that direction, and what do you see about you that shows Huxley to have been mistaken? What aspects of Huxley's world do you secretly find attractive? What about it repels you?

10. Idealists have long dreamed of a universal state, reasoning that war would vanish under such conditions. Huxley attacks that idea in *Brave New World,* arguing that a universal state would eliminate not only war but also those human aspirations and strivings that make life worthwhile. What does Octavio Paz, in *One Earth,* have to say about this proposition? What is your opinion? Must the state always tend to subjugate the individual? Could a form of state be devised to serve the individual instead of vice versa? If so, how? If not, why not? When considering this point, keep in mind the debate in *Brave New World* as well as Mao Tse-tung's discussion of how the Communist version of such a society was to be created in "On the People's Democratic Dictatorship."

11. In "Fifteen Poems Out of Africa" you can get some sense of the resentment of the humiliations imposed upon Africans by colonialism. Can you discern in "Stanley and Livingstone," in Part II, any Western attitudes and approaches that made European colonialism so repugnant? Was there any alternative to colonialism? Would it have been better had the West simply left Africa alone? Did the Africans not, in fact, benefit greatly from the tutelage of the West? Is so, what are the Africans complaining about? Does Mahatma Gandhi's "Statement in the Great Trial of 1922" shed any light on this question?

12. A discussion question in Part II asked what qualities were necessary to a loving and lasting marriage. Could Paul Morel in *Sons and Lovers* have offered those qualities? Why not? What was lacking in him, and why? In some ways his actions and attitudes seems reminiscent of Pao-yu in *The Dream of the Red Chamber* in Part I. How were these two young men similar? Did their personal defects arise from similar causes? Would Paul Bäumer in *All Quiet on the Western Front* have made a good husband? Why not? What was lacking in him, and why?

13. An author's vision of the world is founded on his or her view of human nature. Compare the attitudes of Voltaire, in *Candide* in Part I;

Malthus, in *An Essay on the Principle of Population* in Part II; and Huxley, as expressed by Sir Mustapha Mond in *Brave New World*. Do you feel that there is a continuity of sentiment among these three authors? How does it influence their view of the world and its future? Do you think this view of human nature is justified? Even if it is, do you think that it necessarily leads to a pessimistic view of the world?

14. There is yet another tradition in the Western world regarding human nature. Compare Robespierre, in his "Speech of 17 Pluviôse" in Part I; de Tocqueville, in *Democracy in America* in Part II; and O'Connor, in "Guests of the Nation." How similar are their views of human nature? What reservations do they have about the basic goodness of human beings? How does this affect their view of the future?

15. The conflict between personal morality and civic responsibility is a common one in modern society. How is this conflict presented in "Guests of the Nation"? Do you think that Donovan chose the right course of action? Two selections in Part III—*All Quiet on the Western Front* and *Brave New World*—portray situations in which this conflict is eliminated. How is this accomplished in each, and what is the effect on the human beings involved? How do you think the proper balance between personal morality and civic virtue should be maintained? What would Gandhi, based on his "Statement in the Great Trial of 1922," or Mother Teresa, based on her "Nobel Prize Address," have to say on this subject? Does de Tocqueville, in *Democracy in America* in Part II, have anything to say on this issue?

Copyrights and Acknowledgments

GEORGES BORCHARDT for "Relentlessly She Drives Me" by Leopold Senghor, originally published in *The Heritage of African Poetry*, Longman Group, Ltd., 1985. Reprinted by permission.

CARCANET PRESS, LTD. for "One Earth" by Octavio Paz, excerpted from *One Earth, Four or Five Worlds: Reflections on Contemporary History*, by Octavio Paz, translated by Helen R. Lane, copyright 1985 by Carcanet Press, Ltd. Reprinted by permission.

COLUMBIA UNIVERSITY PRESS for "Yuranosuke at His Revels" from *Cushingura: The Treasury of Loyal Retainers, a Puppet Play*, by Takeda Izumo, Miyoshi Shoraku, and Namiki Senryu, translated by Donald R. Keene, copyright © 1971 Columbia University Press. Reprinted by permission.

DOUBLEDAY for excerpts from *The Dream of the Red Chamber* by Tsao Hsueh-ch'in, translated by Chi-cheng Wang. Copyright © 1958 by Chi-cheng Wang. Reprinted by permission of Doubleday, a division of Bantam, Doubleday, Dell Publishing Group, Inc.

FOREIGN LANGUAGES PRESS for "The Scholars" by Wu Ching-tzu, translated by Yang Hisen-yi and Gladys Yang, copyright 1972 by Foreign Languages Press. For "On the People's Democratic Dictatorship" by Mao Tse-tung, from *Selected Works of Mao Tse-tung*, copyright 1969 by Foreign Languages Press. Both reprinted by permission.

HARPER & ROW for "Brave New World," excerpted from *Brave New World* by Aldous Huxley. Copyright 1932, 1960 by Aldous Huxley. Reprinted by permission of Harper & Row.

INTERNATIONAL AFRICAN INSTITUTE for "Nyagumbe! Nyagumbe!" in "A Chopi Love-song," appearing in *Africa, Journal of the International African Institute*, IV, pp. 475–77, copyright 1931 by the International Language Institute, London. Reprinted by permission.

LONGMAN GROUP for "Choice," by Flavien Renavio; "Dry Your Tears, Africa!" by Bernard Dadié; "For Melba," by Keorapetse Kgositsile; "I Came With You," by Leopold Senghor; "I Will Cling to Your Garment," by Eric Sikujua Ng'Maryo; "I Will Satisfy My Desire," from the Bagirmi of Nigeria; "Love Apart," by Christopher Okigbo; "A Mother to Her First-Born," from the Lango of Uganda; "Nightsong: Country," by Dennis Brutus; "To the Anxious Mother," by Valente Malangatana; "Without You," by Odia Ofeimun; "What a Fool He Is!" from the Amhara of Ethiopia; "Where Has My Love Blown His Horn?" from the Acholi of Uganda. All reprinted from *The Heritage of African Poetry*, edited by Isidore Okpewho. Copyright 1985, Longman Group, Ltd., Essex, U.K.

MISSIONARIES OF CHARITY for "The Nobel Prize Address of Mother Teresa of Calcutta" from *Teresa of Calcutta* by Robert Serrou, copyright 1980, McGraw Hill Book Company.

NAVAJIVAN TRUST for "Statement in the Great Trial of 1922" by Mohandas K. Gandhi, from *The Selected Works of Mahatma Gandhi, Volume VI*, edited by Shriman Narayan, copyright 1968, Navajivan Printing House, India. Reprinted by permission of Navajivan Trust.

NEW AMERICAN LIBRARY for "War and Peace," excerpted from *War and Peace* by Leo Tolstoy, translated by Ann Dunnigan. Copyright © 1968 by Ann Dunnigan. Introduction copyright © 1968 by New American Library. Reprinted by arrangement with NAL Penguin Inc., New York, New York.

W. W. NORTON for "An Essay on the Principle of Population," from *An Essay on the Principle of Population* by Thomas Robert Malthus, A Norton Critical Edition, edited by Philip Appleman, by permission of W. W. Norton & Company, Inc. Copyright © 1976 by W. W. Norton & Company, Inc. For "The Sufferings of Young Werther," reprinted from *The Sufferings of Young Werther* by Johann Wolfgang von Goethe, translated by Harry Steinhauer, by permission of W. W. Norton & Company, Inc. Copyright © 1970 by W. W. Norton & Company, Inc. Both reprinted by permission of the publisher.

OXFORD UNIVERSITY PRESS for "Robespierre's Speech of 17 Pluviôse," from *The Ninth of Thermidor: The Fall of Robespierre*, edited by Richard T. Bienvenu. Copyright © 1968 by Oxford University Press, Inc. Reprinted by permission.

PENGUIN BOOKS for "The Sorrows of Misfortune" by Shen Fu, from *Shen Fu: Six Records of a Floating Life*, translated by Leonard Pratt and Chiang Su-hui (Penguin Books, 1983), copyright © 1983 by Leonard Pratt and Chiang Su-hui. Reprinted by permission of the publisher.

HILDA PETRI, TRUSTEE for "Wounded Knee," from *Black Elk Speaks* by John G. Neihardt, copyright John G. Neihardt Trust, published by the University of Nebraska Press, 1961. Reprinted by permission.

PRYOR, CASHMAN, SHERMAN for "All Quiet on the Western Front," excerpted from *All Quiet on the Western Front* by Erich Maria Remarque, translated by A. W. Wheen. "Im Westen Nicht Neues" copyright 1928 by Ullstein A. G.; copyright renewed 1956 by Erich Maria Remarque. "All Quiet on the Western Front," copyright 1929, 1930 by Little, Brown and Company; copyright renewed 1957, 1958 by Erich Maria Remarque. Reprinted by permission.

RANDOM HOUSE for "Guests of the Nation" by Frank O'Connor, from *Frank O'Connor: Collected Stories*, by Frank O'Connor. Copyright © 1981 by Harriet O'Donovan Sheehy, Executrix of the Estate of Frank O'Connor. Reprinted by permission of Alfred A. Knopf, Inc.

ST. MARTIN'S PRESS for "The Night of a Thousand Suicides" by Teruhiko Asada, from *The Night of a Thousand Suicides*, translated by Ray Cowan, St. Martin's Press, Inc., New York, 1972. Copyright © 1972 by Teruhiko Asada. Reprinted by permission of the publisher.

STATE UNIVERSITY OF NEW YORK PRESS for "The Gaucho: Martín Fierro," by José Hernández, from *Martín Fierro*, by José Hernández, translated by C. E. Ward. Copyright 1967 by the Research Foundation of the State of New York. All rights reserved. Reprinted by permission of the publisher.

UNIVERSITY OF CALIFORNIA PRESS for "Commentary on the Commentator," from *An Islamic Response to Imperialism*, edited and translated by Nikki R. Keddie, © 1983 The Regents of the University of California, University of California Press. Reprinted by permission of the publisher.

VIKING PENGUIN for "Candide" from *Candide*, translated by Richard Aldington, in *The Portable Voltaire*, edited by Ben Ray Redman. Copyright 1949, © 1968 by The Viking Press, Inc. Copyright renewed © 1976 by Viking Penguin, Inc. For "Sons and Lovers" from *Sons and Lovers* by D. H. Lawrence. Copyright 1913 by Thomas Seltzer, Inc. All rights reserved. Reprinted by permission of Viking Penguin Inc.

WADSWORTH for "The Interesting Narrative of the Life of Olaudah Equiano," from *Three Black Writers in Eighteenth-Century England*, edited by Francis D. Adams and Barry Sanders. Copyright © 1971 by Wadsworth Publishing Company, Inc. Reprinted by permission of Wadsworth, Inc.

YALE UNIVERSITY PRESS for "The Tale of Kieu," from *The Tale of Kieu* by Nguyên Du, translated by Huynh Sanh Thông, copyright © 1983, 1987, by Yale University. Reprinted by permission of the publisher.

Illustration Credits

13 Frontispiece from *The Adventures of a Simpleton* by Hans J. C. Grimmels-hausen, London: Heinemann, 1912; 54 Photo by James Araki; 64 Frontispeice by Cheng Shih-fa from The Scholars by Wu Ching-tzu, translated by Yang Hsien-yi and Gladys Yang, New York: Grossett & Dunlap, 1972; 93 Photographie Bulloz; 152 From *The Dream of The Red Chamber*, by Tsao Hsueh-Ch'in, translated by Florence and Isabel McHugh into English from the German Translation by Franz Kuhn. Copyright © 1958 by Pantheon Books. Reprinted by permission of Pantheon Books, a Division of Random House, Inc.; 192 National Portrait Gallery, London; 308 The Bettmann Archive, Inc.;

330 Illustration by Standing Bear from *Black Elk Speaks* by John G. Neihardt, copyright J. G. Neihardt 1932, 1959, 1961. Published by the University of Nebraska Press and Simon & Schuster, Inc.; 352 The Bettmann Archive, Inc.; 364 The Bettmann Archive, Inc.; 388 Culvear Pictures, Inc.; 432 Australian War Memorial; 443 The Bettmann Archive, Inc.; 472 The Bettmann Archive, Inc.

Cover Calligraphy by Brenda Walton.

COPYRIGHTS
AND
ACKNOWLEDG-
MENTS